The Life of
GIOVANNI MORELLI
in Risorgimento Italy

Art direction and cover
Paola Gallerani

Graphic design and layout
Chiara Bosio

Editing
Belinda Nemec

Color separation
Premani s.r.l., Pantigliate (Milano)

Printed by
Monotipia Cremonese, Cremona

Press office
Luana Solla

Officina Libraria
Via Carlo Romussi, 4
20125 Milano
www.officinalibraria.net

ISBN: 978-88-99765-95-8

Printed in Italy

officinalibraria.net Officina.Libraria officinalibraria

Jaynie Anderson

The Life of GIOVANNI MORELLI in Risorgimento Italy

OFFICINA
LIBRARIA

Contents

Chronology

1773 22 October: birth of Morelli's father, Johannes Morell.

1795 3 August: birth of Morelli's mother, Ursula Zavaritt, at Bergamo.

1813 27 January: marriage of Ursula Zavaritt and Johannes Morell at Bergamo; they live in Verona.

1814 15 November: birth of a son to Ursula and Johannes, named Jean Morell.
Johannes Morell is elected president of the Camera Primaria di Commercio del Dipartimento dell'Adige, Verona.

1815 August: death of the infant Jean Morell.

1816 25 February: birth of a second boy to Ursula and Johannes. Named Giovanni Giacomo Lorenzo Morell, later Giovanni Morelli.

1817 May: birth of a third boy to Ursula and Johannes, named Edoardo Morell.

1818 27 September: death of infant Edoardo Morell.

1819 Date unknown: birth of a fourth boy to Ursula and Johannes, also named Edoardo Morell; he dies in infancy, date unknown.

1820 22 November: death of Johannes Morell, aged forty-seven.

1825 Ursula Zavaritt Morell and her only surviving son leave Verona to live in the house of her father (Ambrogio Zavaritt) at Bergamo (Contrada di Prato 1048, now via XX September in the Città Bassa).

1826 "Johann Morell" enrolls in the Kantonsschule, Aarau, Switzerland.

1833–34 Winter semester: "Johann Morell" enrols in the medical faculty at Ludwig-Maximilians-Universität, Munich, where he studies the natural sciences with Ignaz Döllinger and becomes his assistant in comparative anatomy. Morelli enjoys a conspicuous success with his teachers.

1835 Wilhelm von Kaulbach draws Morelli's portrait, as do others. Morelli is deeply influenced by the scientific writings of Goethe and Georges Cuvier, and attends Friedrich Schelling's lectures on Dante.

1836 28 May: "Johann Morell" graduates with a medical degree from Ludwig-Maximilians-Universität, Munich.

Publishes his first booklet, *Balvi magnus*, a pseudonymous joke about his artist friends and their beer-drinking society, in which he reveals an anti-iconological attitude to art.
Meets Buonaventura Genelli, for whom he poses in the life room and begins a lengthy correspondence, which eventually wanes.

1837 Publishes his university thesis, "De regione inguinali. Dissertatio anatomica. Auctore Joanne Morell, medicinae et chirurgiae doctore."
Autumn: leaves Munich to further his studies in comparative anatomy at the Protestant Friedrich-Alexander-Universität in Erlangen, where he becomes more interested in writing than science. Spends seven months at Erlangen, where he attends weekly seminars with Friedrich Rückert, poet and professor of oriental languages, and studies with Johann Veit Engelhardt, who introduces him to journalism. Lives in the former home of August von Platen.

1838 April: meets Louis Agassiz at Neuchâtel.
5 May: visits Meckel's zoological collection at Halle, during a five-week nomadic tour of Germany.
By June: reaches Berlin and frequents the salon of Bettina von Arnim, where he meets the Barons Rothschild, Rumohr, Liphart, and Waagen, and makes his first acquaintance with German art history and the importance of attribution.
August–September: joins Agassiz for fieldwork on the Alpine glaciers, when Agassiz is defining his concept of the Ice Age.

1839 October: arrives in Paris to work at the Jardin des Plantes, where he intends to write a monograph on lizards.
Meets Otto Mündler and Ralph Wornum, with whom he shares Paris lodgings.
Publishes an article in *Kunstblatt* on the drawings of Buonaventura Genelli.
Publishes *Das Miasma diabolicum*, a parody of German mysticism, Protestantism, and the scientific method.
His letters reveal a deep emotional response to Renaissance and Baroque artists, especially Veronese.

1840 Returns to Italy. Italianizes his name. At Florence, becomes part of the circle of Gino Capponi, Giovanni Battista Niccolini, Giovanni Battista Giorgini, Giovan Pietro Vieusseux, and Giuseppe Giusti.

1841 Accompanies Gino Capponi to Germany for an eye operation to arrest Capponi's blindness. Introduces Capponi to his old friends Schelling, Görres, and Döllinger.
Becomes a person of interest to the Austrian police, and thereafter is frequently interrogated by them when traveling.

1842 Begins correspondence with Marchese Niccolò Antinori, to whom he conveys his most intimate thoughts in a lengthy exchange of letters lasting until Antinori's death in 1882. Morelli's first letter (from Rome, 20 April 1842) describes his passion for painting in Roman galleries, and mentions a play he has written, *Gli artisti* (lost).

1844 Helps his aunt's husband, Zanetto (Baron Sebastiano de Reck), nurse his son at Mirano in his final days. Makes fortnightly artistic excursions to Venice.

Acquires a property at San Fermo, Brianza, above the lake of Pusiano, to escape the bourgeois atmosphere of Bergamo.

June–July: the German artist Mende stays with Morelli at Pusiano, drawing, painting, and hunting ducks.

1846 Morelli inherits from his grandfather, Ambrogio Zavaritt, the use of an apartment at Gorle, and another in the lower city of Bergamo, for life.

Writes a play: *Troppa premura nuoce, ossia la prova d'amore.*

1847 Writes a play: *Il Roccocò.*

April (until 7 January 1848): Mende stays with Morelli.

1848 Enlists as a volunteer in the First Italian War of Independence, initially as captain of a legion of volunteers who descend through the Brianza to drive the Austrians out of Monza.

18–22 March: the Cinque giornate di Milano: Morelli leads a company of Bersaglieri to take Porta Comasina, Milan (now Porta Garibaldi).

9 June – 7 August: Morelli is sent on a diplomatic mission by the provisional government of Milan, to the German Diet in Frankfurt am Main, to plead the cause of Italian unity and to refute stories in the German press.

Writes a play, *I Tradimenti*, which includes a scene from the Cinque giornate.

28 October: appointed by Daniele Manin as adjutant to General Solera in Venice.

1849 February: leaves Venice

21–22 March: fights in the Battle of Novara.

13 April – 16 July: in Genoa.

August: at St Moritz, Switzerland.

In exile between his estate at San Fermo near Pusiano and the villa Balbianello, Como, as the guest of Marchese Arconati Visconti.

Writes articles for the *Gazzetta Ticinese.*

19 November: death of his best friend, Giovanni Leonardo Frizzoni. Morelli assumes a paternal responsibility for Frizzoni's five children, especially two of the boys, Teodoro and Gustavo.

At Bergamo he collects money for the Cannons of Alessandria.

1850 By the end of the year has sold his villa at San Fermo and moves to a property acquired at Taronico, near Como.
At the same time begins a loving, intimate relationship with Clementina Frizzoni, widow of Giovanni Leonardo Frizzoni, whom he consoles; writes paternal letters of advice to her son Teodoro about his education.

1853 Morelli sells to Federico Frizzoni (for the price he himself paid for it) a version of Lorenzo Lotto's *Virgin and Child with St Joseph and St Catherine*, which soon disappears from Frizzoni's collection.

1855 Delights in the publication of *Cicerone* by Burckhardt, a writer whom he always admires.
Morelli declines offer of chair of Italian literature at the Politecnico of Zurich, but suggests Francesco De Sanctis, who accepts the post.

1856 5 February: refuses chair of aesthetics at Berne University.
Buys masterpieces by Andrea Mantegna and Andrea Solario, which in 1861 he sells to Gian Giacomo Poldi Pezzoli.
November: spends eight days in Venice, studying its art and architecture.

1857 Becomes increasingly concerned at systematic buying by the National Gallery, London, manifested in annual September visits by the director Charles Eastlake and his travelling agent Otto Mündler (Morelli's old flatmate from Paris), searching out the best Renaissance paintings in Italian private collections for the growing British collection.

1858 12 February: death of Anna Maria Magdalena Morell, Morelli's father's sister (his mother's companion from 1820), who had cared for Morelli like a second mother.

1859 Gives important information on Italian affairs to Sir James Hudson, British ambassador, before the Second War of Independence.
Meets British archaeologist and collector Austen Henry Layard, initiating an important friendship.
June–July: is Comandante della Guardia nazionale di Bergamo (Commander of the National Guard at Bergamo); trains local citizens in gun practice.

1860 25 January: artist-restorer Giuseppe Molteni begins corresponding with Morelli about attribution and conservation; Morelli enters a circle of Milanese and international museum directors and collectors.
5 May: is elected representative for Bergamo in the parliament of the Regno di Sardegna, the first Protestant elected to the Camera dei Deputati.
Is commissioned by Massimo d'Azeglio, president of the Pinacoteca di Brera, Milan, to write a guide to the collections.

1861 27 January: elected to the Camera dei Deputati in the first Italian parliament, despite fierce Catholic opposition to a Protestant deputy. Sits on many government commissions for the next five years. Lives in Turin while the parliament is based there.
April: receives a commission from Quintino Sella to make an inventory of notable works of art in Umbria and the Marches, with Giovanni Battista Cavalcaselle as his assistant. Through his friend Francesco De Sanctis, now minister of public education, he is involved in many such tasks.
Sells the most important paintings he owns, including the work by Mantegna, to Poldi Pezzoli for his house museum in Milan.
Giuseppe Molteni is appointed director of the Pinacoteca di Brera.
11 May–20 June: persuades the Ministry of Public Education to assist Giovanni Secco Suardo with a restoration course in Florence on how to transfer paintings from panel to canvas.
Morelli selects the best paintings from the Lochis collection for the Accademia Carrara, Bergamo.

1862 May: Morelli is disillusioned when minister Carlo Matteucci kills his vision to create an Italian national gallery to display the entire heritage of Italy.
24 June: leads a commission to list every noteworthy work of art in the city of Bergamo, in preparation for conservation.
19 July: gives his only substantial speech to the Camera dei Deputati, a lengthy and passionate address on the subject of museums in Italy and how to preserve the national heritage. This is met with derision; the chamber is unconvinced by his plea for heritage and votes instead for armaments.
September: proposes a museum of Lombardic sculpture for the Castello Sforzesco, Milan, which is realized.

1863 Begins corresponding with Emilio Visconti Venosta, whom he helps form a collection, now in the Museo Poldi Pezzoli, Milan.

1864 Arranges for Clementina Frizzoni's son Gustavo (now aged twenty-four) to study collections in Berlin and Florence, and suggests to Antinori that Gustavo volunteer to make a catalogue of the collections of the Uffizi and Accademia.
Meets Donna Laura Minghetti, embarking on a long and intimate friendship.

1865 Carlo Righetti publishes an account of Morelli's political career to date.
22 October: elected to the Camera dei Deputati for the third time.
Appointed vice-president of the Dante celebrations.
24 December: death of Sir Charles Eastlake, inaugural director of the National Gallery, London.

1866 January: begins to form an outstanding collection of Renaissance painting for his cousin Giovanni Melli, on the understanding that Morelli will later inherit it (Morelli eventually bequeaths the collection to the Accademia Carrara, Bergamo).
February: Sir William Boxall is appointed second director of the National Gallery, London.
2 July–27 September: fights in the Third War of Independence, in the Legion for the defense of the Stelvio and Tonale as a volunteer with Colonel Guicciardi; distinguishes himself in the defense of the Valtellina.
27 September: is appointed Capitano di Stato Maggiore, in a decree from the Colonnello Comandante della Legione.
September: is appointed Commissario ordinatore della Sezione Belle Arti for the Paris Exhibition.

1867 January: death of Giuseppe Molteni, for whom Morelli writes an obituary.
15 September: death of Morelli's mother, Ursula Zavaritt Morell.
12 November: is elected an honorary member of the Istituto di Belle Arti delle Marche, Urbino.

1868 29 March: is elected to the Camera dei Deputati for the fourth and last time.
From 20 July: travels to England for the summer, visiting many English private and public collections and the National Exhibition of Art at Leeds. Returns to Italy via Calais, Lille, Bruges, Antwerp, Rotterdam, and Frankfurt. In the Netherlands he meets the younger artist Edmond Morin, who accompanies him for nine days.
December: serves on a government commission to examine the Pettenkofer restoration method.

1869 Study trip to Germany. In early August he visits Berlin with Count Lodovico Belgiojoso d'Este and Count Alessandro Melzi d'Eril, and from late August with Giuseppe Mongeri he travels to Nuremberg, Prague, Dresden, Weimar, and Kassel.
Death of Giulia Mannelli, wife of Niccolò Antinori.

1870 September–October: travels with Gustavo Frizzoni for fifteen days to Lugano, Locarno, Luino, Arona, Novara, the Valsesia, and the Sacro Monte di Varallo, to study local schools of painting.
13 November: resigns from the Camera dei Deputati.
Becomes member of a government commission to make an inventory of Italian monuments of national and regional interest (Membro della Sottocommissione della Giunta delle belle arti per l'elenco dei monumenti italiani di interesse nazionale e regionale).

1871 Travels in Lombardy, to Pavia, Castiglione d'Olona, and Varese.
1 May: publishes (in *La Perseveranza*) an anonymous article on

the sale of Raphael's Madonna Conestabile to the Tzar of Russia, criticizing the involvement of the Minister Cesare Correnti.
Travels to the Netherlands (Amsterdam, Rotterdam, Leyden), Belgium, and Germany (Berlin, Frankfurt), and at Dresden visits an exhibition of the two versions of Holbein's Madonna del Bürgermeister Meyer.

1872 April: en route to Spain, visits the Louvre in Paris and the Wicar collection in Lille.
24 April–9 June: in Spain (Madrid, Granada, Toledo, Seville, Cordoba), where Austen Henry Layard is now British ambassador; assists Pedro de Madrazo with catalogue of the Prado Museum.
On his return gives his analysis of the political situation in Spain in an audience with Vittore Emanuele II at San Rossore.
Is appointed president of the central committee for the conservation of works of art (Presidente del Comitato centrale per la conservazione delle opere di belle arti).
10 August: sells his large properties at Alserio, near Erba, and at Como, for 91,000 lire, as well as other properties at Brenna and Lurago.

1873 Is nominated as a Senatore del Regno (senator in the upper house of the Republic of Italy).
Inherits part of the collections and estate of his cousin Giovanni Melli.
Spring: travels to Bologna with the restorer Luigi Cavenaghi to examine frescoes by Francia in the Chapel of Santa Cecilia, at the request of Marco Minghetti.
September: accompanies King Vittorio Emanuele II to Vienna and Berlin; they visit the exhibition of Old Master paintings from private Viennese collections at Vienna's World Fair.

1874 Corresponds with Lionel von Donop about Buonaventura Genelli, and includes a short autobiography in a letter.
Is appointed Commissario regio con l'incarico di redigere il catalogo dei dipinti delle scuole classiche di proprietà pubblica e privata e il catalogo delle opere da acquistare per completare la storia dell'arte rappresentata nelle sue scuole (Commissioner with the task of drawing up a list of works of art in public and private collections to represent the Italian Schools of painting).
Is appointed president of the Committee for the Conservation of Works of Art (Conservazione delle opere di belle arti)
Publication of Gino Capponi's *Storia della Repubblica di Firenze*, for which Morelli advised on artistic questions.
Appointment of Sir Frederic Burton as third director of the National Gallery, London.

1874–76 Publishes a series of articles on the Borghese and Doria Galleries in Rome, under the pseudonym Lermolieff, revising the attributions of many famous Renaissance paintings, room by room. The most remarkable is his re-evaluation of the works of Raphael and his account of Leonardo da Vinci and his Lombard followers.

1875 Appointed corresponding member of the Italian Society for Liberal Education and the Social Sciences in Florence (Socio corrispondente della Società italiana di educazione liberale e della Scuola di scienze sociali di Firenze).
Appointed vice-president of celebrations for the 400th anniversary of Michelangelo's birth.
Summer: with Gustavo Frizzoni, follows Dürer's itinerary to Strasburg, Colmar, Berne, Lausanne, Geneva, Besançon, and the lake of Lugano.
August: in Paris with Gustavo Frizzoni, studies the paintings and drawings by Pisanello and Leonardo in the Louvre, as well as the His de la Salle collection of drawings.

1876 Prevents Wilhelm von Bode from buying Giorgione's *Tempesta* for Berlin, by placing it in the collection of Prince Giovanelli in Venice.
February–March: tours Sicily with Gustavo Frizzoni and Lodovico Melzi d'Eril, to compile an inventory of notable works of art.
February: attends salon of Donna Laura Minghetti in Rome.
May: begins keeping an account book, "Spese di Casa," for his Milanese flat, which details expenses, initially for his housekeeper Teresa. The chronology of his travels in these next years is based on this book, as well as from letters.
September: meets Jean Paul Richter, with whom he corresponds until his death.
October: travels with Gustavo Frizzoni to Varallo, Arona, Novara, and Vercelli, to study Gaudenzio Ferrari.
December: attends Senate in Rome.

1877 Travels constantly between Bergamo and Rome, usually stopping either in Florence to visit Niccolò Antinori or in Bologna to visit Laura and Marco Minghetti.
19 February: stays in Florence en route to Rome.
24–31 March: goes to Rome via Florence.
3–14 April: in Rome, where Marco Minghetti gives his first speech about women in Italian art, with Morelli's advice, after which Morelli goes to Naples and Montecassino with Frizzoni for the cataloguing project.
28 April–12 May: Rome, then stays in Florence en route to Milan.
24 May: to Bellagio and back.
1–17 June: at the Albergo della Minerva, Rome.
11–14 August: visits the Zavaritts at Bergamo and Gorle, before leaving for a long study tour in Germany, beginning in Munich.

1–19 September: trip continues to Dresden, where he discovers Giorgione's *Venus* for the first time, then to Berlin, Leipzig, Weimar, Cassel, and Frankfurt.
9 December: leaves Bergamo, staying at Verona (10 December), Bologna (11 December), Rome (12–23 December), Florence (23–26 December), and Rome (27–30 December).

1878 9 January: death of Vittorio Emanuele II, upon which Morelli comments that, despite the monarch's faults, in death he wore the halo of patriotism as the first king of a democratic Italy.
9 January: death of Morelli's good friend General Alfonso La Marmora.
21–24 January: in Rome, where he contributes to the monument for La Marmora.
7 February: contributes 100 lire for a statue of Vittorio Emanuele II for Piazza Matteotti, Bergamo.
9 March: Cecilia Massini da Repito enters Morelli's service.
27 March: leaves Milan to arrive (on 28 March) at the Casa Antinori, thereafter to Rome.
1 April: travels to Bologna (2 April at Modena, then by 5 April returns to Milan).
1–12 May: in Rome, stopping in Florence on his return route.
23–24 May: in Bologna; 25–28 May in Florence; 29 June–11 July in Rome.
14 August–15 September: travels to Munich, Vienna, and with Thausing to Budapest for the first and only time, where Morelli is overwhelmed by the collection.
4 October: in Udine for the cataloguing project.
early December: in Rome, and for Christmas in casa Ginoulhiac with the Frizzoni.

1879 1–8 February in Rome; 9–29 March in Rome; 21 April–3 May in Venice, Urbino, Pesaro, Osimo, Perugia, and Rome.
8–9 July: Bergamo.
1 August: leaves with Mongeri for Munich, to study the Exhibition of Modern Art at the Glaspalast, followed by a visit to Dresden to see the exhibition of Raphael paintings and drawings; on 18 September he consigns his manuscript to Seemann in Leipzig, and moves on to study the permanent collections at Berlin and Frankfurt.
29 September–3 October: at Crella.
1–3 November: with the Layards in Venice.
11–14 November: his first meeting with the German Crown Prince Frederick and Princess Victoria, taking them to see collections in Milan and Bergamo.
6 December: death of William Boxall, director of the National Gallery, London.

1880 1 March: second meeting with Prince Frederick and Princess Victoria (at Pegli, Genoa), then is in Rome for six days, then Florence.

24 April: in Rome; 1 May in Florence; 12 June in Rome.

1 July: in Turin, to see exhibitions, and later to Santena (Cavour's summer house, a villa he detests).

3 July: travels with Donna Laura Minghetti to the Certosa of Pavia, and to Cremona and Mantova; he finds her the most enjoyable travel companion, interested only in the beautiful, never the vulgar.

11–17 July: Morelli is in Rome; 18 July with Antinori in Florence; 19 July at casa Minghetti, Bologna.

August: undertakes serious study in many German collections, checking observations for his forthcoming publication (4 August takes a carriage from Milan to Borgoricco; 5 August through the Spluga pass to Coira, where he stays until 7 August; then to Basel via Zurich until 9 August; to Freiburg and Karlsruhe; 10 August Karlsruhe to Frankfurt; 12 August Frankfurt to Darmstadt; 13–14 August Frankfurt to Kassel; 15 August Cassel to Braunschweig; from 16 August he is a guest in casa Habich; 17–18 August trip to Gotha; 19 August Gotha, Weimar, Leipzig; 20 August Altenberg; 21 August Altenberg, Bamberg, Nuremberg; 22 August Nuremberg to Munich; 26 August Munich to Innsbruck; 27 August Innsbruck to Verona.

By 3–6 September: with the Layards in Venice; 13–17 September with Clementina Frizzoni at Crella.

17–19 October: with Jean Paul Richter at Verona.

November: Morelli publishes with Seemann the first German edition of his opinions on Italian paintings in Germany: *Die Werke italienischer Meister in den Galerien von München, Dresden und Berlin. Ein kritischer Versuch von Ivan Lermolieff.* Lady Layard expresses a wish (seemingly unrealized) to translate it into English.

11–12 December: with Donna Laura Minghetti at Bologna.

1881 26 January: from a photograph he recognizes the St Petersburg Judith as an echt Giorgione.

Relishes reading the polemical reviews of his first book.

March: declines Francesco De Sanctis' invitation to become director of the galleries and museums of Florence, unless he can have Gustavo Frizzoni as deputy director.

9 July: visits the Accademia dei Concordi at Rovigo.

28 July–28 August: travels from Milan to Geneva with Mongeri, then to Dijon, Paris, Lille, Flanders, Stuttgart, returning via the Engadine and Como.

2 September: visits Bergamo with the Vicomte Both de Tauzia, curator of Italian paintings at the Louvre.
September: is appointed honorary associate of the Etruscan Academy of Cortona (Socio onorario dell'Accademia Etrusca di Cortona).
October: travels with Gustavo Frizzoni to Borgo San Sepolcro and Città di Castello; from Bologna to Florence Morelli journeys with Maso Corsini, presumably the Prince Tommaso Corsini, then *sindaco* (mayor) of Florence, before returning to Milan for the Great Exhibition.
29 November–7 December: travels to see works of art and friends at Bologna, Florence, and Perugia.
7–22 December: in Rome, attending the Senate.
22–24 December: in residence at casa Antinori, Florence.

1882 March: travels with Gustavo Frizzoni, looking at private collections in the Marche and Umbria.
May: spends several weeks in Paris; 16 May: goes to London to study British collections.
1 June: studies the drawing collections at Oxford.
2 June: death of Garibaldi (who is deeply mourned in England, to Morelli's surprise).
Until late June: remains in England, where he is welcomed by many. Meets Gladstone at dinner with the collector William Graham, visits Aldermaston, and the Cowper collection.
By 22 June: in Basel, then Lucerne; 24–25 June: travels from Locarno to Milan.
August–September: visits friends between northern Italy and Switzerland: 20–29 August in the Val d'Aosta; 6–9 September with the Frizzoni at Crella; 13–17 September visits the Zavaritts at Gorle; 18–20 September at Baveno with Princess Victoria and Crown Prince Frederick.
1–5 November: with the Layards at Venice, before visiting the Minghetti in Bologna.
19 November: comforts Niccolò Antinori, who dies on 21 November. Morelli stays with the Antinori family in Florence until 30 November.
Publication of 48 drawings from Morelli's collection: *Raccolta di disegni originali dei più celebri artisti tratti dalla scelta collezione del senatore Giovanni Morelli in Milano. Fac-Simile eseguito in eliotipia* (Venice: G. B. Brusa, 1882), and a later illustrated edition in 1886.

1883 Louise Richter publishes her unsuccessful English translation of Morelli's volume *Italian Masters in German Galleries: A Critical Essay on the Italian Pictures in the Galleries of Munich, Dresden, Berlin, by Giovanni Morelli, Member of the Italian Senate* (London: George Bell and Sons, 1883). She receives £50 for the translation.

2 January: Morelli is in Vienna to see his publisher Lützow.
19 January: in Florence to see Antinori daughters, then to Rome at the end of the month for Senate meetings.
September–6 October: in Paris.

1884 13 March: begins a tour of Pisa, Lucca, Pistoia, Florence, Perugia, Foligno, Spello, and Nice, returning to Rome on 27 March, and to Milan by 30 March.
1–18 July: takes a thermal cure from at Levico Terme.
1–4 August at Crella; 15–24 August at Crella with Clementina Frizzoni; 20–21 September visits Esposizione Universale di Torino; 22–28 September at Crella; 15–21 September at Gorle.
12 November: Princess Victoria draws Morelli's portrait in pastels while they are together in the Hotel Austria, Bolzano.
7 December: with the Antinori family in Florence; until 20 December in Rome; then with the Minghetti in Bologna.
22–26 December: with the Antinori for Christmas in Florence.
Gustavo Frizzoni publishes his edition of the *Anonimo Morelliano*, with Zanichelli in Bologna, with much assistance from Morelli, who relishes the author's seeming anonymity.

1885 March: spends much time comforting the Antinori children.
Late April: begins sitting for a series of portraits by Lenbach in Rome.
16–31 July: holidays in the Valtellina at Tirano, Peschiera, and Silvaplana.
15–23 September: at Crella with Clementina Frizzoni.

1886 13 September–4 October: travels to Paris; with the help of Both de Tauzia he examines 40,000 Renaissance drawings, including the sketchbook of Jacopo Bellini.
2–5 November: with the Layards in Venice; 7–9 November with the Minghetti in Bologna; 25–30 November with the Antinori in Florence; 30 November in Rome.
10 December: death of Marco Minghetti.

1887 Morelli is appointed academic advisor to the Brera (Consigliere accademico di Brera).
7–10 June: at Bergamo.
June–July: to England with Frizzoni, Richter, and Koopmann; they visit London, Oxford, Chatsworth, and Windsor (where Morelli has an audience with Queen Victoria).
9–13 September: at Bergamo; 2–5 October at Crella; 7–13 October at Bergamo.
From 6 November: Venice with the Layards, then to Ferrara, Florence, Rome, Florence, Milan.

1888 9 March: Crown Prince Frederick becomes German Emperor and King of Prussia.

1888 15 June: death of German Emperor Frederick William III after a reign of ninety-nine days.
2–26 August: Morelli holidays at Silvaplana.
16–23 October: with the Layards in Venice while the widowed Empress Victoria prepares for her daughter's wedding in Greece.
September: invited by F. A. Brockhaus to publish his writings.
10–25 November: at the Senate in Rome.
26–29 November: at the Antinori villa, Poggio Torselli, near Florence.

1889 Meets Heinrich Wölfflin in Munich.
4 January: Ernesta becomes Morelli's housekeeper.
6 April: Morelli makes his will in his flat in via Pontaccio 14 (casa Ginoulhiac); nominates as his heir his cousin Giovanni Zavaritt, son of his mother's brother Pietro Zavaritt. Asks him to leave all his paintings to the Accademia Carrara: those in his flat at Milan and also those undergoing conservation with Cavenaghi.

1890 Publishes the first volume of his collected works: Ivan Lermolieff, *Kunstkritische Studien über italienische Malerei: Die Galerien Borghese und Doria Panfili in Rom; Von Ivan Lermolieff. Mit 62 Abbildungen* (Leipzig: F. A. Brockhaus, 1890).
12–18 January: the young Bernard Berenson (known as "the Boston Lermolieff") visits Milan; Frizzoni is delegated to show him Morelli's collection.
12–23 April: Morelli is at casa Contini, Florence; 24–26 April: with Antinori's children in Florence.
1–5 July: with the Zavaritts at Bergamo.
25–27 September: with Layard in Venice.
7–11 October: with the Zavaritts at Gorle.

1891 Publishes the second volume of his collected works: as Ivan Lermolieff, *Kunstkritische Studien über italienische Malerei: Die Galerien zu München und Dresden; Mit 41 Abbildungen* (Leipzig: F. A. Brockhaus, 1891).
The last entry in Morelli's account book is for a case of good red wine, Gattinara, in the exceptional vintage of 1876, for 46.80 lire.
28 February: death of Giovanni Morelli.
3 March, at 5 o'clock in the morning, Morelli is buried in the Camposanto, Milan.

1892 Morelli's collection is displayed at the Accademia Carrara, Bergamo, installed by Frizzoni.

1892–93 Morelli's British friends publish the major, carefully edited and translated English edition of his writings by which he is known: *Italian Painters: Critical Studies of their Works, translated by Constance Jocelyn Ffoulkes, with an introduction by Sir Austen Henry Layard, Vol. I: The Borghese and Doria Pamfili Galleries in Rome. Vol. 2: The Galleries of Munich and Dresden* (London: John Murray, 1892–93).

Gustavo Frizzoni publishes the final volume of the collected works in German, which includes his biographical essay on Morelli: *Kunstkritische Studien über italienische Malerei: Die Galerie zu Berlin. Von Ivan Lermolieff. Nebst einem Lebensbilde Giovanni Morelli's heraugegeben von Dr. Gustav Frizzoni. Mit Porträt und 66 Abbildungen* (Leipzig: F. A. Brockhaus, 1893).

1891–94 Edward Habich publishes Morelli's comments on Braun photographs, in *Kunstchronik*.

Genealogies

Giovanni Morelli's Family Tree

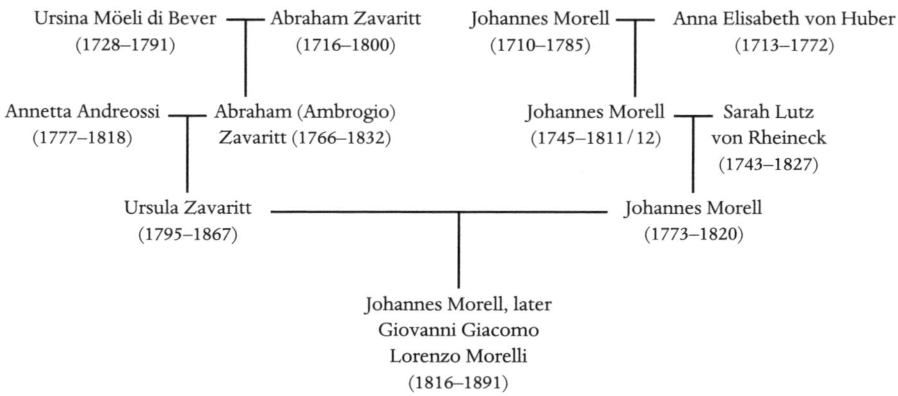

Zavaritt Family

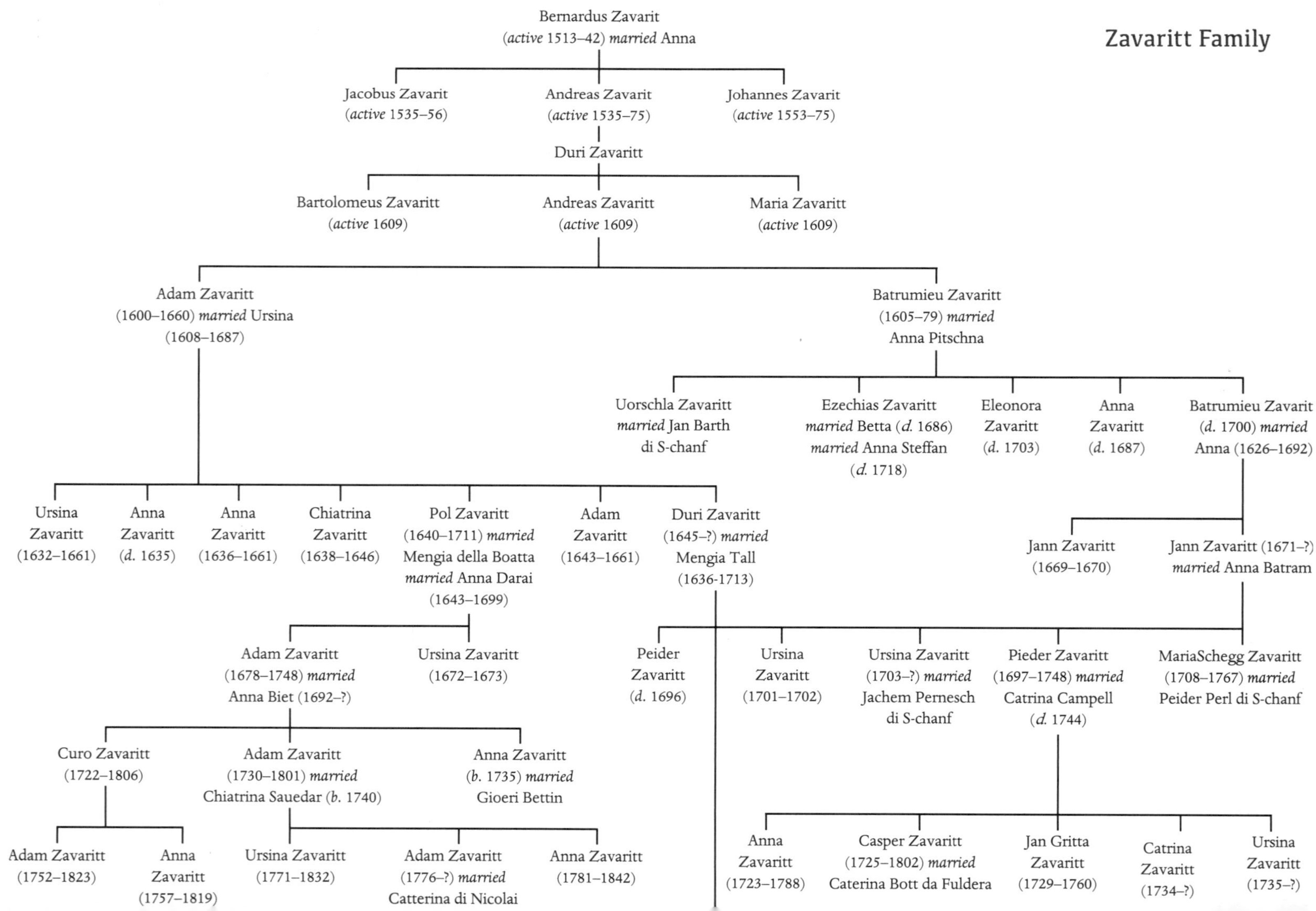

- Adam Zavaritt (1673–1734)
- Flurin Zavaritt (1680–1757) *married* Catrina (1688–1750)
  - Mengia Zavaritt (1714–1719)
  - Abraham Zavaritt (1716–1800) *married* Ursina Moeli di Bever (1728–1791)
    - Catrina Zavaritt (1751–1821) *married* Jachem Travers of S-chanf
    - Maria Zavaritt (1755–1761)
    - Peider Zavaritt (1759–1779)
    - Flurin Zavaritt (1763–1786)
    - Abraham (Ambrogio) Zavaritt (1766–1832) *married* Annetta Andreossi (1777–1818)
      - Ursula Zavaritt (1795–1867) *married* Johannes Morell (1773–1820)
        - **Johannes Morell, later Giovanni Giacomo Lorenzo Morelli (1816–1891)**
      - Margherita (Ghitta) Zavaritt (1797–1820) *married* Sebastiano de Reck
      - Emilia Zavaritt (1798–1833) *married* Ottavio Saluzzi
      - Pietro Luigi Zavaritt (1800–1876) *married* Amalia Steiner (1814–1905)
        - Ambrogio Giovanni Zavaritt (1834–1835)
        - Giovanni Pietro Zavaritt (1837–1913) *married* Rosa Frizzoni (1846–1921)
        - Ambrogio Maurizio Zavaritt (1841–1845)
        - Annetta Zavaritt (1843–1863) *married* Pietro Ginoulhiac
        - Rosina Zavaritt (1846–1847)
      - Luisa Zavaritt (1801–1833) *married* Paolo Enrico Fuzier
      - Giovanni Zaccaria Zavaritt (1803–1840)
      - Carolina Anna Zavaritt (1805–1850) *married* Nicolò Bonorandi
      - Rosa Zavaritt (1807–1832) *married* Enrico Steiner
    - Luci Zavaritt (1769–1773)
  - Catrina Zavaritt (1725–1765) *married* Lüzi

Morell Family

- Hans Morell — Ursula Bächler
  - Johannes Morell (1672–1726) — Helena Hafen
    - Johannes Morell (1710–1785) *married* Anna Elisabeth von Huber (1713–1772)
      - Anna Maria Morell (1737?–1746)
      - Hans Jakob Morell (*d.* 1739)
      - Helena Morell (1740–1795)
      - Anna Elisabetha Morell (1741–1797) *married* Franz Anton Pauli von Maikammer (1728–1789)
      - Hans Jakob Morell (1744–1755)
      - Johannes Morell (1745–1811 / 12) *married* Sarah Lutz von Rheineck (1743–1827)
        - Johannes Morell (1773–1820) *married* Ursula Zavaritt (1795–1867)
          - Johannes (Jean) Morell (1814–1815)
          - **Johannes Morell, later Giovanni Giacomo Lorenzo Morelli (1816–1891)**
          - Edoardo Morell (1817–1818)
          - Edoardo Morell (1819?–1821?)
        - Konrad Morell (1776–1779)
        - Antoni Morell (1777–1778)
        - Anna Elisabeth Morell (1778–1780)
        - Jakob Laurenz Morell (1779–1781)
        - Anna Maria Magdalena Morell (1780–1858)
        - Jakob Laurenz Morell (1782–1862)
        - Johann Konrad Morell (1783–1831)
        - Christian Friedrich Gottlieb Morell (1784–?)
        - Anna Elisabeth Helena Morell (1786–1872)
        - Anna Morell (1788–1870) *married* Heinrich Pauli
      - Eberhard Morell (1747–?)
      - Hans Heinrich Morell (1749–1784)
      - Hans Konrad Morell (1751–1812) *married* Maria Elisabeth Geiering von Biel (1754–1831)
        - Anna Elisabeth Morell (*d.* 1788)
        - Maria Salomea Morell (1790–1796)
        - Marx Morell (1796–1870)
      - Marx Morell (1754–1829)
      - Anna Maria Morell (1755–?)
      - Anna Magdalena Morell (1759–?) *married* Friedrich Adolf Ryffel
    - Anna Magdalena Morell (*d.* 1712)
    - Hans Konrad Morell (1714–1782)
    - Anna Katharina Morell (1716–?) *married* Georg Heinrich Lieb von Bischofszell
    - Anna Ursula Morell (1718–?)
    - Hans Heinrich Morell (1720–1785) *married* Sarah Enderlin von Lindau (?–1753)
      - Hans Jakob Morell (1747–?) *married* Anna Maria Studer
      - Johannes Morell (1748–?) *married* Elise Enderlin von Lindau
      - Hans Heinrich Morell (1749–?) *married* Anna Marg. Bächler von Egelshofen
      - Anna Ursula Morell (1751–?)

Frizzoni Family

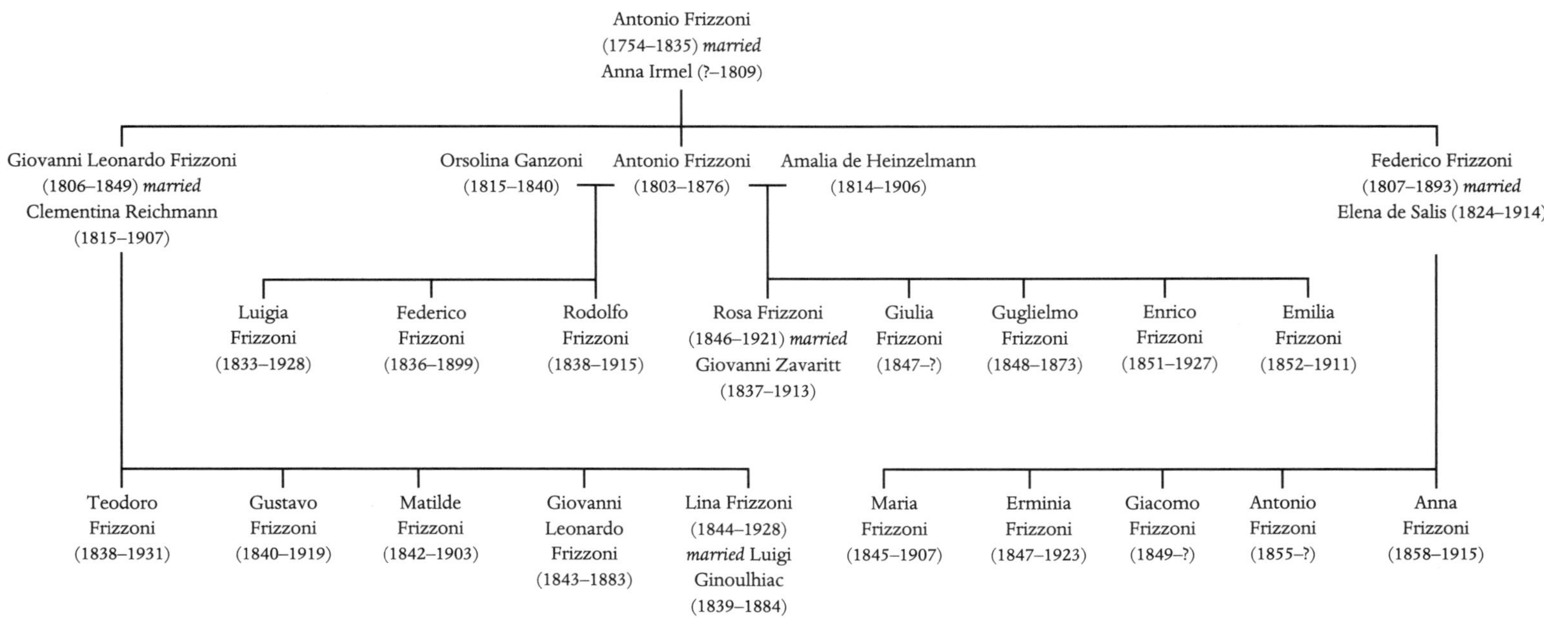

Preface

My interest in Giovanni Morelli was excited during my time as an undergraduate at the University of Melbourne, when I read Edgar Wind's essay "Critique of Connoisseurship" in *Art and Anarchy*.[1] Later, for my Rhodes Scholarship at St Hugh's College, Oxford, I was examined by Wind and met him in the library of his flat in Belsyre Court, North Oxford. I remember the intoxicating experience of working there with sixteenth-century books which in Australia I had known only from microfilms, and discussing our mutual fascination with Morelli. At Oxford I fell in love with my future husband, Richard Pau, who introduced me to his best friend, Willi Zavaritt, a collateral descendant of Giovanni Morelli. The Zavaritt villa at Gorle contained some archival material about Morelli, which led me to many other archives in Italy, Germany, and England. I have published several books of correspondence from that archive, but, as I became more involved with Morelli, his personality became a source of fascination, impelling a biography. Biographies are uncommon in Italian scholarship now, despite contributions by Donata Levi on Morelli's rival Cavalcaselle (1988),[2] and Christopher Duggan's political account of the life of Francesco Crispi (2002).[3]

Giovanni Morelli was the most influential Italian art historian of the nineteenth century, whose books have been constantly in print and cited since his death. When asked about his own life, Morelli always replied that he considered himself a politician, who had lived in Italy and who had worked tirelessly for his country: he saw his involvement with the art world as a marginal and later activity. His participation in the three Wars of Italian Independence, from 1848 to 1866, reveals a patriot who would risk everything—even his life on several occasions—for the love of family, friends, and country. Like many men of the Risorgimento, he pursued romantic visions for the creation of a new democratic state, in which he participated as the popular elected member for Bergamo in the Camera dei Deputati for a decade, and later as a senator.

But after the revolution, disillusionment gradually set in. Many of Morelli's statements about politics are as true now as then, which makes him a surprising commentator on twenty-first century Italy. Morelli's life provides the framework for a new understanding of the culture of the Risorgimento, and reveals why and how connoisseurship, or his famous method of attribution, was invented as a diagnostic instrument that would help to preserve the cultural heritage of Italy. Attracting followers such as Bernard Berenson (whom Morelli hardly knew), connoisseurship was subsequently to become a venal activity in the service of the art market. Nevertheless, Morelli had an intense curiosity about what Berenson did. Other self-professed followers, such as Sigmund Freud, interpreted the Morellian method as predictive of psychoanalysis, when he bought in a Milanese bookshop a copy of the posthumous Italian edition of Morelli's study of Italian paintings in Rome,[4] and claimed that the experience led him to invent psychoanalysis.

A biography, more than any other genre of art historical writing, reveals motivation. Why did Morelli become involved in the politics of art? Why did he create a method of attribution? Why did he contribute to the establishment of Italian national museums, and assist in the understanding of good conservation practice? His name may be more readily associated with a scientific method of attribution—the Morellian method—than with either museology or politics, or with the art market in Risorgimento Italy. Yet the titles of his legendary books—critical studies on Roman princely collections in the Doria and Borghese Galleries, and on the public German galleries of Munich, Dresden, and Berlin—should alert art historians to one of his main concerns as a politician and writer: how to regulate (officially) and manipulate (unofficially) the art market in Risorgimento Italy.

From his youth, Morelli's constant ambition was to become a writer, a poet, and a playwright. This ambition may have been realized in his art-historical writings, which have been in print in different languages and constantly discussed since they first appeared some 150 years ago. The few early plays that survive suggest that he lacked talent as a dramatist, though as a young man he met some of the great writers of his age (in both Germany and Italy), and they believed in him—such was his charm.

The narratives of this biography are constructed from archival material, principally Morelli's correspondence, diaries, and unpublished literary works, and from newspapers.[5] The extant correspondence is only a small part of what Morelli wrote, and even those collections of letters that trace lengthy friendships represent only a portion of what was actually written. A preliminary survey of Morelli's correspondence by Elisabetta Manca and Giacomo Agosti for the Biblioteca Civica Angelo Mai, Bergamo, in 1987 arrived at a figure of 2,200 letters with 121 correspondents, which they realized was only a partial estimate. The many letters that do survive reveal that Morelli enjoyed writing a kind of autobiographical dramatic fiction, perhaps while sitting in a café with a good cigar and a glass of red wine, which he adored. Often sent to friends, they reveal his wit, humor, and sharp and sometimes brutal observation, with sudden flashes of insight. Those to his family are more confessional in tone. In short, he was a brilliant letter-writer.

After Morelli's death in 1891, his executors returned correspondence to the writers or their descendants. For example, Jean Paul Richter's letters reverted to his daughters,[6] while those from Sir Austen Henry Layard went back to him and his wife, and are now in the British Library, all invaluable resources for art historians. The only *carteggi* that have been completely published to date are my editions of Morelli's letters to his cousin Giovanni Melli,[7] and Giuseppe Molteni's letters to Morelli.[8] A potential project for the Italian Senate would be to honor Morelli with a substantial online presence.

On 28 June 1891, Gustavo Frizzoni wrote to Giulio Pietro Ambrogio Zavaritt that he had successfully returned correspondence to Layard and to Richter, and asked if he could do the same with letters from the Antinori family, Edward Habich, and Donna Laura Minghetti, particularly as they were of a personal nature. His wishes were respected. Frizzoni explained that in Germany there was a fashion to publish correspondence, and in his view it was best to leave this matter in the hands of the families of the deceased:

> Poi che gli sono stati grati il Layard e il Richter della restituzione delle loro lettere già dirette al defunto Senatore, io domanderei se Papà tuo consente che a sua mano io ne restituisca altre a persone viventi. C'è in primo luogo il vecchio amico Habich (con assidua corrispondenza), Donna Laura Minghetti, gli Antinori di Firenze, che certo gradirebbero questo riguardo la loro famiglia. Poi che in Germania c'è una grande smania di fare delle pubblicazioni mi sono state chieste a tale scopo le lettere di Minghetti e del defunto Antinori, che sono spesso di carattere affatto privato. Ora mi pare che le persone della famiglia sono le più adatte a decidere in proposito. Ecco perché io chiedo di potere a nome di Giovanni Zavaritt erede rimandare a ciascuno il fatto suo.[9]

During his own lifetime, Morelli was well aware of his friends' publications of collections of their letters, and could have entertained such an ambition for his own.

The personal letters to Morelli that were returned by Giovanni Zavaritt have not survived, and are presumably lost, destroyed, or censored. Similarly, Morelli's correspondence with Gustavo's mother, Clementina Frizzoni, has been edited to remove all personal content. Crown Princess Victoria's letters to Morelli were not returned to the recipient, and represent an extraordinary survival, because almost all of Victoria's other correspondence was intentionally destroyed by her son, Kaiser Wilhelm II, with the exception of her letters to her mother, Queen Victoria, which were smuggled out of the castle Friedrichshof at Kronberg by a British ambassador. Probably this is why the letters in Bergamo were never returned, and nor was Victoria's portrait of Morelli, all testimony to an intimate relationship.

Gustavo Frizzoni mentions that Lionel von Donop was preparing a publication of the correspondence between Morelli and Buonaventura Genelli, the manuscript of which remains unpublished in Leipzig. Frizzoni inherited most of Morelli's correspondence, which informed his writings, but all that he possessed is now lost. Of all writers on Morelli, only Frizzoni has had an overview of his extensive correspondence. His two accounts of Morelli's life, the first published in German in 1893 as a lengthy preface to the third volume of the collected works,[10] gives a detailed account of Morelli's student years in Germany, based on letters written to his uncle, Federico Frizzoni; the Italian version, a preface to Morelli's *Della pittura italiana* (1897),[11] concentrates on Italian material and excludes German. As was always the case with Morelli's books, he changed the content depending on the audience. Significantly, Morelli's correspondence with foreign museum directors is missing, for example that with Karl Woermann, director of the Dresden Gemäldegalerie, with whom he was said to be in daily correspondence when Woermann was preparing the museum's first catalogue (published in 1897, after Morelli's death). From many sources it is known that Morelli corresponded extensively with Sir Charles Eastlake, director of the National Gallery in London, and later with his widow, the wonderful and formidable Lady Eastlake, with whom Morelli enjoyed a friendship long after her husband's death. Only one letter from Morelli to Charles Eastlake survives (in the archive), about the sale of Lorenzo Lotto's Della Torre Portrait. That letter was part of a more extensive correspondence. The National Gallery has a rich archive, which makes this loss surprising. Three letters from Morelli to Lady Eastlake are in the Victoria and Albert Museum.

Gustavo Frizzoni inherited most of Morelli's working notes, which he lent to Morelli's followers, such as Jocelyn Ffoulkes, who quotes them in her monograph on the Lombard painter Vincenzo Foppa. To date, only one of Morelli's working notebooks has been found: that of his famous trip to the Marche and Umbria from 27 April to 9 July 1861, a voyage of hardship which he was commissioned to undertake by his friend the minister of public instruction, Francesco De Sanctis.[12] To my knowledge, no other notebooks survive.

I am primarily indebted to Morelli himself, for the life he led, which has given me so much pleasure to pursue. I have been the recipient of three scholarships, one from the British Academy in 1981 which led to the discovery and re-publication in 1991 of Morelli's pseudonymous works *Balvi magnus* and the *Miasma diabolicum*.[13] They were previously unknown, but have fallen into the literature as naturally as if they had never been forgotten. Other anonymous newspaper writings by Morelli, acknowledged in his letters to

Count Giovanni Battista Camozzi Vertova, have not been accepted in the same way. In 1981 I discovered the correspondence between Morelli and Niccolò Antinori, which the late Marchese Niccolò Antinori made available to me. In 2008 I was a fellow at the Harvard Center for Renaissance Studies at the Villa I Tatti and at the Center for Advanced Study in the Visual Arts at the National Gallery of Art in Washington. I have published four books on Morelli—all documentary studies—and numerous articles.[14]

My knowledge of the Poldi Pezzoli Museum in Milan was inspired by my friendship with two remarkable women, Alessandra Mottola Molfino and Annalisa Zanni, successive directors of the Poldi. More recently, two medical professors from the University of Munich, Adrian Danek and Reinhold Putz, have strengthened my understanding of Morelli's scientific education, and I have included Professor Putz's assessment of Morelli's undergraduate thesis.[15] In 2012 part of the Renaissance collection of the Accademia Carrara at Bergamo was lent to the National Gallery of Australia, Canberra, and my acquaintance with Morelli's collection was intensified during my collaboration with Giovanni Valagussa on the catalogue.[16] This exhibition had an extraordinary visitation, the second-highest to date in the history of Australian museums. On art restoration, I have enjoyed discussing Morellian matters and conservation with the late Joyce Plesters, Lanfranco Secco Suardo, and Giorgio Bonsanti. I am indebted to many others, including David Alan Brown, Adrian Danek, Jill Dunkerton, Anna Flora Eynard, Ornella Frizzoni, Sandra Frizzoni, Eugenio Ginoulhiac, John Griffiths, Leo Kretzenbacher, Elisabetta Manca, Lino Pertile, Dorothea Peters, Reinhold Putz, and Cristina Rodeschini Galati. More recently, my postgraduate students in Melbourne (Paola Colleoni, Angelo Lo Conte, Luca Esposito, and Callum Reid) have helped by reading my chapters, and many others have answered questions.

My interest in Morelli has been generously encouraged by Willi Alberto Zavaritt and Maria Adele Zavaritt, who have studied their family history and discovered many new sources, which they kindly made available to me. They have given me, as Morelli's biographer, ideal conditions in which to pursue this research, often at Gorle, in the villa where Morelli lived and loved. Willi Zavaritt is the custodian of the Morelli collection at the Accademia Carrara in Bergamo, an institution of which he was for twelve years the president. Many of the documents that the family owns were gathered together by the late Elena Zavaritt, without whom this book would not have happened.

My publisher, Marco Jellinek, was remarkable in the last stages of production, an Italian barometer of excellence who helped bring the biography to completion. The team at Officina Libraria, especially Patrizio Aiello, who is a specialist in the art historiography of northern Italy, was a pleasure to work with on the complexities of finishing the volume.

I should like to thank Belinda Nemec for her impeccable copyediting of the English edition. In the last stages of editing this book Monica Fintoni and Andrea Paoletti began their Italian translation of Morelli's biography. Their understanding contributed to the final result of both editions in many positive ways.

I owe a special debt to my late husband, Richard Pau, a molecular biologist, who helped me interpret Morelli's scientific notes from his undergraduate days. Richard was one of the last of his generation to undertake a science degree that included comparative classification as a foundational component, when he studied zoology at the University of Oxford. He catalogued Morelli's drawings, related them to nineteenth-century debates about classification, and sketched his findings in his presentation to the Morelli conference at Bergamo in 1987.[17] It is to him that this book is dedicated.

Jaynie Anderson OSI, FAHA
Professor Emeritus, University of Melbourne, 2019

CHAPTER 1

Assigning Names

Naming, whether it was the way he changed or disguised his own name, or whether it was how he attributed a work of art to an Italian Renaissance artist, was a lifelong preoccupation of Giovanni Morelli. He was born Johannes Morell on 25 February 1816 in Verona, a city that had just unwillingly re-entered the Austrian Empire. Both his parents were of Swiss Protestant origin, from families who, in the eighteenth century, had emigrated from Switzerland to northern Italy: his father's family to Verona and his mother's to Bergamo.[1] His birth name was that of his father, grandfather and great-grandfather, who all came from Wöschbach (now known as Kreuzlingen), in Egelshofen in the Swiss canton of Thurgau. The family of his mother, Ursula Zavaritt (Fig. 1), had emigrated to Bergamo from the village of S-chanf in the Engadine. Unlike most other immigrants, members of the Swiss mercantile elite in Italy returned frequently to their hometowns. The Morell family returned to Egelshofen to record baptisms, marriages and deaths, until the practice died out with Giovanni Morelli's generation.

The Protestant church books of Wöschbach record that the Morell family came there from Lake Constance, beginning with Morelli's great-great-grandfather, Johannes Morell (1672–1726), a church warden, the son of Hans Morell and Ursula Bächler.[2] The Morell family genealogies reveal the insistent use of the same paternal name for the first-born son (see page XXIV). Morelli's great-great-grandfather married Helena Hafen on 3 November 1709, and they had six children. The eldest, Morelli's great-grandfather, was Johannes Morell (1710–1785), who became mayor of the town. He married Anna Elisabeth von Huber on 13 November 1736, and they had twelve children, one of whom was Morelli's grandfather, Johannes Morell (1745–1811/12), who married Sarah Lutz von Rheineck. It was this couple who emigrated from Switzerland to Verona, where Sarah bore eleven children, only six of whom survived to adulthood. The eldest was Morelli's father, Johannes Morell (1773–1820).

The Zavaritts (see page XXII) were among the first foreigners to arrive in Bergamo, in a group that included prominent Swiss mercantile families who intermarried, such as the Andreossi, Bonorandi, Curò, Frizzoni, and Stampa families. Known as the *Engadinesi*, they dedicated themselves to business activities, successfully creating the Banca Popolare di Bergamo, and actively participating in, and directing, the Camera di Commercio. The Engadinesi chose Bergamo because it was a nodal point for commercial activities from Italy across the Alps to the rest of Europe, and the town was governed by Venice, a more liberal commercial city than Milan, with a comparatively secular culture.

The religion of the Engadinesi was a hybrid of Catholicism and Protestantism. They were known generically as the Comunità evangelica riformata,[3] an evangelical form of Protestantism that began in the sixteenth century. Some claimed that their church owed its origin to the controversial Protestant reformer Pier Paolo Vergerio the Younger (1498–1565).[4] Born in Capodistria (now Koper in Slovenia), Vergerio studied law at Padua and was swiftly promoted in the Catholic Church. He first encountered Protestantism when he met Martin Luther, whom he attempted to persuade to recant. Instead he was persuaded by some of Luther's theology. Vergerio was later appointed bishop of Capodistria in 1536, but his developing Protestant sympathies brought him into conflict with the Catholic Church. He fled from the Venetian Inquisition following two sensational trials, and, in exile in the Swiss canton of Grisons, he printed Protestant texts that inspired religious practice in the Swiss evangelical community.

Calvinists from France also arrived in Bergamo: the Blondel, Fuzier, Ginoulhiac, and Mariton families. They were joined by German-Swiss Zwigliani (Zwinglians): the Steiner, Legler, Honegger, Niggeler, and Hefti families. At first these Protestants professed their faith in private homes, but in 1807 they were able to appoint their first pastor, Johann Caspar von Orelli (1787–1849) from Zurich. But under Austrian rule they again became a clandestine religious organization; only after the unification of Italy were they able to commission a church where they could worship (completed in 1876 on Frizzoni property in the center of Bergamo). In 1848 Protestants of Swiss origin fought bravely for religious and political liberty in a "year of miracles" (*anno dei miracoli*), so called because it saw the first significant opposition to Austria. But their success was short lived, ending on 13 August 1848 when the Austrians re-entered Bergamo.

Ursula Zavaritt met her future husband, Johannes Morell, through her father, Ambrogio Zavaritt.[5] Both men were successful silk merchants at the forefront of the Lombardic–Venetian industry of sericulture, the most successful commercial enterprise in northern Italy.[6] Ursula (1795–1867) was the eldest of eight children; she was named after her Swiss grandmother and known affectionately as Ursina (Urzigna in Romansh), Lina, or Orsolina. The older of her two brothers, Pietro Luigi (1800–1876), upon whom Ursula relied for advice, married Amalia Steiner (1814–1905) and was mayor of Gorle for many years. Ursula was less close to the younger brother, Giovanni Zaccaria

(1803–1840), who studied law at Pavia, never married, had a dreadful temper, enjoyed traveling, was fiercely independent, and who successfully directed the Tribunale del Commercio in Bergamo. Her sociable sister Margherita (1797–1820), known as Ghitta, married the Austrian Baron Sebastiano de Reck and lived between Venice and Mirano, where they had a villa. Ursula's other sisters all married within the same Engadine Protestant social network: Emilia (1798–1833) to Captain Ottavio Saluzzi in 1815 at Castasegna, while Luisa (1801–1833) wed Paolo Fuzier and lived in Milan, where she enjoyed the company of the Blondel family. Carolina (1805–1850) was educated at the famous school of Johann Heinrich Pestalozzi at Yverdon-les-Bains, Switzerland, and married Nicolò Bonorandi, who would figure among the Protestants who bravely defended Bergamo in 1848. The youngest sibling, Rosa (1807–1832), was judged the most vivacious and beautiful of all the sisters. She married Enrico Steiner in 1826 and bore two children in her brief life.

From the age of eleven Ursula attended, with her sisters, an Engadine college in Berne. The principal, Signora L'Orsa, reported that Ursula was "ever active and always ready to exert herself for others" (sempre attiva e pronta a spendersi per gli altri), also that she was less sociable than her younger sister Margherita and had a capacity for hard work.[7] Ursula's marriage was contracted between her father and Johannes when the two men met at the annual fair at Bergamo. Ursula and Johannes were engaged on 12 October 1812 and were married in Bergamo by Pastor Orelli on 27 January 1813, after which they traveled to first live briefly in Brescia, then permanently in Verona. Her considerable dowry was 40,000 lire.[8] She was seventeen, and her husband was forty.

Following her wedding, Ursula's letters to her family reveal that she was acutely homesick and often depressed; she confessed that she could not understand why she had agreed to abandon her family in Bergamo, and also admitted to frequent bouts of tears.[9] Yet she wrote that she adored her elderly husband and she entered into the social life of the immigrant Swiss (all successful in the silk trade), arranging dinner parties for eighteen or twenty people, enjoying the theater and musical events, while suffering the military presence of the French and later the Austrians, who made the town the seat of their general command. Six months into the marriage, her husband distracted her with a trip to Switzerland. The desperate tone of Ursula's letters to her family gradually changed when on 27 April 1814 she wrote to her father announcing her first pregnancy.[10] After that, her mood lifted as her days filled with social engagements and preparations for the birth. On 16 November Emilia wrote from Verona to their father with the news that the previous day her sister had given birth rapidly to a boy, whose baptism was celebrated the day after, when all enjoyed hot chocolate, Malaga wine, and bonbons. The infant's godfather, Ursula's brother-in-law the Baron de Reck, gave the new mother a diamond brooch.[11]

After the defeat of Napoleon, and the Congress of Vienna (held from November 1814 to June 1815), Verona again became a city of the Austrian

Empire, some months after Ursula Zavaritt had brought her first child into the world. Ursula Zavaritt and Johannes Morell would have four sons in all, three of whom died in infancy. The first was baptized Johannes, but known as Jean. Described in his first months as handsome, chubby and vivacious, he succumbed to typhus at nine months old, in August 1815.

The following year, on 25 February 1816, Ursula gave birth to the future politician and art historian Giovanni Giacomo Lorenzo Morelli. Her next child, Edoardo, was born in May 1817, only to die on 27 September 1818, aged one year, three months and twenty-seven days, as recorded on his tombstone in the cloister of San Bernardino, Verona, where Jean was also buried.[12] Ursula gave birth to a second Edoardo, probably in 1819, but he did not survive infancy.[13]

Simmering beneath the surface of the newly married couple's life in Verona was their deep resentment and discomfort with the military presence, which was far more evident there than in Bergamo. Writing to her father on 16 July 1813,[14] Ursula complained that her husband, in order to assume the role of president of the chamber of commerce in Verona, had been forced to take an oath before the Viceroy of Italy, Eugène de Beauharnais, and his wife, Augusta Amélie of Bavaria. This was significant because Protestants never swore oaths, but instead promised binding agreements. On the rare occasions when Morelli referred to his childhood in Verona, his memories concerned the unpleasantness of the military.[15]

An amateur family portrait of Ursula Zavaritt playing a lullaby at a square piano, with her husband, Johannes Morell, turning the pages while holding on his lap their first son, Jean,[16] captures a scene in the music room of their elegant palace on the piazza Cittadella, Verona, in 1814 (Fig. 2). The family is dressed in French fashion, Ursula's gown displaying an Empire silhouette, while her husband's hairstyle and boots declare him to be a *filonapoleonico* or supporter of Napoleon. Yet political change was imminent, as Johannes realized, and this is hinted at in the painting: the piano music is Austrian inspired,[17] while on the leg of the instrument is a tiny satyr, suggesting discord. The moment of "playing for change" (*cambio musica*), may signify that it is time to adapt to the political situation of a new regime, a transfer that occurred slowly over some months.

Johannes Morell was enthusiastic and knowledgeable about ornithology; from 1818 to 1820, he was given permission by the Austrian authorities to hunt (normally a prohibited activity), the reason being that he was creating a collection of stuffed birds ("appassionato d'Ornitologia, e proprietario di un fiorito Gabinetto d'Uccelli conservati") and needed to collect rare specimens. Duplicates were given to the Gabinetto di Storia Naturale at the University of Padua.[18] Morell's collection (viewable by appointment) was of some significance: it was described in the first guidebook to Verona (published by a mayor of the city, Giovanni Battista da Persico, in 1820).[19] Giovanni Morelli would inherit his strong interest in science from his father.

Persico's guidebook records the house of the silk merchant Johannes Morell as being to the left of the Dimesse monastery on the elegant piazza Cittadella, which he mentions was used by the military on horseback. A mid-nineteenth-century print records a view of the Brasavola Palace and its front garden. The Morell family palace, on the opposite side, was part of a block of buildings transformed by later owners (Vela and Giuseppe Biasi, who had a famous greenhouse with exotic plants at the back) which now hosts the Istituto Seghetti.[20]

A single letter from Morelli's father survives, from 12 October 1820, sent to his brother-in-law Pietro Zavaritt, in which he writes of his debilitating illness, but from which he believes he is getting better day by day. He writes ironically about how the quantity of wine consumed in Italy increases daily in proportion to the number of foreign troops that arrive, and suggests a price increase. [21]

Johannes Morell died on 22 November 1820, at the age of forty-seven. His marriage to Ursula Zavaritt had lasted almost eight years. It was a union between two upper middle-class families who believed in religious freedom, commercial entrepreneurship, and democratic opportunity, despite the difficult times in which they lived. They were cultured, musical, and well known for their zoological collection.[22] Following the sudden death of her husband, the tone of Ursula's letters changed dramatically. She wrote from Verona to her brothers about the distress of her son Giovanni, whom she always referred to affectionately as Nané (an elision meaning "little one"): "I would like to return to be among my family with whom I was so happy before my marriage. My character should allow me to adapt to different situations, but I live within one room. Poor Nané, who adored his father, cannot forget him, and asks God to allow him to die as well, to join his father, and kisses his portrait."[23] In the same letter, Ursula asks to be comforted by her family, not only for herself but also for her two sons, revealing that she had given birth to a fourth infant, the second Edoardo, mentioned in her husband's will.[24]

A letter from Ursula's sister Carolina, written in October 1821, confirms Giovanni Morelli's childish distress; she describes the five-year-old boy on a visit from Verona to Bergamo, where he came to ride horses, looking as thin as a rake, unwell, and hating being away from his mother.[25] During the years following her husband's premature death, Ursula attempted to continue the family business, but found Austrian rule uncongenial.[26] She was visited by her father, who wrote home to Pietro on 28 October 1822 about a brilliant evening at the theater, where the emperor and empress were present, together with the King of Prussia, princes and ambassadors, though Italian royalty from Piedmont and Sardinia were absent.[27]

Ursula's mother, Annetta Andreossi, had died in 1818, and Ursula's five sisters had left home to be married. Writing to her brother Pietro from Verona on 9 May 1823, she mentions her son Giovanni, who sends his uncle a million kisses. In 1825, some five years after her husband's death, Ursula returned to the Zavaritt family home in via di Prato, Contrada San Leonardo, Bergamo.

Once back in Bergamo with her son, she also looked after her father, assuming the role of *padrona di casa*, and resumed her affectionate relationship with Pietro; this astute businessman would always be a good uncle to Morelli, later advising him on financial matters. In his will, Ambrogio would leave his daughter Ursula a property as a reward for her dedication, and also made provision for his grandson Giovanni. Among Ambrogio's eight children, Ursula was unique in this recommendation.

Most Zavaritt women were married at the age of fourteen or sixteen and had a life expectancy of about forty-five years. By comparison, Ursula lived a long life, as did her late husband's sister, Anna Maria Magdalena Morell (1780–1858), who accompanied Ursula back to Bergamo, and henceforth became her companion, and like a second mother to young Giovanni, as he recalled after her death:

> She died on 12 February at three in the morning. I closed her eyes. Her illness only lasted five days, as her death was unexpected. Her loss is irretrievable, believe me the sadness that I feel is very great. That dear good old lady loved me sincerely, lived only for me, and continually thought of only pleasing me. No one in this world can replace her.[28]

When Giovanni Morelli and his mother left Verona to live in Bergamo, he was aged ten. Like all Zavaritt children he was sent to school in Switzerland, but in his case to the first non-Christian gymnasium in Switzerland, the Kantonsschule at Aarau, in 1828 (Fig. 3). Founded in 1802, this famous school had a progressive syllabus in languages and sciences. Aarau was the center for the Patriotic Swiss Party, and the school's program was inspired by the idealistic and political aspirations of the German Swiss. Its alumni include a surprising number of Nobel Prize winners, one of whom was Albert Einstein.

Like other Italian intellectuals of the Risorgimento—the movement for Italian national unification and independence—Morelli spent many of his formative years abroad. As a child he was trilingual: he spoke Italian at home, his first letters were written in French, and at school in Switzerland German became his primary language. He also excelled in the classical languages of Greek and Latin. The school records from Aarau note that he refused from the age of sixteen to take religious instruction, and wanted to be released from religious duties. Yet later he was to fight for religious freedom, and his Protestant background gave him an unusual sense of independence. The school records also show that he was excellent at science and inadequate at drawing. A pencil drawing by an unknown amateur artist, dating from around the time he was sent to school, shows him as a child with a hammer in hand (Fig. 4).

Morelli's progress at school is recorded in detail in the published syllabus and the class lists of 1830 and 1831.[29] He was already a linguist who had made a promising start in science. In 1830 he won first prize in Latin; came second in Greek and German; fourth in French, oryctology (the study of minerals and fossils), and botany; but only twenty-second in history and geography. In the following year the same pattern emerged: again he received special praise for his scientific studies, the syllabus being about the anatomy and physiology of humans, mammals, birds, and amphibians. Despite his academic ability, he later recalled his school years in Switzerland as being lonely ones.

Morelli's first known letter is in French, to his uncle Pietro,[30] whom he calls "mon ami." The teenage Giovanni is charming, confident, and at ease as he jokes about the young women in Bergamo who flirted for his uncle's attention (in 1832 Pietro would marry Amalia Steiner from Zurich). Morelli laughs at himself as a poor horseman, despite Pietro's lessons. At the same time his mother writes to her brother, thanking him for his generosity to her and her son, emphasizing that Nané is infinitely happy to be in the good hands of his uncles.[31] In just a few years, Nané had been transformed from the painfully thin child mourning his father in Verona to a confident teenager in Bergamo.

Morelli and his mother enjoyed the Zavaritt palace in Bergamo, but in the summer they moved to the family villa at Gorle, situated in idyllic countryside some 4 kilometers away.[32] It was at the centre of a large estate of considerable significance and beauty, which had been the summer palace of the bishops of Bergamo from the thirteenth century until 1798. Gorle was known to have Roman origins, as attested by the strategic Roman bridge across the River Serio, and archaeologists have found traces of a Roman fortress, also indicating that Gorle had been continuously inhabited since antiquity.

The castle dates from the eleventh century, when Gorle became a *ricetto*, a fortified area, constructed to protect the local population from Hungarian invaders. In the early Middle Ages it was a monastery for the Frati Umiliati, a heretical order that specialized in sericulture and which was later suppressed by Carlo Borromeo, the cardinal archbishop of Milan who played a leading role in the Counter-Reformation of the late sixteenth century. By the thirteenth century it was a *possedimento*, a castle with houses, and was acquired by the bishopric of Bergamo as a place of refuge from the bishop's palace in the upper city (Città Alta), to escape either war or the heat,[33] the climate of Gorle being delightfully refreshing in summer. Inside the walls, a medieval palace was constructed for the bishop; this was first occupied by Bishop Giovanni da Scanzo (r. 1295–1309). Around 1300, during the Guelf and Ghibelline wars, the castle's walls were strengthened to defend the bishops' estates.

Successive bishops of Bergamo delighted in their estate at Gorle, although not all were able to visit the place. The legendary Cardinal Pietro Bembo (r. 1539–47) appointed a coadjutant bishop from the Veneto, Vittore Soranzo, who had Waldensian sympathies, to undertake the duties of the bishopric. When Soranzo became bishop (r. 1547–58) he hid cases of heretical books in the castle at Gorle. The later Protestant owners delighted in the fact that Soranzo had defied the Venetian Inquisition by annotating heretical books. Towards the end of his life Soranzo was arrested and charged with heresy. In 1551 he was pardoned, but was condemned by the Inquisition in 1557 and burnt in effigy at Rome for having Lutheran sympathies, before his actual death the following year. Italian evangelism of the sixteenth century, as espoused by Bembo, Soranzo, and Vergerio, was the foundation of the evangelical church of Bergamo.[34]

From 1588 Bishop Gerolamo Ragazzoni (r. 1577–92), inspired by a Tuscan Renaissance model for a villa, redesigned the entire complex of buildings and gardens on the right-hand side of the courtyard. To construct his palace, he took away a medieval church. The palace was built around a courtyard: the medieval structure on the right and on the left Ragazzoni's larger Renaissance building. Extensive landscaped terrace gardens with cypresses were planted in the twentieth century. Another view of the interior courtyard shows the facade of the medieval palace on the left-hand side, and the Renaissance palace on the right. An 1890 photograph gives an idea of the Renaissance side before Luigi Angelini's modifications of 1914–18 (Fig. 6).

The bishop's very large estates (*grandioso possedimento*) at Gorle had been confiscated by the Cisalpine Republic in 1798, just one of many ecclesiastical properties seized to finance Napoleon's military campaigns. It was partly sold in 1801 by Francesco Luigi Blondel to Ambrogio Zavaritt, Lucio Melli, and Enrico and Paolo Luigi Mariton, all Swiss Protestant families from the Engadine. Zavaritt and Melli bought two-thirds of the property for 250,000 lire. In 1803 the Maritons bought from Blondel their one-sixth share. By 1865 the entire property was owned by the Zavaritt family; the division is shown in Fig. 5. In fact, Blondel, the future brother-in-law and business partner of Alessandro Manzoni, better known as the author of the most famous novel in the Italian language, *I promessi sposi* (1827), arranged the sale, as he held an office in the Cisalpine Republic that required him to re-sell the sequestered properties. Only Protestants felt confident enough to acquire a Catholic bishop's summer palace.

The Blondel and Zavaritt families had become major producers of silk, which was known as the gold of Bergamo (*l'oro dei Bergamaschi*).[35] The Zavaritts had been successfully manufacturing this precious textile for generations, beginning with Flurin Zavaritt (1680–1757), who began to trade in it at Chiavenna and co-founded the Zamboni–Zavaritt Company. In the next generation, Abraham Zavaritt (1716–1800) brought the business to Bergamo, where it was located on what is now piazza Pontida, in Borgo San Leonardo. The company's international business consisted of sending bales of raw silk abroad; this rough material, obtained from Bergamesque and Venetian sericulturists, was processed in the Netherlands, England, Germany, and Russia. The company appointed agents in many major cities: Amsterdam, London, Leipzig, Moscow, and St Petersburg. When in the Napoleonic period it became possible to acquire property sequestered from the Church, the directors of the company, Francesco Blondel and Abraham Zavaritt II (Giovanni Morelli's grandfather, later known as Ambrogio, 1766–1832), expanded operations by acquiring the estate at Gorle as a silk factory. In 1812 the property was transformed by the Zavaritt family and Melli brothers into a family-owned enterprise producing its own silk textiles. (The company's activities declined in competition with the cotton industry and later ceased at the onset of the Second World War.)

Zavaritt family correspondence includes frequent discussion of the best methods for cultivating silkworms and producing silk, which became the primary source of the family's wealth. Among their friends and relatives from the Engadine, such as the Melli (or Möeli) family (for whom Morelli would later create the remarkable art collection now in the Accademia Carrara), the conversation was as often about silk as Renaissance paintings. Morelli always relished the success of the family enterprise, as shown in 1856 when he wrote to congratulate his uncle Pietro on the exceptional silk harvest,[36] and he later became a silk producer himself.

Morelli inherited his mother's love for Gorle. He always had rooms there at his disposal, on the side of the Renaissance palace facing the River Serio, with a view of the village of Pedrengo; these rooms were made available to him by his uncle Pietro. There he kept a pair of Swiss watercolors of Romanshorn Castle, near Kreuzlingen, and of the coastline of Lake Constance, as a reminder of his father's Swiss origins. He enjoyed his annual summer holidays (*villeggiatura*) at Gorle, and went there frequently to bathe nude in the river and to picnic with friends, who were a mix of patricians and visiting artists. In addition, he had his own apartment on via XX Settembre 1048, in the lower city, Bergamo Bassa.

When Morelli wrote his books under the pseudonym Lermolieff, the place at which they were composed was given as "Gorlaw," a Russianized version of Gorle.[37] A delightful portrait of Ursula by Morelli's friend Carl Adolf Mende (see Fig. 1), from July 1844, shows a slim, attractive woman, always smiling after her return to Gorle. She is dressed in Dutch fashion, with a white collar and immaculate white apron, her hair arranged in large curls, and accompanied by a vase of roses and wildflowers. Ursula considered the portrait a masterpiece, finely executed and a perfect likeness.[38] She wrote of Mende's daily routine: "He rose at five in the morning, went for a walk, had breakfast with Nané, then went to work either in the studio or the garden."[39]

Among the Swiss emigrant families who came to Bergamo, the Frizzoni, *compaesani* from the Engadine, were good friends of the Zavaritt family over several generations; their connections were strengthened by occasional marriages, as shown in the family trees (see page XXV). The sport of creating Frizzoni genealogies was called Frizzoneria at Bergamo. In order to circumvent the Austrian regime's ban on educating Protestants at Catholic schools in Italy, the Zavaritt sons and daughters went to school in Switzerland,[40] whereas the Frizzoni solved the problem in a different way. The founder of the Bergamo branch of the family, Antonio Frizzoni (1754–1835), was a self-made man who became a wealthy sericulturist.[41] He had three sons, all slightly older friends of Morelli: Antonio (1803–1876), Giovanni Leonardo (1806–1849) and Federico (1807–1893). As their mother, Anna Irmel, had died when they were young, the three Frizzoni brothers were educated primarily at home by a series of tutors (at first evangelical Swiss pastors), but with occasional periods at canton schools at Celerina and Coira in Switzerland. Giovanni and Federico studied the classics, while Antonio as the eldest son was destined to work with his father in the silk business.

Of all their tutors, it was the Saxon Dr Gustav Gündel, who took over the brothers' education in 1818, who would prove the most inspiring. As an alternative to studying in a classroom or attending university, the brothers and their tutor traveled annually, either on the Italian peninsula or to Switzerland or German-speaking countries. In May 1823 they visited the Morell family in Verona, in 1825 they made a study tour to Geneva, and another to Tuscany in 1826. Gündel introduced his charges to many of the great intellectuals of their age. In 1828 Giovanni and Federico traveled with him to universities in Germany, where they met the poet Count August von Platen. In 1829 they met the art historian Carl Friedrich von Rumohr while he was buying works for the Berlin collections. In 1830 they traveled to Dresden, then to Weimar to meet Goethe. In 1831 Antonio and Giovanni went to Vienna. These voyages were extraordinary, and in an often-reproduced contemporary engraving the brothers exude happiness: three elegantly dressed young men in top hats, standing before the Cathedral of Lausanne and holding folio albums of drawings and flowers.

A manuscript account of one of the legendary Frizzoni journeys, written by Giovanni at the age of nineteen, shows the remarkable nature of Gündel's tuition.[42] On this occasion the travels of Giovanni and Federico began on 9 May 1824, when they journeyed to Brescia early in the morning to discover an ancient temple of Hercules (*Capitolium*), which had recently been excavated in the garden of Count Gambara. (A Brescian painter and archaeologist, Luigi Basiletti, was attempting to create a circle of noble friends to sponsor the acquisition and restoration of the monument.) Later in the day they visited Count Paolo Tosio's collection at Brescia, where Giovanni confessed to preferring works of art for their subject matter rather than for their style: mythological fables rather than Catholic martyrdoms—understandable for a Protestant Swiss. It was the contemporary work that most impressed him: Bertel Thorvaldsen's Ganymede and Antonio Canova's bust of Tasso's beloved Eleonora d'Este. In his diary Giovanni gave his impressions of conversations with patrician Lombard collectors; he also recorded Gündel's characteristic expressions and preference for people rather than art, and referred to appropriate classical texts, such as Catullus when they visited Sirmione.

The trio traveled to Verona, Mantua, Florence, and Rome. Their access to distinguished private collections was remarkably easy, and each night the brothers conversed with Gündel about what they had seen. After a visit to the collection of Count Anatoly Demidov, which contained objects of great luxury—including a golden dinner service that had belonged to Napoleon—the brothers debated with their tutor about whether or not they would ever form such a collection. Giovanni remarked that he would find it difficult to invest his patrimony in such unbridled luxury and preciousness, rather than doing good with it. Gündel asked him what he meant by doing good, commenting that, after all, Demidov earned an extraordinary amount of money every day, some two thousand talleri, with which he had to do something. Federico intervened in a sarcastic tone, asking his brother whether he was going to give all his money to the poor, to which Giovanni replied that he would rather do so than spend it in such an egotistical and useless manner. Gündel argued that collecting was not a useless activity, but preserved the fine arts for posterity, and that many men made a living from the collecting activities of Count Demidov. Giovanni recorded that in such delightful conversations they spent many an evening with Gündel, who taught them how to enjoy life.

In 1832 Antonio (Fig. 7) married Orsolina Ganzoni; the following year his father gave him the family silk business to manage, as well as endowing great estates upon the other sons. In 1834 Giovanni (Fig. 8) married Clementina Reichmann (Fig. 10); for their honeymoon they took a cultural tour to Rome, Naples, and Sicily. Eventually all the Frizzoni brothers became collectors of art. The eldest, Antonio, was a remarkable businessman and a significant philanthropist, while Giovanni, to whom Morelli was closest, died tragically young at the age of forty-three, following torture at the hand of the Austrians. Federico (Fig. 9) created the finest collection of all,[43] works from which are now in many celebrated museums: Giovanni Battista Moroni's *Tailor* and Cosimo Tura's *Muse*, both treasures of the National Gallery in London, and Moretto da Brescia's *Pietà* in the Metropolitan Museum of Art in New York. In 1844 Federico married Elena de Salis, a wealthy patrician Swiss, whose family had a collection; as was customary, he took her surname in order to distinguish himself from other Frizzoneria. They lived in Bergamo and Celerina. The collection was referred to as the Frizzoni–Salis Collection and was first housed in his palace in Bergamo, next door but one to the more famous building commissioned by his brother Giovanni from the Brescian architect Rodolfo Vantini between 1825 and 1840. Federico's collection was later moved to the villa Serbelloni at Bellagio on Lake Como, another commission by Vantini, but where Federico seems to have never lived, because according to gossip he had had it built for a ballerina from Milan, of whom his wife disapproved. At that time, the villa (now the Grand Hotel Villa Serbelloni) could only be reached from the lake.

Thus, through travel in Italy, Switzerland, and Germany, Morelli and the Frizzoni brothers were independently introduced to some of the great collectors and writers of German Romanticism, an important cultural legacy for their participation in the Risorgimento. The brothers' youthful correspondence with Morelli reveals their mutual love of German and Italian culture, the emotional component of Romanticism, and the inspirational background to the Risorgimento.

CHAPTER 2

A Scientific Education in Germany

Morelli's schooling in Switzerland prepared him for tertiary study in Germany, where he attended the Ludwig-Maximilians-Universität, Munich.[1] This had all the excitement of a new university, having been reconstituted and relocated from the somewhat provincial city of Landshut to Bavaria's capital by King Ludwig I in 1826. University records show that "Johann Morell ... from Bergamo in Switzerland and the son of a landowner" enrolled in the medical faculty for the winter semester of 1833–34. He received his degree on 28 May 1836 with a thesis on the inguinal hernia, at that time an important topic in surgery.[2] Published in 1837 as *De regione inguinali*,[3] it was judged by contemporaries to be written in elegant Latin, as a clear, but not novel,[4] exposition of the muscular parts of the inguinal region, and considered to be of practical use. Understanding the topography of the human body was one of the major tasks of nineteenth-century medicine, and there was a long and distinguished tradition of the analysis of the inguinal hernia. The small innovations in Morelli's thesis were a detailed description of the origin of the fibers of the *musculus cremaster*, and the comparison of incidence and size of *musculus pyramidalis* in humans and in animals.[5]

These student years in Germany were of crucial significance for Morelli's later practice of connoisseurship. As an undergraduate he lived at Herzogspitalstrasse 9, Munich (Fig. 12).[6] A watercolor (Fig. 11) shows him surrounded by his library and collection of drawings made by friends from the Academy of Fine Arts (Akademie der Bildenden Künste)—a lively institution of even more recent foundation than the university. This depiction is characteristic of many that were commissioned by German undergraduates in the nineteenth century to demonstrate their intellectual life. Sometimes they portrayed the milieu without showing the man himself, his possessions being his still life, as seen in the Romantic representation of his studio in moonlight by Carl Gustav Carus in 1826 (Karlsruhe), or Adolph Menzel's *Bedroom of the Artist* (Berlin), or, most famous of all, Van Gogh's *Chair* (London).[7] No more eloquent visual document could be found to testify to the range of Morelli's scientific education than this watercolor, which was subsequently inscribed: "Gio. Morelli studente a Monaco, da un acquarello del tempo (manoscritt. p. 5)" (Gustavo Frizzoni had intended to reproduce it on page five of his biographical sketch of Morelli).[8] A pencil drawing by Morelli's friend Carl Adolf Mende (Fig. 13) depicts him in the same elaborate dressing gown with a heavy fur collar, though here his handsome, confident features are less idealized than in the watercolor.[9] Other portraits and caricatures from his student years (such as Figs 14 and 15) show Morelli as a charming, witty, assured young man, sensitive to literature and art, open to every experience, yet elusive.

Morelli's room as depicted in the watercolor is luxurious by undergraduate standards, bourgeois rather than bohemian. He enjoyed smoking a hookah pipe of Eastern origin, and preferred to read standing up—in his will he was to bequeath a similar standing desk to Clementina Frizzoni. Morelli's somewhat plump features, especially when compared to the slightly earlier portrait drawing by Wilhelm von Kaulbach (Fig. 14), testify to a genial indulgence in Bavarian cuisine and Pschorr beer (which he would satirize fondly in one of his earliest publications).[10] On the walls are large anatomical drawings of male nudes, seen from the front and back, and of skeletons. Also shown are more works on paper by his artist friends, one an ironic caricature by Ernst Fröhlich, pinned to the back of a door, only partly visible. The skulls of a goat, horse, and humans are placed on a shelf, with further human skulls on a table, while a set of birds' skulls is placed above the taller standing desk, a reminder of his father's ornithological collection in Verona.

It is rare to be able to reconstruct the library of a nineteenth-century intellectual and thus understand how it formed a framework for his education. In Morelli's watercolor the bookshelves are crammed with textbooks, identifiable by their bindings with those that he left to his family, and which he continued to consult throughout his life.[11] In all, some sixty titles are visible, mostly in German, published before or during the time that he was a student. Some anatomical textbooks are annotated.[12] Foremost among them are the works of the most celebrated comparative anatomist of the nineteenth century, Georges Cuvier (1769–1832), whose publications served as textbooks throughout Europe, were translated into many languages, and inspired generations of students. In the right-hand corner of the third shelf of the large bookcase is the 1831 German edition in three volumes of Cuvier's *Le règne animal* (first published in French in 1817),[13] while the four brown books with red labels over the standing desk are Cuvier's lectures on comparative anatomy, again in a German edition.[14] Two volumes on the second shelf above the writing desk are recognizable as Augustin de Candolle's *Théorie élémentaire de la botanique* (first published 1813), in which were expounded certain fundamental principles for the classification of plants.[15]

In immediate proximity are Johannes Müller's *Archiv für Anatomie, Physiologie und Wissenschaftliche Medicin, in Verbindung mit mehreren Gelehrten*

(1834), and Gabriel Gustav Valentin's *Repertorium für Anatomie und Physiologie* (1837), as well as the four volumes of Friedrich Hildebrandt's *Handbuch der Anatomie des Menschen* (1830), located on the left-hand side of the first shelf above the standing desk.

Directly behind Morelli's head (on the upper shelf) are pale-green volumes with a red stripe across the binding: Cotta's collected edition of *Goethe's Werke* (1827–30). Morelli idealized Goethe, as both a writer and scientist, and appropriated his concept of "morphology" as a term for the study of forms in paintings. In 1790 Goethe published *The Metamorphosis of Plants*, in which he recognized that the various parts of plant organs—the stem, leaf, and calyx—are variations of one archetypal form. Later Morelli was to describe his critical method as "art morphology," understanding the outward forms of art as a kind of morphology where everything can be seen on the surface, unlike anatomy, where outward morphology must be aided by dissection for a full understanding of form.

For Goethe, form is not of interest in itself, but only as a manifestation of the inner activity of the living being, the spirit. Morelli echoes Goethe when he writes that it is essentially "through the medium of *form* that we must penetrate to the spirit, in order, through the spirit, to win back to a truer knowledge of form itself."[16] Also, "For my part, I feel daily more and more convinced that it is only through unremitting study of form that one may gradually attain to understanding and recognizing the spirit which gives it life. Such studies, however, are not a matter of weeks, months or even years."[17]

The early ideas of Goethe were elaborated into the philosophy of nature, *Naturphilosophie*, a Romantic vision that influenced the study of anatomy and made some lasting contributions to the development of science. It established the major common plans or types among living organisms, for example, Goethe's demonstration that the petals of flowers are modified forms of leaves. Similarly, scientific discourse about the premaxillary bone, the *Zwischenkieferknochen*, which Goethe had (re)discovered, took place in the context of the correspondence of animal forms. On the other hand, hunting for general patterns could lead to some weird theories that were completely divorced from observation. Many passages in Morelli's critical writings bear the imprint of his acquaintance with Goethe's writings.[18]

The central figure among the Naturphilosophen was Friedrich Schelling (1775–1854). Schelling and the Naturphilosoph biologist Gotthilf Heinrich von Schubert (1780–1860) were teachers at the University of Munich, whom Morelli knew and admired. At that time Morelli was mesmerized by Schelling's charismatic personality, which is conveyed in the portrait by Stieler (Fig. 20). He was particularly fascinated by Schelling's most important statement, *Uber das Verhältnis der bildenden Künste zu der Natur* (The relation of the arts to nature) of 1807, which he subsequently translated anonymously and published.[19] Sometimes Morelli visited Schelling in his study, where the manuscripts of his lectures were available to be read or copied. There he first read Schelling's lecture on Dante, in manuscript, and was struck by the case that Schelling made for Dante as a poet-philosopher; this view was totally novel at that time and it opened up a debate on allegory and history that was to become central to the interpretation of Dante in nineteenth- and twentieth-century Europe. [20] Morelli understood the groundbreaking significance of Schelling's work, for which reason he translated the essay for publication, though he had difficulty in finding a publisher.[21]

Although Naturphilosophie was later discarded, and may seem extraordinary today, Morelli, throughout his art-historical writings, treated the philosophical precept of the relationship between form and spirit as a truism. In his *Lehrbuch der Naturphilosophie* (1809–11), Lorenz Oken states that the whole of philosophy depends upon the demonstration of the parallelism that exists between the activities of nature and the spirit.[22] Morelli drew the same relationship between outward form and the spirit, as he believed that "it is the artist's idea which gives birth to the form." Thus:

> In the declining period of art in Italy, shortly after the death of Raphael, the painter lost all individuality; hence the forms, which are the expression of character, cease to be distinctive. We have, therefore, nothing left to guide us in recognising his work but the general impression and certain external and accidental signs. These mannerisms, which are like flourishes in calligraphy, are, however, very untrustworthy guides, and of small value in identifying pictures.[23]

Accompanying Morelli's library are hundreds of scientific drawings. Most are tracings from definitive examples in the *Annales du Muséum d'histoire naturelle* (1802–07) or Cuvier's *Recherches sur les ossemens fossiles de quadrupèdes* (1812). Among them is a tracing of an elephant skeleton (Fig. 17). Cuvier's most important demonstration of his theory of the "correlation of the parts" was his claim that the essence of an animal was found in the functional integration and correlation of the constituent parts. He concluded that from a fragment you could deduce the whole. If, for instance, you found the fossilized claws of an animal, then you could postulate the form of the shoulder-blade on the basis of your extensive knowledge of comparative anatomy. There is an obvious comparison to be made with Morelli's later anatomical diagrams, where you could begin to identify a Botticelli or a Giorgione by a characteristic detail of high value—perhaps an ear, eye, or foot. A more extensive set of comparative details would allow a connoisseur to suggest an attribution. Cuvier's concept of the subordination of characters, in which some features were considered more reliable than others, was one that Morelli adopted. As a result of detailed osteological comparisons, Cuvier demonstrated that an African elephant was a different species from an Indian elephant, and different again from a fossilized elephant or mammoth. Cuvier thought that the naturalist uses fossils as a historian uses documents, to further their understanding of prehistory.

Another set of tracings shows Morelli's fascination with a newly discovered exotic animal, the tapir. This creature was difficult to classify then, and remains so now, having a pig-like nose (comparable to an elephant's trunk), horse-like hooves, cat-like curved claws, and other characteristics that resemble a wombat or kangaroo (Fig. 18). In the *Annales du Muséum d'histoire naturelle* (1804) Cuvier published fossil bones that appeared to belong to a tapir, but the unusual teeth—molars with transverse ridges—were also common to the kangaroo and the lamantin.[24] Cuvier solved the problem by establishing an empirical relationship between the fossil fragments and the skeleton of a living animal.[25]

The most numerous of Morelli's drawings are tracings of skulls from Johann Baptist von Spix's large folio album *Cephalogenesis: Sive capitis ossei structura, formatio ac significatio* (Munich, 1815). In this, inspired by Cuvier, the conservator of the zoological collections at Munich illustrated the genetic development of the head through the entire animal kingdom, from men to insects, and at all periods of a life cycle, from embryo to old age; the arresting drawings were by Christian Koeck, professor of painting at the Academy of Fine Arts in Munich (Fig. 19). Morelli knew the book thoroughly from his school days at Aarau (and continuing into his postgraduate studies in Erlangen).[26] Morelli's scientific notes, taken from the lectures of his anatomy teacher, Ignaz Döllinger, reiterate the importance of Cuvier, describing the Frenchman as "the ornament of our time ... who suddenly astonished us with a comparative anatomy of which we hardly had any concept. The history of this science will relate how this magnificent person astonished natural scientists, how on every side the desire for knowledge of the structure of animals was awakened, how numerous times he provided a precious contribution for further refinement."[27] Cuvier's influence on Morelli must have been strengthened by the fact that he was a Protestant, and also by the reputation of his salon, which was frequented by such figures as Princesse Mathilde Bonaparte, Stendhal, Chateaubriand, and Alexander von Humboldt.[28]

In his adaptation of Cuvierian principles, Morelli was to insist that all previous art historians, in deciding the authorship of a work of art, had relied on general impressions, whereas a connoisseur had to apply a rigorous method. Even when a work of art was obscured by an inept restoration, a small detail of the original paint surface might still be perceptible, and that detail might allow the connoisseur to understand the whole work and give it an attribution—as a Raphael, for instance. The rigorous comparison of a set of characteristics of high value between a known original Raphael and another painting would in eighty per cent of the case studies prove successful.

At Munich, Ignaz Döllinger (1770–1841), professor of human and comparative anatomy at Ludwig-Maximilians-Universität, and one of the most influential German biologists of the nineteenth century, became Morelli's mentor.

A caricature of this delightful, stout man, taken from an album of drawings that Morelli collected as an undergraduate, reveals a congenial, eccentric personality (Fig. 26). His ill-fitting clothes, shabby top hat, and frock coat (a form of dress that Morelli himself later assumed) testify to an indifference to elegance, as he walks along, his short hands clasped behind his back. It was Döllinger, then rector of the university, who is reputed to have encouraged Morelli to venture beyond the ordinary concerns of a medical student: when Morelli asked him which faculty he should join, he replied *"keiner"* (none), ironically meaning all rather than one.[29]

Morelli became Döllinger's assistant in anatomy, and under his direction gave lectures on the brain and made a study of comparative osteology. Many of Morelli's surviving drawings relate to this subject. Döllinger's career and publications show that he successfully went beyond *Naturphilosophie* and was able to instruct his students in observation and experiment. Initially he was concerned with the application of Schelling's ideas to physiology and embryology. He also contributed to the use and development of the microscope, an instrument Morelli later used to inspect paintings. Like many men of science, Döllinger made pronouncements about theories of the visual arts, as in *Die Baukunst und ihre Bedeutung im Staate erläutert durch die Naturkunde* (1833). Even Döllinger's scientific pronouncements, such as *Ueber den Werth und die Bedeutung der vergleichenden Anatomie* (1814), drew parallels with the visual arts.

Among the students who had slightly preceded Morelli at Munich was the Swiss (later American) Louis Agassiz (1807–1873). One of the few scientists whom Morelli quotes in his writings, Agassiz would soon prove to be a strong influence on him.[30] Towards the end of his life, the renowned zoologist recalled what it was like to study with Döllinger:

> I learned to value accuracy of observation. As I was living in his house he gave me personal instruction in the use of the microscope, and showed me his own methods of embryological investigation ... Döllinger was a careful, minute, persevering observer, as well as a deep thinker; but he was as indolent with his pen as he was industrious with his brain. He gave his intellectual capital to his pupils without stint or reserve, and nothing delighted him more than to sit down for a quiet talk on scientific matters with a few students, or to take a ramble with them in the fields outside the city, and explain to them as he walked the result of any recent investigation that he had made. If he found himself understood by his listeners he was satisfied, and cared for no further publication of his researches. I could enumerate many works of masters in our science, which had no other foundation at the outset than these inspiriting conversations.[31]

Morelli's student years were not exclusively concerned with science and academia. He forged some strong and lasting friendships, and began writing for various audiences. From Munich he published *Balvi magnus*, a parody of iconography and classical archaeology; then as a postgraduate at Erlangen he produced three more: *Miasma diabolicum*, a spoof on scientific method and Protestantism; his translation of Schelling's 1807 lecture *On the Relation of the Arts to Nature*; and an account in *Kunstblatt* of the drawings by his friend and neoclassical artist Buonaventura Genelli (of whom more later)—his first art-historical publication.[32] Each of these disparate works appeared under a different pseudonym, a foretaste of his entire publishing career. For Giovanni Morelli, disguising his identity in print became habitual from an early age, even though he was easily recognized beneath the mask by those who knew him. Pseudonymous writing was a frequent practice in the nineteenth century, and would become especially useful for political subterfuge during the Risorgimento.

With Morelli such disguise began as a form of biographical fiction. His authorship of *Balvi magnus* is acknowledged in the unique complete copy, which belonged to Genelli.[33] It is also described in a letter of 14 October 1836 to Federico Frizzoni,[34] in which he enclosed the title page, featuring a caricature of himself and the artist Ernst Fröhlich (1810–1882), ironically entitled *Dies aber sind die Leiber vom Maler und vom Schreiber* (Fig. 29). Fröhlich was a painter who frequented the Akademie der Bildenden Künste in Munich, and had acquired a reputation as a book illustrator. There were close connections between the Munich anatomists and artists, as students usually employed artists to prepare their anatomical illustrations. Also enclosed in Morelli's letter was the source of his inspiration: a copy of Wilhelm von Kaulbach's publication on the House of Fools, *Das Narrenhaus*.[35]

Balvi magnus was printed in just six days, in a print-run of twenty-five copies, and originated from the lunchtime meetings of an undergraduate drinking society.[36] At the back is a pull-out, mock-classical frieze by Fröhlich, depicting Morelli and his companions: seven painters, an architect, a lithographer, a musician, a young count, a doctor of law, and the secretary (Fig. 31). In Genelli's copy, thirteen of the fourteen names are inscribed in pencil; in order they are: Trentlin, Morell (Morelli), Klotz, Wittenbach, Dorn, Dümolin, Fröhlich, Soltau, Schirmer, *Alligator Hirsutus* (hairy alligator), Wentlin, Seidel, Fries, and Hartmann. Fröhlich portrayed them leaving a brewery before lunch.

This student confraternity, mocking the court of Ludwig I of Bavaria, was constituted as a state in which each member held office, whether as president, secretary, archivist, poet, or court painter. Whoever told an obscene joke had to buy everyone wine as a penalty. The celebration of birthdays was at the expense of the celebrant. Morelli was first given the office of court poet, and later senior medical official. Consequently, he sat to the right of the president, had to give a speech at every birthday, and chose the menu and the wine.

In the text the author describes an Etruscan vase painting discovered by Giovan Pietro Bellori in Sicily, about which there is disagreement among the experts: Johann Joachim Winckelmann and Jonathan Richardson see on the vase a representation of a great Bacchanal, such as had taken place in Sicily. Gotthold Ephraim Lessing doubts this interpretation in the *Laocoön*, and Karl Wilhelm Friedrich Schlegel suggests that the artist has represented the Marriage at Cana. Unbelievably, all this learned exegesis, and two such contradictory opinions on subject matter—one pagan, the other Biblical—relate to Fröhlich's illustration. Thus Morelli, by referring to all the sacred texts of classical art scholarship as absurdities, is writing a parody of archaeological method, as well as satirizing his artist friends.

The pamphlet concludes with further impossible interpretations of Fröhlich's Biedermeier-style advertisement for the most famous brand of beer in Munich, Pschorr, which is given as a Greek inscription. A further text in German proclaims the virtues of the brown liquid: EI DU EDLES BRAUNES BIER WIE VIEL GUTE TUGENDEN HAST IN DIR. Morelli's pamphlet, like the juvenilia of many writers, shows the beginning of his lifelong dislike of iconology, in the first of his many attacks on the pedantry of German art historians. One can only be impressed by the constancy of his position, espoused so firmly when he was still so young. Comparable ironic caricatures appealed to Count Franz von Pocci (1807–1876), who was a member of the Munich club Zwanglose Gesellschaft, founded in 1837 for and by Romantic poets. Morelli's friends Wilhelm and Hermann von Kaulbach, and the chemist who transformed art conservation, Max Joseph von Pettenkofer, were also Zwanglose. The records of this distinguished club and the satirical drawings of the festivities resemble Fröhlich's images in *Balvi magnus*.[37]

All Morelli's drinking companions are given spoof biographies, including an ironic literary self-portrait of Morelli as "Nicholaus Schäffer," aged twenty. Schäffer stresses his reluctance to take a leadership role, but claims to direct political events through effective influence over a leader, again an analysis predictive of his later career in parliament:

> Behind Balvi is his accomplice, wrapped warmly in a coat, freezing like Montgelas' greyhound. He is Nicholaus Schäffer, an ever-watchful amphibian, although it is uncertain, according to Pliny, whether he belongs to the north or the south. He had been a leader in the Corsican rebellion in '92 and '91. But afterwards he saw that a just cause triumphed, and fled to Agosta, where, through intrigues of all sorts, he soon advanced to high rank and was invested with honors, namely senior medical counselor to the State. One thing is certain, according to Stoffel, he is more responsible for the guidance of the State than the great Balvi. Marc Antonio is absolutely under his [Schäffer / Morelli's] control. When someone wishes to obtain office, he needs to press a few ducats into his hand to make it a certainty. What happened to him later is still uncertain, although Stoffel reports he was guillotined by the French in the year '87 at Paris. His whole character is revealed in his bearing, which the artist knew how to interpret superbly well.[38]

Morelli represents himself as the collaborative greyhound to Count Montgelas, Maximilian Josef de Garnerin (1759–1838), a Bavarian politician, and author of the constitution of 1808, who introduced numerous reforms, including obligatory education. Morelli's self-caricature suggests that in his teens he had taken part in revolutionary politics in northern Italy against the Austrian regime.

A few of the revelers went on to have distinguished careers, though information about "Balvi," the leader of the group, whose real name was Trentlin, remains elusive. Immediately behind Morelli, the isolated figure is August Klotz (1808–1858), a history and miniature painter, then studying with Robert von Langer at the Munich Academy. His pseudonym was Lorenz Wanzelgruber (meaning "Lawrence the bed bug who lives in a low-lying place"). Among the printer's errors at the end of the volume, the pseudonym is corrected to Wurzelgraber, "Root-digger." Both names refer to his unusual profile. At his birth, his mother asked what sex her child was, and the midwife replied: "It is a forehead."

Nothing is known of the next two men, Wittenbach and Dorn, but following them in the procession are Hermann Wilhelm Soltau (1812–1861), an artist from Hamburg who specialized in genre and architectural paintings, and the very short Fröhlich. The tall giant in the centre of the composition is Heinrich Ernst Schirmer (1814–1887), an architect who studied at the Dresden Academy between 1831 and 1834, and whose work was informed by Leo von Klenze. Later he became known for his public buildings in Norway. In Balvi's society he was known as Georg Shellebelle, meaning a bell that is prompted to bark.

The small, squat man with the thick head, who follows Schirmer, is Balvi's personal painter, known only by the pseudonym of "Alligator Hirsutus." Next to him, depicted in profile, is a plump, dissipated man, "Wentlin," probably the philosophy student Georg Wendling. The third-last figure could perhaps be one of the brothers Seidel, both landscape painters, either August (1820–1904) or Franz (1818–1903). The penultimate figure is Bernhard Fries (1820–1879), a prodigy who attended the Munich Academy from the age of fifteen. A pupil of Cornelius, he became a distinguished landscape artist. The last figure in the procession is in drag. According to Morelli it is Balvi's love, Anna Bösche, who carries an infant from their union. But if we look closely, we see this figure is a man (identified by Genelli as "Hartmann") dressed as a woman.

Fröhlich produced other drawings to illustrate *Balvi magnus*. Morelli kept these unpublished drawings in an album that he later either gave or lent to his lazy, aristocratic, Florentine friend Niccolò Antinori. The album contains affectionate caricatures by Fröhlich, in which the young Morelli, conversing with a professor, stammers "Excuse me for having contradicted you"—an accurate interpretation of his character, predicting the delight he would later take in contradicting German museum directors (Fig. 28). Another depicts

Morelli having a Spanish lesson with his friend Georg Wendling, who tutored him informally and flamboyantly so that he could read Cervantes in the original.

During this time in Munich, Morelli's typical day involved working for five hours on his thesis (to be ready for Döllinger in March), and spending the rest of his time in museums, either looking at classical sculpture in the Glyptothek, or painting in the Pinakothek, or at contemporary art in the different ateliers of his artist friends.[39] In the evenings he would visit the theater, or draw animals under a microscope. In letters he sometimes mentions his melancholic disposition, which comes and goes.

In December 1836, as a result of the publication of *Balvi magnus*, he met the Berlin-born neoclassical artist Giovanni Buonaventura Genelli (1798–1868). Genelli appreciated the satirical publication, and the pair began to meet daily, sometimes talking for eight hours at a stretch, of their shared love of Don Quixote and other subjects.

The two young men formed an intense friendship at this time.[40] Genelli had a charismatic personality. He had known and corresponded with many intellectuals, including Peter von Cornelius, Ernst Hähnel, Hermann Härtel, Karl Hummel, Franz Liszt, Ernst Rietschel, and Cosima Wagner. He appears as a bibulous, lusty personality in a novel by Paul Heyse (a Zwangloser), first published in 1860 as *Der Kentaur* and republished in 1870 as *Der letzte Kentaur.* Soon after their first encounter, Genelli drew his friend's portrait (Fig. 15), a fine drawing and the most sensitive and romantic image ever made of Morelli. Genelli principally made large contour drawings of ancient Greek subjects, inscribed with innumerable quotations from well-known works by Michelangelo and Raphael. He also made satirical caricatures of the Munich art world. At this time Morelli described him as "the greatest artistic genius of our age," comparable only to Michelangelo[41]—an opinion that he substantially revised years later.

In 1837 Genelli gave Morelli some of his drawings, beginning with a colossal self-portrait as Don Quixote. Morelli claimed that this work had a unique quality about it, conveying a hero from another world.[42] Cervantes' chivalric burlesque had become a cult novel for German artists and writers, especially Schelling, who saw the knight's battle as a symbol of the Romantic conflict between idealism and reality. Friedrich von Schlegel had rediscovered Cervantes somewhat earlier, and made him more accessible by persuading his friend Ludwig Tieck to make a translation, which Morelli owned. (In March 1838, when Morelli was about to leave Erlangen, his friend and mentor Friedrich Rückert would write a letter of introduction for him to Tieck, mentioning that Morelli hoped to learn much about Don Quixote and Shakespeare and intended to show Tieck an interesting picture of Cervantes' hero.) Morelli's article on Genelli also contains brief descriptions of other drawings of artists, the watercolor of an impoverished German artist in Rome, Michael Andersag, plucking a dove with his teeth, and the unfortunate poet Wilhelm Waiblinger, whose personality was that of a beggar, fantasist, and wastrel combined.[43]

Morelli's enthusiasm led him to pose for Genelli as the life-model for a drawing of Prometheus,[44] represented with a powerfully built, athletic body (Fig. 16), in which Morelli took a narcissistic pleasure. Genelli was fond of the composition he had created; it exists in numerous drawings, and he later contemplated using it in larger, more monumental contexts, such as for the ceiling of the Niobidensaal of the Neues Museum, Berlin, in 1850.[45] Genelli described the drawing as representing Prometheus tormented by an eagle, his lament repeated by Echo. Yet Prometheus is not represented as being severely punished for having stolen fire for mankind, as is the convention with other artists. Instead, the eagle is discretely pecking on one side of Prometheus' body, blood unseen, while Echo's admiring gaze is directed at the hero's body.

Morelli, himself a creative and rebellious personality, was also Genelli's model for other drawings of Prometheus, such as *Prometheus Making a Statue at Minerva's Command*, in which the nude Prometheus stands languidly but provocatively to one side, hand on hip, watching as Minerva enlivens the statue by placing a butterfly on its head. Genelli's neoclassical style rarely permitted such a lifelike representation of an individual, but he appears to have been mesmerized by his friend's charisma and powerful stature.

Morelli delighted in his own body. He owned a *macchina innaffiatoia*, a machine in which to take a cold shower, from which he would emerge blue in the morning, a means of improving his circulation, fighting off melancholy, and strengthening his body for whatever daily encounters might take place. In this he imitated his maternal uncle, Pietro Zavaritt, who also enjoyed a daily frisson with the Spartan ancestor of the modern shower, and who had first made the model of the machine that Morelli used daily.

Morelli's youthful enthusiasm for German neoclassical drawing predisposed him to consider collecting and studying Renaissance drawing. Before leaving Munich he purchased drawings for the Frizzoni family by Genelli, Peter von Cornelius, Eugen Napoleon Neureuther, and Friedrich Overbeck (ideas for unrealized scenes from Dante, intended for villa Massimo, Rome), as well as commissioning Kaulbach's portrait of himself (Fig. 14) and obtaining a copy of Kaulbach's print *Das Narrenhaus*. Initially Morelli showed Genelli's drawings to all his acquaintance, including Johann Georg Veit Engelhardt, Friedrich Rückert, and Bettina von Arnim, in the hope of obtaining patronage for his friend. But he later left them in the family villa at Gorle, and did not bequeath them with the rest of his collection to the Accademia Carrara, a sign that he no longer considered them of museum quality. Some drawings in the album that he later gave to Antinori depict Genelli's friends whom Morelli knew in Germany and Rome, who represented a bohemian and irreverent attitude to art that Morelli preferred to the pious and self-conscious refinement of the Nazarene artists. The album contains affectionate caricatures of Bartolommeo Pinelli, Friedrich Müller (otherwise known as Maler Müller), landscape artist Joseph Anton Koch, Johann Martin von Rohden, Philipp Friedrich Rabe, and Michael Andersag.[46] The intensity of Morelli's relationship with Genelli and his family appears to have waned after Morelli returned to Italy in 1840, for although they corresponded until Genelli's death, they rarely met again.[47]

Other artists, such as Carl Adolf Mende (1807–1857), enjoyed a friendship with Morelli that lasted beyond his undergraduate years. A caricature by Fröhlich represents Mende as a hunter, standing at a rudimentary washstand, carrying a gun and a feline game bag, and wearing his habitual beret (Fig. 27). Mende was born at Leipzig and his first degree was in law, but he later turned to painting, and from 1828 resided in Munich, where he concentrated on genre and history pictures, often choosing political subjects interpreted from a liberal viewpoint. His late decision to become a painter meant that he never completely achieved the technical expertise he desired. In the 1840s he spent many months in Italy, returning every year to stay with Morelli. Mende took his own life in 1857, drowning in the river Weser.

□

After graduating at Munich, Morelli undertook further specialization in comparative anatomy on a *wissenschaftliche Reise* to Friedrich-Alexander-Universität in Erlangen, in the Protestant region of Franconia in northern Bavaria.[48] He enrolled in the faculty of *Naturwissenschaften* on 9 November 1837 (at the age of twenty-one), describing himself as a doctor of medicine and the son of a landowner from Bergamo.[49] He intended to stay for three weeks, but remained for seven months,[50] leaving in the spring of 1838. The most interesting among his scientific professors was Lorenz Oken's successor, Rudolf Wagner, who had earlier studied with Cuvier in Paris. Morelli owned Wagner's textbook. At Erlangen Morelli lived in a summerhouse where the poet Count August von Platen had lived as a law student in the summer of 1824, at Burgbergstrasse 92, now known as the Platenhäuschen and home to the local history museum. It was a student's pad, with one room on the ground floor and another on the upper floor, joined by an outside staircase.

At Erlangen Morelli made the acquaintance of two extraordinary intellectuals: Friedrich Rückert (1788–1866), a poet who was professor of oriental languages (Fig. 21), and Johann Georg Veit Engelhardt (1791–1855), a Bavarian politician and Protestant professor of theology and church history (Fig. 22), who encouraged Morelli's journalism as a way to influence political opinion.[51] He corresponded and enjoyed lengthy friendships with both men (though neither correspondence survives). Rückert was a writer who remains in our consciousness as the creator of some of the most memorable love poetry in any language, some of which was set to music by Gustav Mahler as the *Rückert-Lieder* and *Kindertotenlieder* (Songs on the death of children). Morelli described him as a "friend and connoisseur of all that is beautiful" (Freund und Kenner alles Schönen).[52] Then aged forty-nine, and huge in bodily stature as well as intellect, he was the primary Hellenist on the faculty at Erlangen, and he discussed his latest manuscript with the young Italian: a work in progress about the heart-breaking medieval Persian love story of Rostam and Suhrab.[53] For two months Morelli visited Rückert weekly for tutorials in poetry and oriental languages, deeply impressed by his personality.

At Erlangen Morelli wrote his second satirical publication, which bore a long title featuring an even more elaborate set of pseudonyms: *Das "Miasma diabolicum," das ist ein Aufruf an die christlich germanischen Gemeinen, von Traugott Gotthilf Schneck, mit Hülfe der christlichen Brüder Dr. Jonathan Kappelmeier, Physicus, und Fürchtegott Munkeler, Apotheker, herausgegeben mit Anmerkungen und einem gedrängten Lebensabrisse Schneck's versehen durch Nicolaus Schäffer, cand. Theologiae.*[54] Only three copies are known to exist.[55] The book, some 100 pages long, was published in Strasbourg in 1839, by the famous entomologist Henri-Rudolphe-Gustave Silbermann on commission to booksellers Schmidt and Grucker, at their shop on the Grosse Gewerbslaube. "Schneck" (The Snail), and "Nicholaus Schäffer" (Nicholas the Shepherd, the theologian), were Morelli's pseudonyms from his undergraduate drinking society. The text is presented as an edition of an incomplete manuscript with copious and pedantic footnotes by the author and editor that spoof academic conventions: Schneck has been writing the text for more than forty years, and is still revising it at the time of his death; at Schneck's deathbed, Schäffer agrees to publish the work. Despite this satirical tone, the theme of death had a deep personal significance to the young Morelli, who was the only one of four siblings to survive infancy, his three brothers dying during epidemics of typhus or cholera.

While writing, Morelli sent drafts to Genelli; by mid-February 1838 the manuscript was almost complete (only the third section was missing, although the characters had different names, as when "Barbara Pappelmeier" later metamorphosed as "Apollonia"). Genelli made the obvious comparison with Hogarth and Chodowiecki. But unlike Hogarth, who critiqued the libertine lives of the aristocracy, Morelli satirizes the conjugal family life of extreme Protestantism, the Mystics, their cultural prejudices against Shakespeare, Raphael, and Socrates, as well as the inefficacy of their scientific research, and their inability to conceptualize unbiased enquiry. Some of Morelli's uncomfortable experiences of Protestantism, both in Germany and Italy, lie behind the writing, for Genelli remarked: "In order to draw such characters well, you have to have known and studied vermin, which I have not had the opportunity of doing."[56] All Morelli's writings include caricatures of his friends, even if we cannot always identify them.[57]

Schneck's booklet opens with a parody of a sermon by a fundamentalist Protestant pastor. The author promises to present a new discovery concerning the origin of a modern plague, the *miasma* (or *cholera morbus*), but before doing so wishes to discuss worldly concerns that are contrary to the true nature of the German brotherhood. Nothing is more alien to Christianity, he claims, than the study of ancient pagan literature, which cripples the human heart. For what can a baptized Christian soul say, if every hardened sinner today accepts as a model for life the godless heathen, Socrates, who was fearless before justice at the time of his death?

Schneck is obsessed with a particular Morellian theme: recognition, or in this instance how to identify God's chosen few from the children of the world (*Weltkinder*). Unfortunately, he recognizes that the elect and the children of the world all have the same vital organs: a brain, heart, kidneys, spleen, and so forth. Yet it is possible to know what sort of person a man is from his forehead, where the truth is clearly written, because the outer appearance of a man mirrors his soul. Even in the twilight it is thus possible to recognize a true Christian brother from a non-believer. But a much surer way of telling is that a Christian emits a certain Christian odor, while a sinner has a completely different smell. The devout man may also be recognized by his clothing: he wears a black silk short coat over a longer half-length one of the same cloth, and a black velvet hat with a broad brim to protect his eyes from seeing the world and all its sins, while a small white handkerchief is all that a pious man needs for decoration. At the same time he is yellowish, pallid, and lean, with a small, unprepossessing nose, and an extremely large foot.

On the other hand, sinners exhale a stinking gas, which may be avoided by purchasing the Christian Air Visor or plague mask. This is illustrated in two engravings, depicting Apollonia wearing an adult version, and her daughter, Johanna, with an infant's model (Fig. 30). Three successive platelets that lie in the piping of the mouth of the visor give the air a paradisical purity. These Christian Air Visors may be purchased in Munich and Berlin, but the best supplier is Herr Ruprecht Flachkopf (literally "Flathead") in Nuremberg.

The third and last section of the *Miasma* is a forty-page biography of Schneck, purportedly extracted from a longer work by Nicolaus Schäffer. The book ends with a series of illustrations, described in captions rather than in the text, culminating in an image of Schneck in his coffin.

CHAPTER 3
A Young Man Abroad

Although Morelli had qualified as a doctor, he never practiced as one, and could become indignant when described as a medical practitioner. For instance, when Bettina von Arnim asked him "Are you a medical doctor?" His answer was: "I have left the practice of medicine behind and am only concerned with anatomy and the natural sciences."[1] His passion for anatomy and aversion to practicing medicine were consistent throughout his life. Only on occasion would he would give advice to family and friends on medical matters, such as when he accompanied his Risorgimento comrade Gino Capponi to Germany to consult an eye doctor. In his later years Morelli reacted angrily if his method of attribution was considered a medical one, as shown when he was reading an article written by Anton Springer in 1881: Morelli's annotations to the article mostly consisted of "*Bene*" or "*Vero*," but when he read that Springer thought he had practiced medicine ("Auch Morelli hat in seiner Jugend den ärztlichen Beruf ausgeübt"), he objected with furious question marks.[2]

All the evidence confirms that Morelli scientific interest was in comparative anatomy: the scientific books that he bought and copiously annotated, not only as an undergraduate but throughout his life, are almost exclusively concerned with anatomy. Apart from his thesis, there are no medical notes about the human body, and no clinical studies. His notes were carefully kept in book form, reworked as handbooks for his own use in comparative anatomy, never medicine.

Other German authorities on the visual arts, such as architect Gottfried Semper (1803–1879), were also inspired by Cuvier's comparative anatomy in their search for a systematic scheme of interpretation.[3] For Semper, the great innovation that Cuvier had introduced was to shift the emphasis from description by identifiable limbs of a body, and classification by description, to classification by the function performed. In practice, however, Cuvier's method did not rely on the observation of a few details. Like Morelli, he emphasized that a very extensive knowledge was first required. At that time the distinction between an artificial classification system based on a few characters, and a natural one based on the comparison of many characters, was fully appreciated. As Morelli stated, "It has been asserted in Germany that I profess to recognise a painter and to estimate his work solely by the form of the hand, the finger-nails, the ear, or the toes. Whether this statement is due to malice or ignorance I cannot say; it is scarcely necessary to say that it is incorrect."[4]

Many have found it irresistible to follow the distinguished historian Carlo Ginzburg, who in an important article likened Morelli's method to that of Sherlock Holmes.[5] The explanation may be that Morelli and Sir Arthur Conan Doyle shared a common antecedent: Cuvier. In Conan Doyle's short story *The Five Orange Pips*,[6] Sherlock Holmes states:

> the ideal reasoner ... would, when he has once been shown a single fact in all its bearings, deduce from it not only all the chain of events which led up to it but also all the results which would follow from it. As Cuvier could correctly describe a whole animal by the contemplation of a single bone, so the observer ... should be able to accurately state all the other ones, both before and after.

For nineteenth-century intellectuals, Cuvier was omniscient. Since the publication of Morelli's tracings after Cuvier, Ginzburg introduced Cuvier into his account of Morelli's method, gradually excluding Conan Doyle.[7]

Morelli later became acquainted with one of the clearest nineteenth-century discussions on the relationship of "trivial character" to classification, as given by Charles Darwin in *The Origin of Species* (1859), whom Morelli mentions in his later writings on the collections of the Munich and Dresden galleries. As Darwin stated: "The importance for classification, of trifling characters, mainly depends on their being related and correlated with many other characters of more or less importance ... In practice ... if they [naturalists] find a character nearly uniform, and common to others, they use it as one of high value."[8]

□

Morelli's publishing pranks during his undergraduate and postgraduate years were by no means at the expense of his more serious pursuits, and the young Swiss-Italian from Bergamo had made a striking impression on his teachers at Erlangen. When his time there was drawing to a close, in the spring of 1838, Friedrich Rückert wrote a number of letters of introduction for him to friends in Paris. One was to another pupil, who had studied Sanskrit with him, Otto Mündler,[9] thereby initiating a significant friendship with Morelli.

After leaving Erlangen, Morelli spent five weeks traveling in Germany. Firstly he visited the collection of Johann Friedrich Meckel the Elder and his anatomical dynasty in Halle. He went on to Dresden and then to Berlin for several months, where he enjoyed an extremely successful social and intellectual life. Equipped with the letters of introduction from Rückert, he enjoyed the company of art historians and writers, whose conversations he described in his letters to Genelli.

Morelli wrote considerably more than he ever published. Sadly, little of the unpublished work survives, except for his correspondence. Nevertheless, he was a brilliant letter-writer, and in this genre more than any other his literary ability emerges. His letters reveal his aspirations to be a playwright and satirist, modeling himself on Vittorio Alfieri (1749–1803)—an ambition that emerged even before he went to university, as Alfieri's autobiography was his favorite book at both school and university. Alfieri, like Morelli, lost his father when young, was sent away to school at the age of nine, fed his creativity from a melancholy disposition, and enjoyed incessant traveling and many passionate love affairs. When in Paris between 1838 and 1840, Morelli wrote a number of satirical sketches, including one of the Munich contemporary art world, centered around the German writer, philosopher and theologian Johann Joseph von Görres (1776–1848), and his friends, *Die Sage von den drei Schwestern*; and another on the connoisseur: *Der Kunstkenner*. Neither survives.

At times his letters contain theatrical vignettes of famous figures, as if in preparation for one of his comedies, such as his conversations with Bettina von Arnim (1785–1859). Morelli met this renowned figure soon after arriving in Berlin, a siren even in her fifties, still celebrated for her association (as a child) with Goethe.[10] "The ingenious Bettina," whom Morelli described as the eighth wonder of the world, lived on the second floor of an extraordinary palace on the Unter den Linden, which belonged to the Polish Count Raczyński. Here she received visitors while seated before a monument to Goethe, depicted heroically semi-nude (Fig. 36). Dressed in black tails, Morelli first called on her in June 1838, with an introduction from her poet brother, Clemens Brentano, whom he had come to know while studying in Munich.

Bettina—vibrant, only five feet tall, and resembling her brother—greeted Morelli flirtatiously, and conversed while lying on a divan, a black rug over her legs, before a copy of Correggio's ecstatic painting of Jupiter and Io. Brentano had published the visions of an Augustinian nun, Anna Katharina Emmerich (1774–1824), in 1833, while in his pietistic phase;[11] at first the conversation was about this nun, with whom Brentano had spent four years as she recounted her visions to him. (Bettina, who had not grown up with her brother, was skeptical of the nun's holiness.) She then focused on Morelli. "Are you a doctor?" she asked, then, more provocatively: "Hopefully you are also an admirer of homeopathy?" Everyone, she believed, should be concerned with the promotion of this (now discredited) system of healing developed by Samuel Hahnemann (1755–1843). Morelli diverted her chatter with the ironic observation that in her recent book, *Goethe's Correspondence with a Child (Goethes Briefwechsel mit einem Kinde*, 1835), her objective approach to nature had played an important part. Bettina replied that in those letters her views on nature were unconsciously expressed, for she had only been a girl of eighteen when she wrote them, and could give no personal justification for the philosophical views to which she had inadvertently given voice. For Morelli, Bettina was a naïve admirer of Goethe, one who little understood the success of her own epistolary novel. Bettina drew the conversation to an end by saying that she was due at court, but wished Morelli would visit often. Suspecting that he was being dismissed without reason, Morelli departed and concealed himself in a nearby bakery, but was reassured to see Bettina leave, dressed formally, in a carriage.

On a second visit, Bettina's very pretty daughters, Gisela and Armgart, eleven and seventeen years old respectively, were also present, as was the young Mayer Carl von Rothschild. At first their conversation was about philosophy; it then turned to painting, specifically to two French artists whom Bettina especially admired: Paul Delaroche (1797–1856) and Claude Joseph Vernet (1714–1789). Bettina's daughters hoped to engage the heart of the young Rothschild, whom Bettina praised as a kind of "Schelmuffsky" for his many good deeds, his energy, his knowledge, and his wealth—an allusion to the hero of Christian Reuter's 1696 novel whose eponymous title plays on the word *Schelm* (fool or jester). This was a backhanded compliment, as the Schelmuffsky of the novel is a boaster and a charming liar. Eventually the two young men took their leave, Morelli accompanying Rothschild back to his princely abode for an hour's conversation.

On their third visit, on 23 June 1838, Bettina warmly received the young hero (as Morelli described himself) and showed him her drawings and early musical compositions, including *Zu Faust*, in her atelier. The family was at ease with him, the daughters being preoccupied with charming the young Rothschild, while Morelli concentrated on their mother. In exchange for seeing Bettina's cartoons, Morelli ran back home to fetch some drawings that Buonaventura Genelli had given him as a present: a portrait of himself (Fig. 15), a colossal head of Don Quixote, and *Apollo Comforting the Grieving Shepherds*.[12] Bettina was deeply impressed, and recommended patrician patronage for the artist Genelli. Morelli concluded that Bettina was more courageous and imaginative than her brother, and as extravagant in love as in hatred.[13]

At Genelli's request, Morelli provided a lengthy description of another visit to Bettina, when writing from Paris on 12 November 1838. Upon his arrival, Bettina drew his attention to two landscape paintings by her friend Carl Blechen (1798–1840). Morelli saw a picture of a sad young monk seated in front of the sea,[14] which failed to impress him as he did not like transience in painting. Nevertheless, the formality of the occasion and the presence of Rothschild forced Morelli to pronounce it a masterpiece. Rothschild asked Morelli somewhat cheekily if he was a connoisseur (Sind Sie auch ein Kunstkenner?). Morelli wrote: "but I gave no reply, and the young hero threw a smiling glance at Bettina, who was turning a diamond ring on her little finger."[15] "Come with me," said Bettina, as she rose from her armchair, looking at Morelli with a smile, "I must tell you a story that will move you." She threw herself on a sofa and asked Morelli to sit next to her. "I have a special predilection for the Italians," she said, pushing her sidelocks behind her ears.

The same letter to Genelli contains a very lengthy story about Blechen. Originally trained as a bank teller, he preferred art to commercial transactions, and had slowly made his name as an artist, first as a theater designer and later as a landscape painter. He was married to a dressmaker, Henriette Boldt, ten years older than he, but found the marriage unbearable, becoming increasingly melancholic and addicted to tobacco and alcohol. Something of Blechen's dissolute depression is conveyed in Carl Steffeck's portrait sketch of him at a night-time life-drawing class (Fig. 24). Despite Bettina's attempts at a homeopathic cure, Blechen was committed to a psychiatric institution. In Bettina's efforts to save Blechen, she took Morelli (for advice) to the home of the writer Ludwig Tieck and to the extraordinary architect's house of Wilhelm Stier; this was the so-called Stierburg, at Auf dem Carlsbade 11, Berlin-Schöneberg, then just built.

From these conversational vignettes, we see that Morelli moved with ease among artists and intellectuals, despite his distaste for Blechen and Tieck. These letters contain the first Socratic conversational dialogues that prefigure Morelli's later ironic anecdotes as Lermolieff, in which a fictional Russian, his alter ego, engages in conversation with a younger pupil. In fact, Morelli's acquaintance with Bettina von Arnim was more intimate than his letters to Genelli reveal. As he wrote years later, in 1851, to his Florentine friend Niccolò Antinori:

> How I would love to see the Arnim family again, to pass an evening with you in their company. The mother has a good heart, and as a woman she is a real curiosity. When I saw them, Armgart was a beautiful girl, but now would be old, whereas Gisela would have become beautiful. You can create havoc with them; in their house you can commit madness, and you would be certain to never displease them. With them I was as if in my own home. Give them my warmest wishes, and tell them that I would very much like to see them again in Italy, to act as their cicerone.[16]

Morelli's circle in Berlin was wider than is revealed by his correspondence with Genelli. He also knew art historians, scientists, and artists, starting with art historian Gustav Friedrich Waagen (1794–1868), whom he characterized as "an excellent guide, a gossip who always knows what is going on, whether in the palaces or on the street, whether with the great or small, and ... very learned in the history of the Fine Arts."[17] Geologists came next, presaging Morelli's later studies with Louis Agassiz: Alexander von Humboldt, "the most celebrated man in human society today," geographer Carl Ritter, "one of the most distinguished living scientists," and geologist Baron de Buck. Among contemporary artists, he valued Peter von Cornelius highly, followed by the workshops of Ferdinand Kyss and the otherwise unknown portrait painter Pegass. Never forgotten was the incomparable poet Rückert, and he also read the poetry of Goethe, Schiller, Uhland, Hölty, and Heine. Morelli's favorite coffee house was the Spargnapani on Unter den Linden, managed by a Swiss and the chic rendezvous for foreign tourists in Berlin. Morelli also frequented the Museum für Naturkunde (Natural History Museum) and the fish-market, and spent time in the prostitutes' quarter, the Königsmauer.

It was during his time in Berlin that Morelli was introduced to connoisseurship (*Kunstkennerschaft*).[18] In the famous collection of the distinguished publishing house G. Reimer was a painting of the Adoration of the Shepherds, which the reigning sovereigns of the German art-historical world, Gustav Friedrich Waagen and Karl Eduard von Liphart, claimed to recognize as an authentic Correggio. But an art historian who knew more about Correggio than the others, Carl Friedrich von Rumohr, was of another opinion, and he took Morelli aside to explain why Reimer's painting was not by Correggio. Morelli concluded that these Berlin professors were good people (*tüchtige Leute*), but that no judgment could be made without actually seeing the painting, and, in any case, what did it matter whether the Adoration was by Correggio or by one of his pupils, if it was beautiful?[19] (The painting has disappeared from Correggio literature, so Rumohr may have been right.)[20] Of course, Morelli would later revise his opinion as to whether attribution mattered.

From Berlin, Morelli went to Switzerland, to meet his mother and aunt at his father's hometown of Wöschbach (now Kreuzlingen).[21] Then in August and September he met up with the scientist Louis Agassiz (whom he had met in April, at Neuchâtel, finding him extremely friendly and learning much from him in conversation).[22] Agassiz took a group of six students, including Morelli, into the Bernese Oberland to study the Aar, Rosenlaui, and Grindelwald glaciers. This field research involved observations and experiments that would lead Agassiz to define his enduring concept of an Ice Age. The party left Neuchâtel on 12 August on foot, passing through Interlaken and Brienz, arriving at the Grimsel Pass, where days were spent observing the glaciers of the Rhône, Aar being the principal point of observation.[23] The extraordinary landscape is depicted in a lithograph by Hercule Nicolet, showing the hut in which Agassiz and his team lived, known ironically as the Hôtel des Neuchâtelois (Fig. 25). A vast mountainous circle surrounds the Aar glacier. On 9 September the party returned to Neuchâtel and, after twelve days' rest, set out towards Mont Blanc, for the same purpose of observation. One of the other participants on the trip, Agassiz's illustrator Joseph Dinkel, recalled:

> We went not the ordinary way of travelers; Agassiz wanted to see certain parts of the mountains and glaciers of great interest to him. We came to very isolated places and deprived of every comfort we had to sleep on straw and the floor in small rooms and had to live on eggs and potatoes which gave us very little strength to climb up mountains and this lasted three days until we came to Trient near Martigny. The professor cared little for all the privations and fatigues and was always cheerful as he could make many observations of importance to him. We all returned to Neuchâtel on 30 September.[24]

Agassiz published his observations in his *Études sur les glaciers* (1840). The concluding chapters describe "the ancient extension of the Swiss glaciers, and … the former existence of an immense, unbroken sheet of ice, which had once covered the whole northern hemisphere."[25]

Only one letter survives from the extensive scientific correspondence between Agassiz and Morelli. Dated 26 July 1843, written in Lausanne and addressed by Agassiz to his "Lieber Freund," it includes two articles on alpine geology, with which Morelli had assisted in some way.[26] "Take them," Agassiz says, "like a twin's alter ego," as his way of defining their relationship (*nehmen Sie beyde als einen Zwillings alter ego auf*). If only we knew more. During that summer together in Switzerland they formed a friendship, and Agassiz's teaching made a deep and lasting impression on Morelli.[27] Guided by their influential teacher from Munich, Ignaz Döllinger, both men had turned away from medicine to study comparative anatomy, and thereafter applied the principles learnt from a study of comparative anatomy to the definition of new subjects.[28] After undertaking this exhilarating and physically demanding fieldwork with Agassiz, Morelli saw how the methods of his Munich teachers could be successfully applied to another discipline, brilliantly developed by the young Swiss scientist whose friendship he found inspiring.

The influence of Agassiz, as well as other scientists such as Cuvier and Darwin, combined with his developing interest in visual art and exposure to art historians of the calibre of Carl Friedrich von Rumohr, led Morelli to look at the art of the Italian Renaissance with an anatomist's eye. He found much greater satisfaction in the forms (*Gestalten*) of a Raphael, a Correggio, a Titian, a Michelangelo, or a Giulio Romano, than in the comparative demonstrations of osteology.[29]

□

In October 1838 Morelli went to Paris, where he remained until April 1840. His main purpose was to study at the Muséum National d'Histoire Naturelle in the Jardin des Plantes, where Cuvier had once lived. Morelli left no trace of his presence in the extensive archive there, suggesting his relationship was an informal one. Cuvier had died on 13 May 1832, but the Parisian scientific world was still under his spell. There can be no better introduction to Morellian thinking today than a visit to the museum's remarkable galleries dedicated to comparative anatomy and palaeontology (*Anatomie comparée et Paléontologie*). Many of the museum's extraordinary skeletons of animals that remain on display today were crucial in early scientific debates about comparative anatomy, and were the ones that Morelli himself studied, such as Cuvier's elephant. The present display is about comparative classification, and at times selects just those important, but seemingly minor, details that Morelli considered so significant, such as the classification of carnivores by means of the holes at the base of their necks.

Morelli fell in love with Paris and its museums, especially the Louvre, but disliked the French—a Napoleonic hangover from his youth in Verona.[30] His most informative and frank letter from this period was written to his boyhood friend Federico Frizzoni on Christmas Day 1838.[31] It begins with an enthusiastic account of the magical effect that Veronese's *Marriage at Cana* had upon him, as well as his reception of other paintings in the Louvre by Raphael, Ruisdael, Claude,

Poussin, Zurbarán, and Murillo, making it evident that he was as passionate about sixteenth- and seventeenth-century European painting as about the Italian Renaissance. Morelli's love of Baroque art was stimulated by Otto Mündler (1811–1870),[32] whom he met soon after his arrival (armed with one of Rückert's letters of introduction from Erlangen) and with whom he visited the Louvre frequently. Yet Morelli never wrote about the Baroque, and never managed to like Caravaggio. He later wrote that Mündler was "not only a great connoisseur of paintings, but he has a soul that is capable of the most noble aesthetic enthusiasm."[33] Morelli's enthusiasm for Veronese was kindled at Dresden in 1838, when the drama of the artist's historical imagery would strike a chord with his own playwriting. In 1838, *The Marriage at Cana* was the most magical of any work of art that he had ever seen, one that gave him indescribable pleasure: "No other painting until now has had such magic for me" (Kein Bild hat noch bis jetzt einen solchen Zauber für mich gehabt).[34] He visited the Louvre daily, and went to concerts and operas in the evening, enjoying works by Gluck, Rossini, and Mozart (such as *Don Giovanni*).

During these years, Mündler was working on his masterly publication *Essai d'une analyse critique de la notice des tableaux italiens du Musée National du Louvre* (1850). In this, he criticized the attributions in the first catalogues of the Louvre, written by Frédéric Villot. Mündler's critical essay was seminal for Morelli's later books on German and Italian galleries. During Morelli's Parisian sojourn he also met Ralph Wornum, later keeper of the National Gallery in London,[35] who was then working on the first catalogue of the London collection, published in 1847.[36] Wornum's catalogue was regarded as a masterpiece, and owed much to his friendship with Mündler, and maybe to Morelli. All too little is known of the interactions between these three gifted art historians—Mündler, Morelli, and Wornum—at this critical Parisian period in their development, over the course of two years.

In Paris Morelli was more concerned with the study of art and literature than with science, even though he joined the French geological society, where Agassiz was presenting his new theories.[37] Morelli also made the acquaintance of scientists, politicians, and writers, such as François Arago, Alexandre Dumas, and Félix Savart, but none seems to have been as influential on him as those he knew in Germany.

On Christmas Day 1838, Morelli reflected on his life and what might lie ahead. To Federico Frizzoni he declared how proud he was to be an Italian, and how much he looked forward to his return to his homeland. He had not yet thought of marriage (Ans heiraten hab ich noch nicht gedacht), and enjoyed the solitude of his existence, which had always been a part of his life.[38] Any woman would have to have the patience of Job to put up with him, he remarked.

When Morelli did eventually return to Italy, in 1840, it would be to pursue a life on the land, although he also aspired to be a playwright. It was decades later that he would draw upon his youthful experiences in Germany and France, when forming his definition of *la scienza dell'arte*, as an instrument for preserving the patrimony of Italy.

CHAPTER 4

A Return to Italy

In 1840 Morelli returned to make Italy his permanent home, a decision inspired by a deep sense of patriotism. With remarkable purpose and ease he made friends with a group of distinguished Florentines: the legendary linguist and historian Gino Capponi (1792–1876), the poets and dramatists Giovanni Battista Niccolini (1782–1861, Fig. 34), Giuseppe Giusti (1809–1850), and his future friend in the Italian Senate, Giovanni Battista Giorgini (1818–1908). Capponi (Fig. 32) coined the often-repeated definition of Morelli as a man with an Italian soul, but of German education (*italiano d'animo e tedesco di studii*).[1] Morelli went to Florence to satisfy his ambition to be a writer, and to study Tuscan, the preferred model for founding a new Italian language. The latter was one of the shared ambitions of Risorgimento intellectuals, an ambition especially dear to two writers who became Morelli's good friends: Francesco De Sanctis (1817–1883, Fig. 33) and Alessandro Manzoni (1785–1873). The question of a new language for a united Italy continued through the Risorgimento, and was paralleled by Morelli's determination to represent the visual heritage of Italy in newly created secular museums.

For his newly found Florentine friends, Morelli translated German authors, principally Schelling's compelling lectures and Johann Peter Eckermann's conversations with Goethe (*Gespräche mit Goethe*, 1836). In return they read to Morelli drafts of what they were writing: Niccolini's play *Arnaldo da Brescia*, and the first drafts of Capponi's thoughts on education in Lugano, the *Frammento,*[2] a small masterpiece, which he dictated and published anonymously.[3] In letters to Morelli on 30 September 1842 and 17 November 1845, Capponi described the half-satiric text of the *Frammento*, which he was sending to the printer without his name on it (*senza nome*). To Cesare Cantù, Capponi confessed that he felt shabby writing anonymously, but did so as his work was only a fragment.[4]

Writing to Niccolini from Bergamo, on 15 September 1841,[5] Morelli enclosed translations of extracts of writings (*scrittarelli e pensierucci*) by Goethe, a very interesting article defending Manzoni's tragedy *Carmagnola,*[6] and a translation of Goethe's aphorisms from Lawrence Sterne. As always, Morelli was fostering cross-cultural relations between Italy and Germany, and at that moment was enthused by a recent edition of the writings of the Dominican heretic and philosopher Giordano Bruno, edited by Adolph Wagner in Leipzig (1830). All were already known to Niccolini, so Morelli sent an unpublished poem by his friend Count Secco Suardo.[7] As Morelli explained in later years to Niccolini's perspicacious biographer, the formidable scholar and politician Atto Vannucci,[8] their friendship cooled after Morelli's review of *Arnaldo da Brescia* in the *Allgemeine Zeitung*. Morelli received some fifteen letters from Niccolini, of which he gave eight to Vannucci for his book, excluding those that were sour in judgment of their mutual friends. Those eight are published in Vannucci's biography, *Ricordi della vita e delle opere di G.-B. Niccolini* (1866).[9] They contain Niccolini's ironic dismissal of Morelli's articles in Florentine newspapers, stating that they would be available only in coffee houses, to be destroyed by butter and cigar smoke, or crushed in people's pockets. Niccolini promised to find a worthy outlet for Morelli's translation of Schelling's essay on Dante, which eventually appeared in his own writings.[10]

Capponi suffered from a debilitating eye illness; by 1840 it became difficult for him to read, a condition that caused him great pain.[11] In the spring of 1841 Morelli, by then *amicissimo* with Capponi, took him on an impossible mission to find a cure with Philipp Franz von Walther, an eye surgeon in Munich. Capponi, accompanied by his children, also met Morelli's Munich friends from undergraduate days, his anatomy teacher Döllinger, the mystic Görres, and the philosopher Schelling.[12] But Capponi returned disappointed, saying that medicine helped only with small ailments, never the big ones.[13] Morelli confided to Capponi his own health problems, as he did to other friends, provoking concern. At the age of twenty-six, in the full vigor of youth, what could be the cause of such frequent violent illnesses, referred to by Morelli as attacks of the liver and gastric fever, alleviated only by spending weeks in bed?[14] Was it, Capponi speculated, that Morelli led too sedentary a life, interspersed with intense physical activities such as long walks in the mountains? Or was it that he could not cope with the heat? Or what? As Morelli matured, references to these mysterious bouts of illness became less frequent, though he suffered frequently from a cough—the penalty for smoking cigars.

Capponi had introduced Morelli to the Baron Sigismondo Trecchi and Alessandro Manzoni, both of whom Morelli visited in Milan.[15] Trecchi occupied an elegant bachelor nest, where he drank chocolate surrounded by beautifully bound books, English prints, and two little Scottish dogs. At seven o'clock one evening in November 1841, Morelli and Trecchi met up at the Caffè delle Belle Arti to visit Manzoni together. Climbing the stairs to his apartment they encountered an abbot descending. They were received by Manzoni and his wife and children. Trecchi conversed with the family, leaving Morelli free to engage Manzoni, who discoursed at length on the assertion that the Tuscan language is the only language if you want to write in Italian, although it is difficult for a Milanese to know it well. Other dialects are too far away from the prototype and are understood only by those who speak them. The conversation then moved to non-Italian literature. For Manzoni, Goethe was the great hero of modern literature, while Schiller had little historical validity, especially *Don Carlos*. Like Morelli, he hated the French colonizers of Italy, and believed that nothing in modern French literature would last beyond their century.[16] Reading Morelli's letters, Capponi recognized his young friend's ability to write urbane comic scenes mixed with affection and reverence, which he seems to have tossed off in an afternoon, his letters being far more successful than his plays.

Among his Florentine friends, Morelli was closest to the Marchese Niccolò Antinori (1818–1882), a handsome, intelligent, and creative younger son of an aristocratic Florentine family. The two enjoyed an intimate relationship, demonstrated by Morelli's surviving letters, written between 1842 and Antinori's death.[17] A humorous play by Morelli about the Antinori family is in the family archive, entitled *È meglio imbattersi, o cercarsi apposta? Proverbio in tre atti*. As with his other Florentine friends, the two men discussed German literature; with Morelli's encouragement Antinori made a rather pedestrian translation of Goethe's tragedy *Egmont*, which he dedicated to Morelli,[18] and Morelli gave Antinori his album of drawings and caricatures collected when he was an undergraduate in Munich. Antinori was an artist, but an inactive one, and none of his works survive. He occupied various honorary posts, such as the presidency of the Accademia di Firenze, in which official role he collaborated with Morelli on exhibitions and the promotion of conservation. The only likeness of Antinori that survives is in the 1834 group family portrait by Giuseppe Bezzuoli (Fig. 35), in which Niccolò is portrayed as the languid, handsome youth seated on the far left.[19]

In early spring of 1842, Morelli wrote of his ecstasy at being in Rome; this was his first letter of many to Antinori:

> Rome is the only city where an artist can live as an artist, free, without white gloves, and without fear that his own actions will provoke gossip. The ruins are so colossal, and marvellous, the contours of Rome exude such a classical air, they are so serious and so grandiose, that they destroy everything else. Here in this soil thought expands, ideas become greater, nobler, one becomes another man ... Never have I had in my life such emotions, as I have experienced here in Rome, where I am in continual ecstasy ... Every week I visit the Doria Gallery a couple of times to find sublime landscapes by Claude and Poussin. When you are really deeply inspired you can immediately go for a walk in the landscape and try to find what you see in the paintings, and what these artists found, and have more or less imitated. These studies give me great delight, enlarge and purify my soul, and give me a more sublime idea of nature and of art. Blessed is he who lives for ideas, not mere words or

> tradition! I am content with my time, and truly enjoy a most beautiful life. At times such joy enters my body that I would like to embrace everyone I chance to meet, but understand more the beautiful girls than the ugly ones.
>
> I only wish that we could see together Raphael's works. One cannot form a just idea of this great man anywhere else. He is unique among modern artists to equal the ancient—and I will tell you why—because he, like them, penetrates the object represented, while all his other contemporaries, like Leonardo, Michelangelo, Correggio, and even Titian, in as much as they may be great, always repeat themselves in their works, and in their paintings, resembling—more or less—one or the other. All these show the same intention, the same tendency; but Raphael, even though he is always the same, is however at the same time always another, according to the argument that is treated.[20]

Their friendship was intense and complex. They lived parallel lives: both were liberal patriots and fought in the First Italian War of Independence. Antinori served as captain of the Tuscan volunteers at the Battle of Curtatone and Montanara on 29 May 1848, when the Austrian General Radetzky, having been thrown out of Milan after the Cinque giornate (of which more later) managed to reverse his fortune by defeating the Tuscan Division. Like Morelli, Antinori was elected to the parliament of the Kingdom of Sardinia (Regno di Sardegna), at Turin in 1860, and again to the first Italian Parliament in 1861. Like the Zavaritts, Antinori sent his children to school in Switzerland (though in his case to Fribourg). The two men shared artistic interests and had many mutual friends. Both aspired to be writers and discussed literature together, notably German literature. They shared a passion for preserving the patrimony of Italy, for developing new techniques of restoration, and for the emerging use of photography to understand and represent art. When Antinori died, Morelli helped care for his family, especially his children, just as he did when his very good friend Giovanni Frizzoni died. Their friendship transcended normal boundaries, as revealed in the affectionate words of their correspondence:

> My dear Antinori, you do not know how much I love you. This very strong love that I feel for you does not depend on words, like a friendship that I may hold for this and that person, for it is not a rational sentiment, but a spontaneous emotion from my nature towards your own. Our age and emotions join us together. You feel warmly the same need for love as I feel, for those whom friendship is a real cult. In the sad moments of my life, when this enthusiasm continues to diminish, I feel from day to day that I become more miserable and wretched, whereas I am the happiest man alive when the flames of love and friendship are alive in my breast: then I feel beauty in all its fibres, with all my blood, and I find myself capable of every good and magnanimous action. I am certain that you, too, experience the same yourself.[21]

Antinori was the closest of Morelli's Florentine friends. They had many friends in common and often spent time together, as on a summer walking holiday in 1850.[22] Their itinerary involved meeting at the Albergo Feder in Turin (Antinori traveling by sea from Florence to Genova, then by coach to Turin, arriving on 19 or 20 July). From Turin, they planned to walk, equipped with rucksacks and strong, comfortable shoes, to the Valle di Chamonix, to Monte Bianco, and then along Lake Geneva to Berne, Thun, and Interlaken, so as to arrive back at San Fermo between 20 and 25 August, in time to harvest grapes for wine. En route they must have discussed Germany, as the following year Antinori traveled extensively in that country, with guidance from Morelli, when he was translating Goethe's *Egmont*.

□

Morelli's rediscovered Italian paradise was frequently disturbed by the Austrian police presence. He endured constant questioning about his traveling and education (interrogations that he described with ironic humour and quiet indignation in letters to Capponi). At Bergamo in August 1841, Morelli was called by the commissioner of police, who enquired why had he not studied in Austria, why had he stayed so long in Germany and Paris, what he was doing now in Bergamo, what had he achieved in Tuscany, and why was he traveling so much—since he had finished his studies?[23] Finally, the police commissioner stated that the government did not like people who spoke publicly in coffee houses of their travels. Was speaking forbidden? Morelli asked. Not unless it is against the law, the commissioner replied—this is merely a warning from a friend. "I do not have the honour to be your friend," Morelli replied disdainfully, and "from now on, I ask you to treat me like all the others."[24]

Violent episodes were part of the political landscape, though provoked by very different religious motives from those that Morelli stimulated merely by being a Risorgimento patriot, and a Protestant educated in Germany. More disturbing was Morelli's eyewitness account of a violent instance of anti-Semitism that triggered police brutality, occasioned by a riot in Mantua in early July 1842.[25] Returning from Florence, where he had been visiting Capponi, he went from Pistoia to Modena, and at the end of a second day's travel stopped at Mantua. He was awoken by a fight, during which three policemen had interrupted a gang of forty louts who were mistreating a young man of thirty, a Jew, covered in blood and unable to stand, who had run from the ghetto to escape the Mantuan massacre of the Jews. The Mantuans harbored a longstanding prejudice against Jews, whom they considered arrogant and resented for practicing usury—in other words, the usual reasons why the ambitious poor challenge the "arrogant" rich. The riot was provoked by the Jewish population's unsuccessful attempt, a month earlier, to reinstate their civil rights by sending a lawyer to lodge an appeal in Vienna.

At about five o'clock the following afternoon, Morelli was in the Caffè Veneziano, near Mantua's piazza Sant'Andrea, when the hated Austrian police commissioner, Giani, directed the crowd to go home, and called for twelve men to disperse them with bayonets. Morelli withdrew to the interior of the caffè. After three rounds of gunfire, the crowd dispersed, and the coffee house closed. At least twenty people were wounded, including three soldiers, and a woman was killed while drawing her blinds shut, caught by a stray bullet. The next day the ghetto was closed, the Jewish population terrified, the piazza Sant'Andrea occupied by Austrian military. The governor proclaimed that anyone culpable of public disorder would receive a prison sentence of ten or twenty years.

Morelli wrote to Capponi that he had never seen lives lost in such a bestial and stupid manner, without a cause. He left to travel overnight to Brescia, hoping that he would not be considered Jewish. The next day in Mantua stones were thrown at the governor, Count Mazzucchelli, and the commandant Ferraini, while the police commissioner was assassinated. Eight or nine others were killed and many more wounded.

That summer, even Bergamo saw violence: in the following month, August 1842, assassinations occurred on the principal streets, while the police merely laughed.[26] Yet at the same time, as Morelli complained to his sophisticated Florentine friend Giovan Pietro Vieusseux, Bergamo was nothing more than a customs house for silk (*dogana della seta*).[27]

Morelli's lengthiest encounter with police was at Genoa in early August 1843.[28] He arrived at half past six in the morning to find the police expecting him as a person of interest. The commissioner, being eloquent if not learned, read a detailed version of Morelli's biography from a large and weighty volume that resembled the dictionary of the Della Crusca Academy. "To tell the truth," Morelli wrote to Capponi, trying to make light of what must have been a disagreeable experience, "this reading pleased me. Because I found my life written about accurately and with great clarity, for which I hope that this very beautiful work will be like Plutarch for our descendants." Morelli's luggage was searched minutely, after which the police confiscated some letters, and a Bible in the Diodati translation, followed by a body search. The encounter lasted many hours, concluding with a request for Morelli to leave Genoa in the afternoon.

Such incidents were frequent. Morelli was often traveling between Gorle, Bergamo, and San Fermo, as well as staying with friends on the lakes, such as at the sublimely beautiful villa Balbianello that belonged to the Arconati Visconti family. Morelli was in love with this site, located at the point of a peninsula on Lake Como: it was isolated and tranquil, with marvellous vistas over the lake and into the countryside.[29] He suffered frequently from ill health, from some intestinal problems, and was nursed for long periods by his faithful maid, Barbara. Though a voracious reader of newspapers, the classics, and contemporary literature and drama, Morelli loved long and vigorous walking tours in the Swiss mountains, which, he recognised, revived him more than any medicine.

Giovanni Frizzoni's elegant wife, Clementina (Fig. 71) kept a travel diary, which describes their excursions as well as her troubled and unhappy thoughts, interspersed with visits to churches and private collections. Clementina was the daughter of two Swiss from the canton of Grisons, Philippe Reichmann and Anna Jecklin, who kept the famous Reichmann hotel in Milan. In late May 1843 she and Giovanni, their five children, and Morelli, all traveled to Switzerland.[30] The men rode ahead on horseback, while Clementina and the children followed by carriage. During the ride she wrote in her diary, in a depressive mood, that she was not a good mother to her children, nor a good wife to her husband, whom she had never really loved, and implied that there was no sex between them any longer. She lamented that she was unskilled in housekeeping and bored with her life.[31] On another such excursion in August 1843, Clementina described a round of visits in the Engadine, to Swiss families who had emigrated to Bergamo but had kept homes in Switzerland—the Ganzoni in Celerina, the Steiners and Möeli at Bever, and the Zavaritts at S-chanf, where they were received very warmly and where Morelli decided to remain after Clementina and her family left. Her relations with Morelli, her husband's best friend, were at this stage formal, though this would change.

In April 1844 Morelli was in a villa at Mirano, employing his medical skills in looking after the seriously ill thirty-year-old son of his maternal uncle Zanetto (Baron de Reck), who had been widowed early in life by the death of Morelli's aunt Ghitta. Morelli regularly took advantage of the proximity of Venice to take a carriage along the Brenta to visit palaces, especially to study the Manfrin collection, churches, and squares, and to admire sublime paintings.

By the end of 1844 Morelli declared a wish to escape from the narrow-mindedness of small-city life, to enjoy the solitude of the country, intending to produce silk and wine. He intended to buy a property, and deliberated between two places, both extremely beautiful: one near Verona, the other at San Fermo in Brianza.[32] Eventually he bought the latter.

This gracious house, with a columned portico and tree-lined entrance, was located on a little hill overlooking Lake Pusiano, a delightful position (*deliziosissima posizione*) reminiscent of Gorle, with a small vineyard and a vast *giardino inglese*.[33] The air was delightfully fresh (*aria balsamica*), nightingales sang, and Mende hunted ducks that lived on the lakes. The house can still be identified beneath the church of San Fermo and San Rustico, at the border between the towns of Suello and Cesana Brianza. There are spectacular views, one towards the Isola dei Cipressi on Lake Pusiano, and others across the water to smaller towns, and hills of every shape, with superb vegetation. The location was an idyllic nodal point between centers of interest. The house, in which Morelli lived with his mother and his doting aunt Magdalena, was a modest two-story building, with painted furniture, many bedrooms, a salon, a dining room, a billiard room, a large kitchen, a large larder, and a lush orchard, for which he often asked friends for plants and vines. On the second floor were suites for his mother and aunt, six bedrooms, as well as rooms for the concierge and his wife. Morelli also employed a farm manager and two workmen. The property rendered an income: 3,500 lire per year in rent from an adjacent house and 7,000 lire from the production of wine, silk, and fruit. Morelli greatly enjoyed the bucolic solitude of the countryside, where he could be alone with his horse and dogs, reading and writing plays.[34]

Morelli acquired the property with income from his mother's inheritance from her father. Ambrogio Zavaritt had bought for his eight children two huge agricultural properties at Lampugnano (now a suburb of Milan)[35] and Viganone, to provide an income.[36] When Ambrogio wrote his will in 1826 he intended to liquidate the shares of his six daughters, leaving the property to his two sons, Giovanni and Pietro. Upon Ambrogio's death in 1832 the brothers were required to find a huge sum to compensate their sisters for the property, and the will was challenged in a lawsuit, which was not resolved until 1840. In addition, Ursula had been left a bequest of 20,000 lire for having taken care of Ambrogio, as well as a further 51,000 lire (like her sisters).[37]

The villa at San Fermo was within easy reach of Como, taking only three hours by coach or on horseback, or six hours to Bergamo and Milan. Morelli and his mother could visit Leonardo Frizzoni and his family at their villa Crella, near San Giovanni di Bellagio, only a few hours beyond Como. Leonardo had bought this villa in September 1843 from Angiola Vittoria Peverelli Mainoni, for the sum of 71,600 Austrian lire. It was in the exquisite Biedermeier style, built by the Brescian architect Rodolfo Vantini, with charming intimate rooms complemented by Vantini furniture. The villa was in an area that was perpetually in shade and a little cold in the winter, but a delicious refuge from the heat in the summer.

Johann Engelhardt visited Morelli at Bergamo and his country estate in 1846. When they became acquainted during Morelli's time at Erlangen, Morelli was impressed by Engelhardt's uncommon erudition combined with unusual modesty. To Pietro Zavaritt, Morelli reported that although Engelhardt loved Milan, he was in rapture at Bergamo.[38] Engelhardt's impression of the time he spent with Morelli was published as travel articles: an ecstatic account of the landscape of the lakes seen by carriage from Bergamo to Lake Como, and of visits to villa Carlotta and villa Balbianello, where they met the owner, Arconati Visconti.[39]

A few of Morelli's letters to Engelhardt were published anonymously in the Augsburg newspaper *Allgemeine Zeitung*, notably a very long one in 1845 about his friend Gino Battista Niccolini's *Arnaldo da Brescia* (1844); in 1846 another on Niccolini, Manzoni and Gino Capponi; in 1847 one on Pius IX; and in

1848 political articles. Two decades later in a letter to his political mentor, the great patriot Count Giovanni Battista Camozzi Vertova, Morelli recalled that it was through Engelhardt that he began to write for the *Allgemeine Zeitung*, known in Italy as the *Gazzetta d'Augusta*, acknowledging authorship of these few articles.[40] In 1865 Morelli wrote about his authorship of newspaper articles in Germany:

> May I explain how exactly things are. From 1841 until 1855 I was in regular correspondence with my friend, Professor Engelhardt of Erlangen in Bavaria, now deceased. In my letters I threw down all my observations and ideas on scientific, literary and artistic arguments as well as practical experiences of Italy.
>
> My German friend very often used my letters to construct articles for newspapers. Many of these articles were published in the "Gazzetta d'Augusta," while others were published in the "Morgenblatt," others in ephemeral publications in Germany. At times, I know that my friend published my letters, as they were, without additions or modifications. At other times, there was instead some idea taken from my letter, and all the rest of the article was by Engelhardt.
>
> Just as with "Arnaldo da Brescia" I know that I wrote a very long letter to my friend about it, and I know that he used that letter. Thus, I wrote to him that that article was mine, but not knowing in what German newspaper it was published. But if in 1846 I declared to Niccolini that the article in the Allgemeine Zeitung was not mine, that really means that that article was not mine, and that it was probably a writing by a certain Professor Pfeuffer on Arnaldo da Brescia. When I return to the city I will see if I can get hold of the Allgemeine Zeitung for 1848. Upon my arrival I will know precisely if the article is by Engelhardt, and therefore mostly by me, or whether it was that one published by Pfeuffer. I remember precisely an article in the Allgemeine that is my own, which discusses Niccolini, and I will show it to you in Florence.[41]

Morelli's passionate article may be easily identified in an *Allgemeine Zeitung* special supplement on dramatic Italian literature;[42] it reads like a list of his favorite books by Alfieri, Manzoni, and Silvio Pellico, but concentrates on Niccolini's political tragedy *Arnaldo da Brescia*, a bestseller that was prohibited in every Italian state, and sold 3,000 copies in the first week. The play is about a medieval Lombard priest who was martyred. His life is an allegory of the battle for civil and religious liberty that Italians fought in their wars of independence. Morelli claimed that his articles in the 1840s were written to inform the German public about the true nature of the Austrian regime in northern Italy, but at times he hated the newspaper and described it as a lying, prejudiced, Jesuitical rag. He also wrote for the *Gazzetta Ticinese*, the leading newspaper of the Swiss canton of Ticino, in which there are innumerable anonymous articles about the revolutionary years in Italy; some could be attributed to Morelli. This liberal Swiss newspaper was renowned for being moderate and fair and, more importantly, was known as the publisher of the violently anti-monarchist and Republican writer Carlo Cattaneo, one of the leading revolutionaries of the Risorgimento, later exiled to Lugano.

In this decade Morelli wrote many plays, but none was performed. Three survive: *Troppa premura nuoce, ossia la prova d'amore*, a comedy in three acts, written in 1846; *Il Roccocò*, a comedy in five acts, written in 1847; and *I Tradimenti*, another comedy, set in 1848, including one scene set during the revolutionary struggle known as the *Cinque giornate di Milano*.[43] A decade later, Morelli showed them to his friend Francesco De Sanctis, claiming that they were by an anonymous friend. De Sanctis immediately recognized the subterfuge and declared them "mediocre."[44] Morelli reacted with some pride, and at length, saying that he had shown the scripts to Engelhardt, Capponi, and others, who were all complimentary as to their merit, but he ended in agreement with De Sanctis.[45] Morelli's charismatic personality and handsome presence did not persuade De Sanctis. Yet the texts reveal something of Morelli's nationalistic beliefs. The first two comedies are conventional in plot, delighting in comic confusions about identities, hidden beneath masks or disguises, not unlike paintings, whose true worth is hidden beneath discolored varnish. *Troppa premura nuoce* is set in Taranto, Apulia. The play opens with a long soliloquy from the Contessa Sigismonda, who is obsessed with French culture and literature but ignores the Italian classics. She entertains the usual prejudices against Sicilians. Gossips relay the news that the daughter of the Duke of Altamura, Duchessa Carolina, has eloped with her singing teacher to the south of Italy. En route to the south, where Carolina believes she will meet the Prince of Monteforte, Palermo, the man to whom her father has betrothed her, the singing master reveals his true identity. He is the prince, who has disguised himself in order to get to know her before marriage. This Sicilian nobleman embodies all the virtues of the new Italy.

Il Roccocò opens with a discussion set in the Veronese home of an impoverished nobleman, Count Cane della Torre. He is about to be visited by a very rich English lord who is trying to buy all the paintings of Paolo Veronese as well as the entire della Torre family castle, Roccanera, to take back to England. The play concerns the children of Count Cane della Torre and their conventional quest for true love. English lords are consistently portrayed as collectors who would seize the patrimony of Italy, while the French are colonizers.

The later play, *I Tradimenti* (Betrayal), is based on contemporary events at Milan in 1848. At the center of the play is a Lombard, Guido Bentivoglio, an officer in the Piedmont cavalry, with whom Luigia, daughter of Cavaliere Don Donato and his wife, Lucrezia, becomes smitten. As Luigia relates to her uncle, their eyes met at a significant moment: on the first day of the Cinque giornate, on a horrible Monday evening. Thick rain rendered the day miserable, bells sounded like hammers, cannons and guns fired, while Luigia attempted to comfort her distressed parents. She glanced through the window towards the street, to see whether the barricade at the corner of their house was in the hands of the Milanese, only to find the Croatian and Austrian troops in command. More dead than alive, Luigia looked out the window to see a young man throw himself among those fleeing:

> He held them back, he reanimated them. With his left hand he held up the tricolored flag; in his right he held a sword. At his words, by his example, our troops regained their courage and followed him. Around him his brave followers fell dead and wounded; only he appeared invulnerable—a saint. I could no longer breathe, and remained like a stone. He arrived with his small flag at the corner of the piazza, near the Crivelli Palace, and he rallied the others around him, commanding them to recharge their rifles. It was then that he raised his eyes towards our house, towards me. Our eyes met; without realizing it, I waved my handkerchief and he replied, waving his flag. Then he returned enthusiastically to his men, and immediately was at the head of his people, throwing himself against the barricade. A terrible explosion of gunfire occurred! The house shook, and I heard nothing more, did not dare to breathe. My only thought was: is he dead? Will I never see his eyes again? … Finally, I raised my eyes again to see the tricolor flag waving on the barricade, and through the smoke met again Guido's eyes, and that gaze was enough to join us together forever.[46]

The character of Guido is a fictionalized self-portrait of Morelli, mirroring his experiences in the Cinque giornate. The location of the barricade near Palazzo Crivelli (via Pontaccio 12, Milan) was adjacent to the Ginoulhiac building where Morelli later lived. Guido is described as having black hair and a beard, wearing a cape with a beret. Luigia has a second suitor, a painter-soldier Corbelloni, who turns out to be treacherous.

Politics was usually intermixed with art and philanthropy—part of the same culture of romantic heroism. In February 1848 Morelli assisted Giovanni Leonardo Frizzoni with what he believed was a magnificent gift: an oil painting then attributed to Gaudenzio Ferrari, *The Resurrection of Christ between Saints and Donors* (1532), donated to the late-Baroque church of San Giovanni Battista, adjacent to villa Trotti, Bellagio. The archpriest expressed his joy at the benefaction and asked Morelli to help him install the work. "I could not tell you whether the expression of satisfaction on his face was because his bare church was embellished with a masterpiece, or whether it was the pleasure of experiencing your generosity to his parish."[47] It was the best painting Giovanni Frizzoni ever owned, and his only philanthropic gift, inspired by a presentiment of his own death as a consequence of the First War of Independence. Sadly, it is no longer attributed to Gaudenzio.

Upon his return to Italy at the age of twenty-four, Morelli Italianized his name. This was part of a process by which he became increasingly involved in the political battles of the Risorgimento, culminating in the revolution of 1848, where he appeared indifferent even to the loss of his own life, so dedicated was he to the cause of achieving Italian independence and democracy.

CHAPTER 5
Revolution in Lombardy–Venetia, 1848–49

Eighteen forty-eight was the year in which Republican revolutions occurred throughout Europe—in almost all cases against reigning monarchs—in the widest European revolutionary movement ever known. Unlike other European countries, in Italy the revolts were against foreign colonizers, the French and the Austrians, in an attempt to create a united Liberal and democratic country. In Milan a five-day revolt (18–22 March 1848), which became known as the *Cinque giornate di Milano*, was a classless revolution, in which Lombards, whether patricians or workmen, joined forces in an astonishingly successful and seemingly spontaneous push to oust the Austrians from their city. But once this victory was won, the military failed, in what became the First Italian War of Independence, to consolidate its success across the peninsula.

This "year of miracles" in Lombardy began violently. In January 1848 Morelli was in Milan, watching and hoping that the Liberals would increase their strength. There he witnessed violent acts, such as the sickening assassination of the 74-year old jurist Carlo Manganini,[1] at a time when people like the writer Cesare Cantù were fleeing the city, and fear emptied the theaters and streets. Morelli's personal experience confirms Carlo Cattaneo's theory that the revolution in Italy was awakened by the Austrians' constant harassment of the local population.[2] The Austrian military was perpetually on edge.[3] Even if a hundred eyes had seen nothing, a hundred mouths narrated what they imagined would and might happen.

Focusing on Morelli's role in the Risorgimento in northern Italy, we read that he wrote of his involvement in the First Italian War of Independence in letters to his mentor Gino Capponi, and to his friend from boyhood (*amatissimo amico*), Giovanni Leonardo Frizzoni. Both were unable to fight: Capponi was almost blind, and Frizzoni was suffering from an illness brought on by being violently tortured by Austrian troops when he had offered himself as a hostage. During the Cinque giornate, the Austrians abused him in their *caserma* (barracks) at Sant'Agostino, Bergamo, and the long-term effects led to his death in 1849.[4]

At Bergamo on the evening of 17 February 1848, the day after a Bergamasco called Pasini had been shot by a cadet, young Austrian soldiers walked the streets, blowing smoke in the eyes of citizens, with derisory expressions. Their gestures were intentionally irritating, as the Austrians had placed a heavy tax on tobacco. Morelli, who loved cigars, refused to smoke for a few days, so as not to pay the tax. Austrian and Croatian soldiers reacted fearfully when provoked, firing six or eight bullets in the air, as their entire regiment invaded the Borgo San Leonardo, Bergamo. Colonel Salis, adjutant to Archduke Ferdinand I, had recently arrived, increasing nervousness. One Croatian soldier accidentally fell on his rifle, which let out a shot, giving the impression that someone was shooting from a window. In retaliation, the Croatian soldiers forced entry into houses, only to find Bergamasca women feeding their little children at suppertime. The streets were deserted, the shops closed. No one in Bergamo had thought to provoke the military, not even a cat. Two and a half hours later, at 10.30 pm, the Croatian soldiers left, only to return again, very alarmed, when a drunk made a noise in the street.

Any simple action was misinterpreted as a provocation. In late February, Austrian Field Marshall Joseph Radetzky placed Lombardy–Venetia under martial law. On 17 March news of the demise of the Austrian chancellor, Prince Klemens von Metternich, reached Italy. Protests began immediately, with demands for freedom of the press, freedom of religion, and freedom to vote.

In the very first days of this war, Morelli enlisted and was put in charge of a group of volunteers. On 18 March they bravely participated in street fighting, going from town to town in Lombardy, narrowly escaping death in the township of Oggiono in the province of Lecco, not far from his villa in the Brianza. He was then wounded at Monza. In a particularly bloody battle on 22 March they conquered the Porta Comasina in Milan, the second gate in the city to be taken by the revolutionaries.[5] (In the war of 1859 the celebrated general and nationalist Giuseppe Garibaldi would repeat the same conquest, and the gate became the Porta Garibaldi.) Morelli's life changed from one of pessimism to one of optimism:

> From being a misanthropist in a villa I became the leader of an army corps that distinguished itself, then the leader of a battalion of Bersaglieri [highly mobile light infantry], afterwards a simple soldier … At Oggiono, where I stood in a square haranguing a crowd, gendarmes were given the order to shoot me, but they lacked the courage to move close enough to execute their officer's order. At Monza, a rogue bullet left me deaf in one ear, shattering my eardrum. In Milan, at the Porta Comasina, in a charge with only fifteen men I saw three of my who were at my side companions drop dead, without a bullet touching me. And then immediately I found myself among twenty Tyrolese hunters who, instead of killing me, fled via the gate. Then five hours later I had the undeniable pleasure of witnessing the rapid flight of the Austrians—a truly satanic scene. Those ten days lasted a lifetime. I will say nothing about our government, nor about our Ministry of War.[6]

The satanic scenes of fighting and fleeing Austrians described by Morelli were vividly captured by Milanese soldier-artists, who created a new kind of Italian history painting for the events of 1848. More than 1,650 barricades were erected spontaneously throughout Milan, constructed from carriages, furniture of every kind, stairs ripped from buildings, old piano cases, barrels, and whatever other large and bulky object was to hand. Milanese artist Felice Donghi (1828–1887), who later became a scenographer at La Scala, was at the age of twenty a volunteer soldier in the Cinque giornate. During the conflict he made charcoal drawings on the spot, showing these innumerable barricades erected from quotidian, cumbersome stuff; his sketches were then transformed into watercolors, oil paintings, and popular prints.[7] The unexpected objects of the barricades show both the confusion and democracy of the war, the solidarity and brotherhood of the Milanese against the Austrians, irrespective of class or profession (Figs 37 and 38).

After the Austrians fled, Morelli requested permission to form a company of Bersaglieri to keep them perpetually at bay, but his plan was rejected by the generals in charge, Count Pompeo Litta and General Teodoro Lechi, who said that in two weeks it would all be over, and Austria would never again dominate Italy (*in quindici giorni non si parlerebbe più d'Austria in Italia*). Morelli's second request, to send an expedition to Friuli to verify how that territory would be defended, was also spurned, on the grounds that Venice would take care of defenses there.[8]

During the Cinque giornate, similar events occurred in Bergamo as in Milan. Posters throughout the city proudly encouraged the citizens to join their Milanese brothers in the struggle to expel the Austrians,[9] and on the afternoon of 20 March 1848 the Bergamaschi drove the Austrian forces from their caserma in the contrada of Sant'Antonio, and fought them at Sant'Agostino, San Giovanni, and Santa Marta. On 21 March the palaces of the Frizzoni and Camozzi Vertova families became the military headquarters for the revolution in Bergamo, and the Bergamaschi successfully took the Austrian billet at Santa Marta (Fig. 39). Others blocked an Austrian battalion from leaving Bergamo to join Radetzky in Milan. Thirty volunteers were sent from Bergamo to join their Milanese brothers in their heroic assault on the Porta Tosa, on the last day of the Cinque giornate. Two members of the provisional government in Bergamo, Giovanni Leonardo Frizzoni and Giuseppe Zuccala, were used as hostages and tortured badly. Frizzoni managed to escape after a few days, while Zuccala was saved later.[10]

The Protestant women of Bergamo were as dedicated to the struggle for independence as were their husbands. Pietro Zavaritt's wife, Amalia (Fig. 41) was the daughter of a wealthy Zurich silk merchant, Giovanni Steiner. As her portrait shows, she loved luxury, especially furs and jewelry, but she zealously supported the cause of those brutally wounded in the battles of 1848, especially during the fighting at Bergamo, and became president of Bergamo's committee for the wounded (presidentessa del Comitato dei Feriti), an office she filled with great energy.[11] In her mission she was joined by many women from the evangelical Protestant community. Her philanthropic passion continued throughout the Italian Wars of Independence, and resulted in 1859 in forming the organization that subsequently became the Red Cross, Amalia becoming its deputy head for Lombardy.

On the night of 23 March 1848 the Austrians were finally driven out of Bergamo by Piedmontese troops, and the pro-Austrian *podestà* (equivalent to chief magistrate or city administrator), Guglielmo Lochis (better known for his outstanding art collection, now in the Accademia Carrara), was dismissed from office. Those north Italians who, like Lochis, favored the Austrians were known as *filoaustriaci*; they had a predilection for neoclassical art, as shown in the cool portrait of Lochis by Il Piccio (Fig. 42). A provisional government of Bergamo was then formed by Francesco Roncalli, Count of Montorio, composed of patriotic members of the chamber of commerce: Giovanni Battista Barzizza, Giovanni Antonio Piazzoni, Carlo Steiner Salvezzi, and Gabriele Camozzi Vertova (young brother of Count Giovanni Battista Camozzi Vertova).

But independence was short lived. After the retreat of the Piedmontese troops, a lack of Italian leadership meant that Bergamo soon returned to Austrian domination; Camozzi Vertova (Fig. 43) fled to Clusone (under the protection of Countess Clara Maffei, a woman of letters and backer of the Risorgimento), and then to a villa in Genoa, where he gave protection to patriots in exile. (In 1859 Camozzi Vertova would be called back by Garibaldi to join a military corps of volunteers, the Hunters of the Alps, I Cacciatori delle Alpi, and was at Garibaldi's side on 8 June when he liberated Bergamo.)

□

After the Austrian re-taking of Bergamo, Morelli was exiled to San Fermo.[12] By 3 May 1848 he was bored and frustrated in his rural exile, deprived of news and of friends with whom he could divert himself, longing to fight for his country (*pieno zeppo il petto di smania d'agire a pro della patria*), or rather for Lombardy, and irritated by the generals' lack of strategic thought and their failure to act:

> How I suffered from separating myself from the handsome, brave and very ardent youths who should have come with me to the Tyrol. But by order of the new minister of war I had to send them home, because they only wished to have conscripts. Afterwards, the provincial government wanted me to send them to the Veneto, but it was too late—I had already sent them away.[13]

Morelli was continually frustrated by the indecisive politics of King Carlo Alberto, known as "the Italian Hamlet," who intervened in the war exclusively with his Piedmontese armies while barring others, principally volunteers, in a game of power that failed to produce results.[14]

At this time, the provisional government of Lombardy, located in Milan, was keen to appoint international ambassadors. It considered Morelli for the embassy in Paris, but decided instead to send him to Frankfurt, a more important mission. On 17 May 1848 Morelli and his friend Count Alessandro Porro (Fig. 44), a member of the provisional government, were instructed to travel to Germany's newly constituted National Assembly or Diet, "to explain the true spirit of our country and to refute the unjust accusations of mercenary journalists."[15] The Diet, the first elected parliament in the history of Germany (Fig. 46), was inaugurated on 18 May 1848 with 809 elected representatives, and for those Italians who longed for independence and unity it served as a model and symbol of success. The various revolutions across Europe in 1848 had much in common, and different nations looked to one another for inspiration and guidance. Morelli hoped to persuade the Germans that Trieste and the Trentino should belong to Italy, not to Austria. Porro's loyalties and experiences were similar to Morelli's: he too had participated in the Cinque giornate, although Morelli was unusual, perhaps even unique, in having a real knowledge of German and an understanding of German Romantic culture. During this time at Frankfurt Morelli was also accompanied by Mende, his friend from Munich days, who had visited him annually in Italy.

The diplomatic mission began inauspiciously when Morelli was stopped at the Bavarian border because his Milanese passport did not have an Austrian visa—an absurdity, he believed, now that the Austrians had been driven from Milan.[16] Morelli was kept in Frankfurt much longer than he intended to stay (until 7 August, when he was replaced by the patriot and politician Evasio Radice). During his time there he discussed politics with leading German celebrities, aristocrats, and politicians, beginning with the president of the Diet, General Heinrich von Gagern. Those who supported the Italian cause included Friedrich Ludwig Georg von Raumer, Franz Raveaux, Friedrich von Hermann, Johann Gustav Heckscher, and most of all Carl Nauwerk. Resenting the fact that he was not on the Italian battlefield, fighting for what he called the holy cause of independence (*santa causa dell'indipendenza*), Morelli confided impatiently to Giovanni Leonardo Frizzoni that what little he could achieve in Germany had already taken place.[17] He could not wait to return to Italy: as long as the war continued, he wanted to be part of it.

A central executive power had not been created in Germany. Morelli, acting on the suggestion of Nauwerk, suggested that the provincial government of Lombardy–Venetia should take advantage of this fact, and persuade King Carlo Alberto to formally ask the Diet for recognition of the Tyrol, then under Austrian control, as a free and independent state.[18] He also requested that the Milanese demand the withdrawal of Austrian troops from Italy. But these suggestions fell on deaf ears; from the few letters that survive between Morelli, Porro, and the provisional government, we can deduce that the government in Milan rarely even bothered to respond to its two representatives: Porro even asked if the government could send more instructions, as it seemed they had been forgotten.[19]

On 20 June Morelli wrote hurriedly to a member of the provisional government about the sitting of the German Diet that day.[20] The *Allgemeine Zeitung* had reported that there was an Italian blockade of Trieste, to which the Diet's reaction was that any attack on that city—still part of the Austrian Empire—would be considered a declaration of war against Germany, as parts of Austria were considered Germany. Morelli asked for confirmation of these newspaper reports, fearing that such aggression could lead to a European war. He also reported on another dispute: the majority of the Diet wished to give executive power to three reigning princes, while the Left wished for executive power to be in the hands of elected delegates. Count Leopold von Thun und Hohenstein, recently arrived from Vienna, assured him that Italian prisoners taken by the Austrians were being well treated. Morelli concluded with a plea that he be briefed about what was happening in Trieste and the Tyrol.

The following week Morelli addressed the German Diet in its temporary home in St Paul's Church, Frankfurt (Fig. 46), several weeks later publishing an extended version of his speech in a short booklet: *Worte eines Lombarden an die Deutschen* (Words of a Lombard to the German people).[21] Morelli's authorship is unacknowledged in the publication itself, and copies listed in the catalogues of German libraries usually describe it as an anonymous work by a Lombard. Why a pseudonym in this instance, when he was acting in an official capacity? Maybe such literary disguise had become habitual for Morelli, or perhaps it was a decision taken from a prudent political wish for anonymity. In his speech, Morelli's ambitions went far beyond his official brief. In his impeccable German he tried to create sympathy between the two nations, suggesting they were united by a common goal: to turn the German Confederation into a national state and to unite Italy; this could create a new history, in a wonderful way.[22] *Worte eines Lombarden* opened with a claim, followed by an invitation, expressed in Romantic rhetoric:

> The Revolution in Lombardy has come to an end. The yoke of tyranny around our neck has been lifted after thirty-four years. We raise our cap to the sky. Each of us feels a man again. We each feel something moving in our breast: the divine spark of self-esteem. We come to you valiant Germans with outstretched hand.[23]

During the course of this lengthy address, Morelli also spoke of more personal matters: the six years he had spent in Germany as a student, and the intimate friendships and culture that bound him to what he called his second homeland. He lamented that, despite the excellence of education in Austria, the Austrians had ruined all levels of the school system in Lombardy. Religious hatred there was extreme, particularly stimulated by the form of Catholicism practiced by the Austrians. Morelli stressed that his arguments were about the revolution in Lombardy and why and how it had occurred as a protest against the Austrian regime; they were not against the German Confederation, but against the conservative and illiberal system of the Austrian chancellor, Metternich, against whom the Lombards had revolted. He spoke of the Italians' passionate hatred for the Austrian regime, which was in effect a police state, and of his own experience of fighting in the streets against Austrian troops during the Cinque giornate. The behavior in warfare of the Austrian infantry and police contravened morality: volunteers were shot, while wounded prisoners were left to die, their wounds turning gangrenous.

As requested by the government in Milan, Morelli made out a good case for the Italian claim to the South Tyrol, a cause in which he believed ardently (to the extent that he would play a leading role in the fight to take the Valtellina and the Stelvio—areas close to the South Tyrol—in the Third War of Italian Independence in 1866, when he was aged fifty.) He disputed claims that the Austrians shared a common cause with Germany, and that they occupied northern Italy in an alliance with the nobility of Lombardy, a class that in his view was neither large nor clearly definable. He emphasized that the protest against the Austrian regime was driven by the middle class and the Liberal Democrats, widely supported by urban artisans and the Lombard peasantry. He criticized journalists' biased reporting, especially in the *Allgemeine Zeitung*. Morelli's speech ended with fiery, patriotic words: Italy could even forgive old Austria for having spat poison at the Italian nation, for having denigrated and defamed it. He encouraged Germany to follow the Italian example, to become friends, united in a common purpose, and to forget that Germany shared a common language with Austria.

What Morelli proposed was wonderful in ambition, but of course impossible to accomplish by means of a speech or diplomacy. The timidity of the provisional government and the failure of the Piedmontese army frustrated any effective result from his time in Frankfurt. Both Porro and Morelli had formed a low view of the level of debate at the German Diet. Although the two Lombards enjoyed meeting leading German cultural and political figures, throughout their time in Frankfurt they had been plagued by the suspicion that they were wasting their time. Of all the German politicians they encountered, Morelli most admired the self-made man Robert Blum, who is represented as the speaker in Ludwig von Elliott's famous view of the Frankfurt Diet.[24] Tragically, Blum was executed in Vienna at the end of 1848, a symbol of the futility of the German revolt.

In mid-June, Porro left Frankfurt and returned home to Milan, disillusioned. Morelli remained until August. Shortly before he left, he communicated his successes and failures to Capponi in a long letter.[25] He found solace that Capponi supported the views that the provisional government in Lombardy had dismissed in derision. Morelli's judgment foreshadowed a 21st-century historian in his belief that a war led by King Carlo Alberto could only end disastrously.[26] In rage and frustration Morelli wrote:

> Carlo Alberto is the worst general that there is on this earth. He has given us ample evidence—he is a man without faith and without genius, and the camarilla of his tacky generals is composed of men a million times worse than he. When the Austrian army was demoralized, weak, intimidated, he did not attack; he planted himself on the banks of the Mincio, he fortified himself and waited there for three months with the corps of the army. He did not enter the Veneto, nor attack Verona, nor accomplish anything. And his much-vaunted courage is only passive, the most stupid of all forms of courage. After the victory of Goito, he did nothing; a victory is considerable, but you have to know how to profit from it. And what did Carlo Alberto do? He never took the offensive, for he who attacks has half won. At Goito he made the same mistake as at Wurnfer; in short, he acted like a true imbecile.[27]

The three months of Carlo Alberto's inactivity coincided with Morelli's stay at Frankfurt—hence his bitterness when he realized that this one military success had led Italians to forget and lose the potentially greater future victory in idle chatter and speculation.

In his final days at Frankfurt, persistent to the last, and even without instructions, Morelli met again with Gagern, to try to persuade him to make the first elected German parliament act as a mediator between Austria and Italy, as he believed only an armistice could liberate Italy. In these days he also attempted to persuade the Diet to avoid a French intervention.[28] In conversation on 4 August with Archduke John of Austria, the *Reichsverweser* (imperial vicar or regent of the Austrian Empire), Morelli stated that the first act of the new German Diet could be the greatest in history, but the archduke surprisingly confided that the Italians could easily have beaten Radetzky a hundred times.[29] Without authority, Morelli contended that a French intervention must be avoided at all costs, and to prevent one he suggested that the Diet or Radetzky should accept an unconditional amnesty and declare a free and independent Italy. The Diet ignored his suggestions, for they feared Austria. Morelli described the archduke as a wolf from head to foot, false and astute. Be that as it may, on 8 August Radetzky's troops re-entered Milan. Later, on 27 September, Radetzky informed the Diet that a German renunciation of Lombardy would amount to a betrayal of Austria.

For the 32-year-old Morelli, Frankfurt became a banal expression of pan-Germanism, as the Diet would consider only the supremacy of Germany, without regard for any other emerging nation-state. It must have been disillusioning that his first book had no effect on public or political opinion, and that his attempt to form a meaningful connection between two cultures had ended in failure.

As the years went by, Morelli developed an anti-German polemic, a criticism of everything German in science and art—a complete reversal of the love affair with German culture that had been kindled in his student years at Munich and Erlangen.[30] In his best-known works of art historiography he would take joy in publicly challenging and criticizing the work of German curators, museum directors, and scholars.

□

After leaving Frankfurt, Morelli was recommended by Capponi to Daniele Manin (1804–1857), president of the newly created Repubblica di San Marco—an endorsement based on Morelli's experience in the German city.[31] Capponi wrote that Morelli was a lover of all things Italian, who wished to follow closely the good example of constancy and patriotism that Venice gave to Italy.[32]

The Repubblica di San Marco was a revolutionary state in Venice and the Veneto, created under Manin's leadership. It lasted only seventeenth months, from March 1848 to August 1849. The concept of a city-republic played an important role in Risorgimento thinking: Carlo Cattaneo, the intellectual who had done much to inspire the Cinque giornate, believed that Italy should rid itself of foreign invaders and be reunited as a federal republic of city-states, corresponding to the traditional territories of the commune and the signoria. He explained his vision of the city as the ideal principal of Italian federation in his 1849 book *Dell'insurrezione di Milano nel 1848 e della successiva guerra: Memorie di Carlo Cattaneo*, contending that it was a traditional value in Italian history. He praised Italy for having created the ideal of a republic, whether in Rome, Venice, Genoa, Amalfi, Pisa, or Florence, whereas those forces that had "colonized" the Italian Peninsula, such as France and Austria, were without these traditions.

Morelli arrived in Venice in October 1848. On 18 October, while sitting at the Caffè Florian (at that time converted to a command post) on piazza San Marco, he reflected on his initial experience there, while watching the bright lights of the bombs exploding in the distance. A similar scene, *The Bombardment of Marghera on the Night of 25 May 1849*, was captured by the painter and revolutionary Ippolito Caffi: it is a magical representation of a vile act (Fig. 47). In a letter to his literary friend Tommaso Gar, at that time the Manin government's ambassador to Florence, Morelli spoke of his disappointment and of the dreadful conditions, where one lived as if in time of carnival, the enemy having laid siege to the city.[33]

To Manin, Morelli managed to speak only fleetingly, and was greeted coldly. Manin suggested that Morelli join the Marghera artillery, giving him a letter of introduction to its leader, Colonel Giovanni Battista Cavedalis, who was equally chilly, saying there was no lack of men in Venice, but what they needed was money. Morelli's good friend, the writer and jurist Emilio de Tipaldo, promised to help him to be reconsidered by the military, and on 28 October he was appointed lieutenant of infantry (*tenente della fanteria*) to General Francesco Solera, minister of war, by the Venetian provisional government.

Morelli's letters from Venice took three months to reach their recipients, during which time they were opened and censored by the authorities. This was because Morelli, to his surprise, was considered suspiciously conservative. In a long letter to Giovanni Leonardo Frizzoni, written as he prepared to leave in early February 1849, he gave an overview of his Venetian experience. The details of his Venetian military service are unclear to us today, but he was deeply disillusioned:

> Many officials have already resigned, and will go to enlist in Tuscany or Piedmont. In a few days I shall do the same, even though, as adjutant to a general who never does anything, I continue to remain idle, ashamed to wear a uniform. I have been invited to go to Turin, and I will go there shortly, leaving this city where my heart bleeds at seeing our affairs going so very badly.[34]

Nothing much, Morelli observed, could be expected from Venice, with a government composed of rogues and lunatics, and a general who always brought bad luck. The Venetian army was incapacitated, not by lack of courage but by lack of discipline. Appointments were made with ridiculous and overt nepotism, resulting in elderly captains and baby-faced colonels. Reflecting on Italian politics more broadly, Morelli reacted to the declaration of a Roman republic on 9 February 1849, and Pope Pius IX's response to excommunicate all those who had voted for it, by declaring that "the political reform of Italy has to be proceeded by religious reform,"[35] a conviction held by many Protestants in Bergamo and often repeated by Morelli.

At the beginning of 1849 there was chaos across much of Italy; Morelli felt that the only possible way to bring about change was to become a preacher in the desert. The fight for unity would take longer than anyone had imagined, yet never before had Italy been so overtly nationalistic: the will of 25 million people to become a nation was stronger than the power of any army in the world. In February Morelli ridiculed the French for failing to respond to Giuseppe Mazzini's request for support the previous October:

> That France will do nothing for us is natural, and you would have had never to read history to remain ignorant of the fact that that nation is, was, and always will be, our enemy. Nevertheless, I believe that, despite their repugnance, they will eventually make war against Austria, and this will work to our advantage, but to pretend that France comes to Italy to liberate us in knightly fashion from the enemy is as ridiculous as it is undignified, for a people who wish for independence.[36]

The difficult conditions during Austria's siege of Venice from the end of 1848 to 24 August 1849, combined with the poor morale of the troops, are eloquently described in the humorous account written by Johannes Debrunner, a Swiss colonel who formed and led a hundred Swiss volunteers to fight for Venice.[37] They too were disappointed in the Venetian generals, and suffered considerable hardship during the winter, sometimes only able to keep warm by filling their pockets with hot chestnuts. They were joined by Swiss deserters from the Papal Guard, spoke German, and were sometimes unfortunately confused with Austrians.

When King Carlo Alberto and Piedmont denounced the armistice, Morelli enrolled in a Piedmontese regiment. He arrived at Novara on the eve of battle on 21 March 1849, to participate in a very long day of conflict that concluded with a Piedmontese defeat by the Austrians on the morning of 23 March.[38]

Despite constant disillusionment, for Morelli the Risorgimento of the Italian states into one unified, democratic nation was a youthful ideal that he refused to let go.

□

In April 1849 Morelli went to the Republican stronghold of Genoa. He was accompanied by Niccolò Antinori, who stayed with him for his first three weeks there. The two patriots arrived in the immediate aftermath of the sack of the city (5–11 April). After the armistice that had been signed on 24 March by King Carlo Alberto's successor, Vittorio Emanuele II, and the Austrian General Radetzky, a popular revolt had taken place in Genoa, brutally put down by General Alfonso La Marmora and his troops. (A decade later Morelli would work with La Marmora to formulate legislation against the *brigantaggio* in the south; they may well have encountered one another at this time.) Exactly why Morelli went to Genoa is unclear, except that during the brutal fighting the Genoese had urgently requested volunteers who had fought in the Cinque giornate. But these reinforcements arrived too late, and Morelli may have been among them. From Genoa he also observed events such as the French siege of Rome. "I do not know whether I will remain here or rather move to another place," he declared on 4 May. "I am well and for some days now I have begun to interest myself in poetic things and have taken up the work that for months and months I lacked."[39]

On 27 April Morelli's good friend Massimo d'Azeglio, a Romantic landscape artist and liberal monarchist politician, was in Genoa. Morelli believed that d'Azeglio was one of the few who had a good grasp of politics, for he had no desire to recommence a war of desperation without disciplined soldiers. D'Azeglio had just been invited by the new king to form a cabinet, which he was to lead for the next three years. (It was d'Azeglio who in 1860 would invite Morelli to write a guide to the Pinacoteca di Brera, for in his view there was no one more able to do so.)[40]

From the vantage point of Genoa, Morelli reflected with urbane cynicism on the European revolutions of 1848 and 1849, what had led to them, and how they might change societies. The ambition of his compatriots was to release

Europe from the chains of institutions and beliefs inherited from the Middle Ages, to create new laws, a new philosophy, a new morality—one inspired by the Gospels. Is it civilization that propels us forward, he pondered, as every discovery in science is revolutionary? Yet he opined that the conservative press of every country had no idea: their syllogisms were defective; they threw the dust of big words in people's eyes. France, he believed, would become more and more decadent, and would eventually lose all influence—a prediction that would be disproven by events in 1859.

While in Genoa Morelli reported in the press and in his letters on the noble defense of the Roman Republic as the French army bombarded the city into submission. On 29 April he wrote of a skirmish between eighteen French cavalry and Garibaldi's men, in which the Romans took one prisoner and shot four of the cavalry, losing only one of their own men. On 30 April the general called all troops, and the cannons thundered from eight o'clock in the morning until two in the afternoon. Together with the Carabinieri, Garibaldi took out four of the French cannon, and the French army was completely beaten outside the walls of Rome, in a battle damaging and bloody. The French left 600 dead or wounded on the battlefield and took 452 prisoners. On the Italian side, about 200 died, and Garibaldi's army retreated too soon. Morelli received a report that in Rome there were more than 60,000 armed men (almost certainly an exaggeration), while the fighting was at its most ferocious in the pope's garden in the Vatican, where even women were firing weapons.[41]

From Genoa on 21 May 1849 Morelli detailed to Giovanni Leonardo Frizzoni (then unable to fight) the movements of Austrian and French troops in different Italian cities, principally watching General Charles Oudinot, commander of the French expedition that besieged the new republic in Rome in order to reinstate Pius IX:

> The news that arrived in Genoa today is that:
>
> At Civitavecchia 25,000 French reinforcements have already arrived, camped only 4 or 5 miles from Rome.
>
> At Livorno arrests and executions continue. Two Austrian officials were assassinated a few days ago, and it was falsely rumored that the patriot [Francesco] Guerrazzi had been shot—though I do not believe it. On the recommendation of the Austrians, 150 men, many Lombards, were shot by the Austrians without trial. Livornesi wrote that after the occupation of Livorno many Lombards were arrested. The damage from bombs to the city is not serious so far.
>
> At Palermo it is said that complete anarchy reigns. A description of that city made to me weeks ago by d'Azeglio's brother, the Jesuit [Luigi] Tapparelli, makes me believe it must be true.

> Austria has taken Bologna, even though the resistance has been bold and courageous, the keys sent to the pope. (In Italy we have unfortunately only single cities!)
>
> 40,000 soldiers are to be concentrated here in Genoa, the number already surpassing 30,000.[42]

On 3 July reports reached Genoa of extraordinary cannon fire in Rome. It was remarkable that an unfortified city of only 160,000 inhabitants maintained itself without internal disorder during two months of fighting. So far the French had spent 1.2 million francs on destruction. By 30 June much of the city had been destroyed by French projectiles: at San Pancrazio there was hardly a house that still had a roof on it, while the church of San Pietro in Montorio, with an altarpiece by Sebastiano del Piombo, was in a disastrous state, riddled with French bullets. Reliable rumour had it that Roman deputy Michele Accursi came home after a meeting in Paris with Oudinot, to ask the Roman Assembly to surrender, in order to save the monuments of the city from worse damage. Difficulties, Morelli predicted, would begin for the French when they entered Rome, and for Pope Pius IX as well.

In the next decade, 1849–59, Morelli and many of his democratic friends would overcome the reservations about the monarchy that had resulted from the failure of 1849. Patriots of all kinds converged, because the monarchy represented the only possibility of success after the repeated failures of the Mazzini republic.

□

After the fighting, Morelli retreated in August 1849 to St Moritz in Switzerland to stay with the Frizzoni family; then he went to villa Melli at Bever, and finally to his own villa at San Fermo, where he received news of the death of his old friend Giovanni Leonardo Frizzoni:

> Poor Giovanni … In the revolution of 1848 he was sent from the city as a parliamentarian to the Austrian garrison, where he was locked up in the barracks, and held hostage for thirty-six hours, continuously threatened by a fusillade. That experience hastened his death. He died of a nervous fever, fifteen days after a successful cataract operation on his eyes.[43]

Frizzoni's widow, Clementina, who had nursed her husband in his last illness, was desolate, as were their five children (see Frizzoni family tree on page XXV). Morelli's letter to his then favourite among them, the eldest, Teodoro (1838–1931), expresses his condolences in a way that transcends a commonplace expression of grief: "Here is a son who promises to become worthy of his father … Next Spring I hope to spend some time with you, then we will speak of your studies, we will speak of your future and most of all we will speak of your father." Morelli promises to send the lad a Newfoundland dog to comfort and protect him in his grief.[44] Teodoro's brother Gustavo (1840–1919) would later became Morelli's protégé, first biographer, and most devoted follower.[45]

Impoverished by the First War of Independence, during which he had received no income, Morelli retreated to San Fermo, which he referred to as his *Sanssouci*. He was helped financially by his maternal uncle, Pietro Zavaritt. At a practical level he looked to replenish his garden, and requested from Gorle cuttings of fruit and flowers, *pipi d'orati*, *beurrès gris*, Spanish vines, strawberries, pineapples, *reseda* (mignonette) seeds, and beautiful white roses. As his funds were limited he employed people on a day-to-day arrangement, and in this way tried to return his bank balance to credit.[46]

At San Fermo Morelli lived with his mother and aunt in relative solitude. They received no visits, nor made any. Morelli divided his time between managing his estate, with short visits to Milan, and reading Alphonse de Lamartine's *Histoire des Girondins* (1847), an eight-volume page-turner that gave an account of French revolutionary politics over the last fifty years, with unforgettable vignettes of the leading figures, from the imprisoned king to the assassins. Later recognized as a literary classic, it may have inspired Morelli's thoughts on how to achieve democratic government. In the Lombard revolution Morelli had fought in companies composed of volunteers, some from old patrician families with liberal monarchist principles, supported by urban artisans, hunters, and mountaineers. In the aftermath of 1848–49, those who had caught a glimpse of the potential for change longed for more, but saw that it would be difficult to achieve. As Morelli wrote:

> Nationalism is huge in all the Peninsula—religious reform is urgent, and this in my opinion is the principal thing to be gained, because as long as there exists a leonine Rome in Italy one cannot speak of national independence. Our Rome belongs to the Middle Ages and will be destroyed from head to foot. We will remake a Rome that is truly Italian—Piedmont, at the forefront of Italian nationalism, is very democratized and will become more worthy of directing the national movement. I have great admiration for the Piedmontese—they are colder, more moral, more conscientious.[47]

In his mature years Morelli would become instantly recognizable as a magnificent character from a noble past age in Italy, the Risorgimento, one that by the time of his death in 1891 was fast disappearing. For when the young Viennese art historian Julius von Schlosser met the elderly Lombard, he characterized Morelli as unforgettable, not only for his liveliness, his spirit, and his culture, but because he had played an active part in the Risorgimento, an experience that had helped shape his entire being.[48]

CHAPTER 6
A Decade in Waiting for a Unified Italy

For most of the 1850s, Morelli enjoyed country life at San Fermo. When war and politics became impossible, simply being a good rural citizen was something to be embraced. Nevertheless, throughout this time he believed that eventually he would participate in the liberation of his country.[1] Every period of Italian history re-invents the Renaissance. During the Risorgimento, Morelli and his friends did just that, in preparation for Italian independence. The word "risorgere," meaning "to rise again," implied a national Renaissance. Allied with the political imperative to free Italy from foreign rule or intervention was Morelli's ambition to preserve and display the patrimony of Italy by establishing new museums across the nation.

Exile in the aftermath of 1848–49 was also sweet for Morelli in the sense that he escaped frequently to villa Balbianello at Bellagio, owned by the Arconati Visconti family and said to be the most magical villa on Lake Como. Here he fell in love with Clementina Frizzoni, the young widow of his best friend Giovanni Leonardo—a woman whose company he had always enjoyed. Clementina described her first years with Morelli as *anni volcanici*, but the details of their relationship have been censored by the Frizzoni family, who destroyed the intimate content of their letters. We do know that they enjoyed a lengthy, amorous friendship that lasted until Morelli's death. It began as an exciting sexual experience, but was as much about caring for the five Frizzoni children.

From 1850 Morelli and Clementina were in contact while on vacation in separate holiday retreats in the vicinity of Bellagio: Clementina at Crella and Morelli at Taronico, where he bought a villa in 1856. His move from the idyllic but isolated San Fermo to this small village near Como, where many wealthy Milanese families spent their leisure hours, repositioned Morelli in the larger theater of Milanese politics, and put him in contact with European royalty. Neighbours included King Leopold II of Belgium, Archduke Maximilian I of Austria (then viceroy of Lombardy–Venetia before leaving to become emperor of Mexico in 1864) and Maximilian's wife, Carlotta. From the Sommariva villa at Tremezzo on Lake Como they could hear the sounds of the Saxon court of Meiningen-Hildburghausen-Gotha, band music, and the whistle of rockets and fireworks. Morelli enjoyed the garden at Crella even more than the proprietors did, spending from seven to nine o'clock every evening there with his "buon' amica" Clementina.[2]

Glimpses of the rapport between Morelli and Clementina may be seen in a manuscript that survives in copies among some six Frizzoni archives in Bergamo, containing passages from letters written by Morelli to Clementina from 1854 to 1855.[3] The quotations reveal what Morelli was reading as he wrote about them to Clementina. They range from newspaper articles, to plays, classical texts, and literature about Christianity and Protestantism. While reading a review of the Le Monnier edition of *The Imitation of Christ* by Thomas à Kempis, with parallel texts in Latin and Italian, Morelli thought of Clementina and her *bimbi*.[4] He confessed that he would willingly re-read this deeply moving text, "not alone, but with you all, my dear" (*e non da solo, ma insieme con voi tutti, amica mia*). What survives of the letters reveals an intense meeting of minds, an intellectual intoxication with ideas, as Morelli communicates his thoughts.

The letters also played an educational role, whether consciously or unconsciously, in the lives of the five Frizzoni children. The first fragment from the correspondence is a highly individual comparison of the ways in which two French authors create and confront irony: Blaise Pascal (1623–1662) and the lesser-known revolutionary Paul Louis Courier (1772–1825). For Morelli, Courier's images are more popular, more natural, conveyed in a warmer style, whereas Pascal is an honest Catholic, more malicious, less liberal, but a better writer. The comparison is followed by a lengthy extract from an unpublished rare manuscript by Gino Capponi, the beginning of his *History of Christianity*, unfinished due to the misfortune of the author.[5] The quotation is about the pure beginnings of Christianity, and analyzes five reasons for the success of the early Church given by Edward Gibbon in his *Decline and Fall of the Roman Empire*. Throughout the correspondence there is discussion of the beginnings of new periods in Christianity, with Morelli always expressing admiration for early Christianity and for Martin Luther.

The next fragment is a discussion of the plays of the Spanish dramatist Pedro Calderón de la Barca (1600–1681), arguing that they would be incomprehensible without a knowledge of the period in which the playwright lived. Morelli then moves on to Lord Byron's 1821 play *Marino Faliero*, emphasizing his personal dislike of Byron's portrayal of the doge's wife, Angiolina, a blue-stocking whose defense of her husband reminds him of those pompous professors of unhappy memory (*infelice memoria*) whom he endured at the Diet of Frankfurt. From there he expresses his dislike of Pierre Daru's *Histoire de la République de Venise* (1797), written, he realizes, by a courtier of Napoleon, and with no credibility.

At times Morelli reflects on his disillusionment with the battles of 1848–49, and laments that these struggles brought no significant change. He expressed to Clementina one such complaint about Count Gabrio Casati, a Lombard patrician who for many decades had attempted to secure freedom for

Lombardy through his political dealings with the Austrian regime, and most importantly had been president of the provisional government of Lombardy when Morelli was at the Frankfurt Diet. By chance, in 1854 Casati invited Morelli to visit him at home, which gave Morelli the chance to observe him personally. Morelli concluded that Casati was only capable of seeing politics in the most trivial manner, and explaining them in an even more trivial way, with inflated vanity and puerile humour. Morelli suddenly understood how, under the direction of such a man, Italian affairs went so badly in 1848.

In this way Morelli poured out his heart to Clementina, communicating his thoughts about Austrian politics, expressing his antipathy to all things French, avowing his belief in Montaigne's view of friendship, responding to her many questions, and occasionally communicating his frank feelings about art. On this last topic, he constantly admired Vasari, despised Giovanni Paolo Lomazzo, and believed that Carl Friedrich von Rumohr, whom he had met when a young student in Berlin, was the most important art historian after Winckelmann:

> Rumohr is a real Teutonic Baron, full of haughtiness, arrogance, and prejudice. But he has a very fine and sophisticated sensibility and many followers. His style is more that of a diplomat than a philosopher or artist. No one knows better than he how to impress, and to his bravura one may attribute this extraordinary fame, that he knew how to acquire in Europe.[6]

Morelli confessed to Clementina that he had had spent an entire morning with Rumohr's book. He thought it unlikely that anyone would read an Italian translation of the three volumes, the first being only about abstract theories of the beautiful, thus dismissing Rumohr's *Italienische Forschungen* (Berlin, 1827–31), always considered the foundation of modern art history. Even though Rumohr, Morelli noted, was considered the "pope of art," his discoveries would be overturned in a few years.

By contrast, Jacob Burckhardt's *Cicerone*, just published in 1855,[7] delighted Morelli, partly because it was the product of a Swiss Protestant sensibility, but more because he recognized the quality of the writing and Burckhardt's idiosyncratic knowledge. "In much I am not in agreement with him," he wrote to Clementina, "but in others his judgment and way of observing art (*ravvisare l'arte*) appear fine and beyond what one normally reads. The most beautiful passages in this book, or those that seem so to me, I shall note, in order to read them to you, when we will meet again."[8] Morelli's admiration for all of Burckhardt's writings would prove constant. When asked in August 1864 to recommend someone to advise on the restoration of Florence Cathedral, he suggested to Niccolò Antinori that Burckhardt, then professor at Basel, be appointed, asserting that *The Civilization of the Renaissance in Italy* was the most pleasurable influence on his own writing.[9]

□

Morelli never considered marrying Clementina, although from 1872 until Morelli's death they lived in separate but adjacent apartments at via Pontaccio 14, Milan, in a house belonging to Swiss relatives, the Ginoulhiac family. But he supported the education of her sons as if he were their father. Beginning with eleven-year-old Teodoro (pictured as an adult in Fig. 49), on 15 December 1849 Morelli wrote: "I was most pleased to receive your dear letter, and even more so when reading it to experience the beautiful and precious inheritance that your poor father left to me with you. Be assured, dear one, that I will be always your sincere and true friend. And were you not always, dear Teodoro, my favourite?"[10] After Christmas, on 2 February 1850, Morelli received from Teodoro his translation of the *Fables of Fedro*. Dissatisfied that the boy had not brought out the moral of the story, Morelli gave an extensive criticism of his translation. It must have been at this time that Morelli gave to Teodoro three portraits of himself as a young student in Munich, by Mende (Fig. 13), by Kaulbach (Fig. 14), and the intellectual portrait in his study (Fig. 11).

Teodoro, like his father, studied extensively abroad when he was a young man. From Taronico, on 26 September 1857, Morelli wrote to him in Paris, complimenting him on his study of the fine arts (*arti belle*), pleased that he was not merely concentrating on transferable skills (*lo studio dell'utile*), but was involved in the history of a subject that in Italy had been shrouded in darkness. Morelli relished the description that Teodoro sent him of a three-quarter-length, three-figure painting, then attributed to Giorgione, which had been bought by Wilhelm II of the Netherlands for his collection of Italian Old Master paintings.[11] At that date Morelli had not seen the work (it had not been sold with the rest of Wilhelm's collection at the auction held in August 1850), so his words are taken from Teodoro's (missing) letter to him. Teodoro's description of the painting reminded Morelli of his hatred of German philosophy and aesthetics, as Teodoro wrote: "There is no action in this painting, but those three faces represent a series of actions—the woman is present reality—the husband represents the past, the doctor, the prophet, the future," to which Morelli responded: "This way of looking at and interpreting art is contrary to art itself, because if the artist had ever had such an allegorical idea while he stood before his canvas, it is certain that he would have made one of those insipid clumsinesses that the modern German School regards as high and profound history painting."[12] The Venetian painting depicts a young woman swooning, supported by her companion, who holds her full and nearly nude breasts, while a man (the presumed doctor) looks on. There are many versions of this composition (now called *The Lovers*); the best-known is in the British Royal Collection, while another is at Casa Buonarroti, Florence.[13] The composition remains puzzling, and without a convincing interpretation the attribution to Giorgione impossible. But the raw sexuality must have appealed to the young Teodoro, as it did in recent times to Diana, Princess of Wales. In the 2017 television documentary *Diana: In Her Own Words*, the version from the British Royal Collection appears above the princess—presumably chosen by her for her rooms—when she speaks of the breakdown of sexual relations in her marriage.

In the same letter, Morelli advises Teodoro on what to do in an art gallery, with a view to creating his own collection. In the Louvre, for instance, he recommends concentrating on looking at only Leonardo, Raphael, and Correggio:

> Consider them one by one, then compare them with one another (*Considerale prima a una a una da sé, poi confrontale l'una coll'altra*) ... Another thing that I would like to recommend, as I have practiced it for some time, is that when you enter a gallery, before noting the judgment in the catalogue, you should baptize the works in your own mind (*E un'altra cosa che vorrei raccomandarti, perché da me praticata con non piccolo mio vantaggio. Usati, quando entri in una galleria di quadri, prima di ricordare il giudizio stampato nel Catalogo, di battezzarli "mente tua"*).[14]

Teodoro is also encouraged to indulge in the many pleasures of Paris, including patisserie at Felix, Ostend oysters with a glass of Chablis, and dinner at either Les Frères Provençaux or the Café Français. As the letters continue, Morelli becomes more passionate about his paternal role, remarking on 24 November 1857 that Burckhardt, who had known Teodoro, has been in Italy for three weeks but has not visited him, even though he would have loved to have met him.

□

In the 1850s Morelli and his mother and aunt were living on income derived from rent on his mother's estates at Viganone, near Lodi, and Lampugnano, which totalled about 8,000 lire per annum. In the earliest of his surviving books of accounts from this time (it stops in November 1856),[15] he meticulously recorded payments to his mother and aunt; local travel to the Brianza, Bergamo, Cernobbio, Lecco, and Milan; payments to an expensive tailor for shirts, gloves, shoes, boots, and hats; and occasional expenses such as book purchases, binding of manuscripts, a subscription to the *Allgemeine Zeitung*, and considerable tips to the staff in the Frizzoni home at Crella. The Morelli property was administered by Angelo, Giuseppe, two unnamed domestics, and Antonietta.

From the 1850s Morelli began acquiring paintings, from private collections in Bergamo.[16] Some of these purchases were for himself, others on behalf of friends who were forming collections. But although this activity involved both buying and selling, Morelli was never an art dealer.

Among Morelli's list of expenses is an entry for March 1853 for the purchase of a Lorenzo Lotto from the heirs of the bishop of Bergamo (presumably from the estate of Carlo Gritti Morlacchi, who had died the previous December).

The price was 326.5 lire, a reasonable sum for a good-sized religious painting.[17] On the next page it is recorded that Morelli sold the work to Federico Frizzoni (younger brother of the late Giovanni Leonardo) for the same price (Fig. 50). The only Lotto that Federico ever owned is recorded by Eastlake in his notebook on 14 September 1855, as a variant of the composition of *The Virgin and Child with St Joseph and St Catherine*, which Eastlake had seen in the Lochis collection and was to select for Bergamo.[18] There are five or six versions of the composition and Federico may have sold his, as it is not recorded on Eastlake's later visits, nor in the inventory that Morelli made of his friend's collection, a sign of a negative judgment.[19]

Three years later Morelli mentions paintings again: in February 1856 he had a carpenter build some cases built for their transport,[20] as he rather liked to travel with a few paintings.[21] These particular expenses relate to a Madonna and Christ Child by Mantegna that Morelli bought for himself in 1856, and until he sold it in 1861 often took with him on his travels, protected by a specially made box.[22]

Morelli developed an informal policy to find masterpieces for important collections belonging to his friends. For instance, to the Lombard patriot Gian Giacomo Poldi Pezzoli (Fig. 53) he sold five significant Renaissance paintings that had been in his possession since 1856, beginning on 14 September 1861 with the Mantegna *Madonna and Christ Child* for 2,000 lire; on 1 August 1862 he sold three works to Poldi—two by Andrea Solario (St Catherine and St John the Baptist) and a third, possibly a Head of St John the Baptist by Solario—all said to have a Bergamesque provenance, for 1,132.4 lire; and on 9 June 1866 a portrait of a young boy said to be by Domenico Puligo, now attributed to Francesco Salviati, for 440 lire.[23] The paintings were then sent for restoration with the renowned Giuseppe Molteni in Milan, and the works by Solario were transferred from wood panel to canvas by Antonio Zanchi.

The 2,000 lire for the Mantegna was a very high price for Poldi to pay for a painting; he only once paid more than that: some 5,750 lire for two works by Lorenzo Lotto and Luini. To put these figures in perspective, Poldi's total yearly income was 27,000 lire, while a subscription to a box at La Scala cost 360 lire. Probably the price of the Solario works was lower because of their condition. As for the exquisite portrait of a boy, believed then to be by Puligo, 440 lire was what Poldi often spent on an acquisition. Morelli had recognized the quality of the Mantegna when he bought it in May 1856, describing it as a real jewel, a marvel (*meraviglia*), even though the head of the Madonna had been retouched and the dealer had failed to recognize the authorship.[24]

A few acquisitions remained in Morelli's collection, such as a Cariani portrait, and a *St Jerome* by Bartolomeo Montagna, now in the Accademia Carrara. Morelli was proud of pictures by Bergognone, the Lombardic equivalent of Fra Angelico. He speculated that Charles Eastlake would have liked to buy them for the National Gallery in London, but Morelli would never sell them, because every gentleman should retain rare and beautiful works of art for the national heritage: he believed they belonged to the nation, and the owner was merely a custodian.[25]

It may have been the artist, restorer, and museum director Giuseppe Molteni who introduced Morelli to Poldi, as the first reference to their friendship is in Molteni's letters, when by 1861 they are already "amici," and dedicated to the same cause: to create a superb collection of Renaissance paintings that could serve as a political show of power, a demonstration of Italian genius, at a period when Italy was subject to the repressive regime of the Austrian empire.[26] The father of Gian Giacomo Poldi, Giuseppe, had inherited a considerable estate from his father's family, the Poldi of Parma, and an even larger one from his mother's family, from Count Pezzoli d'Albertone of Bergamo, a collector of taxes for Empress Maria Theresa of Austria. The family's Milanese residence was a seventeenth-century palazzo, with an internal garden in the English style, recognized in old guidebooks as one of the most beautiful in Milan. Gian Giacomo's mother, Rosa Trivulzio, was the daughter of an outstanding intellectual, the Marchese Gian Giacomo Trivulzio, a leading figure in neoclassicism and the Enlightenment, and his wife Beatrice Serbelloni, who had created a legendary Romantic salon which brought together patriots and poets like Silvio Pellico and Federico Confalonieri.

Poldi grew up in this privileged milieu of culture allied with patriotism in the 1820s and 1830s. His mother was widowed in 1831, and she expanded the family's art collection, often taking advice from Molteni. When Poldi came of age in 1846 (at twenty-four, according to Austrian law), he immediately constructed an apartment for himself in a separate wing of the palazzo, and formed an armory of ancient and modern weapons, on the advice of dealer Giovanni Colombo. In 1847 this collection was displayed in the Sala d'Arme, in an installation designed by La Scala scenic painter Filippo Peroni. As in sixteenth-century Venice, the armory was meant to impress foreign visitors with a show of strength. This was a period of incandescent Romanticism, when operas by the young Verdi were first performed at La Scala: *Nabucco* (1842), *I Lombardi alla prima crociata* (1843) and *Giovanna d'Arco* (1845). Though traditional in form, these operas were interpreted by Italian patriots as stories paralleling contemporary politics. Similarly, the armory was meant to empower Italians in that period of bitter fighting for individual rights that had culminated in the Cinque giornate. When Poldi's armory was sacked by the Austrians in retaliation against him as a young Liberal, and Marshall Radetzky re-established Austrian rule over Milan, Poldi was heavily fined 600,000 Austrian lire and expelled from Milan. He took refuge in Switzerland, and traveled throughout Europe, adding to his collection. By the 1850s the Poldi Pezzoli was the most-imitated house museum in the world, inspiring the creation of the Musée Jacquemart-André in Paris, the Isabella Stewart Gardner Museum in Boston, and the Frick Gallery in New

York. The motivation was different, however: these French and American collectors valued Italian Renaissance art for art's sake, without espousing any of the values of the Risorgimento.

An alliance that developed during this decade between Morelli and Francesco De Sanctis (who in 1861 was appointed Ministro dell'Istruzione Pubblica, a portfolio that included cultural affairs), was unusually productive. They had known one another from at least the 1850s, when De Sanctis was in poverty and exile. Morelli had lent him books, arranged for the sale of those De Sanctis had written, and in 1855 helped him obtain his first appointment (as professor of Italian literature at the Politecnico of Zurich, a position first offered to Morelli). Shortly after the appointment Morelli wrote to his uncle, Pietro Zavaritt: "I went on my autumnal journey. I spent four days at Belgirate on Lago Maggiore in company with De Sanctis, Manzoni, De Meis and other friends. That brief sojourn and intimate experience of life was true manna for my mind and heart."[27] De Sanctis' impression of the same trip was of Morelli promising the group of friends a walk (*passeggiata*) that became a forced march of six hours (*marcia forzata di sei ore*). But he also recalled Morelli reducing them all to laughter with his impersonation of the gestures and accent of their southern colleague, Diomede Marvasi, reciting a dictionary of Neapolitan obscenities.[28]

□

Across Europe, many national galleries were founded to house and display the art of the Italian Renaissance, rather than to preserve the cultural heritage of the countries where they were located. These new institutions sought out the best Italian Old Master paintings, wherever they could find them. After the battles of the Risorgimento, conservation played an important role in preserving Italian patrimony throughout Italy, but especially in Lombardy and Tuscany, because many monuments had been damaged and neglected, whereas for these foreign national galleries conservation was valued as a diagnostic instrument for judging quality and condition. When, for instance, nine recently cleaned pictures were placed on view at the National Gallery in London in November 1852, their appearance caused considerable controversy in the press, leading to a parliamentary enquiry the following year.[29] The 900-page report is a revealing study of attitudes to art restoration in mid-nineteenth-century England.[30] Due to the emergence of national museums, a critical public, the appearance of restoration manuals, and programs for the education and ethics of restoration, a more modern concept of restoration was gradually developing. One of the few Italians who contributed to the British parliamentary enquiry was the relatively unknown writer and critic Giovanni Battista Cavalcaselle (1819–1897), then sharing London lodgings with Joseph Archer Crowe (1825–1896) while working together on the first of their many joint publications, on early Flemish painting (1857). The parliamentary report contains a ferocious letter from the 34-year-old Cavalcaselle, written on 9 June 1853, in which he charged Charles Eastlake, then aged sixty, and recently appointed as the first director of the National Gallery, with vandalism. To prove his point, Cavalcaselle described Claude's *Landscape with Hagar and the Angel* as ruined (*rovinato*), claiming that blue underpainting on the dress of the angel had been revealed by the removal of a greater part of a hypothetical superimposed orange-yellow glaze, which he detected in touches of color on the dress and shoulder. Cavalcaselle also alleged that the color of the angel's wings had been cleaned away down to the white preparation. Current opinion does not support Cavalcaselle's analysis,[31] but rather reveals that the shoulder and wing are particularly well preserved parts of the painting, which is in much better condition than most works by Claude. The yellow on the angel's shoulder is solidly brushed in, for Claude conceived the dress as shot coloring—yellow in the lights and blue in the shadows—while the tips of the wings are in impasto. Cavalcaselle must have been misled by his painter's theory that Hagar's blue dress needed to be complemented by an angel in yellow.[32]

To his credit, Eastlake tried to reconcile these differences of opinion, but his friends, especially the archaeologist Austen Henry Layard and his wife, Lady (Enid) Layard, always held reservations about Cavalcaselle.

What has surprised today's art historians about Eastlake's restorations of Renaissance paintings is the care that he took to cover up erotic details. When Eastlake visited the collection of Federico Frizzoni at Bellagio he was very taken by Moretto da Brescia's last work, *The Entombment of Christ* (now in the Metropolitan Museum of Art, New York), except that the position of the Virgin's fingers, outlining Christ's prominent navel, made the picture too sexy, and hence ineligible for London, unless it could be covered up or changed.[33] Similarly, the deletion of details on Bronzino's famous *Allegory* (a work that Eastlake did accept for the National Gallery), such as the hiding of a tongue kiss, and the obscuring (by a restoration) of Cupid's hand squeezing his mother's nipple, affected the interpretation of the painting until very recently.[34]

From 1855, when he began as director of the National Gallery, Eastlake adopted an energetic acquisitions policy, and appointed Otto Mündler, Morelli's friend from his postgraduate days in Paris, to assist him as travelling agent for the gallery.[35] It was from Mündler that Morelli heard about Eastlake's policies. Mündler occupied the post from 1855 to 1858, when it was abolished by the House of Commons, due to persistent anti-German criticism in the press. During that time, Mündler kept diaries of all the works of art he saw and considered for acquisition for the gallery—many, many more than those acquired.[36] Eastlake and Mündler would take their acquisitions to Molteni's studio in the Brera, where they were examined, restored, repainted, and sometimes re-attributed, before being exported to England.[37]

The urge to create national museums, whether in Berlin or London, introduced serious problems for patriotic Italians. While the best Italian Old Master paintings were being hunted down by other nations, in Italy public museums were being formed from old aristocratic collections, such as the Uffizi, or from enforced ecclesiastical requisitions, like the Brera. Before 1861 it was comparatively easy to take paintings out of Italy. Morelli feared that Eastlake was an *"indefesso accaparratore,"* an indefatigable searcher of paintings.[38]

□

Nevertheless, Morelli would form strong and long-lasting friendships with a number of British men and women. He had met the first of his true English friends, diplomat James Hudson (1810–1885), at the Diet of Frankfurt in 1848, and renewed the acquaintance when Hudson was the English representative at Turin between 1852 and 1864.[39] From the moment of his appointment, Hudson was recognized as a passionate Italophile, by both British and Italian politicians. Though born to an aristocratic Yorkshire family, he was rumored to be the bastard son of King George IV. People who visited his office at the British legation at Turin, such as Eastlake and Morelli, were impressed by his art collection, which made manifest his sophisticated connoisseurial understanding of Lombard painting, demonstrated by his ownership of the most gorgeous Moretto da Brescia portrait of a young man, luxuriously dressed with an inscription in Greek on his cap: "Alas, I desire too much." The image reveals much about the collector.[40]

Hudson was tall, very handsome, eccentric, and fascinating to everyone who met him. He was given a succession of brilliant diplomatic postings: to Washington in 1838, The Hague in 1845, Rio de Janeiro in 1850, and then to Italy, where the British prime minister, Lord Palmerston, reported to Cavour that Hudson was the very best British diplomat there was. His instructions were to put his heart into the Piedmontese, a brief that he exceeded, on his own initiative.[41] Inevitably Hudson became friendly with Cavour and with a group of Italian politicians who were also Morelli's friends and political colleagues, including the first prime minister of Piedmont, Massimo d'Azeglio, as well as Marco Minghetti, later prime minister of Italy. Hudson was a Liberal, who was against the despotic politics of Austria. He was supportive of Protestants in Italy and opposed to the Roman Curia—political sympathies similar to Morelli's. His diplomatic career ended rather abruptly when he left Turin in 1864, and it became a matter of speculation why this happened. After his death in 1885, one explanation was offered by his good friend Austen Henry Layard: that Hudson was *not* removed to make room for Sir Henry Elliot, as some had claimed, but had resigned for personal reasons. He was deeply in love with a Milanese woman, Signora Eugenia, who was already married. Hudson retreated to Salò, where he received his pension and lived happily with her in retirement. According to Layard, Hudson was disliked because he would "not submit to the routine of office, rarely answered dispatches and never took any notice of 'circulars' and was altogether too independent. He always received the most cordial support from [prime minister] Lord Russell who was an advocate of the Italian cause as every Italian gratefully recognizes."[42]

In any case, the surviving correspondence between Hudson and Morelli dates from the time Hudson retired and is all about his pure enjoyment of the Morellian method, looking at pictures, and only occasionally about politics. In April 1859 Morelli was planning an artistic study tour accompanied by Hudson, whom he believed was very interested in the fine arts (*il quale s'interessa pare molto di Belle Arti*);[43] they would go to Moncalieri to meet a learned Barnabite who was an expert on the school of Piedmont, to Vercelli, and to Vigevano, in all a trip of eight days. At the same time, Morelli was in communication with Cavour, noting the increasing presence of troops and reserves. On 1 April he stated his belief that, by the end of May, war would break out.

□

Morelli's prediction proved correct. The Second Italian War of Independence erupted at the end of April 1859. It saw the French allied with Piedmont and the Kingdom of Sardinia, against a weakened Austrian Empire. Morelli's role in June and July was to head the National Guard of Bergamo (he was Comandante della Guardia Nazionale), which was in charge of defense and security for the city, a position to which he was elected after the Austrians left Bergamo. The war finished in mid-July. As long as there was an element of danger, Morelli was animated by the office, but once the danger had passed he attempted to resign, which he eventually succeeded in doing on 3 August.[44] Liberated, Morelli went to the Engadine, where he regained his sanity and energy by walking in the mountains.

Public proclamations throughout Bergamo chart the fast-moving events of these months. On 8 June 1859 Garibaldi invited all men of Bergamo between the ages of twenty-one and fifty-five to enlist in his Cacciatori degli Alpi. With powerful and emotive words, echoing Manzoni, Garibaldi summoned his compatriots:

> All young men who can carry a rifle are called to surround the tricolor flag. None of you would wish to be inert and cowardly in this holy war; no one would wish one day to confess, blushing, that they had not participated. Now is the time to say that you were not lying when you said that you hated Austria. To arms then. No sacrifice seems impossible to us, because we are the generation who will achieve the task of Italian Independence.[45]

Practical as always, Morelli published a proclamation (on 18 June) asking all citizens who were in the National Guard to practice shooting, and created a *bersaglio* (firing range) in the square beneath the church of Sant'Agostino, previously reserved for football. To supervise the bersaglio, he set up a commission, consisting of his own friends and relatives: Conte Giovanni Spini, Pietro Zavaritt, Conte Luigi Albani, and Attilio Vimercati. Bergamo had 2,300 men and 400 reserves in its National Guard. They were prepared to fight, although in the end they did not see action. On 7 June the Austrians abandoned Bergamo. On 8 June Garibaldi led his troops through the city's Porta San Lorenzo. A few days later, Count Giacomo Lupi was named *podestà* (mayor or administrator).

On 8 July Vittorio Emanuele II and Napoleon III announced an armistice, preliminary to the Peace of Villafranca (11 July) that Napoleon III negotiated with Franz Joseph I of Austria. Under the latter treaty, Lombardy went from Austrian to French rule. The French later passed Lombardy to Sardinia–Piedmont but retained Venetia. It was a controversial peace; though closing the war in Italy's favour, it was disliked by many, especially the Venetians and Sicilians, who were still under Austrian occupation. For Morelli, it meant the end of Austrian domination of Italy, the creation of a powerful new Piedmont–Lombardy, and the majority of Italians recognizing Vittorio Emanuele as their king. On 12 August Vittorio Emanuele II visited Bergamo and was acclaimed by the citizens. By mid-April 1860, Garibaldi had enrolled more than a 170 men from Bergamo among the thousand he took to assist Sicily, which led to Bergamo becoming known as *La città dei Mille*, in recognition of their most significant contribution to the Risorgimento.

□

In the aftermath of this military success, in December 1859 Morelli wrote ecstatically to Teodoro of a wintry excursion to Parma, Modena, Bologna, and Ferrara, giving a personal account of sixteenth-century Emilian art, in which Correggio emerges as his favourite genius. When Correggio came to Parma in 1516 it was a cultural desert, and Morelli suggests that he visited Venice in 1512 to encounter the Giorgioneschi, Lotto, and Titian, for his coloring is very close to Giorgione's:[46]

> Correggio is one of those fascinating geniuses whose work either fascinates or repulses you. He is perhaps the freest soul that art has ever known. And as for the feeling of beauty in the forms of the human body, he goes beyond Raphael, Michelangelo, science, and general culture. At times his sensitivity borders on the nauseating; there is not a fibre in the limbs of his figures that does not quiver with life, everything is in movement, everything is interpenetrated with an electric, nervous fluid. The air that circulates in his paintings is marvellous (I remember only having seen something similar in the works of Velazquez). Correggio achieves this air by means of chiaroscuro. In this

respect, there is nothing more miraculous than the head, hand, and arm in Saint Mary Magdalen in the painting of [The Madonna of] St Jerome (Galleria Nazionale, Parma). Correggio is the most liberated representative of art that has broken away from the Church. He moves towards anarchy, in every work going beyond the boundaries that are assigned to art. This is a characteristic that he shares with other geniuses, brought up like him in the august life of the provinces, far from the great centre of culture ... No one is as capable as Correggio of conveying palpitating life and reality. He is sensual, it is true, indeed very sensual, the most sensual of all artists—but his sensuality is eternal, I would say transparent, the sensuality of nervous beings, extremely sensitive ethics. If you would like to find a comparison among plants, he is comparable to a *mimosa sensitiva*.[47]

Morelli's passionate tone when communicating to Teodoro his views on Emilian art is unmatched in his later published writings on art. Here he reveals how in the 1850s he was putting together local histories of various regional schools of art, part of a grand plan beginning with Piedmont and then Emilia-Romagna. The ideas are sophisticated and developed, the language exuberant. To Antinori he recounts days spent in Bologna, escaping the snow and rain, visiting churches, private collections, and galleries. At night in his hotel room he commits to paper his thoughts on Emilian art.[48]

On 10 February 1860, De Sanctis wrote to mutual friend Angelo Camillo De Meis, regretting that he seemed to have lost touch with Morelli:

I hear that Emiliani Giudici has been elected professor of fine arts and aesthetics—how Morelli would have laughed at that. What does one hear about Morelli? Is he in Bergamo or Milan? I have not heard from him in a long time. I know he intended to live in Milan. It is strange that in this changing movement of men and things, that no one thinks of him.[49]

But by the following year, 1861, when De Sanctis was appointed Ministro dell'Istruzione Pubblica by Cavour, he and Morelli (old allies, and committed to the same cause), embarked on a series of artistic reforms, for in his short-lived ministry De Sanctis would repeatedly ask for his friend's advice.

CHAPTER 7

Representing Bergamo in the Camera dei Deputati

In the aftermath of the 1848–49 revolution, Italy in the 1850s had enjoyed a mood of positivism and a belief that everything that had been fought for in the battles of the Risorgimento could now be achieved. The Italian-speaking people were moving towards unity and democracy. In the elections held in 1860, Morelli became the representative of Bergamo in the Camera dei Deputati in the Parlamento del Regno di Sardegna, which from 1848 had been a constitutional monarchy. Although the Camera dei Deputati was said to be democratic, only literate men over the age of twenty-five and who paid taxes were allowed to vote, representing a small selection of the population (and in the upper house, senators were appointed, not elected). Nevertheless, Morelli's election was testimony to his popularity and exceptionally distinguished military service, and was achieved despite the Catholic Church's hostile opposition to a Protestant candidate. This was the beginning of an extraordinary decade in Morelli's life.

The opening of the 1860 parliament, held in Turin on 2 April, was memorably recorded by Dutch artist Peter Tetar van Elven, a specialist in Italian Risorgimento history painting and official war artist to King Victor Emmanuel II.[1] In the painting (Fig. 51), the king is surrounded by deputies, a club that included Morelli and many friends, such as Camillo Cavour, Alessandro Manzoni, Marco Minghetti, and Francesco De Sanctis, to name only a few—all celebrated intellectuals.[2] The venue is a hall that is in fact surprisingly intimate (despite the representation in the history picture), resembling an eighteenth-century opera house, in the Palazzo Carignano, an extraordinary late-Baroque palace designed by Guarino Guarini for the Savoy royal family. Because parliament would continue to sit in Turin for the next five years, Morelli based himself there for the duration.

Morelli took considerable pride in his position as the elected representative for Bergamo, and would be elected again on 27 January 1861, 22 October 1865, and 29 March 1868. In 1861 the opposing candidate for Bergamo was the conservative Count Giacomo Lupo, but Morelli won by a huge majority, again despite Catholic hate speech against him.[3]

Few enjoy bureaucracy, and Morelli was no exception. Yet he realized that, to create a new Italy, it was essential to spend time on boards and on formulating new legislation, even if the results were unpredictable. By 1865 Morelli had participated in more than twenty-two demanding parliamentary commissions about education, the budget, heritage, conservation, architectural construction, the establishment of new museums, and the creation of a national inventory of works of art, as well as serving on political committees that assisted Alfonso La Marmora's fight against the *briganti*, who were opposed to Italian unity.[4]

He continued to make friends—and enemies—with collectors, restorers, museum directors, and royalty from all over Europe, in what became a political game to determine who should have the best paintings, and how the patrimony of Italy should be preserved and interpreted. In 1874 Morelli was the first Italian politician to effect change in this area at the highest level, by introducing legislation to protect the patrimony of Italy. Later, when he declined the directorship of the Uffizi in 1874, he did so in the realization that it would be much more difficult to bring about change when working at the lower level of a museum directorship. He preferred to continue with the national inventory: "a gallery director without this inventory would be like a warrior without arms. He would need to know what we need in order to complete the collections."[5]

In 1865 a journalist, playwright, and novelist Carlo Righetti (1828–1906), writing under the anagram Cletto Arrighi, published an account of Morelli's political career, as one in a series of biographies of 450 notable deputies.[6] Righetti knew Morelli, had undergone similar experiences in the Risorgimento—having fought in the Wars of Independence—and his informed political biography may have helped with Morelli's re-election in 1865[7] (although it was largely forgotten in later scholarship).[8] Righetti emphasized that Morelli was one of the most active of all the deputies in the Camera dei Deputati, a man who could never be seduced by private interest (*uomo superiore a qualunque seduzione di privato interesse*),[9] who refused to be paid a salary for anything he did, and that even though he addressed the Camera only once, he was always present unless he was away on a commission.

Of the many committees on which Morelli sat, the most important was one on educational reform, which involved daily meetings for four months.[10] Another senator records that Morelli was one of the most assiduous deputies, and that his vote always had value, because he was conscientious and influential.[11] Morelli only ended his role as deputy by resigning in protest in 1870 when the parliament was to be relocated from Florence to Rome.

□

The 1860s also brought a significant change to Morelli's personal life. In 1864 he first met the wife of his friend and fellow politician Marco Minghetti,

Donna Laura, with whom he would embark on an intimate relationship that continued for many decades. Surprisingly, this liaison appears not to have affected his friendship with Marco, although Morelli on occasion judged him very harshly, as when he wrote to Antinori that, despite all his literary and parliamentary qualities, Minghetti lacked the nerve to have a virile soul. It was not only his soul that lacked virility, for contemporary satirists suggested that he was timid in bed, and neglected Laura to go hunting. For Morelli, Minghetti was not really a man, and so could never be a statesman; rather, he was like a baby who had to have icing sugar sprinkled on his illusions.[12]

Laura was born into the Acton family at Naples on 2 March 1829.[13] She was a woman of uncommon beauty and intelligence, both patriotic and cultured, as well as being a fine musician. Her first marriage was to Domenico Beccadelli of Bologna, the Prince of Camporeale, the couple living at Palermo, Germany, and Paris, where she shone at the court of Napoleon III, a dark beauty, passionate and much admired (*bruna, bellissima, ardente, ammirata*). Her husband died in January 1863 and the promiscuous young widow was courted by many Englishmen, including Lord Palmerston. Instead she chose Minghetti, whom she wed in September 1864. Minghetti (born at Bologna in 1818) was then prime minister of Italy (a post he held twice), a politician known for his oratory, but who would be remembered most for his writings on politics and art, in which he was greatly assisted by his friend Morelli. Nevertheless, he is considered to have been a brilliant statesman, who held numerous ministerial positions, and followed Cavour's ideas with enthusiasm in the 1850s, until he took a leadership position. Minghetti was the last Italian president from the historical Right.

Another introduction to Laura Minghetti is given by Countess Walburga Ehrengarde Helena de Hohenthal, later Lady Paget (1839–1929), in her racy memoirs written in Vienna in the 1880s.[14] Before Walburga's marriage to Sir Augustus Berkeley Paget in 1860 she was lady-in-waiting to Crown Princess Victoria, and throughout her life moved with ease among diplomats and royalty. In 1867 her husband became British ambassador in Florence (then the capital of Italy), where she encountered Donna Laura at a party at the Belgian legation, and described her thus: "She wore a cream-coloured satin dress, with creamy coloured lace about it, out of which her beautiful creamy shoulders did more than peep. Her eyes and hair were jet black, her face very long and narrow in shape and colouring like that of a Byzantine saint in expression, more French than Italian." Walburga characterized Laura as "very calculating and ambitious," and:

> it was a severe blow to her when Minghetti was hurled from his post of Prime Minister, ten days after their marriage, in consequence of the September convention, by which the Capital was removed to Florence. After trying to marry Lord Granville, who said he loved her in every capacity except that of a

> wife, and then Sir James Hudson, who also politely but firmly declined, she had chosen Minghetti out of the circle of her adorers. He belonged to a middle-class family of Bologna, and his way of living was of the very simplest.[15]

Lady Paget's take on Donna Laura's appearance at social gatherings and her courting by an infinite number of admirers, one of whom was Morelli, is rather wicked. As Morelli later confided to Niccolò Antinori, he enjoyed meeting with Donna Laura a few times a year, as she had many qualities, but not more often, as she dominated, even tyrannized, him.[16] Nevertheless, he often enjoyed traveling with her, as "she took a lively interest in everything that was beautiful, and never in the vulgar."[17] For instance, when in Rome on 18 March 1879 Morelli wrote to the painter Franz von Lenbach to enquire whether his portrait of Marco Minghetti was finished, mentioning that he had the pleasure of seeing "the life-loving Donna Laura" daily.[18] Corresponding with his friend Jean Paul Richter in November 1881 he referred to his "dearly beloved friend Laura Minghetti," who had just spent three days with him in Milan, to be joined on the last day by her husband;[19] Morelli spent only a half a day with the married couple. Leaving aside the cold cynicism that is often evident in Morelli's accounts of his personal relations, when writing to others he revealed that he valued Laura's friendship, which continued until the end of his life.

□

Morelli's motivation to be a politician is confirmed by his only speech to the Italian parliament. This passionate and lengthy address, delivered on 19 July 1862, was prompted by his concerns about the inadequate care of the Italian Royal Collection of the Sabauda family, prompted by its transport from the Pinacoteca di Torino in the Palazzo Madama to the Palazzo dei Musei.[20] More broadly, he was alarmed that Italy could lose much of its cultural patrimony. While the British parliament had granted the National Gallery in London large sums for acquisitions, each Italian gallery received only 8,000 lire from the government for its annual budget, usually spent on a useless bureaucracy. The catalogues of Italian museums were confused and with erroneous attributions, a lack of order mirrored in muddled display installations. Morelli also objected to the government spending large sums on commissioning works from living artists for parliamentarians' offices, while Italian monuments were in such a sorry state of neglect, and many important works had been sold abroad. Morelli described a broad vision for a total reform of art legislation; the installations, staffing and conservation of Italian museums; the teaching of art in academies; and the re-writing of art literature, guides and catalogues, to ensure that the patrimony of Italy was understood and appreciated. But his speech was met with incomprehension, and the house voted in favor of expenses for arms instead of culture.

Meanwhile, Francesco De Sanctis as minister for public instruction had been keeping him busy. In July 1861 he asked Morelli to outline reforms for the Florentine Academy. Morelli's response included a recommendation to abolish the study of history, geography, and engraving, the latter because he believed it had been supplanted by photography. The history of art as it was taught in Italy was then only about names, not concepts. Instead he recommended teaching the history of art in front of works of art.[21] Many of his proposals were implemented. Morelli favored taking works of art away from churches and other religious institutions to place them in museums. From 1866 he initiated a general inventory of works of art in Italy, intended to record every work of art from the classical periods of art history, whether in public or private collections, that should not leave the country.

In the spring of 1861 Morelli accepted De Sanctis' commission to travel for three months, with Giovanni Battista Cavalcaselle, to the Marche and Umbria, to systematically describe the Renaissance art of those regions, the first time that such a task had been undertaken.[22] Their intention was to identify masterpieces, often unrecognized, which were in monasteries that had been suppressed during the Napoleonic period. The lengthy report that resulted listed pictures by Piero della Francesca, the young Raphael, Lorenzo Lotto, and many "minor" artists.[23] The Marche region (whose cities include Ancona, Ascoli Piceno, Fermo, Macerata, Pesaro and Urbino) was in particular danger of losing treasures to foreign museums. Morelli hoped that as a result of this project and his earlier efforts to gather information about the other regional schools of Italy, whether the Emilia Romagna, Lombardy, or Piedmont, a great national museum would be created—an ambition that was never realized.

The Marche–Umbria trip was not without its dangers: the militant *brigantaggio* still existed in the Marche as well as in Rome. Morelli deplored this state of affairs, believing that such opposition to Italian unity could only be eradicated by separating church and state, something that he hoped would happen the following year in Rome and Venice.[24] Also, he and Cavalcaselle met with some clerical opposition, such as priests hiding works of art among bales of hay.

Before the excursion began, Morelli knew of Cavalcaselle by reputation and looked forward to their collaboration. A few years earlier, Morelli had described him as very intelligent about art ("un altro grandissimo intelligente dell'arte, un certo Cavalcaselle veneziano").[25] On closer acquaintance, however, their relationship soon soured, their personalities being so very different: Morelli the German-educated scientist turned charismatic Lombard politician, Cavalcaselle the introverted artist-turned-critic with a morbid preoccupation with death. How could they have enjoyed one another's company for three months? Indeed, they suffered one another. Morelli even qualified his early view of Cavalcaselle's connoisseurship, concluding that although Cavalcaselle had a very practiced eye—the best that Morelli had encountered—and knew a lot about technique, he failed to understand the interior life of a work of art. There was no love lost between them in years to come, as shown by Morelli's observation to Mündler in 1866: "Cavalcaselle, the surly lay brother, came here to see me yesterday; Unfortunately, I cannot do anything for him."[26] Morelli remarked wryly that everyone attributed his distaste to envy on his part, which was far from the truth.

One might have expected that these two men would have bonded, given their mutual love of art and commitment to the Risorgimento. Many of Morelli's friends, and they were numerous, shared common experiences in the battles of the Risorgimento. But even in the most recent telling of Cavalcaselle's life,[27] his participation in the Risorgimento is limited to the sentimental account by his English collaborator, Crowe, who depicts him in tatters, a refugee from the battles, when he meets him for the second time.[28] According to Crowe, Cavalcaselle did work with Manin in Venice in 1848 and with Giuseppe Mazzini in the short-lived Roman Republic of 1849, but did not participate in the second battles of 1859. What passed between Morelli and Cavalcaselle may remain mysterious, but most likely Morelli was disappointed in Cavalcaselle's half-hearted participation in the wars of the Risorgimento.

Morelli's own diaries of this excursion are the only surviving account of his famous method in practice.[29] As a scientist, never an artist (his drawing skills were poor), Morelli recorded in words visual characteristics of high value. A description exemplifying the Morellian method occurs in his account of a tondo in the church of San Francesco at Pesaro. Indifferent to the religious content or the horror of the image, Morelli makes a formal analysis:

> By Marco Zoppo a tondo representing a head drawn from life of St John the Baptist, with the head cut off bloodied, in foreshortening, in the style of Mantegna; the beard and the hair, as in the other painting, highlighted with grey—the hair as if made like pappardelle [large, flat, egg pasta noodles]—there is very great reality in the drawing and expression—in tempera—in good condition—24 centimeters high and 25 wide—blue background. On the back of the frame: "The painter who made this head was Marco Zoppo of Bologna (1415)."

Morelli's words, though seemingly simple—even banal—concentrate on the essential characteristics of this small, violent tondo, and isolate memorably the way in which Zoppo represents hair—like broad strands of pasta—rather than being a predictable analysis of hands and ears. He notes an inscription on the reverse in seventeenth-century handwriting. The method was flexible in practice, enviable in its simplicity, and amazingly successful in its accuracy. Morelli himself estimated that his attributions were correct eighty per cent of the time, which tallies with modern estimates.[30]

The sad aftermath of the Marche–Umbria excursion is best conveyed by Morelli's words to Antinori in May 1862, revealing his frustration. At just this moment De Sanctis was replaced as minister by Carlo Matteucci (1811–1868), a famous physicist. Matteucci ignored Morelli's vision to create a truly national gallery of all Italian art, one that would have overturned Vasari's Florentine-centric view of the Renaissance. But even today, no truly national museum of art has been created in Italy:

> Matteucci deceived me—even though I have no doubt he did not know what he was doing when he presented the decree to the King to sign ... It is a decree signed by the King on 21 April in which all the books and works of art that belong to religious institutions suppressed in Umbria will remain the property of the communes in which they are to be found. With one stroke of a pen the King has destroyed my work of 68 consecutive days—which I undertook with such love and which I brought to a conclusion with the intimate conviction that I had rendered my country a service—even if not even a dog had thanked me ... But that does not matter—what does matter is that with that decree Matteucci has condemned many works of art of great importance to be lost to the history of Italian art ... First of all that decree is unconstitutional—neither Pepoli [Gioacchino Pepoli, minister for Umbria], nor the provincial government for Umbria, nor the king's government have the power to arrange as they wish the goods of the nation—this prerogative belongs only to parliament. Secondly, there could be nothing more contrary to wisdom, to say anything else to such a gift. Why limit such outbursts to books and works of art? I do not see why they do not give away the land of the supressed convents to these communes? Those Communists would know what to do with land, but not with Old Master paintings, as in time they will convert them into foreign gold. After such a precedent, all Italian communes that have suppressed convents, or convents to be suppressed, would want to enjoy equal privileges. Our beautiful dreams of founding a truly national gallery are dead. I cannot tell you how much I am venomously against that idiot Matteucci. Poor Italy, to be governed by that race of man.[31]

Nevertheless, Morelli remained undeterred, and pursued his agenda in Bergamo, with some success. On 24 June 1862 the prefect of that province issued an edict for the conservation of monuments and works of art in the city and its territory, and entrusted responsibility to a committee of like-minded patriots: Dr Alberico Gerli, Count Ottavio Lochis, Dr Giovanni Morelli, Prospero Arrigoni, Count Paolo Sozzi Vimercati, Giuseppe Maria Bonomi, and Count Antonio Roncalli.[32] Much of Bergamo's patrimony had been destroyed by foreigners during the wars of the Risorgimento, and the restoration of objects and buildings was urgently required.

Also in 1862, Morelli was appointed by minister Brioschi to head a commission to prepare legislation about conservation. In May–June the previous year he had persuaded the Ministry of Public Education to help his aristocratic friend from Lurano, Count Giovanni Secco Suardo, hold the first modern course in art conservation, in Florence. Antinori, in his role as president of the Florentine Academy, had assisted with the arrangements. The topic was the transfer of paintings from panel to canvas, and examples included a work that had belonged to the Frizzoni family, the so-called Gaudenzio Ferrari (an artist whom Morelli passionately pursued). Both Suardo and Morelli believed that conservation work should not be undertaken by creative artists but by professional restorers. Their view was that a painter has an instinctive urge to "modernize" the productions of previous eras; unable to tolerate the "blemishes" of the past, he is incapable of subordinating his taste to an earlier artist.

Morelli and Suardo first met in the 1840s through a mutual friend in Milan, Count Girolamo D'Adda, when Morelli returned from Germany as a young student.[33] Though Suardo was some twenty years older than Morelli, they became close friends, united by their concern with the politics of art conservation. Morelli played a role in Suardo's great achievement: publication of the first modern manual for restoration, *Manuale ragionato per la parte meccanica dell'arte del restauratore dei dipinti* (1866), later republished in an expanded version by his sons as *Il restauratore dei dipinti* (1894), which is still in print today. Morelli was involved in the conceptualization and distribution of the book, while Suardo supervised the restoration of paintings from Morelli's collection. At one point Suardo compares the treatment by two restorers of related portraits of patrician women (then attributed to Piero della Francesca, but now to Piero del Pollaiuolo): one in the Uffizi, the other in the Poldi Pezzoli. Suardo concludes that in treating the Florentine version, the restorer Acciai has changed the painting's original character by stippling it all over, while the Milanese counterpart has been treated by Luigi Cavenaghi in such a manner that no hint that it had been touched could be found, so ably has the talented young man respected what survived.[34] Today the Poldi Pezzoli version is recognized as being in exceptionally fine condition.[35]

Throughout 1862 Morelli continued his quest to create Italian museums, now turning his attention to sculpture. For Milan, he proposed a museum of Lombard sculpture, corresponding closely to the collection now in that city's Castello Sforzesco.[36] Following Leopoldo Cicognara's *Storia della scultura dal suo Risorgimento in Italia fino al secolo di Canova* (1823), where sculpture was defined as the art form that best demonstrated Italian genius, Morelli too contended that sculpture was Lombardy's greatest extant regional art form. The choice of the Castello was highly symbolic of Italy's new freedom: for a century before the Milanese took it back in 1859 it had been an Austrian military fortress.

Just as with the creation of painting collections, for sculpture Morelli was galvanized by the competitive collecting of the British, particularly Sir Henry Cole and his assistant John Charles Robinson at the South Kensington Museum in London (later the Victoria and Albert Museum). The policy of that museum was to create a collection of works of manufacture as a model for British design. Under this mandate Robinson, as curator or superintendent of art collections, had managed in 1854 to buy the important collection of terracottas and wax sculptural sketches belonging to the Gherardini family of Florence. Morelli was informed of Cole and Robinson's collecting activities by Austen Henry Layard, an informal advisor to Cole. But no secret was made of the new museum's acquisition policy for sculpture, which was self-consciously proclaimed in the introduction to Robinson's 1862 catalogue of its Italian holdings:

> To this day, none of the great continental museums have any systematic collections of renaissance sculpture; even in Florence, the Athens of the revival, only a few marbles, of great value and importance it is true, and a more numerous, but still inadequate collection of bronzes, are to be found dispersed amidst the vast galleries of the Uffizi; whilst in our country, till very recently, the art-student might have sought in vain for any examples of Italian sculpture.[37]

Robinson also bought and sold for many private clients, a practice unusual among British museum men, and one that brought him into constant conflict with Cole, who as museum director was publicly accountable.[38] Robinson even took opportunities to add to his own personal collection. For instance, in these years he acquired three sculptures, *Strength*, *Charity*, and *Justice*, two for the national collection, but the third, the most interesting, he kept for himself. It was eventually acquired by the Victoria and Albert in 1903, but the incident reveals a certain dishonesty, which made Robinson unacceptable to some of his colleagues, not only Cole but also Austen Henry Layard, and which eventually led to his resignation. Indeed, since Robinson bought and sold on his own account not only sculpture, but also a considerable number of Italian Renaissance and Spanish seventeenth-century paintings, after leaving South Kensington he was considered unacceptable for the directorship of the National Gallery of London.

In the first part of his report of September 1862, Morelli gives his version of the history of Milanese museums. At the suggestion of his friends Alessandro Manzoni and Massimo d'Azeglio, he had been commissioned in 1860 to write the first catalogue of the painting collection of the Accademia di Brera, and in 1863 was asked to extend it to the archaeological collection.[39] He was convinced that the Brera held enough sculpture to form a separate collection, independent of Renaissance painting yet complementary to it, the jewel being Bambaia's exceptional monument (1515–22) to Gaston de Foix from the monastery of Santa Marta. Morelli points out that the idea of a museum of Lombard sculpture was not new, having been proposed by earlier Italian and Austrian governments since 1808, following the depositing in the Brera in 1806 of a small group of important Lombardic sculptures that illustrated the development of the school, namely the monument to Gaston de Foix, the equestrian monument to Bernabò Visconti, the funerary monument of the bishop of Bobbio (Battista Bagarotti of Piacenza), and the funeral monument of the poet and Renaissance humanist Lancino Curzio. In 1818 the Brera had been enriched with the collection of artist Giuseppe Bossi, bought for the paltry sum, even then, of 7,500 lire, which Morelli estimated was worth at least 100 million lire in 1862. In 1819 Milan's municipal government gave the Brera fragments of sculpture from the gates of the city. In 1857 the Brera, returning to the project of 1808, asked the Austrian governors to formulate a plan for a museum of archaeological antiquities, and this eventuated in the Castello Sforzesco.

In the next section of his 1862 report, Morelli speculates on the cultural significance of museums in Risorgimento Italy,[40] shifting his position from wanting one large national gallery to a regional approach. Every region of Italy, he argues, has its own characteristic physiognomy and concept of beauty. Every kind of museum and collection should be about provincial or regional art, which is intimately connected with language, architecture, and public building in every town. If each Italian town operated in this way, together they could boast that they possessed more than museums and collections of sculpture in London, Paris, and Berlin. In conclusion he lists in detail the most important sculptures, reliefs, ancient statues, ancient fragments of marble, and lapidary inscriptions that should be reserved for a new museum of scultpure. He identifies some fragments as being in other collections, namely that of the Arconati family, and the Ambrosiana.

The museum complex in the Castello Sforzesco was born with a ministerial decree of 13 November 1862. It was a unique conception in Italy for the period. The Museo Nazionale del Bargello in Florence, housing medieval and Renaissance Italian sculpture, opened a few years later, in 1865. Two decades after the Sforzesco a sister institution, the Museo Civico in Bologna, would be founded (in 1881). This too housed sculpture from the city gates and tombs from suppressed churches and monasteries; as in Milan, these were the most significant ecclesiastical and civic commissions for Renaissance sculptors. When he made his suggestions Morelli had in mind international examples: the Glyptothek in Munich, which he had known when he was an undergraduate: Le Noir's short-lived Museo dei Monumenti Francesi (which created great nostalgia for sculpture), and the newly created South Kensington Museum.

In November 1862 Morelli was alerted by Giuseppe Molteni, director of the Brera, to a crisis concerning the celebrated marble door of the Medici Bank, a work described by Filarete, and attributed by Vasari and later writers to Michelozzo Michelozzi.[41] The famous door, then located at via de' Bossi 4, Milan, had been sold to well-known Milan art dealer Giuseppe Baslini, who immediately found a foreign buyer, presumably Vicomte Pierre-Paul Both de Tauzia, curator of the Louvre. Baslini's actions prompted a public outcry. A mutual friend of Molteni and Morelli, Giuseppe Mongeri, professor of aesthetics at the Reale Accademia di Belle Arti in Milan, protested vehemently against such an important monument being sold abroad, in a series of passionate and delightfully indiscrete articles in the Milanese newspaper *La Perseveranza*.[42] The article published on 17 June 1863 contains an interesting discussion of Baslini's involvement in the transaction, and explains why Molteni and Morelli accused him of nefarious practices.

Another member of this Milanese club of like-minded connoisseurs, the painter Giuseppe Bertini, was similarly disturbed about the door, and in January 1863 he wrote directly to Robinson, leaving him in no doubt about Milanese feeling on the subject, and reminding him that there was now a museum of Lombard sculpture in Milan, of which he was one of the curators.[43] Bertini reported that Baslini was also selling Renaissance sculpture and maiolica in large quantities (*all'ingrosso*) to French collectors. The famous door is now in the Castello Sforzesco, but the "affresco Leonardesco" (Vincenzo Foppa's *Young Cicero Reading*) found its way to the Wallace Collection in London, sold by Baslini to Both de Tauzia, who sold it to Sir Richard Wallace.

In 1863 Mongeri, Morelli, d'Azeglio, and De Sanctis discussed possible ways to control by legislation the exportation of works of art from Italy. Although these laws were enacted, there were still some experts in evasion—even among Morelli's friends, especially Jean Paul Richter, who decades later explained to Layard how he managed to extract himself from accusations of dirty dealing concerning the later activities of the Victoria and Albert Museum.[44] That particular incident reveals that any system, then and now, can be abused if the local authorities underestimate the value of a work of art, whether honestly or dishonestly. It is unlikely that Layard received Richter's explanation and indignation with any sympathy.

A few years later, in 1866, the initial effects of the new laws could be judged by a lengthy report written by Sir William Boxall, Eastlake's successor at the National Gallery, London, when he wrote to Layard as a trustee:

> The Italian Government has set its seal and has inventoried every work of art in every church or fraternity worthy of having! Every significant work of art must be first offered to the Italian government. Morelli says that when the government has collected together all the fine things from all the Churches … and made its selection for a great National Gallery in Florence (a wild vision) we shall be the first to whom a specimen of any particular school we may require shall be offered.[45]

The one major picture that Boxall tried (unsuccessfully) to buy, from the mayor of Pesaro, was Giovanni Bellini's famous altarpiece, while he considered Signorelli's *Judgment of Pan* (then in the collection of Janet Ross) too hedonistic for the British public. It was later acquired by Berlin, only to be lost in the Second World War. Morelli's view of Boxall was given in confidence to Sir James Hudson:

> Boxall is an excellent gentleman, a very fine connoisseur with an appreciation of what is beautiful in art. I consider that his taste is more exquisite than that of the late Sir Charles, but he does not understand our schools of painting, nor does he appreciate the historical part of a work of art. For these reasons, he is less qualified than Sir Eastlake for the position of Director of the National Gallery of London. Besides, he is too meticulous, and thus he would allow the best bargains to escape.[46]

Morelli's grand plans for museums in Italy was connected to his view of the role of private collections. A few of these were being created by patrician Milanese and Bergamasque families with his help, and would eventually enter public galleries. Morelli specialized in creating small collections, for example the one he assembled for his friend the Marchese Emilio Visconti Venosta (1829–1914), minister of foreign affairs for eight terms between 1863 and 1901. Still remembered as the longest-serving foreign minister in the history of Italy, Visconti Venosta was an extraordinary diplomat, even if a little slow to act. He and Morelli had met by 1861 at the latest, when they spent some fifteen days together at Silvaplana.[47] The two friends shared a patriotic political dedication to a democratic Italy, and a deep involvement in Italian Renaissance art. Upon Visconti Venosta's election to the presidency of the Brera, Morelli was jubilant. His friend was charming and handsome, tall and thin, with long hair and reddish side whiskers, which underlined an impression of being cool and considered.[48] He admired Morelli personally, and also adopted his famous method of art attribution—of which he wrote one of the most understanding accounts,[49] and kept his own notebooks modeled on Morelli's observations. Visconti Venosta was responsible for the 1895 commission of the bust of Morelli for the Brera (Fig. 90).

Together with Bertini, Morelli occasionally suggested acquisitions to Visconti Venosta, such as a tondo by Fra Bartolomeo della Porta of the Virgin worshipping the Christ child accompanied by St Joseph. (Morelli discusses the tondo in his book on the Borghese Gallery: he came across it at Bertini's workshop, where he saw Bertini's student Emilio Cavenaghi liberating the painting from previous unfortunate restorations, thus revealing a "jewel.")[50] The tondo was subsequently bequeathed by Margherita Visconti Venosta, the widow of Emilio's son, to the Museo Poldi Pezzoli, together with other works including a youthful drawn portrait of Visconti Venosta by Bertini, showing a refined young man with a floppy bow tie.[51]

Another such collection, now a part of the Castello Sforzesco's holdings, was that of Morelli's friend Count Lodovico Belgiojoso d'Este, in which a taste for seventeenth-century Dutch painting is particularly evident. Morelli bought Gerbrandt van den Eeckhout's *Granida and Daifilo* (dated 1652) for Lodovico at the pawn shop Monte di Pietà, Rome, as Belgiojoso states in his manuscript catalogue of his collection. According to the same manuscript, two small paintings on canvas, both Italian landscapes though originally with an uncertain attribution to one of the Berchem, were reattributed to Marco Ricci by his friend Morelli. Flemish and Dutch painting of the Seicento was a special characteristic of the Belgiojoso collection, some examples of which (according to the notes on provenance in the manuscript catalogue) were acquired by the count on his travels in Germany, Holland, and France, while others came from patrician Lombard collections. At least one, and perhaps more, were bought at the pawn shop Monte di Pietà in Rome, with help from Morelli.

□

Beginning on Christmas eve 1864, the *Gazzetta di Bergamo* published a series of articles arising from a public discussion about "Who must we elect?," comparing the relative merits of rival candidates Giovanni Morelli and Francesco Cucchi.[52] Morelli stood for the Liberal majority, while Cucchi, a Garibaldino and about twenty years younger, stood for change. Some of the few criticisms levelled against Morelli (which some others considered virtues) were that he was too ministerial and that he supported the death penalty. Both candidates were exemplary patriots, and both were anti-clerical, which counted a great deal with the Bergamo electorate. The newspaper suggested that Cucchi should stand for another seat (to no avail, as he was determined to represent the city of Bergamo). Although Cucchi was unsuccessful in the next two elections, in 1870 he succeeded Morelli, and would remain in the Camera dei Deputati until 1892, when he became a senator.

The strategist for Morelli's re-election was Count Pasino Locatelli (1822–1894), a patriot who, like Morelli, had fought in the Cinque giornate in 1848 and defended Bergamo in 1859. He also shared Morelli's passion for art, having published an account of the lives of Bergamo's artists, sculptors, and architects: *Illustri Bergamaschi* (1867). For most of his career he directed the humanities at the high school in Bergamo. In his frank correspondence to Locatelli, Morelli revealed much soul-searching about politics, and Locatelli acted during the election as a conduit between the Liberal Association and the candidate, Morelli.[53] Grateful for the count's support for his return to parliament, Morelli affirmed that he would stand as an act a love for his country, and because he shared Locatelli's political principles; like d'Azeglio, Morelli believed that it was the duty of honest men to occupy political office. The Liberal Association had defined a program without consulting the potential candidate, but which they wished Morelli would implement when elected. Skeptical about the real effects of their proposals, Morelli questioned the Liberals' demands: they wanted freedom of the press, but would that be possible, Morelli argued, in a country that published such extreme newspapers as *L'Unità italiana*, *L'Unità Cattolica*, *Lo Zingaro*, and *Il Contemporaneo*? Secondly, the Liberal Association asked for a widening of the right to vote; why not, proposed Morelli, ask for universal suffrage? In a country dominated by a theocracy for many centuries, freedom could not remain merely with the cultured classes. He doubted that Italy was ready for such an honor.

There were other requests, but with these two reservations Morelli accepted the program of the Liberal circle, and proceeded to clarify his own intentions as a candidate. He declared that he would never have proposed himself, never having done such a thing in his life, nor intending to do so in the future. Nor could he have predicted who the other candidates might be. Then there was the delicate question that he was the only Protestant (at least by birth) to have had the honor of sitting in the Italian parliament; for this reason alone he was unique among the proposed candidates.[54] Would this not pose problems for the electorate, he mused, especially when considering the Roman question (whether Italy's capital should be in Rome)? Might the voters doubt his motives? After five years as a deputy, he realized his own faults: that he was not good at making speeches, and was not personally ambitious, though very proud to contribute to the Italian cause. He maintained that from his youth he had been indolent, and to explain his character quoted a Latin proverb beloved of Montaigne: *Fugax rerum, securaque in otia natus* (Fleeing affairs and born in idle ease). This may have made him unsuitable for public office, or so he reasoned.

But the voters of Bergamo had other views, and Morelli was re-elected by a large majority. After his return, in November 1865 Morelli reported (as requested) to Locatelli about the state of the new Camera. He was bitterly disillusioned: Urbano Rattazzi could create a majority by combining his so-called Moderates (*moderati insensati*) with other votes from the Left. La Marmora was on the verge of resigning as prime minister, and the king was on the point of asking Rattazzi to form a cabinet, an act that could endanger the monarchy. Rattazzi, in Morelli's view, was corrupt, his incompetent hands sullied even further by policies that would lead to misadventure. Indeed, Morelli was correct: by March 1866 La Marmora would make peace with Rome, and war with the Austrians. Morelli, quoting his friend Massimo d'Azeglio, concluded: "Italy is created, but now we need to think seriously and create the Italians" (*Italia è fatta—ora bisogna pensare sul serio e fare anche gli Italiani*).[55]

CHAPTER 8
Creating Modern Italy

The last campaigns in the movement for Italian Independence were fought between late June and late July, when the Austrians were retreating from Venice. They took place in the Valtellina valley on the Swiss border, specifically on the Spondalunga, a zig-zag mountain highway which over the centuries has been contested in every war along the Italian frontier. The battle of the Stelvio was later acknowledged as the most brilliant military operation of this concluding conflict, achieved with minimal resources other than the devoted patriotism of local men.

Morelli played an important part in this decisive conflict. A photograph of him in military uniform, as part of the 44th Battalion of the Guardia Nazionale Mobile, shows him leaning forward to advise Colonel Enrico Guicciardi, surrounded by local patriots from Milan, Bergamo, and Como (Fig. 55). Together such men achieved a sensational victory on the difficult terrain of the Stelvio Pass.

Guicciardi (1812–1895) came from a patrician family in the Valtellina. Like Morelli he had fought in the Cinque giornate and had been elected to Italy's first national parliament in 1860, as the representative for Cosenza, a challenge for a northerner as Cosenza was in the south. He had led troops in the Stelvio in his home territory in 1848, an experience that prepared him for this last battle. In 1866, at the age of fifty-three, he approached the minister of war, Ignazio de Genova di Pettinengo, and General La Marmora in Florence, proposing the formation of a group of volunteers, to be called the Bersaglieri of the Alps, to defend the upper valleys of Lombardy—the Valtellina and Valcamonica—well aware of the difficulties and dangers of the task ahead. Eventually the minister agreed to send two battalions of the Guardia Nazionale. Guicciardi, though realizing that the force was inadequate, accepted the rank of colonel and led the mission to defend the Sondalo valley.

The colonel enlisted brigades of volunteers from various social strata and walks of life—aristocrats, local government officials, policemen, customs guards, mountaineers, and foresters—bringing what weapons they could find; after three months of fighting they defeated the Austrian General

Alexander von Metz and his more numerous forces. Following the victory, Morelli kept as souvenirs twelve French Saint-Étienne rifles used by his compatriots, examples of the weapons they were obliged to use. Each weighed 5 kilograms and measured 1.9 meters long, including a vicious bayonet at the end (1.5 meters without). Each was dated with its year of manufacture: 1842, 1849, or 1851; after being refurbished for fighting they had probably been sold by the French to the Italian government in about 1861.

In Fig. 55, seated on the ground at Guicciardi's right is Aristide Caimi, a passionate advocate for social justice in the Valtellina.[1] He published an account of the defense of the Valtellina based on his own experience of fighting in the battles, in which he describes the role played by Morelli as commander-in-chief (*Capitano di Stato Maggiore*), second only in command to the colonel.[2] In the photograph, Caimi, Guicciardi, and Morelli form a triumphant trio. Behind them is a line of soldiers, their names inscribed below: Pietro Pedranzini (1826–1903), Enrico Panci, Giuseppe Colombo, Cesare Beruto, Innocente Regazzoni, Bertolini, Giovanni Baiotti, and Romualdo Bonfadini (1831–1899). Equipped with swords and hunting rifles, uniforms crumpled from fighting, the troops are exultant. Another photograph of largely the same group (Fig. 54) shows a proudly jubilant Morelli, head held high, though his right hand is tucked into his uniform, as if wounded and in a sling. As before, the names of the soldiers are recorded below. The commander, Pedranzini, secretary of the town of Bormio, was particularly praised for his fearlessness. Some of the men went on to have distinguished careers, such as Giuseppe Colombo (1836–1921), an engineer and entrepreneur who built continental Europe's first centralized electric power plant (in Milan's via Santa Radegonda); and Cesare Beruto (1835–1915), a civil engineer and architect who was one of the creators of successive plans for the city of Milan.

Caimi's narrative of the conflict begins on 19 June, with a description of the preparations on both sides as they jockeyed for position on the mountains, the Italians poorly armed and without official uniforms. On 28 June Guicciardi sent a telegram to the mayor of each local town, asking for those citizens capable of bearing arms to defend their country. Many young men had already enlisted in Garibaldi's army, but others arrived at Tirano that same evening.

On 3 July the Austrian army was weakened and demoralized by its massive defeat by the Kingdom of Prussia at the Battle of Königgrätz (Hradec Králové and Sadová, in the present-day Czech Republic). The battle for the zig-zag Stelvio Pass began on 11 July. The Austrian encampment was at the Rocca dei Bagni Vecchi, the key to the Stelvio, some 4 kilometres from the town of Bormio. On 11 July there was combat at the Serra on the Ponte del Diavolo, followed by the Austrian attack on the Stelvio valley. Guicciardi's plan was for a multi-pronged offensive: Morelli and his troops were the *avant guardia*, who would cross the mountains to attack the Austrians from behind, cutting off any retreat. Other columns confronted the enemy in different ways.

Caimi wrote a thrilling story of outstanding bravery, in which he described Guicciardi's brilliant tactical leadership, and Morelli's fearlessness when on 12 and 13 July he led a patrol along the crest of the Glandadura mountain. The column of fifty men marched by night beyond Bormio to the valley of Santa Caterina; then, conquering their trepidation, they climbed Mount Reit, the highest in the Stelvio, which peaks at more than 3,000 meters. They entered tunnels between the first and second roadmen's houses (*cantoniere*), which they feared would be occupied by Austrian troops. Instead they found Austrian corpses and abandoned equipment. The second house had been burnt down by the Austrians in 1859, remaining a charred ruin.

They later encountered Austrian soldiers, whom they fought off successfully. Garibaldi and others sent telegrams of praise, but the minister and his generals were not co-operative in other ways, especially when it came to telegraphic communication and resources. On 18 July Morelli sent an angry note to Giovanni Battista Camozzi Vertova, mayor of Bergamo, written in pencil from the front line:

> They day before yesterday we attempted an attack with guns and rockets that lasted from four in the morning until after midday. The rockets were discharged and dislodged from our cannons with extraordinary competence. Many were wounded, but none of us, which seemed a miracle. I beg you to send, daily by telegraph, our news to Colonel Guicciardi at Bormio, as the minister of war and even the general in charge treat us as abandoned. It is a disgrace![3]

On 30 July hostilities were suspended, and Colonel Guicciardi took a few days' absence, leaving the troops in Morelli's charge. Later, Morelli recalled his exhilaration during the magnificent walks of seven or eight hours' duration that he took with Guicciardi during the cease-fire, such as on 20 August when they crossed the awe-inspiring glaciers of Monte Cristallo and the Stelvio, to descend from the top of the Stelvio pass, only to find Italian and Austrian sentries staring at one another from ten feet apart. Wanting to assess whether it would be possible to surround the enemy and take them prisoner at the second and third roadhouses, they recognized that such a trek would only be feasible for robust and practiced walkers, but relished the thought of a unique battle on a glacier, the enemy disappearing beneath the snow in the face of the locals' winning advantage (*Un combattimento sopra il ghiacciaio sarebbe del resto cosa originale*).[4] (Such a battle did in fact take place, but much later—in the First World War.) In order to remain active during the armistice, or so Morelli wrote, they walked 16 miles from Bormio to the Forno glacier to hunt bears in the mountains.

In the Alps, the silent beauty of long days on guard duty and long nights on sentry duty became something of a passion for Morelli, even during the twelve or fifteen days of ceasefire which he spent commanding the outposts on the treacherous highway known as La Spondalunga.[5] Morelli considered that the successful operation he had directed in the tunnels would have failed against French or Italian soldiers, but the Austrians were unable to cope with surprise attacks executed boldly on bleak nights. He delighted in seeing the imperial hunters (*Kaiserjäger*) terrified by the mountaineers from the Valtellina. After they captured the third and fourth roadhouses, Morelli and Guicciardi visited the outposts, and realized that more than a thousand Austrian men had been employed in this form of guard duty, sometimes on the summit of mountains, in dangerous places that took many hours on foot to reach.

After the final victory, on 22 September, Morelli left Bormio to stay with Emilio Visconti Venosta, Italy's foreign minister, in his family villa at Tirano (now the Museo Civico). On 25 September the troops were feted in a triumphal procession at Sondrio, the footpath strewn with flowers. Morelli, always true to that part of his Protestant self which was ill at ease with ceremony, disliked the speeches, and fled to stay with the Frizzoni family at Bellagio, then went home to Milan.

A few weeks later, Caimi told Morelli that the three months on the Stelvio had been the best of his entire life,[6] and sent him a draft of his *Giornale* for comment, as well as asking to see the letter that Austrian General Francesco Nestor had sent at the conclusion of hostilities, congratulating Morelli on his conduct. During the writing, Morelli assisted Caimi in many ways.[7] In 1881 Colonel Guicciardi re-edited the book;[8] it doubled in size with the addition of 140 telegrams, many original documents by Guicciardi, a new introduction, and a conclusion. Despite the bravery of all involved in the battle of the Stelvio, the troops had been given relatively little recognition at the time, and were awarded one-third fewer honours than any other legion.

To celebrate Italy's hard-won freedom from the Austrians, spectacular liberation ceremonies took place in November 1866 in Venice, where Morelli went to stay with Austen Henry Layard at Ca' Capello on the Grand Canal, among many distinguished British visitors.[9] Morelli's thoughts returned to his youth. It was a dream come true, for instance, to see Verona, the incarnation of Austrian militarism, taken back by Italy, though it had cost his nation terrible bloodshed and many thousands of lives. "Verona with all its fortresses and strongholds in the hands of our soldiers!"

□

Once Italy had proven victorious in battle and finally gained its independence, Morelli soon redirected his energies back to art. During his Venetian sojourn he wrote of the restorers there who scrubbed paintings, and lamented Layard's acquisition from the Costabili collection in Ferrara of some twenty-two paintings as yet another case of an old family collection of Italian art being broken up for sale and dispersed abroad, though he understood the underlying reasons, as rich Italian collectors were yet to appreciate the Emilian Quattrocento.

In January 1866, before entering the military fray, Morelli had begun buying paintings for an older Swiss cousin, Giovanni Melli. The Zavaritt and Melli families had a long business association in sericulture, from at least 1801, when they had become joint proprietors of the villa at Gorle. Both of Morelli's parents were related to Melli's parents. As Morelli acknowledged:

> I am indeed fortunate to have you as a cousin, one who combines a love of the Fine Arts with money, without which nothing may be achieved, nor concluded in this world. But you too are fortunate to have a cousin like me, who is furnished with a pair of excellent eyes and who moreover is helped by good fortune to achieve miracles! Let us shake hands and consider ourselves both fortunate. Now you should know that yesterday morning I discovered three real jewels for your collection, and I hope that tomorrow I shall be able to obtain a fourth. Put your spectacles on your nose and read attentively the names of the artists, whose works will very soon enrich your Gallery.[10]

Morelli's gratitude was often repeated:

> To have found a cousin such as you on the path of my life is the most beautiful gift that Divine Providence could have given. And if I think that without the powerful help of your wallet all these masterpieces would at the end of the day have gone to foreign countries. I can only feel a profound sense of gratitude towards you, for having had faith entirely in my eyes and my conscientiousness, as you have procured for me the great satisfaction of saving all these beautiful and rare masterpieces for Italy.[11]

Giovanni Melli was by this time a modest and unassuming bachelor. He was born Johannes Möeli in 1803 at Bever, an idyllic Engadine village in the Swiss canton of Grisons. The family home is still the most imposing building in Bever, a rustic patrician palace built in around 1590, now a luxurious hotel, the Chesa Salis. Giovanni's father, Lucio Möeli, when aged sixty married Anna Caterina Boringhieri, aged twenty-four, and they had three children: the eldest, Pietro, was mentally impaired; the second was Giovanni; and a third died in infancy. Little is known of Giovanni's youth, except that he had fallen in love with a ballerina who did not return his affection, and that he enjoyed hunting chamois. He was not particularly interested in sericulture as his father had been, but lived as a rentier, and invested in the building of an early railway line between Monza and Milan.

Melli enjoyed good food and luxurious clothing, took a daily walk along via Monte Napoleone to drink coffee, perhaps discussing the latest performance of an opera by Verdi, or the latest art book he had bought at a Milanese bookshop (in the last years of his life at the Libreria Hoepli). He was an easy-going but not very robust man, with a particular fondness for his dynamic younger cousin, Giovanni. Like their handsome friend Poldi, both men firmly intended to remain bachelors. Morelli would tease his cousin about his landlady, who fancied him. He had read in the newspapers that she was to hold dancing soirées, to which neither men would accept an invitation. Morelli suggested that Melli invite the landlady to see his paintings, and more slyly recommended that she see his statue of a satyr, since satyrs were always the widow's Benjamin (or younger object of desire).[12] While at Venice in February 1872 Morelli wrote to Melli to say how happy he was to be in Venice studying, that he received many invitations, some from very beautiful women, without replying to a single one. "I want to preserve my perfect freedom, and that would be lost if I were to make visits and accept invitations to lunch, etc. etc. I do not care a damn if they call me a bear."[13] In these letters his references to marriage were always cynical, as an institution that millions entered into, but rarely happily. As Layard remarked, Morelli exerted an extraordinary fascination over women, "amongst his most attached and warmest friends were some of the most highly-endowed and charming of his countrywomen."[14]

Morelli's letters to Melli open with affectionate greetings, phrased to suggest that Melli was a thoughtful and reserved man, disinclined to communicate or write: "Mio caro e generoso Mecenate delle belle arti" (My dear and generous patron of the fine arts), "Cugino amico, Amico cugino" (My cousin-friend and friend-cousin), "Caro filosofo" (Dear philosopher), "Caro e taciturno Giannino" (Dear and taciturn little Giovanni). Sometimes his cousin needed firm persuasion, as when Morelli wrote his last letter to him, on Christmas Eve 1872, suggesting Melli acquire the wonderful Madonna and Child by Giovanni Bellini (Fig. 76) from the Countess Noli at Alzano Maggiore. The countess was surrounded by creditors, and depended on a "hunchback" as the go-between to negotiate. Morelli asks Melli to leave his armchair (situated beneath the Molenaer portrait of a man smoking (Fig. 57), whom he resembled smoking in his dark flat), go to his desk, take out the money, and put it in an envelope to pay for the picture. The work is now recognized as one of the most remarkable of all Bellini's Madonna paintings, and one of the few with an early provenance. It was part of the dowry of the Abbess Lucrezia Agliardi-Vertova when she founded the Carmelite convent of St Anna in Albino at Alzano. The painting may have been commissioned directly from Bellini in Venice by her father, the architect Alessio Agliardi.[15] There are no copies or variants of it from Bellini's studio, suggesting that it was a unique commission, only copied twice (and much later) by Giovanni Battista Moroni.[16]

Morelli's first letter to Melli was written from Florence, on 23 January 1866, where the Camera dei Deputati was sitting. The writer was looking at a shop of one of the many antiquarian dealers, thinking of the collection that he was forming for Giuseppe Arconati Visconti, in whose magical villa at Bellagio he often stayed.[17] Would it not be better to enrich the collection of another friend, he mused, and give the paintings to his cousin for the same price that he paid for them? But the offer should be taken up quickly, otherwise he would offer them to his friend Senator Carlo Cagnola, whom he also helped form a collection (now in his villa at Gazzada, near Varese).[18] The letter had the desired effect.

Morelli generally preferred to avoid dealers, with the exceptions of Giuseppe Baslini in Milan and Michelangelo Guggenheim in Venice. He rediscovered a significant number of paintings in a Roman pawn shop, the Monte di Pietà, where they were often misattributed and inexpensive.[19] He enjoyed taking collector friends there on shopping expeditions. As a politician, Morelli confessed that he could have felt unscrupulous for not informing the authorities of the correct attributions so that the state could derive money, but he was entirely cynical and believed that the best way of acquiring a picture for the nation was to place it in the collection of a patriotic friend. And in almost all cases, Morelli's friends *were* reliable patriots, these acquisitions having now gravitated to national collections (although in a few families, such as the heirs to the Andreossi and Arconati Visconti collections, the friends' sons later proved unreliable). The finds from the Roman pawn shop were noted by an international audience of collectors and reviewed in the *Deutsches Kunstblatt* (1853) by a Roman correspondent, the archaeologist and historian Ernst aus'm Weerth.

The most sensational of Morelli's acquisitions at the Monte di Pietà was Botticelli's *History of Virginia the Roman* (Fig. 56). Morelli bought the painting in 1871, when the subject was described in the pawn shop catalogue as "Horsemen and a rape of nuns." The narrative panel has since been recognised as a complex and compelling painting in Botticelli's late style, with more than fifty figures in a scene of judicial atrocity and murder, set against the harmonious proportions of classical architecture, based on Livy (*Ab urbe condita*, III, 4–49). Morelli was the first to associate the panel with a description in Giorgio Vasari's *Lives* of many very lively and beautiful paintings with multiple figures, framed in a *spalliera* in a room in the palace of Giovanni Vespucci in Florence. He described to Melli how the Botticelli had been brought to the pawn shop in 1851 by a monsignor's servant, to whom the shop had paid 980 Roman scudi, while Morelli had paid slightly more: 15,000 lire, which was still not very much considering the picture's importance. Morelli managed to snatch the picture from under the nose of an English collector, who was trying to finalize a contract for it—but was struggling to obtain an export licence to take the painting out of Rome, for which a fee of 20 per cent of the purchase price was charged.

Eventually Morelli inherited his cousin's collection, which he in turn bequeathed to the Accademia Carrara in Bergamo.[20] But the most exquisite painting owned by Morelli at the time of his death was acquired not for his cousin, but for himself. This was Pisanello's portrait of Leonello d'Este

(Fig. 58), the most cultivated of all Renaissance princes. It was in Alexander Baker's collection in England until 1871, after which Morelli bought it, at some cost.[21] He certainly knew of the panel's existence much earlier, when it was in the Costabili collection at Ferrara. A recent restoration (2016) has revealed it to be of considerable significance and beauty, confirming Morelli's judgment, and supporting the interpretation that the portrait had been made for Leonello's wedding.[22]

Ever since his undergraduate years in Munich, Morelli had nurtured a passion for northern European painting; at least one admirer, Jacob Burckhardt, thought that this part of his collection was more important than the Italian.[23] For of all authorities on Dutch painting, it was Théophile Thoré (the great Republican journalist and art critic who had rediscovered the work of Vermeer, Franz Hals, and others) whom Morelli most admired, and to whom he referred most frequently in letters, principally to Thoré's two volumes on Dutch collections, *Musées de la Hollande* (Paris, 1858 and 1860), which he owned. Morelli imagined himself as an Italian Thoré, rediscovering lost works by little-understood Dutch masters, and snapping them up for trivial sums at the pawn shop.

In fact, Morelli proved remarkably successful in finding paintings at reasonable prices. He argued that, to acquire unrecognized masterpieces, one could always depend on the gross ignorance of contemporary artists of the Roman academy, who generally made haphazard guesses at the attributions and monetary values of Old Master paintings. In January 1871 Morelli bought for his cousin (at the pawn shop) a representation of La Fontaine's fable of the satyr and the traveler by Barent Fabritius (together with other paintings, including a portrait by Rembrandt's pupil Govaert Flinck).[24] The fable recounts a confrontation between a traveler and a peasant who has lost his way on a cold wintry day. To the satyr's astonishment the peasant warms his chilly fingers in his mouth, and then blows on his spoon to cool his soup, at which the satyr exclaims in disgust: "From this moment I renounce your friendship, for I will have nothing to do with one who blows hot and cold with the same breath." There is something of the brash humour of the proverb in the representation by Fabritius that chimes with the undergraduate Munich beer-drinking culture of *Balvi magnus*. Morelli relished the wild comedy of the piece, the Rembrandtesque quality of the light and coloring, and the vibrant style that contributes to its satirical quality. Uncharacteristically, Morelli pursued the painting's iconographic theme enthusiastically in his travels, noting another example by Jordaens in Munich.[25]

Melli's collection was housed in a villa at Rogoredo in the Brianza and in several Milanese apartments (via Clerici 4, and via Bigli 15), close to Poldi Pezzoli's house and to the Brera. Morelli recommended the large Italian canvases for Rogoredo, and the small Flemish, Dutch, and Italian works for Milan. The works were then examined by Molteni's successor, the restorer

Luigi Cavenaghi. Conservation treatments were undertaken, signatures were discovered, and attributions made.

In terms of personal taste, one work in Morelli's collection is arresting. Bought not for his cousin, but for himself, it is a real connoisseurial tease. For Federico Zeri and Francesco Rossi, who wrote an account of Morelli's collection, there is nothing like it in all of Italian painting.[26] Described as an allegorical man's head, both Morelli and Frizzoni attributed the panel to Sodoma (1477–1549), or to his son-in-law, Bartolomeo Neroni (1505/10–1571). The picture is a half-figure of a mature man, with leaves and flowers crowning his head, a wild expression on his face. To the spectator he makes two obscene gestures, his right arm raised with the sign of "up yours" (*fa le fiche*) and the left with a gesture signifying "Get fingered" (*manichetto*). It has been associated with a sixteenth-century academy in Siena, but remains an enigma.

Melli died at the age of seventy on 14 February 1873 in Milan. His will, made in 1866, the year in which he and Morelli began forming the collection, nominated Morelli as his heir.[27] But the will was unexpectedly challenged by some relatives from Turin, the Boringheri family, on behalf of Melli's elder brother, Pietro, who was in a psychiatric hospital in Milan. By December a settlement was reached. According to the laws of the canton Grisons (Giovanni Melli was a Swiss citizen), Melli could dispose to Morelli only one-fifth of his estate, which he had inherited from his parents. Morelli chose as his share the paintings, the art books, and a collection of ancient coins. The irony was that Pietro, who was well looked after, died shortly after his younger brother, on 14 May 1873. Although the ostensible reason for challenging the will was removed, the case continued. Had Giovanni Melli become an Italian citizen, his will could not have been challenged.

An inventory of Melli's paintings was prepared in May 1873 by Giuseppe Baslini,[28] inevitably a close friend of Morelli's. In this exercise Baslini's attributions were uncharacteristically vague, even imprecise, and his valuations low, presumably in an effort to minimize inheritance tax. For instance, he described Botticelli's *History of Virginia* as a "rape of nuns ... Tuscan School said to be by Botticelli," giving it a value of only 2,000 lire. All of this is a little hard to believe, given Morelli's ecstatic account of the restoration done by Cavenaghi and witnessed by Boxall, an Englishman famous for his painful reticence and hesitancy, who is said to have exclaimed on seeing it: "I am prepared to commit madness for this painting" (*io per questo quadro sono pronto di fare una pazzia*).

After Melli's death and the disappointment of receiving only part of his cousin's estate, Morelli sold a number of the pictures, and the ancient coins and silver. With the proceeds he rented a Ginoulhiac apartment in Milan at via Pontaccio 14, a building where Clementina Frizzoni and her son Gustavo also lived, close to many friends and to the Brera. He still had an apartment in the lower city of Bergamo and one at Gorle, and intended to build a villa at Taronico, strategically located near the Frizzoni at Crella, the villa Melzi d'Eril, the villa Trotti, and Balbianello. Nothing came of that ambition, though he retained his *cascina* (farmhouse) there.

In via Pontaccio Morelli constructed a little museum, which he and Gustavo Frizzoni would show to visitors, and even Layard took guests there, sometimes without Morelli. Some enjoyed the experience, others hated it. The art historian Adolfo Venturi, for instance, still ached with discontent years after a visit to the collection, during which his abilities as a young connoisseur were tested by Morelli's amanuensis, Frizzoni. Venturi (presumably choosing an anecdote favorable to himself) described his experiences before a depiction of the Presentation of Christ in the Temple:

> I expressed surprise that the artist was unknown, and, once informed of a Modenese provenance, proposed a hypothesis concerning the artist, which produced an indignant shrug of the shoulders from Frizzoni, who declared, "Rather it is by his compatriot, Francesco Bianchi Ferrari." Having failed to persuade me that he was right, Frizzoni changed his tone of voice, and coldly allowed me to leave. I departed, humiliated, but increasingly unconvinced that the wretched picture was by Bianchi Ferrari, under whose name it appeared in Morelli's book of 1880, a battlefield for Lombardic criticism. I continued my trip from Milan to Brescia, Verona, Vicenza, Padua, Rovigo, and Ferrara. In this last city, which has become precious for my research, I found some ugly little paintings in Enea Cavalieri's collection that corresponded to Morelli's Presentation: the same emaciated figures with long fingernails, painted by a third-rate artist, Michele Coltellini (*le stesse figure allampanate con lunghe dita, dipinte da un pittore di terzo ordine*), far away from the refinement and idealization of Bianchi Ferrari. I reconstructed the corpus of this dull and fallible maker of images, and took revenge on Morelli, by demonstrating in the Prussian *Jahrbuch* that the fantastic Bianchi Ferrari was not the author of his painting, nor of the many other pictures which had been wrongly assigned to him.[29]

When the collection went to the Accademia Carrara, the attribution to Coltellini was accepted, and still is today. Venturi's vignette reveals the function of Morelli's collection as the setting for a kind of rite of passage: any future Morellian neophyte would be examined in an initiation ceremony (often conducted by Frizzoni in Morelli's absence), in which he would be put to the test of attributing works by many minor and difficult to identify artists.[30]

The collection also served as an advertisement for Morelli's abilities, and he would show it to many visitors to Milan, including European royalty, foreign scholars, collectors, and museum directors. More importantly, it had a direct bearing on Morelli's writings, for he used works in his own collection as the touchstone when evaluating an artist's other works. For example, in his lopsided account of the oeuvre of Botticelli, he exaggerated the importance of his own painting, the *History of Virginia*, neglected to mention any of the celebrated mythologies in the Uffizi, and concentrated instead on deleting works from Botticelli's corpus. More significantly, in the case of minor masters Morelli could be alternately assisted and misled by works in his own collection.

When planning the eventual distribution of his collection, Morelli left only the best pictures to the Accademia Carrara, where they would hang near those he had chosen for the museum from the estate of Count Lochis. In Morelli's correspondence are references to other paintings he owned, usually without an attribution, as "quadri di simpatia" (sympathetic pictures); these were considered less important, and he used them to decorate his country houses. Examples included a large painting of Venus seated on the knees of Adonis, with a little cupid in the air, holding a wreath of flowers; a portrait of a Spanish official with a red scarf and long hair; and a portrait by Murillo.[31] None survived as permanent objects in his collection.

One of Morelli's last major discoveries was to attribute the *Madonna di Piazza* in the cathedral at Pistoia, a work previously documented as being by Andrea del Verrocchio, to a member of Verrocchio's workshop, the young Lorenzo di Credi—an attribution that has stood the test of time. Morelli owned three works that he believed may have constituted the predella for the altarpiece. One eventually went from his apartment in Milan to the Accademia Carrara, while the other two remained with the Zavaritt family at Gorle and are now on loan to the Accademia Carrara.[32]

□

On 15 September 1867 Morelli's mother died at Bellagio. He wrote to Antinori of Ursula's last illness: a three-day battle with death as she struggled with catarrh, which was hell for him to experience. "Dear friend I cannot tell you how unhappy I am ... There is no longer anyone in this world who will follow my journey with a loving eye, a dear and affectionate voice who will call me home, who greeted me always with affectionate words. A mother's affection cannot be re-experienced ever again."[33]

Having lost her husband and three children at a young age, Ursula had been free to devote herself to her surviving son's welfare, which she did for the rest of her life. She remained Giovanni Morelli's intimate confidante until her death. All of Morelli's friends were impressed by her geniality; she was the soul of the household.[34] On the evening of 16 September Ursula's body was transported to Bergamo for burial, and the mourning Morelli went to stay with his uncle Pietro at Gorle for a few weeks.

To distract him, Layard suggested a trip to England, where Morelli had never been. He arrived on 20 July 1868. He spent his first weekend as the guest of the very beautiful watercolorist Anne-Margaretta Higford Burr, at Aldermaston Manor in Berkshire, and subsequently was her guest in London.

Her husband, Daniel Higford Davall Burr, was an eccentric member of parliament, who kept monkeys and snakes in the garden at Aldermaston. She had traveled extensively with Layard, in the East and in Italy, copying ancient art and Renaissance frescoes for the Arundel Society.

Soon after Morelli's arrival in England he visited the national exhibition of Italian art from British private collections at Leeds, where the poet and parliamentarian Lord Houghton (Richard Monckton Milnes) was his host.[35] Lady Eastlake, recently widowed, took Morelli to visit the galleries of Lord Hertford (Richard Seymour Conway, the Fourth Marquess) to view what we now know as the Wallace Collection, and also to the gallery of pictures belonging to Francis Egerton, the First Earl of Ellesmere, who had inherited the Bridgewater paintings. Lady Eastlake, although brutally critical of many people, was fascinated by Morelli. Three years earlier she had written:

> We have seen a good deal of Signor Morelli here, the Deputato for Bergamo, one of those extraordinarily clever men whom even the slavery of Italy did not extinguish. His conversation is most charming, both on Art and Italy, and many other things. He is a great statesman and politician by nature, by education a physician, by taste a connoisseur; but with power and memory for everything, and a grand-looking man besides. His account of various signs of progress in Italy is full of interest—the rise of wages; the education of the most elementary kind; the difficulties which they find in getting teachers for schools; the Neapolitan soldiers, who, when they have their furlough, return before it expires, not able to endure the filth, misery and disorder of their old homes. As he expressed it "no end of dirty linen to wash."[36]

She remained enchanted with Morelli for the rest of her life, while the few surviving letters he wrote to her (in German) are a testimony to his great respect for her judgment and eye.[37] In turn, she wrote very well informed and deeply enthusiastic reviews of his writings.

Sir William Boxall, Eastlake's successor as director of the National Gallery, together with the writer and historian Janet Ross, took Morelli to see the Royal Collection at Hampton Court Palace, and later to the print room at Windsor, where he saw Prince Albert's extraordinary Raphael collection. On 14 and 15 August Morelli traveled to Oxford, where he was hosted by Albert Osliff Rutson, a fellow of Magdalen College. He enjoyed the medieval appearance of the town, and was curious about the monastic life of the fellows. He spent a day at Blenheim Palace with the Duke of Marlborough's collection, where he much admired Raphael's Ansidei altarpiece, Reynold's large group portrait of the Marlborough family, and the many little copies by David Teniers after Italian paintings. He was astonished by the Raphael drawings at the Ashmolean and at Christ Church, which to his eyes were authentic and deserved to be better known.[38] Never was a man in mourning so brilliantly distracted by wonderful collections and loyal English friends. From England Morelli moved on to study collections in Bruges, Ghent, Antwerp, Rotterdam, Amsterdam, and Frankfurt.

Free train-travel was one of the perquisites enjoyed by Italian politicians, and Morelli traveled incessantly. In Autumn 1869 he spent time in Berlin with Count Lodovico Belgiojoso d'Este and Count Alessandro Melzi d'Eril. He regretted not accompanying his friends on a study tour to Munich and other German galleries to examine Dutch and Italian painting, especially to see the first international exhibition of works of art, all from private collections, at Munich.[39] The most important were works by Van Eyck, and the very rare Vermeer, from the collection of Barthold Suermondt. Abroad he discovered the authors of the paintings he had bought for his cousin Melli, such as his attribution of the portrait of the young man smoking in Amsterdam to Molenaer (Fig. 57). Later in Dresden he spent at least four or five hours in the Gemäldegalerie, which he considered the "best gallery in Germany," but where he found many paintings falsely baptized with the wrong names.[40]

□

Aware that in 1871 the Italian parliament was to move from Florence to Rome, home of the Catholic Church, on 13 November 1870 Morelli announced his retirement from politics. In his statement to the Bergamo electorate his Protestant opposition to Catholicism is manifest:

> Now the upcoming elections are imminent, two reasons force me to withdraw from political life. The main question the new parliament will be called upon to resolve is the most serious, the most significant, ever put forward. It proposes the establishment of a new relationship between Church and State, to establish guarantees for the pope. Should some of you, either for reasons of personal friendship or from habitual benevolence, wish to vote for me this time, I cannot accept such a mandate for such a nuanced and consequential matter. The Roman question concerns the religious sentiment of our nation. If one does not belong to the Catholic faith and believes himself to be free of prejudices, I believe that person cannot be a free and authoritative judge of such a question. But aside from the faith into which I was baptized, there are political reasons against my re-election. It is true that in 1860 I voted for Rome to become the political capital of Italy; it is also true that many hopes have become illusions. Then it seemed to me that the magic strength of freedom would have solved all problems, and that after a moral regeneration of our nation, our entry into the Eternal City would only have been the confirmation of the Risorgimento of our country. Forget heaven, for I do not want to deny the great and multiple progress that Italy has made in the last ten years, but this progress, unless I am deceived, is more material than moral. In my opinion,

> it is only with moral force, with lively debate, constant daily engagement, that Italy can go ahead and, more importantly, remain in Rome. What moral strength is there? Who could respond to the idea of the implementation of a free church in a free state or to the transfer of the capital to Rome, or that the pope may be murdered, or became the supreme person in a theocratic government? Who can believe in any of these parties? Deeply convinced that these moral questions will not find their solution, except with time, I do not know how to decide to follow the actual course of events that is imposed by the sentiments of the moment.[41]

After his resignation, Morelli became ever more deeply immersed in the fine arts, content to have left his political life behind him[42] (though he was extremely depressed by the capture of Rome on 20 September 1870, the last episode of the Risorgimento). He was happy to be among paintings of the Madonna and saints, men and women of another age, to have understood the relationship between nature and art, to have seen twenty-eight galleries in a trip of two months, and to enjoy his solitude studying art, as he wrote to Antinori in 1871:

> These studies make the hours pass peacefully, make me experience pure joy, and enable me to forget the bitter disillusion in my soul. This Italy that I have so loved from my youth until 20 September of the last year, for which I would have given my life a hundred times, disgusts me. I know no sentiment more humiliating, more depressed, than that which I experience among foreigners. To you who understand me, I would say frankly that I am ashamed of my country. I have spent two months in the mountains without speaking to anyone, thinking of retreating to some small abode on the lake of Geneva to finish my days there.[43]

CHAPTER 9

A Friendship: Austen Henry Layard

Giovanni Morelli's most enduring and perhaps surprising friendship was with Sir Austen Henry Layard (1817–1894),[1] the British archaeologist who excavated the Assyrian cities of Nimrud and Nineveh, the results of which are immediately apparent to any visitor to the British Museum.[2] Layard was an unconventional Englishman, an autodidact and an Italophile, deeply involved in the study of of Italian art since his boyhood in the Palazzo Rucellai, Florence (Fig. 59). Born in Paris to Huguenot parents, at the age of eighteen he became friendly with Cavour, who introduced him to the world of Risorgimento Liberal politics.

Both Morelli and Layard were intemperate in their passion for Liberal politics; their outspokenness as members of parliament, whether in Italy or England, meant that, although they achieved some success at the broader level of government, neither was ever appointed a cabinet minister. In his biographical memoir of Morelli (the first in any language, written shortly after his friend's death), Layard paid eloquent tribute to "that remarkable and highly-gifted man, with whom I was in constant correspondence, and to whom I owe, to a great extent, such acquaintance as I have with Italian art."[3] When Morelli and Layard first met, they were both bachelors. For many years Layard was in love with his cousin, Lady Charlotte Guest, but his love was unrequited, even though he left his portrait carved on the stairs at her home, Canford Manor. When Charlotte's husband died, she became free to marry, but she rejected Layard to marry a younger man: her children's tutor, Charles Schreiber. In 1869, at the age of fifty-one, Layard married Charlotte's daughter, Enid (Fig. 60). The marriage was intensely happy, as revealed repeatedly in Lady Layard's journal.[4]

Under Layard's influence, Morelli disclosed his real name in the first English edition of *Italian Masters in German Galleries*, published in 1883.[5] This translation by Louise Richter (Fig. 61) had been considered a failure by both Morelli and Layard, in part because Richter was not a native English speaker. Layard's account of Morelli's life for the second English edition (1892–93) was carefully constructed from his conversations with Morelli over many years. The text was shown in draft to Morelli's closest friends, Gustavo Frizzoni and the Kaiserin Friedrich, who suggested additions and improvements, as well as to Henrietta Hertz, who financed its publication. The short biography elicited admiration from everyone, including Elizabeth, Lady Eastlake (Fig. 62), who had admired Morelli at least as long as Layard had done. She congratulated him:

> Dear Layard,
>
> Your proof sheets so kindly sent have been a *great* treat to me, and I laid them down with the comforting conviction that dear Morelli had at length received *thorough* justice; indeed you tell even those who thought they knew him well much more than they knew—as for instance myself. How true it is that a man is known by his friends. His comprised a group of the choicest characters—our Empress and *you* at the top. There is no accident in such a fact—the noble and intelligent gravitate together.[6]

Encouraged by Layard, Lady Eastlake had written her own tribute to Morelli, for the July 1891 issue of the *Quarterly Review.* In the same year, when Layard wrote his memoir, he recalled that their friendship had extended "over nearly forty years," and that he had first met Morelli at the British legation in Turin, in the company of James Hudson, a close friend of both men, for they frequently corresponded and traveled together in search of pictures.[7] Layard was in Italy almost every year between 1855 and 1859, picture hunting and making copies of Quattrocento frescoes for the Arundel Society, an organization formed in 1848 to popularize Italian art in England. He made Morelli's acquaintance in 1859, when both are known to have been at Turin.

Yet their friendship did not blossom until 1862, when Morelli was consulted by Giuseppe Molteni at the Brera about the attribution of a painting of the Entombment that Layard had recently purchased from the celebrated Manfrin collection in Venice and brought to Molteni for restoration (now, together with the major part of Layard's collection, in the National Gallery, London).[8] Molteni asked his "arcicarissimo amico," Morelli, for help.[9] The work was signed on a prominent, but much-damaged, *cartellino,* which he hoped his friend could decipher.[10] Morelli obliged, but had considerable difficulty reading the signature; eventually, after much hesitation, he misread it as "Bastianus," meaning Sebastiano del Piombo.[11] He was perplexed that this painting, which was so like Cima da Conegliano's *Lamentation* (Moscow), could have anything to do with Sebastiano, whose language was Giorgionesque in Venice, and later Michelangelesque in Rome.[12] Nevertheless, it gradually became known as a work by Sebastiano del Piombo, and the uncharacteristic manner was interpreted as evidence of Sebastiano's youthful eclecticism.[13]

While its attribution was being discussed, the painting underwent an extensive and unnecessary restoration. According to Layard's catalogue:

"Before the picture was cleaned by Molteni there were two figures of putti seated on the cornice which had been added to the original picture."[14] In 1980 the National Gallery in London conserved the painting, revealing precisely how freely Molteni had indulged in overpainting. Before the 1980 work began, X-ray photography revealed that Molteni had painted over the angels; there was no doubt that they were part of the artist's original conception, as they had been executed directly over the preparatory ground. These angels were the artist's own invention, added by him to the Cima composition that he had copied almost exactly. It was presumably for this reason alone that Molteni, perhaps in company with Morelli, Mündler, and Eastlake, considered the angels to be an earlier restorer's additions. Molteni also repainted many other sections of the picture, changing large areas of the sky and landscape, especially the rocks, and reducing the size of the women's headdresses, notably that of the Magdalen. (Molteni's overpainting was easily removed in 1980.) Crowe and Cavalcaselle had questioned Morelli's attribution to Sebastiano, and slyly argued that "the barbarous form of this signature suggests suspicions," as the lettering of the cartellino had been slightly reinforced by Molteni.[15] Many years later, the signature, though still difficult to read, was correctly interpreted as Andrea Busati, one of Giovanni Bellini's eighty-six students.[16]

After Morelli had studied Layard's acquisitions from the Manfrin collection, he asked Molteni if he could meet the famous archaeologist again. Layard readily agreed.[17] They met in October 1862, and from the following year corresponded in French, until Morelli's death in 1891.[18] Henceforth, Layard and Morelli traveled together regularly, visiting private collections in Brescia and Bergamo, as well as dealers in Milan, with the understanding that Morelli would advise Layard on the purchase of Lombard paintings. After one such trip in 1862, they were already close friends, although Morelli initially appears to have been intentionally very slow to send Layard news of possible acquisitions. Their friendship was formed on a mutual love of Italian painting, the study of which they both pursued as an escape from politics. Although it has been suggested that Morelli introduced Layard to Lombard art,[19] there is considerable evidence that, well before he met Morelli, Layard had an extensive knowledge of Italian painting, and had even been captivated by the relatively conservative Ambrogio Bergognone.[20] Rather, Morelli may be given credit for introducing Layard to the work of Moretto da Brescia and his pupil Giovanni Battista Moroni.

During his boyhood in Florence, Layard had grown up in the Palazzo Rucellai, where his parents entertained poets and painters, including the English painter and antiquarian Seymour Kirkup, who gave young Austen drawing lessons. At the same time he met the writer and activist Walter Savage Landor, who introduced him to Greek, as well as to the radical democratic beliefs that would remain with him for life.[21] In Florence he was surrounded by Italian Renaissance art, growing especially fond of an altarpiece by Filippino

Lippi of the Virgin and the Child between St Jerome and St Dominic, which hung at the foot of his bed (and is now in the National Gallery, London).

Many years later, after he had excavated Nineveh, Layard returned to Italy to study Italian narrative fresco cycles, with the same intensity as he had recorded Assyrian reliefs. By the end of 1855 he could claim: "I have now a pretty complete illustration of the history of fresco painting from Giotto to Fra Bartolommeo."[22] Indeed, it could be argued that Layard's lifelong concern was the study of Italian art, while the discovery of Nineveh and the contribution to Assyrian archaeology for which he is remembered (most conspicuously in the British Museum) was merely a brilliant interlude.

On these annual trips to Italy in the early 1850s, Layard was usually accompanied by Anne-Margaretta Higford Burr, an accomplished amateur artist who made watercolor copies of the frescoes, while Layard made tracings of figures or groups. Dante Gabriel Rossetti described Higford Burr, at the age of thirty-two, as "refined and very nearly beautiful, energetic withal to an extraordinary degree in Ruskin's style, but quite mild and feminine—ten hours at the top of a ladder to copy a Giotto ceiling being nothing to her."[23] Rossetti also recorded the extraordinary effect of their copies in Victorian England:

> She has been travelling all over Italy with Layard, and they together have given one one's first real chance of forming a congruous idea of early art without going there … It is fearful to hear them describe the havoc going on among the originals of their tracings, etc. In one instance, specially admiring a glorious fresco by Pietro della Francesca—I was told that while the tracing was being made, some demons came with an order to knock it out of the wall to make a window—which was done![24]

Recording fresco cycles, which was in some ways a continuation of his meticulous archaeological records, took Layard not only to major monuments like the Arena Chapel in Padua, but also to lesser-known places such as the sanctuary of the Madonna dei Miracoli at Saronno, to make copies of frescoes by Bernardino Luini. Sometimes Italian friends introduced him to masterpieces in remote churches, as when the distinguished archaeologist Count Giovanni Carlo Conestabile took him to see Perugino's fresco of St Sebastian at Panicale, which he subsequently arranged to have copied by a local artist, Marianecci.[25] Layard's copies were exhibited, in May 1857, at a meeting of the Arundel Society.[26] He persuaded the meeting that the society should be responsible for copying and publishing reproductions of Italian Quattrocento frescoes, an urgent task in view of their destruction and neglect. Every fresco was to be reproduced in two ways: as a chromolithograph based on a careful watercolor copy, and as an outline engraving based on a tracing.[27] After Layard's address, Ruskin spoke enthusiastically in favor of the enterprise.

In the early years of their friendship, Layard sent Morelli some chromolithographs as presents, after frescoes by Filippino Lippi and Masaccio in the Brancacci Chapel, and Mantegna's Eremitani frescoes in Padua,[28] as well as the Luini cycle at Saronno.[29] In return, Morelli found Italian subscribers, who received the reproductions and publications, many of which were written by Layard, some with help from Morelli.[30] "La benemerita Società Arundel di Londra," as Morelli described it, was a lifelong concern for Layard, and one of his last letters to Morelli is a request concerning the society's publication of frescoes at the Castello di Malpaga, where Bartolomeo Colleoni had lived in the fifteenth century.[31] These were then attributed to Girolamo Romanino, now to Marcello Fogolino. Morelli arranged to have the society's copyist, Luigi Desideri, gain access to several portraits of the famous *condottieri* (mercenaries) in private collections, to illustrate Oscar Browning's memoir of Colleoni.

While working on his ambitious project to record Italian fresco cycles, Layard also began to collect Italian paintings. He discovered rare works by minor masters in out-of-the-way collections, which he bought at modest prices, well before he met Morelli. In 1855 he had discovered fragments of a fresco cycle by Spinello Aretino in an abandoned church of the Compagnia di Sant'Angelo, Arezzo, which he brought back to England.[32] In the following year he purchased Bartolomeo Montagna's *Three Saints* from the Tanara family chapel in San Giovanni Ilarione, a small village between Vicenza and Verona.[33] He wrote enthusiastically to John Murray: "it is one of the best specimens I have seen of this rare and interesting master. At Milan, too, I picked up two Ambrogio Bergognones, parts of an altarpiece … works of the master are so very rare."[34] These two panels by Bergognone were acquired from a Milanese dealer, Bruschetti, on the advice of Saverio Cavallari, a professor of archaeology from Palermo.[35] As early as 1856 Layard was also investigating the possibility of acquiring works from the celebrated Costabili collection in Ferrara, "which contains a most interesting series of Ferrarese masters—quite unique. Many painters of a high order of merit are to be met with in Ferrara—Ercole Grandi, Panetti, Tura to say nothing of Garofalo—who in some pictures take a very high position … the Costas delight me. Fancy Sir Joshua Reynolds neglecting them for those wretches the Carracci."[36]

The Costabili collection was of interest to everyone, including Eastlake, who wrote to Layard:

> The pictures you name in the Casa Costabili are precisely those which I have proposed to buy. I had written again to Sgherbi about them and had even invited the Sig. Marchese to name his price—Sgherbi in reply to my first offer (that is my first this year, for I had made proposals for the same thing two years since) intimated that the price offered—doubtless considering the state of the picture—was not "inconveniente," but that the proprietor declined to deal on

> so small a scale. I certainly begin to fear that my repeated applications may induce Costabili to estimate the pictures in question more highly, and that he may speak of my offer to others. If, however, those seemingly worthless things are still unsold when you return to England, I shall be glad to confer with you as to the possibility of making up a larger group of pictures so as to make a more tempting offer.[37]

By December 1860 Eastlake had succeeded in buying a major work from the Costabili collection, Pisanello's *Virgin and Child with St George and St Anthony Abbot* (National Gallery, London),[38] but the marchese had only agreed to sell it to him on condition that he also acquire two other paintings, by Bono da Ferrara and Cosimo Tura, both representations of St Jerome.[39] Together with a huge altarpiece by Garofalo that Eastlake had acquired on behalf of the National Gallery from Count Antonio Mazza of Ferrara, they were sent to Molteni for restoration.[40]

Layard was at times extremely dissatisfied with his acquisitions, and wrote to his friend Janet Ross that he had been "rummaging about in various holes and corners in search of something to throw away my money upon. I have only succeeded in finding one picture which is worth having and within my means. It is attributed to Palma Vecchio[41] … I have seen one or two things I should like to have, but travellers spoil the market by giving absurd prices for worthless things."[42] By 1862 his luck had changed, and he made two excellent acquisitions from the Manfrin collection, purely on his own initiative. The first was the so-called Sebastiano, previously discussed, and the second was an Adoration of the Magi by Bramantino, both of which he took to Molteni. In the Manfrin collection the Adoration had been attributed to Mantegna, but it was reattributed to Bramantino by Mündler. Both Eastlake and Morelli agreed. Once the triumvirate had decided, Molteni wrote to Morelli expressing his deep regret that the Pinacoteca di Brera had not made the acquisition of this rare youthful work by the Milanese artist.[43] It is now one of the best works from the Layard collection in the National Gallery.

Following their meeting in Molteni's studio, Layard wrote to Morelli confirming his request that he make acquisitions on his behalf.[44] Mündler had already sold him a head of Christ by Previtali, but he wished for further Bergamesque pictures.[45] After several months' hesitation Morelli replied in February 1864, with the promise that he would try to find something by next autumn.[46] In December, after lengthy negotiations with Count Angelo Averoldi in Brescia, Morelli arranged a contract to purchase a Moretto portrait for the considerable sum of 4,000 francs, as well as an early Moretto—a Madonna and Child with Saints—for a further 2,500 francs.[47] These were the most expensive acquisitions that Layard had made to date, but in quality they could hardly rival those he had bought on his own at far less expense. The portrait is especially disappointing, in view of its price. Morelli considered that it had been over-cleaned, and it was sent to Molteni to gain "a little patina"—a layer of dark varnish. The pictures were then exported to England, together with a further curious painting, a present from Morelli to Layard, of Pegasus and the Muses, ascribed to Romanino in an inscription on the reverse.[48]

Layard and Morelli visited north Italian collections together, including the celebrated gallery of a Napoleonic general, Teodoro Lechi, in Brescia, where a St Catherine by Lorenzo Lotto had appealed to Layard. Repeatedly he wrote to Morelli asking him to acquire it, but in May 1865 was cynically counseled to wait: "Remain calm, this saint will not escape us—Lechi is old—he is 88, and sooner or later he will pay his tribute to nature, and then it will be easy to buy."[49] No such work by Lotto is described in the extensive inventories of the collection, but there was a half-length St Catherine among the *anonimi* that Morelli presumably pounced upon, to Layard's delight.[50] After revisiting Brescia, Morelli reported that Lechi had substantially increased his prices following the Pourtalès sale in Paris, so the Lotto was out of the question, but he had managed to acquire in Brescia a further Moretto, of Christ blessing St John the Baptist. In January 1866 Morelli suggested to Layard that he acquire a third Moretto, but if he decided otherwise Morelli could offer it to his friend Marchese Giuseppe Arconati Visconti, for whom he was also forming a collection.[51]

Morelli had already bought the Moretto painting of Christ blessing St John months earlier, for in October 1865 Molteni had reported its arrival in his studio, and judged it to be "the most gracious and beautiful Moretto I have seen in my life" (*il più grazioso e bel Moretto che ho visto in vita mia*). Amusingly, the Milanese restorer complained to Morelli that, since he had been forced to restore a "weak" Botticelli for him, he should in recompense be allowed to work on the Moretto, even at a reduced fee.[52] (This "weak" Botticelli, *Christ the Redeemer*, has recently been shown to be a superb "late" work of great power and emotion, to Morelli's credit.)[53]

Morelli must have asked Molteni to finish the Moretto restoration quickly, for in January 1866 Molteni reported that he was working day and night in order to have the picture ready.[54] Layard agreed to the acquisition on 1 February, but presumably Morelli had not told Molteni that the painting he was restoring so quickly and cheaply was on offer to Layard, as on 25 February Molteni proudly reported that a foreign collector, the Emperor Napoleon III, had seen it in the atelier and had asked to buy it, whereupon Molteni declared that this Moretto would never be exported to England or France, but was destined for the city of Bergamo.[55]

Morelli did much to establish the reputation of Moretto da Brescia (Alessandro Bonvicino, c. 1498–1554), both in his critical writings and in his letters to collectors.[56] Layard readily concurred with Morelli: "I do not know another master who gives me more pleasure—above all in his silvery paintings."[57] Under Morelli's guidance Layard acquired portraits by Moretto's pupil Giovanni Battista Moroni (c. 1525/29–1578), including one from Count Lupi's collection in Bergamo, which passed through the ritual expensive restoration at Molteni's studio. Morelli wrote to Layard: "Molteni finds your little Moroni very beautiful, and it is in effect. Consequently, we have decided that he must not only correct this young man's body, which seems to be bandaged in swaddling clothes, but must also join a piece of canvas three fingers long to the top of the picture to give it correct proportions."[58] The painting still has Molteni's additional piece, a strip along the top edge, but the corrections to the so-called swaddling clothes were removed in 1975. A comparison of the picture before and after restoration reveals that Molteni tried to correct that audacious foreshortening of the right shoulder, which like many a correct rendering of perspective may have appeared unconvincing to an academic theoretician.[59]

To Layard, Morelli gave an extremely perceptive analysis of Molteni's restorations, which may explain why he corrected the shoulder:

> This Molteni is a strange fellow. He is a truly outstanding restorer, endowed, as he is, with a fine artistic sensibility and a passion for ancient art. But because he is a pupil of our Academies, he occasionally takes part, just as your excellent director of the National Gallery [Eastlake] often does, in the battle the Academies wage to correct the naïve inaccuracies of the Old Masters, which are almost always merely the result of their engaging, easygoing manner. The naïve imprudence [*disinvoltura*] of genius will never be understood by the pedantry of our academicians. But apart from that, Molteni is a good chap and very conscientious.[60]

Molteni's career as a restorer was impressive by any standards. He was *conservatore* not only at the Brera, but also from 1861 for the Reale Pinacoteca in Turin. Many collectors, whether Italian, French, or English, who acquired Renaissance paintings in northern Italy brought them to him for restoration. Sometimes his role was more than the conventional restorer, for he acted as an advisor to Gian Giacomo Poldi in the crucial years when he was creating his collection.[61] Molteni owed his success not only to his skill, but also to his very real knowledge, personal charm, and wit. Something of this is conveyed in Lady Eastlake's impression of a visit to his studio:

> He is a most interesting man of about fifty, high-bred to look at, though the son of a peasant, acutely sensitive to art, honest, honourable, and the wittiest creature. He is adored by numerous friends, who drop in at all times to his studio, and can't live without Molteni. His restorations are just what one may expect from a man of exquisite feeling and a thoroughly good artist. He has carriages perpetually at our service and declares that his friends allow him so much a year to keep their horses exercised. One of these friends is

> a Conte Taverna; another a young Marchese Poldi, famed for his enormous wealth, who would never know how to kill time without Molteni's jokes. I told the Marchese that it was my greatest ambition to see the Casa Poldi, and he instantly took us there.[62]

When Molteni died in January 1867, Morelli was profoundly distressed, and wrote that the loss of the Milanese restorer was more irreparable than that of Ingres and of the French philosopher Victor Cousin, who had both died in the same year.[63] Layard, too, had found Molteni congenial, always anticipating with pleasure his annual visit to the Brera studio.[64]

In assisting Layard with the formation of his collection, Morelli introduced him not only to private collectors but also to Giuseppe Baslini and his shop on the Corso Porta Venezia 10, Milan. Baslini was one of the most successful dealers in Italy and enjoyed an international clientele among German and English museum directors. In 1865, Layard bought from Baslini a Madonna by Luini,[65] as well as an altarpiece of the Virgin and four saints by Francesco Bonsignori (c. 1460–1519).[66] As Morelli explained to Layard, the price of the Bonsignori was extremely low, for Molteni (also a close friend and consultant to Baslini) had dismissed it—unbelievably—as a seventh-century [*sic*] work.[67] Layard accepted Morelli's attribution to Bonsignori and wrote to him thankfully: "I do not forget that I owe these two precious paintings to your friendship, for without your expertise I would not have decided to take them ... I am really beginning to find myself in possession of a Pinacoteca."[68] Further acquisitions from Baslini, made presumably with advice from Morelli, were an Annunciation by Gaudenzio Ferrari,[69] later retouched by Molteni, and Giampietrino's Christ Carrying the Cross.[70]

In October 1865 Layard bought a number of pictures in Venice, all acquired extremely cheaply in comparison to his purchases through Morelli. From an old man living in Venice (son of an Englishman), Layard bought Gentile Bellini's Portrait of Mehmet II for a mere five pounds,[71] while from the dealer Favenza he purchased a Carpaccio Adoration of the Kings,[72] as well as Moroni's portrait of Leonardo Salvagno,[73] both of these last works originating from the Thiene collection in Vicenza. At the same time, Layard may have acquired the rare signed painting by Girolamo da Vicenza, the Death and Assumption of the Virgin.[74] In the following year Layard acquired (also from Favenza) a Cimesque altarpiece on wood of the Virgin and Child with Saint Paul and Saint Francis,[75] which Morelli was to praise enthusiastically. These acquisitions parallel the charming but modest little portrait by Raffaellino del Garbo bought in Bergamo with Morelli's assistance.[76]

In 1866 Layard bought twenty-two paintings from the Costabili collection, both for himself and for the collection of Lady Layard's brother, Sir Ivor Guest. Layard had been visiting the collection since 1856, and the large number of paintings involved must have been due to Marchese Giambattista Costabili's expressed wish to sell a group rather than individual works, a condition with which Eastlake had earlier been forced to comply. In 1872, what remained of the Costabili collection of Ferrarese Old Masters was made publicly available for sale, and by 1885 the collection was dispersed.[77] When Layard informed Morelli of his purchases, Morelli sent him a copy of a valuation he had made some eight years earlier, with the following comment:

> I had it made … with the intention of saving, if it were possible, a good number of rare and sometimes even unique works of the Ferrarese School—but my project was not to be realized, for neither the Government, nor private collectors would support me. I have at least the satisfaction that the greater number of pictures from this interesting collection can now be found in possession of people who know how to appreciate them, and who take pleasure in showing them and allowing others to enjoy them. Allow me, then, my very good friend, to repeat my congratulations on the magnificent acquisitions that you have just made in Ferrara as well as in Venice, for as I have already had occasion to tell you, the painting by Cima da Conegliano on wood is really a work of the highest quality. I am happy that this pearl fell into your hands.[78]

In a much franker letter to Antinori, Morelli expressed his chagrin that Layard had bought so well and so cheaply, while Italian collectors were too stupid (*troppo imbecilli*) to appreciate the artworks.[79] However, by Layard's standards the Costabili pictures had been expensive, and the price had almost doubled after they had been restored by Molteni.[80] Between 1863 and 1866 Layard had bought extensively, and it has sometimes been claimed that all his acquisitions were made with Morelli's advice, and that during this period Layard's taste changed from the early to high Renaissance, and from the Florentine and central Italian schools to the upper Italian schools, under Morelli's tutelage.[81] A different interpretation is presented here: the best of Layard's acquisitions were made on his own initiative, although he kept Morelli informed of everything he was buying. On many occasions Morelli inhibited him from buying pictures that were of significance. Nor did Layard's taste change so dramatically, although it is true that he was introduced to the charm of Bergamesque painting through Morelli. After the expensive Costabili acquisitions, Layard lost interest in increasing his collection. After several hints to Morelli that it was not a good time to sell pictures in England, Layard wrote to him firmly on 1 June 1869, stating that he had neither the space nor the money for more pictures.

Morelli expressed his opinion of the worth of Layard's collection to his soul-mate Antinori in July 1875, when he and Luigi Cavenaghi (Molteni's successor) were helping Layard with the display of his collection at Ca' Cappello. "Yesterday I was occupied with the installation of fifty paintings in four rooms, and tomorrow I will concentrate on their arrangement, among which there are half a dozen that are very important and rare."[82]

Morelli's reputed role as an advisor to Layard, and also to their mutual friend James Hudson, was ambiguous. He was prepared to tell his English friends about modest masterpieces by provincial masters, but when it was a question of a painting by a major artist, a Botticelli or a Giorgione, Morelli would suggest the acquisition to an Italian collector, to ensure that masterpieces of national importance remained in Italy. This interpretation is undeniable if we briefly survey the works Morelli was advising his Italian friends to buy in the same period in which he was helping Layard form his collection. Then and now, Italian museums had no budget for acquisitions, and this was the only way for a patriot to keep pictures in Italy. After Layard's death his collection remained in Italy, where it was curated by Lady Layard.[83]

When it came to the possible loss to Italy of a famous private collection, Morelli acted in the interests of his city, rather than those of his English friends. Count Guglielmo Lochis had built a neoclassical villa at Crocetta di Mozzo, on a hill west of Bergamo, the last of the Pre-Alpi Orobiche. The collection was housed in a separate building, a copy of the Pantheon in Rome, built at one-tenth the size of the original. Morelli appears not to have been the slightest bit concerned that Lochis was pro-Austrian (*filoaustriaco*). Both Eastlake and Mündler had repeatedly visited Lochis in the 1850s. On 4 February 1856, Eastlake had reported to the trustees of the National Gallery that Lochis was willing to sell the entire collection for 16,000 lire.[84] Lochis changed his mind, and when he died in 1859 the collection was left to Bergamo, but with the proviso that it be kept intact in the villa where his heirs resided.

In October 1861 Morelli insisted to the *sindaco* (mayor) of Bergamo, Count Giovanni Battista Camozzi Vertova, that two-thirds of the collection be transported to Bergamo immediately, because the Lochis heir, Count Carlo Lochis, had intimated to Eastlake's agents that he was willing to sell a few choice pieces.[85] When the division was finally made, Morelli made the selection. In May 1865 James Hudson wrote to Layard: "Are you aware that the Lochis Gallery—which you saw near Bergamo is to be divided one ½ to Bergamo and the ½ to be sold for the benefit of the heirs of Lochis? It will be a good chance for you—if you want anything out of it write to Morelli who is to make the decision."[86] Layard promptly wrote to Morelli asking for information, who replied that he had presented his selection for the division to the mayor of Bergamo, and although it was not known whether the heirs would accept, he thought they would be obliged to agree. Morelli listed the pictures that remained: some beautiful Bassano, an ugly Buonconsiglio, a retouched Marco Palmezzano, two so-called Paolo Veronese, two paintings by Basaiti, some works by the Carracci, and a few Guido Reni that were probably not authentic—in short, nothing worthy of Layard's collection.[87]

In his own copy of the 1858 catalogue of the Lochis collection,[88] Morelli's brutally frank annotations reflect his judgment. On the first page, he notes his choice of 169 paintings from 524: "Scelti 169. Tutti 524." Frequently there is a large "0" in the margin when he dismisses a work. The first enthusiastic comment concerns a portrait by Cariani of Giovanni Benedetto Caravaggi: "bellissimo, val. 100. Conservato," then in the margin he puts a value of 1,000 lire—ten times higher. Opposite Cariani's Christ the Reedemer he asks himself whether this is the painting described by the *Anonimo Morelliano* as belonging to Leonino Brembati, and sees much of Lotto's influence, especially in his use of light: "Ha molto del Lotto massime nel lumeggiare." He gives Lotto's masterpiece of the Flight into Egypt (which he already knew from the version he sold to Federico Frizzoni) a high valuation. At times he dismisses a work as a weak copy or "un lavoro dozzinale." In all, Morelli's judgment is impeccable, as the Lochis collection now in the Accademia Carrara demonstrates.

The conclusion to the story was summed up by Gustavo Frizzoni while traveling in England in 1867. Frizzoni wrote to Count Carlo Lochis of his low opinion of the English as artists and architects, but praised them highly as collectors:

> But what can I tell you about London? Here you have to find resources in things other than the pleasure of beautiful architecture or buildings, for the English have no taste in these matters, as they generally succeed in everything other than being good artists. But in making collections of art and science they are second to nobody, especially since they know no limits in their expenses, when they make acquisitions that contribute to making their museums more complete and interesting. I am certain that the National Gallery would please you enormously, since it has only well-chosen work, acquired mostly with much money. I tell you the truth that my heart cries to see the Perugino from the Melzi collection, banished from its home, also the painting of the Family of Darius before Alexander by Paolo Veronese, formerly the property of the Pisani family. Also there are some very beautiful works by those dear Tuscans, and of the highest quality by Giovanni Bellini. One of the first questions that the director of the gallery, Boxall, asked, was if I knew of any good collections for sale in Italy. You can well imagine that I did not forget your own, inspiring him to visit it the next time he returns to Bergamo.[89]

Morelli was playing a careful game, weighing the interests of English friends and Italian patrimony. In January 1866, for instance, he bought for Arconati Visconti a very beautiful tondo, which he attributed to Domenico Ghirlandaio (now more plausibly assigned to Francesco Botticini). He made a point of telling Layard that if the Englishman had been in Florence at the right moment he would have sold the tondo to him.[90] Another significant masterpiece that Morelli rediscovered in the Monte di Pietà pawn shop in

Rome was a Magdalen by Piero di Cosimo, which he subtly persuaded his friend the Barone Barracco to buy.[91] But the best example of this complicated balancing act involved his good friend Hudson. In May 1871 Morelli complained to his cousin, Giovanni Melli:

> Hudson overwhelms me with letters. I have had two in the last eight days, because he wants me to acquire works by Titian or Lotto or Pordenone or Giorgione for his friend in London. He says that it does not matter how expensive they are. If I am so fortunate again as to acquire works by these artists, his London friend may rest assured that I would not acquire them for him. The British are a curious people![92]

A couple of months later, Morelli cynically dissuaded Hudson from buying Giorgione's *Tempesta*, then in the Manfrin gallery, Venice, advising him to concentrate instead on less expensive works by Lombard artists:

> The little picture on canvas by Giorgione (at least the connoisseurs describe it thus) is now for sale in the Manfrin collection, Venice ... It is a very beautiful thing, nor is the state of conservaton bad, but the price asked—30,000 lire—is exaggerated. The subject however appears to me too arcane for that public, and then it is a little painting that would have never appealed to anyone's taste, except for the true connoisseurs of art. The portrait of Bernardo Licinio da Pordenone, of which I send you a poor photographic facsimile, is certainly to my eyes the best painting of that period, but it is not a painting to compare with the Moroni portrait—a canvas, my dear friend, that would not be easy to find anything similar.[93]

Morelli's strategy worked, and Hudson opted for the Moroni portrait, known as *Il Gentile Cavaliere*, which he acquired for the English collector John Samuel, and which is now in the National Gallery, London.

Both Layard and Hudson understood how their friend Morelli's patriotism influenced his advice, but they were content to accept Morelli's judgment on these north Italian artists he wished to promote. After all, Eastlake had acquired directly from Morelli the very first Lorenzo Lotto for the National Gallery, the magnificent Della Torre double portrait (Fig. 63).[94] In the past some Italian scholars have considered that Morelli was a dealer, but this cannot be argued when we compare the pictures that he occasionally recommended to his English friends with what he bought for his cousin Melli, where with restricted means he built a superb collection. Morelli occasionally bought and sold pictures, but when it came to a major painting like Giorgione's *Tempesta*, he did everything in his power to keep the picture in Italy, and to prevent museum directors from abroad taking such an important work back to their nascent museums.

CHAPTER 10

The National Gallery, London

After the death of Sir Charles Eastlake in 1865, Austen Henry Layard predicted to Morelli that the artist Sir Edwin Landseer would be elected his successor as director of the National Gallery.[1] But to Layard's surprise, the British prime minister, Lord John Russell, wrote to him on 28 December 1865: "Landseer has not the qualifications necessary. To my mind there is no one so fit as yourself."[2] Several days later Russell wrote again, expressing his fear that artists would consider Layard's appointment a political one, and mentioning that Queen Victoria had proposed J. C. Robinson, then superintendent of the South Kensington Museum, whereas Gladstone (then chancellor of the exchequer, under Lord Russell) had suggested the painter William Boxall. On 6 January 1866 Layard replied to Russell, enclosing a letter he had received that morning from Morelli, suggesting that he could rely on Morelli's assistance if he were appointed. Referring to Morelli's letter, he regretted Eastlake's death, by which England had lost a patriot, an artist, and a distinguished connoisseur. The same letter contained an impressive list of pictures, some of which Morelli had already bought for Layard, others that he was proposing to him, including an Andrea del Sarto, a Giampietrino, works by Moretto and Catena, and—to whet Layard's appetite—a detailed description of the so-called Ghirlandaio (mentioned in Chapter 9) offered to the Marchese Arconati Visconti.[3]

Layard then told Morelli in confidence that Russell had begged him to accept the directorship, but that a difficulty had arisen concerning the salary: he could not receive two stipends (the other was his parliamentary stipend). Even though the possibility of an unsalaried directorship had been considered, he would have to resign from the House of Commons, which he was unwilling to do.[4]

In any case, a few weeks later Russell informed Layard that the Queen had approved Boxall's appointment, and formally requested that Layard "offer him your assistance in the business of his office."[5]

Layard was appointed a trustee, as his expertise would be of value to the institution. He wrote to his old friend Morelli:

> As for me it would have been sweetly satisfying to have helped you in such a position. With us, unfortunately, a man who loves the Fine Arts is the most useless being in the world. In this regard, my country is at the same level as Turkey. Can you imagine that our new Minister of Public Instruction, [Domenico] Berti, has just nominated as director of the Uffizi Gallery in Florence, the most important museum in Italy, but also the most neglected, a certain [Aurelio] Gotti, a young man who is completely vulgar, who has only been concerned with grammar until now, and who understands painting as much as a Chinese would understand the politics of Schleswig Holstein![6]

In response to the prime minister's request, Layard wrote Boxall a letter of introduction to Morelli.[7] As a result Boxall, on his annual visits to Italy, would be taken by Morelli to see what was for sale at Baslini's studio and elsewhere in Lombardy.[8] Those paintings with a Baslini provenance purchased during Boxall's directorship were probably viewed under these circumstances, such as the painting of Tobias and the Angel by a follower of Verrocchio, and a Botticelli studio picture of the Virgin and Child, both purchased in 1867.[9]

Layard also introduced Boxall to James Hudson, who in November 1867 took him to see a supposed Titian that was for sale in the Guicciardini collection in Florence. After much prevarication, Boxall concluded that the picture was merely a copy (certainly a correct assessment; the work they saw was presumably the seventeenth-century copy after Titian's famous *Bacchanal of the Andrians*). Yet Hudson wrote to Morelli that he was mortified: "I promised myself it would be the last time that I would take that gentleman to see paintings."[10] Both Morelli and Layard agreed with Hudson.

An enthusiastic letter from Morelli to Boxall about Solario's *Man with a Pink*, then with Baslini, reveals the sort of advice Morelli gave.[11] After Morelli's first visit to England (in September 1868), Boxall wrote to Layard:

> You have doubtless heard from Morelli and know all the things he saw. I did my best as cicerone and he left England with the highest estimate of the treasures we possess of the works of great painters. I was delighted to find that he relished as thoroughly the best of our own painters and I never before met with an Italian who did more justice to the Dutch School. We parted sincere friends and I shall always think of him with the warmest feelings of affection.[12]

The warmth of their correspondence suggests they enjoyed one another's company, as when Boxall invited Morelli to stay with him in London for several weeks in August 1869. Morelli was unable to accept the invitation, but declined it in such a way that suggests real friendship, explaining that for at least a year he had had an aversion to writing letters (hard to believe, given the quantity that survive), but that after spending fifteen days walking on glaciers in the Swiss mountains he felt reborn, rejuvenated, unlike when he lived his sedentary city existence.[13]

Following his appointment, Boxall had written to Layard, "Morelli and Cavalcaselle I find are both enemies to our carrying off fine pictures and I cannot tell you how impossible such acquisitions are become throughout the country."[14] But in October 1872 Morelli took Boxall to see the collection that he had formed for his cousin, Giovanni Melli, where Boxall was uncharacteristically enthusiastic about Botticelli's *Virginia*, which he offered to buy. On the same day, however, elsewhere in Milan Boxall was unimpressed by a Boccaccino Annunciation, which he declined.[15]

Morelli was to be of assistance to Boxall's successor as director of the National Gallery, the Irish painter Sir Frederic Burton, despite holding him in relatively low regard. After meeting Burton for the first time (in March 1875), Morelli conveyed his impression to Layard: "I went on a brief excursion with him to the Brera, but it seemed to me that Mr Burton had not yet obtained that familiarity with our great painters that would be necessary to successfully direct a collection like your own."[16] In England Burton was considered somewhat touchy, even fiery, but in Morelli's presence (which could be intimidating), he appears to have been reserved. In the following year, Morelli reported to Layard that Burton was in Milan to buy four superb portraits—three by Moroni and another by Moretto—from the collection of Count Fenaroli in Brescia; the intermediary was Baslini.[17] Morelli's judgment of Burton was mistaken, as the Irish painter bought some 500 works during his directorship, including Leonardo da Vinci's *Madonna of the Rocks*, and Raphael's Ansidei Altarpiece.

Moroni became "a particular favourite of the English," as was amply demonstrated in the fine exhibition organized by the National Gallery in 1978 to mark the 400th anniversary of his death,[18] and again in 2014 at the Royal Academy. This was largely due to the way in which Morelli stimulated English taste, firstly with Layard and Hudson, and later with the successive directors of the National Gallery. It is surely not accidental that the first scholarly study of Moroni's oeuvre was written by another of Morelli's closest friends, Carl von Lützow,[19] in whose periodical Lermolieff published his *Kunstkritische Studien*.

At the same time that Morelli was advising Burton, he found himself again obliged to act to prevent the sale overseas of Giorgione's *Tempesta*—this time to Wilhelm von Bode, who was negotiating on behalf of the Gemäldegalerie in Berlin. Morelli persuaded the Italian government to intervene, and arranged for Prince Giovanelli, a Venetian collector whom he also advised, to acquire the *Tempesta* for his own collection, at the same price of 30,000 lire.[20] For many years Morelli had been compiling a general inventory of paintings in Italian private collections, listing notable masterpieces that he hoped the Italian government would make every effort to retain in Italy. Occasionally he would become seriously annoyed when one of these paintings was sold abroad, as when Hudson negotiated with a member of the Rothschild family the sale of a painting (formerly in the Sciarra collection in Rome) of a violin player (then attributed to Raphael but now ascribed to Sebastiano del Piombo), which he considered a shameful loss to Italy.[21]

In the last decade of his life, Morelli continued to advise Layard, and to assist Burton on his trips to Italy. After the death of his lifelong friend Niccolò Antinori in 1882, Morelli suggested to Layard that the National Gallery acquire Ridolfo Ghirlandaio's *Procession to Calvary*. Burton had already been advised by his agents in Florence that the Antinori heirs wished to sell, and Layard informed Morelli that the painter, dealer and collector Charles Fairfax Murray was to buy the painting.[22] Morelli's part in these negotiations was not made public, as he wrote to Layard that his position as a senator did not allow him to be involved in the matter directly (*ma position ne me permettait pas de me mêler directement dans l'affaire*).[23] Morelli's further suggestion that the National Gallery acquire an Albertinelli tondo from the Antinori collection was disregarded.

A few weeks later, Layard asked Morelli for his opinion of several works for sale in the Prinetti collection, Milan. Morelli advised against the acquisition of a Lorenzo di Credi (the Virgin adoring the Christ Child with two angels and St Joseph, location unknown), but wrote enthusiastically in favour of a Madonna and Child by Gaudenzio Ferrari (now in the Brera, Milan).[24] To Morelli's astonishment, Burton rejected it, on the grounds that it had been ruined by restoration. Morelli retorted indignantly to Layard:

> Do you know that Mr Burton is sometimes bizarre? How could he have found the Gaudenzio Ferrari belonging to the Prinetti ruined by restoration! I assure you that it is one of the best preserved paintings that I know, and you shall be persuaded of that when you see it. But alas there are very few people, even among those who know the Old Masters, who have the least knowledge of that which is restored and that which is original. And if collectors and gallery directors know so little what can one expect of the public ... I am indignant that those boasters, who occupy such high positions, are not worthy of them. In the science of art there are those things that one can learn by studying and there are others that cannot be learnt, because they are a gift of nature. I count among those things that can be learnt the science of restoration.[25]

With Renaissance paintings, distinguishing between what was original and what was restored, often hidden beneath darkened varnish or the dignifying filth of patina, was a task that caused many museum directors difficulty. Molteni's studio in the Brera had provided a forum for discussion, as well as the opportunity for many collectors and museum directors to examine paintings while they were being restored. Molteni had been director of the

Brera since 1861, and he and Morelli had studied pictures together over many years. After his election to the Camera dei Deputati, Morelli persuaded the Italian government to give financial assistance to the Brera for long-overdue restoration, to be carried out by Molteni, who—like many museum directors of his generation—was a highly gifted and successful artist and restorer. Even such an able judge as Sir Charles Eastlake frequently revised his opinion of a painting when he had examined it before and after restoration. For example, when Eastlake first saw Lorenzo Lotto's portrait of Giovanni Agostino and Niccolò della Torre (when Morelli acquired it in 1859), he considered the work "heavy and opaque and on the whole ineligible" for the National Gallery.[26] But he revised his opinion after Molteni had removed the varnish and repainting, making Morelli an offer that amounted to twice what it had cost, restoration included. Molteni had repainted the picture to Eastlake's taste (Figs 63 and 64).

After Burton's refusal to buy the Gaudenzio Ferrari, Morelli wrote to Layard about five pictures that he had acquired for his own collection (all now in the Accademia Carrara, Bergamo): Botticelli's portrait of Giuliano de' Medici (Fig. 65); two cassone panels by Pesellino representing scenes from the *Decameron*; and two saints (the wings of a triptych) attributed by Morelli to Mariotto Albertinelli. Morelli claimed that he had not offered these works to Burton, as he would have rejected them, since they were covered by a dark patina, beneath which he could not have seen the true colors.[27]

Morelli discovered a Marco d'Oggiono Madonna and Child in the Manfrin collection, and, after encouragement from Layard, Burton finally made the acquisition.[28] Sometimes Morelli wrote to Layard to ascertain whether his suggestions had been accepted, as when he enquired in November 1883 whether Burton had bought anything in Venice, though expressing doubt: "J'en doute fort, car l'homme procède avec beaucoup de circonspection."[29] A few weeks later, after having spent many hours with Burton examining paintings in the Borghese Gallery, Morelli wrote to Layard: "C'est un très brave homme mais d'un prudence vraiment excessive, et je suis sûr que sans vos conseils, il n'avrait peut-être jamais pris la résolution d'acheter le tableau de Marco d'Oggiono."[30]

Morelli had visited England on three separate occasions and had made extensive notes on the contents of English private collections. When there was a possibility that these collections were to be offered for sale, he was consulted by Layard, and his views were presented to the Trustees of the National Gallery. On 12 June 1883 he strongly recommended the acquisition of Raphael's Ansidei Altarpiece, then in the collection of the Duke of Marlborough at Blenheim. Occasionally Morelli would tease Layard when some sensational masterpiece was successfully exported from England by a foreign museum, as when the Berlin museum bought Botticelli's illustrations to Dante, or again when Morris Moore's painting of Apollo and Marsyas, alternatively attributed to Perugino or Raphael, was sold to the Louvre.[31] Before the William Graham collection was sold on 9 April 1886, which he had earlier visited in Layard's company, Morelli forwarded to the trustees of the National Gallery a list of twelve paintings, among which was a tondo that he especially recommended, with a new attribution to Fungai.[32] In the same year he drew Layard's attention to three important paintings in Lord Methuen's collection, two histories of Joseph by Bachiacca, and a Virgin and Child by Andrea di Aloigi, all of which the National Gallery acquired.[33]

More or less concurrently, Morelli suggested to Layard that Burton might be interested in two paintings from the estate of his distant cousin, Enrico Andreossi: an interesting work by Cariani of the Madonna and Child accompanied by saints, and a Bonifacio de' Pitati of a similar subject. The restorer Luigi Cavenaghi took Burton to see the collection, which Morelli had helped his cousin acquire, and Burton decided in favour of both after an independent valuation had been made. As executor of the Andreossi estate, Morelli was not directly involved.[34]

At other times Morelli was freely critical of Burton's purchases. He was suspicious of the attribution to Giorgione of the Adoration of the Magi that Burton had bought from the Miles collection at Leigh Court[35] (a judgment not borne out by later scholarship—Morelli had misattributed the work to Catena). Similarly, Morelli considered that Burton had paid far too high a price for the Florentine tondo of the Virgin and Child with St John the Baptist and an Angel, purchased at Baslini's studio.[36] Here Morelli accurately assessed the acquisition of a piece that has always been thought to come from an unnamed painter's workshop.

On 31 March 1887 Baslini died. Although Morelli and his friends considered that Baslini had practiced unethical dealing by selling whatever masterpieces he could lay his hands on to the highest bidder, without thinking of Italy's national heritage, Morelli commented to Layard: "C'était un brav'homme et il valait mieux que la plus part de ses confrères."[37]

In the 1880s Morelli's most successful pupil, Jean Paul Richter, editor of Leonardo da Vinci's writings, was also actively involved in the art market. Morelli kept Layard informed of everything that passed through Richter's hands. For example, on 20 June 1887 Morelli warmly recommended an Adoration of the Magi by Dosso Dossi, as well as Mantegna's Holy Family with St John, but neither can have appealed, as they were much later acquired by Ludwig Mond.[38] Several months later Morelli drew Layard's attention to two canvases by Gerolamo Mocetto: fragments of a cycle of the Massacre of the Innocents, which the National Gallery purchased from Richter the following year.[39] In the same letter Morelli mentioned the Mantegna again, as well as a portrait of a young man, then ascribed to Sebastiano del Piombo, but now known as Giorgione's *Giustiniani Portrait*, at Berlin. Layard failed to respond to either suggestion. On another occasion Layard was seriously displeased when

Richter initially offered a Palma il Vecchio portrait to the trustees, but later sold the work to Mond for a better price, pretending he had never received the gallery's letter of acceptance.[40] As a consequence their relations soured, and Layard was never friendly with Richter as might have been expected.

Over the many years of their acquaintance, Layard and Morelli frequently traveled together and shared ideas. It was largely due to Layard that Morelli's discoveries were publicized in England. Layard had been extremely critical of Louise Richter's translation of Morelli's writings: "La traduction n'est pas ce qu'elle aurait du être. Madame Richter n'écrit pas trop bien l'anglais—j'en suis très fâché."[41] At Layard's suggestion the second translation was made by a young English scholar, Jocelyn Ffoulkes (1858–1950), who in her monograph on Foppa would prove herself one of the most able art historians of her generation.[42] The task of rendering Morelli's prose into English was not an easy one, and many drafts were corrected extensively by Layard, Lady Eastlake, and the curator and critic Sidney Colvin. At Layard's suggestion, and with Morelli's approval before he died, the venomous polemic against German art historians such as Bode was deleted, in order to make the text acceptable to English taste. Layard frequently urged Morelli to write his account of Italian art in a way that was both more readable and more explicit about his scientific method, which he had discussed with Morelli in galleries when they traveled together all over Europe, as when in 1883 Layard wrote: "In my view one cannot exaggerate the importance of your book for the history of art, and criticism. And for that reason, I desire that you rewrite it, and create another work more about method. You do not do yourself justice as Lermolieff."[43]

Layard failed to convince Morelli to change his way of writing, but the English edition, which eventually appeared posthumously, when compared closely with the earlier German editions bears the imprint of Layard's concerns. Layard also attempted to incorporate all of Morelli's discoveries into the popular and influential travel literature that English tourists carried abroad, much of it commissioned by John Murray, whose publishing house Layard advised. For this reason, Layard undertook to rewrite Franz Theodor Kugler's *Handbook of the History of Painting in Italy*, which had been published in English translation in 1842, and in a revised version by Eastlake.[44] Layard's revisions amounted to a Morellian rewriting, and many of the chapters bear little resemblance to either Kugler's original text or Eastlake's edition. In a certain sense Morelli almost dictated his views to Layard, not only about the great masters of the Renaissance, such as Giorgione, Raphael, and Correggio, but he also illuminated many provincial figures who had been barely mentioned in previous writings. When the project was conceived in 1884, John Murray sent Morelli an interleaved copy of Kugler for him to make editorial suggestions. Subsequently many letters from Morelli to Layard, clearly written from Morelli's notes, with lists of artists' works, were used by Layard. Morelli also assisted him with the correction of several sets of proofs.[45]

When the correspondence between Layard and Morelli is read in its entirety it is apparent that the friendship was always more of Layard's seeking than Morelli's. Initially the excuse was to ask Morelli to buy pictures for him, but neither of them had the financial means to form a truly great collection. Morelli would alight on a previously unattributed work hung in the dark corner of a private gallery, which he would persuade the owner to part with for as little money as possible. This had both a financial and intellectual appeal to Layard. It must have been extraordinarily exciting to see these new acquisitions transformed in the studios of Molteni and Cavenaghi, when signatures reappeared and the dark layers of patina were taken away. Layard's lifelong passion for Italian art, which he had at various times tried to fulfil, either in his projected history of Italy, or in the formidable task he undertook to record the history of Italian fresco painting in archaeological copies, made him susceptible to Morelli's form of connoisseurship. It was as if Morelli held for Layard the secret that would lead him to an understanding of Italian art. The experience of spending hours in a gallery with Morelli, which Layard enjoyed repeatedly, was unforgettable, and not only for Layard. Nothing in Morelli's writings, sensational though the results certainly were, ever approximated the reality of the experience of discovering original works of art with him. In some magical way Morelli communicated an inner understanding of artistic psychology—an understanding that Layard felt never really came through in his friend's writings—those indigestible lists of artists' works, full of venomous asides against the artistic establishment, and prefaced by curious Socratic dialogues.

CHAPTER 11
Senator and Connoisseur

In 1873 Morelli received his greatest honor, one reserved for those who were especially eminent—such as Alessandro Manzoni and Giuseppe Verdi. Morelli was appointed by the king of Italy, Vittorio Emanuele II, as a Senatore del Regno, for life. This was an appointment to the upper house of the Italian parliament in the bicameral system initiated in 1861. Not many members of the Camera dei Deputati achieved this distinction, unless they had been ministers, a role that the outspoken deputy from Bergamo had never occupied.

As a senator, Morelli was extremely active, serving on numerous committees, many to do with the patrimony of his country. His account book shows that he travelled to Rome frequently when the Senate was in session. In the 1870s he also began to publish his writings on art, the fruit of decades of study. After leaving the Camera dei Deputati in 1870, he had devoted himself more than ever to "scientific looking." This was never to be confused with art history, nor philosophy, both of which subjects he detested, but was rather the direct experiencing of works of art, like a scientist examining a specimen in a laboratory. He travelled to Spain to visit Austen Henry Layard, to Sicily to continue the national inventory, and as Lermolieff he published his first articles on connoisseurship for serious art periodicals,[1] leading up to his first book, on Italian paintings in German museums.[2] In 1876 he also began a significant new friendship, with Jean Paul Richter (Fig. 66), which would last until the end of Morelli's life.

The effect of Morelli's first articles as Lermolieff, published in the *Zeitschrift für Kunstgeschichte* between 1874 and 1876, was considerable. They would become among the most quoted articles of any nineteenth-century writer on art. Though they are unmentioned in their correspondence, Morelli must have discussed them with Gustavo Frizzoni, who in 1869 had begun to publish—slightly ahead of his mentor—discoveries that must have been made in mutual agreement. Morelli had known Carl von Lützow, librarian of the Akademie der bildenden Kunst at Vienna and editor of the *Zeitschrift*, since at least the 1860s. Judging from the contents of his journal since the year of its foundation (1866), Lützow was already acquainted with many of Morelli's friends, for he had published articles by Mündler and Frizzoni, as well as articles about Buonaventura Genelli.[3]

These articles were the first publications for which Morelli used the pseudonym Lermolieff, derived from an anagram of his own name. From the beginning Morelli had always written under pseudonyms, and would do so all his life. On this occasion there may also have been a serious political reason, for as a senator Morelli could not be seen to be attacking the Roman princely families, the Borghese and Doria, nor the Vatican. Morelli feared that with the abolition of the hated *fedecommessi*, that is by dispensing with the legal obligation to keep the patrimony of families intact, the nobility would be inclined to sell all their treasures abroad. Layard gave a psychological explanation for Morelli's use of pseudonyms: that he "had a kind of horror of appearing in print." Moreover, he contended that Morelli's love of fun and delight in mystifying pretentious pedants induced him to assume the character of an ignorant and simple "son of the Steppe," who, having commenced in his own country the study of art, sought in Germany and Italy instruction from learned professors and professional art critics.[4] The ruse was intended to be deeply irritating to the German art-historical world.

Before Morelli, art historians had merely "ascribed" pictures to famous artists, but after the publication of these first articles it became fashionable to dramatize acts of connoisseurship. He put into print a practice for which he was known. In October 1873 Morelli boasted to Antinori he had been taken by his friend Moritz Thausing, director of the Albertina Museum in Vienna, to an exhibition of 260 Dutch and Flemish paintings from private collections, dating from the Quattrocento to the Settecento, and that he had attributed them all correctly before six German professors of art. About three-quarters were signed, but he claimed he was too far away to see the signatures.[5] This was not an isolated act of bravura.

An exchange of letters in October and November 1873 between the pair whom Morelli dubbed "the Siamese twins," Sir Joseph Archer Crowe and Giovanni Battista Cavalcaselle (Figs 67 and 68), demonstrates that his articles were being discussed even before they appeared. Writing from Munich on 5 October 1873, Cavalcaselle reported to Crowe on Morelli's activities in the German galleries, about which he had heard when gossiping on the stairs with museum curators and directors in Berlin, Dresden, and Munich.[6] News of Morelli's de-attribution of a painting of St Sebastian in Dresden, said to be by Antonello da Messina, to a follower of Antonello da Messina, instigated a flurry of activity, and a folder of blue paper drawings was sent by Cavalcaselle to Crowe, entitled: "Antonello osservazioni intorno ai fondi di quadri" (Observations on the backgrounds of Antonello's paintings). Then Cavalcaselle underlined the instruction, "If they are of no use, throw them all away (*Se non serve gettate via tutto questo*)."

Crowe must then have asked Morelli directly about these attributions, who replied at some length.[7] Taken aback that his opinions had been discussed before he had published them, Morelli gave freely a list of works he had attributed to Pietro da Messina. Morelli regarded the St Sebastian in Dresden, previously attributed to Giovanni Bellini, as the most important work by Pietro da Messina. Yet the condition of the painting made it difficult to ascribe: "This painting has suffered a great deal; the sky, the clouds, the saint's hair, and almost every detail in the shade has been repainted in a way that makes it very difficult to see the actual state of the painting and to recognize the hand of the artist."[8] In fact, the condition misled Morelli.[9]

In Munich Cavalcaselle had met Adolf Bayersdorfer (later curator of the Alte Pinakothek), who told him that Morelli, in the presence of Carl von Lützow, had pronounced that the Antonello da Messina in Dresden was a fine painting, but was not by the master himself. Instead Morelli considered it a work by his follower Pietro da Messina. Bayersdorfer told Cavalcaselle that Morelli had written an article for Lützow's periodical, which would appear next year. A later conversation with the artist Julius Hübner, director of the Gemäldegalerie, Dresden, revealed to Cavalcaselle that Dresden had acquired the Antonello because Crowe and Cavalcaselle had publicly endorsed the attribution.[10] If there should be trouble with journalists, Hübner asked for their help in defending his acquisition. At the same meeting, with Morelli in mind, Hübner went on to discuss with Cavalcaselle the picture we now know as the Dresden Venus, which he believed to have all the qualities of a Cariani. Cavalcaselle reported to Crowe: "I then replied that I believed it to be by a follower of Palma or Lotto, who was an imitator of the Giorgionesque style, but not by Giorgione ... I am displeased that a storm is brewing. I hope that with prudence we will survive even this."[11] In this particular instance, Morelli's judgment about the St Sebastian has not survived the test of time; the painting is now given to Antonello, whereas the Venus in Dresden is accepted as canonical by the directors and curators of the Gemäldegalerie, although Titian's participation is now better understood.[12]

Although their books are jointly signed, this exchange confirms, and as Crowe himself boasted, that Cavalcaselle was not responsible for the text. The literary style is in the pedantic manner of Crowe. The obsequious tone of Cavalcaselle's letter to Crowe, and rather prosaic lists of paintings in a guided tour style in other texts,[13] confirm Crowe as the author. Cavalcaselle usually sent Crowe information, which he then edited. Nor was Cavalcaselle responsible for the Italian translations of the books. As Crowe wrote in his autobiography:

> Crowe and Cavalcaselle remained inseparable. The world tried to get at the secret of our collaboration. In Italy people said that Cavalcaselle was nobody; in England many extolled Cavalcaselle and sneered at the ignorance of Crowe.

> I was obliged at last to protest publicly against the theories broached all round us on the subject of authorship, and at a later period I allowed Cavalcaselle to put his name first to an Italian translation of the *History of Italian Painting*.[14]

Crowe was responding to criticism from Ruskin, who had written ironically of the "inspiring observations by the rapturous Crowe" and the "more cautious Cavalcasella [*sic*]." The personalities of both were so unimpressive that it was difficult for their compatriots to credit either with the remarkable achievements of their new history of Italian painting, but extraordinary and important it was—and is. Both men began as artists: Crowe studied with Paul Delaroche in Paris, who taught him how to distinguish one painter from another by examining his peculiarities of drawing, touch, finish, and general execution, whereas Cavalcaselle studied in Padua with persons unknown, and seems to have had little interest in contemporary art or in becoming a painter. Both made drawings after paintings, as an aide to connoisseurship. The first book they published together was on Flemish painting, surely Crowe's choice, of which he was later dismissive in his *Reminiscences*. In a patronizing way Crowe explained that Cavalcaselle helped him "at the British Museum in copying extracts and was full of zeal at this sort of work."[15] This account appears to be accurate. Crowe's biography ends chronologically in 1860 and does not mention Morelli. It would have surprised Morelli to see Cavalcaselle's abbreviated and often inept drawings after Renaissance pictures so frequently reproduced as a connoisseurial guide to their attribution. In his books Morelli described Crowe and Cavalcaselle as the foremost critics of their age, but as the indices to the volumes demonstrate, he doubted many of their attributions.

The most dramatic and frequently discussed of all Morelli's discoveries was his reattribution of a painting of a Sleeping Venus in the Gemäldegalerie, Dresden (Fig. 69). In the gallery handlist of 1872, compiled by the director Julius Hübner, the picture was listed among several undistinguished copies after Titian, as a "Schöne Copie wahrscheinlich von Sassoferrato." Morelli proclaimed the work to be by Giorgione. Yet it was only accepted as such in the later scholarly catalogue of 1887, written by Hübner's successor, Karl Woermann, who was an ardent disciple of the Morellian method.

Morelli not only reattributed anonymous works, but also challenged many generally accepted attributions, including one of the most famous treasures of the Dresden collection, a *Magdalen Reading*, always accepted as a Correggio, which he declared to be merely a late Flemish copy (Fig. 70). Giorgione's Sleeping Venus, once renamed, became one of the most loved paintings in Dresden, while the so-called Correggio was hidden away in a storeroom, and was eventually destroyed in the Second World War. These two examples, one positive, the other negative, are indicative of the range of Morelli's achievements, which resulted in the systematic rewriting of numerous gallery catalogues. Morelli dramatized the role of the connoisseur, for he placed a greater emphasis than ever before on the act of attribution, referring to each new naming of a painting as a baptism.

In 1992 the condition of the Dresden Venus was examined closely in the conservation laboratories of the Doerner Institute in Munich, where analysis of the pigment layers, combined with X-radiography, revealed, as Marcantonio Michiel has led us to believe, precisely where and how Titian had repainted parts of the surface.[16] To summarize the results of complex research: Giorgione first defined the position of the body of Venus, using a white ground that corresponds to her figure. Giorgione's small *pentimenti* may be seen in the repositioning of her head, which he turned towards the spectator. Michiel said that Titian finished the landscape and cupid, but Titian's retouchings were in fact more extensive than Michiel realized. Titian reworked the extant landscape, totally invented the red drapery, and increased the rocky area behind Venus' head, so that her countenance is framed by the contour of the cave. The conservation history of the painting was known to Morelli when he made his discovery. As early as 1789, Daniel Chodowiecki noted the poor condition of the picture. Perhaps this may explain the extensive alterations by Titian. By 1837 it was decided to paint over the figure of Cupid and to cover part of the landscape, which happened in 1843 with Martin Schirmer's restoration, the painting at that date considered to be by an unknown Venetian. Later Karl Woermann considered reconstructing the lost Cupid, but it would be too difficult, and too little remained. Modern conservators make the same evaluation. Despite clear evidence of two hands on the painting, some scholars attribute the painting to Titian, but the true evaluation of the painting confirms the testimony of the *Anonimo Morelliano*.

□

In the early years of democratic government in Italy, when Morelli wrote to Francesco De Sanctis that every town in every region of Italy should have a museum where regional schools could be displayed and studied, he had envisaged a wide series of reforms for all Italian museums. In February 1870 Morelli traveled to Naples with Giuseppe Mongeri at the request of Cesare Correnti, minister of public instruction, to formulate new laws for the installations of art galleries, to reform art teaching, and to institute a conservation policy.[17] He was reluctant to undertake the task, but did so because he hoped the minister would accept his proposed legislation restricting the exportation of works of art. The report resulting from this trip described some 760 paintings, 100 of which the authors believed had incorrect attributions.

Morelli was continually preoccupied with the state of Milanese collections, especially that of the Pinacoteca di Brera. In 1870 it was at his suggestion that Giuseppe Mongeri and Gustavo Frizzoni were asked to compile an inventory of some eighty-two paintings that had been given to the Brera in December 1864 after the suppression of religious institutions, but which had temporarily been left neglected in Milanese churches. Morelli wanted a number of these pictures deposited in the Brera, because of their importance and their sometimes sorry condition.[18] The president of the Accademia di Brera, Count Carlo Barbiano di Belgiojoso, replied that the actual number of paintings was many more than those listed in Mongeri and Frizzoni's inventory, in fact exceeding 400, that they were all recorded in a catalogue conserved in the archive, but that proper administration of the collection had been impeded by the fact that all the inventories of the Brera had been lent to Morelli in 1866 to compile a catalogue, and were only returned after the death of the director Molteni in 1867. The national inventory had been an ambition over many decades:[19] Morelli had even refused an official post from the Italian government to direct all Italian museums, in order to create (with Frizzoni's assistance) an inventory of those works of art that should be in public collections.

□

In 1872 Morelli was invited to Spain by Austen Henry Layard. His old friend had also left politics, in his case for an ambassadorial career, and Madrid was his first appointment. Morelli traveled in late April and early May along the Riviera from Genoa to Montpellier, where he spent some days studying the Fabre collection.[20] Ignoring the dangers of Spanish Carlists, he traveled by coach and train, staying a few days in Barcelona, to arrive at Madrid, where he met King Amadeo I of Spain. The king was in fact Italian, the Duke of Aosta, son of Vittorio Emanuele II. He had been elected King of Spain in 1870, but had failed to find local support. As a result he was living alone in an enormous palace, as if in a convent, and was represented as a devil by the press. At the time of Morelli's visit the king had only one supporter, his Italian secretary, and was surrounded by enemies and traitors, his position no longer tenable. Nevertheless the visit was fruitful for Morelli; through Layard he met and exchanged ideas with the most interesting Spanish politicians: Llorente, Moret, Gómez, Signela, Ríos Rosas, and General Milans del Bosch.

The art that he saw in Spain was a different matter: Morelli was lost in admiration for the Royal Collection, which included forty-two masterpieces by Titian, including his equestrian portrait of Charles V—in Morelli's view the most beautiful portrait in the world. Among more recent artists, Goya appealed to him as the most original of the nineteenth century. Morelli's arrival had been eagerly awaited by Pedro de Madrazo, director of the Prado, who had not finished writing his catalogue. There were in all some 2,100 paintings to study, and Morelli spent three or four hours there every day. Among his students were ambassadors, lords, and ladies, who examined and studied the pictures with him. He also made trips to Toledo, Granada, Valencia, and elsewhere.

On his return from Spain, Morelli requested an audience with Vittorio Emanuele II. Their meeting took place near Pisa on 18 June 1872 at the king's villa, Gombo, San Rossore. He made notes about the encounter, interspersed with jottings on the characteristic colors of Trecento frescoes by the Altichiero school at the Santo in Padua.[21] The notes are written with Morelli's sense of ironic wit, as if drafting a play: a brigadier accompanied him to a courtyard, where he found the king dressed in country style. Morelli gave him a letter from Camillo de Barral, addressed to Antonio Aghemo. The king enquired whether he had been sent to Spain by the Italian government. Morelli replied that he had not, but that he understood Spanish politics. The king asked: "you are no longer a member of parliament?," to which Morelli replied "I left politics when I could no longer be persuaded of what the government had done to enter Rome" (*Lasciai la politica quando non ero più persuaso della strada seguita dal Governo per entrare in Roma*). A second, lengthier meeting, of more than an hour, took place on 20 June in the second little room on the first floor of the villa at San Rossore, as the king wished to learn more about the situation of his son. Many Italians, such as their foreign minister, Visconti Venosta, were against the election of Amadeo I, as they feared Spain would relapse into Republicanism.[22]

At this second meeting the king offered Morelli a Havana cigar and, once the two men were seated on a sofa, enquired why he had visited Spain. Morelli responded that he had been invited by Layard to study art, but once there everyone had spoken to him of King Amadeo as a foreigner. Morelli briefed Vittorio Emanuele on Spanish political parties, and on the irreverent attitudes to Amadeo that endangered his kingship. Vittorio Emanuele reflected: "I did not advise him to accept the crown of Spain—he repudiated it the first time—but shortly after the war with France he told me that now I have decided to accept it."[23] The king decided to send an envoy to Madrid to persuade his son to leave Spain, if and when the majority of Parliament turned against him, even though he might be reluctant to do so on account of his love for the Duchess La Saavedra. Vittorio Emanuele was curious to know more of La Saavedra, if she were beautiful, or small. He noted her name in a diary.

□

In Spring 1876 Morelli went to Sicily to continue the national inventory of art. He usually traveled in company, often including Gustavo Frizzoni. A series of letters from Gustavo to his mother, Clementina, and his brother Teodoro reveal what it was like to travel with the senator.[24] Writing from Genoa, Frizzoni imagined his mother in the foggy streets of Milan, wearing her fur (Fig. 71), eating a solitary frugal meal, while he, from the moment they left the Po valley, was enjoying spring, with no fire needed in the evening. He traveled with Duke Lodovico Melzi d'Eril for the first few weeks. Signor Nané, as Gustavo called Morelli, was as happy as a spring lamb at the change of climate. At Genoa they stayed in the Grand Hotel de France, and visited the private patrician collections of the Brignole, Balbi, and Doria. They also discovered an odd painting of an *Ecce Homo*, then attributed to Sodoma, in a public collection at Genoa, which resembled one that Morelli had acquired for his own collection, and which they remembered having cleaned together in Morelli's apartment. In fact, Morelli's *Ecce Homo* panel is now regarded as from Sodoma's workshop or anonymous.[25]

On 5 February they learnt of the death of Gino Capponi after a short illness. Morelli left hurriedly to attend the funeral in Florence (Fig. 73), a last tribute to one of his dearest friends, staying with Antinori. After this, Morelli and Frizzoni resumed their tour. They attended a wonderful soirée in the Minghetti palace in Rome, where Donna Laura Minghetti (Fig. 72) shone among many men, including the minister for foreign affairs, Emilio Visconti Venosta, and Admiral Simone Antonio Saint Bon. "Our Senator," wrote Gustavo to his mother,

> spoke very little, but seemed to have found himself very much in his element, even though, if I am not deceived, the gravitas of the Admiral imposed a little even on him. But maybe you are wondering: what kind of impression does your son himself make? In my own judgment: in the main discrete and prudent, allowing himself to mingle, giving some opinions when the conversation was about the fine arts, and listening when the talk was about politics, history or literature.[26]

The architecture of the famous Salon of the Signora was very beautiful, furnished with luxurious materials and tapestries. The next night they were invited back for a performance of vocal quartets by Mendelssohn, sung without accompaniment. In this company "Signor Nané" was reborn as a politician. Marco Minghetti, who left politics a month later, was not mentioned.

The next stage of the tour took Morelli and Frizzoni to Naples. They were struck by the extraordinary beauty of the landscape, whether in Sorrento, Capri, or Santa Chiara, but found walking around Naples like purgatory, especially given the task in hand: in no other place had they found such an anti-artistic population; the Neapolitans were different from other Italians, and had no sense of decorum. Gustavo disliked the imprint of Spanish culture evident in the over-decorated Baroque churches—a very Risorgimento, and also Bergamesque, reaction to the Baroque style, betraying a belief that the Spanish were colonizers.[27]

By 1 March the two men had reached Palermo, where Frizzoni viewed everything by contrast as very beautiful, especially the Cathedral of Monreale, comparable to St Mark's in Venice. Their principal research was in churches; every evening Frizzoni and Morelli would compile a list of what they had found for their inventory. They met the poet Bernardino Zendrini (a friend of Gustavo's brother Teodoro), and more frequently Sidney Sonnino (later prime minister of Italy), with other men, all armed with rifles in preparation for a visit to the perilous interior of Sicily. At Taormina, Morelli chanced upon an old acquaintance, Don Ciccio Floresta, with whom he had enjoyed hunting game on Lake Pusiano with Mende in 1842. They discovered works by Antonello da Messina in Syracuse, as well as a many-figured Last Judgment said to be by Fra Angelico, and at Bari a wonderful work by Paris Bordone. Sometimes they were accompanied by a cicerone or guide, who usually annoyed them. Clementina regularly sent copies of the Milanese newspaper *La Perseveranza* to keep them in touch with current events.

In all, Morelli and Frizzoni spent a month and a half cataloguing paintings, visiting all the major Sicilian towns as well as some in Campania and Puglia, the most important being Bari, Barletta, Caserta, Capua, Catania, Messina, Palermo, Taormina, Trani, and Syracuse.[28] By 18 March they were back in Rome, staying at the Hotel Minerva, and saw Minghetti's right-wing government fall from power on that very day—in their view a disastrous event for Italy. About 420 deputies gathered to vote. Morelli watched on while Frizzoni mingled with the crowds on the Piazza di Montecitorio.[29]

□

One result of Morelli's articles for Lützow was a request for a meeting from the German art historian Jean Paul Richter (1847–1937), who is best known for his work on the notebooks of Leonardo da Vinci. This encounter resulted in an intense collaborative friendship between the two scholars. Many art historians regarded Morelli's new assessment of Leonardo da Vinci and his Lombard followers as the most original part of his research,[30] and it was this that caught the attention of Richter, who discovered the true identity of Lermolieff from Lützow.[31] Richter was the son of a Lutheran pastor from Leipzig, which meant they shared a Protestant background, and over time their relationship extended to their families: Morelli was named godfather to Richter's elder daughter, Irma Anne (1876–1956), who became a painter and art historian. She and her sister Gisela Marie Augusta (1882–1972), who would become a curator of Greek art at the Metropolitan Museum of Art in New York, later edited and published (in 1960) the Morelli–Richter correspondence. In this volume the daughters omitted all personal content, to concentrate on matters relating only to painting. They also removed any unpleasant judgments that Morelli made about other art historians. Understandably, they were prone to include more about their father than about Morelli. The Richters were a remarkable family: Jean Paul's wife, Louise Richter, was also an art historian (and novelist and translator), while one of his nephews was the noted Giorgione scholar George Martin Richter.

The two men began corresponding in September 1876,[32] and the friendship developed with the exchange of books, as Richter moved from the study of ancient mosaics to Correggio. On 1 July 1877 Richter confessed that he had begun the difficult task of researching Correggio's works, but discovered that Morelli had written essays on Correggio in the Borghese Gallery, and he left Correggio aside. Richter had already begun thinking about producing an edition of Leonardo's writings, an artist whom Morelli had studied intensely but with a different connoisseurial purpose. In the summer of 1877 they visited public and private collections in Leipzig and Dresden. The traveling was mutually enjoyable, and Richter sent Morelli an effusive letter of thanks,[33] to which Morelli replied that he hoped studying art would grant Richter many joyous hours, discovering many gold mines that would invite investigation and research.[34] In these years Morelli sent Richter his visiting cards for three significant players in the English art world: Ralph Wornum, William Boxall, and Lady Eastlake, the last of whom he adored and admired.[35] Morelli considered Wornum (keeper at the National Gallery, London) to be a dry man who had read and written a lot, but failed to understand art. "Lady Eastlake, on the other hand, is a very clever lady, well versed in art history. She is a kind of manly woman, energetic and absolute in her views, but very good and ready to serve."[36] Boxall was always an excellent friend to Morelli, but perhaps by that date too ill to be of much help to Richter.

A few months after their trip, Morelli wrote to Richter a long letter about how to become a connoisseur. He advised: "If one really wants to achieve results in the science of art, one must not study documents on paper, but the works of art themselves, which takes a great deal of effort, time, and perseverance, but ultimately gives infinite satisfaction and results."[37] This may appear to be an ironic piece of advice, as Richter was then preparing his edition of the literary works of Leonardo da Vinci (1883),[38] in which he would thank Morelli in the preface, but it was not. As Claire Farago has shown in a study that significantly deepens our understanding of the relationship between Morelli and Richter, Morelli's way of examining works of art as a kind of autopsy was an inspiration to Richter, who established a chronology of Leonardo's manuscripts by an analysis of his handwriting, another form of autopsy.[39] Richter's volume was, and remains, extraordinarily successful and enduring, as it introduced Leonardo as a writer to the nineteenth century.

In 1880 the Leipzig publisher E. A. Seemann produced a German edition of the writings of Lermolieff.[40] Richter assisted Morelli with corrections to the German text and with the index. This editorial assistance did not affect the originality of Morelli's style of writing in German, which Richter saw as a unique parody of the official academic style of writing.[41] Morelli believed that his writings were not for the general public, yet he denied that they were for a learned readership. Seemann found the style overly ornate, and Morelli's method of referring to pictures by numbers and locations difficult to follow. Yet the books were astonishingly popular, eventually available in three languages, and still discussed passionately today. Louise Richter undertook the English translation of the Seemann volume (for a fee of £50),[42] and the publisher George Bell persuaded Morelli to drop the pseudonym when the book appeared in 1883.[43] Layard told Morelli that an English writer living in Venice, Browning, was so enthusiastic about Lermolieff that he declared that he had never read a book that gave him so much pleasure.[44]

Louise Marie Richter (née Schwab, 1852–1938), was born in Turkey, daughter of the American consul in Bursa. She was an excellent linguist (though a trivial and sentimental novelist, as shown by her 1886 romance *Melita: A Turkish Love Story*). Louise met Jean Paul after a lecture given by Heinrich Schliemann in London; they married; and later she translated her husband's articles from German into English. When Richter published *The Literary Works of Leonardo* he received only £100, according to his wife, thus convincing him that he needed to earn his living as a dealer, and writer of catalogues of private collections. Richter sold paintings to the National Gallery, London, during the tenure of various directors, until he retracted the offer of a portrait in 1889 which he sold privately for a higher price.[45] Richter was also in trouble with the Ministry of Public Instruction in Italy for illegally exporting works of art, charged by the Tribunale of Venice in March 1890 for his role in the sale of the Malaspina monument to the South Kensington Museum. Although he vindicated himself (with some difficulty), his reputation suffered.[46] Most of Morelli's friends were perplexed by his involvement with Richter, as they considered him dishonest in his dealings on the art market, and as having no eye, despite his expertise in archaeology and palaeography. But Morelli enjoyed his friendship, especially in their pursuit of Leonardo da Vinci.[47] More than that, Morelli was creating disciples, among whom there was sometimes rivalry. The competition between Richter and Frizzoni, for instance, became the subject of an amusing novel by Bernard Berenson's friend Carlo Placci, *Un furto: Romanzo* (1892), concerning the theft of a Botticelli to prove an attribution.[48] There were other Morellians, such as the charming translator of his works, Jocelyn Ffoulkes, with whom Morelli spent time, and to whom he gave presents of Renaissance drawings.

In fact, Morelli and Frizzoni were involved in the creation of Placci's novel. A serious young student, Piero Tavolino, recognizes an unattributed painting in a dark corner of the Galleria Tornabuoni as worthy of study. He muses whether it is by an obscure member of Botticelli's workshop (*oscuro compagno*) or an undistinguished follower (*allievo dozzinale*), or even Botticelli himself. The owner of the gallery dismisses the picture as "an ugly thing." The Galleria Tornabuoni is a barely disguised portrait of the Galleria Corsini in Florence. The picture in question is now in the National Gallery of Art, Washington,

D. C. Lermolieff, who appears in the novel, is described as "old, with a silver beard, wrinkled and bronzed skin, penetrating dark eyes;" he has invented an experimental system of observation derived from zoological and botanical systems of classification, resulting in the continual observation of minute details and their interrelationship, until he was able to distinguish a genuine painting from a forgery, the development of a local school of painters, or the chronology of an individual artist. Lermolieff in the novel disapproves of that form of art criticism which is imaginative, poetic, descriptive, or literary, as exemplified in the writings of Ruskin, Gauthier, Taine, and Pater. Tavolino is assisted in his studies by a spinster from Leipzig, Henrietta Hertz, the benefactor of the Bibliotheca Hertziana. Lermolieff takes Tavolino on a study trip to Umbria, but in the end his only discovery is the painting in Florence. Tavolini steals the picture, has it restored, then replaces it in the gallery, only to be too scared to make the attribution. Instead, another odious follower of Lermolieff, Dr Preller (a recognizable portrait of Richter; "Preller" means a fraud in German) attributes the picture correctly.

□

Though he came from a wealthy family, Morelli had frugal Protestant habits—except for the constant luxury of foreign travel, which involved good hotels. A notebook from the last fifteen years of his life gives a reasonably detailed account of how he spent his money, as well as documenting some of his incessant traveling.[49] He spent relatively modest amounts on clothing, toothpaste, carpentry, cigars, visiting cards, photographs of himself, photographs of paintings and drawings,[50] stamps for his innumerable letters, telegrams, an account at the Hoepli bookshop in Milan, an annual subscription to *Perseveranza*, and small amounts for provisions to his housekeeper (Teresa from March 1878, who was succeeded by Cecilia Massini da Repito, and from 1889 Ernesta, who looked after him in his final illness). The rent on his apartment in Milan was 835 lire, paid twice yearly to Luigi Ginoulhiac, totalling 1,670 lire annually. At the end of 1876 he calculated that he had spent 6,248.43 lire on his household in that year.

Traveling abroad was Morelli's biggest expense, whether to Germany, Switzerland, England, or France. There were periods during which he made an annual trip from mid-August to mid-September. A month's excursion in August–September 1877 to Dresden, Berlin, Leipzig, Weimar, Kassel, and Frankfurt cost 600 lire, almost half a year's rent. On that trip he paid quite a lot of money (143 lire) for photographs of drawings. While en route to and from Rome he usually dropped in at Florence to visit his friend Niccolò Antinori. At Bologna he stayed with Marco and Donna Laura Minghetti. Traveling in Italy was free—a perquisite for being a senator. The following year he spent an expensive month in Munich and Vienna, buying catalogues and photographs, in all amounting to 767 lire. In 1880 he traveled through Switzerland and Germany, altering his usual pattern: he left on 4 August to arrive on 6 August at the Spluga, where he had fought in the last act of the Risorgimento, ending the day at Coira. The next day to Zurich and then Basel, where he stayed a day, followed by Freiburg and Karlsruhe on 10 August, from Karlsruhe to Frankfurt, then on 12 August from Frankfort to Darmstadt, 13–14 August in Frankfurt and Kassel, then on 15 August from Kassel to Braunschweig. On 16 August he was a guest of Edward Habich, staying until 19 August, when he went to Weimar, Leipzig, then on 20 August from Gotha to Altenburg, 21 August Bamberg to Nuremberg, then Munich for a few days, where he bought Schopenhauer's volume of philosophical essays *Parerga and Paralipomena* (1851). He made his way back to Verona via Innsbruck. In all this trip cost 659.13 lire. In early September he was staying with the Layards in Venice, and from 14 to 17 September with Clementina at Crella.

Sometimes Morelli recorded where he stayed, as when in Rome from 1–17 June 1878 he was at the luxurious Albergo della Minerva, overlooking the Pantheon, with a view of Bernini's elephant with obelisk. He sometimes mentions tips (*mancie*) to staff in his friends' houses, or acts of philanthropy as when on 7 February 1878 he contributed 100 lire to the cost of a statue of Vittorio Emanuele II for the piazza Matteotti at Bergamo. He enjoyed good red wine, and there are entries every now and then for a dozen bottles of Chianti, often from Antinori, who came from a famous family of winemakers. Morelli was an excellent horseman, but also a great walker, recording many payments to his shoemaker, Raimondi. He loved *panettone* for himself and his friends and on one occasion bought a very expensive one as a present for Count Seckendorff: it cost 32 lire, when the usual price was 1.5 lire. In Milan he often lunched, either alone or with friends, at the Cova restaurant on via Monte Napoleone.

Towards the end of the account book the handwriting becomes wobbly and frail. Morelli details some of the books he buys, and the many copies of Marco Minghetti's *I ricordi* (1888) that he gave as presents.

A comparison between Morelli's account book and his correspondence reveals that he did not describe all his travels in the book of expenses, and never mentioned his traveling companions. In 174 pages of the account book there is never a mention of a painting being bought or sold, which contrasts markedly with the diary of Jean Paul Richter, who records very extensive dealings on every page. This suggests that Morelli was never a dealer, though he occasionally did buy paintings.

CHAPTER 12
Morelli and the Princess

In the last decade of his life, Morelli met Crown Prince Frederick William of Prussia, in waiting to become Kaiser Friedrich Wilhelm III (Fig. 74), and his wife. She was the very beautiful, politically radical, and deeply intelligent Victoria, Princess Royal of Great Britain and subsequently Crown Princess of Prussia, eventually Empress Frederick of Germany (1840–1901, Fig. 75).

The first-born child of Queen Victoria and Prince Albert of Britain, "Vicky," as she was known in her family, was gifted linguistically from a very young age, and her father's favorite. She was married in 1858, aged just seventeen, to Frederick William, in what was said to be a love match, but which was equally importantly a political union. Victoria was a Liberal in politics, and her father hoped—somewhat naively—that she would have an important role influencing opinion in Germany. Though groomed by her father to realize his ambitions, once in Berlin Victoria became isolated in an alien environment, ostracized by the German court. Her first child, William ("Willy"), the future Kaiser Wilhelm II, was born in 1859; the labor was a difficult one and Wilhelm's left arm was damaged in delivery, for which he never forgave his mother, nor she herself.

Victoria's husband is remembered as the emperor who ruled for ninety-nine days. He is often portrayed as a weak figure, failing to confront his father, Kaiser Wilhelm I, with his Liberal beliefs, and being too indulgent towards his wife.[1] The imperial chancellor, Otto von Bismarck, disliked the royal couple, as they disagreed with his politics. Crown Prince Frederick's main duty was to act as Protector of the Berlin Museums, a title he held for decades.[2] He was involved in the conceptualization of the Renaissance museum for Berlin's Museum Island, to be realized decades later (1897–1904) as the Bode Museum.[3]

Morelli's rival in museology and collecting, Wilhelm von Bode, the distinguished director of the department of sculpture, had a formal but friendly relationship with the crown prince and princess.[4] The newly created Kunst und Gewerbe Museum, in a building designed by Martin Gropius and Heino Schmieden, was opened on Victoria's birthday in 1881 as a tribute to her. Much later, when she was widowed, as the dowager empress she invited Bode to write a catalogue of her collection at Friedrichshof, where he spent a week working on the task.[5]

On one matter Victoria was determined to defy Bode: she wished to obtain two portraits of women, by Rubens and Paris Bordone, which had been owned by her favorite portrait painter, Franz Xaver Winterhalter. Winterhalter was given these two pictures in 1866 in return for painting the portraits of Barthold and Nancy Suermondt, and treasured them in the last six years of his life.[6] Victoria had adored Winterhalter from the time she was a child. She and her husband saw the Rubens and Bordone pieces in his studio around 1867, most likely when they were negotiating a commission for their pendant portraits (painted that year, and now in the British Royal Collection). Winterhalter, the most fluent and popular portrait painter of the nineteenth century, had been best friends with the connoisseur Otto Mündler in his Parisian days, when he had shared lodgings with Morelli. When Winterhalter died, the portraits were left to his brother, and after the brother's death Victoria managed to buy the Paris Bordone from his estate for a very large sum—to Bode's chagrin. It remains at Friedrichshof, while the Rubens is now in the Gemäldegalerie, Berlin.[7]

The friendship between Morelli and the royal couple was initiated by an introduction from Austen Henry Layard and Marco Minghetti in 1879, when the crown princess's private secretary and close confidant, Count Götz Burkhard von Seckendorff, wrote to Morelli to advise him that the prince and his wife intended to travel to Milan and Bergamo between 10 and 15 November and would be charmed if they could meet him.[8] On 10 November Seckendorff wrote again to inform Morelli that the royal couple would travel incognito to Milan on 11 November.[9] Morelli was initially irritated by the request, but eventually decided to meet them, as in his position of senator he could ill afford to be evasive. As he confided to Antinori, he hoped it would not be a boring, wasted day (*una giornata di noia me la sarò cavata*).[10]

Morelli's fear of boredom evaporated into enchantment, though what actually occurred during their meetings may only be guessed—during their visits the princess failed to write her daily letter to her mother. They would have discussed art, but they had other mutual interests, such as Darwin's *Origin of the Species*, a book the princess admired—much to her mother's chagrin—as did Morelli. On 11 November 1879 Morelli hired a brougham for the "*Signori Principi*,"[11] and the next day in Bergamo he bought some sugared almonds (*confetti*) for the "*Principessa*," as he called her.[12] Two days later he hired two carriages and took the royals to lunch at the Caffè Cova on Milan's via Monte Napoleone.[13] He also took them to see the private collections of Poldi, Trivulzio, and Borromeo, as well as his own. He confessed to finding Victoria magical, with a deep and intelligent interest in art. Such was her charm that he gave her a drawing by Cristofano Allori,[14] and gave other drawings from his own collection to the couple.[15]

Victoria and Frederick were impressed by the *"petit musée"* in Morelli's house at Milan, the princess especially by a portrait of a Medici prince.[16] A mention of this work in the royals' letter of thanks of December 1879 may be the first reference to Morelli's acquisition of the Botticelli portrait of Giuliano de' Medici (Fig. 65, now in the Accademia Carrara, Bergamo), though the usual date of purchase given is May 1883, as there is a letter from Morelli to Jean Paul Richter, where the picture is mentioned.[17] As there is no other portrait of a Medici prince in Morelli's possession, perhaps he acquired it earlier and could not resist showing it to the royal couple.[18]

A few weeks later the princess wrote a more personal and effusive letter of thanks in French, and another emphasizing that, although their first letters were in French, when they realized Morelli had excellent German, they preferred to use that language.[19] Glimpses of Morelli's conversations with the princess may be read in Victoria's letters to her mother, Queen Victoria. For instance, on 8 December 1879 she expressed her regret that professors in Oxford (meaning Ruskin among others) were criticizing the restoration of St Mark's in Venice, and causing much offence: "There are so many competent people who would do anything to protect all their grand works of art from destruction that private letters to anyone like Minghetti, Morelli and Boni would have been quite sufficient."[20] Nor, she wrote, were the English without fault in these matters, citing the sorry condition of Temple Bar, Northumberland House, and Westminster Abbey, ending with a suggestion that her mother's collection of Old Masters should be given permanently to the National Gallery in London, as the pictures were not being cared for properly at Hampton Court:

> Dozens are misnamed—the good and the bad are muddled together many in dark rooms where one cannot see them properly ... The Hampton Court Gallery wants fresh varnish and fresh frames for some pictures, then a great weeding out of the very valuable and beautiful pictures from the trash and the right names and dates put on the pictures, because there are some awful blunders in the names and it only misleads the public, besides being a disgrace in our day, where learning and science have done so much for gaining an accurate knowledge of art and artists of bygone days.[21]

Vicky's Morellian advice that her mother conduct an inquiry into the Royal Collection appears to have been ignored.

In May 1880 Morelli accompanied the royal couple again,[22] and looked after their daughters when they came to Milan.[23] As a token of her appreciation, Victoria sent him a gift of some antique Persian carpets, intended for the floor of his apartment "museum." On occasion Morelli helped the princess acquire furniture: chairs in Milan, and with Antinori's help a beautiful bed from Florence. Sometimes she would delegate correspondence: for instance, Seckendorff conveyed to Morelli that the crown princess missed the south more than words could express (*mehr denn Worte sagen können*), and continuously thought of Italy.[24]

From the beginning, the royal couple sent their children and friends to meet Morelli. One of the latter was Pauline, Countess Kalckreuth, lady-in-waiting to Victoria and a painter: while on holiday from the Prussian court in 1880, she visited Morelli's collection in Milan and was deeply impressed by Bellini's Alzano Madonna (Fig. 76). She acquired a photograph of the work to display in her residence, to be placed so that she could constantly contemplate it. In her letter of thanks the countess professed a great sympathy for Italians, and confessed that, since her Italian experience, recording a conversation with Morelli, she saw Germans differently: as big, strong-boned figures (*Unsere große starkknochige Gestalt*) who now looked clumsy and rough, lacking grace.[25]

When Frederick and Victoria visited Italy, they met and traveled with Morelli, stayed at the Zavaritt villa at Gorle, visited Bergamo and numerous galleries and monuments, and enjoyed his company as their cicerone. He regularly advised them on what to see on their travels. Morelli was triumphant at receiving, in late May 1880, a ten-page letter from Victoria (Fig. 77),[26] stating that all she desired was to return to Italy to meet his Florentine friends.[27] The empress-in-waiting was a passionate Italophile, as Morelli explained to Antinori: "That wonderful woman cannot live without seeing the blue sky of Italy, something which the Prussians cannot forgive her."[28] Indeed, Victoria's long letter speaks of her yearning for all things Italian: her new friends to whom Morelli has introduced her (Niccolò Antinori, the Prince and Princess Corsini, the Princess Borromeo); the sweet Italian language; and Renaissance artists, including Botticelli, Filippino Lippi, Ghirlandaio, and Andrea del Sarto. She is in ecstasy when she remembers the Palazzo Vecchio and the Cappella Ricciardi in Florence, the Cambio in Perugia, the lower church in Assisi, and the Borgia apartments in the Vatican. But above all it was the experience of Morelli's collection in his Milanese apartment, and the hours spent with him, that delighted the royal couple and which they hoped to repeat.

The recent electoral success of the Liberal party in Italy, winning seventy seats, gave the princess considerable pleasure, politics providing another bond between her and Morelli. Most movingly of all she wrote of the death of her eleven-year-old son Waldemar from diphtheria, a tragedy that happened in 1879, before she met Morelli. Victoria was unable to express her suffering publicly, but Morelli had almost immediately become a confidant whom she trusted. As she confessed to him, she had come to Italy in the autumn of 1879 heartbroken, her health shattered, for the child had been the life and sunshine of the royal household. Morelli's gift to her of a most beautiful drawing by Tiepolo (Fig. 78) gave her great pleasure, as Seckendorff reported: "Die schöne Zeichnung besonders hat der hohen Frau große Freude gemacht."[29]

Right from the beginning, this was an extraordinary friendship: Morelli the brilliant conversationalist, a patrician, at ease with European aristocracy, proved a charming friend, forging a bond strengthened by his remarkable knowledge of Italian art.

At Schloss Fasanerie at Fulda, now a museum that houses collections of the House of Hesse, there are four drawings with Morelli's collector's mark, "M°." These were gifts from him to the princess. Two are of eighteenth-century Venetian subjects: Giacomo Guardi's *Capriccio*, and a drawing by Giovanni Battista Tiepolo of *Death Giving an Audience* (Fig. 78). The third is a Baroque portrait drawing by Cristofano Allori, with an inscription from Morelli, and the fourth is a portrait study by Francesco Furini.[30]

The Tiepolo drawing is the most significant.[31] The skeletal figure of Death, wearing a cap and cloak, is seated in the foreground of a landscape, reading from a large folio album, with a horse's skull nearby. On the left a rider bursts into the scene, pointing dramatically with his left hand towards a group of old men and two young women, who discuss the interpretation of a sculptural fragment of a ruin. To the right is a group of women, and foot-soldiers with long lances, led by a hunter with a dog, who appears literally to smell Death (probably a reference to the often-expressed belief that dogs can sense when a person is about to die). Together these protagonists provide an audience for Death. Tiepolo imagined four variations of this subject for his series of etchings *Capricci* of 1743 (the other three in the Victoria and Albert Museum), though none is exactly preparatory to any of the prints.

The gift is also significant because Morelli, who unlike Victoria never really admired Tiepolo, understood that the subject would have had a personal meaning for the princess, given her dominating mother's obsessive grief for Albert, which preoccupied her children and the British nation for decades, and more recently the death of the princess's young son. In return, Victoria's first gift to Morelli (given in 1882) was one of her own works: a somber, muted still life, also a meditation on death, and her most moving painting (Fig. 79).[32] She gave this in return for the charming head by Francesco Furini and the Guardi drawing, as well as photographs of newly acquired works from Morelli's collection. In her accompanying letter she states that no modern work of art is comparable to the Old Masters in his collection.[33] Later she writes that her work is dark and melancholic, and needs to be displayed in a good light, and asks for a photograph of it.

Morelli described this *Vanitas* to Maria Antinori: "The German Princess sent me, as a gift, a large painting she had made, representing a large bronze cross, at the foot of which is a human skull, books, a crown, and a rosary, as well as other things—it is painted with great skill and signed Victoria 1882."[34] Other still lives by Victoria in the Royal Collection at Windsor, and those in the collection of the House of Hesse,[35] confirm Morelli's judgement that his *Vanitas*, painted in a deeply melancholic Spanish chiaroscuro, with a funereal frame, was of exceptional quality. Victoria was no mere amateur, for she had taken lessons with artists in England and Germany, including Anton von Werner and Heinrich von Angeli.[36]

From 6 to 14 August 1882 Morelli stayed with the royal couple at the Hotel Bellevue at Baveno on Lake Maggiore, in company with Donna Laura and Marco Minghetti, Alessandro Trotti (a patriotic, eccentric artist and a grandchild of Manzoni), and some other charming friends.[37] After this Morelli gave the princess a stunning portrait drawing of himself by Franz Seraph von Lenbach, which Victoria then had specially mounted in a beautiful old frame to hang in her room in Berlin.[38] The corners of the frame have four conspicuous and vibrant satyrs that complement Morelli, different from the usual frame that Lenbach gave his portraits.[39]

In 1883 the princess and her husband went on a very Morellian art-historical excursion, from Trento, through the Trevigiana, to Bassano, Castelfranco, and the Villa Maser.[40] She also mixed with other collectors and diplomats, such as Sir James Hudson, "Mr Robinson," and "Mr Malcolm."[41] She and Morelli continued to exchange works of art. In November 1883 Morelli gave Victoria and her husband another expensive drawing; they responded by expressing their regret at being unable to buy a charming small Pinturicchio painting which, although not expensive, was too much for them.[42]

The most sympathetic and informal portrait that we have of Morelli is a colored chalk drawing by Victoria (Fig. 80). In making this she may have intended to rival Lenbach, by creating a lively, sympathetic image. It is inscribed and dated (in Morelli's hand) 12 November 1884, a date on which she was staying (without her husband) in Bolzano, at the Hotel Austria.[43] The portrait is exceptionally fine, the most accomplished she ever executed. She kept it with her until 1890, when she sent it to Morelli as a gift when he was ill.[44] This suggests that the date of 12 November 1884 signified an important experience in their relationship, one that they both treasured.

In Morelli's mature years his favored portrait painter was Franz Seraph von Lenbach, whom he had first met in the company of the princess. Several Lenbach portraits of Morelli exist in the Castello Sforzesco, Milan (one being Fig. 83) and in the Accademia Carrara, Bergamo (Fig. 81). In the latter example, to portray the grand Italian senator, now in his seventies, Lenbach appropriated a formal three-quarter-length pose from paintings by Titian and Tintoretto. The portrait was executed in the artist's studio at the Palazzo Borghese, Rome;[45] Morelli began sitting for the genial Lenbach on 29 April 1885.[46] By 7 June the portrait was nearly complete, the resemblance judged convincing. Ironically, Morelli noted how Lenbach had taken particular care to render his large and very prominent nose.

There is also an informal photographic portrait of Morelli from this period, made by a friend from the fighting days in the Cinque giornate: the great patriotic Milanese photographer and painter Giulio Rossi (1824–1884). It shows

Morelli as a more relaxed, Bohemian figure, in a crumpled suit, smiling, at home in his bachelor pad in Milan (Fig. 82).

Morelli wrote to mutual acquaintances about his friendship with the prince and princess. For in October 1886 he was their guest at Portofino in Liguria; he confided to Emilio Visconti Venosta that the more he knew the royal couple, the more he admired them, though he found the warmth of their welcome embarrassing.[47] A year later, when the princess was in Milan, she spoke at length to Morelli about Marco Minghetti, who was about to publish his memoirs (*Ricordi*), and insisted that Morelli persuade Visconti Venosta to write a preface—a plea that seems to have come to nothing.[48]

In January 1887 Crown Prince Frederick caught a cold, which led to a persistent sore throat. A small growth was discovered, but doctors disagreed on whether to operate. In June the royal couple traveled to England for Queen Victoria's golden jubilee, then to Venice and on to villa Clara at Baveno on Lago Maggiore. In September Frederick was still unwell; they went to villa Zirio at San Remo,[49] where his condition deteriorated. At this time Frederick's father, the ninety-year-old Kaiser Wilhelm I, was also seriously ill, and the younger royals' escape to their beloved Italy was much criticized by their own children and by the German public—as was almost everything they did.[50]

In the summer of 1887 Morelli traveled at Princess Victoria's suggestion to England, to study private collections of Renaissance drawings in preparation for a planned fourth volume of *Kunstkritische Studien*, which would be purely on drawing. While there he met Queen Victoria. Morelli believed that Renaissance drawings had suffered less than paintings had from the injuries of time and of man (the latter through ill-advised restoration efforts). He contended that it was especially in preparatory studies and drawings that the painter manifests his "constructive bony framework" (*ossatura costitutiva)*: a comparison of paintings and their preparatory drawings would be always revelatory. Morelli's interest in the study of drawing was usually considered a secondary activity, although his travels in his last years were often motivated by his ambition to become an expert in that field. Bernard Berenson was to take up the study of drawings very seriously, and interpreted this pursuit as a Morellian legacy.

In October 1887 Morelli, accompanied by Laura Minghetti (who was in mourning for her husband), visited the prince and princess at Baveno. Victoria wrote to her mother that Morelli was "still so delighted at having been presented to you and at having seen Windsor. He says you have some great treasures at Hampton Court which are but little known."[51] But the crown prince's illness was pitiless, as Morelli lamented to Emilio Visconti Venosta:

> One could not imagine a crueler destiny than this. After so much happiness, so much success, after so many sublime pleasures, to be condemned all of a sudden to a long death. What a dark, terrible horizon to be presented with

> every morning, when you wake up with your eyes drowned in tears from the night before! What a tragedy. If I knew that I could be of some help, to provide some comfort to those excellent and sympathetic people, I would go immediately to San Remo. But persuaded as I am that my presence would provide more bother than satisfaction, I will wait for another invitation to go to visit them.[52]

At the end of the year Seckendorff wrote to Morelli to thank him for his Christmas greetings, which he returned on behalf of "*unser ganzes Haus.*" He reassured Morelli that all the royal household, including the princess, understood his silence at such a difficult time (*schwerer sorgenvoller Zeit*) as reflecting a deep compassion that can hardly find expression (*tiefen Mitgefühl, dass kaum einen Ausdruck finden kann*). Seckendorff refused to give in to useless hopes (*unnöthigen Hoffnungen*), but said that everyone should be thankful that, for the time being, it was not so bad. They implored God that the new Kaiser might enjoy life, while he showed a touching devotion.[53] At that time many members of the imperial family were visiting, and Seckendorff invited Morelli to come in the New Year.

After the new growth was discovered, Morelli visited the prince and princess at Sanremo; Frederick walked with him, holding Morelli by the arm and trying to smile at the fleeting nature of life.[54] The old Kaiser, Wilhelm I, died on 9 March 1888, followed by his son, now Kaiser Frederick William III, on 15 June 1888, the few months of his reign destroyed by cancer of the throat, which doctors had failed to treat adequately.[55] Victoria was said by all accounts to be distressed that thirty years of marriage should end in widowhood (Fig. 87), at the very moment that her life should have been coming to fruition, now that she had become Empress of Germany. As she wrote to her mother: "I disappear with him."

Queen Victoria's eldest daughter, now reduced to the unimportant role of dowager empress, was the most remarkable English princess of modern history. She had the political acumen of her father, expressed in radical ways, the impetuosity of her mother, and a rare understanding of the arts. During her husband's last illness she was very lonely. Her friendship with Morelli had become an intimate and loving one (from the time she drew his portrait), as attested in a confidential letter Morelli wrote to his cousin Giovanni Zavaritt following a meeting in 1889, when Victoria, now widowed, was resting with her family in Venice:

> I reply to your welcome letter, which reached me in Venice where I went to greet the poor Empress Frederick, whom I had not seen again since her loss. I spent almost all of 36 hours with her, while she rested in Venice before embarking with her four daughters to travel to Greece. I found her very depressed and dejected.

I saw and met on this occasion the Prince of Wales, with his family, his wife, two daughters, and two sons, with whom I lunched at Layard's. I found them affable and easy to get along with. They too were in Venice en route to Athens to attend the wedding of their niece Sofia with the hereditary prince of Greece.[56]

After a stay of six days in the lagoon city I returned to my nest, where I awaited a stack of proofs to correct, a tedious task that takes up a lot of time, especially to me since I emend and change much, to the despair of my publisher. Now, however, I am working on the last changes before the first volume goes to press, which will be published in the middle of November and which will elicit a tempest of venomous criticism on the part of professors and directors of galleries, and I am already pleased in anticipation.[57]

The letter reveals the depth of Morelli and Victoria's sympathy for one another, and also Morelli's complete discretion, for he confided only in his country cousin Giovanni and his old friend Austen Henry Layard, with whom he was staying in Venice.[58] Maybe the shared pain of having comforted Morelli after the death of his very close friend Niccolò Antinori in December 1882 created the spark of intimacy that led to the affair that blossomed after Empress Frederick was widowed. Following the lengthy, traumatic experience of the emperor's death, Morelli must have consoled her deeply, in a country that fascinated her more than any other.

The public spectacle of the empress, in deep mourning, arriving in Venice by special train at three o'clock on the afternoon of 21 October 1889 was recorded by Lady Layard in her diary.[59] A distinguished group met the princess and her entourage at the station, from which they were all escorted by gondola to the steamer *Imperatrix*. That evening there was a spectacular festival between the Riva degli Schiavoni and the Salute, and San Giorgio, on boats from Chioggia decorated with Chinese lanterns. The next morning Layard, Morelli, Laura Minghetti, and Count Seckendorff accompanied Victoria to various bric-à-brac shops. They all lunched at Ca' Capello, and in the afternoon attended a ceremony at the Greek Church in honor of Princess Sophie. That evening they all dined on the *Imperatrix*, together with the Greek Orthodox patriarch and the Greek consul, as well as many others, including the Princess Hatzfeld.

Little of Victoria's correspondence survives, with the remarkable exception of her daily letters to her mother, which were smuggled out of Friedrichshof by the Honorable Frederick Ponsonby when he and her brother, King Edward VII, visited the dying empress in March 1901.[60] Thus when she died no papers or letters were found, despite extensive searches and questioning, as her son wished to destroy any negative comment about his relationship with his mother. They were published, in part, twenty-seven years later, in order to fulfil Victoria's express wish that extracts be published. So her letters to Morelli, now in Archivio Zavaritt in Bergamo, are an exceptional survival.

Austen Henry Layard, as Morelli's confidant, knew when Morelli was meeting Victoria.[61] But despite Morelli's discretion, his friendship with the princess excited jealousy among others, as shown for instance by Adolfo Venturi's dry comment that princesses and ladies surrounded Morelli when he accompanied Princess Victoria in Italy: "He tried to educate her to acquire a collection; but that august woman thought a great deal about spending a million lire for a little picture by Girolamo da Santa Croce."[62] Venturi failed to understand that the Dowager Empress Victoria already possessed an extraordinary collection, which became a permanent museum at Schloss Friedrichshof, the castle in the Taunus mountains near Frankfurt that she built to live in after her husband's death. It includes remarkable examples of English royal portraiture, as well as significant Italian Renaissance paintings, which Victoria had brought with her as a bride from England. It remains intact, as she left the castle and collection in trust—an example of the noble sense of freedom and culture in which she and Frederick believed.

Some intimation that Morelli and Princess Victoria were already romantically involved *before* her husband died might be deduced from an 1887 portrait of Morelli painted by their mutual friend Lenbach (Figs 83 and 84). Morelli gave this head-and-shoulders view to Gustavo Frizzoni, who used it as the preferred image for Morelli's publications; Frizzoni bequeathed it to the Museo Civico, Milan, where it went in 1916, together with Morelli's drawing collection. The preparatory drawing for it was in Victoria's possession. On the reverse of the painting is a drawing by Lenbach, verging on caricature, of a woman who may be identified as Victoria, whom he also portrayed at this time. Next to her is Lenbach's drawing of a man's head in a square box, resembling Victoria's husband. Perhaps Lenbach's doodles represent a divided couple, and are a comment on the relationship between the three people. It is not hard to imagine that Victoria, who had enjoyed an extraordinarily happy and privileged childhood, followed by a difficult marriage and an unbearable relationship with her eldest son, eventually found happiness with Morelli.

The correspondence between Morelli and the crown princess began in French and then proceeded in German. Five letters are from the princess herself, but the majority, some thirty-five dating from 1880 to 1890, are from Count Seckendorff, who saw himself as Victoria's confidant, presented himself as such to Morelli, and acted as her amanuensis. In his first letters the "*wir*" plural, emphasized between quotation marks, refers to the entire royal entourage, but after the death of Frederick it refers increasingly to Victoria and Seckendorff as a unit, separate from the court. For a man in Seckendorff's position, the letters reveal an unusual intimacy with Victoria, as well as with Morelli. This is exemplified by Seckendorff's barely concealed expressions of sympathy for Victoria in respect to her harsh treatment by her son as Kaiser Wilhelm II, when for instance she was bitterly hurt by being thrown out of the great Baroque Schloss at Potsdam, where she had lived for twenty-nine years in October 1888, forced to find another residence (Friedrichshof).[63] Seckendorff's very sympathetic and hardly secretarial or distanced depiction of Frederick's final illness and of Victoria's suffering with her husband was written by a close confidant to both the princess and Morelli.[64] The address and leave-taking formulas in Seckendorff's letters to Morelli are usually much fonder (and grow more so over time) than those of other correspondents.[65] He begins by addressing Morelli as *Bester Herr Morelli*, then *Lieber Herr Morelli*, then *Lieber Freund und Gönner*, then *Verehrter Gönner*, and finally *Verehrter Freund*. By comparison, the Countess Kalckreuth is much more formal: *Verehrter Herr Morelli* in her first letter, and *Lieber Signor Morelli* in her second.

When Morelli died, Layard considered the dowager empress to be the most perceptive person to comment on the obituary he was preparing. To seek her views he visited her at Trento for her fifty-first birthday, where he found her extremely beautiful, with only one "defect": that she liked walking at length in the mountains, jumping up and down hills with great agility, which he was unable to equal, though Morelli certainly would have enjoyed it.[66] Among the many flowers on Morelli's grave there was a majestic wreath from Victoria.[67] Layard also sent his short biography in proof to Lady Eastlake, who remarked:

> I laid them down [flowers on his grave] with the comfort and conviction that dear Morelli had at length received *thorough* justice; indeed you tell even those who thought they knew him well much more than they knew—as for instance myself. How true it is that a man is known by his friends. This comprised a group of the choicest characters—our Empress and *you* at the top. There is no accident in such a fact—the noble and intelligent graduate together.[68]

Morelli's last gift to Victoria is described in his will as "a little portrait by Francesco Pourbus, representing a boy holding an apple in his hand."[69] Though the portrait has disappeared, this remembrance sent a clear message of regret that they had not spent their lives together. In her widowhood Victoria was increasingly preoccupied with art. She wrote to her mother: "Each time I leave Italy I feel more and more how little I really know about art history. It is a vast study."[70] In her final letters to her mother she offered advice on how to hang the Venetian pictures at Buckingham Palace, especially works by Titian. Her library at Friedrichshof reveals that she bought all of Morelli's books on the Italian and German galleries, remaining to her last days a true Morelli *Kennerin*.

CHAPTER 13

Endgames and Black Nomenclature

In his last decade, Morelli wrestled with his publications, improved his collection, enjoyed the company of friends, and avoided bureaucratic responsibilities. In 1880, as Ivan Lermolieff, he published *Italian Masters in German Galleries*, focusing on the state art galleries of Munich, Dresden, and Berlin. The book came out in three languages: first in German with Seemann in 1880,[1] then in the clumsy English translation of Louise Richter in 1883,[2] and finally in Italian with Zanichelli in 1886.[3] In March 1881 he was again offered the directorship of the Florentine galleries by Francesco De Sanctis, once more minister of public instruction. Morelli made it known that he would only accept such an appointment subject to certain conditions, which he then set down (principally that Gustavo Frizzoni would assist him as deputy director), knowing that they were so outrageous that the government would find his candidature unacceptable. His reason for not wishing to take on the post was that he felt too old, in his sixties, to undertake such a position: it would be a burden, take away his personal freedom, and inhibit him from writing.[4] At the same time, he was acquiring paintings, most significantly the portrait of Giuliano de' Medici by Botticelli (Fig. 65), which he bought privately in Florence in 1883 for a modest sum.[5] His eye was also struck by contemporary works, such as a portrait by Giuseppe Bertini of the flamboyant Countess Casati, related by marriage to the Camozzi Vertova family, which he thought was one of Bertini's most significant achievements, perhaps due as much to the subject's eccentric personality as to the artist. Restraining himself, he did not buy it, concentrating only on Renaissance art.

□

In 1878 Morelli showed three of his essays on the collections in German art museums to Jean Paul Richter, who aroused the interest of the Leipzig publisher E. A. Seemann. In preparing the volume for publication, Richter assisted Morelli with corrections to the manuscript, and later with proofs. Morelli was uncertain about publishing in German, so Richter's help in editing his text was of the greatest importance. Morelli took the manuscript to the publisher in early August 1879.

As on many previous occasions, Morelli attempted to hide his identity through word-games, anagrams, and puns. The published volume was by "Ivan Lermolieff," supposedly translated from Russian into German by "Dr Johannes Schwarze." The English edition of 1883 was published under Morelli's own name, but in the 1886 Italian edition Morelli reverted to the fiction of Lermolieff, claiming that the translation was by an unknown baroness of initials "A. K." The nomenclature is consistently "black," based on the etymology of the author's surname, which is derived from a Latin word for brown or dark-colored: the fictional Russian Lermolieff (based on an anagram of Morelli), the translator Schwarze, or in the English edition where Giovanni Morelli or John Black is cited as the author.

In the preface to the German edition, Lermolieff describes visiting galleries in Munich, Dresden, and Berlin, before returning to Russia to write at "Gorlaw" (recognizable as villa Zavaritt at Gorle). Morelli's youthful love affair with German culture re-emerges when he describes the importance of the collection in Munich's Alte Pinakothek, and even more so with Dresden's Gemäldegalerie Alte Meister, for him the richest picture gallery in the world, the most precious of all collections, which cannot be rivaled anywhere for its beauty. Finally, he concentrates on Berlin's Gemäldegalerie, a museum of later foundation but nevertheless impressive, which owed much, as he states, to the connoisseurship of Edward Solly. Rudolf Marggraff's 1866 catalogue of the Munich Pinakothek had been a highly publicized disaster, critiqued by Otto Mündler in a series of reviews for the Heidelberg journal *Recensionen und Mittheilungen über bildende Kunst*. This inadequacy gave Morelli the opportunity to showcase his method, changing many an attribution.

The preface contains a dialogue reminiscent of Morelli's early pseudonymous publications, but this time the central protagonist is Lermolieff, a Russian who has retreated to Gorlaw, where he is visited by two Russian gentlemen, recognizable as highly unflattering caricatures of Joseph Archer Crowe (tall, large, with blonde hair and an exaggerated moustache), and Giovanni Battista Cavalcaselle (small, dark-skinned, toothless, and with very large hands). The elder of the two, Crowe, recounts to Lermolieff that he had made his living as a political journalist, but became bored and decided to write about art. Cavalcaselle is characterized as a failed artist who has studied painting to become a house painter, but was then unable to earn his living. A dialogue ensues, in which the two visitors ask for elucidation about Italian art; their lack of preparation, and Cavalcaselle's unfamiliarity with the Italian language (a snide remark, for it was Crowe the journalist who had actually written these two men's numerous publications) is the fiction that prompts Lermolieff to publish his own findings.

Like his undergraduate caricatures, Morelli's depiction of the well-known pair of art historians was a little too close to reality to be funny. Morelli was a brilliant mimic, but what was amusing in conversation failed on the printed page. These caricatures were omitted from the English translation. On 29 November 1880, Morelli remarked to Layard: "Until now it seems to me that nobody among these good Germans has perceived the poison that is hidden in the preface to my book."[6] To Antinori he had earlier confessed that, although he experienced a sense of satisfaction at having published his stuff, the hailstorm could not fail to land on his head.[7]

Despite his use of pseudonyms, Morelli longed both for recognition and for a full-scale polemical battle with German art historians. He had sent a copy of Lermolieff to Lady Eastlake, but she told Layard that she had received a volume by a Russian, translated into German, and that she had no idea who the author was. Nevertheless, the author was immediately recognized by many German art historians, and indeed by Crowe and Cavalcaselle. Through the grapevine Morelli heard that they were furious with him: Princess Victoria laughingly told Layard that her friend Crowe "saw nothing of value in the book," while Cavalcaselle thought Morelli "a bit naughty." The princess laughed even more when Layard told her that Morelli was living in fear of conspiracy and even assassination.[8]

Morelli thrusts into the consciousness of his readers the importance of restoration as a diagnostic instrument for attributing paintings:

> By far the greater number of pictures which have descended to us from the best periods have been subjected to barbarous restorations, so that instead of beholding the physiognomy of a master in his work the connoisseur sees only the black mask with which the restorer has covered it, or at best a skinned and utterly disfigured surface. In such a ruin there is no possibility of distinguishing an original from a copy. Only a close observation of the forms peculiar to a master in his representation of the human figure, can lead to any adequate results.[9]

Like the scientist Cuvier, Morelli looked closely, searching for parts of a painting that had not been daubed by the restorer's brush, where the hand of a master could be detected, and from that an attribution could be made. In the book he makes frequent reference to the condition of paintings being "injured by modern restoration," "repainted," "daubed," or "the face has been cleaned entirely off and then repainted." The benefit of years of study with his restorer friends Giuseppe Molteni and Luigi Cavenaghi—and not least Giovanni Secco Suardo—is evident throughout. Anatomical details were also important, as part of a set of characteristics of high value in determining authorship. For instance, with Titian the thumb is given a high rating, because Morelli identifies fifty works by that artist in which the base of a man's thumb is abnormally developed.

Even more than in his earlier writings, Morelli emphasizes the importance of drawings in defining an artist's style. Significantly, the only illustrations in the volume are drawings. Over the years Morelli had built up his own collection of drawings,[10] and from 1868 he collected numerous catalogues of drawings, which he annotated on his incessant travels. His extant library contains seventeen catalogues for the Louvre drawings, five for Berlin, six for Dresden, as well as innumerable others with extensive marginal annotations about authorship.[11] He had his own collector's stamp: a large blue "M" capped by an "o" (the first two letters of his surname). Morelli happily contributed to a small book called *Fagan's Collectors' Marks* (1883) by Louis Alexander Fagan, an Anglo-Italian who worked in the department of Prints and Drawings at the British Museum.[12] Morelli lauded the publication, which recorded 671 collectors' stamps, commented favorably that the Uffizi was about to adopt a collection stamp, but regretting that other institutions, such as the Biblioteca Ambrosiana, the Biblioteca Reale di Torino, and the Accademia in Venice, had failed to do so.

Morelli's volume on German galleries contains an overview of Giorgione's oeuvre: a restricted rather than an expansive one, with which few would quarrel today. It is here that he proposes that the Venus in the Dresden Gemäldegalerie is by Giorgione—his most famous attribution.[13] Despite his broad knowledge of the collections of Europe, he does reveal some local bias: there is a rather disproportionate quantity of (very passionate) discussion of painters from Bergamo and Brescia, including Previtali, Jacopo Palma, Moretto, and Moroni.

Morelli's attributions of works in the Dresden Gemäldegalerie received public acknowledgement several years later in Karl Woermann's catalogue (published 1887), in which no less than fifty-six paintings are re-baptized. Woermann explains how art-historical studies have achieved the status of an independent science in the years since Hübner published the museum's first catalogue (1856). Following his appointment as director in 1882, Woermann undertook many *Studienreisen* in preparation for his catalogue, consulted numerous experts (Crowe and Cavalcaselle among them), but most importantly Morelli: "one of the finest and most methodical of all living connoisseurs" (*einem der feinsten und methodischsten aller lebenden Kenner*). After Morelli's death, Woermann met Gustavo Frizzoni in Milan, who helped him with acquisitions for the gallery. Decades later, he described his friendship with Morelli at much greater length in his autobiography, recalling his first encounter with Morelli's writings while researching his history of Italian painting, and his particular debt to Morelli's knowledge of the northern Italian schools. Woermann then declares:

> Personally, I first learnt to know and love him in Dresden, and then repeatedly visited him in Milan, where he lived. Though not large in stature, his handsome lively Italian head with a greying Van Dyck beard stood out from the crowd. He was one of the most sociable and inspiring personalities I have ever met. As long as he lived, we remained in friendly contact by letter and in person.[14]

In Morelli's section on Dresden there is a brief encounter between Lermolieff and one "Elise von Blasewitz," accompanied by her father. (This character was based on a widow Morelli knew, and he later said that, like most widows, she was a blue-stocking). Lermolieff and Elise discuss the attribution of a painting of Mary Magdalen reading, then attributed to Correggio, but which Lermolieff considers to be by Adriaen van der Werff. Lermolieff gives his reasons, outlining certain characteristics:

> "Look at the dazzling, glaring ultramarine of the mantle. Why, that is the Van der Werff color all over; see the affected form of the fingers, the long nails, with all that light thrown on the cut edges, a thing no Italian ever did ... compare the foliage in Van der Werff's pictures, and lastly the cracks in this painting with the cracks in the paintings of Van der Werff and his contemporaries. Then observe all these little stones in the foreground, how minutely they are executed". "Never" said the irritated lady with an ironical smile "you will not convert me," for as she recounts how Mengs thought it the best Correggio ever, and Wilhelm von Schlegel agreed in a poem.[15]

There is much that is surprising in the book, such as Morelli's singling out the seventeen plates of a majolica dinner service as the most valuable treasure of the Museo Correr at Venice. He attributes these to Timoteo Viti,[16] and even though they are now attributed to Nicola di Urbino, he throws into the critical limelight the refinement of the majolica and identifies their manufacture as Urbino. His judgment was accepted for a long time.[17]

When Morelli published the Italian edition in 1886, the writer Gabriele D'Annunzio arranged for the brilliant young scholar Corrado Ricci to review it for his chic periodical *Cronaca Bizantina*.[18] The book caused a sensation, even though the title reads like an undergraduate prank—even more in Italian than in German: *Iwan Lermolieff, Le opere dei maestri italiani nelle gallerie di Monaco, Dresda e Berlino: Saggio critico di Jvan Lermolieff tradotto dal Russo in Tedesco per cura del Dott. Giovanni Schwarze e dal Tedesco in Italiano dalla Baronessa di K. A.* Adolfo Venturi tried to restrain Ricci:

> Do not be in such a hurry to publish your criticisms of Morelli's book, if you want to achieve something that is not only good but excellent. You are right, the arrogance of the honorable Senator is annoying. However, you must take into account the good results he arrived at, especially regarding the Milanese school, which he knows well from within and without.[19]

In his review Ricci asks: why, in a book of historical research, the claim is made to previous fake editions and a fictive translator, especially when the earlier English edition bears the author's real name? He questions whether these fictions might lead readers to question the seriousness of the book, yet he never doubts that Senator Giovanni Morelli is one of the most authoritative art critics of all time.[20] Ricci imagines Morelli writing in the rooms of his Milanese apartment, seated before the Alzano Madonna by Giovanni Bellini (Fig. 76), or the tragic end of Virginia as portrayed by Botticelli (Fig. 56), or in front of Timoteo Viti's St Catherine, and Ercole de' Roberti's St John the Evangelist. The review attempts to demolish the value of anatomical diagrams of hands and ears as a means of determining authorship, Ricci claiming that such elements are never consistent even within the work of an individual artist, and that a portrait represents the ear of the sitter rather than of the artist. Grudgingly, he admits that Morelli's perception of details in a work of art is always extraordinary, though they may not be anatomical. Who would disagree? At the end of the review Ricci claims that the book makes one of the greatest contributions to an understanding of Italian art, though because of Morelli's intellect, not his method. D'Annunzio drew the review to the attention of their mutual publisher, Zanichelli, with some pride.[21] When Ricci grew old, he, like Morelli, became a senator, and his first speech to the senate, titled "Sempre per l'arte" (Always art, 15 May 1925), argued, not unlike Morelli, that art was not merely an object of luxury, but was of fundamental moral importance to the Italian state.[22]

The pseudonym "Lermolieff" perplexed Morelli's family and social circle, especially his British friends. In his carefully worded explanation to Lady Eastlake, his tone is deeply reverential (as he was towards her late husband).[23] Writing with brutal frankness to someone he considers his equal—a kindred spirit—he explained that he assumed the identity of a Tartar from Russia to shame the arrogance of German art historians when they spoke about Italian art.[24] He still respected German science—a result of his early scientific education in Germany—but detested the smug pretensions of the Berlin clique in art history. For a Tartar to know more than they did about Italian art was the ultimate ironic insult. He also intended to reveal flaws in the writings of Crowe and Cavalcaselle, whom the Germans held in high regard.

The correspondence between Morelli and Lady Eastlake touched on such things as Morelli's attribution of a canvas of St Sebastian by Timoteo Viti in the Palazzo Ducale at Urbino, of which he attached a sepia photograph; a discussion of how Raphael died, which Morelli thought was caused by *febbre perniciosa*, a form of virulent malaria, rather than through his love affair with the Fornarina, because Raphael was just too busy with commissions to have spent time with his lover—or so Morelli thought. Morelli claimed to be ignorant of literature on Raphael, though his library suggests otherwise, and one of the leading scholars on Raphael judges that Morelli had more influence on Raphael studies than did any other connoisseur of the nineteenth century.[25] Usually Morelli's opinions were given simply as lists, but in his letters with Lady Eastlake he reasoned in some detail about why he made an attribution.

The most sensational of Morelli's attributions to Raphael was the *Donna Velata* in the Palazzo Pitti (Fig. 89), discussed at some length in Lermolieff's dialogue, as well as the double portrait of Andrea Navagero and Agostino Beazzano (Fig. 88), covered in his dialogue on the Doria Gallery. In modern literature Morelli's role in establishing the attribution of these works is usually forgotten.[26] At the same time, Morelli radically and unwisely took away from Raphael many drawings. He theorized that the young Raphael spent some time in Timoteo Viti's studio, an important discovery which he was honored to have had accepted by Lady Eastlake, a "connoisseur of the highest rank" (*Diesen für die Kunstgeschichte wichtigen Punkt von einem Kunstkenner Ihres Gewichtes bestätigt zu sehen, ist für mich von der höchsten Bedeutung*).[27] Morelli also refuted the authorship of the so-called Raphael Sketchbook in the Gallerie dell'Accademia, Venice, which was collected by Giuseppe Bossi, and considered by Crowe and Cavalcaselle (among others) to be Raphael's. Most scholars today would agree with Morelli that only one drawing in the collection is an autograph Raphael, while the others are Umbrian drawings, sometimes copies after the young Raphael.[28] Morelli studied the drawings themselves at length, and to Lady Eastlake he gave references to the photographs of Antonio Fortunato Perini—evidence that he sometimes judged works based on photographs, while purists would claim that it was essential to see the original. He ridiculed the argument that a watermark is a guarantee of Raphael's hand; after all, he surmised, there was only one supplier of paper in Perugia.[29]

At this time Lady Eastlake was writing a critical overview of recent literature on Raphael for the *Edinburgh Quarterly*, which appeared in March 1883. Lermolieff had charmed her, and she accepted many of his suggestions:

> "Ivan Lermolieff" is more to be trusted for the veracity of his conclusions than for that of his own identity. Though neither Russian nor German, we may not precisely call him a wolf in sheep's clothing, for the disguise covers a generous animal who hurts no one, shows neither teeth nor claws, but deals out sure and vigorous strokes with a great magnanimous paw ... the secret could but escape, that under this Muscovite "alias"—an anagram of his own name with a Russian tail in it, and in the garb of a faultless German style—we have here the work of Il Senatore Giovanni Morelli, an Italian gentleman well known in England; one of the most gifted representatives of political as well as pictorial science—certainly the most widely accomplished man—in the modern Italian nation.[30]

□

In the summer of 1887 Gustavo Frizzoni accompanied Morelli to England,[31] where they were joined by Wilhelm Koopmann, then preparing a book on Raphael's drawings, published a decade later.[32] Their first day in England was a quiet Sunday, and Frizzoni observed the many devout churchgoers. He chose to attend a Unitarian Chapel (possibly Rosslyn Hill in Hampstead), but, not speaking English, understood little, despite his intense curiosity about their cult. To profit from a day without fixed appointments, the three men went to the ancient city of Oxford to study drawings. Frizzoni found it an intense but tiring intellectual activity, which led to unpleasant negative results, for in attempting to establish what should have been gold among the drawings, they in fact turned them into pinchbeck. In Frizzoni's eyes, criticism should have the noble intention of searching for truth, wherever it lay and in whatever form, whereas Koopmann performed a demolition job, eliminating many of Raphael's drawings, destroying any illusions. Raphael was eclipsed by his followers and pupils or, in the worst scenario, by vulgar forgers. To justify this approach, Koopmann maintained that the quantity of drawings attributed to Raphael would be enough for twelve artists, and that he had been imitated by many. Among the drawings they saw in Oxford was the collection at Christ Church, where Morelli's attributions were recorded by the librarian, Thomas Vere. All have proved enduring,[33] revealing how Morelli created new traditions of attribution just by giving his opinion, despite Koopmann's negativity.

Back in London they were invited to dine with the Layards, where Gustavo gave a letter to Signor Nané from his mother, as he acted as a go-between for their correspondence. Morelli's health, Gustavo told Clementina, was much better, but like Figaro he was pulled here and there, and never got a quiet moment; he saw and observed continually. One considerable distraction was a visit to the collection of the parliamentarian, landowner, and garden enthusiast Robert Stayner Holford, at his palatial London home, Dorchester House on Park Lane. Holford's wife received them warmly and led them to the rooms where were hung some paintings that had been acquired from the Frizzoni family, tactfully leaving them alone to wander where they wished. Unfortunately, according to Frizzoni, the family had sold "our" Moretto for a miserable sum, though to a good home.

Frizzoni's favourite building in London was the National Gallery, where on this trip he studied again for a re-edit of his rather long article on the collection.[34] He found the gallery as rich and attractive as ever, and noted a new installation and many new acquisitions for Queen Victoria's Jubilee. He concluded that England seemed to be a country that was truly independent, and whose many regions warranted visiting.

They saw many private collections, the most significant belonging to Sir Richard Wallace. Layard forced them to visit the Manchester Jubilee Exhibition of the last fifty years of British art, which they tolerated. The admirable institution of the British Museum never failed to impress, with large sections about India, Asia Minor, and Greece, as well as the best library in the world, for which Gustavo had taken out a reader's ticket for life in 1878.

But for him and his two companions, the most important department was the print room.

In July they attended a sumptuous banquet at the home of the German-born chemist and industrialist Ludwig Mond, The Poplars, on Avenue Road near Regent's Park, where Jean Paul Richter and his wife were staying. Then the group journeyed by train to Chatsworth, some four hours from London, to study the collection of the Duke of Devonshire. When they arrived at the princely residence, located in idyllic countryside resembling a Dutch landscape, they were at first unable to find lodgings. There was an easy remedy: the porter led them from house to house in the village, where one by one they each found a place to stay. The men were enchanted by the tiny cottages, each surrounded by a small garden, with very beautiful flowers, all carefully cultivated. Inside were murals with Biblical mottos. They ate at the hotel nearby.

At the ducal residence they found two ample corridors in which the walls were covered top to bottom with Old Master drawings under glass; these could be individually removed for close scrutiny. Among this abundance could be found the very rare hand of Giorgione, as well as works by Titian, Giovanni Bellini, Raphael, Parmigianino, and many others. Each found something that appealed to him: "Sig. Nané," related Frizzoni, "was always at the centre of the group, his character being both authoritative and friendly. Richter was always close by his side, literally, hugging his rib bones, to make himself safe, and adopted a mocking tone."[35] Frizzoni's account of Morelli was always given respectfully, but it is clear that he detested the extreme negativity of Koopmann, and the unctuous grovelling of Richter. He was discomforted to find that he preferred paintings to drawings, and was amazed by the contents of the private collections in England.

After two-and-a-half days they returned to London via Windsor, where they saw more drawings, the sumptuous royal apartments, and the Gothic chapel with its funerary monuments. Morelli had an audience with Queen Victoria, a meeting arranged by her daughter, which may be only imagined in its detail.

The group left England on 1 August and parted ways: Morelli returned to Italy to accompany Clementina from Crella to the Engadine, while Frizzoni and Koopmann went to Paris to study drawings.

□

In 1889 Morelli met the Swiss art historian Heinrich Wölfflin at Munich, who then sent him his book on the early work of Michelangelo (*Die Jugendwerke des Michelangelo*, 1891), an artist about whom Morelli wrote rarely, because he felt his critical method did not work with mannerists, or the proto-Baroque. Wölfflin proudly transcribed in his diary a compliment from Morelli's letter of thanks: "You appear to me to be an unusually fine and sharp observer." Indeed it was no mean compliment, especially given that Morelli was nothing if not critical.[36] Both Morelli and Wölfflin were Swiss, and both avoided social history to concentrate on questions of form. They must have continued to correspond, as the following year Wölfflin suggested to Emil Sulger-Gebing that he and Morelli were locked in mutual admiration, a rare state for both men. Wölfflin went on to describe Morelli as "the best connoisseur," said that he had written to him from Milan, and accepted Wölfflin's writing, sentence by sentence, in the belief that Germans should keep their hands away from Italian art, leaving it to the Italians.[37]

□

In the autumn of 1888 the Leipzig publishing house F. A. Brockhaus invited Morelli, at the suggestion of Jean Paul Richter, to commit to a new critical edition of his writings. This project would bring to an end Morelli's longstanding frustration as an author, although the process would not be easy. In his last years Morelli struggled with ill health, traveled incessantly, and spent much time at the Senate in Rome—all obligations that resulted in successive delays in delivering the manuscript with which he hoped to complete his legacy to the art world. He was assisted in the project by Richter and Gustavo Frizzoni.[38]

The publishing house had been founded early in the century by Friedrich Arnold Brockhaus; Morelli's contact was probably his grandson [Heinrich] Eduard Brockhaus (1829–1914, Fig. 86), who by this time had principal responsibility for the business. The family had a strong background in art history: Eduard's son Albert was famous as *the* German expert on netsuke (he visited Morelli in Italy in May 1889), while another son, Heinrich, became the first director of the Kunsthistorisches Institut in Florence. Brockhaus teased the books out of Morelli, persuading him to produce the finest writing of which he was capable, and encouraging him to send the results to Leipzig as work proceeded: section by section, illustration by illustration, photograph by photograph, anatomical drawing by anatomical drawing. The correspondence between the publisher and Morelli reveals much about the vocation of writing art history: the private ecstatic triumphs, the public battles, and the critical reception of reviewers.

The planned new edition of Morelli's works would be in three volumes, each of about 400 pages, for which Brockhaus calculated a price of 8 marks, or 24 marks for the set. Brockhaus suggested four months' interval between them, so that people would buy each book individually, rather than having to spend 24 marks all at once. He proposed a print run of 1,000 copies, with a payment of 2,000 marks on publication, another 2,000 marks once 750 copies had been sold, and a final 2,000 after the entire print run of 1,000 had sold. If the idea of issuing each volume separately was agreed to, the profits would be split 50/50 between publisher and author, with an additional payment of 1,000 marks to Morelli immediately after publication of each volume. Brockhaus calculated that in this way the total payment to Morelli would amount to 6,300 marks. Editions in other languages could come out after the German one. Their publication would be, in effect, a new work, not merely a re-issue of earlier texts. Morelli confessed himself flattered by the invitation. As the volumes were published separately, a payments of 1,000 marks was given for each.

The contract was signed at the end of March 1889. The first volume was on the Borghese and Doria galleries in Rome, to which Morelli added much material on drawings by Raphael and others that he had seen on his trip to England in 1887. The second volume was to be about Italian pictures in Munich's Alte Pinakothek, with new excurses into galleries in Vienna, Budapest, Paris, Madrid, and England. The third would be a critical study of the Gemäldegalerie in Berlin, accompanied by his articles on Raphael. The author's name was to remain Ivan Lermolieff, the translator Johannes Schwarze. Morelli had permission to republish the articles from Lützow's journal (1874–75), as well as the book printed by Seemann, for which he had never signed a contract or received royalties. Nevertheless, Morelli emphasized that the book would have significant new content, and was not merely a second edition. Richter's role was limited to compiling the admirable indexes (which he signed),[39] making editorial suggestions, and proofreading.

Great care was taken with the sixty-two illustrations (and line drawings of new anatomical details) for the first volume, which Morelli agreed to pay for himself. He wanted them larger than in the Seemann edition, so that the reader would have a clear picture of what he was writing about. Their model was a recently issued publication by Paul Müller-Walde on Leonardo, which was elegant and generously illustrated.[40] They even considered color reproductions, but in the end went for *Autotypien*, half-tone photo-engraving, a process developed by Georg Meisenbach around 1880.

By early May 1889 the manuscript for the first volume was two-thirds complete, but Brockhaus realized that Morelli was making innumerable alterations to the proofs. He advised that such late changes would be expensive, as typesetters would have to be compensated. As a result Morelli brought the manuscript to Berlin, meeting Brockhaus for the first time. He spent the rest of May traveling, to look again at collections in Schwerin, Oldenburg, Dresden, and Vienna, returning to Milan on 3 June. The first set of galley proofs arrived on 7 June, even though Brockhaus had not yet received the entire manuscript by that date. In the end there were at least five sets of proofs. Brockhaus suggested that Morelli eliminate a few words against Bode,[41] which he did.[42] Wilhelm von Bode was one of the most extraordinary museum directors ever known, as is shown by the outstanding quality of the Berlin museum collections of Italian Renaissance painting and of sculpture. Morelli perceived him as a danger to the patrimony of Italy, but also had a petty personal view of his antagonist, which was returned in equal measure by Bode. Morelli avoided meeting him, and did his utmost to prevent him obtaining works like Giorgione's *Tempesta*.

The first volume was published on 5 December 1889.[43] Complimentary copies were sent to colleagues such as Adolphe Braun in Dresden, Carl von Lützow and Franz Wickhoff in Vienna, Wilhelm Lübke in Karlsruhe, Oscar Eisenmann and Edward Habich in Kassel, Carl Justi in Bonn, William Cosmo Monkhouse at the Royal Academy in London, Sidney Colvin in London, Paul von Delaroff in St Petersburg, and Jocelyn Ffoulkes, then working in Dresden on the English translation. Of all these recipients, Wickhoff had the greatest understanding of the visual culture of the sciences, for he too had been formed in this way. Through him and Moritz Thausing (who had died in 1880), Morelli's influence was felt on the entire Vienna school of art history.[44] The first volume was reviewed in two international journals, *La Perseveranza* and *The Academy*, while other reviews were for the German art-historical world: the *Deutsche Rundschau*, Von Seidlitz in *Janitschek's Repertorium für Kunstwissenschaft*, and negatively by Oskar Eisenmann in Lauser's *Allgemeine Kunstchronik*.

On publication Brockhaus reported the accounts. Production had been more expensive than anticipated, due largely to the illustrations, which alone cost about 3,400 marks. Late changes during the typesetting stage amounted to an extra 244.30 marks. If all copies were sold, the profits of the first volume would be about 3,750 marks, of which 1,000 marks would be paid to Morelli as an advance.[45] Despite the cost over-runs, Morelli was enthusiastic about the initial critical reception.[46] The first letters praised the book's beautiful appearance (*die schöne Ausstattung*), especially the illustrations over which they had taken so much care. Brockhaus, though happy to hear from Morelli about positive reactions to the book, predicted that museum director Wilhelm von Bode and his followers and supporters (*Anhänger*) would speak out against Morelli, and suggested they should brace themselves for a heated fight (*so daß man sich auf einen lebhaften Kampf gefaßt machen darf*).[47] But views on this point were mixed: one correspondent said that Morelli had been overly considerate to Bode,[48] while others reported that he had caused quite a hullabaloo among Bode's followers and clients:

> As long as those attacks are just regarding my thesis, I'll endure them calmly; should however the facts reported by me be denied, I will defend them—should I consider the adversary worthy of a reply. Had Dr Bode not been continuously stepping on my feet for years, as strongly as I felt compelled to refute his (in my eyes completely wrong) interpretation of Italian art history—but I have to attack his thesis with much more consideration. By the way, the noise that Bode's party makes will just promote book sales.[49]

In fact there are more than sixty critical references to Bode in Richter's index to Morelli's first volume, many more than to Vasari, or to any artist, or indeed to any other art historian. Even Crowe and Cavalcaselle are mentioned a mere forty-eight times. Morelli, the Risorgimento hero, who had defended the Stelvio with such courage, emphasized the drama of his new attributions by underlining each one with a prominent baptismal cross, their ubiquity revealing the pride and aggressive ambition of a book by a soldier art historian. In the later English edition, Layard eliminated all the crosses, and all references to Bode, as unsuited to English taste, and perhaps of no interest. That version was published posthumously under Morelli's real name in 1892.

Over Christmas Morelli read some negative reviews, the ones that always hurt. Brockhaus sent him copies of the *Münchener Neuesten Nachrichten* with articles by Adolf Bayersdorfer, curator of the Alte Pinakothek and friend and henchman (*Helfershelfer*) to Bode, and a review by Woldemar von Seidlitz, also aligned with Bode. Morelli dismissed them as harmless. He considered Bayersdorfer lazy, and von Seidlitz an innocent aesthetician. He predicted that his opponents would portray him as "someone who eats Germans for breakfast" (*Deutschenfresser*), a colloquial way of saying the he had a pathological hatred of Germans, "since I had the courage to attack their main leader, Dr Bode, or to put it more correctly, since I dared to defend myself against his constant attacks." From others in Vienna, Prague, Dresden, Munich, Mainz, Bonn, and Stuttgart, he received complimentary letters, including one from an unnamed but most distinguished German art historian, who observed: "You certainly have hit the sore spot of German art studies." From Munich, the painter Lenbach wrote jubilantly: "With a courageous hand, you have poked that damned wasps' nest and have castigated the impudence of that one in Berlin with striking sarcasm." Another critic wrote:

> Accept my sincere thanks for the enjoyable hours I spent reading your book, as well as for the instruction I have gained from it, and will continue to do so, for a long time to come. Charming, how you dress up the bitter truths addressed to Berlin. All sincere friends of art welcome the publication of your work no less than I do, as they welcome the beneficial tranquility after a thunderstorm that has come down from heaven to drench the Infallibles' heads in Berlin.[50]

From London, Sidney Colvin wrote, among other things: "I have read it with the greatest interest and admiration."

One review hurt more than the others: that of Wilhelm Koopmann,[51] with whom Morelli had corresponded for more than seven years, and with whom he had traveled to study drawings just two years earlier. Koopmann's review, he confessed to Brockhaus, showed that even with the best will and diligent study it is not given to everyone to gain a proper understanding of art. Morelli had tried to achieve this, but "the seed had fallen on dry sand."[52]

Brockhaus was eager to begin work on the second volume, which would be about the German galleries. The text arrived in Leipzig on 23 May 1890, and typesetting began immediately. Brockhaus was pleased to learn from Morelli's preface that, in Dresden, art lovers (*Kunstfreunde*) were reluctant to reject attributions that had been unchallenged for centuries, but not the incoming director, Karl Woermann.[53]

Brockhaus made a final suggestion for the second volume: that Morelli eliminate from his preface the polemic against Bode and other German art historians. Although Brockhaus had defended Morelli, both in private and in public, because he believed in him, he asked for the personal attacks to be eliminated in the interest of the book, as they would detract from his achievement.[54] In publishing Lermolieff, the respected firm of F. A. Brockhaus was taking a position in the politics of German art museums, releasing a text whose intention was to influence public opinion, just as this publishing house had conceived a brilliant and highly influential encyclopaedia, the *Conversations-Lexikon*, on which Morelli had advised.[55]

Volume Two appeared on 4 January 1891.[56] The production costs were the same as for volume one. Again, the typesetter had to be paid for late corrections, so Morelli received only 700 marks upon publication. Volume One had sold 317 copies by 31 December 1890, and a year later this had risen to only 495 copies, bringing in 3,969.90 marks, less than what had been spent (5,063.75 marks), so there was no profit.[57]

Morelli maintained his fighting spirit against what he considered Bode's clique, until his last letter to Brockhaus, written a month before he died:

> And now please allow me to express my most sincere thanks for the very kind advice that you have given me. You will see in the relevant passage that I have followed it in accordance with your wishes. It is unfortunately, very true that, in my innermost conviction to defend truth against falsity, I do all too often, as they say, run riot—thus, as you remark correctly, damaging rather than helping the noble cause which I am defending. This weakness is in my blood. Alas, it has, at times, also caused some frustration in my political life.[58]

The importance of an enlightened commissioning publisher, *Die Herren Brockhaus*, cannot be underestimated, for without this company's firm and judicious support we would not have Morelli's writings in their final form. Despite the seeming anonymity of Die Herren Brockhaus, they must have knowingly espoused a position in the politics of German art history that was critical of the powerful and influential figure of Bode. The company's list of publications reveals the Brockhaus publishing house to be an extraordinary phenomenon; the *Conversations-Lexikon* strongly influenced German culture, but *every* Brockhaus publication was of importance.

This was especially true for Morelli, who had received other offers to publish his works in Germany. That a third volume in the series appeared was due to the efforts of Gustavo Frizzoni. He had inherited Morelli's papers, and painstakingly worked with his mentor's fragmentary notes (with the help of a young German from Mainz), to produce an expanded version of the 1880 book—a most difficult task.[59] Sadly, the material that Frizzoni inherited—all of Morelli's working notes, and his correspondence with museum directors—no longer exists. As an introduction to the third volume, Frizzoni wrote the first considered biography of Morelli, which also appeared in Italian, in a considerably modified form.[60]

Brockhaus planned an English edition of Morelli's writings, as the earlier translation by Louise Richter, not a native English speaker, was widely considered to be inadequate. A younger Welsh scholar and devoted Morellian, Jocelyn Ffoulkes, was engaged for the task, though she was painfully hesitant about her considerable abilities. Nevertheless, she was given Morelli's notes on early Lombard painter Vincenzo Foppa and later wrote an outstanding monograph, which remains the most authoritative work on that artist. On 9 February 1890 Ffoulkes had finished translating Morelli's section on the Borghese Gallery and asked Layard for his opinion of her translation, saying: "Signor Morelli's works are too valuable to be put before the English public in a garbled version."[61] Lady Eastlake was another guiding force, though as Ffoulkes remarked it was difficult to find a publisher: "It is very strange that all the publishers should be so afraid of it."[62] By June 1890 the manuscript was being considered by Macmillan, and Ffoulkes wrote to Layard: "Signor Morelli has authorized me to leave out all his 'Polemik mit Bode und der gleichen,' and Lady Eastlake says she will remodel 'Princip und Methode.' Lady Eastlake adds: 'a publisher ought to know that the text will be much curtailed and that an introduction will be written—tho' he need not be told by whom but only by an old hand'."[63] (It was Lady Eastlake who eventually persuaded John Murray to publish the English edition.) But a few days later, Ffoulkes was worried about Morelli's health:

> Signor Morelli has been ill since the 22nd May. It began with influenza and most severe rheumatic pains and was followed by complete lack of strength and appetite and sleeplessness. When he was better the Doctor ordered him to Monte Generoso [Ticino], but he did not feel up to that, and in his last card to me dated June 24th he says he is going to his relations [the Zavaritts] near Bergamo.[64]

For the last ten or eleven months of his life, Morelli suffered from failing health. He died on 28 February 1891. The cause was a heart complaint, and for his final three weeks he was wretched, having difficulty breathing.[65] Nevertheless, the last entry in his account book was made in that same month: twelve bottles of the most exquisite Piedmontese wine, Gattinara, in a noble vintage.[66]

□

On 10 March 1891 the president of the Italian Senate, Domenico Farini, announced the death of his illustrious colleague, Giovanni Morelli:

> Although his nature prohibited him from engaging in the daily riot of politics, he never missed solemn debates of major interest. He had a secure sense of reality, noble strength, was moderate without appearing weak, and remained faithful to his principles and friends, in a way that informed his conduct in both seats of government. He interrogated the treasures of Italian art, especially painting, about which he was passionate, in every Italian city and in Germany. He left a famous book, which informed opinion. He was so modest that he published under a pseudonym and in German ... Modesty, strength, sensitivity all made Morelli's life one of morality ... His will was an epilogue worthy of a man with an excellent mind, generous heart, and patriotic to the core, whose departure we mourn.[67]

Morelli's senate colleague from Bergamo, Count Giovanni Battista Agliardi, concluded the tribute by emphasizing that Morelli had also served four times as elected deputy for Bergamo, and had generously left his extraordinary art collection of more than a hundred paintings and several sculptures to the Accademia Carrara in Bergamo.

Morelli's specific instructions for his funeral reflected his modesty, and his Protestant disrespect for everything that was pompous and rhetorical:

> I wish to be buried in the Camposanto, Milan, among Italian compatriots, not with foreign Protestants. I want the burial of my body to take place at 5 o'clock in the morning, without any official recognition or pomp; nor do I want speeches given at my tomb, nor that acquaintances should be sent notices of my death. It is enough to have a simple announcement in the Gazette of my hometown, Bergamo.[68]

He was buried in accordance with his wishes, in the Camposanto (the monumental cemetery) in Milan. His gravestone bears this epitaph: *Dottor Giovanni Morelli. Senatore del Regno. Della Patria e delle Arti benemerito.* There were tributes of affection and admiration but, given the early hour, the burial was attended by only true and faithful friends, and representatives of the government—there were no curious onlookers.[69]

As well as the bequest to the Accademia Carrara, his will specified many other legacies. He left his drawings to Gustavo Frizzoni, with the obligation that at Frizzoni's death they would go to the Museo Civico of Milan. He also left money for a scholarship for a young Bergamasco to study science in one of the German universities. There were many individual legacies. One, to his friend Donna Laura Minghetti, was a painting said to be by Leonardo da Vinci, which Morelli had calculated she would know how to dispose of to her advantage. He did not underestimate her. She showed it to Bernard Berenson who, mesmerized by Donna Laura's beauty and flamboyant personality, but most of all by her amorous relationship with Morelli, was very taken by the painting, accepting it as being by Leonardo. Nevertheless, he remarked to Isabella Stewart Gardner that he had not selected it for her collection, as it seemed unfinished and repainted,[70] and he did not buy it. (Instead Jean Paul Richter, who was capable of being a tacky dealer, must have realised it was not authentic yet helped Donna Laura sell it to the American collector Theodore Davis for 5,000 francs, an enormous sum.) A diary entry by Lady Layard on 22 February 1899 relates Laura's version of the story:

> Richter must have known as well as Mme Minghetti what had been Morelli's real opinion of the picture, but he did not scruple to sell it to the American for this enormous sum—Henry always said that when once a man took to picture dealing or to antiquaries he was morally ruined. Richter had behaved so dishonestly to the Trustees of the [National] Gallery formerly that they (Henry & Sir Wm Gregory) & Sir F. Burton had long ago broken off relations with him. I used to tell Morelli in former days jokingly that he was made use of by a German who picked his brain for his own advantage.[71]

But as Morelli had confided to Layard, in Richter he thought he was training a domestic pussy cat, but instead he was transformed into a lion.

Frizzoni was in charge of installing Morelli's collection at the Accademia Carrara, where it arrived on 3 April 1892, more than a year after his death. It was displayed in two large rooms on the second floor, in chronological order of the Italian schools of painting—possibly reflecting its arrangement in Morelli's Milan apartment. Frizzoni's accompanying catalogue is a goldmine of impeccable information about the collection.[72] Berenson perceptively assessed the significance of Morelli's collection:

> His collection has more than the interest of an ordinary collection of good pictures. It was the laboratory of a specialist who devoted a long life to the scientific study of Italian painting. Its value is not so much in the number of extraordinary masterpieces it contains, although it is not lacking in masterpieces, as in the fact that is has excellent examples of all the Italian schools, and a great variety of painters in these schools.[73]

In fact, Morelli's collection was a micro version of his wild vision of 1860, when he had wished to create a truly national museum, representing all the Italian schools of art.

EPILOGUE

The Critical Aftermath: Followers and Frenemies

Since their first publication, Morelli's writings have been continually discussed, firstly by his intimate friends, followers, and translators, then by many others who hardly knew him, such as the young Bernard Berenson. Morelli considered his method most effective in attributing Quattrocento painting, particularly with artists whose representations of physiognomy were rather bony, such as Botticelli and Filippino Lippi. He believed his method was eighty per cent accurate, and recent attempts to evaluate his success would confirm this estimate.[1]

But there are many other areas of art history and archaeology where scholars are faced with attribution problems for art histories without names. Classical archaeologists and scholars of Asian art, for instance, working in fields where the name of an artist was rarely recorded or known, have looked to the Morellian method as a way of creating biographies for anonymous artists, and imposing an interpretative order on the visual world based on the evidence before their eyes. Many different interpretations of his method were developed among art historiographers, though Morelli would perhaps have been perplexed to learn that his method became useful to archaeologists. Nevertheless, there is evidence for such a claim. For instance, the analyses of Sir John Davidson Beazley (1885–1970), professor of classical archaeology at Oxford between 1925 and 1956, underwent a change following his encounter with Morelli's writings, in such a way as to imply a real understanding of how the method might be used for the analysis of linear drawing on Attic vase painting. This was discussed in Bernhard Ashmole's obituary of his teacher.[2] Beazley's debt to Morelli has been questioned by Mary Beard and others, who see the Morellian method as being merely about detail.[3] Yet Ashmole's testimony is persuasive and informed, especially when considered in relation to the development of Beazley's writings. There is a change between a classic article by Beazley such as "The Master of the Berlin Amphora" (1911),[4] and his later style, where Morelli's method is evident, beginning with Beazley's preface to *Attic Red-Figured Vases in American Museums* (1918). More recently, the Morellian method has even been applied to ancient Australian rock art.[5]

Morelli's volume on Roman galleries, which of all his writings was—and remains—of greatest interest to the Italian public, did not appear in an Italian edition until six years after his death, in 1897.[6] Sigmund Freud encountered Morelli when he bought a copy of this version in a Milanese bookshop. That the edition was published at all was due to the initiative and dedication of Gustavo Frizzoni, who assumed editorial responsibility, without any form of recompense other than the intellectual satisfaction of making Morelli's works accessible to an Italian readership.[7]

Morelli invented connoisseurship for the modern world, but by the mid-twentieth century connoisseurship had been rejected, often seen as a mere instrument of the art market, associated with the venality of Berensonian activities. However, in the last decades of the twentieth century the connoisseurship of details revealed in the conservation process began to be seen as an essential scientific tool of the discipline of art history. Images of under-drawing revealed in restoration laboratories using new methods and technologies provided another way of understanding Renaissance painting, and another set of criteria for attribution. Morelli was one of the pioneering figures in analytical conservation in Italy, and even though conservation has since changed beyond all recognition, he set the precedent for the close looking at art in laboratories.

□

Morelli's loyal friends were mostly politicians—Hudson, Layard, Minghetti, and Visconti Venosta—with whom he spent considerable time traveling and looking at paintings. The exceptions were Richter, Boxall, and the most devoted of all: Gustavo Frizzoni, who was like a son to him. Layard was stricken by the death of his friend:

> Yesterday, a telegram from Milan informed us of Morelli's death. Our friendship—a very intimate one—has lasted for so many years that I am greatly distressed at his loss. I shall miss him terribly—and the void is not one to be filled up. We were in constant correspondence, and his letters—chiefly concerning matters of art, were always highly interesting. I have a large collection of them. He was one of the best type of Italian gentleman. Highly cultivated, a most delightful companion and a most upright, honest and independent man. Altho' he never took a prominent part in public affairs, he was highly esteemed, and his advice constantly sought by the principal statesmen of the "Right"—Minghetti, Visconti Venosta, Alfieri and others.[8]

Equally, among the British Morelli had a following, as when Claude Phillips observed that it would be impossible to return to a pre-Morellian state of thinking to understand art.[9] Franz Wickhoff's relationship with Morelli was based on their mutual understanding of scientific method, which—as Julius von Schlosser recognized—led to a special understanding of collections, as well as helping to interpret individual works of art (though for Schlosser mere attribution or *Attribuzlerei* was dead erudition).[10]

Bernard Berenson and Morelli only met twice.[11] Morelli was curious about the activities of someone he called "the Boston Lermolieff,"[12] but observed him from a distance. Berenson professed himself a loyal follower, and learnt about Morelli through Frizzoni. Morelli may have found the young Berenson boring, hence he avoided meeting him. Lady Layard's opinion (though expressed in 1910), echoed their circle's view: "He is a most unattractive little man ... He is a mine of art information and goes up and down the land altering the ideas hitherto received on the authors of different pictures. A pupil of our dear friend Morelli, he exaggerates all his master's theories and methods and has not his modesty."[13]

It has become somewhat of a cliché to evaluate Morelli in terms of one or two of his attributions. But when his life is surveyed, what is extraordinarily impressive is the *extent* of his renaming of pictures, which in the nineteenth century created a revolution in the understanding of Italian Renaissance art, his most authoritative achievements being about Leonardo da Vinci and the Lombard school of his followers, in Venetian art, and in our understanding of Raphael. He started a revolution whose aftershocks we still feel today. Much of his legacy can be found in his books and articles, but a lot was created by oral tradition, when he gave his opinion on works that he saw in Oxford, Madrid, or elsewhere.

A telling example of the way in which Morelli transformed our understanding of Renaissance art concerns a portrait of a man that hangs in the Borghese Gallery in Rome. This work is reproduced in the posthumous Italian edition of his writings, where he attributes it to Raphael.[14] Before Morelli's time, the portrait had languished under an attribution to Hans Holbein, later revised by Otto Mündler as a self-portrait by Perugino, until it was attributed by Lermolieff to Raphael and dated to 1502. At the same time, Marco Minghetti in his book on Raphael attributed it to the master, following Morelli's suggestions.[15] During Morelli's lifetime its true qualities were hidden by tacky repainting by past restorers who had invented a misleading fur coat, painted over the background to eliminate the Italian landscape, changed the shape of the hat, and added heavy jowls. In 1911, when Cavenaghi restored the portrait, this overpainting was removed. Paintings usually had a different appearance in the nineteenth century before modern scientific conservation, making it all the more remarkable that Morelli could detect a Raphael beneath the heavy-handed alterations. Like Cuvier, or like an antiquary of a new kind, Morelli concentrated on those parts of the painting that were not obscured, to detect that it was a Raphael. Though most writers have focused on the anatomical diagrams that he believed in, his method involved focusing on highly characteristic details of all kinds which he considered of high value for an artist. Morelli was determined to destroy the cultural mentalities of nineteenth-century Italian restorers and their publics, promoting a different form of investigative conservation, predictive of 21st-century practice, though the means at his disposal—usually just a microscope—were much simpler. Today connoisseurship matters as a fundamental skill in art history, and it is due to Morelli that it became scientific.

Most art historians possess a Morellian understanding, though it is sometimes found in the least expected places, as noted by Gertrude Bing, director of the Warburg Institute, when writing to Kenneth Clark on the publication of his autobiography in 1957:

> I found your "autobiographical extravagances" very interesting as a kind of genealogy of historians of art; and in that connection I thought one point that occurred to me might please you. It is that Saxl, in the full knowledge of what nonsense has been made of the method, appreciated his Morellian training as much as you do. He always defended Morelli against his detractors and I think the manner had become such a part of his makeup that he used it quite unashamedly.[16]

As art historians, we are all now Morellians to some degree.

Notes

Notes to Preface

1 Edgar Wind, "Critique of Connoisseurship," in *Art and Anarchy* (London: Faber and Faber, 1963), 32–51.

2 Donata Levi, *Cavalcaselle: Il pioniere della conservazione dell'arte italiana* (Turin: Einaudi, 1988).

3 Christopher Duggan, *Francesco Crispi, 1818–1901: From Nation to Nationalism* (Oxford and New York: Oxford University Press, 2002).

4 Giovanni Morelli, *Della pittura italiana: Studii storico-critici di Giovanni Morelli (Ivan Lermolieff); Le Gallerie Borghese e Doria-Pamphili in Roma. Prima edizione italiana preceduta dalla biografia e dal ritratto dell'autore, e illustrata da 81 incisioni* (Milan: Fratelli Treves, 1897).

5 All translations from German, French, and Italian are my own.

6 Louise Richter recounts how Morelli's heir and executor, Gustavo Frizzoni, returned to her the letters that her husband, Jean Paul Richter, had written to Morelli (Louise Richter, Diary no. 5, 1891, Richter Papers, New York, Metropolitan Museum of Art, Onassis Library for Hellenic and Roman Art).

7 Jaynie Anderson, *Collecting, Connoisseurship and the Art Market in Risorgimento Italy: Giovanni Morelli's Letters to Giovanni Melli and Pietro Zavaritt (1866–1872)* (Venice: Istituto Veneto di Scienze, Lettere ed Arti, 1999).

8 Jaynie Anderson, *The Restoration of Renaissance Painting in Mid Nineteenth-Century Milan: Giuseppe Molteni in Correspondence with Giovanni Morelli*, Teoria e Storia del Restauro 21 (Florence: Edizioni Edifir, 2014).

9 Gustavo Frizzoni to Giulio Pietro Ambrogio Zavaritt, 28 June 1891, Archivio Zavaritt, Gorle.

10 Gustavo Frizzoni, "Giovanni Morelli: Ein Lebensbild," in *Kunstkritische Studien über italienische Malerei: Die Galerie zu Berlin. Von Ivan Lermolieff. Nebst einem Lebensbilde Giovanni Morelli's herausgegeben von Dr. Gustav Frizzoni. Mit Porträt und 66 Abbildungen* (Leipzig: F. A. Brockhaus, 1893), xi–lxiii.

11 Gustavo Frizzoni, "Cenni biografici intorno a Giovanni Morelli," in Giovanni Morelli, *Della Pittura Italiana: Studii storico critici di Giovannni Morelli (Ivan Lermolieff); Le Gallerie Borghese e Doria Pamphili in Roma* (Milan: Fratelli Treves Editori, 1897).

12 Jaynie Anderson, ed., *I taccuini manoscritti di Giovanni Morelli*, Le Marche Disperse, Fonti 1 (Milan: Motta, 2000).

13 *Balvi magnus, das ist kritische Beleuchtung des balvischen Missale* (Munich, 1836); and Traugott Gotthilf Schneck, F. Munkeler, and Nicolaus Schäffer, *Das "Miasma diabolicum," das ist ein Aufruf an die christlich germanischen Gemeinen, von Traugott Gotthilf Schneck, mit Hülfe der christlichen Brüder Dr. Jonathan Kappelmeier, Physicus, und Fürchtegott Munkeler, Apotheker, herausgegeben mit Anmerkungen und einem gedrängten Lebensabrisse Schneck's versehen durch Nicolaus Schäffer, cand. Theologiae* (Strasbourg: Schmidt und Grucker, 1839); reprinted in Jaynie Anderson, ed., *Balvi magnus und Das Miasma diabolicum: Giovanni Morellis erste pseudonyme Veröffentlichungen: Balvi magnus und Das Miasma diabolicum* (Würzburg: Königshausen und Neumann, 1991).

14 See Selected Bibliography.

15 See Chapter 2.

16 *Renaissance: 15th & 16th Century Italian Paintings from the Accademia Carrara, Bergamo*, exhibition catalogue (Canberra: National Gallery of Australia, 2011).

17 Richard Pau, "Le origini scientifiche del metodo Morelliano," in *Giovanni Morelli e la cultura dei conoscitori: Atti del convegno internazionale, Bergamo, 4–7 giugno 1987*, ed. Giacomo Agosti, Maria Elisabetta Manca, and Matteo Panzeri, vol. 2 (Bergamo: Pierluigi Lubrina, 1993), 301–19.

Notes to Chapter 1: Assigning Names

1 For an overview of Swiss emigration to Bergamo, see Silvio Honegger, *Gli Svizzeri di Bergamo: Storia della comunità svizzera di Bergamo dal Cinquecento all'inizio del Novecento* (Bergamo: Junior, 1997); and Giorgo Mollisi, ed., *Svizzeri a Bergamo: Nella storia, nell'arte, nella cultura, nell'economia dal '500 ad oggi* (Lugano: Società Editrice Ticino, 2009).

2 The books may be consulted at the Evangelical Church at Kreuzlingen, and on microfilm at the Staatsarchiv, Frauenfeld.

3 Maria G. Girardet Soggin, Thomas Soggin, Rita Gay, and Salvatore Ricciardi, *Una presenza riformata a Bergamo: La comunità cristiana evangelica nel corso di due secoli* (Bergamo: Sestante, 2007).

4 Anne Jacobson Schutte, *Pier Paolo Vergerio: The Making of an Italian Reformer* (Geneva: Édition Droz, 1977).

5 For a complete history of the Zavaritt family, see Willi Alberto Zavaritt, *Zavaritt: Cinquecento anni di storie e memorie* (Bergamo: privately printed, 2017).

6 Paul Ginsborg, *Daniele Manin and the Venetian Revolution of 1848–49* (London: Cambridge University Press, 1979), 1–47.

7 Signora L'Orsa (principal of the college at Berne) to Ambrogio Zavaritt, 1810, Archivio Zavaritt, Gorle.

8 Ambrogio Zavaritt, "Libro della famiglia," Archivio Zavaritt, Gorle.

9 In these letters Ursula repeatedly mentions how difficult it is to leave Bergamo: "Car je ne puis prononcer le nom chéri de Bergame, sans avoir les yeux tout remplies de larmes." Ursula Zavaritt Morell (at Brescia) to Ambrogio Zavaritt, 13 February 1813, Archivio Zavaritt, Gorle.

10 "Moi je crois d'être enceinte; les maux de cœur me font passablement souffrir." Ursula Zavaritt Morell to Ambrogio Zavaritt, 27 April 1814, Archivio Zavaritt, Gorle.

11 Emilia Zavaritt (at Verona) to Ambrogio Zavaritt, 16 November 1814, Archivio Zavaritt, Gorle.

12 Ottavio Cagnoli, *Iscrizioni in Verona con cenni statistici e con tavole a tutto il MDCCCLI* (Verona: Vicentini e Franchini, 1852), vol. 1, 8–9.

13 We know of the birth of another Edoardo only because a child of this name is mentioned in the last will and testament of his father, Johannes Morell, written on his deathbed in November 1820.

14 Ursula Zavaritt Morell (at Verona) to Ambrogio Zavaritt, 16 July 1813, Archivio Zavaritt, Gorle.

15 Jaynie Anderson, *Collecting, Connoisseurship and the Art Market in Risorgimento Italy: Giovanni Morelli's Letters to Giovanni Melli and Pietro Zavaritt (1866–1872)* (Venice: Istituto Veneto di Scienze, Lettere ed Arti, 1999), 136.

16 Ursula Zavaritt Morell (at Verona), postscript to Emilia Zavaritt on a letter to Ambrogio Zavaritt, 29 November 1814, Archivio Zavaritt, Gorle: "Cavalier … nous fera le portrait de mon petit Jean."

17 I am grateful to John Griffiths for his interpretation of the music. The artist has depicted guitar music, written on a single stave (rather than piano music, which is written on two staves), presumably because it is more legible from a distance.

18 Governo, S. 1718, XLVIII 3/1, Archivio di Stato di Venezia, Venice.

19 "Alla sinistra, del monastero delle dimesse, s'è fatto domicilio il sig. Morell, negoziante di sete, e il va fornendo d'uno scelto gabinetto d'ornitologia," Giovanni Battista da Persico, *Descrizione di Verona e della sua provincia* (Verona: Società Tipografica Editrice, 1820), 142.

20 Giuseppe M. Rossi, *Nuova guida di Verona e della sua provincia* (Verona: Tip. Friziero, 1854), 103; Francesca Venuto, "Giardini a Verona e provincia nell'Otto e nel Novecento," in *L'architettura a Verona dal periodo napoleonico all'età contemporanea*, ed. Pierpaolo Brugnoli and Arturo Sandrini (Verona: Mondadori, 1994), 301.

21 Johannes Morell to Pietro Zavaritt, 12 October 1820, Archivio Zavaritt, Gorle.

22 Despite research generously undertaken by Dr Roberto Mazzei, director of the Archivio di Stato, Verona, nothing more is known of the circumstances of the Morell family in Verona.

23 Ursula Zavaritt Morell (at Verona) to her brothers, 21 December 1820, Archivio Zavaritt, Gorle: "Mes bien chers frères! … Mon pauvre petit Nanè [*sic*], qui adorait son père, ne peut pas l'oublier … il prit le bon Dieu de le faire aussi mourir pour aller trouver son papa: il dit aussi: 'Dieu m'a ôté un si bon homme, qui m'aimait tant!! À présent je n'ai plus personne qui me contente, e qui me donne de l'argent.' Presques tous les jours il vient baiser son portrait. Non, vous ne pouvez vous imaginer, quel cœur tendre a ce petit."

24 In the same letter to her brothers (21 December 1820), Ursula asks for sympathy "pour moi et mes deux pauvres enfants sans père." Ursula is presumably referring here to a fourth son, about whom nothing else is known, apart from a reference in his father's will. She would then have been pregnant four times during the almost eight years of her marriage. This last son appears also to have died in infancy: on 9 May 1823 Ursula writes from Verona to her brother Pietro, to tell him about a visit she had received from Gündel, tutor to the Frizzoni brothers. She writes of only one surviving son (Giovanni Morelli), who sends his uncle Pietro a million kisses.

25 Carolina Zavaritt to Pietro Zavaritt, October 1821, Archivio Zavaritt, Gorle.

26 Johannes Morell made his will on 21 November 1820, the day before his death (Tribunale Provinciale di Verona, Filza IV, 332, Archivio di Stato di Verona, Verona). His most important possession was a shop, which he left to his wife to carry on as a business with advice from friends, especially his cousin Enrico de Pauli Morell. Two sons are mentioned, Giovanni and Edoardo: "Erede usufruttuaria in unione delli miei figlioli Giovanni, ed Edoardo Morell, ordino e voglio sia la Signora Orsola Zavaritt." The second Edoardo must have died in infancy, soon after his father.

27 Ambrogio Zavaritt to Pietro Zavaritt, 28 October 1822, Archivio Zavaritt, Gorle.

28 Giovanni Morelli to Niccolò Antinori, 19 February 1858, Archivio Antinori, Florence: "La mia buona vecchia zia Maddalena è morta. Tranquilla e serena quale sempre fu in vita e quale tu la conoscesti ella spirò il 12 di questo mese alle ore 3 del mattino. Io ebbi il mesto conforto di chiuderle gli occhi, d'aver ancora l'ultima Sua parola. La sua malattia non durò che cinque soli giorni, talché la repentina sua morte ci colse tutti all'improvviso. La perdita è per me irreparabile, credimelo pure—e il dolore che ne provo è grandissimo. Quella buona cara vecchierella m'amava svisceratamente, non viveva che per me, e il continuo suo pensare non era diretto che a farmi piacere, a usarmi ogni sorta di tenere attenzioni."

29 "Rangordnung der Schüler der Aargauischen Kantonsschule am Ende des Schuljahrs 1830," and the same title for 1831, Archive of the Kantonsbibliothek, Aarau. On the school's history, see *Die Aargauische Kantonsschule in den vergangenen 150 Jahren: Festschrift im Auftrage des Aargauischen Regierungsrates verfasst von Dr Th. Müller-Wolfer* (Aarau: H. Sauerländer, 1952).

30 This letter is from Morelli's teenage years and before the marriage of Pietro Zavaritt to Amalia Steiner in 1832. Giovanni Morellli to Pietro Zavaritt, 28 July n.d., Archivio Zavaritt, Gorle.

31 Ursula wrote to her "carissimo fratello," overwhelmed by his generosity to her and her son "della sua bontà": "Nanè si correggerà dei suoi difetti, e le ha scritto come si sia trovato felice nell'abbracciare i suoi cari zii e di capire quale fortuna gli sia toccata nel trovarsi nelle loro buone mani." Ursula Zavaritt Morell to Pietro Zavaritt, 27 March 1828, Archivio Zavaritt, Gorle.

32 Giovanni Beretta, *Gorle: La sua storia* (Gorle: La Stamperia di Gorle, 1983).

33 Gianmario Petrò, "Il castello vescovile di Gorle," *La Rivista di Bergamo*, n.s., no. 1 (May 1995): 12–21.

34 On Italian evangelism in the sixteenth century, see Lino Pertile, "Un testo in movimento: Le 'Annotationi nel Dante' di Trifon Gabriele dal 1527 al 1565," *Rivista di studi danteschi* 6 (2006): 142–53; and Lino Pertile, "A text in movement: Trifon Gabriele's *Annotationi nel Dante*, 1527–1565," in *Interpreting Dante: Essays on the Traditions of Dante Commentary*, ed. Paola Nasti and Claudia Rossignoli (Notre Dame, IND: University of Notre Dame, 2013), 341–58.

35 For an overview, see Alberto Cova, *Storia economica e sociale di Bergamo. Vol. 4: Dalla fine del Settecento all'avvio dello Stato unitario* (Bergamo: Fondazione per la Storia Economica e Sociale di Bergamo, 1994).

36 Giovanni Morelli (at Taronico) to Pietro Zavaritt, 27 June 1856, Archivio Zavaritt, Gorle: "E cosa ti dirò del tuo raccolto 'galette'? La tua solita modestia non mi permette di farne lode, che anzi cerchi di diminuirne il valore. Ma io che ti capisco e intendo attraverso il tuo linguaggio convenzionale, non posso fare a meno di congratularmi teco e meco insieme, non esclusi i parenti e amici—perché tutti godiamo di vederti stare a contento lungo i dodici mesi dell'anno."

37 The villa and surrounding gardens were radically restored by the architect Luigi Angelini for the Zavaritt family between 1914 and 1918, a restoration that masked the architectural presence of the contrasting medieval and Renaissance palaces.

38 Ursula Zavaritt Morell to Pietro Zavaritt, 21 July 1844, Archivio Zavaritt, Gorle: "Il mio ritratto poi, è un capolavoro, tutti ne sono sorpresi per la rassomiglianza perfetta ed il lavoro finissimo."

39 Ursula Zavaritt Morell to Pietro Zavaritt, 17 April 1844, Archivio Zavaritt, Gorle: "Il caro Jean si fa fare il ritratto dal famoso Mende. Si alza alle cinque del mattino, fa la passeggiata, colazione con Nané e si mette all'opera in seguito, sia nello studio sia nel giardino."

40 Giorgio Spini, *Risorgimento e protestanti* (Milan: Il Saggiatore, 1989), 374–75.

41 Sergio Brofferio, Anna Flora Eynard Ginoulhiac, and Sandra Zavaritt Frizzoni, *Da Celerina a... Bergamo: Biografia e carteggio di Antonio Frizzoni (1754–1835)* (Bergamo: privately printed, 2004).

42 The manuscript exists in six versions belonging to members of the Frizzoni family. The one quoted here is from the archive of the late Gian Carlo Eynard, "Diario di un viaggio di studio di Giovanni Frizzoni compiuto nel 1824 con il fratello Federico e il Signor Gündel."

43 For a full account of this important collection, see Jaynie Anderson, "Frizzoneria in Bergamo," in *Ex Fumo Lucem: Baroque Studies in Honour of Klára Garas: Presented on her Eightieth Birthday*, ed. Zsuzsanna Dobos and Peter Ujvari, vol. 2 (Budapest: Museum of Fine Arts, 1999), 233–52, for the inventory made by Morelli.

Notes to Chapter 2: A Scientific Education in Germany

1 Some of the material in this chapter was first presented in Jaynie Anderson, "Giovanni Morelli et sa définition de 'la scienza dell'arte'," *Revue de l'art* 75 (1987): 49–55.

2 Morelli's thesis was cited in the medical handbooks of Krause (1841) and Arnold (1845), and in a dissertation on a related subject by Jacob Schütz (Landau, 1842).

3 The bare details of Morelli's enrolment may be consulted in the archive of Ludwig-Maximilians-Universität, Munich. His thesis, "De regione inguinali. Dissertatio anatomica. Auctore Joanne Morell, medicinae et chirurgiae doctore" (Munich: J. Rösl, 1837), is held in the Universitätsbibliothek, Munich; Bibliothèque Nationale, Paris; and several other German academic libraries.

4 I am grateful to Professor Reinhard Putz of the University of Munich for his assessment of Morelli's thesis.

5 Those famous scientists who preceded Morelli were Astley Cooper, *Ligamentum inguinale* (1809); Franz Caspar Hesselbach, *Ligamentum interfoveolare* (1814); and the first-ever discussion by Antonio Scarpa, *Sull'ernie: Memorie anatomico-chirugiche* (1809).

6 Morell is described as coming from "Bergamo in der Schweiz." *Verzeichniß des Lehrer-Personals und der sämmtlichen Studirenden an der königl. Ludwigs-Maximilians-Universität in München im Studien-Jahre 1836* (Munich: Karl Wolf, 1836).

7 Donat de Chapeaurouge, "Das Milieu als Porträt," *Wallraf-Richartz-Jahrbuch* 22 (1960): 137–59.

8 Gustavo Frizzoni, "Giovanni Morelli: Ein Lebensbild," in *Kunstkritische Studien über italienische Malerei: Die Galerie zu Berlin. Von Ivan Lermolieffl Nebst einem Lebensbilde Giovanni Morelli's herausgegeben von Dr. Gustav Frizzoni. Mit Porträt und 66 Abbildungen* (Leipzig: F. A. Brockhaus, 1893), xi–lxii.

9 The drawing belonged to Teodoro Frizzoni, and was first published in *Giovanni Morelli: Da collezionista a conoscitore: Catalogo della mostra, Bergamo 4 giugno–31 luglio 1987* (Bergamo: Accademia Carrara, 1987), 77.

10 Anonymous [Giovanni Morelli], *Balvi magnus, das ist kritische Beleuchtung des balvischen Missale* (Munich, 1836).

11 Today, Morelli's library is divided. His scientific books are with the Zavaritt family in their villa at Gorle. Gustavo Frizzoni gave Morelli's art library and photographic collection to the Biblioteca dell'Accademia di Belle Arti di Brera, Milan (now renamed Biblioteca d'Arte Contemporanea, though still located in the Accademia di Belle Arti). Morelli's literary library was bequeathed to the Biblioteca Civica Angelo Mai, Bergamo.

12 On Morelli's scientific education, see Richard Pau, "Le origini scientifiche del metodo Morelliano," in *Giovanni Morelli e la cultura dei conoscitori: Atti del convegno internazionale, Bergamo, 4–7 giugno 1987*, ed. Giacomo Agosti, Maria Elisabetta Manca, and Matteo Panzeri (Bergamo: Pierluigi Lubrina, 1993), vol. 2, 301–19, esp. 314–16.

13 Georges Cuvier, *Das Thierreich, geordnet nach seiner Organisation: Als Grundlage der Naturgeschichte der Thiere und Einleitung in die vergleichende Anatomie*, trans. F. S. Voigt (Leipzig: F. A. Brockhaus, 1831).

14 Georges Cuvier, *Vorlesungen über vergleichende Anatomie* (Leipzig: Kummer, 1809).

15 Augustin-Pyramus de Candolle, *Regni vegetabilis: Systema naturale sive ordines genera et species plantarum secundum methodi naturalis normas digestarum et descriptarum* (Paris, 1818–21).

16 Giovanni Morelli, *Italian Painters: Critical Studies of their Works*, trans. Constance Jocelyn Ffoulkes, with an introduction by Sir Austen Henry Layard. Vol. I: *The Borghese and Doria-Pamphili Galleries in Rome* (London: John Murray, 1892), 73–74.

17 Morelli, *Italian Painters ... The Borghese and Doria-Pamphili Galleries*, 70.

18 Later art historians, such as Heinrich Wölfflin, were also influenced by the idea of Goethe's morphology. See Evonne Levy, *Baroque and the Political Language of Formalism (1845–1945): Burckhardt, Wölfflin, Gurlitt, Brinckmann, Sedlmayr* (Basel: Schwabe, 2015), 110–11.

19 "Sopra la relazione tra l'arti belle e la natura, discorso di Federigo Schelling tenuto nell'Academia di Monaco, il dì onomastico di S. M. il Re Massimiliano di Baviera, traduzione del dottor G. M.," *Lo Spettatore industriale. Studi e notizie di tecnologia, igiene e letterature* 3 (1845): 285–320. Republished by Valentini, Milan, 1845.

20 For Schelling's reading of Dante, see Wolfram Hogrebe, "Schelling und Dante," *Deutsches Dante-Jahrbuch* 62 (1987): 7–31; and Johannes Bartuschat, "Dante in Germania in età romantica," in *Letture e lettori di Dante: L'età moderna e contemporanea*, ed. Marcello Ciccuto, Letture Classensi 39 (Ravenna: Longo, 2011), 47–70.

21 It appeared much later, in Niccolini's collected works, as "Considerazioni filosofiche di F. G. G. Schelling sopra Dante", in *Opere di G. B. Niccolini* (Florence: Le Monnier, 1858).

22 "Die gesammte Philosophie beruht mithin in der Nachweisung des Parallelismus der Natur und der Geisteshätigkeit."

23 Morelli, *Italian Painters ... The Borghese and Doria-Pamphili Galleries*, 4n1.

24 Georges Cuvier, *Annales du Muséum d'histoire naturelle* 3, 1804, plate XI, fol. 1.

25 On Cuvier's thoughts about the tapir, see Martin J. S. Rudwick, *Georges Cuvier, Fossil Bones, and Geological Catastrophes* (Chicago: University of Chicago Press, 1997), 39–41.

26 A sheet with a comparative analysis of four monkey heads was shown in 1979 in an innovative exhibition on connoisseurship: see David Alan Brown, *Berenson and the Connoisseurship of Italian Painting: A Handbook to the Exhibition* (Washington, D. C.: National Gallery of Art, 1979), 34.

27 Morelli's notes were copied from Döllinger's lectures; see Pau, "Le origini scientifiche del metodo Morelliano," 315.

28 Raymond Schwab, *La Renaissance orientale* (Paris: Payot, 1950), 320.

29 An anecdote told by Jean Paul Richter in his obituary of Morelli in *Beilage zur Allgemeinen Zeitung* 6 (April 1891): 1–4.

30 Morelli, *Italian Painters... The Borghese and Doria-Pamphili Galleries*, 74, where he quotes a passage about their mentor Döllinger's teaching methods.

31 Elizabeth Cary Agassiz, ed., *Louis Agassiz: His Life and Correspondence* (Cambridge, MA: Macmillan, 1885), vol. 1, 150–51.

32 A Dilettante, "Handzeichnungen von Genelli: Von einem Dilettanten," *Kunstblatt* (6 June 1839): 181–82.

33 Nachlass 255, Universitätsbibliothek, Leipzig. The text was republished in Jaynie Anderson, ed., *Balvi magnus und Das Miasma diabolicum: Giovanni Morellis erst pseudonyme Veröffentlichung: Balvi magnus and Das Miasma diabolicum* (Würzburg: Königshausen & Neumann, 1991).

34 The letter is transcribed in Anderson (ed.), *Balvi magnus*, 33–34n32.

35 Guido Görres, Wilhelm von Kaulbach, and H. Merz, *Das Narrenhaus von Wilhelm Kaulbach, gestochen von H. März erläutert von Guido Görres nebst Ideen über Kunst und Wahnsinn* (Regensburg: Friedrich Pustet, 1836).

36 Giovanni Morelli to Federico Frizzoni, 14 October 1836. The text of the letter in German is given in Anderson, *Balvi magnus*, 33–34.

37 For Zwanglose chronicles and drawings, see *Archiv der Zwanglosen*, Bd. 1: 1837–1844. BSB Cgm 8026, Bayerische Staatsbibliothek, Munich, https://opacplus.bsb-muenchen.de.

38 "Ihm zur Seite erblicken wir tief im Mantel eingehüllt, frierend wie Montgela's Windspiel, seinen Helfershelfer. Es ist Nikolaus Schäffer, das stets lauernde Amphibium, von dem man nicht weiß, ob er dem Süden oder Norden angehöre. Er hatte in den Jahren 92 und 91 die Corsicanerrebellionen mitgemacht und war ein Häuptling derselben. Nachdem er aber sah, daß die gerechte Sache siegte, flüchtete er sich nach Agosta, wo er sich bald durch Intriguen aller Art zu der Würde emporzuschwingen wußte, die er zu derselben Zeit bekleidete. Er war nämlich Obermedizinalrath im Michel'schen Staate, und so viel ist gewiß, sagt Stoffel, daß die Führung des Staates mehr durch ihn, als durch den großen Balvi geschah; denn Antoni stand ganz und gar unter seinem Pantoffel, und wollte einer zu einem Amte kommen, so brauchte er bloß einige Ducaten ihm in die Hand zu drücken und er war seiner Sache gewiß. Was später aus ihm geworden, ist noch zweifelhaft, obwohl Stoffel behauptet, er sey, von den Franzosen gefangen, im Jahre 87 zu Paris guillotinirt worden. Sein ganzer Charakter liegt in der Stellung, die der Künstler wieder ganz vortrefflich aufzufassen wußte." The original text of Morelli's mini biography is on pp. 10–11 of the original *Balvi magnus*, and pp. 132–33 of Anderson, ed., *Balvi magnus*.

39 Morelli to Frizzoni, 14 October 1836, in Anderson, ed., *Balvi magnus*, 33–34.

40 Genelli's eighty-three surviving letters to Morelli date from Christmas Eve 1837 to 1856 (Archivo Zavaritt, Gorle). Twenty letters from Morelli to Genelli, dating from his student days in Erlangen in 1838 until 1855, are conserved among Genelli's own voluminous archive (Nachlass Genelli 255, Universitätsbibliothek, Leipzig).

41 Giovanni Morelli to Federico Frizzoni, 1 January 1837, formerly in the archive of Giovanni Frizzoni, Bergamo.

42 A Dilettante, "Handzeichnungen von Genelli."

43 Many of these drawings are illustrated in Anderson ed., *Balvi magnus*.

44 Frizzoni, "Ein Lebensbild," xvi–xvii.

45 Hans Ebert, *Buonaventura Genelli (Maler und Werk)* (Dresden: Verlag der Kunst, 1987), 109–13, 117.

46 Many of these drawings are reproduced in Anderson, ed., *Balvi magnus*.

47 Only a few years after Genelli's death in 1868, a biographer emerged: Lionel von Donop, a Berlin museum curator and art historian who, like a squirrel, collected from Genelli's estate all the original manuscript material in the artist's possession at the time of his death, and then amassed an equally vast amount of material in correspondence with Genelli's friends. In response to von Donop's enquiries, Morelli described his friendship with Genelli in letters in 1874 and 1875. When questioned about past friendships, everyone has a selective memory: Morelli neglected to mention his anonymous article about Genelli's drawings, published under the pseudonym "A Dilettante" in *Kunstblatt* on 6 June 1839. Morelli owned all the drawings discussed in that article. But von Donop became increasingly fascinated with his source, and eventually elicited from Morelli a short biography, in which he characterized his career as having been primarily in politics, referring only briefly to his late interest in art; it read: "Ich wurde also in Verona geboren wo mein seliger Vater Präsident 'del Tribunale di Commercio' war und in hohen Ehren stand. Nach dem 1821 erfolgten Tode des Vaters kam ich, eine kleines Kind noch, nach Bergamo in die Vaterstadt meiner Mutter. Im Jahre 1836, als Genelli von Leipzig nach München über siedelte, befand ich mich auf der Universität daselbst, wo ich als Assistent des Anatomen Döllinger speziell mit anatomischen Studien mich beschäftigte, und woselbst ich im selben Jahre die Doctorwürde erhielt. Ein satyrischer Scherz, 'die Beleuchtung des Balvischen Missale' für eine Privatgesellschaft hingeworfen und nur in 50 (sic.) Exemplaren abgedruckt und worin das Künstlerleben in München etwas grell persiflirt wird, machte mich bekannt mit Genelli, welcher an jenem Scherze große Freude fand; und von jener Zeit an datirt die Freundschaft zwischen uns beiden.

"Im Herbst 1837 verließ ich München, besuchte für einige Zeit Erlangen und Berlin und kam endlich im Herbste 1838 nach Paris, um daselbst meine naturwissenschaflichen Studien zu vollenden. Ein Versuch, den ich während meines Aufenthaltes in Erlangen machte, durch Friedrich v. Rückert den Herzog von Coburg für Genelli zu

interessiren, schlug fehl. Nach einem zweijährigen Aufenthalte in Paris kehrte ich im Jahre 1840 nach Italien zurück, und seit jener Zeit hab' ich meine Heimath nie mehr auf längere Zeit verlassen, mit Ausnahme des Jahres 1848, wo ich als Abgeordneter der revolutionären Regierung zu Mailand mich nach Frankfurt am Main begeben mußte, um daselbst so gut als möglich, zuerst bei der deutschen Nationalversammlung, später beim Reichsverweser für die lombardisch-venetianischen Angelegenheiten zu plaidiren. Nach der Schlacht von Custoza gieng ich direkte nach Venedig, wo ich durch die Vermittlung Manin's zum Adjutanten des Generals Solen ernannt wurde. Nach der Amnestie kehrte ich in die Lombardei zurück, wo ich drei Jahre lang auf dem Lande zugebracht, immer thätig für die Befreiung meines Vaterlandes vom Joche der Fremdherrschaft. Vom Jahre 1860 bis 1870 saß ich als Abgeordneter der Stadt Bergamo in der Nationalversammlung—zog mich dann vom politischen Leben zurück; wurde aber 1872 von unserm König in den Senat erhoben. Nebst der Politik beschäftigen mich seit langen Jahren Studien und Forschungen in der heimatlichen Kunstgeschichte. Und somit hätte ich also meine Pflicht gethan! Sie sehen, daß das Einzige, was für einen Deutschen in meinem Leben einiges Interesse haben kann, meine Freundschaft mit Genelli ist."
("So, I was born in Verona, where my late father was president of the Tribunale di Commercio and held in high honor. After the death of my father in 1821, I came as a small child to Bergamo, my mother's home town. In 1836, when Genelli moved from Leipzig to Munich, I found myself at the city's university, where, as an assistant to the anatomist Döllinger, I was specifically doing anatomical studies, and in the same year I obtained my doctorate. A satirical joke, 'The Illumination of Balvi's Missal,' written for a private society and reprinted only in fifty [*sic*] copies, and in which the artistic life in Munich is somewhat garishly satirized, led to my acquaintance with Genelli, who took great joy in that joke; we have been friends ever since.
"In the autumn of 1837 I left Munich, visited Erlangen and Berlin for some time, and finally came to Paris in the autumn of 1838 to complete my studies there in natural sciences. During my stay in Erlangen, an attempt was made by Friedrich von Rückert to interest the Duke of Coburg in Genelli, but failed. After a two-year stay in Paris, I returned to Italy in 1840, and since then I have never left my home for any length of time, with the exception of the year 1848, when I, as a member of the revolutionary government of Milan, left for Frankfurt am Main in order to plead for Lombard affairs in the best way possible, first at the German National Assembly and later with the Imperial Regent. After the battle of Custoza, I went directly to Venice, where through Manin's agency I was appointed adjutant to General Solen. After the amnesty I returned to Lombardy, where I spent three years in the countryside, always working for the liberation of my country from the yoke of foreign rule. From 1860 to 1870 I sat as a member of parliament for the city of Bergamo in the National Assembly—then withdrew from political life, but was raised in 1872 by our King to the Senate. In addition to politics, I have been involved in studies and research in the history of art for many years. And so, I have done my duty! You see, the only thing that can interest a German in my life is my friendship with Genelli.") Giovanni Morelli to Lionel von Donop, autobiographical letters, 1874 and 1875, Genelli Nachlass 255, Universitätsbibliothek, Leipzig.

48 The best account of Morelli at Erlangen is in his own letters to Federico Frizzoni, quoted extensively by Federico's nephew Gustavo Frizzoni in "Ein Lebensbild."

49 Universitäts-Archiv der Friedrich-Alexander-Universität, Erlangen.

50 Giovanni Morelli (at villa Balbianello) to Niccolò Antinori, 5 August 1851, Archivio Antinori, Florence.

51 Giovanni Morelli (at Erlangen) to Buonaventura Genelli, 26 February 1838, Nachlass Genelli, 255, C460, Universitätsbibliothek, Leipzig. Morelli corresponded with Engelhardt from 1838 until his death in 1856, creating a *carteggio* of some 200 letters from Engelhardt to Morelli, though none survive.

52 Morelli to Genelli, 26 February 1838.

53 On 15 October 1837, shortly after arriving at Erlangen, Morelli wrote to Federico Frizzoni about his encounters with writers on the faculty. See Frizzoni, "Ein Lebensbild," xix–xxx; and Friedrich Rückert, *Rostam und Suhrab: Eine Heldengeschichte in zwölf Büchern* (Stuttgart: J. Kreuzer, 1846). Frizzoni, having visited Germany as a young man with his tutor Gustav Gündel, and even met Goethe, was the ideal correspondent to understand Morelli's German experiences.

54 Traugott Gotthilf Schneck, F. Munkeler, and Nicolaus Schäffer, *Das "Miasma diabolicum," das ist ein Aufruf an die christlich germanischen Gemeinen, von Traugott Gotthilf Schneck, mit Hülfe der christlichen Brüder Dr. Jonathan Kappelmeier, Physicus, und Fürchtegott Munkeler, Apotheker, herausgegeben mit Anmerkungen und einem gedrängten Lebensabrisse Schneck's versehen durch Nicolaus Schäffer, cand. Theologiae* (Strasbourg: Schmidt und Grucker, 1839).

55 See Anderson ed., *Balvi magnus*.

56 Buonaventura Genelli to Giovanni Morelli, 16 February 1838, Archivio Zavaritt, Gorle; copy by von Donop in Universitätsbibliothek, Leipzig.

57 When Morelli wrote to Genelli about the identities of the characters in another of his writings, *Saga von den drei Schwestern*, which has been lost, he identified the characters, each represented under a rather thin disguise: Johann Joseph von Görres, Clemens Brentano,

Joseph Ignaz von Döllinger, and many others (Morelli to Genelli, 24 April 1839, Nachlass Genelli 255, C463, Universitätsbibliothek, Leipzig).

Notes to Chapter 3: A Young Man Abroad

1 "Die practische Medizin hab' ich liegen lassen und beschäftige mich dafür speziell mit Anatomie und den Naturwissenschaften." See Jaynie Anderson, "'Die geniale Bettina': Giovanni Morelli in Conversation with Bettina von Arnim," *Oxford German Studies* 18–19 (1989/90): 45–59.

2 Morelli's copy of Springer's article "Kunstkenner und Kunsthistoriker," *Im neuen Reich* 11, no. 46 (1881): 737–58, is still in his library collection: Q.VI.86, Biblioteca dell'Accademia di Belle Arti di Brera, Milan.

3 Michael Podro, *The Critical Historians of Art* (New Haven and London: Yale University Press, 1982), 44; Joseph Rykwert, "Semper and the Conception of Style," in *Gottfried Semper und die Mitte des 19. Jahrhunderts: Symposion vom 2. bis 6. Dezember 1974*, ed. Eva Börsch-Supan and Gottfried Semper (Basel: Birkhäuser, 1976), 68–81.

4 Giovanni Morelli, *Italian Painters: Critical Studies of their Works*, trans. Constance Jocelyn Ffoulkes, with an introduction by Sir Austen Henry Layard. Vol. I: *The Borghese and Doria Pamfili Galleries in Rome* (London: John Murray, 1892), 32.

5 Carlo Ginzburg, "Spie: Radici di un paradigma indiziario," first published in *Rivista di storia contemporanea* 7 (1978): 1–14, then in expanded versions in *Crisi della ragione: Nuovi modelli nel rapporto tra sapere e attività umane*, ed. Aldo Gargani (Turin: Einaudi, 1990), 58–106. English translation by Anna Davin, "Morelli, Freud and Sherlock Holmes: Clues and Scientific Method," in *The Sign of Three: Dupin, Holmes, Peirce*, ed. Umberto Eco and Thomas A. Sebeok (Bloomington: Indiana University Press, 1984), 81–118. Since my publication in 1987 of Morelli's tracings after Cuvier ("Giovanni Morelli et sa définition de 'la scienza dell'arte'"), Ginzburg has increasingly concentrated on Cuvier, in his publication *Wooden Eyes: Nine Reflections on Distance* (New York: Columbia University Press, 1998), 127–28.

6 First published in *The Strand* (November 1891).

7 Ginzburg continued to develop his arguments about Morelli in successive versions of his famous article, and introduced Cuvier for the first time as "un modello conoscitivo nello stesso tempo antichissimo e moderno," in "Spie: Radici di un paradigma indiziario," in *Miti, emblemi, spie: Morfologia e storia* (Turin: Einaudi, 1986), 183.

8 Charles Darwin, *The Origin of Species* (London: John Murray, 1859), chapter 14, 209.

9 For the letters of introduction for Morelli from Rückert to Ludwig Tieck and Otto Mündler, see Friedrich Rückert, *Briefe*, ed. Rüdiger Rückert (Schweinfurt: Rückert-Gesellschaft, 1977), vol. 2, 690 and 740. Rückert characterizes Morelli as "Hr. Doktor Morell, dem ich einen Brief schuldig geblieben bin. Kennen Sie ihn, oder können ihn kennen lernen, was Sie nicht gereuen wird, so bringen Sie ihm statt jenes Briefes meine schönsten Grüße. Er ist von Geburt Italiener, von Erziehung Schweizer, von Gesinnung und Geist Deutscher, was er hoffentlich auch in Paris bleiben wird." Morelli corresponded with Rückert after he left Erlangen; see Rüdiger Rückert, ed., *Briefe an und über Friedrich Rückert: Korrespondenz insbesondere von Familienmitgliedern*, vol. 2 (Schweinfurt: Stadt Schweinfurt, 1987), 485.

10 The full text of Morelli's letters referring to von Arnim was first published in Anderson, "'Die geniale Bettina'."

11 Anna Katharina Emmerich, *Das bittere Leiden unseres Herrn Jesu Christi*, ed. Clemens Brentano (Sulzbach: Seidel, 1833).

12 For Morelli's collection of drawings by Buonaventura Genelli, see Giulio Bora, *I disegni della collezione Morelli* (Cinisello Balsamo: Amilcare Pizzi, 1988), 335–39.

13 An Englishwoman who met Bettina for several hours in 1843, Sarah Austin (aunt of Morelli's friend Austen Henry Layard), was less impressed than Morelli, and recalled Bettina's conversation as "that of a clever woman, with some originality, great conceit, and vast unconscious ignorance." See Sarah Austin's diary, 18 January 1843, in Janet Ross, *Three Generations of Englishwomen: Memoirs and Correspondence of Mrs John Taylor, Mrs Sarah Austin and Lady Duff Gordon* (London: John Murray, 1888), vol. 1, 176–77.

14 Blechen's landscape, formerly in the Nationalgalerie, Berlin, was destroyed in the Second World War.

15 Anderson, "'Die geniale Bettina'," 52.

16 Giovanni Morelli to Niccolò Antinori, 22 August 1851, Archivio Antinori, Florence, published in Giacomo Agosti, "Giovanni Morelli corrispondente di Antinori," in *Studi e ricerche di collezionismo e museografia Firenze 1820–1920*, Quaderni del Seminario di Storia della Critica d'Arte 2 (Pisa: Scuola Normale Superiore, 1985), 25–27: "Quanto desidererei riveder la famiglia Arnim e esser con te una serata nella loro compagnia! La madre è d'un cuore eccellente, e come donna una vera curiosità. Ai miei tempi l'Armgarth era una bella ragazza, ora sarà vecchia—ma Ghisely sarà diventata bella intanto. Fa' pur del chiasso con loro; che in quella casa si può far ogni pazzia, ed essere certo di non dispiacere. Io era lì come in casa mia. E salutamele tutte caramente e di' loro ch'io desidererei tanto di vederle in Italia e di poter loro fare il Cicerone."

17 Morelli to Antinori, 22 August 1851: "Waagen … ottimo cicerone, pettegolo e sempre *au fait* di tutto quello che succede nei palazzi come nelle strade, in relazione

con tutti, grandi e piccoli e dottissimo nella storia delle belle arti."

18 Giovanni Morelli (at Paris) to Buonaventura Genelli, 24 April 1839, Nachlass Genelli, C 463, Universitätsbibliothek, Leipzig.

19 Morelli to Genelli, 24 April 1839: "Ich sage nur dieses, damit Sie sich nicht darauf verlassen, eh Sie es selbst sehen. Doch, was liegt am Ende soviel daran, ob es von Correggio oder einem seiner Schüler sei, wenn es nur schön ist."

20 Others followed von Rumohr; see Franz Kugler, [Untitled], *Kunstblatt* 3 (1845): 11.

21 Ursula Zavaritt Morell (at Wöschbach) to Pietro Zavaritt, 28 July 1838, Archivio Zavaritt, Gorle.

22 Giovanni Morelli (at Neuchâtel, Switzerland) to Federico Frizzoni, 15 April 1838, quoted in Frizzoni, "Ein Lebensbild."

23 A letter from Agassiz's illustrator, Joseph Dinkel, records the journey (Joseph Dinkel to Elizabeth Cary Agassiz, n.d. MS Am I, 1419, 293, seq. 1136–1138, Louis Agassiz Correspondence and Other Papers, Houghton Library, Harvard University, https://iiif.lib.harvard.edu/manifests/view/drs:12379926$1114i). Dinkel does not give the names of the students, but the date corresponds with other evidence that Morelli accompanied Agassiz, and there is no correspondence to show that Morelli was anywhere else during these months.

24 Dinkel to Cary Agassiz. Agassiz's biographer and wife, Elizabeth Cary Agassiz, explains the significance of the 1838 expedition: "Following the same comparative method, he intended to track the footsteps of the ice as he had gathered and put together the fragments of his fossil fishes, till the scattered facts should fall into their natural order once more and tell their story from the beginning to end.

"In his explorations of 1838 he found everywhere the same phenomena: the grooved and polished and graven surfaces and the rounded and modeled rocks, often lying far above and beyond the present limits of the glaciers; the old moraines, long deserted by the ice, but defining its ancient frontiers; the erratic blocks, transported far from their place of origin and disposed in an order and position unexplained by the agency of water.

"These excursions, though not without their dangers and fatigues, were full of charm for men, who, however serious their aims, were still young enough to enter like boys into the spirit of adventure. Agassiz himself was but thirty-one; an ardent pedestrian, he delighted in feats of walking and climbing." Elizabeth Cary Agassiz, ed., *Louis Agassiz: His Life and Correspondence* (Cambridge, MA: Macmillan, 1885), vol. 1.

25 Cary Agassiz, ed., *Louis Agassiz*, vol. 1, 296.

26 Louis Agassiz to Giovanni Morelli, 26 July 1843, Archivio Ginoulhiac, Milan. Photocopy, MMB 993/10–15, Biblioteca Civica Angelo Mai, Bergamo. The letter was presumably given by Gustavo Frizzoni to his sister Lina, who, like her mother, was widowed young with many children and was always in need of money; selling autograph letters was one means of increasing her income.

27 Constance Jocelyn Ffoulkes, "Giovanni Morelli," in *Encyclopaedia Britannica*, 11th edn, 1910–11, 829.

28 As Agassiz wrote: "During the years I passed at Munich I devoted myself almost exclusively to the different branches of natural science, neglecting more and more my medical studies, because I began to feel an increasing confidence that I could fight my way in the world as a naturalist, and that I was therefore justified in following my strong bent in that direction." Elizabeth Cary Agassiz, ed., *Louis Agassiz*, vol. 1, 150.

29 Giovanni Morelli to Federico Frizzoni, n.d., Archivio Zavaritt, Gorle.

30 On the Louvre in these years, see Marie-Claude Chaudonneret, "Historicism and 'Heritage' in the Louvre, 1820–1840: From the Musée Charles X to the Galerie d'Apollon," *Art History* 14 (December 1991): 488–510; also Marie-Claude Chaudonneret, *L'Etat et les artistes: De la restauration à la monarchie de Juillet (1815–1833)* (Paris: Flammarion, 1999).

31 Giovanni Morelli to Giovanni Frizzoni, 25 December 1838, Archivio Zavaritt, Gorle.

32 See David Mandrella's account of Mündler's life, in *Dictionnaire critique des historiens de l'art* (Paris: Institut National d'Histoire de l'Art, 2010), https://www.inha.fr/fr/ressources/publications/publications-numeriques/dictionnaire-critique-des-historiens-de-l-art/mundler-otto.html.

33 Giovanni Morelli to Niccolò Antinori, 16 October 1857, Archivio Antinori, Florence: "Mündler ... è persona colta e galantuomo; lo conosco dal 1838 in qua e a Parigi feci con lui i miei studi sui pittori del Louvre; egli è certamente non solo gran conoscitore delle scuole pittoriche, ma è anima pur capace del più nobile entusiasmo estetico."

34 Giovanni Morelli (at Paris) to Buonaventura Genelli, 12 November 1838, Nachlass Genelli, 255, C 462, Universitätsbibliothek, Leipzig.

35 Jean Paul Richter, obituary of Morelli, *Beilage zur Allgemeinen Zeitung* (6 April 1891): 1–4.

36 Ralph Nicholson Wornum and Charles Lock Eastlake, *Descriptive and Historical Catalogue of the Pictures in the National Gallery: With Biographical Notices of the Painters* (London: W. Clowes and Sons, 1847), subsequently revised and reissued.

37 Morelli wrote to the Frizzoni family in Bergamo that he was preparing a monograph on lizards.

38 "... Allein zu sein ist für mich nicht nur—Genuß, sondern auch ein Bedürfniss, wenn ich es nicht mit mir selbst und allen meinen Freunden verderben will." Giovanni Morelli to Federico Frizzoni, 25 December 1838, formerly in the archive of Giovanni Frizzoni.

Notes to Chapter 4: A Return to Italy

1 As recorded by Gustavo Frizzoni; see Giacomo Agosti, "'Un'italiano d'animo e tedesco di studi' a Firenze: Giovanni Morelli e i suoi interlocutori in Toscana," in *L'Idea di Firenze: Temi e interpretazioni nell'arte straniera dell'Ottocento*, ed. Maurizio Bossi, Lucia Tonini, and Francis Haskell (Florence: Centro Di, 1989), 117–26.

2 Anonymous [Gino Capponi], *Pensieri sull'educazione: Frammento inedito, 1841* (Lugano: Tipografia della Svizzera Italiana, 1845).

3 Eugenio Garin, "Il pensiero di Gino Capponi," in *Gino Capponi: Linguista, storico, pensatore*, ed. Giovanni Nencioni. Studi (Accademia toscana di scienze e lettere La Colombaria) 50 (Florence: Olschki, 1977), 41–45.

4 *Lettere di Gino Capponi e di altri a lui raccolte e pubblicate*, ed. Alessandro Carraresi (Florence: Felice Le Monnier, 1882), vol. 2, 218 (letter 24, November 1845).

5 Giovanni Morelli (at Bergamo) to Giovanni Battista Niccolini, 15 September 1841, Carteggi Vari 60, 84, Biblioteca Nazionale Centrale di Firenze, Florence.

6 Goethe, "Graf Carmagnola gegen die englischen Critiker vertheidigt," *Kunst und Alterthum* 3 (1831).

7 Giovanni Morelli (at Gorle) to Giovanni Battista Niccolini, 2 November 1841, Collezione d'Autografi, V. 60, 85, Biblioteca Nazionale Centrale di Firenze, Florence.

8 Giovanni Morelli (at Bellagio, Lake Como) to Atto Vannucci, 3 November 1865, and at Bergamo, 3 March 1865, Collezione d'Autografi, 10, 101, Biblioteca Nazionale Centrale di Firenze, Florence.

9 See Atto Vannucci, ed., *Ricordi della vita e delle opere di G.-B. Niccolini. 1, Vita e opere. Amici, critici e nemici. Pubbliche testimonianze di stima e d'affetto. Notizie bibliografiche. Lettere dal 1798 al 1823*, vol. 2 (Florence: Felice Le Monnier, 1866): 258, 261, 267, 272–73, 279, 309–11, 362–64, 379.

10 Vannucci, ed., *Ricordi della vita e delle opere di G.-B. Niccolini*, 201.

11 Marco Tabarrini, *Gino Capponi: I suoi tempi, I suoi studi, I suoi amici; Memorie raccolte* (Florence: Barbèra, 1879), 244–46.

12 *Lettere di Gino Capponi*, vol. 2, 24–26, 35–37, 41–46, 60–62, 68–69, 90–92, 105–106, 123–24, 142–50, 150–52, 156–57, 385–86, 417–27, 503, and vol. 3, 15–17, 68, 309–10.

13 Tabarrini, *Gino Capponi*, 244–46.

14 Gino Capponi (at Florence) to Giovanni Morelli, 30 September 1842, in *Lettere di Gino Capponi*, vol. 2, 105.

15 Giovanni Morelli (at Bergamo) to Gino Capponi, 3 November 1842, Capponi, X, 7, Biblioteca Nazionale Centrale di Firenze, Florence.

16 Morelli to Capponi, 3 November 1842.

17 Significant extracts from the correspondence are published in Giacomo Agosti, "Giovanni Morelli corrispondente di Niccolò Antinori," in *Studi e ricerche di collezionismo e museografia: Firenze 1820–1920*, Quaderni del Seminario di Storia della Critica d'Arte 2 (Pisa: Scuola Normale Superiore di Pisa, 1985), 1–83.

18 *Il Conte Egmonte: Tragedia di Wolfango Goethe; Prima versione dal Tedesco di Niccolò Antinori* (Florence: Le Monnier, 1853).

19 Ettore Spalletti, "La pittura dell'Ottocento in Toscana," in *La pittura in Italia: L'Ottocento*, ed. Enrico Castelnuovo and Gioacchino Barbera (Milan: Mondadori/Electa, 1997), vol. 1, 306.

20 Giovanni Morelli to Niccolò Antinori, 20 April 1842, Archivio Antinori, Florence: "Roma ... l'unica città, mi pare, dove un artista possa vivere veramente da artista; libero, senza guanti bianchi e senza il timore che alle tue azioni segua una coda di pettegolezzi. Le ruine sono così colossali, così maravigliose, i contorni di Roma spirano un'aria così classica e sono tanto serii e grandiosi che ammazano ogni altra cosa. Qui in questo suolo il pensare s'allarga, le idee divengon più grandi, più nobili; insomma si diventa un altr'uomo ... Mai in vita mia non ho avute tante emozioni quante n'ho avute qui in Roma, sono in continua estasi. Ma t'assicuro che ne traggo assai profitto da questo mio soggiorno, almeno mi pare così. Visito ogni settimana un paio di volte la galleria Doria, dove trovansi de' sublimi paesaggi di Claudio e di Poussin, e quando mi vi son ben bene inspirato vo subito a passeggiare nella natura e cerco di trovarvi ciò che ne' quadri ho veduto, e che quegli artisti trovarono e che hanno più o meno imitato. Questi studi mi danno sommo diletto, m'allargano e purificano l'animo, e gli danno una più sublime idea della natura e dell'arte. "Beato quello cui tutto è viva idea e non più mera parola e tradizione! Sono contento de' miei giorni, e godo veramente di questa bellissima nostra vita e talvolta m'entra tal'allegrezza in corpo, che vorrei abbracciare tutti quanti mi capitan innanzi; s'intende però da sé, le belle ragazze sempre più volontieri che le brutte. Vorrei solamente che potessimo insieme vedere le opere di Raffaello; fuori di qui non si può farsi un'idea giusta di questo grand'uomo. È l'unico tra gli artisti moderni che raggiunga affatto gli antichi—e ti dirò il perché—perché egli, come quelli, penetra sempre nell'oggetto che rappresenta—mentre tutti gli altri suoi contemporanei, come Lionardo, Michel'Angelo, Coreggio, e poi Tiziano, per quanto grandi siano, sempre mai vanno ripetendosi nelle loro opere, e i loro quadri si rassomigliano più o meno uno all'altro. Tutti questi mostrano lo stesso volere, la medesima tendenza; ma Raffaello è bensì anche lui sempre lo stesso, però allo stesso tempo sempre un altro, secondo l'argomento che viene a trattare."

21 Giovanni Morelli (at Bergamo) to Niccolò Antinori, 15 December 1844, Archivio Antinori, Florence: "Caro mio Antinori, tu non sai quanto io ti amo, questo mio fortissimo amore che sento per te non dipende, come l'amicizia che porto o a questo o a quello, dal raziocinio—no, è un sentimento spontaneo della mia natura verso la tua. L'età e i sentimenti ci congiungono—tu senti lo stesso bisogno d'amore caldamente come lo sento io, per cui l'amicizia è un vero culto, e ne' tristi momenti della mia vita quando questo entusiasmo andava diminuendo io mi sentiva di giorno in giorno divenire più miserabile e meschino—mentre che sono l'uomo il più felice quando la fiamma dell'amore e dell'amicizia è viva nel mio petto —allora sento il bello con tutte le fibre, con tutto il mio sangue e mi trovo capace d'ogni buona e magnanima azione. Sono certo, che tu pure proverai lo stesso in te."

22 Morelli enthusiastically outlined the plan to Antinori in a letter from San Fermo, 4 July 1850, Archivio Antinori, Florence.

23 Giovanni Morelli (at Bergamo) to Gino Capponi, 10 August 1841, Capponi, X, 7, Biblioteca Nazionale Centrale di Firenze, Florence.

24 Morelli to Capponi, 10 August 1841: "Io non ho l'onor di esser il suo amico, gliel dissi alquanto sdegnoso, e la prego di trattarmi d'or innanzi come tutti gli altri."

25 Giovanni Morelli (at Bergamo) to Gino Capponi, 6 July 1842, Capponi X, 7, Biblioteca Nazionale Centrale di Firenze, Florence.

26 Giovanni Morelli (at Bergamo) to Gino Capponi, 20 August 1842, Capponi X, 7, Biblioteca Nazionale Centrale di Firenze, Florence: "Qui da noi si continua ad ammazzare la gente sulle strade maestre, e non passa quasi giorno che non si sente un nuovo assassinio—e la Polizia ne ride."

27 Giovanni Morelli (at Verona) to G. B. Vieusseux, 3 May 1841, Carteggio Vieuss. 72, 206, Biblioteca Nazionale Centrale di Firenze, Florence.

28 Giovanni Morelli (at Bergamo) to Gino Capponi, 6 August 1843, Capponi X, 7, Biblioteca Nazionale Centrale di Firenze, Florence.

29 Giovanni Morelli (at Bergamo) to Gino Capponi, 21 November 1845, Capponi X, 7, Biblioteca Nazionale Centrale di Firenze, Florence.

30 The manuscript in German, "Clementina Reichmann, diario di viaggio 1839–1846," is in the archive of Anna Flora Eynard, Bergamo. A transcription made by Professor Christian Grawe of the University of Melbourne is in the Biblioteca Civica Angelo Mai, Bergamo.

31 "Meinen Kindern bin ich keine Mutter wie ich sollte—meinem Mann gewähre ich nicht was ich könnte—meiner Haushaltung verstehe ich nicht vorzustehn—Niemandem bin ich nöthig und eine nagende Unzufriedenheit mit mir selbst gewährt mir bittere unmuthvolle Stunden, ohne daß ich den Muth und die Willenskraft in mir fühlte, mich aus diesem zerstreuten, kraftlosen Gemüthszustand loszureißen. Ein unruhiger Geist treibt mich ohne zu wißen wohin; meine Gedanken sind selten bey dem Gegenstande den ich betreibe." Or in English translation: "I am not the mother to my children that I should be—I do not give my husband what I could—I do not have the skills to manage my household—I am not needed by anyone, and a nagging dissatisfaction with myself grants me bitter hours full of discontent, without feeling the courage and willpower in me to break away from this distracted, feeble state of mind. A spirit of unrest is driving me I know not where; my thoughts are rarely on the subject that I am dealing with at the time."

32 Giovanni Morelli (at Bergamo) to Niccolò Antinori, 15 December 1844, Archivio Antinori, Florence.

33 This description is taken from letters that Morelli's mother wrote to her brother Pietro (Archivio Zavaritt, Gorle).

34 Giovanni Morelli (at Bergamo) to Gino Capponi, 14 September 1845, Capponi, X, 7, Biblioteca Nazionale Centrale di Firenze, Florence.

35 The property at Lampugnano, and another at Bollate Milanese, were bought from Dr Pecchio for 20,000 lire, and measured 1,080,420 square meters. I have been unable to identity their locations.

36 The Viganone property, in Borghetto Lodigiano, Provincia di Lodi, was bought by Ambrogio on 19 November 1818, through the notary Bianchi di San Colombano, for 278,208.50 lire, and measured 918,160 square meters.

37 Archivio Zavaritt, Gorle.

38 Giovanni Morelli (at Milan) to Pietro Zavaritt, 22 September 1846, Archivio Zavaritt, Gorle.

39 Johann Georg Veit Engelhardt, "Aus einer Reise durch Tyrol und einen Theil der Lombardei," in three parts, in *Monatsblätter zur Ergänzung der Allgemeinen Zeitung*: "I: Villegiatur am Comersee" (February 1846): 73–77; "II: Porta's Gedicht: Die Wahl eines Caplans" (April 1846): 195–97; "III: Villegiatur am Comersee" (November 1846): 542–49.

40 Giovanni Morelli (at Taronico) to Giovanni Battista Camozzi Vertova, 5 September 1865, Fondo Risorgimento italiano, Sala 24, Cassa 1, Faldone 28, no. 413, Biblioteca Civica Angelo Mai, Bergamo. The passage where Morelli acknowledges authorship of his letters and articles reads: "Della qual cosa moltissime fra le sue lettere a me dirette potrebbero fare fede. Nel 1846 passò un mese presso di me, parte a Bergamo parte qui al lago. Molte fra le mie lettere a lui indirizzate (nel 1845, vedo, quella lunghissima sull'Arnaldo da Brescia di G. Battista Niccolini; nel 1846 altra sopra Niccolini,

Manzoni e Gino Capponi—nel 1847 una su Pio IX—nel 1848 alcune di argomento politico) furono da lui fatte inserire nella *Gazzetta d'Augusta*."

41 Giovanni Morelli (at Bellagio, Lake Como) to Atto Vannucci, 3 November 1865, Collezione d'Autografi, 10, 101, Biblioteca Nazionale Centrale di Firenze, Florence: "Ecco come stanno precisamente le cose. Dal 1841 al 1855 io ... tenni carteggio regolare col defunto mio amico Professore Engelhardt di Erlangen, in Baviera. In quelle mie lettere io gli andavo buttando giù tutte le mie osservazioni e idee che noi si presentavano alla mente sopra argomenti scientifico-letterari e artistici, come pure sulle cose pratiche d'Italia".
"Ora, di quelle mie lettere l'amico Tedesco si serviva spessissimo per farne degli articoli da Gazzetta. Molti di codesti articoli furono pubblicati nella *Gazzetta d'Augusta*, altri nel *Morgenblatt*, altri in altre Efemeridi della Germania. Alle volte so che la mia lettera veniva stampata tal quale, senza aggiunte o modificazioni da parte dell'amico – alle volte invece non v'era che qualche idea presa dalla mia lettera, e tutto il resto dell'articolo apparteneva all'Engelhardt.
"Siccome *sull'Arnaldo da Brescia* so d'avere scritto all'amico una lunghissima lettera e so anche che di quella lettera egli se n'è servito, così io le scrissi che quell'articolo era mio, non sapendo però più in che giornale Tedesco fosse comparso. Ma se nel 1846 io dichiarai al Niccolini non essere mio l'articolo dell'*Allgemeine Zeitung*, vuol dire che realmente quell'articolo non mi appartiene, e che sarà probabilmente uno scritto da certo Prof. Pfeiffer sull'*Arnaldo da Brescia*. Tornato in città vedrò se riuscirò a procurarmi l'annata del 1848 dell'*Allgemeine*, e al mio arrivo costì il saprò dire precisamente se l'articolo è quello dell'Engelhardt e quindi in gran parte mio, oppure se è quello pubblicato dal Pfeiffer. Di un articolo nell'*Allgemeine* tutto mio, che tratta di Niccolini, ma ne ricordo benissimo, e glielo mostrerò a Firenze."

42 "Italienische dramatische Literatur: Niccolini's *Arnold von Brescia*," Part 1 in *Allgemeine Zeitung* [Augsburg] 52 (21 February 1844): Beilage, 25–27; Part 2 in *Allgemeine Zeitung* [Augsburg] 53 (22 February 1844): Beilage, 419–20.

43 They are in the Archivio Zavaritt, Gorle.

44 Francesco De Sanctis to Camillo De Meis, 19 July 1856, in Francesco De Sanctis, *Epistolario (1856–1858)*, ed. Giovanni Ferretti and Muzio Mazzocchi Alemanni (Turin: Einaudi, 1965), 110: "Morelli mi ha mandato le tre commedie dell'anonimo, e le trovo mediocri. Foss'egli l'autore? Sono imbarazzato nel darne giudizio."

45 Giovanni Morelli to Francesco De Sanctis, 4 August 1856, in De Sanctis, *Epistolario*, 127–29.

46 *I Tradimenti*, Act I, Scene 7: "Ecco che vedo un giovane lanciarsi in mezzo ai fuggenti—egli li trattiene, gli rianima. Colla sinistra alzava una bandiera tricolore, nella destra teneva una spada. Alle sue parole, al suo esempio, i nostri riprendono coraggio e lo seguono. Intorno a lui i bravi suoi seguaci cadevano morti e feriti, egli solo pareva invulnerabile, pareva un Santo. Io non respirava più, stavo lì come un sasso. Arrivato col suo piccolo drappello alla cantonata della piazza, lì alla casa dei Crivelli, e' raduna intorno a sé tutti gli altri e comanda loro di ricaricare i fucili. Fu allora ch'egli alzò lo sguardo verso casa nostra, verso me. I nostri occhi s'incontrarono, senza accorgermene, io gli sventolai il fazzoletto, egli mi risponde facendo sventolare la bandiera tricolore, poi con entusiasmo si rivolge a' suoi e subito dopo lo veggo alla testa della sua gente precipitarsi contro la barricata ... Un terribile scoppio di fucilate! Ne tremò tutta la casa, io non sentiva più nulla, non osava fiatare. È morto, non vedrò più il suo occhio, fu l'unico mio pensiero ... Alfine alzo gli occhi e vedo la bandiera tricolore che sventolava sulla barricata, e attraverso il fumo incontro l'occhio di Guido—e quell'occhiata bastò per legare le anime nostre per sempre—sì per sempre!"

47 Giovanni Morelli to Giovanni Leonardo Frizzoni, 13 March 1848, Archivio Zavaritt, Gorle.

Notes to Chapter 5: Revolution in Lombardy–Venetia, 1848–49

1 Giovanni Morelli (at Milan) to Gino Capponi, 29 January 1848, Capponi, X, 8, Biblioteca Nazionale Centrale di Firenze, Florence.

2 *Antologia degli scritti politici di Carlo Cattaneo*, ed. Giuseppe Galasso (Bologna: Il Mulino, 1962), 73.

3 Giovanni Morelli to Niccolò Antinori, 20 February 1848, Archivio Antinori, Florence.

4 Fifteen letters from Morelli to Giovanni Leonardo Frizzoni between 9 February 1847 and 8 November 1849 (Archivio Zavaritt, Gorle) give a picture of Morelli's political and military activities in the battles of the First Italian War of Independence.

5 Based on Emilio Visconti Venosta, Obituary of Morelli, *L'Illustrazione Italiana* (22 March 1891): 180–81.

6 Giovanni Morelli (at Frankfurt am Main) to Gino Capponi, 4 July 1848, Capponi X, 8, Biblioteca Nazionale Centrale di Firenze, Florence: "Da un misantropo ritiratosi in villa io prima divenni d'un corpo franco, che si distinse, organizzatore d'un battaglione di bersaglieri, poscia semplice soldato, e nel momento che dovea movere al campo di battaglia, ecco il governo Provvisorio che mi ordina di levarmi d'indosso l'uniforme e di dirigermi alla volta di Francoforte in qualità di diplomatico. Chi sa che ne sarà di me da qui un mese! Del resto l'ho scampata bella, e pare che il cielo non mi voglia per ora morto, quando però il cielo scomunicasse delle controversie di noi altri miseri mortali.
"In Oggiono mentre ch'io stavo in piazza, arringando il popolo i Gendarmi ricevevano l'ordine di fucilarmi;

ma non ebbero il coraggio d'avvicinarsi non che poi di seguire l'ordine del commissario. A Monza una palla nemica mi rese sordo d'un orecchio lacerandone il timpano; a Milano nel prender d'assalto con soli 15 uomini dei miei la porta Comasina vidi cader morti tre compagni, che mi stavano ai fianchi, senza che palla m'avesse toccato, e subito dopo mi trovai solo in mezzo ad una ventina di cacciatori tirolesi i quali invece d'ammazzarmi si misero a fuggire, lasciandone la porta—e cinque ore di poi l'innegabile gioia d'assistere alla precipitosa fuga degli Austriaci—scena veramente satanica. Quei 10 giorni valgono tutta una vita."

7 Paolo Peluffo, Maria Canella, and Paola Zatti, *Cronaca di una rivoluzione: Immagini e luoghi delle Cinque giornate di Milano* (Milan: Silvana, 2011).

8 Morelli to Capponi, 4 July 1848.

9 For an overview, see Bortolo Belotti, *Storia di Bergamo e dei Bergamaschi* (Bergamo: Poligrafiche Bolis, 1959), vol. 6.

10 Ippolito Negrisoli, "Bergamo alla riscossa: L'insurrezione del marzo 1848 (19–22) ed i rapporti con Milano nelle gloriose Cinque giornate," *Bergomum* 42, nos 1–2 (1948): 1–27; Giuseppe Locatelli Milesi, "Gli ostaggi nella caserma di S. Agostino: Episodio della rivoluzione di Bergamo del marzo 1848," *Rivista di Bergamo* (1922): 447–51.

11 Giorgio Spini, *Risorgimento e protestanti* (Milan: Il Saggiatore, 1989), 239–40.

12 Giovanni Morelli (at San Fermo) to Giovanni Leonardo Frizzoni, 3 May 1848, Archivio Zavaritt, Gorle.

13 Morelli to Frizzoni, 3 May 1848: "Quanto non ho io sofferto del separarmi da quella bella e brava gioventù, che doveva venire meco nel Tirolo, e che per ordine del nuovo Ministro della Guerra dovetti mandare a casa—perché questi non vuole sapere d'altri che di coscritti. Dopo, il Governo provinciale mi voleva mandare sul Veneto—ma fu troppo tardi—avea già licenziata la mia gente."

14 Christopher Duggan, *The Force of Destiny: A History of Italy since 1796* (London: Penguin, 2007), 171–76.

15 His commission, on 17 May 1848, was to present "lo spirito vero del nostro paese e a confutare le ingiuriose accuse del giornalismo prezzolato" (Governo provvisorio di Lombardia, Carte Casati, 174, Fascicolo 15, V, Archivio delle Civiche raccolte storiche del Comune di Milano, Museo del Risorgimento, Milano). For a full account of the importance of the Italian mission, see Pietro Pedrotti, Enrico Brol, and Bice Rizzi, *L'Azione parlamentare del Trentino nel 1848–49 a Francoforte e a Vienna* (Trento: Tipografia Editrice Mutilati e Invalidi, 1948), 102ff. Morelli's mission is discussed in Federico Curato, "L'Insurrezione e la guerra del milleottocentoquarantotto," in *Storia di Milano. 14: Sotto l'Austria (1815–1859)* (Milan: Fondazione Treccani degli Alfieri per la Storia di Milano, 1960), 410–11, a. The documents have been published by Federico Curato, ed., *Le relazioni diplomatiche tra la Gran Bretagna ed il Regno di Sardegna dal 1852 al 1856: Il carteggio diplomatico di Sir James Hudson* (Turin: Industria Libraria tip. ed., 1956), 417–30 (no. 179).

16 Federico Curato, "Il Parlamento di Francoforte e la prima Guerra d'indipendenza italiana," *Archivio storico italiano* 110 (1952): 276n66.

17 Giovanni Morelli (in Frankfurt) to Giovanni Leonardo Frizzoni, 9 June 1848, Archivio Zavaritt, Gorle.

18 Giovanni Morelli to Anselmo Guerrieri Gonzaga, 16 June 1848, Governo Provvisorio di Lombardia, Carte Casati, 33.1, Fascicolo 15–V, c. 179, Archivio delle Civiche raccolte storiche del Comune di Milano, Museo del Risorgimento, Milan.

19 Alessandro Porro to Anselmo Guerrieri, 8 June 1848, Governo Provvisorio della Lombardia, Carte Casati, 1848, no. 177, Archivio delle Civiche raccolte storiche del Comune di Milano, Museo del Risorgimento, Milan.

20 Giovanni Morelli to an unknown, 20 June 1848, Biblioteca Comunale, Forlì.

21 *Worte eines Lombarden an die Deutschen* (Frankfurt am Main: Streng und Schneider, 1848). A rare copy of this tract is in the Biblioteca Civica Angelo Mai, Bergamo; it was given by Morelli to Giovanni Battista Camozzi Vertova and is inscribed "*Johan Morel al Parlamento di Francoforte 1848 sulla rivoluzione Lombarda.*"

22 Frank Eyck, *The Frankfurt Parliament 1848–1849* (London: Macmillan, 1968), esp. chapter 7.

23 The passionate opening lines of *Worte eines Lombarden an die Deutschen*: "Die Revolution der Lombardei ist zu Ende. Das Joch einer vierunddreißigjährigen Tyrannei drückt nicht mehr unsern Nacken. Wir erheben wieder unser Haupt frei zum Himmel; ein Jeder von uns fühlt sich wieder Mensch, fühlt daß in seiner Brust sich etwas rührt und regt, von dem er bisher kaum eine Ahnung haben konnte: es ist dies der göttliche Funke der Selbstachtung. In diesem erhebenden Gefühle treten wir nun zu euch, ihr deutschen Männer, und bieten euch unsere Hand."

24 Giovanni Morelli (at Frankfurt) to Buonaventura Genelli, 21 June 1848, Genelli Nachlass, Universitätsbibliothek, Leipzig: "Der beste—ich möchte sagen, der einzige wahre hervorragende Redner ist Robert Blum—er hat alle Gaben dazu, schade, daß ihm die Feinheit einer soliden Durchbildung abgeht."

25 Giovanni Morelli to Gino Capponi, 5 August 1848. This important letter is published in Capponi's correspondence, *Lettere di Gino Capponi e di altri a lui raccolte e pubblicate*, ed. Alessandro Carraresi (Florence: Successori Le Monnier, 1884), vol. 2, 420–27, and in part in Gustavo Frizzoni, "Cenni biografici intorno a Giovanni Morelli," in Giovanni Morelli, *Della pittura Italiana: Studii storico critici di Giovannni Morelli (Ivan Lermolieff); Le Gallerie Borghese e Doria Pamphili in Roma. Prima edizione*

italiana preceduta dalla biografia e dal ritratto dell'autore, e illustrata da 81 incisioni (Milan: Fratelli Treves Editori, 1897), x–xi.

26 Duggan, *The Force of Destiny*, 170–75.

27 Morelli to Capponi, 5 August 1848.

28 Federico Curato, "Il Parlamento," Part II, *Archivio storico italiano* (1953): 109.

29 Morelli's second report to Milan, dated 16 June 1848, no. 179, described the arrival of the archduke in Austrian uniform in some detail.

30 Luigi Santini, *La comunità evangelica di Bergamo: Vicende storiche* (Torre Pellice: Claudiana, 1960), 140–41.

31 *Lettere di Gino Capponi*, 459.

32 Gino Capponi to Daniele Manin, October 1848, in *Lettere di Gino Capponi*: "Oggi peraltro voglio sodisfare il debito di cortesia che tengo con Lei, prendendone occasione dal raccomandarle il signor Morelli di Bergamo, il quale, amantissimo delle cose d'Italia, delle quali fu parte in ogni fortuna, vuol veder da vicino il bell'esempio di costanza e di patriottismo che dà oggi a tutta Italia Venezia."

33 Giovanni Morelli to Tommaso Gar, 18 October 1848, Archivio Tommaso Gar, b. E/9, fasc. 5, Fondazione Museo Storico del Trentino, Trento. See Sergio Benvenuti, *Le lettere di Tommaso Gar negli archivi e nelle biblioteche del Trentino* (Trento: Istituto per la storia del Risorgimento italiano, 1963).

34 Giovanni Morelli (in Venice) to Giovanni Leonardo Frizzoni, 5 February 1849, Archivio Zavaritt, Gorle: "Molti ufficiali hanno dato però la loro dimissione ed anderanno ad arruolarsi in Toscana o in Piemonte—e pochi giorni or sono feci ancor io lo stesso, giacché come Aiutante d'un Generale che non faceva mai nulla, io mi stava di continuo inoperoso, e mi vergognava di portar l'uniforme. Sono invitato d'andare a Torino e vi anderò fra breve—e lascio volentieri questa città dove mi piangeva il cuore di vedere andar le cose nostre così infamemente male."

35 Morelli to Frizzoni, 5 February 1849: "... questo imbroglio Romano ci taglia le gambe più che mai, almeno per adesso, benché io sia come te della più ferma convinzione, che alla riforma politica d'Italia abbia a precedere una riforma religiosa."

36 Morelli to Frizzoni, 5 February 1849: "Che la Francia, in cui molti italiani avevan ed hanno tuttora riposto tutta la loro speranza, che la Francia dico non faccia nulla per noi è naturale, e bisognerebbe non aver mai letto la storia per ignorare che quella nazione è, fu e sarà sempre la nostra nemica; credo bensì ch'essa nonostante le sue ripugnanze dovrà far la guerra contro l'Austria, e che quindi opererà a vantaggio nostro—ma il pretendere ch'essa venga in Italia a cavallerescamente liberarci dal nemico è cosa tanto ridicola quanto indegna d'un popolo che vuole rendersi indipendente."

37 Debrunner's lively and witty account was written in 1849 from Frauenfeld, the town of Morelli's ancestors, and published in German, French, and Italian: Johann Debrunner, *Venezia nel 1848–1849: Avventure della compagnia svizzera durante l'assedio fatto dagli Austriaci* (Turin: Presso tutti i librai, 1851).

38 Emilio Visconti Venosta makes reference to Morelli in Novara in his manuscript for a biography of Morelli (Mazza 16, archivio della Fondazione Cavour, Santena). The text corresponds closely to Layard's biographical essay on Morelli (discussed in Chapter 9), but with much additional material.

39 Giovanni Morelli to Giovanni Leonardo Frizzoni, 4 May 1849, Archivio Zavaritt, Gorle: "Io non ho ancora deciso nulla, né so se mi fisserò qui o piuttosto in qualche altro sito. Di salute sto bene e da qualche giorno ho di nuovo cominciato a interessarmi di cose poetiche e a riprendere quella lena, che già da mesi e mesi mi mancava."

40 Massimo d'Azeglio to Giovanni Morelli, 20 July 1860, 35 R 5, Biblioteca Civica Angelo Mai, Bergamo.

41 Morelli to Frizzoni, 4 May 1849.

42 Giovanni Morelli to Giovanni Leonardo Frizzoni, 21 May 1849, Archivio Zavaritt, Gorle:
"Le notizie giunte quest'oggi a Genova sono incirca queste—
1) A Civitavecchia giungeranno sempre nuovi rinforzi francesi che già in numero di 25,000 stavano accampati a circa 4 o 5 migliaia da Roma.
2) A Livorno si proseguiranno gli arresti e le fucilazioni. Due Ufficiali austriaci avevano stati assassinati giorni sono—dicesi fucilato anche Guerrazzi—non lo credo però. Per disposizioni dell'Autorità Governativa austr. senza processo di sorta furono fucilati (scrivono Livornesi a casa di Genova) più di 150 individui, fra i quali si parla di molti lombardi che si credono arrestati dopo l'occupazione della città. Il danno che la città ha avuto dalle bombe non è per cosa di gran momento.
3) In Palermo dicesi regnare completa anarchia—una definizione di quella città, fattami settimane sono dal fratello di Azeglio (il Gesuita Tapparelli) mi far creder vero questo dicesi.
4) Bologna presa dagli Austriaci—le chiavi inviate al Papa—la resistenza dei bolognesi essere stata assai gagliarda e coraggiosa. (In Italia noi non abbiamo purtroppo che singole città!)
5) Qui a Genova saranno concentrati più di 40,000 soldati—il numero di questi già ora sorpassa i 30,000."

43 Giovanni Morelli to Niccolò Antinori, 12 December 1849, Archivio Antinori, Florence.

44 Giovanni Morelli to Teodoro Frizzoni, 15 December 1849, Archivio Zavaritt, Gorle.

45 The life of Frizzoni's youngest son, also named Giovanni Leonardo (1843–1883, Fig. 48), demonstrates

how the family's love of country dictated the education of the succeeding generation, as they endeavoured to acquire military competence. As a five-year-old the younger Giovanni Leonardo went to live in Milan with his grandmother at Palazzo Reichmann, via Corso di Porta Romana 3, in which city he subsequently began his military career, before attending the military college in Florence and later the military academy in Turin. He fought in the Third War of Independence in 1866, distinguishing himself at the Battle of Custoza and winning a silver medal for valor. The war over, he left the military, went to Turin University and graduated in mineral engineering. He then studied geology and mineralogy at the Accademia delle Miniere, which he practiced successfully for the rest of his life, and settled in matrimony with Erminia, with whom he had four children.

46 Giovanni Morelli (at San Fermo) to Pietro Zavaritt, 7 December 1849, Archivio Zavaritt, Gorle.

47 Giovanni Morelli (at Geneva) to Giovanni Leonardo Frizzoni, 3 July 1849, private archive, Bergamo, quoted by Santini in *La comunitá evangelica di Bergamo*, 112: "Il sentimento nazionale è grande in tutta la Penisola—la riforma religiosa è urgente, e questo è a mio parere il principale de' guadagni, poiché finché esisterà in Italia la Roma leonina non si può parlare d'indipendenza nazionale—questa Roma, che appartiene al medio evo, va distrutta da capo a fondo; vi risorgerà una Roma veramente italiana—il Piemonte, baluardo della nazionalità italiana, s'è democratizzato di molto e si renderà qui ogni dì più degno di dirigere il movimento nazionale. Io ho grande stima di queste popolazioni piemontesi—sono più fredde delle nostre, ma più morali, più coscienziose."

48 Julius von Schlosser, *La storia dell'arte nelle esperienze e nei ricordi di un suo cultore* (Bari: G. Laterza e Figli, 1936), 13–14.

Notes to Chapter 6: A Decade in Waiting for a Unified Italy

1 Giovanni Morelli to Lionel von Donop, autobiographical letters, 1874 and 1875, Genelli Nachlass 255, Universitätsbibliothek, Leipzig.

2 Giovanni Morelli (at Taronico) to Pietro Zavaritt, 29 June 1856, Archivio Zavaritt, Gorle: "Il mio giardino a Crella—lo chiamo mio perché ne godo più io de' suoi proprietari reali—s'è fatto veramente bello in questa primavera; tutte le piante hanno fatto getti straordinari, anco quelle che già da molti anni non davano segno di vita. Vo tutte le sere a passarvi un paio d'ore dalle 7 alle 9."

3 The handwriting of the transcriber and editor is that of Bice Eynard, wife of Clementina's grandson Ugo Frizzoni. Of the many versions that exist among the Frizzoni family, I quote from the one in the Archivio Zavaritt, Gorle: "Brani da lettere del Signor Morelli alla Nonna Clementina," 1854–55, transcribed by Bice Eynard, Archivio Zavaritt, Gorle. The few marginal comments by Bice Eynard are banal.

4 Alessandro Torri, *Della imitazione di Gesù Cristo di Giovanni Gersenio: Anonima traduzione antica corrispondente all'originale Latino secondo il codice De-Advocatis del secolo XIV pubblicato la prima volta in Parigi nel 1833 dal cavaliere Gaspare De-Gregory. Nuova edizione del volgarizzamento ridotto a corretta lettura e prima italiana del vero testo con illustrazioni per cura del dottore Alessandro Torri* (Florence: Le Monnier, 1855).

5 "Un passo di un manoscritto raro assai, che è l'incominciata Storia del Cristianesimo di G. Capponi sgraziatamente troncato lì per la sventura toccata al suo autore." Capponi's understanding of Christianity appears in some of his publications, but no manuscript exists of this text.

6 From "Brani da lettere del Signor Morelli alla Nonna Clementina": "è un vero Barone teutonico, pieno zeppo di boria, d'arroganza e di pregiudizi. Ma ha un senso finissimo ed esercitatissimo, e molti sagacia. Il suo stile è più quello d'un diplomatico che d'un filosofo o d'un artista. Nessuno conosce meglio l'arte d'imporre che lui, e a questa sua bravura credo sia da ascriversi non tutta, ma gran parte di quella straordinaria fama ch'egli seppe acquistarsi in Europa."

7 Jacob Burckhardt, *Der Cicerone: Eine Anleitung zum Genuss der Kunstwerke Italiens* (Basel: Schweighauser'sche Verlagsbuchhandlung, 1855).

8 From "Brani da lettere del Signor Morelli alla Nonna Clementina": "Mi sono dato a percorrere qua e là il libro del Burckhardt—in molte cose non so essere d'accordo con lui, in altre invece il suo giudizio e modo di ravvisare l'arte parvemi fino e al di sopra di quanto si sente e si legge al solito. I più bei passi di questo libro, cioè quelli che a me sembrano tali, voglio notarmeli per poterveli leggere un giorno, quando ci ritroveremo nuovamente."

9 Giovanni Morelli to Niccolò Antinori, 13 August 1864, reprinted in Giacomo Agosti, "Giovanni Morelli corrispondente di Niccolò Antinori," in *Studi e ricerche di collezionismo e museografia Firenze 1820–1920*, Quaderni del Seminario di Storia della Critica d'Arte 2 (Pisa: Scuola Normale Superiore, 1985), 41–42.

10 Giovanni Morelli (at San Fermo) to Teodoro Frizzoni, 15 December 1849, Private archive, Bergamo: "La cara tua letterina mi fece grandissimo piacere. Nel riceverla e meglio ancora nel leggerla sentivo vieppiù la bella e preziosa eredità, che in te mi lasciò il povero tuo padre. Sii certo, mio caro, che ti sento sempre sincero e buon'amico. E non fosti tu forse sempre il prediletto mio Teodoro?"

11 Erik Hinterding and Femy Horsch, ""A Small but Choice Collection:" The Art Gallery of King Willem II of the Netherlands (1792–1849)," *Simiolus: Netherlands*

Quarterly for the History of Art 19, nos 1–2 (1989): 4–122, see no. 161, pp. 105–6.

12 The passage about the presumed Giorgione, from Giovanni Morelli (at Taronico) to Teodoro Frizzoni, 26 September 1857, Archivio Zavaritt, Gorle, reads: "E che tu, battendo questa via, abbi ad arrivare lontano m'è prova la bella e viva descrizione che mi facesti di quel Giorgione dall'Aja; vi hai lasciato fuggirti alcune osservazioni che sono davvero finissime—ve n'ha poi altre che rammentano un po' di soverchio l'estetica tedesca come per esempio quando dici: non c'è azione in questo quadro, ma quelle tre faccie ti presentano tutt'una serie d'azioni—la donna è la realtà presente—il marito mi rappresenta il passato—ed il medico è il profeta dell'avvenire ecc. Siffatto modo di guardare ed interpretare l'arte è certamente il più contrario all'arte stessa, che se all'artista forse mai occorse tale idea allegorica, mentre ch'egli stava dinanzi alla sua tela, puoi esser certo che avrebbe fatto una di quella insipide goffaggini che la scuola tedesca moderna spaccia per opere altissime e profondissime di "pittura storica". E quello che in quel quadro del Giorgione t'avrà colpito il più è certamente la verità con cui il pittore ha saputo rappresentare in quelle faccie e attitudini li diversi moti dell'animo tanto nel marito quanto nel medico, non che lo svenimento nella donna." Morelli possessed the catalogue of the Dutch Royal Collection, listed by Giacomo Agosti and others in "Il fondo Morelli nella Biblioteca dell'Accademia di Brera," in *G. Morelli: Materiali di Ricerca*, ed. Eleonora Bairati (Bergamo: Biblioteca Angelo Mai, 1987), 143, but it is unlikely that Morelli had seen the painting at this date. He travelled briefly to The Hague in 1868, on return from his first trip to London.

13 On the Hampton Court version, which has been attributed at various times to Titian, Cariani, and others, see John Shearman, *The Early Italian Pictures in the Collection of Her Majesty the Queen* (Cambridge: Cambridge University Press, 1983), 69–72.

14 Morelli to Teodoro Frizzoni, 26 September 1857.

15 "Conto corrente dei fittabili del Viganone e Lampugnano di Lina Morell Zavaritt 1841," Archivio Zavaritt, Gorle.

16 In a lively letter to his very closest friend, Morelli discussed a significant number of paintings he had bought for himself: Giovanni Morelli (at Bergamo) to Niccolò Antinori, 23 May 1856: "Sappi, mio caro amico, ch'io sono ora circondato da' più preziosi quadri che immaginar ti puoi, e fra questi ve ne sono due che sono veri gioielli: un ritratto di giovinetto ch'io acquistai e pagai per opera di Marco d'Oggionno, ma che mi pare sappia più del maestro che dello scolare, e una Madonna del Mantegna (a tempera forte) col bambino che dorme, che è una meraviglia davvero; la testa della Madonna pur troppo è stata ritoccata. A me fu venduto per quadro 'della scuola Mantegnesca'—ma è indubitato Andrea Mantegna. Oltre questi due mi fu dato rinvenire in una delle nostre quadrerie di Bergamo due tavole di 'Andreas Mediolanensis' col nome e coll'anno 1499—(S. Gio. Battista e Santa Catterina) e un'altra tavola dello stesso artista rappresentante la testa di S. Giovanni Battista sopra bacile d'argento—stupenda cosa. Qui gli intelligenti ritenevano questo A. Mediol: per Andrea Salaino—mentre che invece è Andrea Solari, coetaneo quasi a Lionardo da Vinci, e che nel 1503 fu chiamato dal Cardinale d'Amboyse in Francia, dove dipinse vari quadri che sono fra i principali del Louvre e di altre raccolte—e dove morì incirca nel 1510. Il Solari, di cui non mi sovvengo aver visto opera nelle gallerie di costì, è uno de' più bei pittori di quell'epoca d'oro! E quando ritornerai da noi vedrai come sono belle e care queste tre tavole che di lui ho acquistato—e a poco prezzo, vedi. Così ho pure trovato nelle mie indagini fatte altri bei quadri: un magnifico ritratto d'uomo del Cariani (affatto Giorgionesco)—una bella tavola di Perin del Vaga, rappresentante Lucrezia romana e un magnifico S. Giovanni apostolo di Bartolommeo Montagna. Insomma al primo acquisto che feci per caso della tavola del Lotto feci sì che mi sono sentito una tale smania di rinvenire al Lotto de' compagni degni di lui, che per più mesi non mi sono d'altro occupato che delle vite e delle opere de' pittori nostri bergamaschi, e in tal modo visitando e chiese e quadrerie private sono pervenuto ad acquistare e cognizioni e quadri; e spero che tirando avanti così e secondato sempre dalla medesima fortuna io riuscirò a formarmi una bella piccola galleria. Ma Niccolino mio, ancor tu devi porgermi aiuto in tale ardua impresa—e se mai ti venisse fatto di scoprire un qualche del quadretto di pittore del 1400—se vuoi pure un Raffaello—che costì sia acquistabile a prezzo moderato, pensa a me e fammelo sapere, sai!"

17 "Conto corrente dei fittabili del Viganone e Lampugnano di Lina Morell Zavaritt 1841." This entry stands out as the only note about a work of art, and is under the heading "DARE" (to give).

18 Susanna Avery-Quash, *The Travel Notebooks of Sir Charles Eastlake*, The Volume of the Walpole Society 2011/73 (Huddersfield: The Walpole Society, 2011), 242: "Bergamo—14 September Lochis Gallery, Laurentius Lotus 1533 ... Joseph lifts veil from the sleeping C. reclining (entire fig) on couch, to show him to St Catherine—Virgin appears to caution him not to disturb the Infant—with her right hand—she holds a book in her left—landscape bk. Ground—Jasmine on rt side –different from specimens in Carrara Museum and Frizzoni collection."

19 Morelli's undated inventory is published in Anderson, "Frizzoneria in Bergamo." Other versions are in the Accademia Carrara, Bergamo (provenance 1632, Collection Canonici di Ferrara); the Osmitz Collection,

Rome; Hermitage, Leningrad; two private collections—at Bergamo, and Houston, Texas, a version from 1540 said to be the painting begun by Lotto's student, Coriolano, from Lotto's design and finished by Lotto for his student's wedding.

20 "trasporto di casse di quadri," lire 27; "Pagato la fattura d'una cassa," and "Per trasporto da Milano a Bergamo di 2 casse quadri, lire 4."

21 Giovanni Morelli to Pietro Zavaritt, 19 June 1856, Archivio Zavaritt, Gorle.

22 On 25 May 1856 Morelli informed Mündler of his acquisition (for which he had paid 23 golden Napoleons), and confided that "the head of Christ is a true jewel, but the Madonna's head and eyes are overpainted and might profit from a restoration with Fumagalli," Rolf Kultzen, "Giovanni Morelli als Briefpartner von Otto Mündler," *Zeitschrift für Kunstgeschichte* 52 (1989): 379.

23 Poldi's acquisitions from Morelli are documented in his "Libro dei conti," in "La cassa mia particolare," in *Appendice documentaria* of the exhibition catalogue *Gian Giacomo Poldi Pezzoli: L'uomo e il collezionista del Risorgimento*, ed. Lavinia M. Galli Michero and Fernando Mazzocca (Turin: Allemandi, 2011), 161–72. The third painting is there, identified as perhaps a Madonna and Child by Solario, inv. 1627 (see "Andrea Solario: Madonna con il Bambino," on the website of the Museo Poldi Pezzoli, http://www.museopoldipezzoli.it/#!/it/scopri/collezioni/577). For a recent account of the relationship between Morelli and Poldi, see A. Di Lorenzo, "Giovanni Morelli, Gian Giacomo Poldi Pezzoli e il collezionismo privato in Italia nella seconda metà dell'Ottocento, patriottico e risorgimentale," in *Giovanni Morelli tra critica delle arti e collezionismo, atti della giornata di studi (Pavia, Collegio Ghislieri, 24 marzo 2015)*, ed. G. Angelini (forthcoming). Di Lorenzo argues that the third painting, mentioned in the often-cited letter from Morelli to Niccolò Antinori of 23 May 1856, where three of his paintings are described (two now certainly being in the Poldi), could be by Giovanni Francesco Maineri, while a head of St John the Baptist is now in the Bob Jones University Museum and Art Gallery, at Greenville, South Carolina. Morelli's pioneering understanding of Solario is discussed at length in David Alan Brown, *Andrea Solario* (Milan: Electa, 1987).

24 Giovanni Morelli to Niccolò Antinori, 23 May 1856, cited in Agosti, "Giovanni Morelli corrispondente di Niccolò Antinori," 30–31.

25 Giovanni Morelli (at Taronico) to Niccolò Antinori, 16 October 1857, quoted by Agosti, "Giovanni Morelli corrispondente di Niccolò Antinori," 31–34.

26 Jaynie Anderson, ed., *The Restoration of Renaissance Painting in Mid Nineteenth-Century Milan: Giuseppe Molteni in Correspondence with Giovanni Morelli*, Teoria e Storia del Restauro 21 (Florence: Edifir, 2014), 40.

27 Giovanni Morelli (at Taronico) to Pietro Zavaritt, 29 October 1856, Archivio Zavaritt, Gorle: "Ma ancor'io ho fatto il mio viaggietto autunnale, sai! Sono stato per 4 giorni a Belgirate al Lago Maggiore in compagnia di De Sanctis, Manzoni, De Meis e di alcuni altri amici. E quel breve soggiorno e quella vita di intima espansione fu vera manna per la mia mente e pel mio cuore."

28 Elena Croce and Alda Croce, *Francesco de Sanctis* (Turin: Unione Tipografico-Editrice Torinese, 1964), 246: "Che gusto a vedere quel Morelli contraffare i gesti e la voce di Diomede Marvasi, e ripetere tutto il suo dizionario di bestemmie napolitane!"

29 Jaynie Anderson, "The First Cleaning Controversy at the National Gallery 1846–1853," in *Appearance, Opinion, Change: Evaluating the Look of Paintings*, ed. Victoria Todd (London: United Kingdom Institute for Conservation, 1990), 3–7.

30 *Report from the Select Committee on the National Gallery Together with the Proceedings of the Committee, Minutes of Evidence* (London: The House of Commons, 1853).

31 These are observations based on an analysis by the late Joyce Plesters, who pioneered our understanding of artists' colors.

32 In her biography of Cavalcaselle, Donata Levi supports his judgment, as being "hypercorrect" (Donata Levi, *Cavalcaselle: Il pioniere della conservazione dell'arte italiana* (Turin: G. Einaudi, 1988), 31–34.

33 First noted by Anderson in her "Introduction: Otto Mündler and his Travel Diary," in *The Travel Diaries of Otto Mündler 1855–1858*, ed. Carol Togneri Dowd, The Volume of the Walpole Society 51 (London: The Walpole Society, 1985): 23–24.

34 Jaynie Anderson, "'A most improper picture': Transformations of Bronzino's Erotic Allegory," *Apollo* 139 (February 1994): 19–28.

35 For an extended account, see Anderson, "Introduction: Otto Mündler and his Travel Diary," 7–67.

36 As Eastlake predicted, Mündler's notebooks (much more than those of Eastlake) preserve invaluable information about collections, the art market, the early working methods of connoisseurs, and the diagnostic importance of conservation for galleries. The published version of the diaries (*The Travel Diaries Of Otto Mündler 1855–1858*, ed. Togneri Dowd) is an English summary from the lengthier unpublished version in Berlin museum archives.

37 Jaynie Anderson, ed., *The Restoration of Renaissance Painting in mid Nineteenth-Century Milan: Giuseppe Molteni in Correspondence with Giovanni Morelli*, Storia e Teoria del Restauro 21 (Florence: Edifir, 2014).

38 A letter of condolence from Morelli to Lady Eastlake suggests that they knew one another well and enjoyed each other's company. Morelli recalls spending a most beautiful evening in Bellagio with Eastlake, whom he describes as an excellent and amiable man (*trefflichen und so liebenswürdigen Mann*). Giovanni Morelli to Lady Eastlake, I, 1868, MSS English 86, M.39, Letters to Sir Charles and Lady Eastlake, 1823–1882, 25–3–22 L. 416, Victoria and Albert Museum, London.

39 Federico Curato, "Profilo biografico di Sir James Hudson, G.C.B.," in *Le relazioni diplomatiche tra la Gran Bretagna ed il Regno di Sardegna dal 1852 al 1856: Il carteggio diplomatico di Sir James Hudson*, vol. 1 (Turin: Industria Libraria tip. ed., 1956), xi–cl.

40 This portrait of Fortunato Martinengo Cesaresco is now in the National Gallery, London.

41 Curato, "Profilo biografico di Sir James Hudson", xiv.

42 Austen Henry Layard to Lord Arthur Russell, 29 September 1885 (following publication of Hudson's obituary in *The Times* a few days earlier), Add. MSS 39, 039, British Library, London.

43 Giovanni Morelli (at Turin) to Ursina Zavaritt Morell, 1 April 1859, Archivio Zavaritt, Gorle. This is the only surviving letter from Morelli to his mother.

44 Giovanni Morelli (at Bergamo) to Niccolò Antinori, 4 August 1859, Archivio Antinori, Florence.

45 Garibaldi's proclamation is in the Museo del Risorgimento, Bergamo:

"Tutti i giovani che possono prendere un fucile sono chiamati intorno alla bandiera tricolore.

"Nessuno di voi vorrà assistere inerte ed imbelle alla guerra santa; nessuno vorrà un giorno confessare, arrossendo, di non avervi preso parte. Ora è il tempo di mostrare che non si mentiva quando dicevamo d'odiare l'Austria.

"All'armi dunque!

"Nessun sacrificio ci sembri grave, perché noi siamo quella generazione che avrà compito l'impresa dell'Indipendenza Italiana."

46 Giovanni Morelli to Teodoro Frizzoni, 21 December 1859, private archive, Bergamo. He justifies Correggio's presumed Venetian education: "Fatto sta che l'arte del colorire di Correggio, se bene tutta sua particolare, non s'accosta a nessun'altra tanto quanto a quella de' Giorgioneschi, e particolarmente a quella di L. Lotto."

47 Morelli to Teodoro Frizzoni, 21 December 1859: "È forse l'animo *più libero* che abbia avuto l'arte—e quanto al sentimento del bello nelle forme del corpo umano egli va innanzi, almeno nel credere mio, non solo a Raffaello, ma Michelangelo pure, i quali però gli soprastavano di molto nella scienza e nella cultura generale. La sua sensitività confina alle volte col malaticcio; non v'ha fibbra nelle membra delle figure sue che non getti scintille di vita; tutto è mobile, tutto è compenetrato nelle sue opere di un fluido elettrico, nervoso o magnetico, se vuoi. L'aria poi che gira ne' suoi dipinti è cosa meravigliosa; solo in un'opera di Velazquez mi ricordo aver osservato qualcosa di simile. E quest'aria il Correggio l'ottiene mediante il suo chiaroscuro. A questo riguardo non v'ha nulla di più miracoloso della testa e braccio e mano di S. M. Maddalena nel quadro del S. Girolamo. Correggio è il rappresentante più libero dell'arte staccatasi dalla Chiesa. Egli accenna dovunque all'anarchia, trasgredisce in ogni sua opera i confini assegnati all'arte. E anco questo è un tratto ch'egli ha comune con molti altri geni, allevati come lui nella vita augusta della provincia, lontani da un gran centro della cultura ... Nessuno non ti rende il momento dell'essere così palpitante di vita, di realtà quanto il Correggio. Egli è sensuale, è vero, anzi tutto sensuale, il più sensuale degli artisti—ma la sua sensualità è eterna, trasparente direi, è la sensualità di esseri nervosi, estremamente sensitivi etici. Se vuoi trovargli un paragone fra le piante, paragonalo con una mimosa sensitiva."

48 Giovanni Morelli (at Nice) to Niccolò Antinori, 13 March 1860, Archivio Antinori, Florence.

49 Francesco De Sanctis to Angelo Camillo De Meis, 10 February 1860, in Francesco De Sanctis, *Epistolario (1859–1860)*, ed. Giuseppe Talamo and Carlo Muscetta, Opere di Francesco De Sanctis 20 (Turin: Giulio Einaudi, 1965), 139–40: "Sento che Emiliani Giudici è stato nominato professore di Storia delle Belle Arti e di Estetica. Che gran risata ne ha dovuto fare Morelli. E che ne è di Morelli? Sta a Bergamo o a Milano? Ti scrive qualche volta? Io non ne ho avuto più notizia. So però che aveva intenzione di risiedere a Milano. *È strano che in questo rimescolamento d'uomini e di cose nessuno pensi a lui*."

Notes to Chapter 7: Representing Bergamo in the Camera dei Deputati

1 Together with his father, Tetar had moved to Turin in 1851. He was with Garibaldi on his military campaigns in 1859 and 1860. In 1861, he moved to Paris to work for *L'Illustration*. Maurizio Corgnati, *Soldati e pittori nel Risorgimento Italiano* (Milan: Fabbri Editore, 1987), 229.

2 I am grateful to the curators of the Museo del Risorgimento in Turin for their identification of Morelli.

3 See the discussion of Morelli's election in the *Gazzetta di Bergamo* 48, no. 15 (2 February 1861): front page: "In questi giorni, alcuni tristi vanno insinuando alle orecchie dei creduli, che Morelli per principio politico avversa l'unità italiana. Ed è questa una di quelle raffinate calunnie che entrano facili nella mente di tutti ..."

4 A list of the twenty-two boards on which Morelli served during his first term, prepared for his re-election in 1865 for the Bergamo electorate, reveals the extent of his dedication. In 1861 he was a member of a committee that extended conscription to 18,000 Neapolitans; he made his important three-month journey in the spring to the Marche and Umbria to list every notable work

of art; and by September was on the jury for the 1861 *Esposizione di Firenze* and vice-president for the section on painting, drawing, and printmaking. In 1862 he investigated extraordinary expenses for the budget of 1861 from the Ministry of War, and served on a committee to recognize military pensions conferred by the government of Sicily in 1848. In 1863 he served on committees or boards that evaluated treasury spending: supervised bridges; managed the transport of the Archivio Palatino to Modena; evaluated the stipends of professors in Naples; and arranged the agricultural industrial exhibition in Naples. In 1864 he spent four months on a commission of senators and deputies to recommend to parliament reforms to Italian education. In 1864 he worked with Massimo d'Azeglio and Professor Mongeri to formulate laws for the conservation of works of art. In that year he contributed to commissions relating to the postal service; the transfer of parliament to Florence; an enquiry to disallow inheritance; and many more to his credit.

5 Giovanni Morelli (at Rome) to Austen Henry Layard, 5 June 1874, Add. MSS 38963.British Library, London.

6 Cletto Arrighi [Carlo Righetti], *I 450 deputati del presente e i deputati dell'avvenire per una società di egregi uomini politici, letterati e giornalisti diretta da Cletto Arrighi*, vol. 6 (Milan: Presso gli Editori, e presso l'ufficio della Cronaca Grigia, 1865), 177–81.

7 Morelli thanks Pasino Locatelli, who in 1864 was shepherding his re-election, for sending him the *opuscolo* by Arrighi. Giovanni Morelli to Pasino Locatelli, 14 August 1864, 35 R 5, Biblioteca Civica Angelo Mai, Bergamo.

8 With the notable exception of Telesforo Sarti, who copies much of this source in his authoritative dictionary *Il parlamento subalpino e nazionale: Profili e cenni biografici di tutti i deputati e senatori eletti e creati dal 1848 al 1890* (Terni: Tipografia Editrice dell'Industria, 1890), 683–84.

9 Arrighi [Righetti], *I 450 deputati*, 180.

10 Arrighi [Righetti], *I 450 deputati*, 179–80.

11 Sarti, *Il Parlamento subalpino e nazionale*, 684.

12 Giovanni Morelli (at Bellagio) to Niccolò Antinori, 25 September 1864, Archivio Antinori, Florence: "Con tutte le belle anzi le splendide qualità letterarie e parlamentari di cui è fornito, manca però alla mente sua quel nerbo che è il fondamento d'animo virile. Il Minghetti non è uomo di stato; è leggiero di carattere come una bimba, e sopra ogni cosa che ha a trattare non può a meno di metterci lo zucchero delle illusioni."

13 *Genealogia degli Acton a cura di Ferdinando e Francesco E. Acton in ricordo del loro padre Alfredo Acton che raccolse dati e documenti della famiglia alla storia della quale aggiunse Gloria e prestigio con la sua mente e le sue opere* (Naples: privately printed, 1969). My thanks to Peter Acton for granting me access to this source.

14 Walburga Paget, *Embassies of Other Days and Further Recollections*, vol. 1 (London: Hutchinson, 1923), 226–87.

15 Paget, *Embassies of Other Days*, 227.

16 Giovanni Morelli to Niccolò Antinori, 20 July 1873, reprinted in Giacomo Agosti, "Giovanni Morelli corrispondente di Niccolò Antinori," in *Studi e ricerche di collezionismo e museografia, Firenze 1820–1920*, Quaderni del Seminario di Storia della Critica d'Arte 2 (Pisa: Scuola Normale Superiore di Pisa, 1985), 56.

17 Giovanni Morelli to Niccolò Antinori, 3 July 1880, reprinted in Agosti, "Giovanni Morelli corrispondente di Niccolò Antinori," 74.

18 Giovanni Morelli (at Rome) to Franz von Lenbach, 18 March 1879. Morelli's letters to Lenbach are held in a private collection in Cologne; photocopies are in MS MMB 993/4, Biblioteca Civica Angelo Mai, Bergamo.

19 Giovanni Morelli to Jean Paul Richter, undated, November 1881, Bibliotheca Hertziana, Rome.

20 Giovanni Morelli, "Discussione del disegno di legge concernente il trasporto della Pinacoteca di Torino dal Palazzo Madama al Palazzo dei Musei," in *Atti del Parlamento Italiano: Sessione del 1861–1862*, ed. Giuseppe Galletti and Paolo Trompeo, *Discussioni della Camera dei Deputati* (Florence: Botta, 1882), 3413–23.

21 Giovanni Morelli (at Turin) to Niccolò Antinori, 19 July 1861: "la storia dell'arte, come viene insegnata in Italia, non serve che a riempire la testa dei giovani di nomi cui non corrisponde concetto alcuno. Converrebbe, se mai, insegnar loro la storia dell'arte di faccia alle opere dei grandi maestri, dei quali tiensi loro discorso."

22 "Penetrato quale sono già da molto tempo del sacro dovere che incombe ad un governo nazionale di tutelare seriamente, e assai più di quanto fu fatto fino al giorno d'oggi, quel preziosissimo patrimonio che ci lasciavano i gloriosi nostri avi in opera di mosaico, scultura, cesellatura, niello, in affreschi, nonché in tavole e tele dipinte ecc.—io non potevo se non accogliere con animo lietissimo e molta soddisfazione quell'invito fattomi." Published in Jaynie Anderson, "Giovanni Morelli, museologo del Risorgimento," in *Giovanni Morelli: Collezionista di disegni: La donazione al Castello Sforzesco*, ed. Giulio Bora (catalogue of exhibition at the Castello Sforzesco, Milan, 9 November 1994 – 8 January 1995), (Milan: Silvana, 1994), 38–39.

23 Giovanni Morelli and Giovanni Battista Cavalcaselle, "Catalogo delle opere d'arte nelle Marche e nell'Umbria," in *Le gallerie nazionali italiane: Notizie e documenti*, ed. Adolfo Venturi, year 2 (Rome: Ministero della Pubblica Istruzione,1894–95), 191–349.

24 Giovanni Morelli (at Ascoli Piceno) 1861, quoted by Margherita Ginoulhiac, "Giovanni Morelli (Lermolieff): La vita, l'opera, il metodo critico," *Bergomum* 14 (1940): 55.

25 Giovanni Morelli to Niccolò Antinori, 16 October 1857, Archivio Antinori, Florence.

26 Giovanni Morelli to Otto Mündler, 20 June 1866, cited in Rolf Kultzen, "Giovanni Morelli als Briefpartner von Otto Mündler," *Zeitschrift für Kunstgeschichte* 52 (1989): 398–99: "Cavalcaselle, der mürrische Laienbruder ist hier—und hat mich gestern aufgesucht; ich kann aber leider vorderhand nichts für ihn thun."

27 Susanne Müller-Bechtel, *Die Zeichnung als Forschungsinstrument: Giovanni Battista Cavalcaselle (1819–1897) und seine Zeichnungen zur Wandmalerei in Italien vor 1550* (Munich: Deutscher Kunstverlag, 2009), 7–22.

28 Joseph Archer Crowe, *Reminiscences of Thirty-Five Years of My Life* (London: John Murray, 1895), 87–88.

29 For the full text, with reproductions of every work of art listed, see Jaynie Anderson, ed., *I taccuini manoscritti di Giovanni Morelli*, Marche Disperse 1 (Milan: Federico Motta, 2000).

30 Valentina Locatelli, "Italian Painters, Critical Studies of their Works: The Gemäldegalerie Alte Meister in Dresden. An overview of Giovanni Morelli's attributions," *Journal of Art Historiography* 13 (December 2015): 1–22, https://arthistoriography.wordpress.com/13-dec15/.

31 Giovanni Morelli to Niccolò Antinori, 8 May 1862, Archivio Antinori, Florence. "Il Matteucci me l'ha fatta grossa—sebbene non dubiti ch'egli non si sapesse neppure quel [che] facesse quando presentò quel decreto alla firma del Re ... È un decreto, firmato dal Re il 21 Aprile p.p., per cui i libri e gli oggetti di belle arti già appartenenti alle case religiose e collegiate soppresse nell'Umbria resteranno proprietà del Comune in cui si trovano. Ecco con un sol tratto di penna del Re distrutto quell'indefesso mio lavoro di 68 giorni consecutivi—nel quale io avea posto tanto amore e che avea condotto a termine coll'intimo convincimento d'aver reso un servizio al mio paese—sebbene neppur un cane non me n'abbia ringraziato ... Ma ciò non importa—quel che importa è che con quel decreto Matteucci sono condannate a perdita sicura molte opere di grandissima importanza per la storia dell'arte italiana ... Prima di tutto quel decreto è incostituzionale—né il Pepoli [Gioacchino Pepoli, allora commissario generale dell'Umbria], né il consiglio Provinciale dell'Umbria, e nemmeno il Governo del Re hanno facoltà di disporre a lor talento dei beni della Nazione—questa prerogativa spetta al solo Parlamento. In secondo luogo non ci poteva [essere] nulla di più contrario alla sapienza per non dir altro, come un dono siffatto. E perché limitare gli slanci di generosità ai soli libri e oggetti d'arte? Non vedo ragione perché anco le terre di quei conventi soppressi non abbiano ad essere regalate a quei Comuni? Delle terre almeno quei Comunisti ne saprebbero che farsene—de' quadri antichi no certo, se non se, col tempo e coll'astuzia convertirli in oro straniero. Dopo un precedente di questa natura tutti i Comuni Italiani dove troveransi conventi soppressi o da sopprimersi vorranno naturalmente godere di un egual privilegio.
"A morte dunque i nostri bei sogni di fondare costì una Galleria veramente Nazionale! Non so dirti quanto io sia inviperito contro quello scimunito del Matteucci ... Povera Italia, da che razza d'uomini ha sempre ad essere governata."

32 Prefettura della Provincia di Bergamo, No. 10748-1397 P. Circolare no. 21.

33 Cristina Giannini, "Giovanni Morelli e il Conte Suardo," in *Giovanni Morelli e la cultura dei conoscitori*, Atti del Convegno Internazionale, Bergamo, 4–7 giugno 1987, vol. 1, ed. Giacomo Agosti (Bergamo: Pierluigi Lubrina, 1993), 199–220.

34 Giovanni Secco Suardo, *Il ristauratore dei dipinti*, vol. 2 (Milan: Hoepli, 1894), 293ff, 307ff. The archive of the Suardo family remains in the family castle at Lurano, and is the most important existing source for our understanding of nineteenth-century conservation. A nucleus of letters from Morelli to Suardo dates from 1864, addressed to the Conte *amabilissimo e carissimo*.

35 Associazione Giovanni Secco Suardo, Archivio Storico Nazionale e Banca Dati dei Restauratori Italiani, ASSL (Archivio Secco Suardo Lurano), Censimento, 80, 1.2–54, a–9.

36 Giovanni Morelli (at Bellagio) to Francesco De Sanctis, 18 September 1862. The full text is published in Jaynie Anderson, "Giovanni Morelli, museologo del Risorgimento," in *Giovanni Morelli: Collezionista di disegni*, 38–39.

37 J. C. Robinson, *Italian Sculpture of the Middle Ages and Period of the Revival of Art. A Descriptive Catalogue of the Works ...* (London: South Kensington Museum, 1862), introduction.

38 For a fuller account, see Anderson, "Giovanni Morelli, museologo del Rinascimento," 25–39.

39 He did not fulfil these commissions.

40 Morelli to De Sanctis, 18 September 1862.

41 Giuseppe Molteni to Giovanni Morelli, 12 November 1862, quoted in full in Jaynie Anderson, *The Restoration of Renaissance Painting in Mid Nineteenth-Century Milan: Giuseppe Molteni in Correspondence with Giovanni Morelli*, Teoria e Storia del Restauro 20 (Florence: Edizioni Edifir, 2014), 49–50.

42 Giuseppe Mongeri, "La porta nella via de' Bossi in Milano," *La Perseveranza*, 5 and 7 November 1862 and 17 June 1863; Giuseppe Mongeri, "Un'ultima parola intorno alla porta dei Bossi," *La Perseveranza*, 27 January 1864.

43 Giuseppe Bertini to J. C. Robinson, 30 January 1863, Fasc. 48, Papers of J. C. Robinson, Department of Western Art, Ashmolean Museum, Oxford: "Comincio dal dirvi che voi avete male capito o male interpretato ciò che vi diceva nella mia lettera riguardo alla porta de' Medici. Vi avevo detto che speravo farla comperare al nostro futuro Museo—ed ora il Museo è fondato ed io formo parte della Direzione. Questo monumento dunque, non partirà certamente da Milano; e neppure le bellissime terre cotte del Caradosso—a tal uopo furono già fatte delle trattative. A proposito di Museo, essendo, noi componenti la direzione, affatto novi in questa partita, desidereremmo sapere da voi se il vostro Museo ha uno Statuto—e se esiste, mi fareste un regalo a spedirmene tosto una copia, sotto fascia, per la posta." No other part of the correspondence between Bertini and Robinson exists, at least among Robinson's papers, suggesting that they may have been laundered of any reference to personal dealing, a practice applied to the papers of many nineteenth-century art historians.

44 Jean Paul Richter to Austen Henry Layard, 5 March 1890, Add. MSS 39045, British Museum, London: "The Italian Ministry of Public Instruction has summoned me to appear at the Tribunale of Venice for having sent out there the Malaspina monument in 1886. You recollect perhaps that you had recommended it to Mr Armstrong. It is now in the South Kensington Museum. On February 27th the case had to come on, but I obtained postponement until March 27, as only a few day's time had been given me to prepare the defense. In Venice, I had to go through the very numerous documents collected by the prosecution, with the result of finding, that all the requirements of old and new laws, Austrian as well as Italian, had been fulfilled by me. Comm. Leopoldo Brizio, my *solicitor* wrote to me: 'credo di potermi ripromettere con buon fondamento un felice esito, parendomi che risulta evidente la di lei buona fede e la linea condotta correttissima da lei tenuta.' The monument had been bought by me for fr. 6,000 and the Italians evidently intend to get out of me double that money for having sent out those sculptures 'occultandone la vera consistenza ed eludendo la vigilanza della Commissione governativa.' But the Accademia delle Belle Arti at Verona had declared to the Prefetto that the monument was not worth keeping, and among the deeds collected by the prosecution are the very certificates of the Accademia of Venice for the shipment of all the cases. "I have applied for protection in proper quarters in London. Lord Salisbury has telegraphed about the matter to Lord Dufferin. An Italian version of my memorandum on the merits of this case has been given to Signor Crispi by Lord Dufferin, who told me the other day that he hopes to have the case settled amicably. If not I shall return to Venice a few days before the trial comes on. Prof. Helbig in Rome of the Imperial Archaeological Institute, Prof. Rodolfo Lanciani and others have of late been annoyed with similar lawsuits." Richter's reputation with the British was that he had always been dishonest in the art market.

45 Archive of the National Gallery, London.

46 Giovanni Morelli (at Bergamo) to Sir James Hudson, 26 November 1867, Archive of the late Piero Malvezzi, Milan: "Boxall è un eccellente galantuomo e finissimo conoscitore e apprezzatore del Bello nell'arte—io ritengo il suo gusto più squisito ancora di quello del defunto Sir Charles—ma egli non conosce le scuole pittoriche nostre, né apprezza punto la parte storica di un'opera d'arte. Per queste ragioni io l'ho per meno adatto del Sir Eastlake al posto di Direttore della Galleria Nazionale di Londra. Inoltre è uomo troppo meticoloso: si lascierà sfuggire le migliori occasioni." For a later reassessment, see Michael Levey, "A Little-known Director: Sir William Boxall," *Apollo*, no. 159 (May 1975): 354–59.

47 Morelli's correspondence with Visconti Venosta begins, rather formally, in 1863; his letters to Venosta from 19 May 1863 until 21 October 1889 are in the archive of the Fondazione Cavour at Santena.

48 As confirmed by a *carta da visita* that he gave to Morelli. For a perceptive portrait of Visconti Venosta as a diplomat, see Federico Chabod, *Italian Foreign Policy: The Statecraft of the Founders, 1870–1896*, trans. William McCuaig (Princeton: Princeton University Press, 1996), 467–95.

49 Morelli complimented Emilio on the publication as being one of the best, in which the author's ideas are clearly explained: "… fra i molti articoli tedeschi sul libro del Lermolieff non ve ne sia alcuni in cui le idee dell'autore siano esposte con tant'ordine, fedeltà e chiarezza come nel bellissimo articolo di E. Visc. Venosta," Giovanni Morelli to Emilio Visconti Venosta, 14 August 1884, Fondazione Cavour, Santena. Visconti Venosta would write one of the most informative obituaries of Morelli (published in *L'Illustrazione*), based on an unpublished manuscript account of his life.

50 Giovanni Morelli to Emilio Visconti Venosta, 3 August 1888, quoted in Giovanni Morelli, *Della pittura italiana: Studii storico-critici di Giovanni Morelli (Ivan Lermolieff). Le Gallerie Borghese e Doria Pamphili in Roma*, ed. Jaynie Anderson (Milan: Adelphi, 1991), 424.

51 Gianpaolo Angelini, *La patria e le arti: Emilio Visconti Venosta patriota, collezionista e conoscitore* (Pisa: Edizioni ETS, 2013).

52 "Chi dobbiamo eleggere?" *Gazzetta di Bergamo* (24 December 1864): 2.

53 See Morelli's lengthy and reflective letter to Pasino Locatelli, written at "Taronico, presso Bellagio" on 20 September 1865, MSS 35 R, Biblioteca Civica Angelo Mai, Bergamo.

54 Morelli to Locatelli, 20 September 1865: "Io sono l'unico protestante, almeno di nascita, che ebbe l'onore

di sedere al Parlamento e che trovasi forse fra i nuovi candidati. Ora, le questioni principali intorno alle quali un candidato dovrà manifestare l'opinione sua agli Elettori sono quelle di Venezia e di Roma. So bene che di quest'ultima pure un candidato assennato parlerà da uomo politico e non da teologo o da filosofo—ma in tutto ciò a molti Elettori la cosa potrebbe forse sapere assai di strano, il sentirsi cioè parlare da un protestante della questione romana, e chi non mi conosce a fondo sarebbe forse condotto a sospettarmi o furbo o illiberale, e in tutti i modi poco sincero. Ed io invero so di non essere né l'uno né l'altro. Per l'ultima mi permetta di farle un'altra confessione. Le due prime nomine a deputato mi giunsero proprio affatto inaspettate. Io in coscienza sentivo di non meritarmi per nulla un sì alto onore. L'ho riguardato come un dovere impostomi della nazione ed io ho fatto quanto stava in me per compiere il mandato affidatomi dai miei Elettori. Ora, dopo una prova di cinque anni devo confessare ch'io non sono punto tagliato per fare degnamente e utilmente il deputato politico. Mi ci mancano troppe cognizioni, mi ci manca il dono della parola, mi ci manca la nobile ambizione di voler essere qualche cosa a questo mondo. Per questo non è ch'io voglia presentarmi a Lei privo d'amor proprio—anzi, senza ch'io glielo dica, Ella può immaginarsi come io dovrei riputarmi fortunato di potere assistere al trionfo finale della Causa italiana e continuare ad adoperarmi per contribuirvi in quella misura che le poche mie forze me lo consentirebbero."

55 Giovanni Morelli (at Florence) to Pasino Locatelli, 29 November 1865, MS 35, R 5, Biblioteca Civica Angelo Mai, Bergamo.

Notes to Chapter 8: Creating Modern Italy

1 Aristide Caimi, *In Valtellina: Chiaroscuri* (Milan: Presso Giuseppe Bernardoni di Gio., 1858).

2 Aristide Caimi, *Giornale delle operazioni di guerra eseguite dalla legione di guardia nazionale mobile a difesa dello Stelvio e Tonale nella campagna del 1866 redatto da Aristide Caimi già Capitano Aiutante Maggiore in primo della Legione* (Turin: Tipografia G. Cassone, 1868), 36.

3 Giovanni Morelli (at the roadhouse at Stelvio) to Giovanni Battista Camozzi Vertova, Fondo Risorgimento italiano, Sala 24, Cassa 1, Faldone 28, no. 413, Biblioteca Civica Angelo Mai, Bergamo: "Dai posti avanzati fra la 1a e 2a Cantoniera dello Stelvio, 18 Luglio 1866. Caro amico—L'altroieri fecero un tentativo d'attacco; la fucilata, accompagnata da razzi, durò dalle 4 a.m. fino dopo il mezzodì; vennero scacciati e sloggiati dovunque dai nostri cannoni diretti con una maestria straordinaria. Ebbero vari feriti—noi nessuno, e pare proprio un miracolo. Ti prego a volere mandare *quotidianamente* per telegrafo le notizie del giorno al nostro Colonnello E. Guicciardi a Bormio, poiché il Ministero della Guerra non che il Quartier Generale, ci trattano da Corpo abbandonato; è una vergogna!"

4 Giovanni Morelli (at Bormio) to Niccolò Antinori, 23 August 1866, Archivio Antinori, Florence.

5 Giovanni Morelli to Niccolò Antinori, 2 September 1866, Archivio Antinori, Florence.

6 Aristide Caimi to Giovanni Morelli, 7 October 1866. Caimi's letters to Morelli from 1866 to 1869 are in the Archivio Zavaritt, Gorle.

7 This included introducing Caimi to the very beautiful Lady Virginia Somers, with whom Caimi promenaded through Venice on his first visit there in January 1867 while collecting material for his writing.

8 *Giornale delle operazioni di guerra eseguite dalla legione di guardia nazionale mobile a difesa dello Stelvio e Tonale nella campagna del 1866 redatto da Aristide Caimi già Capitano Aiutante Maggiore in primo della legione. Seconda edizione corredata da documenti aggiunti dal già comandante della legione, Senatore Enrico Guicciardi* (Rome: Tipografia dell'Opinione, 1881).

9 Giovanni Morelli to Niccolò Antinori, letter quoted above, 4 November 1866: "A Venezia mi trovai alloggiato sul Canale Grande in compagnia di molti Inglesi, l'entusiasmo dei quali per quanto vedevano o credevano vedere, mi divertì assai. Fra questi v'erano anche i nostri amici Layard e Lady Burr Highford [*sic*], v'era il generale Cadogan, tanto pericoloso ai nemici che alle donne, v'era una Miss Ross, gran domatrice di cavalli, un bel capo ameno, e v'erano infine Lord e Lady Sommers [*sic*], due amabilissime e care persone, che certo avrebbero rubato a te pure il cuore. Per il giorno 28 s'aspettava in quell'albergo Lord John Russell e famiglia, cui Layard voleva assolutamente presentarmi, ma per molte ragioni trovai ch'era tempo di tornarmene a casa e partii da piazza S. Marco."

10 Anderson, *Collecting, Connoisseurship*, 87.

11 Anderson, *Collecting, Connoisseurship*, 114.

12 Anderson, *Collecting, Connoisseurship*, 150.

13 Anderson, *Collecting, Connoisseurship*, 157.

14 Austen Henry Layard, Introduction to Morelli, *Italian Painters ... The Borghese and Doria Pamfili Galleries in Rome*, 35

15 Anderson, *Collecting, Connoisseurship*, 172–73.

16 See Anderson in the exhibition catalogue *Renaissance: 15th & 16th Century Italian Paintings from the Accademia Carrara, Bergamo*, ed. Ron Radford, Giovanni Valagussa, Jaynie Anderson, Attilio Pizzigoni, and David Wise (Canberra: National Gallery of Australia, 2011), 142; and also the lengthy catalogue entry by Giovanni Valagussa in his *Accademia Carrara, Bergamo: Dipinti italiani del Trecento e del Quattrocento: Catalogo completo* (Milan: Officina Libraria, 2018), 314–19, n. III.24.

17 For a detailed account of the collection that Morelli formed for Arconati, which is now mainly in the Louvre,

see Anderson, "Giovanni Morelli et la collection Arconati-Visconti," *La Revue du Louvre et des Musées de France* 40, no. 3 (1990): 205–11.

18 Anderson, *Collecting, Connoisseurship*, 65–67.

19 There were two major catalogues of the collection: *Catalogo de' quadri, sculture in marmo, musaici, pietre colorate, bronzi ed altri oggetti di belle arti esistenti nella Galleria del Sagro Monte di Pietà di Roma* (Rome: Gigli, December 1857) and another in 1875.

20 Morelli's letters to Melli were published in Jaynie Anderson, *Collecting, Connoisseurship and the Art Market in Risorgimento Italy: Giovanni Morelli's Letters to Giovanni Melli and Pietro Zavaritt (1866–1872)* (Venice: Istituto Veneto, 1999).

21 Giovanni Morelli (at Milan) to Jean Paul Richter, 22 April 1878, Bibliotheca Hertziana, Rome.

22 See the remarkable publication after the portrait's restoration at the Opificio delle Pietre Dure, Florence: Cecilia Frosinini and Maria Cristina Rodeschini, eds, *Il ritratto di Leonello d'Este* (Florence: Edifir), 2016. Subsequently a different date (1441–44) has been proposed by Valentina Locatelli in Valagussa, *Accademia Carrara, Bergamo: Dipinti italiani*, 232–37.

23 Burckhardt, "Die Gemälde des Senators Giovanni Morelli in Bergamo," reported by his pupil, Albert Gessler, *Basle National-Zeitung*, 26 March 1892.

24 Giovanni Morelli to Giovanni Melli, 28 January and 14 February 1871, in Anderson, *Collecting, Connoisseurship*, 99, 106.

25 Anderson, *Collecting, Connoisseurship*, 91, 99–101, 133.

26 Federico Zeri and Francesco Rossi, *La raccolta Morelli nell'Accademia Carrara* (Milan: Amilcare Pizzi, 1986), 197–98.

27 For a full account, see Anderson, *Collecting, Connoisseurship*, where a more extensive documentation of these events is presented, especially pp. 24–31.

28 Published in Anderson, *Collecting, Connoisseurship*, 197–206.

29 Adolfo Venturi, *Memorie autobiografiche* (Milan: Hoepli, 1911), 39–40; Adolfo Venturi, "Unbekannte oder vergessene Künstler der Emilia," *Jahrbuch der Königlich Preussischen Kunstsammlungen* 11 (1890): 183–94.

30 Venturi also visited Morelli's home with the senator himself (Donata Levi, "Appunti su Corrado Ricci e la sua attività museografica," in *Corrado Ricci: Storico dell'arte tra esperienza e progetto*, ed. Andrea Emiliani and Donatino Domini (Ravenna: Longo Editore, 2004), 51–63).

31 Giovanni Morelli (at Florence) to Pietro Zavaritt, 26 April 1869, Archivio Zavaritt, Gorle.

32 The three panels have been discussed together for the first time by Giovanni Valagussa in *Accademia Carrara, Bergamo: Dipinti italiani*, 79–82, who does not state that the three panels have the same provenance (the Monte di Pietà, Rome). The *Annunciation* in the Louvre also shares this provenance. Morelli was interested in the *Annunciation* to the extent that he asked for it to be copied. On 4 December 1885 Lady Layard recorded in her journal that "Henry arranged with the Director of the Louvre Mr Gruyer that I should go to his private room to copy a picture wh. he removed from the gallery on purpose for me. It is a small tiny picture an Annunciation with Lorenzo da Credi's name on the frame but wh. Morelli says is by Leonardo da Vinci," (Armstrong Browning Library, *The Brownings: A Research Guide*, Baylor University, Waco, Texas, 2001–14, https://pops.baylor.edu/layard/xml.php?fn=18851204.xml&h=Leonardo%). See also the catalogue of the exhibition held at the Palazzo Strozzi in Florence in 2019, curated by Francesco Caglioti and Andrea De Marchi, *Verrocchio, Master of Leonardo* (Venice: Marsilio Editori, 2019). Verrocchio's workshop, where Leonardo da Vinci had been apprenticed, has long been the subject of intense debate, most recently in a 2018 exhibition at the Worcester Art Museum, Massachusetts, where the museum's Miracle of St Donatus at Arezzo, together with an Annunciation from the Louvre, has been accredited to Leonardo da Vinci.

33 Giovanni Morelli (at Bellagio) to Niccolò Antinori, 16 September 1867: "O, amico mio, non ti so dire quanto infelice io mi senta; il centro di mia vita con lei è tramontato. Non v'ha più a questo mondo occhio che con amore seguirà i miei passi, voce cara e affettuosa che mi richiamerà a sé, e che mi offra il primo saluto quando rientrerò in casa mia, e che abbia sempre una buona parolina a darmi—o, l'affetto della mamma non lo ritroverò certo mai più!"

34 These included Morelli's old friend Francesco De Sanctis, who wrote: "La madre di Morelli è un'amabile e gentile signora, e m'ha accolto benissimo." Francesco De Sanctis to Diomede Marvasi, 19 August 1859, in Francesco De Sanctis, *Epistolario (1856–1858)*, ed. Giovanni Ferretti and Muzio Mazzocchi Alemanni (Turin: Einaudi, 1965), 86 (letter no. 446).

35 Austen Henry Layard to Giovanni Morelli, 15 July 1868, British Library, Add. MSS, 38,966.

36 Lady Eastlake (at Bellagio), diary note, 4 September 1864, in Elizabeth Eastlake and Charles Eastlake Smith, *Journals and Correspondence of Lady Eastlake* (London: John Murray, 1895), vol. 2, 187.

37 For an account of Lady Eastlake's ambitions after the death of her husband, and a questioning of her abilities, see Julie Sheldon, "'His Best Successor': Lady Eastlake and the National Gallery," in *Museums and Biographies: Stories, Objects, Identities*, ed. Kate Hill (London, Boydell & Brewer, 2012), 61–74.

38 My account is based on Morelli's letters to Layard, 16 August and 21 September 1868, Add. MSS 38,995, British Library, London.

39 *Katalog zur 1. Internationalen Kunstausstellung im Königlichen Glaspalaste zu München, Eröffnung am 20. Juli, Schluss am 31. Oktober 1869* (Munich: Verl. des Ausstellungscomités, 1869).

40 Giovanni Morelli (at Dresden) to Pietro Zavaritt, 5 September 1869, Archivio Zavaritt, Gorle.

41 Giovanni Morelli, statement to his electorate, *Gazzetta di Bergamo*, 13 November 1870, p. 1: "Ora in presenza delle prossime elezioni, due ragioni mi obbligano a ritirarmi dalla vita politica. La questione principale che il nuovo Parlamento italiano sarà chiamato a risolvere, è, non vi ha dubbio, la più grave, la più decisiva, che mai gli venisse posta innanzi. Si tratta di stabilire le nuove relazioni fra lo Stato e la Chiesa, non che di fissare le guarentigie da darsi al Pontefice. Ebbene, ammesso pure che ad alcuno di voi sia per amicizia personale, sia per una benevola consuetudine, non ripugnasse di confermarmi il suo voto anco questa volta, io per parte mia sento l'obbligo di dichiarare che non potrei accettare un mandato di tanta delicatezza, di tanta conseguenza. Nella questione romana, checché se non [ne] possa dire in contrario, è interessato il sentimento religioso della Nazione; e chi non appartiene al culto cattolico, scevro di pregiudizi egli si voglia reputare, a me pare non possa entrare giudice libero e autorevole in una quistione di tanto momento.
"Ma estrazione fatta dalla mia fede di battesimo, vi sono eziandio delle ragioni politiche che questa volta dovrebbero rendervi titubanti alla mia rielezione. Se è vero che nel 1860 io pure partecipai alla votazione di dichiarare Roma capitale d'Italia, egli è altresì vero che da quegli anni a questa parte molte speranze mi sono tramutate in illusioni. Allora sembravami che la forza magica della libertà avrebbe a provvedere a tutto, e che dopo un rivolgimento morale della Nazione il nostro ingresso nella Città eterna non sarebbe stato che il suggello della rigenerazione del paese nostro. Tolga il cielo che io voglia negare il grande e multiforme progresso dall'Italia fatto in questi ultimi dieci anni; ma questo progresso è se non m'inganno, più materiale che morale. A mio aviso però non è se non colle forze morali, col concorso vivo, costante, quotidiano di tutta quanta la Nazione che l'Italia potrebbe andare e sopratutto restare a Roma. Codeste forze morali ci sono? Chi potrebbe rispondere che coll'attuazione leale del principio della libera Chiesa in libero Stato o col trasferimento della Capitale a Roma, o il Papato non vi rimanga ucciso, o si arrivi al supremo dei Governi teocratici? Chi può desiderare qualunque di codesti partiti? Intimamente convinto che certe questioni morali non possano trovare la loro soluzione che dal tempo non saprei decidermi in modo alcuno di seguire il corso attuale degli eventi quale è imposto dalle passioni del momento."

42 Gustavo Frizzoni to William Boxall, 24 June 1871, NGA1/1/57/9, National Gallery Archive, London.

43 Giovanni Morelli (at Bergamo) to Niccolò Antinori, 24 September 1871, Florence, Archivio Antinori: "Codesti studi mi fanno passare piacevolmente le ore, mi fanno provare alle volte delle gioie purissime e trovare non di rado un salutare contraveleno alle amare disillusioni, di cui è pieno l'animo mio. Quest'Italia, che ho tanto amata da' miei anni giovanili fino il 20 Settembre dell'anno scorso, per cui avrei dato non una ma cento volte la mia vita, ora, lo dico con dolore, mi fa ribrezzo. Non conosco sentimento più umiliante, più triste di quello che ho provato io in mezzo agli stranieri ... mi vergognai della mia patria—ho passato due mesi di là dai monti senza mai affiatarmi con nessuno, e quante volte non mi s'affacciò il pensiero di ritirarmi in qualche cantuccio al lago di Ginevra e finire colà i miei giorni."

Notes to Chapter 9: A Friendship: Austen Henry Layard

1 For an earlier version of this chapter, see Jaynie Anderson, "Morelli and Layard," in *Austen Henry Layard tra l'Oriente e Venezia*, ed. Frederick Mario Fales and Bernard Hickey (Rome: "L'Erma" di Bretschneider, 1987), 109–37.

2 Layard's relationship with Morelli is charted in their lengthy though fragmentary exchange of letters, now in the Manuscripts Department in the British Library, London.

3 Sir Austen Henry Layard, "Introduction," in Giovanni Morelli, *Italian Painters: Critical Studies of their Works*, trans. Constance Jocelyn Ffoulkes, vol. 1: *The Borghese and Doria Pamfili Galleries in Rome* (London: John Murray, 1892), 1–39, part. 1, 10.

4 Now conveniently online: "Lady Layard's Journal," in Armstrong Browning Library and Museum, *The Brownings: A Research Guide* (Waco, Texas: Baylor University), http://www.browningguide.org/browningscircle.php.

5 Giovanni Morelli, *Italian Masters in German Galleries: A Critical Essay on the Italian Pictures in the Galleries of Munich, Dresden, Berlin, by Giovanni Morelli, Member of the Italian Senate. Translated from the German by Mrs Louise M. Richter* (London: George Bell and Sons, 1883).

6 Elizabeth, Lady Eastlake, to Austen Henry Layard, 22 February 1892, John Murray Archive, National Library of Scotland, Edinburgh.

7 John Fleming argues that although Layard was in Italy in 1855, 1856, and 1858, he is not known to have visited Turin until 1859, when he may have first met Morelli (John Fleming, "Art Dealing and the Risorgimento—I," *The Burlington Magazine* 115, no. 838 (1973): 7n33). In this he contradicts Adolfo Venturi, who states that they met in 1862, based on *notizie* supplied by Lady Layard, but unfortunately Molteni's letters to Layard are missing—Venturi's article shows that he had access to correspondence between Layard and dealers

that no longer survives (Adolfo Venturi, "La formazione della Galleria Layard a Venezia," *L'Arte* 15 (1912): 449–51).

8 Giovanni Morelli to Jean Paul Richter, 20 March 1878, in Irma Richter and Gisela Richter, eds, *Italienische Malerei der Renaissance: Im Briefwechsel von Giovanni Morelli und Jean Paul Richter 1876–1891* (Baden-Baden: Grimm, 1960), 36. The substance of this letter, which contains Morelli's view of the development of Sebastiano del Piombo, was edited and published by Richter in the same year, in a curious article in which he claims to be reporting a conversation with Lermolieff: Jean Paul Richter, ed., "Ueber Sebastiano del Piombo und Giulio Romano von Iwan Lermolieff," *Zeitschrift für bildende Kunst* 13 (1878), Beiblatt (supplement), cols 553–56.

9 Anderson, ed., *The Restoration of Renaissance Painting*, 49.

10 Giuseppe Molteni to Giovanni Morelli, 2 November 1862, cited in Anderson, ed., *The Restoration of Renaissance Painting*, 49: "Il Signor Layard mi portò un quadro da restaurare ch'io desidero mostrarvi e farvi emettere un giudizio sul medesimo che sebbene sia in possesso di un bel cartellino io lascerò a Voi a decifrare. Venite a tri a tri a tri-onfar!"

11 Molteni's subsequent letter of 12 November, 1862, indicates that Morelli was in difficulty; see Anderson, ed., *The Restoration of Renaissance Painting*, 49–50.

12 As Molteni reported to Layard: "Morelli non leggeva con certezza *Bastianus*, anche perché non si capacitava che il 'quadro tutto Cima' avesse 'a che fare con frate Sebastiano tutto giorgionesco a Venezia, tutto michelangiolesco a Roma'," quoted in Venturi, "La formazione della Galleria Layard," 450.

13 Giovanni Frizzoni, "La Galerie Layard," *Gazette des Beaux-Arts* 16, no. 2 (1896): 461; Georges Lafenestre and Eugène Richtenberger, *Venise* (Paris: Quantin, Librairies-Impremeries Réunis, 1896), 311.

14 Archive of the National Gallery, London, dossier on the painting.

15 Joseph Archer Crowe and Giovanni Battista Cavalcaselle, *A History of Painting in North Italy: Venice, Padua, Vicenza, Verona, Ferrara, Milan, Friuli, Brescia, from the Fourteenth to the Sixteenth Century*, vol. 3 (London: John Murrary, 1912), 204n2.

16 The signature was correctly deciphered by Georg Gronau; see Martin Davies, *National Gallery Catalogues. The Earlier Italian Schools* (London: National Gallery Publications, 1961), 130–32.

17 Morelli said that he would like to meet Layard again, and wrote to Molteni: "io lo assicurai, che dal canto suo non è minore la voglia," as summarized by Venturi in "La formazione della Galleria Layard," 451.

18 Add. MSS 38, 963, British Library, London. An edition of the correspondence was begun by the late Miss Sybille Pantazzi, and was inherited by Dr Madeline Lennon.

19 Fleming, "Art Dealing and the Risorgimento," 8.

20 See Layard's letters to his aunt, Mrs Austen, especially those of 12 August and 7 September 1856, in which he describes his tour of Lombardy and his discovery of many artists, reprinted in Austen Henry Layard, *Autobiography and Letters from his Childhood until His Appointment as H. M. Ambassador at Madrid*, vol. 2, ed. W. N. Bruce (New York: Scribner's, 1903), 209–10.

21 The best account of Layard's childhood is given by Gordon Waterfield, in *Layard of Nineveh* (London: John Murray, 1963), 13–14.

22 Layard, *Autobiography and Letters*, 208.

23 Gabriel Rossetti to William Allingham, Friday, n.d. April 1856, in Oswald Doughty and John Robert Wahl, eds, *The Letters of Dante Gabriel Rossetti* (Oxford: Clarendon Press, 1965), vol. 1, letter no. 240.

24 Rossetti to Allingham, n.d. April 1856.

25 Layard often attempted to introduce Morelli to his Italian friends, sometimes without success, as is shown in a letter from Conestabile to Layard: "Malheureusement je n'ai jamais pu faire connaissance personnelle de M. Morelli, qui je connais bien de nom. Par un malentendu, que je regrette toujours, l'année passée il a eu la bonté de venir chez moi un journée, et il n'a pas pu entrer, n'ayant pas voulu laisser sa carte. J'espère d'avoir l'occasion de le voir, et de causer avec lui [...] C'est un de nos plus grands connaisseurs," Giovanni Carlo Conestabile (at Livorno) to Austen Henry Layard, 26 September 1868, Add. MSS 38, 995, British Library, London.

26 See the excellent account of Layard's activities for the Arundel Society, in Tanya Ledger, "A Study of the Arundel Society 1848–1897," (PhD thesis, University of Oxford, 1978), 74–77. See also her discussion of some of the chromolithographs published by the Arundel Society, in Christopher Lloyd, ed., *Art and its Images: An Exhibition of Printed Books Containing Engraved Illustrations After Italian Painting*, exhibition catalogue (Oxford: Bodleian Library, 1975), 121–33. Robyn Cooper gives a more general appraisal of Layard's role in the society in "The Popularization of Renaissance Art in Victorian England: The Arundel Society," *Art History* 1, no. 3 (1978): 263–92. Layard was not involved in the society at its inception, nor were his copies after Italian frescoes commissioned, although they were later to become of great importance for the society.

27 See Layard's own article, "Fresco-Painting," *Quarterly Review* (October 1858), partly reprinted in Layard, *Autobiography and Letters*, vol. 2, 204–6.

28 Austen Henry Layard to Giovanni Morelli, 30 November 1863, Add. MSS 38, 966, British Library, London.

29 Austen Henry Layard to Giovanni Morelli, 5 December 1864, Add. MSS 38, 966, British Library, London.

30 On 12 August 1865 Layard wrote to Morelli to ask for information about the Luini frescoes at Saronno, because the Arundel Society had asked him to write an introduction to its publication. On 6 September 1865 Morelli sent Layard some material, but it was insufficient, and nothing came of it (Add. MSS 38, 966 and Add. MSS 38, 963, British Library, London).

31 Layard's letter to Morelli from Ca' Capello, Venice, 8 January 1891, is not among the Layard papers at the British Library. It was enclosed by Morelli in a letter to his friend in Bergamo, Conte G. B. Camozzi Vertova, now in Sala 24, Cassa 1, Faldone 28, no. 413, fondo Risorgimento italiano, Biblioteca Civica Angelo Mai, Bergamo.

32 National Gallery, London: no. 1216, A–B.

33 National Gallery, London: no. 3074.

34 Austen Henry Layard (at Bologna) to John Murray, 25 September 1856, John Murray Archive, London (now at National Library of Scotland, Edinburgh).

35 Francesco Saverio Cavallari is mentioned by Otto Mündler in his travel diary on 20 January 1856, fol. 24: "Went to dine with Cavaliere Molteni, made the acquaintance of another member of the Academy, Professore di Archeologia, Cavallari, a Sicilian, who comunicates to me most interesting and important notices on Sicilian artists, and a Florentine, Venetian and other pictures to be found in Sicily, in the Abruzzi ecc."

36 Layard to Murray, 25 September 1856.

37 Charles Eastlake to Austen Henry Layard, 24 October 1860, John Murray Archive.

38 Dillian Gordon, *The Fifteenth Century Italian Paintings*, National Gallery Catalogues (London: Yale University Press, 2003), 296–309.

39 National Gallery, London: Pisanello no. 776; Bono da Ferrara no. 771; Cosimo Tura no. 773.

40 Molteni reported this in a letter from Milan on 3 December 1860 to Morelli, whom he addresses as "caro e poi caro il mio amato Morellissimo." See Anderson, *The Restoration of Renaissance Painting*, 43–44.

41 *St George and a Female Saint*, no. 3079, acquired from "the Grimani family at Venice, purchased from the dealer, Richetti," according to Layard's notes in the National Gallery, London.

42 Quoted by Waterfield in *Layard of Nineveh*, 304n.

43 "Che sfortuna, è proprio un vero peccato che non sia per la nostra Pinacoteca, giacché in essa non abbiamo di questo nostro valentissimo artista che l'affresco da lui eseguito appena ritornato da Roma, e purtroppo già il nostro bravo artista incominciava a lasciarsi andare ad una maniera più moderna, più floscia e più leziosa," quoted by Venturi in "La formazione della Galleria Layard," 450.

44 Austen Henry Layard to Giovanni Morelli, 30 November 1863, Add. MSS 38, 966, British Library, London: "Je retiendrai toujours le souvenir le plus agréable de ma trop courte visite [à Bergamo …] N'oubliez pas, je vous en prie, mon désir de posséder quelque morceau de vôtre école Bergamasque. M. Mündler a eu la bonté de me céder une fort belle tête du Christ par Previtale qu'il a trouvé chez le pharmacien pendant sa dernière visite à Bergamo."

45 *Salvator Mundi*, National Gallery, London: no. 3087.

46 Giovanni Morelli to Austen Henry Layard, 20 February 1864, Add. MSS 38, 963, British Library, London: "Per l'autunno prossimo io vorrei sperare caro Signor Layard, di poterle fare acquistare alcune altre cose dei nostri pittori lombardi."

47 Giovanni Morelli to Austen Henry Layard, 26 December 1864, Add. MSS 38, 963, British Library, London: "[…] après de longues négociations je lui ai fait l'offert de 4,000 francs pour le beau portrait de Moretto (dit de Morone et évalué 8,000 francs) et de 2,500 francs pour le charmant petit tableau sur bois du même maître, et représentant la Vierge avec l'Enfant Jésus, et S. François et S. Antoine en tout donc 6,500 francs. M. Averoldi s'est obligé de maintenir ce contrat pout tout le mois de Janvier. Or c'est vous à le sanctionner. Le petit tableau de Moretto a en quelques parts des couleurs soulevées, mais c'est un mal facilement réparable—du reste c'est une belle composition et l'œuvre dite, il me semble, de la plus charmante époque du grand maître, c'est à dire de 1530 à 1540; on l'avait évalué 5,000 francs et je sais positivement que M. Averoldi a plusieurs fois refusé 2,000 francs que lui ont été offerts par des marchands de tableaux. Quant au portrait de Moretto on l'a un peu trop nettoyé et il lui faudrait un peu de patina. Molteni s'en chargerait de cela."

48 The painting, dubiously attributed to Romanino, is National Gallery, London: no. 3093.

49 "Mais soyez tranquille, cette Sainte ne nous échappera pas—Lechi est vieux, il a 88 ans, et tôt ou tard il voudra lui aussi payer le tribut à la nature, et alors il sera plus facile d'acheter." Giovanni Morelli to Austen Henry Layard, 19 May 1865, Add. MSS 38, 963, British Library, London.

50 See Fausto Lechi, *I quadri della Collezione Lechi in Brescia* (Florence: Olschki, 1968), 166, no. 7, among the anonymous works: "Santa Caterina della ruota. Mezza figura. In legno, m. 0.73 × 0.51. Mostra S. Caterina d'esser rassegnata ai voleri dell'Altissimo. Tiene essa nella mano sinistra la palma, simbolo del martirio. Ricco abito verde guarnito d'oro, con manto color simile." In later inventories it was attributed to Callisto Piazza da Lodi. Morelli delighted in dramatically baptizing anonymous works hanging in dark corners of private collections, and this was probably what happened when he visited the Lechi collection. Layard, who was always

after a bargain, may have hoped to obtain the painting cheaply. Fleming surmised that the Lechi panel was bequeathed, many years later, by Gustavo Frizzoni to the Museo Poldi Pezzoli, Milan (Fleming, "Art Dealing and the Risorgimento," 8n47), but unfortunately the measurements do not correspond. Most scholars now consider it a variant of a more famous autograph work, Lotto's *St Catherine of Alexandria*, National Gallery of Art, Washington, D. C.

51 Giovanni Morelli to Austen Henry Layard, 3 January 1866, Add. MSS 38, 963, British Library, London; see also Layard's acceptance, 1 February 1866, Add. MSS 38, 966.

52 Giuseppe Molteni to Giovanni Morelli, 25 October 1865, in Anderson, ed., *The Restoration of Renaissance Painting*, 56–57.

53 For the first evaluation of the high quality of the *Cristo dolente*, see Everett Fahy in *Botticelli nelle collezioni lombarde*, exhibition catalogue (Milan: Museo Poldi Pezzoli, 2010) 80–82; also Anderson in *The Restoration of Renaissance Painting*, 150, and Valentina Locatelli, in Jaynie Anderson et al., *Renaissance: 15th & 16th Century Italian Paintings from the Accademia Carrara, Bergamo*, exhibition catalogue (Canberra: National Gallery of Australia, 2011), 82–86.

54 Giuseppe Molteni to Giovanni Morelli, 25 June 1866, in Anderson, ed., *The Restoration of Renaissance Painting*, 59: "Al Battesimo di Cristo del Moretto, ci lavoro giorno e notte e pel tempo che avete avuto la degnazione di fissarmi il che significa comando, per me, sarà ultimato, dunque calcolateci pure."

55 Giuseppe Molteni to Giovanni Morelli, 25 February 1866, in Anderson, ed., *The Restoration of Renaissance Painting*, 59–60: "Il Principe era smanioso di avere il vostro Moretto, ma io lo distolsi subito da quell'idea dicendogli francamente che era vostra e che quindi *ghera su tanto de gatt* sia per l'Inghilterra sia per la Francia. L'unica città degna di possedere una simile preziosa gemma è la gran città di Bergamo." Molteni also informed Morelli that he had in his studio for restoration two portraits recently acquired by Sir W. R. Drake. One was Bronzino's portrait of Piero de' Medici, left by Drake to the National Gallery, London (no. 1323), in 1891.

56 Giovanni Morelli to Austen Henry Layard, 8 January 1865, Add. MSS 38, 963, British Library, London: "Pour mon goût Moretto c'est un des peintres les plus purs, les plus harmonieux, les plus nobles du seizième siècle et, j'ajoutera, l'un des peintres les plus originaux que je connaisse."

57 Austen Henry Layard to Giovanni Morelli, 6 September 1865, Add. MSS 38, 966, British Library, London: "Je ne connais pas de maître qui me fait plus de plaisir surtout dans ces tableaux *argentés*."

58 Giovanni Morelli to Austen Henry Layard, 21 October 1865, Add. MSS 38, 963, British Library, London: "Molteni trouve vôtre petit Moroni très beau, et il l'est effectivement. Nous avons donc décrété qu'il doit non seulement corriger le corps de ce jeune homme, qui semble emmailloté dans des langes, mais joindre à la partie supérieure du quadre trois doigts de toile, pour donner au tableau de plus justes proportions. Vous verrez que ce portrait vous ferà grand plaisir."

59 See Mina Gregori, *Giovan Battista Moroni: Tutte le opere* (Bergamo: Poligrafiche Bolis, 1975), 278–79.

60 Giovanni Morelli to Austen Henry Layard, 3 January 1865, Add. MSS 38, 963, British Library, London: "C'est un drôle d'homme que ce Molteni—doué, comme il est, d'un sentiment très fin pour l'art et passionné pour l'art ancien, c'est un restaurateur vraiment incomparable, mais élève de nos Académies il lui arrive ce qu'arrive souvent aussi a vôtre excellent directeur de la Galerie Nationale [Eastlake], c'est-à-dire de montrer parfois la guerre coordonnée de l'Académie, en voulant corriger les naives incorrections des anciens maîtres—les quelles presque toujours, ne sont que l'effet de leur aimable laisser-aller, de cette naïve 'disinvoltura' du génie qui ne sera jamais comprise par la pédanterie des nos Académiciens. Du reste Molteni est un bon enfant et très consciencieux dans son art."

61 See the introductory essay by Alessandra Mottola Molfino in *Museo Poldi Pezzoli: Storia del museo*, 15–61, Musei e gallerie di Milano (Milan: Electa, 1982), and also the manuscript account of Molteni's restorations in the archive of the museum: "Elenco e rispettivo prezzo dei restauri eseguiti da Giuseppe Molteni ai quadri di proprietà del Nobile Signor Cavaliere Don Giacomo Poldi dall'anno 1853 in avanti."

62 The visit was on 22 August 1858. See Elizabeth Eastlake, *Journals and Correspondence*, ed. Charles Eastlake Smith, vol. 2 (London, 1895), 98–100. Molteni's correspondence contains references to Sir Charles Eastlake, whom he knew well, and for whom he worked as a restorer, as when on 10 October 1860 Molteni wrote to Morelli: "Sappiate adunque che il Signor cavaliere Eastlake in questo momento di ritorno dal suo viaggio mi annuncia che riceverò da ristaurare due Antonio Vivarini firmati e una Madonna e Bambino di Gentile Bellini, aggiungendo che sono bellissimi ma rovinati." Eastlake had bought all three pictures for his own collection. The panel of Saints Jerome and Peter went from his collection to the National Gallery, London (no. 768). One Antonio Vivarini of the Virgin enthroned was later acquired by Poldi (no. 1570), and the Virgin and Child by Gentile Bellini was later bought by Richter from Lady Eastlake's sale for his client, Ludwig Mond, and is now in the National Gallery, London (no. NG3911). For full documentation, see Anderson ed., *The Restoration of Renaissance Painting*, 62–63, n33–35.

63 Giovanni Morelli to Austen Henry Layard, 31 January 1867, Add. MSS 38, 963, British Library, London. Morelli's moving letter to Layard is almost an obituary: "La mort de nôtre bon Molteni a aussi contribué de me rendre plus taciturne encore de mon ordinaire. J'en ai été profondément affligé. C'était en Italie à peu près le seul homme avec lequel je pouvais m'entretenir de nos chers peintres anciens, le seul dont l'intelligence *alla au de là* des bornes où arrivent la plupart des amateurs et soi-disant connaisseurs de beaux-arts.—Hélas, cet homme rare n'existe plus, et l'Italie, j'ose dire même l'Europe, a fait une grande perte en lui. C'était un homme qui avait encore conservé le bon goût italien traditionnel, et dont le nombre maintenant est presque réduit a zéro. De ces jours-ci la France a perdu aussi deux de ses illustrations, le philosophe Cousin et le peintre Ingres, dont on fera certainement plus de cas que de la mort de Molteni, qui est passé presque inaperçu—mais quant à moi je pense que la perte de ce dernier soit plus irréparable que celle des deux français. Vous en aurez été touché, car outre un bon enfant qui vous chérissait, vous avez perdu en Molteni l'habile médecin à la cure du quel vous avez confié vos beaux tableaux de Ferrare."

64 Austen Henry Layard to Giovanni Morelli, 4 February 1867, Add. MSS 38, 966, British Library, London: "Sa perte est grande pour ses amis, et pour l'art—l'était un homme que j'aimais et que j'estimais beaucoup. Les heures que je passais dans son atelier étaient parmi les plus agréables de l'année, et j'anticipais toujours avec plaisir ma visite périodique à Milano parce que j'y trouvais Molteni—l'était un de ces homme vraiment 'simpatici' dont on en trouve rarement—mais dont j'ai eu le bonheur de connaître plusieurs parmi mes amis Italiens."

65 National Gallery, London: no. 3090.

66 National Gallery, London: no. 3091.

67 Giovanni Morelli to Austen Henry Layard, 3 January 1865, Add. MSS 38, 963, British Library, London: "Son jugement sur vôtre Bonsignori est faux—son extrême vanité ne lui permet pas de convenir avec nous que cette belle et intéressante prédella soit l'œuvre d'un des meilleurs écoliers de Mantegna, car l'ayant jugé, il y a deux ans, une peintre du VII siècle il devrait confesser d'avoir dit alors un *grosso sproposito*. Mais c'est grâce à ce mécompte de Molteni que Baslini vous a rendu à si bon marché la toile de Bonsignori."

68 Austen Henry Layard to Giovanni Morelli, 30 December 1864, Add. MSS 38, 966, British Library, London: "Je n'oublie pas que je dois aussi ces deux tableaux précieux a vôtre amitié, car sans vôtre opinion je ne m'avrais guère décidé à les prendre … Je commence vraiment à me trouver en possession d'une Pinacothèque." And in a later letter (Austen Henry Layard to Giovanni Morelli, 29 January 1865, Add. MSS 38, 966, British Library, London): "Le Bonsignori est, pour moi, un véritable chef d'œuvre. Ce grand style, un peu dur et sec, a un grand charme pour moi. Peu à peu je me fais une Galerie. C'est mon plus grand plaisir d'avoir de beaux tableaux dans ma chambre."

69 National Gallery, London: no. 3068, 1–2. Cecil Gould, *The Sixteenth-Century Italian Schools*, National Gallery Catalogues (London: National Gallery, 1975), 97, draws attention to extensive retouching in the angel's white robe, face, and right hand, as well as on the Madonna panel, which may be from Molteni's restoration; see Giovanni Morelli to Austen Henry Layard, 26 December 1864, Add. MSS 38, 963, British Library, London: "Molteni travaille aux deux petites planches de Gaudenzio Ferrari, et il y réussit parfaitement."

70 National Gallery, London: no. 3097, mentioned in Giovanni Morelli to Austen Henry Layard, 3 January 1866, Add. MSS 38, 963, British Library, London.

71 National Gallery, London: no. 3099; see Austen Henry Layard to Giovanni Morelli, 24 October 1865, Add. MSS 38, 966, British Library, London: "Je l'ai acheté chez un vieillard ici pour peu de chose."

72 National Gallery, London: no. 3098; believed to be a Gentile Bellini when Layard discovered it; see Austen Henry Layard to Giovanni Morelli, 13 October 1865, Add. MSS 38, 966, British Library, London.

73 National Gallery, London: no. 3124.

74 National Gallery, London: no. 3077. This work is not mentioned in Layard's correspondence.

75 According to Layard (16 December 1866), Molteni wrote pages (now lost) describing his "miraculous" restoration of the Cima (National Gallery, London: no. 3112).

76 National Gallery, London: no. 3101. Molteni attributed the portrait to Foppa when he was restoring it (see Layard to Morelli, 13 October 1865), while the current attribution was proposed by Morelli.

77 This unique collection was formed by Giambattista Costabili (1756–1841) in an attempt to preserve the artistic heritage of Ferrara from dispersal during the Napoleonic period. Of the 624 paintings he acquired, 358 were by Ferrarese Old Masters, as can be seen from the first inventory made of the collection: Camillo Laderchi, *Descrizione della Quadreria Costabili* (Ferrara: Negri, 1838–41). His heir, his great-nephew Giovanni (1815–1882) was a fervent patriot, who spent much of his time away from Ferrara in political and military office during the Risorgimento. By the 1850s the Costabili family was in grave financial difficulty, and attempted to sell the collection to the Comune of Ferrara, but without success. It was probably at this time that Morelli made his valuation. Subsequently, Giovanni sold some of the best pieces to Eastlake and Layard, thereby hoping to arouse English interest in acquiring the rest of the collection intact. According to Layard (20 October 1866), he kept the smaller works from the Costabili collection for himself, while the larger, more important works he sold to his cousin, Sir Ivor Guest, later First Lord Wimborne. Layard's paintings are now in the National Gallery, London, while the others are fulsomely described in *A Catalogue of the Pictures at Canford Manor in the Possession of Lord Wimborne* (Edinburgh: privately printed, 1888); see also the catalogue of the Wimborne collection (Christie's, 9 March 1923). Three of the paintings that Layard acquired for Guest were included in the exhibition *From Borso to Cesare d'Este: The School of Ferrara, 1450–1628* (London: Matthiesen Fine Art, 1984), nos 13, 28, 42. By 1872 Giovanni Costabili had commissioned a sale catalogue from Gaetano Giordani, director of the Bologna Pinacoteca: *Catalogo de' quadri di varie scuole pittoriche nella Galleria Costabili in Ferrara* (Ferrara: Tipografia dell'Eridano, 1872). In that year Morelli and many of his friends, including Venetian dealer Michelangelo Guggenheim, bought a substantial number of paintings from the collection. On the history of the dispersal of the collection, see Laura Benini, "Descrizione della Quadreria Costabili," *Musei ferraresi: Bollettino annuale* 7 (1977): 79–96; also Emanuele Mattaliano and Amalia Mezzetti, *Indice ragionato delle "Vite de' Pittori e Scultori Ferraresi" di Gerolamo Baruffaldi* (Ferrara, 1981), passim.

78 Giovanni Morelli to Austen Henry Layard, 3 November 1866, Add. MSS 38, 963, British Library, London: "Je vous envoie aussi la copie d'une appréciation (approssimativa) des quelques tableaux que vous avez eu le bon goût d'acquérir de Mons. Costabili. Je l'avais faite il y a huit ans [Morelli's evaluation is missing from the correspondence] et dans le but de sauver si c'était possible, un bon nombre d'œuvres rares et quelques unes même uniques de l'école ferraraise—mais mon projet d'alors n'a pas pu se réaliser, n'ayant ni le gouvernement ni les particuliers voulu m'appuyer. J'ai au moins la satisfaction que la plupart des tableaux de cette intéressante collection se trouvent maintenant en possession de personnes qui les savent apprécier e qui se font un plaisir de les montrer et de les faire agréer aussi aux autres. Permettez-moi donc, mon très cher ami, des vous répéter mes congratulations de la magnifique acquisition que vous venez de faire tant à Ferrare qu'à Venise—car comme j'ai déjà eu occasion de vous le dire le tableau de Cima da Conegliano sur bois [National Gallery, London: no. 3112] est vraiment un'œuvre de premier ordre. Je suis heureux que cette perle soit tombée dans vos mains [...] Pour mon goût les tableaux plus simpathiques de vôtre acquisition resteront toujours (1) les tempere et (2) la petite Madonne avec les deux Saints d'Ercole Grandi, (3) les deux portraits de Garofalo, et (4) l'Adoration avec les deux anges de Lorenzo Costa." All these pictures are now in the National Gallery: (1) The works in tempera were two episodes from the story of Moses, now attributed to a follower of Lorenzo Costa (nos 3103 and 3104). They formed part of a set of eight, one of which Morelli owned, and is now in the Accademia Carrara, Bergamo (no. 951), where it is attributed to Boccaccio Boccaccino, at Longhi's suggestion. A further five were purchased by Morelli from Costabili in 1872, and later sold to his friend Emilio Visconti Venosta. Another painting from the same series, "a single figure of Moses to whom God is speaking," is lost, though Morelli thought it was in England during his lifetime. Venturi identified the series in the Gonzaga inventories as "Otto pezzi di quadri con l'opera del Testamento Vecchio di mano del Costa Vecchio," *Storia dell'arte italiana* 7, no. 3, 807. Originally Layard gave these two *tempere* to Sir Ivor Guest, but, as Morelli considered them especially valuable, he later swapped them for a Romanino Marriage of the Virgin. (2) The Ercole Grandi is the charming altarpiece of the Virgin and Child with Saints Dominic and Catherine of Siena, no. 3102, now catalogued simply as Ferrarese School. (3) The Garofalo portraits are a double portrait of a married couple, no. 3117, previously attributed to Garofalo in Layard's manuscript catalogue, but now in the limbo of the Italian school. (4) The last painting praised by Morelli, once attributed to Costa in Laderchi's catalogue, is Mazzolino's *Nativity*, no. 3114. Layard's acquisitions were sent to Molteni, whom Morelli described as "l'habile médecin à la cure du quel vous aviez confié vos beaux tableaux de Ferrare" (31 January 1867). According to Morelli, Dosso Dossi's St John the Baptist, which was for Lord Wimborne (later in the Gnecco collection, Genoa), was to be subjected to the most extensive restoration, but it is uncertain whether Molteni completed the work, for he died in 1867, and the painting was transferred from board to canvas by Pinti, an Italian restorer in England, in 1867. An interesting account of Layard's collection, mentioning his Costabili acquisitions, is given in his letter to Cavalcaselle, from Cornford, 25 January 1867, among the Cavalcaselle papers, MS. IT. IV. 2035 (12276), Fasc. 2, Epistolario, Biblioteca Marciana, Venice. Cavalcaselle was especially critical of Molteni's restoration of Gentile Bellini's *Mehmet II*, a criticism that Layard effectively censored (to Crowe's chagrin) when he acted as an advisor to John Murray, correcting the proofs of Crowe and Cavalcaselle's *History of Italian Painting*. They described the collar of the cloak of Mehmet II as "entirely new," but it was changed at Layard's insistence to "restored," (see Crowe's angry letter to John Murray, 26 September 1868, John Murray Archive). In fact, Molteni's restoration *was* much more extensive than Crowe and Cavalcaselle realized.

79 Giovanni Morelli (at Bergamo) to Niccolò Antinori, 4 November 1866, Archivio Antinori, Florence: "Layard purtroppo ha acquistato preziosi quadri della Galleria Costabili di Ferrara. 22 per 38.000 lire—ve ne ha 3 o 4 che soli valgono più di quella somma. Ma qui da noi i ricchi sono troppo imbecilli per sapere apprezzare e gustare siffatte cose."

80 Austen Henry Layard to Giovanni Morelli, 6 November 1866, Add. MSS 38, 966, British Library, London: "Je vous remercie de la copie de l'appréciation des tableau de la Galerie Costabili. Je vois que vous avez noté presque tous les tableaux que j'ai pris, ce que me fait plaisir car d'une preuve, que me choix a été bonne. Vos prix sont aussi à peu près les mêmes que j'avais fixé—seulement j'estime l'Ortolano [a magnificent altarpiece of St Joseph presenting the Infant Christ to the Virgin, now attributed to Niccolò Pisano, Worcester Art Museum, USA] à presque le double—c'est un magnifique tableau ... Il a beaucoup gagné quand je l'ai vu descendant de ce coin obscur où il était suspendu. Je le trouve aussi bien qu'un beau Garofalo. Mais, comme vous dites, depuis que vous avez fait l'appréciation les prix des tableaux sont doublés et quoique j'ai payé une somme assez forte pour ceux que j'ai pris à Ferrara—je crois que so me les ai fait payé cher, et que quand ils sortent des mains de Molteni ils vaudraient certainement le double."

81 For example, Fleming, "Art Dealing and the Risorgimento," 8–9.

82 Giovanni Morelli (at Venice) to Niccolò Antinori, 4 July 1875, Archivio Antinori, Florence: "Ieri mi occupai della distribuzione di questi 50 quadri nelle 4 sale, e domani si darà principio al collocamento di essi, fra i quali ve n'ha mezza dozzina di molto importanti e rari."

83 Recently discovered documentation about the Layard collection when it was in Venice is presented by Cecilia Riva, "La Collezione Layard nel catalogo dattiloscritto 1896," *Predella: Journal of the Visual Arts* 35 (2014): 53–78.

84 David Robertson, *Sir Charles Eastlake and the Victorian Art World* (Princeton, N. J.: Princeton University Press, 1978), 143, 151. See also Gregori, *Giovan Battista Moroni*, 226.

85 Giovanni Morelli to Count Giovanni Battista Camozzi Vertova, 20 October 1861, Biblioteca Civica Angelo Mai, Bergamo.

86 James Hudson (at Pistoia) to Austen Henry Layard, 8 May 1865, Add. MSS 38, 991, British Library, London.

87 Morelli to Layard, 19 May 1865.

88 *La Pinacoteca e la Villa Lochis alla Crocetta di Mozzo presso Bergamo, con notizie biografiche degli autori dei quadri*, 2nd edn (Bergamo: Tipografia Natali, 1858), annotated by Giovanni Morelli, D III 4, Biblioteca dell'Accademia di Brera.

89 Gustavo Frizzoni (at London) to Count Carlo Lochis, 13 July 1867, Carteggio Lochis, MMB, 933, I, Biblioteca Civica Angelo Mai, Bergamo: "Ma che ti dirò di Londra? Qui davvero bisogna trovare risorse in altre cose che nel piacere che possono recare gli edifici di bella architettura: gusto sotto questo punto di vista gl'Inglesi non ne hanno, poiché in pratica riescono in generale tutt'altro che buoni artisti; ma per fare raccolte di oggetti d'arte e scienza non sono secondi a nessuno, tanto più poi che non conoscono limite alle spese, quando si tratti di fare degli acquisti che contribuiscono a rendere vieppiù completi ed interessanti i loro musei. La Galleria Nazionale sono certo piacerebbe a te pure immensamente, poiché non ha che roba scelta, acquistata, come sia in gran parte a peso d'oro. Dico la verità che mi piangeva il cuore a vedere il Perugino già di casa Melzi, bandito così lungi da casa sua e così pure lo storico quadro della famiglia di Dario davanti ad Alessandro di Paolo Veronese, già proprietà Pisani. Anche di quei cari toscani ve ne sono di bellissimi e alcuni Gian Bellini di primo ordine. Una delle prime domande che mi fece il direttore della galleria, Signor Boxall fu, se non conoscessi delle buone raccolte in vendita in Italia, e ti puoi bene immaginare che non mi scordai della tua animandolo a tornare a visitarla la prossima volta che tornerà a Bergamo."

90 Morelli to Layard, 3 January 1866: "... mon ami Arconati, auquel j'ai procuré il y a trois semaines, un des plus beaux *tondi* de Domenico Ghirlandaio que j'ai jamais vu. C'est une peinture de la jeunesse du maître, et le grand nigaud qui la possédait la retenant toujours—sur l'opinion des professeurs florentins un'œuvre de l'école de Ghirlandaio, a cru de faire une très bonne affaire en la vendant au marquis Arconati pour le prix de L. 4,500—je vous assure qu'elle en vaut les L. 55,000. Le tableau (*tondo*) est parfaitement conservé et a une magnifique guirlande de fruits en bois coloré qui en formant la corniche; il représente la Vierge adorant l'enfant Jésus qui git par terre devant elle; derrière le Christ vous voyez deux anges charmants agenouillés. C'est une veritable perle. Si vous avez été a Florence ces jours là au lieu de l'offrir à Arconati j'aurais eu le plaisir de la dédier a Vous sûr que vous auriez eu l'apprécier bien autrement que le jeune Marquis Milanais. Mais l'affaire pressait et il falut la résoudre sur le champ." Layard replied: "Je porte envie à M. Arconati. Un vrai Ghirlandaio! Mais c'est un trésor. Je n'en connais pas un seul en Angleterre." (Austen Henry Layard to Giovanni Morelli, 11 January 1866, Add. MSS 38, 966, British Library, London). The tondo, now attributed to Botticini, is in the Musée du Louvre.

91 See Morelli's delightful letter to the Barone Giovanni Barracco, in which he persuaded him to buy the picture, in Giovanni Barracco, *La Maddalena di Pier di Cosimo* (Rome, 1910), 5–8.

92 Giovanni Morelli to Giovanni Melli, 25 May 1871, quoted in Anderson, *Collecting, Connoisseurship*, 124–5.

93 Giovanni Morelli (at Munich) to James Hudson, 1 August 1871, Malvezzi MSS, Milan: "Il quadretto in tela del Giorgione (dai conoscitori almeno ritenuto tale) si trova tuttora invenduto nella raccolta Manfrin di Venezia … È una gran bella cosa, né lo stato di conservazione parvemi cattivo, ma il prezzo, che se ne chiede—di 30.000 lire—è esagerato. L'argomento però parmi troppo lubrico per quella gente, e poi è un quadretto che non sarà mai gustato, se non da' veri conoscitori d'arte. Il ritratto di Bernardo Licinio da Pordenone, di cui ti mandai un pessimo facsimile in fotografia, è certo negli occhi miei una buona pittura della bell'epoca, ma non è opera da potere fare al pari del ritratto di Moroni—tela, caro mio, che non sarà tanto facile di rinvenire una simile."

94 In a fascinating letter (the only remaining one from the correspondence between Morelli and Eastlake), Morelli demanded that his name be mentioned in the National Gallery's annual report as the former owner, rather than accepting Eastlake's suggestion of substituting another; clearly, Morelli wished to claim the credit for having introduced Lorenzo Lotto to the National Gallery. He wrote: "V. S. mi domanda inoltre se io preferisco forse di vedere al mio sostituito altro nome in codesto Rapporto che Ella pubblica tutti gli anni? So purtroppo che non commetto un'azione troppo patriotica nel privare il proprio paese di un capo d'opera qual è questo quadro del Lotto che io Le ho ceduto—ma giacché la colpa è mia che io pure e non altri ne porti la pena! Per fare piacere a me, pregherei quindi V. S. a non volere minimamente alterare la verità dei fatti, e lasciare correre che il mio nome figuri in mezzo a quelli degli altri disgraziati, che al pari di me furono costretti a privarsi de' migliori tesori loro." Giovanni Morelli (at Bergamo) to Charles Eastlake, 29 December 1862, Lotto dossier, Archive of the National Gallery, London.

Notes to Chapter 10: The National Gallery, London

1 As in the previous chapter, some of this material was published in Jaynie Anderson, "Morelli and Layard," in *Austen Henry Layard tra l'Oriente e Venezia*, ed. Frederick Mario Fales and Bernard Hickey, Fenice 8 (Rome: "L'Erma" di Bretschneider, 1987), 109–37.

2 The correspondence between Lord John Russell and Austen Henry Layard is in the archive of the National Gallery, London. However, the copy of Morelli's letter that Layard mentions in his letter of 6 January 1866 is missing.

3 Austen Henry Layard to Lord John Russell, 6 January 1867, Add. MSS 38, 963, British Library, London.

4 Austen Henry Layard to Giovanni Morelli, 11 January 1866, Add. MSS 38, 966, British Library, London.

5 Lord John Russell to Austen Henry Layard, 9 February 1866, Add. MSS 38, 966, British Library, London.

6 Giovanni Morelli to Austen Henry Layard, 18 May 1866, Add. MSS 38, 963, British Library, London. Minister Berti, a moral philosopher and historian, occupied his post for more than a year, while his appointee to the Uffizi, Gotti, was a linguist who specialised in Tuscan proverbs. Gotti is remembered for having added the collection of self-portraits for the Corridorio Vasariano, and for finding new spaces for exhibiting Florentine collections.

7 Austen Henry Layard to William Boxall, 26 April 1866, Add. MSS 38, 966, British Library, London. He gave Boxall the letter to give to Morelli, presumably.

8 For example, on 17 September 1869 Layard wrote to Morelli: "J'ai vu des tableaux de Baslini. J'ai trouvé l'un des Marco Marziale très beau et j'ai écris ledessus a Boxall qui doit se trouver actuellement à Milan." These were two altarpieces by Marco Marziale, which Boxall subsequently acquired for the National Gallery (nos 803 and 804), his attention having been drawn to them by Layard, on Morelli's advice. In the same letter, Layard mentioned a painting of Christ going to Calvary, and very gently ventured to disagree with Morelli's attribution: "Baslini m'a dit que vous l'attribuez à Boccaccino. Je n'ose émettre une opinion au contraire à la vôtre—autrement je l'aurais cru de cet école lombarde venant du Foppa que nous (c'est à dire moi) connaissons du peu." Nevertheless, the work that Boxall bought from Baslini at the same time is still ascribed to Boccaccino (National Gallery, London, no. 806). Several years later, on 30 November 1870, Morelli complained to Layard that he had not seen Boxall for more than a year, as if this were unusual: "Boxall, ma quel caro e brav'uomo, imitando l'esempio mio, non mi diede segno di vita da più d'un anno a questa parte."

9 For an assessment of Boxall's acquisitions, see Michael Levey, "A little-known director: Sir William Boxall," *Apollo: The International Magazine of Arts* 101, no. 159 (May 1975): 354–59.

10 Sir James Hudson (at Pistoia) to Giovanni Morelli, 16 November 1867, Cassetta G. Morelli, Fondazione Cavour, Santena.

11 Giovanni Morelli (at Bergamo) to William Boxall, 9 December 1873, Archive of the National Gallery, London.

12 William Boxall wrote to Austen Henry Layard, 21 September 1868, Add. MSS 38, 995, British Library, London.

13 Giovanni Morelli (at Munich) to William Boxall, 24 August 1869, Archive of the National Gallery, London.

14 Quoted from a letter in an English private collection, which Mrs Angelina Bacon drew to my attention.

15 Giovanni Morelli to Austen Henry Layard, 8 October 1872, Add. MSS 38, 963, British Library, London.

16 Giovanni Morelli to Austen Henry Layard, 25 March 1875, Add. MSS 38, 966, British Library, London: "J'ai fait avec lui une petite excursion à Brera, mais il m'a semblé que Mr Burton n'avait pas encore cette familiarité avec nos grands peintres qui serait pourtant nécessaire pour diriger avec succèss une collection telle que la vôtre. Pourtant je pourrais m'être trompé, car Mr Burton parle très peu!"

17 Giovanni Morelli to Austen Henry Layard, 2 June 1876, Add. MSS 38, 963, British Library, London. The pictures by Moroni were *Il cavaliere col piede ferito* (no. 1022), *Canon Ludovico Terzi* (no. 1024), Portrait of a Lady (no. 1023), and one of the only surviving dated portraits by Moretto (no. 1025).

18 See Allan Braham's catalogue for *Giovanni Battista Moroni: 400th Anniversary Exhibition* (London: National Gallery, 1978), 3.

19 Carl von Lützow, "Giovanni Battista Moroni," *Die Graphischen Künste* 14 (1891): 21–26.

20 Morelli wrote to Layard describing his part in the transaction: "Mon gouvernement ayant appris par Mons. Barozzi que la Prusse traitant l'achat de tableaux de Giorgione de la collection Manfrin, a prié la Prince Giovanelli de prévenir les délégués prussiens, et de s'emparer du tableau pour la Pinacothèque de Venise. Giovanelli a donc acheté le petit tableau pour la somme de 30.000 livres—à présent il se trouve dans les mains de Cavenaghi qui l'a déjà nettoyé et l'a trouvé beaucoup plus conservé qu'on ne s'y attendait. Mais le prix est très fort" (Giovanni Morelli (at Rome) to Austen Henry Layard, 16 January 1876, Add. MSS 38, 963); see also Layard's reply, 11 February 1876, Add. MSS 38, 966, British Library, London. When Giovanelli died, Morelli reported to Layard that he expected the prince would leave his collection to the Accademia, of which he was president (Giovanni Morelli to Austen Henry Layard, 12 September 1866, Add. MSS 38, 965, British Library, London); but on 6 October Morelli wrote to Layard that the prince's will was a scandal, for his had bequeathed everything to his illegitimate son, and nothing to the Accademia, not even the *Tempesta*.

21 "Et à présent l'ami Hudson voudrait faire acheter a une dame Rothschild le Violiniste de Rafael—il me dit, qu'il préfère le voir à Londres qu'à St. Pétersbourg. Il s'agit de 350 où 400,000 francs. Le tableau est superbe, mais très repeint. Mais en tout cas, c'est une honte pour l'Italie de laisser partir tous ces splendides œuvres d'art." Giovanni Morelli to Austen Henry Layard, 17 February 1877, Add. MSS 38, 963, British Library, London.

22 Austen Henry Layard to Giovanni Morelli, 9 March 1883, Add. MSS 38, 667, British Library, London.

23 Giovanni Morelli to Austen Henry Layard, 2 April 1883, Add. MSS 38, 964, British Library, London. Ghirlandaio's *Procession to Calvary* (no. 1143) had been seen by Eastlake in 1856 and 1864. Before it was exported from Italy, Luigi Cavenaghi transferred the painting from board to canvas (see Austen Henry Layard to Giovanni Morelli, 30 March 1883, Add. MSS 38, 964, British Library, London).

24 Austen Henry Layard to Giovanni Morelli, 23 May 1883, Add. MSS 38, 964, British Library, London. These two pictures were in the collection of the landscape artist Prinetti and were described admiringly by Otto Mündler in October 1856, especially the Virgin and Child by Gaudenzio Ferrari, whose "loveliness increases on repeated inspection," *The Travel Diaries of Otto Mündler 1855–1858*, ed. Carol Togneri Dowd, The Volume of the Walpole Society 51 (London: The Walpole Society, 1985), 136.

25 Giovanni Morelli to Austen Henry Layard, 29 June 1883, Add. MSS 38, 964, British Library, London: "Mais savez-vous que ce homme de Mr. Burton est quelquefois drôle? Comment peut-il avoir trouvé le Gaudenzio Ferrari des Prinetti tout-à-fait abimé par la restauration! Je vous assure que c'est une des peintures les mieux conservées que je connaisse, et vous vous en persuaderez quand vous vendrez ici. Mais hélas! il y a si peu de gens, même parmi les amateurs des tableaux anciens qui aient la moindre connaissance de ce qui est restauré et de ce qui est original … Et si les amateurs et les directeurs des galeries en savent si peu que voulez-vous en attendre du gros public? … J'en suis indigné de ces *'hâbleurs'*, qui occupent de hautes positions, dont ils ne sont pas dignes. Dans la science des arts il y a des choses qu'on peut apprendre avec l'étude, il y en a d'autres qu'on ne peut pas apprendre, car elles sont un don de la nature. Mais parmi celles qu'on peut apprendre je compte aussi la science de la restauration."

26 Charles Eastlake to the trustees of the National Gallery, 13 September 1859, Archive of the National Gallery, London. For a contemporary criticism of Molteni's restoration of the portrait, see Roberto Bassi Rathgeb, "Le postille di Antonio Piccinelli alle 'Vite dei pittori, sculturi ed architetti bergamaschi' di F. M. Tassi," *L'Arte* 58 (1959): 123–24.

27 Giovanni Morelli to Austen Henry Layard, 14 September 1883, Add. MSS 38, 964, British Library, London: "Tous ces cinque tableaux ont un véritable mérite et feraient honeur tant au Louvre qu'à la Galerie Nationale de Londres. Il faut de la chance pour trouver encore aujourd'hui de ces trésors d'art—mais Mr Burton n'en avrait acheté aucun de ces 5 tableaux, tous les cinque étaient couverts d'une couche de couleurs à l'huile noirçies, œuvre du même restaurateur du dernier siècle—et ce masque avrait probabilment empeché Mr Burton d'y reconnaitre les véritables auteurs."

28 National Gallery, London, no. 1149.

29 Giovanni Morelli to Austen Henry Layard, 23 November 1883, Add. MSS 38, 667. British Library, London.

30 Giovanni Morelli to Austen Henry Layard, 14 December 1883, Add. MSS 38, 964, British Library, London.

31 Giovanni Morelli to Austen Henry Layard, 10 June 1883, Add. MSS 38, 964, British Library, London: "Le petit tableau connu sous le nom de Raphael de M. Moore, et dont il y a le dessin à Venise dans l'accademie représente Apollon et Marsyas; Mr Moore qui l'avait acheté il y a peu près 35 ans à Londres a un très bel prix, en demandait 500,000 frcs. Pour moi c'est un'œuvre de la jeunesse de Pérugin (opinion que j'ai manifestée, il y a un an publiquement), mais c'est beau comme si c'était de Raphael. Mr. Gruyer a eu donc raison de l'acheter pour le Louvre (un prix de 200,000 francs), mais il a tort a vouloir soutenir somme que le tableau appartient à Raphael." On Morelli's part in this celebrated controversy, see Francis Haskell, "Un martyr de l'attribution: Morris Moore et *L'Apollon et Marsyas* du Louvre," *Revue de l'art* 42 (1978): 77–88.

32 See Austen Henry Layard to Giovanni Morelli, 17 January 1886, and Morelli's replies, 25 January and 7 February 1886. At least four works from the Graham collection are now in the National Gallery: after Benozzo, no. 2863; Fungai, no. 1331; Milanese school, no. 2089; Venetian school, no. 4250.

33 On Lord Methuen's collection, see Austen Henry Layard to Giovanni Morelli, 26 July 1886, and Morelli's reply, Add. MSS 38, 965, British Library, London.

34 See Giovanni Morelli to Austen Henry Layard, 8 July, 30 September, 14 and 20 October 1885, Add. MSS 38, 964, British Library, London. Richter described the paintings in a letter to Morelli, 1 July 1886, after they had been installed in the National Gallery, exhibited under glass (*Italienische Malerei der Renaissance*, 474).

35 On 24 July 1884 Layard wrote to Morelli concerning Burton's acquisition, which elicited the following response: "Si Crowe et Cavalcaselle ont cru attribuer à Giorgione le petit tableau du Leigh Court, vous pouvez être sûr que ce n'est pas un'œuvre de Giorgione—car Cavalcaselle n'a jamais compris ce grand maître." Richter had also communicated his view to Morelli that the painting at Leigh Court was not a Giorgione, although today no one would doubt that it is.

36 See Giovanni Morelli to Austen Henry Layard, 21 December 1885, where he attributes the tondo to Fra Diamante, an attribution not recorded in the National Gallery catalogue.

37 Giovanni Morelli to Austen Henry Layard, 1 April 1887, Add. MSS 38, 965, British Library, London.

38 Now in the National Gallery, London: Dosso Dossi, no. 3924; Mantegna, no. 5641.

39 Giovanni Morelli to Austen Henry Layard, 18 November 1887, Add. MSS 38, 965, British Library, London.

40 Austen Henry Layard to Giovanni Morelli, 27 September 1889, Add. MSS 38, 968, British Library, London.

41 Austen Henry Layard to Giovanni Morelli, 31 October 1883, Add. MSS 38, 667, British Library, London.

42 Constance Jocelyn Ffoulkes, *Vincenzo Foppa of Brescia, Founder of the Lombard School: His Life and Work* (London: John Lane, 1909).

43 Austen Henry Layard to Giovanni Morelli, 10 October 1883, Add. MSS 38, 667, British Library, London: "On ne peut pas selon moi, exagérer l'importance de vôtre livre sur l'histoire de l'art et sur la vrai critique—et c'est justement pour cela que je désire tellement que vous le refassiez, et que vous mettiez dans un autre travail plus de méthode. Vous ne vous rendez pas justice dans Lermolieff. Avec vos vastes connaissances vous pourriez dans quelques mois produire un livre qui satisfairait à vos amis, et qui aurait une vrai influence sur l'histoire de la peinture."

44 Franz Kugler, *Handbuch der Geschichte der Malerei in Italien seit Constantin dem Grossen* (Berlin: Duncker & Humblot, 1837). Layard's title accurately conveys what had happened: *Handbook of Painting: The Italian Schools. Based on the Handbook by Kugler. Originally edited by Sir Charles Eastlake, P.R.A., Sixth edition. Thoroughly Revised and in Part Rewritten, by Austen Henry Layard, G.C.B.* (London: John Murray, 1891). The section of Kugler's *Handbook* that discussed German, Flemish, and Dutch painting was also revised in a series of editions published by John Murray, the first in 1842, translated again by Mrs Hutton, subsequently edited by Sir Edmund Head in 1846, and again in 1860 by Waagen, and finally in 1874 by J. A. Crowe.

45 Layard also contributed to other guidebooks, such as *A Handbook of Rome and its Environs, 15th edn., Carefully Revised On the Spot ... Picture Galleries, Edited by the Late Rt. Hon. Sir A. Henry Layard. General Editor, the Rev. H. W. Pullen* (London: John Murray, 1894). In this volume some of the entries for individual galleries, namely the Palazzo Doria, Palazzo dei Conservatori, Palazzo Barberini, and Palazzo Corsini, refer to Morelli's attributions, which contradicted the labels on the paintings. Morelli's discoveries were denoted (M), although there was no list of abbreviations to tell the innocent tourist what this meant.

Notes to Chapter 11: Senator and Connoisseur

1 Iwan [*sic*] Lermolieff, "Die Galerien Roms. Ein kritischer Versuch von Iwan Lermolieff. I: Die Galerie Borghese. Aus dem Russischen übersetzt von Dr. Johannes Schwarze. Mit Illustrationen," *Zeitschrift* *für bildende Kunst* 9 (1874): 1–11, 73–81, 171–78, 249–53; 10 (1875): 97–106, 207–11, 264–73, 329–34; 11 (1876): 132–37, 168–73; Iwan [*sic*] Lermolieff, "Über Sebastiano del Piombo und Giulio Romano von Iwan Lermolieff," *Zeitschrift für bildende Kunst*, Beiblatt 13 (1878): coll. 553–56.

2 Ivan Lermolieff, *Die Werke italienischer Meister in den Galerien von München, Dresden und Berlin. Ein kritischer Versuch von Ivan Lermolieff. Aus dem Russischen übersetzt von Dr. Johannes Schwarze* (Leipzig: E. A. Seemann, 1880).

3 In 1884 Lützow dedicated a book to Morelli, *Die Kunstschätze italiens in geographische-historischer Übersicht*, and in the preface gave a moving tribute to his friend: "Wenn sein Name auf dem Widmungsblatte dieses Buches steht, so wolle darin ausser dem Zeugnisse der Verehrung, welche ich ihm persönlich entgegenbringe, auch ein neuer Beweis für den innigen geistigen Verkehr zwischen der italienischen und deutschen Wissenschaft erblickt werden, zu dessen fruchtbringender Entwicklung beigetragen zu haben, nicht das geringste Verdienst unseres berühmten Mailänder Freundes ist."

4 Introduction to the English edition, ed. 1892, p. 28.

5 Giovanni Morelli to Nicolò Antinori, 14 October 1873, Archivio Antinori, Florence. He also described this show of bravura in a letter to Layard on 11 December 1873, Add. MSS 38, 995 (British Library, London).

6 "Notes on Italian Painters, No. 1," Giovanni Battista Cavalcaselle (at Munich) to Joseph Archer Crowe, 5 October 1873, 86 ZZ 51-55, Crowe and Cavalcaselle papers, National Art Library, Victoria and Albert Museum, London.

7 Giovanni Morelli (at Gorle) to J. A. Crowe, 2 November 1873, 86 ZZ 51–55, Crowe and Cavalcaselle papers, National Art Library, Victoria and Albert Museum, London.

8 "Cette peinture comme vous savez a beaucoup souffert, le ciel, les nuages, les cheveux du saint et presque toutes les parties dans l'ombre ont été repeintes de manière que c'est très difficile d'y voir, dans l'état dans lequel elle se trouve avec quelque sureté la main de l'auteur."

9 For a detailed account of the changing attributions, see Andreas Henning, "Il *San Sebastiano* di Antonello da Messina a Dresda: Iconografia e restauro," in *Antonello da Messina*, ed. Mauro Lucco and Giovanni Carlo Federico Villa (Milan: Silvana, 2006), 75–89.

10 Cavalcaselle to Crowe, 5 October 1873: "Ma di qui Hübner terminando diceva perché il Sig. Rossmann ha scritto che lei e il Sigr. Crowe ritenevano il quadro di Antonello e fu dietro a tale dichiarazione che ne fu fatto l'acquisto."

11 Cavalcaselle to Crowe, 5 October 1873: "Io rispondeva che quanto a me lo credevo d'un seguace del Palma, e del Lotto, ed un'imitatore di quella maniera Giorgionesca, ma non del Giorgione—e così finì ... [che] esso se ne andò da una parte ed io dall'altra. Mi dispiace che si prepara una burrasca. Spero che colla prudenza si passerà anco questa."

12 Jaynie Anderson, *Giorgione: The Painter of "Poetic Brevity," Including Catalogues Raisonnés* (Paris and New York: Flammarion, 1997), 217–30, esp. 307–8.

13 Such as Guido Curto, ed., *Cavalcaselle in Piemonte: La pittura nei secoli XV e XVI* (Torino: Centro Studi Piemontesi, 1981), on Macrino d'Alba and Piedmontese painting, which is not unlike Mündler's notebooks for the trustees of the National Gallery.

14 Joseph Archer Crowe, *Reminiscences of Thirty-five Years of My Life*, 2nd edn (London: John Murray, 1895), 232–33.

15 Crowe, *Reminiscences*, 103.

16 M. Giebe, "Die Schlummernde Venus von Giorgione und Tizian: Bestandaufsnahme und Konservierung—neue Ergebnisse der Röntgenanalyse," *Jahrbuch der Staatlichen Kunstsammlungen Dresden* (1992): 91–105.

17 Giovanni Morelli (at Florence) to Giovanni Melli, 14 February 1870, Archivio Zavaritt, Gorle.

18 Giovanni Morelli (at Florence) to Cesare Correnti (Minister of Public Instruction), 30 April 1870, Archivio della Biblioteca dell'Accademia di Belle Arti di Brera, Milan.

19 Giovanni Morelli to Austen Henry Layard, 6 June 1874, British Library, London.

20 Giovanni Morelli (at Madrid) to Giovanni Melli, 8 May and 6 June 1872, and Giovanni Morelli to Pietro Zavaritt, 21 April–5 June 1872, published in Anderson, *Collecting, Connoisseurship*, 164–69, 177–87.

21 Morelli's notes, "Udienza di S. M. avuta a Pisa," were kept by Emilio Visconti Venosta, and are now in the archive of the Fondazione Cavour, Santena.

22 Federico Chabod, *Italian Foreign Policy: The Statecraft of the Founders* (Princeton: Princeton University Press, 1996), 372–73.

23 "Io non l'ho mai consigliato di accettare la corona di Spagna—egli la respinse la prima volta—poi dopo la Guerra di Francia mi disse un bel poco: ora sono deciso di accettarla," Victor Emmanuel II talking of his son, according to Morelli's notes, "Udienza di S. M. avuta a Pisa."

24 Private archive, Bergamo.

25 See the Brogi photograph in the Fototeca Zeri, Bologna, inv. 87315.

26 Gustavo Frizzoni (at Rome) to Clementina Frizzoni, 11 February 1876, Private archive, Bergamo: "Nostro Senatore parlava poco, ma pareva trovarsi abbastanza nel suo elemento, tutto che la gravità del Ministro della Marina, se non mi inganno imponga un poco anche a lui. Ma il tuo figliolo, penserai, che figura vi

faccia? A giudicare da me stesso, per lo meno discreta e prudente, permettendosi di frammischiare qualche parere quando il discorso cadeva sulle belle arti ed ascoltando quando si parlava di politica, di storia o di letteratura."

27 Gustavo Frizzoni (at Naples) to Teodoro Frizzoni, 18 February 1876, Private archive, Bergamo.

28 Frizzoni's notes for the Sicilian catalogue are conserved in the Biblioteca Ambrosiana, Milan.

29 Alessandro Rovetta, "Tracce del 'doppio catalogo' di Giovanni Morelli nei manoscritti di Gustavo Frizzoni all'Ambrosiana: Le collezioni milanesi," *Arte Lombarda*, nuova serie, no. 146/148 (1–3), 50 anni (2006): 220–26.

30 See Lermolieff, "Die Galerien Roms: Ein kritischer Versuch. 1. Die Galerie Borghese," *Zeitschrift für bildende Kunst* 9 (1874): 249–53.

31 Morelli and Richter's surviving correspondence is reasonably complete, because Giovanni Zavaritt, via Gustavo Frizzoni, returned Richter's letters to his widow, Louise Richter, after Morelli's death. The letters are now in the Bibliotheca Hertziana, Rome (Archiv Nachlass Jean Paul Richter). They have been published in part as *Italienische Malerei der Renaissance im Briefwechsel von Giovanni Morelli und Jean Paul Richter 1876–1891*, ed. Irma Richter and Gisela Richter, foreword by Paola Della Pergola (Baden-Baden: Bruno Grimm, 1960). When Richter's daughters were preparing the correspondence for publication, they transcribed all the letters in the Bibliotheca Hertziana, Rome, now consultable in the manuscript "Ungekürzte Transposition des Briefwechsels Jean Paul Richter–Giovanni Morelli sowie Giovanni Morelli–Jean Paul Richter, 1876–91 auf Typoskript in Vorbereitung der Publikation." For the first very detailed biography of Richter, see Dietrich Seybold, *Das Schlaraffenleben der Kunst: Eine Biografie des Kunstkenners und Leonardo da Vinci-Forschers Jean Paul Richter (1847–1937)* (Munich: Wilhelm Fink, 2014).

32 The correspondence opens with a letter from Richter (at Venice), 14 September 1876, asking to meet Morelli, as he has heard about Lermolieff from Lützow. Morelli replied immediately (16 September), inviting him to via Pontaccio 14, Milan: "the earlier you come the better." Archiv Nachlass Jean Paul Richter, Bibliotheca Hertziana, Rome.

33 Jean Paul Richter to Giovanni Morelli, 1 September 1877, Archiv Nachlass Jean Paul Richter, Bibliotheca Hertziana, Rome: Richter signs his letter: "Mit dem ergebensten Danke für Ihre grosse mir erwiesene Güte zeichnet in der bestimmten Hoffnung Sie noch in Deutschland widersehen zu dürfen, in ehrerbietiger Hochschätzung, hochverehrter Herr."

34 "Und nun leben Sie wohl—von deutschem Boden aus ist dieser Gruss der letzte den ich Ihnen wohl in diesem Jahre zusenden werde. Mögen Ihnen Ihre Kunststudien eben so viele heitere schöne Stunden gewähren als ich denselben verdanke, Se aber sind jung—die ganze herrliche Welt der Kunst mit ihren unentdeckten Goldgruben steht offen vor Ihren Blicken und ladet Sie ein zum Forschen und Nachsuchen. Frisch ans Werk also und seien Ihnen die Götter gnädig."

35 Giovanni Morelli to Jean Paul Richter, 10 October 1877, Archiv Nachlass Jean Paul Richter, Bibliotheca Hertziana, Rome.

36 "Lady Eastlake dagegen ist eine sehr gescheite und in der Kunstgeschichte wohlbewanderte Dame. Sie ist eine Art Mannweib, energisch und absolut in ihren Ansichten, aber dabei sehr gut und dienstfertig," Giovanni Morelli to Jean Paul Richter, 10 October 1877, Archiv Nachlass Jean Paul Richter, Bibliotheca Hertziana, Rome.

37 Giovanni Morelli to Jean Paul Richter, 19 November 1877, Archiv Nachlass Jean Paul Richter, Bibliotheca Hertziana, Rome: "Und will man in der Kunstwissenschaft wirklich zu einem Resultate kommen, so muss man dieselbe nicht in Documenten von Papier studiren, sondern in den Werken der Kunst selbst. Das kostet freilich viel Mühe, Zeit und Beharrlichkeit, aber man hat zuletzt doch die unendliche Genugtuung sich auf festem Boden zu fühlen, und seine Zeit und seinen Witz nicht umsonst, gespendet zu haben."

38 Jean Paul Richter, *The Literary Works of Leonardo da Vinci: Compiled and Edited from the Original Manuscripts* (London: Sampson Low, Marston, Searle & Rivington, 1883).

39 Claire Farago, "Re-Reading Richter and MacCurdy: Lessons in Translation," in *Leonardo in Britain: Collections and Historical Reception*, ed. Susanna Avery-Quash and Juliana Barone, Biblioteca Leonardiana: Studi e documenti 7 (Florence: Olschki, 2019).

40 Ivan Lermolieff, *Die Werke italienischer Meister in den Galerien von München, Dresden und Berlin. Ein kritischer Versuch von Ivan Lermolieff. Aus dem Russischen übersetzt von Dr. Johannes Schwarze* (Leipzig: E. A. Seemann, 1880).

41 Jean Paul Richter to Giovanni Morelli, n.d. 1881, Archiv Nachlass Jean Paul Richter, Bibliotheca Hertziana, Rome.

42 Giovanni Morelli, *Italian Masters in German Galleries: A Critical Essay on the Italian Pictures in the Galleries of Munich, Dresden, Berlin, by Giovanni Morelli, Member of the Italian Senate. Translated from the German by Mrs Louise M. Richter* (London: George Bell and Sons, 1883).

43 Bell's letter is quoted in Jean Paul Richter to Giovanni Morelli, 30 April 1881, Archiv Nachlass Jean Paul Richter, Bibliotheca Hertziana, Rome.

44 Austen Henry Layard, cited by Giovanni Morelli in his letter to Jean Paul Richter, 28 October 1881, Archiv Nachlass Jean Paul Richter, Bibliotheca Hertziana, Rome, repeated in Layard's introduction

to Giovanni Morelli, *Italian Painters: Critical Studies of their Works* (1892).

45 Jaynie Anderson, "Richter, Jean Paul," *Oxford Art Online*, s.v. Richter.

46 See Richter's detailed letters to Layard about the matter: Jean Paul Richter (at Florence) to Austen Henry Layard, 5 March 1890, Add. MSS 39045, British Museum, London.

47 Morelli's last letter to Richter testifies to the warmth of their relationship until the end: Morelli chose to reply to Richter rather than answering the other thirty-seven letters on his desk that awaited a response. Giovanni Morelli (at Milan) to Jean Paul Richter, 5 February 1891, Archiv Nachlass Jean Paul Richter, Bibliotheca Hertziana, Rome.

48 Discussed extensively in Anderson, *Collecting, Connoisseurship*, 59–61.

49 Giovanni Morelli, "Libro di spese di casa 1876–1891," Archivio Zavaritt, Gorle. No earlier account books survive.

50 On 9 October 1871 Antinori opened an exhibition in Florence of photographs by Adolphe Braun of Dornach, demonstrating Morelli's commitment to reproducing works of arts.

Notes to Chapter 12: Morelli and the Princess

1 Victoria was well aware of her husband's reputation, as shown in her letters to her mother: *Dearest Mama: Letters Between Queen Victoria and the Crown Princess of Prussia, 1861–1864*, ed. Roger Fulford (London: Evans Brothers, 1968), 211–12.

2 For an account of Crown Prince Frederick as Protector of Berlin Museums, see Tilmann von Stockhausen, *Gemäldegalerie Berlin: Die Geschichte ihrer Erwerbungspolitik, 1830–1904* (Berlin: Nicolai, 2000).

3 It was not until 1880 that Crown Prince Frederick was able to appoint a properly trained archaeologist as director, Richard Schöne, so for most of the time the museum was directed by aristocrats, such as Count Guido von Usedom. On the fiftieth anniversary of the Royal Museums in 1880 the Crown Prince delivered a speech that endorsed the vision of Wilhelm von Humboldt. Katrin Wehry, in *Kaiser Friedrich III (1831–1888) als Protektor der Königlichen Museen: Skizze einer neuen Kulturpolitik*, Jahrbuch der Berliner Museen 54; Jahrbuch der Preussischen Kunstsammlungen (Berlin: Gebr. Mann, 2013), argues for a positive interpretation of his role as protector of museums; this view has been disputed by Bernhard Schulz in "Too Little, Too Late: An Attempt, Not Entirely Successful, to Rescue the Reputation of Emperor Friedrich III of Prussia," review in *The Art Newspaper*, no. 261 (October 2014): 92.

4 Wilhelm von Bode, *Mein Leben*, ed. Thomas W. Gaehtgens and Barbara Paul (Berlin: Nicolai, 1997).

5 Wilhelm von Bode, *Die Kunstsammlungen Ihrer Majestät der Kaiserin und Königin Friedrich in Schloß Friedrichshof* (Kronberg, 1886).

6 Eugene Barilo von Reisberg, "A Slight Case of Bartering," in *The Winterhalter Catalogue*, 13 August 2014, https://franzxaverwinterhalter.wordpress.com/2014/08/13/a-slight-case-of-bartering/. For further information on the Suermondt portraits, see Eugene Barilo von Reisberg, "Franz Xaver Winterhalter: Portraiture in the Age of Social Change" (PhD dissertation, University of Melbourne, 2016), 429, nos 827–29.

7 von Bode, *Mein Leben*, vol. 1, 305–6.

8 Count Götz Burkhard von Seckendorff to Giovanni Morelli, 4 November 1879, Archivio Zavaritt, Gorle. Little of Victoria's correspondence survives outside the Archivio Zavaritt, Gorle, with the notable exception of her letters to her mother, Queen Victoria, now in the Royal Archives at Windsor Castle.

9 Count Götz Burkhard von Seckendorff to Giovanni Morelli, 10 November 1879, Archivio Zavaritt, Gorle.

10 Giovanni Morelli (at Milan) to Niccolò Antinori, 9 November 1879, Archivio Antinori, Florence.

11 This cost him 1 lire.

12 These cost 2.5 lire.

13 Giovanni Morelli, "Libro di spese di casa 1876–1891," Archivio Zavaritt, Gorle.

14 Giovanni Morelli to Jean Paul Richter, 17 November 1879.

15 Count Götz Burkhard von Seckendorff to Giovanni Morelli, 10 December 1879, Archivio Zavaritt, Gorle.

16 Princess Victoria (at the Grand Hôtel de la Mediterranée, Pegli, near Genoa) to Giovanni Morelli, 10 December 1879, Archivio Zavaritt, Gorle: "... à plusiers reprises, cité le portrait en question représentant un prince de la famille des Médicis ce que vous prouvera que ce tableaux a fait une certaine impression à S. A. S."

17 Giovanni Morelli and Jean Paul Richter, *Italienische Malerei der Renaissance im Briefwechsel von Giovanni Morelli und Jean Paul Richter 1876–1891*, ed. Irma Richter and Gisela Richter, foreword by Paola Della Pergola (Baden-Baden: Bruno Grimm, 1960), 216.

18 Morelli had found this portrait of Giuliano de' Medici in Florence, claiming it was the primary version, only to be challenged by Bode in 1887, who had acquired a version from Bardini for the Gemäldegalerie, Berlin. Another more detailed portrait (on board) of Giuliano, now in the National Gallery, Washington, was later discovered in the 1940s. In a recent exhibition the three portraits have been subject to subtle connoisseurial analyses, but there is still no agreement as to which is the primary one. See Stefan Weppelmann, catalogue entry in *The Renaissance Portrait: From Donatello to Bellini*, ed. Keith Christiansen and Stefan Weppelmann (New York: Metropolitan Museum of Art, 2011), 174–77.

19 Princess Victoria to Giovanni Morelli, 24 and 25 December 1879, Archivio Zavaritt, Gorle. I am grateful to my colleague Dr Leo Kretzenbacher from the University of Melbourne for his transcription of Victoria's three letters to Morelli, and the thirty-five letters from Götz Burkhard von Seckendorff between 1880 to 1890.

20 Roger Fulford, ed., *Beloved Mama: Private Correspondence of Queen Victoria and the German Crown Princess, 1878–1885* (London: Evans, 1981), 58–9.

21 *Beloved Mama*, 58–9.

22 Götz Burkhard von Seckendorff (at Genoa) to Giovanni Morelli, 10 May 1880, Archivio Zavaritt, Gorle.

23 Götz Burkhard von Seckendorff (at Baden Baden) to Giovanni Morelli, 18 May 1880, Archivio Zavaritt, Gorle.

24 Götz Burkhard von Seckendorff (at Neues Palais, Potsdam) to Giovanni Morelli, 22 June 1880, Archivio Zavaritt, Gorle.

25 Gräfin Kalckreuth (at the Crown Prince's Palace, Berlin) to Giovanni Morelli, 31 December 1882, Archivio Zavaritt, Gorle.

26 Princess Victoria (at the Neues Palais, Potsdam) to Giovanni Morelli, 29 May 1880, Archivio Zavaritt, Gorle.

27 Giovanni Morelli to Niccolò Antinori, 3 July 1880, Archivio Antinori, Florence.

28 Giovanni Morelli to Niccolò Antinori, 8 June 1882, Archivio Antinori, Florence, published in Giacomo Agosti, "Giovanni Morelli corrispondente di Niccolò Antinori," in *Studi e ricerche di collezionismo e museografia Firenze 1820–1920* (Pisa: Scuola Normale Superiore di Pisa, 1985), 82.

29 Götz Burkhard von Seckendorff to Giovanni Morelli, 19 August 1882, Archivio Zavaritt, Gorle.

30 *Im Lichte Venedigs: Tiepolo-Zeichnungen und venezianische Gemälde des 18. Jahrhunderts aus Eigenbesitz* (Eichenzell bei Fulda: Museum Schloss Fasanerie, 1996), 36–37 and 84–85.

31 Reproduced in Eduard Sack, *Giambattista und Domenico Tiepolo: Ihr Leben und ihre Werke* (Hamburg: H. v. Clarmanns, 1910), 258, no. 194, illus. 286, as being still at via Pontaccio 14, Milan.

32 Sent from Neues Palais, Potsdam: Götz Burkhard von Seckendorff to Giovanni Morelli, 10 October 1882, Archivio Zavaritt, Gorle. Morelli has made Victoria very curious (*I. K. H. haben Sie den Mund wässrig gemacht*) to experience the natural beauty of Mont Blanc and Aosta with them.

33 Princess Victoria (at Baveno) to Giovanni Morelli, 19 August 1882, Archivio Zavaritt, Gorle.

34 Giovanni Morelli to Maria Antinori, 24 October 1882: "La Principessa di Germania mi spedì in dono in questi giorni un gran quadro dipinto da lei stessa—rappresenta una così detta *Vanitas* cioè a dire un crocefisso di bronzo, al piè del quale vedesi un cranio umano, de' libri, una corona per dire il Rosario e altre cose simili—il tutto dipinto con molta maestria; il quadro è segnato Victoria 1882", Agosti, "Giovanni Morelli corrispondente di Antinori," 15n30.

35 On Princess Victoria as an artist and collector, see the catalogue of the exhibition held at the Museum Schloss Fasanerie: *Im Schatten der Krone: Victoria, Kaiserin Friedrich: 1840–1901. Ein Leben mit der Kunst* (Eichenzell bei Fulda: Michael Imhof, 2001.

36 See the account of Princess Victoria as an artist in Jane Roberts, *Royal Artists: From Mary Queen of Scots to the Present Day* (London and Glasgow: Grafton Books, 1987), 121–38.

37 Agosti, "Giovanni Morelli corrispondente di Antinori," 83n34.

38 Princess Victoria to Giovanni Morelli, 13 October 1882, Archivio Zavaritt, Gorle: "Ihre schöne Handzeichnung von dem Kopf—habe ich in einen hübschen alten Rahmen gesteckt, u. er hängt in meinem Zimmer in Berlin, wo Sie ihn hoffentlich einmal sehen werden."

39 The drawing was deaccessioned by the House of Hesse, and its present location is unknown.

40 Princess Victoria (at Florence) to Queen Victoria, 29 April 1883, in *Beloved Mama*, 138.

41 Princess Victoria (at Florence) to Queen Victoria, 14 May 1883, in *Beloved Mama*, 139.

42 Prince Frederick and Princess Victoria to Giovanni Morelli, 20 November 1883, Archivio Ginoulhiac, Bergamo; photocopy in the Biblioteca Civica Angelo Mai, Bergamo. Presumably given by Gustavo Frizzoni to his sister Lina.

43 Crown Princess Victoria's letters to her husband make this clear. I am grateful to the archivist for the House of Hesse at the Schloss Fasanerie, Christine Kloessel, for identifying where the empress was on the date the portrait was drawn. Victoria's letters to her mother confirm the location, although there is a gap of several days to 12 November 1884.

44 Götz Burkhard von Seckendorff (at Palais Kaiserin Friedrich, Berlin) to Giovanni Morelli, 7 February 1890, Archivio Zavaritt, Gorle: "Nur ein Wort um Ihnen zu sagen, daß heute ein Kistchen an Sie abgeht—nach Mailand—durch die Botschaft in Rom—ein Pastell-Portrait von Ihnen von der Hand der Kaiserin enthaltend."

45 The process is described in Morelli's letters to Jean Paul Richter.

46 Morelli and Richter, *Italienische Malerei der Renaissance im Briefwechsel*, 398, 412–13.

47 Giovanni Morelli (at Portofino) to Emilio Visconti Venosta, 26 October 1886, Maz. 12, fas. M., Fondazione Cavour, Santena: "Ne' giorni che tu eri a Milano io me la godevo a Portofino, ospite dei Principi di Germania … T'assicuro che più imparo a conoscere codesti Principi e

più sono costretto a stimarli e a volergli bene. Mi fecero delle accoglienze sì cordiali e m'usarono tante gentilezze che ne fui quasi imbarazzato."

48 Giovanni Morelli (at the Senate, Rome) to Emilio Visconti Venosta, 26 November 1888, Maz. 12, fas. M., Fondazione Cavour, Santena.

49 Among Victoria's biographers, Hannah Pakula gives the best account of the period leading up to the emperor's death: Hannah Pakula, *An Uncommon Woman: The Empress Frederick; Daughter of Queen Victoria, Wife of the Crown Prince of Prussia, Mother of Kaiser Wilhelm* (New York: Simon and Schuster, 1995), 479–94.

50 Franz Herre, *Kaiserin Friedrich, Victoria, eine Engländerin in Deutschland* (Stuttgart and Leipzig: Hohnheim, 2006), 241–57.

51 Crown Princess Victoria (at Baveno) to Queen Victoria, 17 October 1887, in *Beloved and Darling Child: Last Letters Between Queen Victoria and her Eldest Daughter, 1886–1901*, ed. Agatha Ramm (Stroud, UK: Alan Sutton, 1990), 58.

52 Giovanni Morelli (at the Senate, Rome) to Emilio Visconti Venosta, 26 November 1887, Maz. 12, fas. M, Fondazione Cavour, Santena: "Destino più crudele di codesto non saprei immaginarmelo—dopo tante felicità, tante glorie, dopo tante sublimi soddisfazioni—eccoti tutt'ad un tratto la condanna a morte a lunga sentenza. Che orizzonte buio, terribile, non ha a presentarsi tutte le mattine [indecipheral word] sapessi di svegliarsi a quegli occhi bagnati ancora dalle lagrime della sera! Che tragedia. Se sapessi di poter essere di qualche utilità, di qualche sollievo a quella brava e simpatica gente, anderei subito a San Remo—ma persuaso qual sono, che la mia presenza riuscirebbe loro forse più di disturbo che di soddisfazione, aspetterò un secondo invito per andare a visitarli."

53 Götz Burkhard von Seckendorff (at villa Zirio, Sanremo) to Giovanni Morelli, 26 December 1887, Archivio Zavaritt, Gorle : "... daß es zur Zeit nicht schlecht geht und Gott um seinen Segen anflehen, daß er ein kostbares Leben erhalte. Der hohe Herr zeigte eine rührende. ja geradezu erhebende Ergebenheit und ein Vertrauen das nur Seelengröße einflößen kann."

54 Emilio Visconti Venosta, obituary for Giovanni Morelli, *L' Illustrazione Italiana*, 22 March 1891: "Ritornando all'uomo, non si può dimenticare che fra gl'illustri amici ch'egli ebbe si contava quel Principe generoso e sventurato che fu l'Imperatore Federico III. Nei frequenti viaggi che il Principe Federico faceva in Italia, soleva, passando per la nostra città, recarsi in casa sua e insieme alla Principessa sua moglie, lo desiderava compagno e maestro nelle visite alle città italiane, alle gallerie e ai monumenti."

55 For an account of the crown prince's illness and death, see *The Letters of Queen Victoria*, ed. George Earle Buckle, vol. 1 (London: John Murray, 1930), 369–71.

56 The royal party consisted of Victoria's four children; her brother "Bertie," then Prince of Wales, later King Edward VII; his wife Alexandra; and their children. Victoria's daughter Sophie of Prussia married Crown Prince Constantine of Greece on 27 October 1889.

57 Giovanni Morelli to Giovanni Zavaritt, 28 October 1889, Archivio Zavaritt, Gorle: "Rispondo alla gradita tua che mi raggiunse a Venezia, dove era andato per salutarvi la povera Imperatrice Federico, che non avevo più riveduta dopo la sua disgrazia. Passai quasi tutto il tempo con lei durante le 36 ore, ch'ella si fermò a Venezia prima d'imbarcarsi colle sue 4 figlie per recarsi in Grecia. L'ho trovata molto abbattuta e sconfortata. Vidi e conobbi in quest'occasione anche il Principe di Galles con tutta la sua famiglia, la moglie, due figlie e due maschi; pranzai da loro dai Layard e li trovai tutti gente molto affabile e alla buona. Anche loro si recarono da Venezia ad Atene per assistere alle nozze della loro nipote Sofia col principe ereditario di Grecia. Dopo un soggiorno di sei giorni nella città delle Lagune ritornando qui nel mio nido, dove mi stava aspettando un mucchio di bozze di stampa da correggere—lavoro uggioso e che porta via del gran tempo, specialmente a me che emendo e cambio molto, a dispetto del mio Editore. Ora però sono agli sgoccioli colla stampa del primo Volume, che escirà verso la metà di Novembre e che mi tirerà addosso una tempesta di vituperi da parte dei professori e direttori delle Gallerie e me ne rallegro già anticipatamente."

58 As recorded in Morelli, "Libro di spese di casa 1876–1891," October 1889.

59 "Lady Layard's Journal: 21 October 1889—Ca' Capello, Venice," in Armstrong Browning Library and Museum, *The Brownings: A Research Guide* (Waco, Texas: Baylor University), http://pops.baylor.edu/layard/xml.php?fn=18891020.xml.

60 *The Letters of the Empress Frederick*, ed. Frederick Ponsonby (London: Macmillan, 1928), esp. the introduction, ix–xix.

61 For example, in 1887 Layard wrote to Sir William Gregory, director of the National Gallery in London, that Morelli "went on Sunday to Baveno to see the Crown Princess, but he was able to return on Tuesday" in order to accompany Gregory to Bergamo and Brescia. Austen Henry Layard to Sir William Gregory, 17 October 1887, Add. MSS 38, 950, British Library, London.

62 Adolfo Venturi, "La formazione della galleria Layard a Venezia," *L'Arte* 14 (1912): 460.

63 Götz Burkhard von Seckendorff (at the Palais Kaiserin, Berlin), to Giovanni Morelli, 14 October 1888, Archivio Zavaritt, Gorle: "Zunächst muß ich Ihnen also mitteilen, daß wir Friedrichskron und somit Potsdam am 1. Oct. verlassen haben. Der Aufbruch aus dem Hause wo die arme Kaiserin 29 Sommer verlebte war bitter hart. Allein

ich hoff die Zukunft soll 'Ihr' auf dem kleinen Gut welches 'Sie' bei Frankfurt erworben hat Ruhe und Arbeit mit Genuß (für die Zukunft) gewähren. Das Haus mit einem Areal von 200 Morgen liegt bei dem malerischen Örtchen Cronberg am Fuß des Taunus, 40 Minuten zu fahren von Homburg. Klima und Lage scheinen vortrefflich. Es wird im kommenden Jahr noch manches zu thun geben zu bauen etc. allein je mehr Arbeit desto beßer. Es wird das alles die arme Frau auf andere Gedanken bringen."

64 Götz Burkhard von Seckendorff (at Sanremo) to Giovanni Morelli, 26 December 1887, Archivio Zavaritt, Gorle.

65 For these linguistic observations, I am again grateful to my colleague Leo Kretzenbacher.

66 Austen Henry Layard to Sir William Burton, 20 November 1891, Add. MSS 38, British Library, London.

67 Gustavo Frizzoni, "Ein Lebensbild," in *Kunstkritische Studien über italienische Malerei: Die Galerie zu Berlin* (Leipzig: F. A. Brockhaus, 1893), lxiii.

68 Lady Eastlake to Austen Henry Layard, 22 February 1892, John Murray Archive, London (now at National Library of Scotland, Edinburgh).

69 "Ritrattino di Francesco Pourbus rappresentante un ragazzo che tiene una mela in mano." There is a portrait of a boy, attributed to Pourbus, in Victoria's collection at Friedrichshof in the Taunus, but neither the description nor the attribution allows it to be identified as Morelli's posthumous gift.

70 Crown Princess Victoria (at Trento) to Queen Victoria, 9 November 1892, in *Beloved and Darling Child*, 149.

Notes to Chapter 13: Endgames and Black Nomenclature

1 Ivan Lermolieff, *Die Werke italienischer Meister in den Galerien von München, Dresden und Berlin. Ein kritischer Versuch von Ivan Lermolieff. Aus dem Russischen übersetzt von Dr. Johannes Schwarze* (Leipzig: E. A. Seemann, 1880).

2 Giovanni Morelli, *Italian Masters in German Galleries: A Critical Essay on the Italian Pictures in the Galleries of Munich, Dresden, Berlin, by Giovanni Morelli, Member of the Italian Senate, Translated from the German by Mrs Louise M. Richter* (London: George Bell and Sons, 1883), 2.

3 Jvan Lermolieff, *Le opere dei maestri italiani nelle gallerie di Monaco, Dresda e Berlino: Saggio critico di Iwan Lermolieff tradotto dal Russo in Tedesco per cura del Dottore Giovanni Schwarze e dal Tedesco in Italiano dalla Baronessa di K. A.* (Bologna: Nicola Zanichelli, 1886).

4 As he explained to his old friend Giovanni Battista Camozzi Vertova, he hoped that the response would be negative: "Quanto a me ti posso assicurare che spero in una negativa—giacché mi vedo troppo innanzi negli anni per sobbarcarmi ad un'opera che di necessità mi leverebbe gran parte della mia libertà personale." Giovanni Morelli (at Rome) to Giovanni Battista Camozzi Vertova, 16 March 1881, Fondo Risorgimento Italiano, Sala 24, Cassa 1, Faldone 28, no. 413, Biblioteca Civica Angelo Mai, Bergamo.

5 Giovanni Morelli (at Milan) to Giovanni Battista Camozzi Vertova, 10 January 1884, Biblioteca Civica Angelo Mai, Bergamo: "Mesi or sono ebbi la buona sorte di rinvenire in una casa privata a Firenze il ritratto di Giuliano de' Medici, fratello di Lorenzo dipinto dal Botticelli. Dalla medaglia di Antonio del Pollaiuolo infuori è il solo ritratto del padre di Clemente VII che si conosca. L'acquistai a prezzo discreto ed ora è mio e può dirsi una delle più preziose perle della mia raccolta."

6 Giovanni Morelli to Austen Henry Layard, 29 November 1880, British Library, London.

7 Giovanni Morelli to Niccolò Antinori, 2 November 1880, Archivio Antinori, Florence: "Finora non posso che provare soddisfazione di aver pubblicata la mia roba—ma la grandinata non potrà però mancare di scaricarsi sul mio capo, poiché la mia torcia (se è torcia) deve aver bruciato molti nasi e incendiate molte parrucche."

8 Austen Henry Layard (at Potsdam) to Giovanni Morelli, 7 June 1881, Add. MSS 389, 67, British Library, London: "Elle m'avoué, en riant, que son ami M. Crowe était furieux contre vous, et qu'il avait tort, et qu'il n'y avait rien dans vôtre livre que aurait du lui blesser—mais pour Cavalcaselle vous étiez un peu méchant. Je lui ai donné les explications dont vous m'aviez fourni, et elle en a été parfaitement satisfaite. Elle a beaucoup rit quand je lui ai dit que vous craigniez une conspiration artiste-critique, et l'assassinat."

9 Morelli, *Italian Masters in German Galleries*, 2.

10 Reassembled by Giulio Bora in his book *I disegni della collezione Morelli* (Bergamo: Credito Bergamasco, 1988).

11 A full account of the titles in Morelli's library is given in *La figura e l'opera di Giovanni Morelli: Materiali di ricerca*, ed. Giulio Orazio Bravi and Matteo Panzeri (Bergamo: Biblioteca Civica Angelo Mai, 1987); for the section on the art-historical books, including the drawing catalogue, see the same volume, 115–204. An attempt to construct Morelli's view of drawings from the marginalia in these catalogues has been made by Giacomo Agosti, "Gli studi del Kunstkenner. Le passioni del marchand-amateur. Uno sguardo alla Biblioteca di Morelli sui disegni antichi," in Bora, *I disegni della collezione Morelli*, 31–49.

12 Giovanni Morelli (at Milan) to Louis Alexander Fagan, 27 May 1881, CG DCCXLVIII.309, Biblioteca Marucelliana, Florence.

13 Morelli, *Italian Masters in German Galleries*, 151–68.

14 Karl Woermann, *Lebenserinnerungen eines Achtzigjährigen* (Leipzig: Bibliographisches Institut, 1924), 474–75: "Persönlich lernte ich ihn erst später in Dresden kennen und lieben und suchte ihn auch wiederholt in Mailand auf, wo er wohnte. Nicht gross von Gestalt, fiel er durch seinen schönen, lebhaften italienischen Kopf mit ergrauendem Knebelbart auf. Er war eine der umgänglichsten und anregendsten Persönlichkeiten, der mir begegnet sind. Solange er lebte, blieben wir brieflich und persönlich in freundschaftlichem Verkehr."

15 Morelli, *Italian Masters in German Galleries*, 129–37.

16 Lermolieff, *Die Werke italienischer Meister*, 348.

17 Timothy Wilson, "Nicola da Urbino," in *Majolique: La faïence italienne au temps des humanistes, 1480–1530* (Paris: Musée National de la Renaissance, 2012), 157–95.

18 Corrado Ricci, "Critica d'Arte," *Cronaca Bizantina* (17 January 1886): 3–4.

19 "Non avere tanta fretta a pubblicare le tue critiche intorno all'opera del Morelli, se vorrai fare cosa non solo buona ma ottima. Hai ragione: quella sicumera dell'onorevole Senatore infastidisce! Ma però tieni calcolo dei buoni risultati ai quali è arrivato, massime a riguardo della scuola milanese, ch'egli conosce più davvicino e più addentro," Adolfo Venturi to Corrado Ricci, quoted in Giovanna Bosi Maramotti, "Gli anni bolognesi di Corrado Ricci," in *Annali della Scuola Normale Superiore di Pisa: Classe di Lettere e Filosofia* 4 / 5, no. 2 (2000): 497.

20 Ricci, "Critica d'Arte."

21 Gabriele D'Annunzio (at Rome) to Zanichelli, 10 March 1886, F. S. Zanichelli, carte V. fasc. 48, no. 6, Biblioteca Comunale dell'Archiginnasio, Bologna.

22 Andrea Emiliani, "La politica delle arti prima di Maria Vittoria Brugnoli. Dibattiti parlamentari tra gli anni '20 e '40 del Novecento," in *Maria Vittoria Brugnoli: Storica dell'arte, funzionaria dell'amministrazione dei beni culturali e docente universitaria: Atti della Giornata di studio in ricordo di Maria Vittoria Brugnoli*, ed. Enzo Borsellino and Federica Papi (Rome: Tre-Press, 2017) 139–49.

23 Giovanni Morelli (at Milan) to Lady Eastlake, 31 August 1882, 25-3-22 L. 416, letters to Sir Charles and Lady Eastlake, 1823–1882, Victoria and Albert Museum, London: "In dieser mit Charlatan's aller Art erfüllten Welt von einer Dame Ihres Schlages geachtet zu sein ist wahrlich keine geringe Genugthuung, und ich bin Ihnen daher zu großem, innigem Danke verpflichtet für alle die liebenswürdigen Beweise von Wohlwollen, die Sie mir in London gegeben und die Sie nun mit Ihren an mich gerichteten Blättern noch haben besiegeln wollen."

24 Morelli to Lady Eastlake, 31 August 1882: "Da Sie nun die Güte haben wollen sich mit dem Büchlein des Lermolieff eingehend zu beschäftigen, so erlauben Sie mit Ihnen einige Winke zu geben. Daß ich große Achtung vor der deutschen Wissenschaft hege, brauch' ich Ihnen nicht erst zu sagen; hätte ich doch sonst nicht so lange Jahre auf deutschen Universitäten studiert. Was mich jedoch, als Italiener, sehr oft kränken und ärgern müßte, war das oberflächliche, wegwerfend süffisante Urtheil, der [crossed out: "starke," replaced with "pedantische"] Schulmeisterton, den sich so viele deutsche Schriftsteller, und vor allem die Berliner, Italien gegenüber erlaubten, ohne unsere Sprache zu kennen, und ohne je Gelegenheit gehabt und gesucht zu haben, mit unserer besseren Gesellschaft in nähere Berührung zu kommen. Ich habe daher gewünscht, daß einmal ein Tatare nach Deutschland käme und daß derselbe den prahlsüchtigen Söhnen des Arminius bewiese, daß, wenn die heutigen Italiener allen Grund haben über ihre Unwissenheit zu weinen, Deutschland, wenigstens in der Kunstwissenschaft, doch nicht in der Lage ist darüber stolz und selbstzufrieden zu lächeln und mit seiner Allwissenheit groß zu thun. Das war der Stachel, der hauptsächlich mich antrieb, das Buch des Lermolieff in die Welt zu senden."

25 Sylvia Ferino Pagden, "Raffaello come *test-case* della validità del metodo morelliano," in *Giovanni Morelli e la cultura dei conoscitori*, vol. 2 (Bergamo: Pierluigi Lubrina, 1993), 331–49.

26 As, for instance in the exhibition catalogue: Davide Gasparotto, *Pietro Bembo e l'invenzione del Rinascimento* (Venezia: Marsilio, 2013), 260–61.

27 Giovanni Morelli to Lady Eastlake, 11 November 1882, National Art Library, Victoria and Albert Museum, London.

28 See the catalogue by Sylvia Ferino Pagden: *Disegni umbri: Gallerie dell'Accademia di Venezia* (Milan: Electa, 1984), esp. pp. 150–51, where the drawing by Raphael, from his Roman period, of a horseman fighting two nude figures, and on the reverse a standard-bearer.

29 The correspondence between Morelli and Lady Eastlake ends abruptly with the statement that the last general elections in Italy were very questionable. We will never know why, as only these few pages remain, the rest of the letter censored.

30 Lady Eastlake, "The Life and Works of Raphael," *Edinburgh Review* (March 1883): 175–76.

31 The narrative of their excursion is in letters that Gustavo Frizzoni wrote from the Fine Arts Club on Hanover Square to entertain his mother Clementina, alone (*sola, soletta*) at the family Villa at Crella, and his brother Teodoro. These letters are in a private archive in Bergamo.

32 Wilhelm Koopmann, *Raffaels Handzeichnungen in der Auffassung von W. Koopmann* (Marburg: N. G. Elwert, 1897).

33 Christopher Baker, "Connoisseurs at Christ Church: Morelli, Fry and Berenson," *Journal of the History of Collections* 13, no. 2 (2001): 163–73.

34 Gustavo Frizzoni, "L'arte italiana nella Galleria nazionale di Londra," *Archivio storico italiano* 4, no. 113 (1879): 246–81. The article was developed into a book: Gustavo Frizzoni, *L'arte italiana nella Galleria nazionale di Londra* (Florence, 1880).

35 Gustavo Frizzoni (at London) to Clementina Frizzoni, 28 July 1887: "Il Sig. Nane naturalmente formava sempre il centro della compagnia, pel suo carattere autorevole e famigliare ad un tempo. Il Richter che gli sta sempre alle costole per quanto possibile, s'è fatto però esso molto provetto e sicuro e ha preso un certo tono canzonatorio, dal quale male si difendono i compagni più timidi, quale lo scrivente e l'ottimo dott. Koopmann: i quali però non si lasciano confondere e tirano non ostante diritto per la loro strada."

36 Giovanni Morelli to Heinrich Wölfflin (via Ackermann), in the last months of 1890, in Nachtrag 73, Notizheft 26, fol. [26] r, Nachlass Heinrich Wölfflin, Universitätsbibliothek, Basel: "Sie erscheinen mir als ein ungewöhnlich feiner und scharfer Beobachter." I am grateful to Giovanna Targia for the information about Morelli and Wölfflin.

37 Heinrich Wölfflin to Emil Sulger-Gebing, 2 December 1890, quoted in *Heinrich Wölfflin, 1864–1945: Autobiographie, Tagebücher und Briefe*, ed. Joseph Gantner (Basel: Schwabe, 1984), 76–77: "Dagegen schrieb mir Morelli (Lermolieff) in Mailand, der beste Kenner dieser Dinge, er nehme Satz für Satz an, und das will umso mehr heißen, als der Betreffende sonst der Ansicht ist, die Deutschen sollten die Hände von der italienischen Kunst fern halten, sintemal die Italiener allein mit ihr fertig würden."

38 The correspondence between Morelli and Brockhaus is reasonably complete. Letters from Brockhaus to Morelli are in the Archivio Zavaritt, Gorle, and those from Morelli to Brockhaus in StA-L, 21083, F. A. Brockhaus, No. 281, Sächsisches Staatsarchiv, Leipzig. Morelli's letters are all addressed *An Herrn F. A. Brockhaus*, without naming a correspondent, while the letters from Brockhaus to him are all signed "F. A. Brockhaus," with one exception signed "Eduard." Morelli's letters have brief comments from Brockhaus in the margins. I am most grateful to my colleague Dr Leo Kretzenbacher for providing a transcription of their correspondence.

39 Morelli praised the indexes to Brockhaus as being executed with great expertise and admirable industriousness ("mit großer Sachkenntnis und mit bewunderungswürdigem Fleiße ausgeführt"). After persuasion, Richter reluctantly agreed to make an index for the second volume.

40 Paul Müller-Walde, *Leonardo da Vinci: Lebensskizze und Forschungen über sein Verhältniss zur florentiner Kunst und zu Raffael* (Munich: Hirth, 1889).

41 F. A. Brockhaus to Giovanni Morelli, 5 November 1889, Archivio Zavaritt, Gorle: "Inwiefern Sie in der Polemik gegen Director Bode noch eine kleine Änderung eintreten lassen wollen, stelle ich Ihrem Ermessen anheim; meines Erachtens dürfte es sich wol empfehlen, den Schluß des von S. IX auf S. X überlaufenden Satzes wegzulassen, weil doch anzunehmen ist, dass auch den Gegner [einige] sachliche Gründe leiten."

42 For an account of the polemics between Morelli and Bode, as seen from their publications, see Catherine B. Scallen, "Wilhelm Bode's and Giovanni Morelli's Debates about Connoisseurship," in *Rembrandt, Reputation and the Practice of Connoisseurship* (Amsterdam: Amsterdam University Press, 2004), 89–102.

43 Ivan Lermolieff, *Kunstkritische Studien über italienische Malerei: Die Galerien Borghese und Doria Panfili in Rom; Von Ivan Lermolieff. Mit 62 Abbildungen* (Leipzig: F. A. Brockhaus, 1890).

44 On Morelli and the Vienna school of art history, see Julius von Schlosser, *Die Wiener Schule der Kunstgeschichte: Rückblick auf ein Säkulum deutscher Gelehrtenarbeit in Österreich* (Innsbruck: Wagner, 1934), 164–71.

45 On Christmas day 1889, Morelli in Milan received 800 marks in payment, plus copies of the book.

46 Giovanni Morelli to F. A. Brockhaus, 20 December 1889, Archivio Zavaritt, Gorle.

47 F. A. Brockhaus as quoted in Giovanni Morelli's letter of 20 December 1890.

48 "ich wäre zu rücksichtsvoll gegen Herrn Bode verfahren," [underlined in the original]. Giovanni Morelli to F. A. Brockhaus, 20 December 1889, Archivio Zavaritt, Gorle.

49 Morelli to F. A. Brockhaus, 20 December 1889: "sagte man mir andererseits, daß über meine Polemik gegen den Berliner Director unter den Anhängern und Clienten desselben ein Hallo entstanden sei. Ich darf also auf sehr bittere Angriffe von Berlin aus gefasst sein. Solange dieselben nur meine These betreffen, will ich sie in aller Ruhe über mein [one word illegible] Haupt ergehen lassen; sollten jedoch die von mir berichteten Thatsachen bestritten werden, dann werde ich auch zur Vertheidigung derselben schreiten—falls ich nämlich den Gegner einer Antwort würdig erachten sollte. Hätte Dr. Bode mir nicht schon seit Jahren stets auf die Füsse getreten, so stark ich zwar im immerhin gegen seine, nach meiner Überzeugung, ganz verkehrte Auffassung der ital. Kunstgeschichte aufzutreten mich verpflichtet gefühlt habe—allein ich muß gegen seine These weit rücksichtsvoller vorgehen. Übrigens wird der Lärm der Bode'schen Partei dem Absatze der Bücher nur förderlich sein."

50 Giovanni Morelli to F. A. Brockhaus, 18 January 1890, StA-L, 21083, 281–44, F. A. Brockhaus, Sächsisches Staatsarchiv, Leipzig.

51 Wilhelm Koopmann, "Iwan Lermolieff's Experimentalmethode, ein unfehlbares Mittel zur Bestimmung von Kunstwerken," *Preußischer Jahrbucher* 65 (1890): 467–74.

52 Giovanni Morelli to F. A. Brockhaus, May 1890, StA-L, 21083 F. A. Brockhaus, No. 281, Sächsisches Staatsarchiv, Leipzig: "Die Kritik des letzten ist wirklich sehr unschuldig und liefert mir einen ferneren Beweis,

daß auch beim besten Willen und beim anhaltendsten Fleiß es nicht jedermann gegeben ist, ein richtiges Veständniß der Formen zu gewinnen. Ich habe in einem über siebenjährigen Briefwechsel mit Dr. W. Koopmann mir alle erdenkliche Mühe gegeben, ihm meine Formenlehre an Beispielen auseinanderzusetzen und begreiflich zu machen—allein wie ich zu meinem gesagten Bedauern auch aus dieser seiner Kritik an meinem Buch ersehen muß, fiel meine Saat auf Sand."

53 More seriously, Brockhaus questioned Morelli's statement about the minister of culture, Carl Friedrich von Gerber, as to whether he had actually spoken about Morelli's previous book in parliament in the way he was quoted here. He asked whether Morelli had the original of von Gerber's speech or could indicate the date when the speech was given, so that the original quote could be verified. Woermann was consulted but was unable to prove the matter one way or the other, and Brockhaus asked Morelli to delete this part of the text. The only time von Gerber had spoken about the Dresden Gallery was in a meeting of the Second Chamber on 7 February 1882, when the report of a parliamentary subcommittee was discussed that dealt with the attacks by Dr. Oskar Eisenmann, director of the Kassel Gallery, in the *Kölnische Zeitung*, against the previous management of the Dresden Gallery (before Woermann). Von Gerber's speech was reported verbatim in the stenographic protocol, but Morelli's name was never mentioned. Brockhaus suggested that Morelli delete all references to von Gerber, as his enemies would pounce on this as an attack against the minister. Morelli agreed. No record of what Morelli originally wrote survives.

54 F. A. Brockhaus to Giovanni Morelli, 12 December 1890, Archivio Zavaritt, Gorle: "Ich habe mir erlaubt, auf dem einen Abzug einige Bemerkungen zu machen, welche ich Ihrer gefälligen Beachtung anheimgebe. An den speciell bezeichneten zwei Stellen auf Seite VIII und XI habe ich doch den Eindruck, daß es gerathsam sein dürfte, durch Wegfall des Angestrichenen die Polemik zu mildern. Sie wissen, daß ich aus Überzeugung Ihren Standpunkt öffentlich und privatim vertrete und deshalb auch eine gewisse Berechtigung zur Abwehr gegen Angriffe anerkenne, allein es erscheint mir im Interesse des Buches und seiner ganzen Tendenz selbst angemessener, jetzt nicht nochmals so direkt in die persönlichen Hinweise einzugehen. Ich möchte Ihnen daher empfehlen, die von mir angedeuteten Streichungen vorzunehmen."

55 Kirsten Belgum, "Documenting the Zeitgeist: How the Brockhaus Recorded and Fashioned the World for Germans," in *Publishing Culture and the "Reading Nation": German Book History in the Long Nineteenth Century*, ed. Lynne Tatlock (Rochester, NY: Camden House, 2010), 89–117.

56 Ivan Lermolieff, *Kunstkritische Studien über italienische Malerei: Die Galerien zu München und Dresden. Mit 41 Abildungen* (Leipzig: F. A. Brockhaus, 1891).

57 F. A. Brockhaus to Giovanni Zavaritt, c. 19 November 1891, Archivio Zavaritt, Gorle.

58 Giovanni Morelli (at Milan) to F. A. Brockhaus, 8 May 1890, Sächsisches Staatsarchiv, StA-L, 21083 F. A. Brockhaus, Leipzig, Nr. 281: "Und nun gestatten Sie mir daß ich Ihnen meinen verbindlichsten Dank ausspreche für den überaus freundlichen Rath, den Sie mir zu geben die Güte hatten. Daß ich denselben Ihrem Wunsche gemäß befolgte, werden Sie an der betreffenden Stelle sehen. Es ist leider sehr wahr, daß ich in der innigsten Überzeugung, das Wahre gegen das Falsche zu vertheidigen, gar zu oft in meinem Eifer wie man zu sagen pflegt über die Schnur haue—und damit, wie Sie richtig bemerken, einer [one word illegible, "noblen"?] Sache, die ich vertheidige, eher schade als nütze. Diese Schwäche liegt mir halt im Blute und hat auch in meinem politischen Leben nicht selten Verdruß bereitet."

59 *Kunstkritische Studien über italienische Malerei: Die Galerie zu Berlin. Von Ivan Lermolieff. Nebst einem Lebensbilde Giovanni Morelli's herausgegeben von Dr Gustav Frizzoni. Mit Porträt und 66 Abbildungen* (F. A. Brockhaus, Leipzig, 1893). This volume also contains three essays on Raphael: "Perugino oder Raffael?," "Raffael's Jugendentwickelung," and "Noch einmal das venetianische Skizzenbuch").

60 See the bibliography of Morelli's publications.

61 Jocelyn Ffoulkes to Austen Henry Layard, 9 February 1890, Add. MSS 39098, British Library, London.

62 Jocelyn Ffoulkes to Austen Henry Layard, 28 July 1890, Add. MSS 39098, British Library, London.

63 Jocelyn Ffoulkes to Austen Henry Layard, 25 June 1890, Add MSS 39046, British Library, London.

64 Jocelyn Ffoulkes to Austen Henry Layard, 30 June 1890, Add MSS 39046, British Library, London.

65 "Lady Layard's Journal: 1 March 1891—Ca' Capello, Venice," in Armstrong Browning Library and Museum, *The Brownings: A Research Guide* (Waco, Texas: Baylor University), http://pops.baylor.edu/layard/xml.php?fn=18910301.xml.

66 For the wine he paid 46.80 lire (Giovanni Morelli, "Libro di spese," Archivio Zavaritt, Gorle).

67 Senato del Regno, *Atti parlamentari. Discussioni*, 10 March 1891: "Quantunque natura nol trasse alle giornaliere zuffe della politica non mancò mai ai solenni dibattimenti intorno ai maggiori interessi. Sicuro senso della realtà, nobile fermezza, moderazione senza debolezza, fede salda nei propri principi, nei propri amici, informarono la condotta sua nei due rami del Parlamento. Dello studio dell'arte e sopratutto della pittura appassionatissimo, i tesori dell'arte italiana aveva interrogati in ogni nostra città ed in Germania; della messe

sapiente lasciò un volume che andò famoso e diedegli riputazione di caposcuola di un'alta critica, la quale infirmò molti giudizi e molte opinioni anteriori. Eppure tant'era modesto, che nel dare alla luce quegli studi, quasi non bastasse il duplice pseudonimo, che il dettato in lingua tedesca meglio ancor nascondeva, si scusava di non aver voluto con essi, egli nano, atteggiarsi a gigante. Modestia, fortezza, dirittura d'animo indirizzarono tutta la vita di Giovanni Morelli ad una mirabile unità morale ... Il suo testamento fu un epilogo degno dell'alta mente, del cuore generoso e del patriottismo dell'uomo di cui rimpiangiamo la dipartita."

68 Morelli's will is reprinted in Matteo Panzeri, "La Raccolta Morelli nell'Accademia Carrara di Bergamo: Un'ipotesi ricostruttiva del primo allestimento (1892)," *Archivio storico bergamasco* 8 (1985): 78–79.

69 *La Perseveranza*, 2 March 1891 and 3 March 1891.

70 *The Letters of Bernard Berenson and Isabella Stewart Gardner, 1887–1924, With Correspondence by Mary Berenson*, ed. Rollin van N. Hadley (Boston: Northeastern University Press, 1987), 135–36.

71 "Lady Layard's Journal: 22 February 1899—Ca' Capello, Venice," in Armstrong Browning Library and Museum, *The Brownings: A Research Guide* (Waco, Texas: Baylor University), https://pops.baylor.edu/layard/xml.php?fn=18990222.xml.

72 Gustavo Frizzoni, *La Galleria Morelli in Bergamo: Descritta ed illustrata con 24 tavole fototipiche* (Bergamo: Bolis, 1892).

73 Bernard Berenson, "The Morelli Collection at Bergamo," *The Connoisseur* 4, no. 15 (November 1902): 145–51.

Notes to Epilogue:
The Critical Aftermath: Followers and Frenemies

1 Valentina Locatelli, "Italian Painters, Critical Studies of their Works: The Gemäldegalerie Alte Meister in Dresden. An Overview of Giovanni Morelli's Attributions," *Journal of Art Historiography* 13 (December 2015).

2 Bernard Ashmole, "Sir John Beazley," *Proceedings of the British Academy* 56 (1972): 453–54.

3 Mary Beard, "Mrs Arthur Strong, Morelli, and the Troopers of Cortés," in *Ancient Art and Its Historiography*, ed. Alice A. Donohue and Mark D. Fullerton (Cambridge: Cambridge University Press, 2003), 148–70. Beard has a simplistic view of the Morellian method as being concerned only with detail.

4 J. D. Beazley, "The Master of the Berlin Amphora," *Journal of Hellenic Studies* 31 (1911): 276–95.

5 R. G. Gunn and Susan Lowish, "The Morellian Method and its Potential in Rock Art Research," *Rock Art Research* 34, no. 2 (2017): 193–205.

6 Giovanni Morelli, *Della pittura italiana: Studii storico-critici di Giovanni Morelli (Ivan Lermolieff); Le Gallerie Borghese e Doria-Pamphili in Roma. Prima edizione italiana preceduta dalla biografia e dal ritratto dell'autore, e illustrata da 81 incisioni* (Milan: Fratelli Treves, 1897).

7 On 19 May 1894, Frizzoni wrote to Giovanni Zavaritt, Morelli's executor and cousin, to ask for permission to publish an Italian version, and mentioned an existing Italian translation by the secretary to the Palazzo Ducale, Clotaldo Piucco, who was also a well-known Venetian journalist specializing in theatrical criticism and translation.

8 Austen Henry Layard to William Gregory, 2 March 1891, British Library, London.

9 Claude Phillips, "Signor Morelli's New Book," *The Academy* (3 May 1890): 306.

10 Julius von Schlosser, *La storia dell'arte nelle esperienze e nei ricordi di un suo cultore*, trans. Giovanna Federici Ajroldi (Bari: Giuseppe Laterza & Figli, 1936), 13–14, 36, 93–94.

11 For the best account of their relationship, see David Alan Brown, "Giovanni Morelli and Bernard Berenson," in *Giovanni Morelli e la cultura dei conoscitori*, vol. 2 (Bergamo: Pierluigi Lubrina, 1993), 389–97.

12 As shown by Morelli's letters to Jean Paul Richter in January 1890, Bibliotheca Hertziana, Rome.

13 Cited by Angela Emanuel in "Enid Layard and Julia Cartwright," in *Austen Henry Layard tra l'Oriente e Venezia*, ed. Frederick Mario Fales and Bernard Hickey (Rome: "L'Erma" di Bretschneider, 1987), 169.

14 Morelli, *Della pittura italiana*, 136.

15 For the history of the attribution, see Paola Della Pergola, *Galleria Borghese: I Dipinti*, vol. 2, (Rome: Istituto Poligrafico dello Stato, 1959), 113–14.

16 Gertrud Bing to Kenneth Clark, 5 February 1957, 8812.1.3.354, Clark papers, Tate Gallery Archive, on the occasion of the publication of Clark's autobiography.

List of Plates

1. Carl Adolf Mende, Portrait of Ursula Zavaritt Morell (1795–1867), 1842. Oil on board, 30.5 × 39.5 cm. Archivio Zavaritt, Gorle.

2. Anonymous Veronese artist, Jean Morell as an infant with his parents, Ursula Zavaritt (1795–1867) and Johannes Morell (1773–1820), at the piano in Verona, 1814. Oil on board. Zavaritt Collection, Gorle.

3. Friedrich August Wärtli and A. Bertschinger, *Ansicht des Cantons-Schul-Gebäudes in Aarau 1835 (The Kantonsschule,* Aarau), 1860. Colored lithograph, 34.6 × 21.0 cm. © Staatsarchiv, Aarau.

4. Anonymous artist, Giovanni Morelli as a boy aged about ten, with a hammer, c. 1826. Drawing on paper. Archivio Zavaritt, Gorle.

5. Map of the ground plan at the villa Zavaritt, 1802, showing the division of property. Inscribed: *Pianta terra della Casa Civile e rustici annessi, che serve ad indicare la divisione della medesima tra il Sigr. Ambrogio Zavarit, e Fratelli Moëli, e li Signori Enrico e Paolo Luigi Fratelli Meriton*. Archivio Zavaritt, Gorle.

6. View of the Renaissance side of Villa Zavaritt, Gorle, c. 1910 (before the Angelini transformation). Photograph. Archivio Zavaritt, Gorle.

7. Anonymous artist, Portrait of Antonio Frizzoni (1803–1876), 1839. Oil on canvas. Private collection, Bergamo.

8. Anonymous artist, Portrait of Giovanni Leonardo Frizzoni (1806–1849), 1839. Oil on canvas. Private collection, Bergamo.

9. Anonymous artist, Portrait of Federico Frizzoni (1807–1893), 1839. Oil on canvas. Private collection, Bergamo.

10. Friedrich Nerly the Elder, Portrait of Clementina Frizzoni (née Reichmann, 1815–1907), with a view of the Frizzoni house at the Colle dei Pasta, c. 1836. Oil on canvas. Private collection, Bergamo.

11. Anonymous Bavarian artist, Giovanni Morelli in his undergraduate lodgings at Munich, 1835. Watercolor, 21 × 30 cm. Inscribed by Gustavo Frizzoni: *Gio. Morelli studente a Monaco, da un acquarello del tempo (manoscritt. p. 5)*. Archivio Zavaritt, Gorle.

12. View of the Herzogspitalstrasse, Munich. Photograph by Georg Böttger, 1875. Morelli had his lodgings here, with the hospital tower on the right, and the tower of St Peter's Church in the background. Stadtarchiv, Munich.

13. Carl Adolf Mende, Portrait of Giovanni Morelli, 1835. Pencil on paper, 27.0 × 22.8 cm. Signed and dated: *A. Mende f. 1835 / München*. Inscribed verso in pencil: *Ritratto di Giovanni Morelli / Dono sign. Comm. Teodoro Frizzoni / febbraio*. Accademia Carrara, Bergamo, bequest of Giovanni Morelli 1891.

14. Wilhelm von Kaulbach, Giovanni Morelli as an undergraduate in Munich, c. 1835. Drawing. Previously collection of Teodoro Frizzoni. Location unknown. Photograph by Jaynie Anderson.

15. Buonaventura Genelli, Portrait of Giovanni Morelli, c. 1837. Drawing. Archivio Zavaritt, Gorle.

16. Buonaventura Genelli, *Prometheus*, 1836. Drawing. Archivio Zavaritt, Gorle. Photograph by Jaynie Anderson.

17. Giovanni Morelli, *Elephas indicus 1/16* (Elephant skeleton), c. 1833–36. Ink on paper, 19.5 × 21.5 cm. Tracing after Georges Cuvier, *Recherches sur les ossemens fossiles* (Paris: Dufour, 1821–23), vol. 1, 204. Archivio Zavaritt, Gorle.

18. *The Tapir Skeleton*, from M. & G. Cuvier, *Recherches sur les ossemens fossils*, vol. 2 (Paris, 1822).

19. Christian Koeck, Comparison of the skulls of a man (I), an ape (II), a lion (III), an ostrich (IV), a tortoise (V), a crocodile (VI), a boa constrictor (VII), a frog (VIII), and a pike (IX). Engraving from Johann Baptist von Spix, *Cephalogenesis, sive capitis ossei structura, formatio et significatio per omnes animalium classes, familias, genera ac aetates digesta, atque tabulis illustrata, legesque simul psychologiae, cranioscopiae ac Phyiognomiae inde derivatae* (Munich: 1815), Plate 1.

20. Joseph Karl Stieler, Portrait of Friedrich Wilhelm Joseph von Schelling (1775–1854), 1835. Oil on canvas, 71.8 × 57.7 cm. © Bayerische Staatsgemäldesammlungen—Neue Pinakothek München.

21. Carl Barth, *Friedrich Rückert* (1788–1866), 1859. Engraving. Universitätsbibliothek Erlangen-Nürnberg, Friedrich-Alexander Universität, Erlangen.

22. Johann Georg Veit von Engelhardt (1791–1855). Photograph by Johann George Gattineau, Erlangen. Universitätsbibliothek Erlangen-Nürnberg, Friedrich-Alexander Universität, Erlangen.

23. Buonaventura Genelli (1798–1868), Self-portrait, c. 1835. Drawing. Archivio Zavaritt, Gorle.

24. Carl Constantin Heinrich Steffeck, Portrait study of Carl Blechen (1798–1840), 1837. Graphite on paper, 109 × 87 cm. Ashmolean Museum, University of Oxford.

25. Hercule Nicolet and J. Bettannier, *Hôtel des Neuchâtelois, sur la Mer de glace du Lauter Aar et Finster Aar. Côté Méridional*, 1840. Lithograph, 19.4 × 29.7 cm. This shelter, dubbed the "Hôtel des Neuchâtelois" was built by Louis Agassiz. Musée d'art et d'histoire, Neuchâtel.

26. Ernst Fröhlich, Caricature of Ignaz Döllinger (1770–1841), professor of anatomy at the University of Munich. Pen, ink and watercolor on paper, 25 × 20 cm. Album Antinori, fol. 21. Collection of the Marchese Niccolò Antinori, Florence. Photograph by Jaynie Anderson.

27. Ernst Fröhlich. *Grosse Toilette von A. Mende* (The "great toilette" of the painter Carl Adolf Mende, 1807–1857). Pencil on paper, 28.5 × 21.5 cm. Collection of the Marchese Niccolò Antinori, Florence. Photograph by Jaynie Anderson.

28. Ernst Fröhlich, Morelli arguing with one of his professors in Munich, exclaiming "Excuse me for having contradicted you" (*Perdonatemi di avervi contraddetto*), 1835. Pencil on paper, 21 × 24.5 cm. Inscribed: *da da da da Sie verzeihn wenn ich Ihnen widerspreche spreche ich glaube positiv dgl. e. e.* Album Antinori, fol. 23. Collection of the Marchese Niccolò Antinori, Florence. Photograph by Jaynie Anderson.

29. Ernst Fröhlich (1810–1882), Caricature of Giovanni Morelli and Fröhlich on the title page of *Balvi magnus*, 1836. Inscribed: *Dies aber sind die Leiber vom Maler und vom Schreiber*. Genelli Nachlass, Universitätsbibliothek, Leipzig.

30. Illustrations to *Das Miasma diabolicum*, 1839. Fig. I: Portrait of Apollonia Kappelmeier, the devout sister of Jonathan, with her "Christian Air Visor". Fig. II: The Christian Air Visor for children, worn by Apollonia's youngest child, Johanna, aged ten years.

31. Ernst Fröhlich, Caricature of Morelli and his beer-drinking friends, 1836. Pull-out tailpiece from Morelli's *Balvi magnus*. Inscribed: *EI DU EDLES BRAUNES BIER WIE VIEL GUTE TUGENDEN HAST IN DIR*. And below in Greek: *MISSA* and *PSCHORR*. Genelli Nachlass, Universitätsbibliothek, Leipzig.

32. Marchese Gino Capponi (1792–1876). Carte-de-visite photograph by Alphonse Bernoud, c. 1860s. © National Portrait Gallery, London.

33. Francesco Saverio Altamura, Portrait of Francesco De Sanctis (1817–1883), 1890. Oil on canvas, 78 × 64 cm. Museo Nazionale di San Martino, Naples.

34. Stefano Ussi, Portrait of Govanni Battista Niccolini (1782–1861), 1864. Oil on canvas, 68 × 74 cm. Galleria d'arte moderna di Palazzo Pitti, Florence.

35. Giuseppe Bezzuoli, *La famiglia Antinori*, 1834. Oil on canvas. Collection of the Marchese Niccolò Antinori, Florence.

36. Ludwig Emil Grimm, *Bettina* (Portrait of Bettina von Arnim (1785–1859) with statue of Goethe), 1838. Etching, 28.8 × 22.4 cm. The British Museum, London. © The Trustees of the British Museum.

37. Felice Donghi and Gaetano Bonatti, *Barricate nella contrada in S. Giuseppe* (Barricades at San Giuseppe, Milan), 1848. Hand-colored lithograph. Civica Raccolta delle Stampe Achille Bertarelli, Milan.

38. Felice Donghi and Gaetano Bonatti, *Barricate mobile di Porta Tosa* (Barricades at Porta Tosa in Milan), 1848. Hand-colored lithograph. Civica Raccolta delle Stampe Achille Bertarelli, Milan.

39. Anonymous artist, *La cacciata delle forze Austriache dalla Caserma di St Marta, Bergamo 1848* (Attack of the Austrian forces of the barracks of Santa Marta, Bergamo, 1848). Watercolor. © Biblioteca Civica Angelo Mai e Archivi storici comunali Bergamo.

40. Giacomo Trecourt, Portrait of Pietro Luigi Zavaritt (1800–1876), 1842. Oil on canvas, 45 × 55 cm. Private collection, Bergamo.

41. Giacomo Trecourt, Portrait of Amalia Steiner Zavaritt (1814–1905), aged twenty-eight, 1842. Oil on canvas, 45 × 55 cm. Private collection, Bergamo.

42. Giovanni Carnovali (called Il Piccio), Portrait of Count Guglielmo Lochis (1789–1859), 1835. Oil on canvas, 49 × 42 cm. © Accademia Carrara, Bergamo.

43. Giovanni Battista Camozzi Vertova (1823–1869). Photograph by Rodolfo Masperi. Museo del Risorgimento, Bergamo.

44. Conte Alessandro Porro (1814–1879). Photograph. Archivio Civico Fotografico, Milan.

45. Marchese Anselmo Guerrieri Gonzaga (1817–1879). Photograph. Archivio Civico Fotografico, Milan.

46. Franz Heister and J. B. Bauer, *Eröffnung der National-Versammlung, in der Paulskirche zu Frankfurt a/M, den 18 Mai 1848* (Opening of the National Assembly, in the Church of St Paul, Frankfurt am Main, on 18 May 1848). Lithograph. © Historisches Museum, Frankfurt am Main. Photograph by Horst Ziegenfusz.

47. Ippolito Caffi, *The Bombardment of Marghera by the Austrians on the Night of 25 May 1849*. Oil on canvas. Galleria d'Arte Moderna, Ca' Pesaro, Venice.

48. Giovanni Leonardo Frizzoni (1840–1919). Carte-de-visite photograph by A. Mauri, Bergamo. Private archive, Bergamo.

49. Teodoro Frizzoni (1838–1931). Carte-de-visite photograph by A. Mauri, Bergamo. Private archive, Bergamo.

50. Page from Morelli's household account book (*Libro di spese*), showing the entry on the painting by Lorenzo Lotto that he sold to Federico Frizzoni. Archivio Zavaritt, Gorle.

51. Peter Tetar van Elven, *Inaugurazione del Parlamento il 2 aprile 1860*, 1860. Oil on canvas. © Museo Nazionale del Risorgimento Italiano di Torino, Proprietà Città di Torino–Galleria Civica d'Arte Moderna e Contemporanea.

52. Detail of Morelli in Fig. 51 (*Inaugurazione del Parlamento il 2 aprile 1860*), among the Cavouriani.

53. Francesco Hayez, Portrait of Gian Giacomo Poldi Pezzoli (1822–1879), 1851. Oil on canvas, 120 × 93.5 cm. Museo Poldi Pezzoli, Milan.

54. Colonel Enrico Guicciardi (1812–1895) with his troops, including Morelli. Photograph, 1866. Archivio Zavaritt, Gorle. Names inscribed by Morelli: *1. Panci. 2. Bertolini. 5. Beruto. 7. Guicciardi. 9. Morelli. 11. Regazzoni. 3. Baiotto. 4. A. Caimi. 6. Pedranzini. 8. Colombo. 10. Paravicini. 12. Bonfadini.*

55. Colonel Enrico Guicciardi (1812–1895) with his troops, including Morelli. Photograph, 1866. Archivio Zavaritt, Gorle. Names inscribed by Morelli: *1. Pedranzini. 2. Panci. 3. Colombo. 4. Beruto. 5. Regazzoni. 6. Bertolini. 7. Baiotto. 8. Bonfadini. 9. A. Caimi. 10. Guicciardi. 11. Morelli. 12. Paccacini.*

56. Sandro Botticelli, *The History of Virginia the Roman*, c. 1500. Tempera and gold on panel, 83.3 × 165.5 cm. Accademia Carrara, Bergamo, bequest of Giovanni Morelli 1891.

57. Jan Miense Molenaer, *Young Man Smoking*, c. 1635. Oil on board. Accademia Carrara, Bergamo, bequest of Giovanni Morelli 1891.

58. Antonio Pisano, called Pisanello, Portrait of Leonello d'Este, c. 1441. Tempera on panel, 29.5 × 19.7 cm. Accademia Carrara, Bergamo, bequest of Giovanni Morelli 1891.

59. Sir Austen Henry Layard (1817–1894). Albumen carte-de-visite photograph by Maull & Polyblank, London, c. 1860. Given by Layard to Morelli. Archivio Zavaritt, Gorle. © National Portrait Gallery, London.

60. Lady Layard (Mary Enid Evelyn Guest, 1843–1912). Photograph by Julia Margaret Cameron, 1869. Victoria and Albert Museum, London, given by Alan S. Cole in 1913.

61. Louise Marie Richter (née Schwab, 1852–1938). Photograph, c. 1880. Richter Papers, Archives of Duke University, North Carolina. Photographed by Jaynie Anderson.

62. Lady Eastlake (née Elizabeth Rigby, 1809–1893). Calotype by David Octavius Hill and Robert Adamson, c. 1843–48. National Portrait Gallery, London.

63. Lorenzo Lotto, Giovanni Agostino Della Torre and his Son, Niccolò, c. 1515–16. Oil on canvas, 85.0 × 68.2 cm. National Gallery, London, purchased 1862. Shown before conservation.

64. Fig. 63 shown after conservation.

65. Sandro Botticelli, Portrait of Giuliano de' Medici, c. 1478–85. Tempera and oil on wood panel, 59.5 × 39.3 cm. Accademia Carrara, Bergamo, bequest of Giovanni Morelli 1891.

66. Jean Paul Richter (1876–1891). Photograph, c. 1879. Collection Jaynie Anderson.

67. Louis Kolitz, Portrait of Sir Joseph Archer Crowe (1825–1896), 1877. Oil on canvas, 78.1 × 66.0 cm. National Portrait Gallery, London.

68. Giovanni Battista Cavalcaselle (1820–1897). Engraving. Source: Wikipedia.

69. Giorgione, *The Sleeping Venus*, c. 1508/10. Oil on canvas, 108.5 × 175.0 cm. Gemäldegalerie Alte Meister, Dresden.

70. Engraving after painting attributed to Correggio, *The Reading Magdalen*. Painting formerly in Gemäldegalerie, Dresden (lost in the Second World War).

71. Clementina Frizzoni (née Reichmann, 1815–1907). Photograph. Private archive, Bergamo.

72. Franz Seraph von Lenbach, Donna Laura Minghetti, née Acton (1829–1915), 1874. Drawing. Private collection, Naples.

73. The funeral of Gino Capponi, 1876. Engraving after drawing by Tancredi, published in *L'Illustrazione Italiana* 3, no. 17 (20 February 1876).

74. Crown Prince Frederick of Prussia (1831–1888, Emperor Frederick III). Photograph by Reichard & Lindner, Berlin, 1879. Carte-de-visite given to Morelli. Archivio Zavaritt, Gorle.

75. Crown Princess Victoria of Prussia (1840–1901, Empress Frederick). Photograph by E. Bambocci, Bari, 1879. Carte-de-visite given to Morelli. Archivio Zavaritt, Gorle.

76. Giovanni Bellini, *Madonna and Child (The Alzano Madonna)*, c. 1485–87. Oil on wood panel, 84.3 × 65.5 cm. Accademia Carrara, Bergamo, bequest of Giovanni Morelli 1891.

77. Crown Princess Victoria, letter to Giovanni Morelli, 29 May 1880: the first sheet of ten pages. Archivio Zavaritt, Gorle.

78. Giovanni Battista Tiepolo, *Death Giving an Audience*, c. 1740. Pen drawing with wash in brown ink on white paper, 29.2 × 42.7 cm. Gift of Giovanni Morelli to Crown Princess Victoria. Morelli's stamp is in the lower right corner. Schloss Fasanerie, Kulturstiftung des Hauses Hessen, Eichenzell.

79. Crown Princess Victoria, *Vanitas*, 1884. Oil on canvas, 122.8 × 72.4 cm. Accademia Carrara, Bergamo, bequest of Giovanni Morelli 1891.

80. Crown Princess Victoria, *Giovanni Morelli*, 1884. Pastel on paper. Dated in Morelli's hand: 12 November 1884. Executed at the Hotel Austria, Bolzano. Archivio Zavaritt, Gorle.

81. Franz Seraph von Lenbach, Portrait of Senator Giovanni Morelli, 1886. Oil on canvas, 125.5 × 90.2 cm. Accademia Carrara, Bergamo, bequest of Giovanni Morelli 1891.

82. Giovanni Morelli. Photograph by Giulio Rossi, Milan, 1887. Archivio Zavaritt, Gorle.

83. Franz Seraph von Lenbach, Portrait of Giovanni Morelli, 1887. Oil on paper, 60 × 48 cm. Galleria d'Arte Moderna, Milan, gift of Gustavo Frizzoni 1916.

84. Franz Seraph von Lenbach, drawings (chalk and pastel) on verso of Fig. 83 (Portrait of Giovanni Morelli, 1887), showing a woman resembling Crown Princess Victoria and a man, whose face is fading out, a discrete image of Crown Prince Frederick. Chalk and pastel.

85. Queen Victoria (1819–1901) with her eldest daughter, Empress Frederick (1840–1901), both dressed in mourning in 1888, with a photograph of Emperor Frederick III, who died in June that year. Gelatin silver photographic print pasted on card. Royal Collection, Windsor, RCIN2105953.

86. [Heinrich] Eduard Brockhaus (1829–1914). Photograph, 1905. Süddeutsche Zeitung Photo / Alamy Stock.

87. Gustavo Frizzoni (1840–1919). Photograph. Archivio Zavaritt, Gorle.

88. Raphael, Double portrait (Andrea Navagero and Agostino Beazzano), 1516. Oil on canvas, 77 × 111 cm. Galleria Doria Pamphilj, Rome.

89. Raphael, *Donna Velata* (Woman with a Veil), c. 1512–15. Oil on canvas, 82.0 × 60.5 cm. Palazzo Pitti, Florence.

90. Lodovico Pogliaghi, *Giovanni Morelli*, 1895. Pinacoteca di Brera, Milan.

Plates

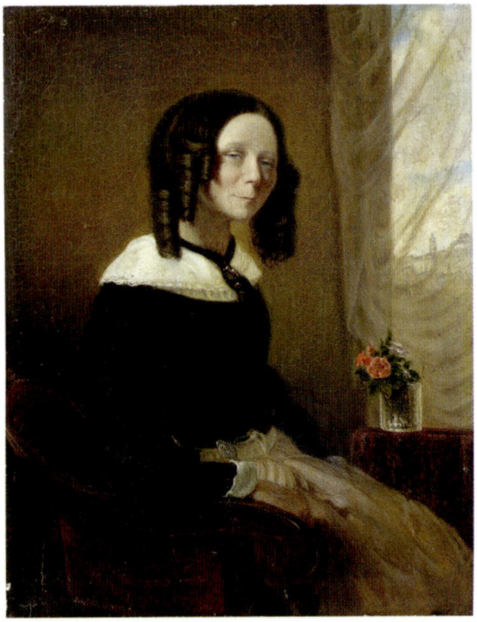

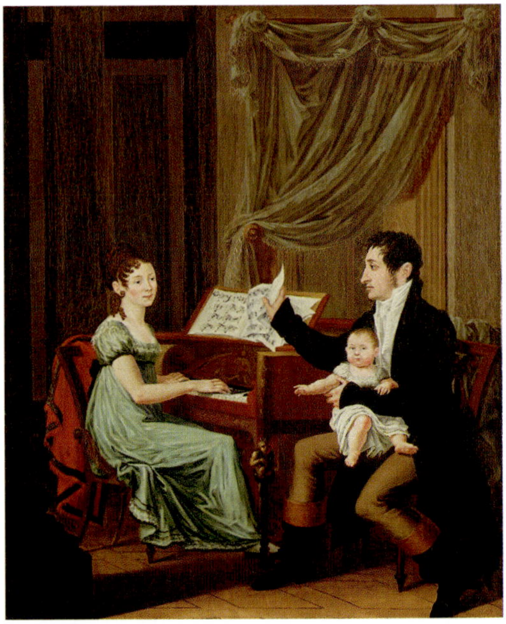

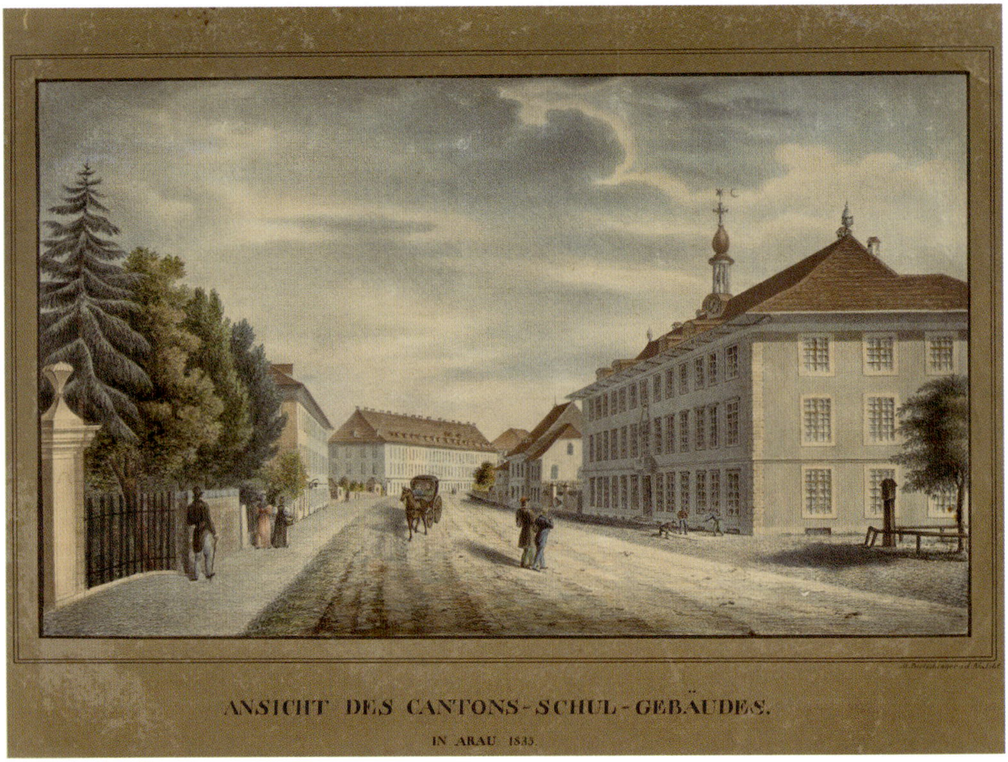

1. Carl Adolf Mende, Portrait of Ursula Zavaritt Morell, 1842.

2. Jean Morell as an infant with his parents in Verona, 1814.

3. *Ansicht des Cantons-Schul-Gebäudes in Aarau 1835*, 1860.

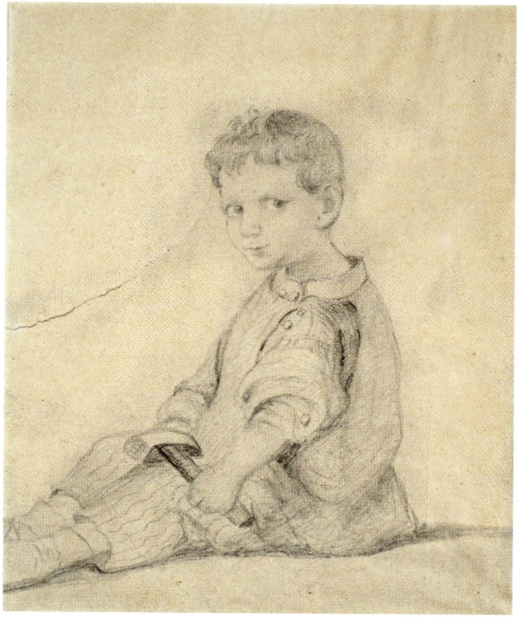

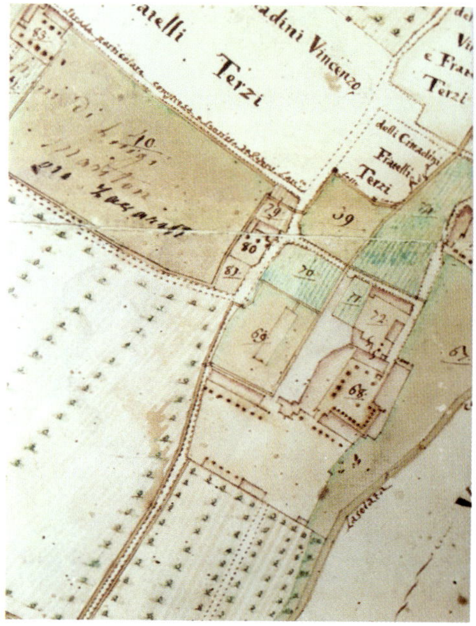

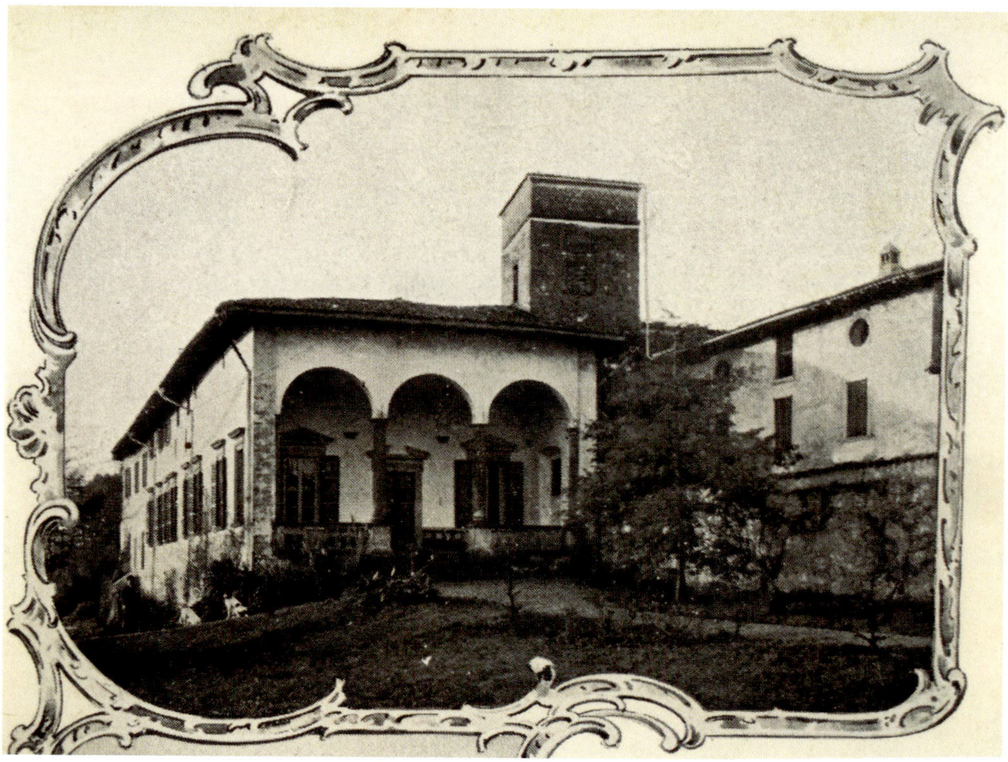

4. Giovanni Morelli aged about ten, c. 1826.

5. Map of the ground plan at the villa Zavaritt, 1802.

6. View of the Renaissance side of Villa Zavaritt, Gorle, c. 1910.

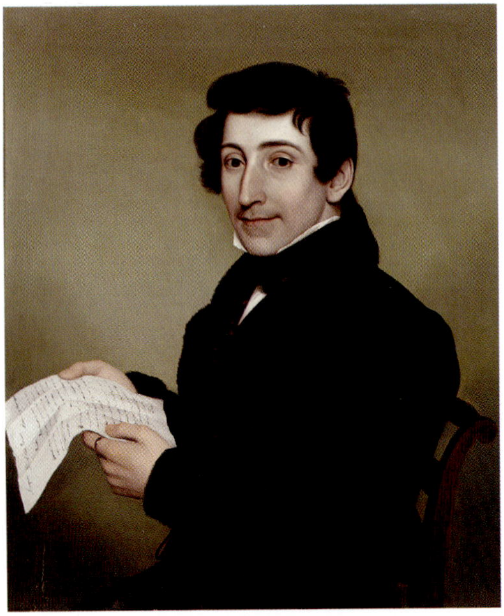

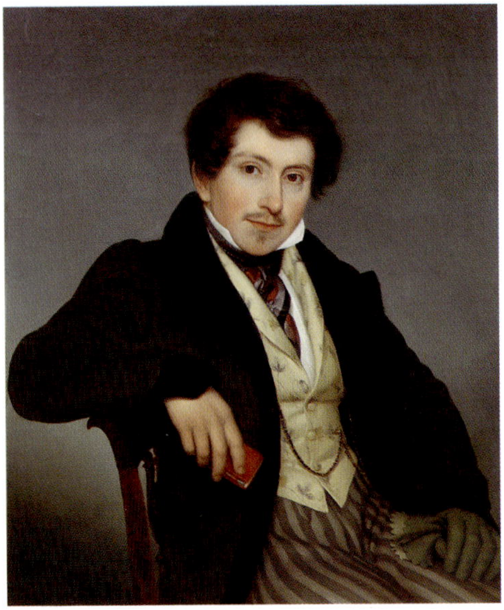

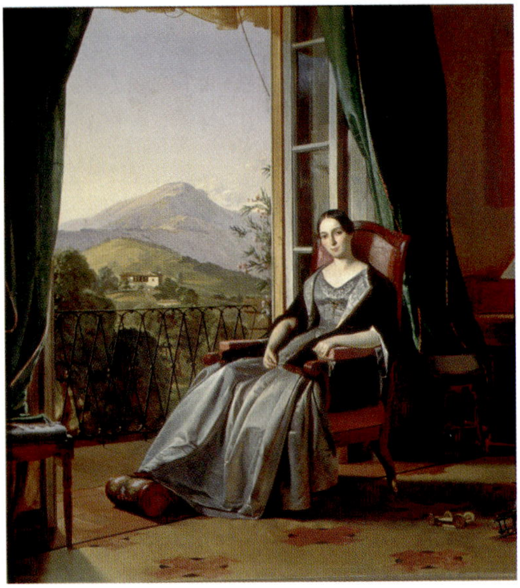

7. Portrait of Antonio Frizzoni, 1839.

8. Portrait of Giovanni Leonardo Frizzoni, 1839.

9. Portrait of Federico Frizzoni, 1839.

10. Friedrich Nerly the Elder, Portrait of Clementina Frizzoni, c. 1836.

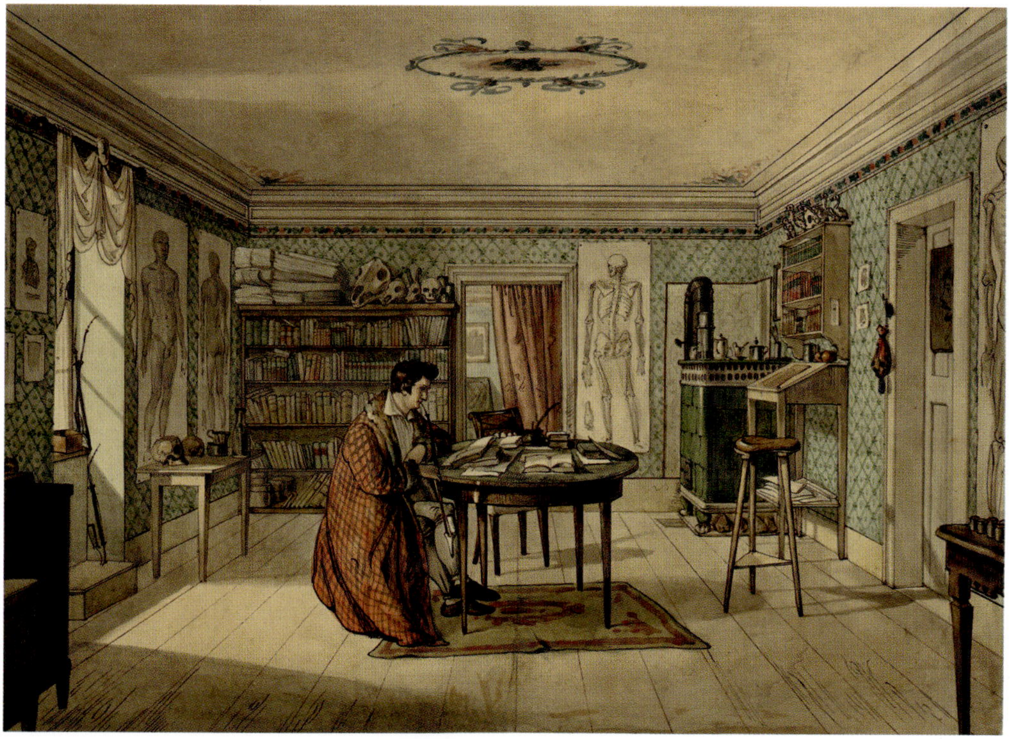

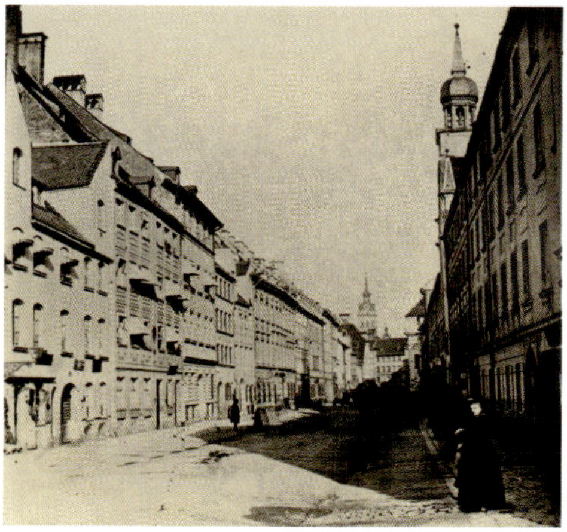

11. Giovanni Morelli in his undergraduate lodgings at Munich, 1835.

12. View of the Herzogspitalstrasse, Munich, 1875.

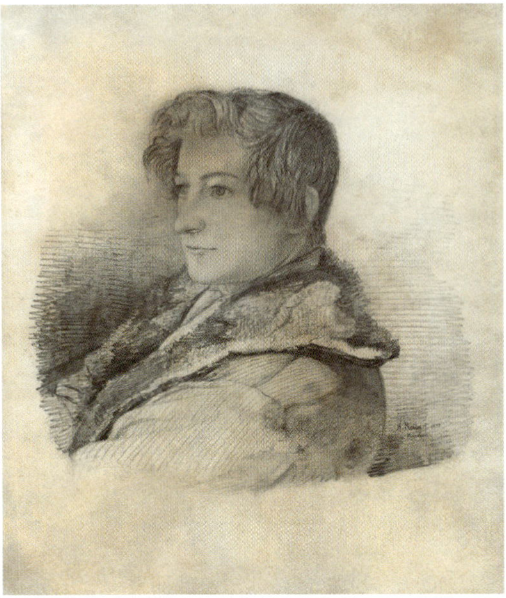

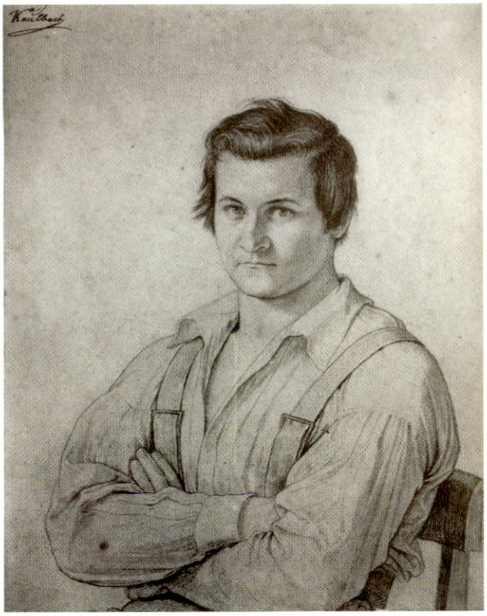

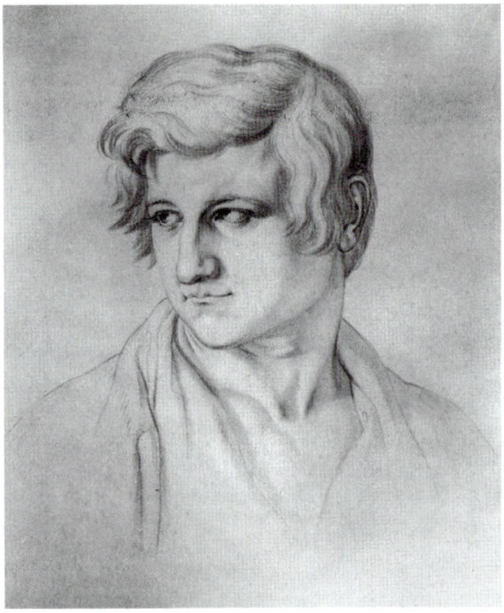

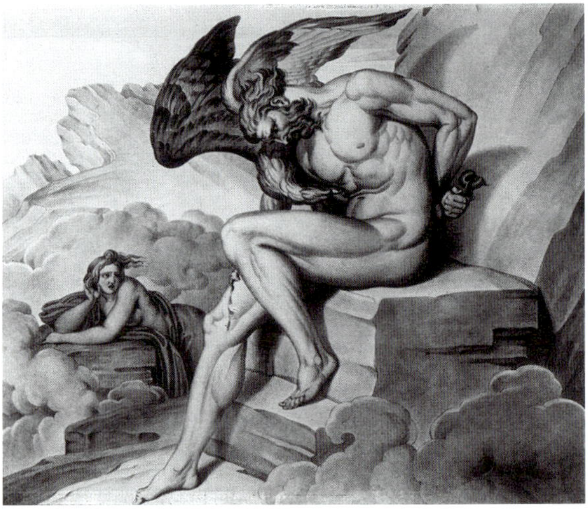

13. Carl Adolf Mende, Portrait of Giovanni Morelli, 1835.

14. Wilhelm von Kaulbach, Giovanni Morelli as an undergraduate in Munich, c. 1835.

15. Buonaventura Genelli, Portrait of Giovanni Morelli, c. 1837.

16. Buonaventura Genelli, *Prometheus*, 1836.

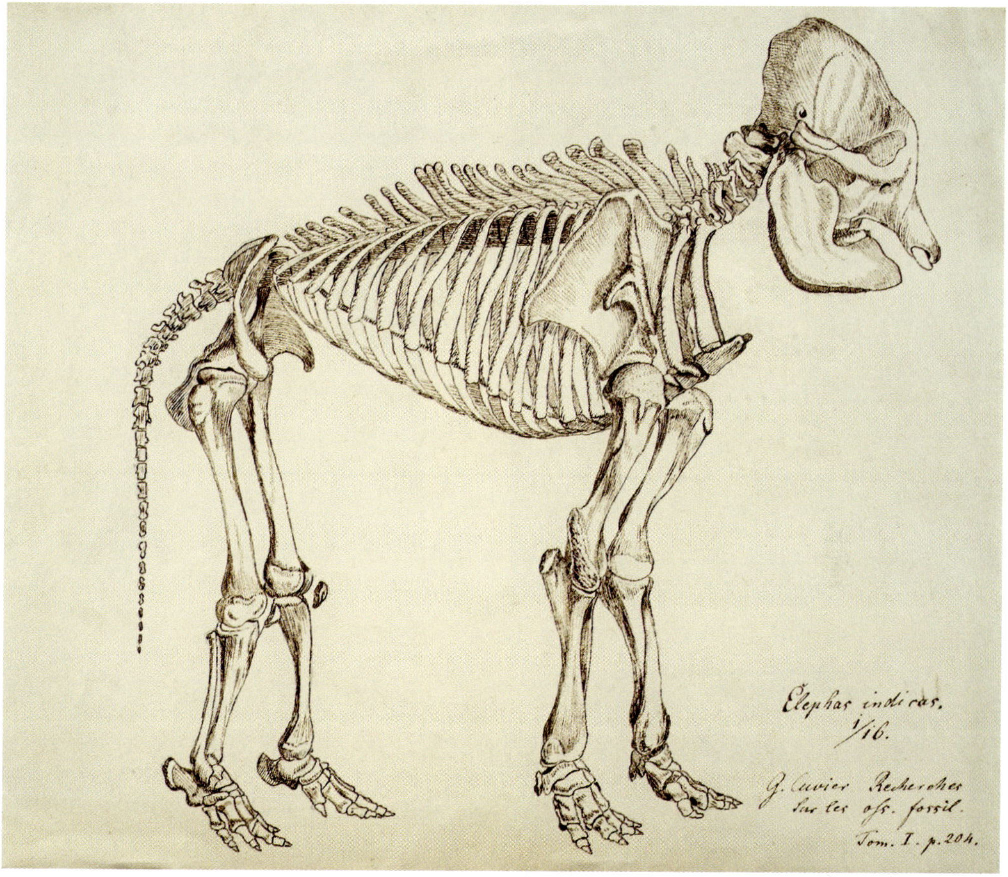

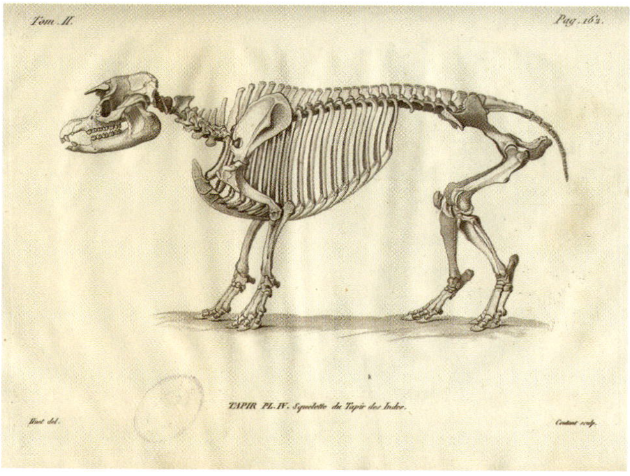

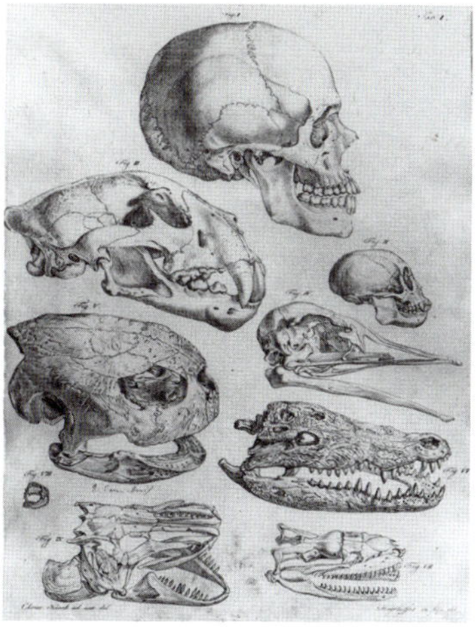

17. Giovanni Morelli, *Elephant skeleton*, c. 1833–36. Tracing from G. Cuvier, *Recherches sur les ossemens fossiles*.

18. *The Tapir Skeleton*, from G. Cuvier, *Recherches sur les ossemens fossiles*, 1822.

19. Christian Koeck, Comparison of skulls, 1815.

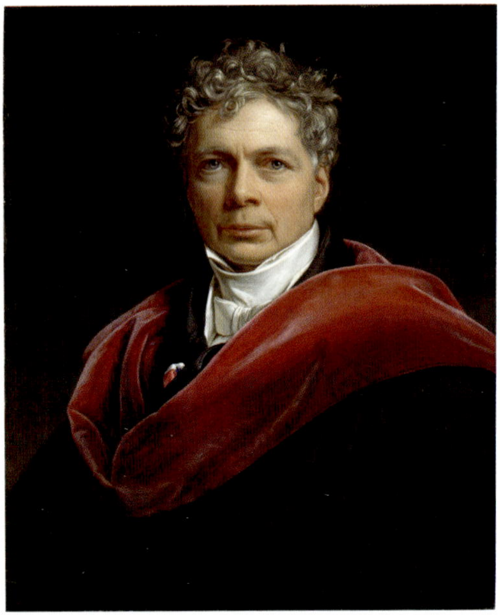

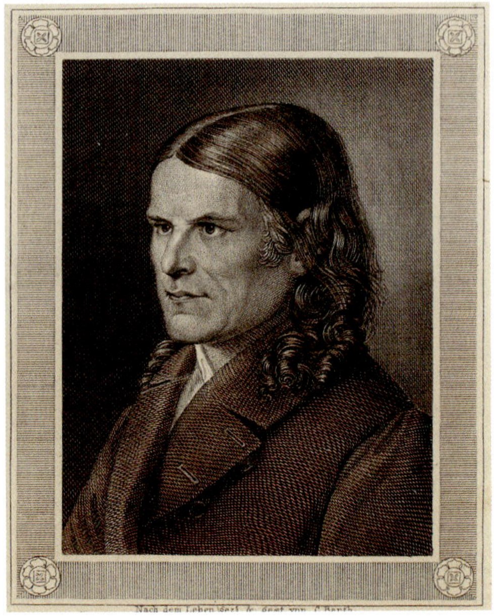

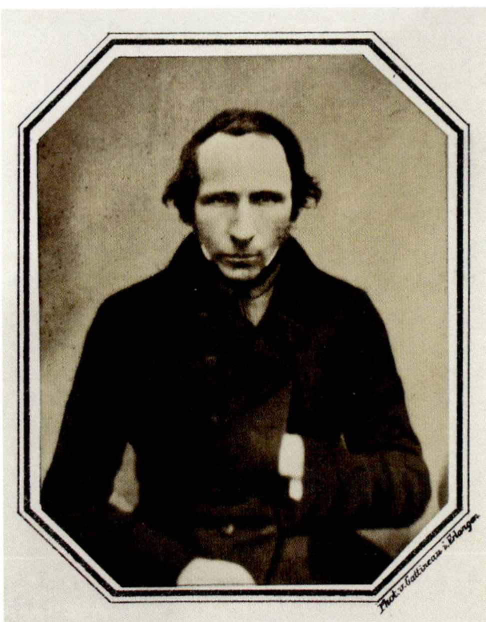

20. Joseph Karl Stieler, Portrait of Friedrich Schelling, 1835.

21. Carl Barth, *Friedrich Rückert*, 1859.

22. Johann Georg Veit Engelhardt. Photograph by Johann George Gattineau, Erlangen.

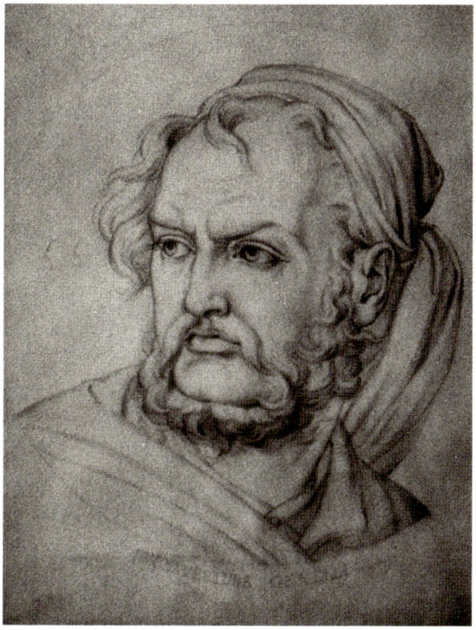

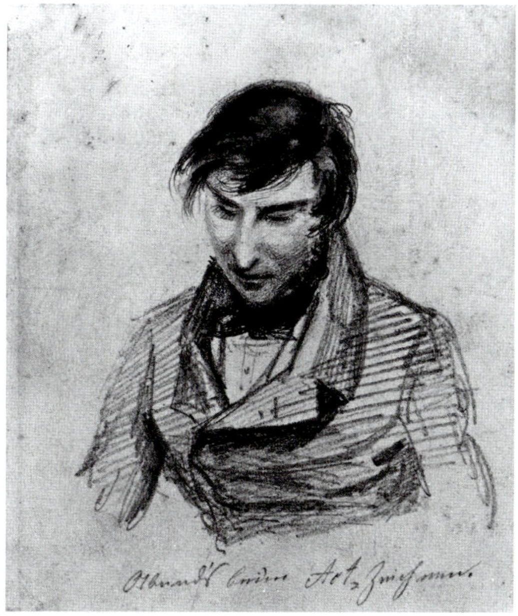

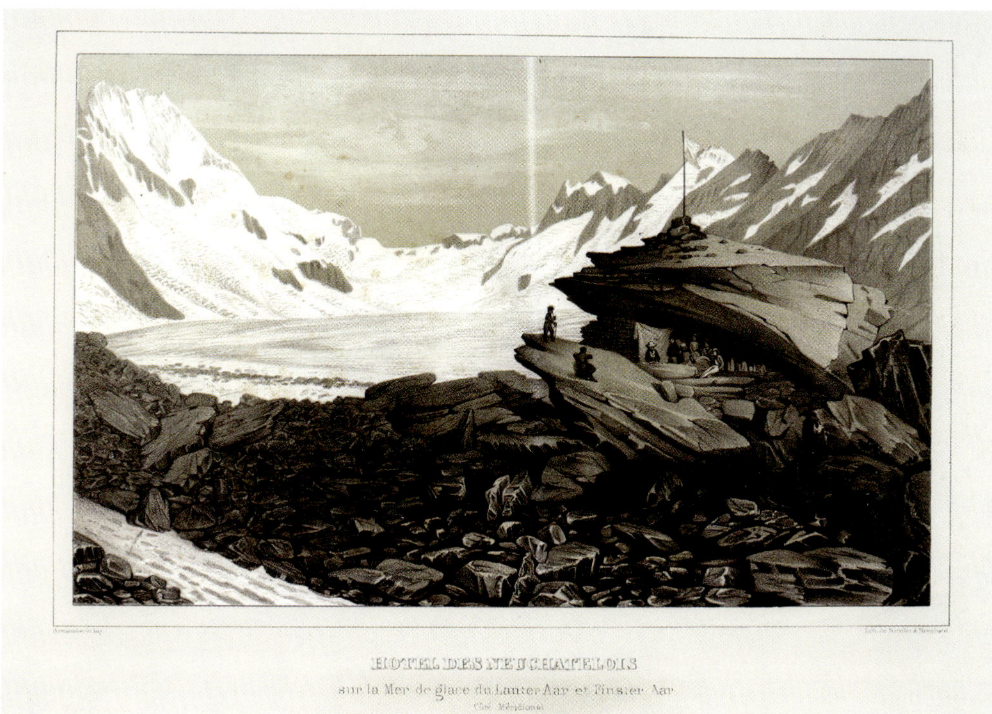

23. Buonaventura Genelli, Self-portrait, c. 1835.

24. Carl Constantin Heinrich Steffeck, Portrait study of Carl Blechen, 1837.

25. Hercule Nicolet and Joseph Bettannier, *Hôtel des Neuchâtelois*, 1840.

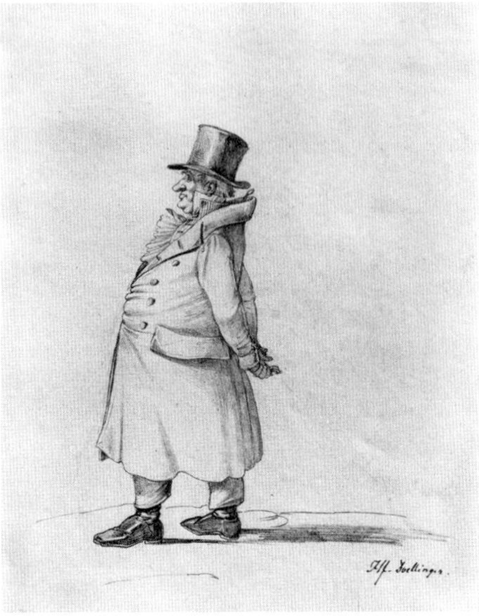

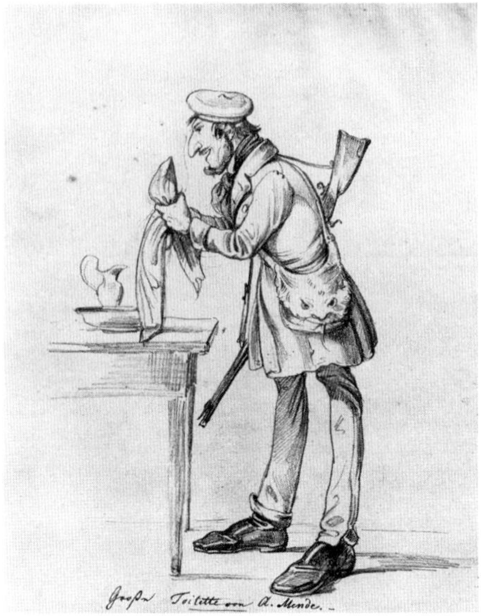

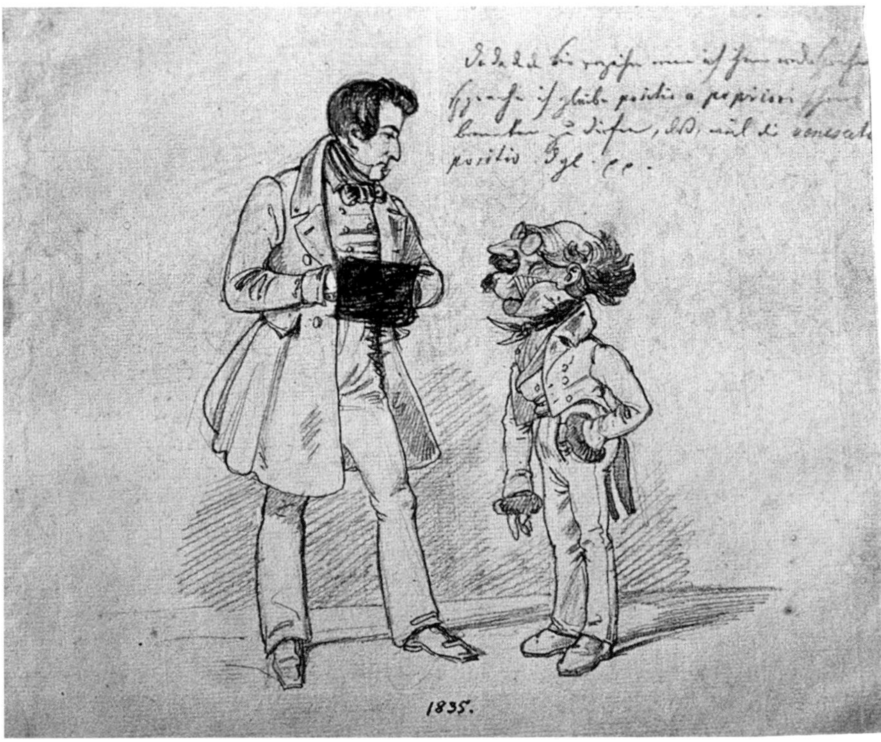

26. Ernst Fröhlich, Caricature of Ignaz Döllinger.

27. Ernst Fröhlich. *Grosse Toilette von Carl Adolf Mende.*

28. Ernst Fröhlich, Morelli arguing with one of his professors in Munich, 1835.

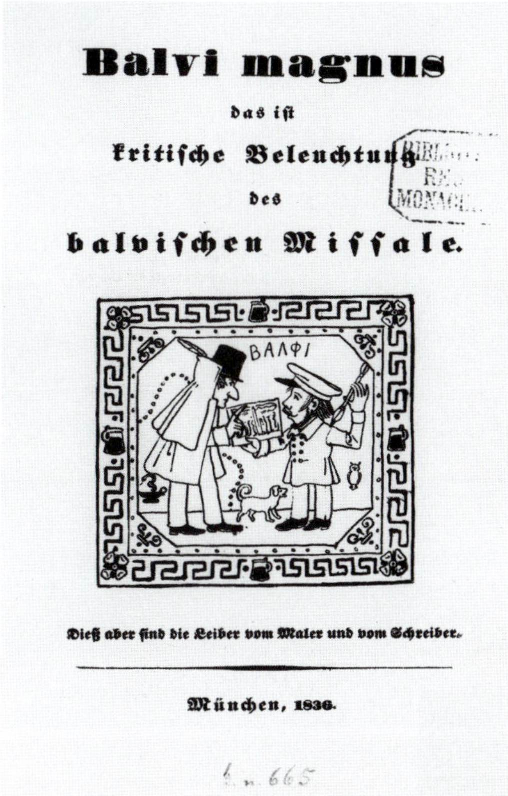

Balvi magnus

das ist

kritische Beleuchtung

des

balvischen Missale.

Dieß aber sind die Leiber vom Maler und vom Schreiber.

München, 1836.

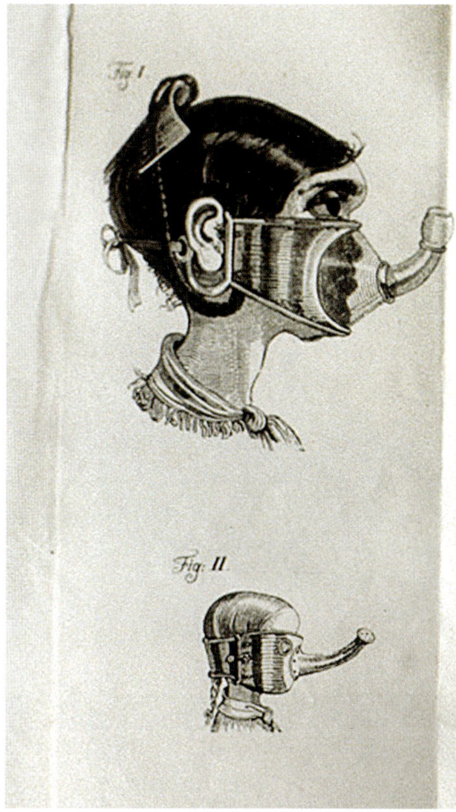

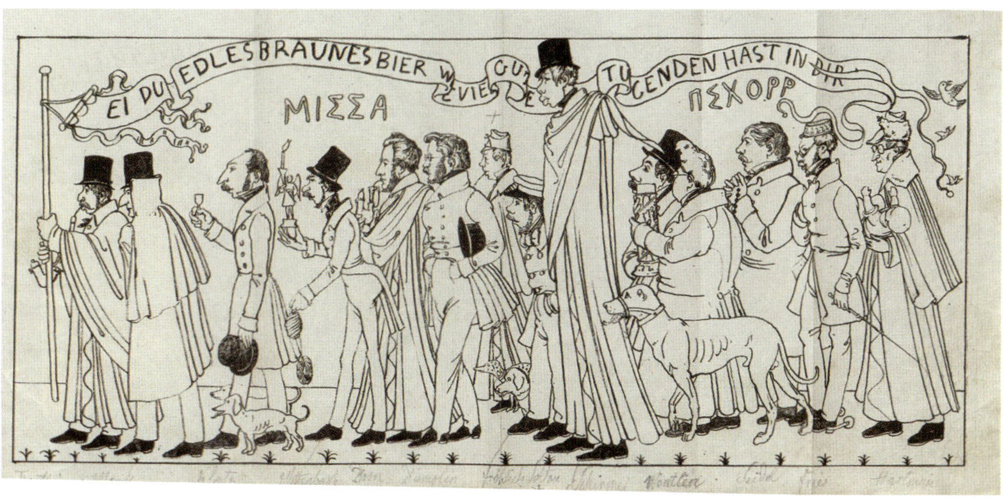

29. Ernst Fröhlich, Caricature of Giovanni Morelli and Fröhlich, *Balvi magnus*, 1836.

30. *Das Miasma diabolicum*, 1839: "Christian Air Visor."

31. Ernst Fröhlich, Caricature of Morelli and beer-drinking friends, *Balvi magnus*, 1836.

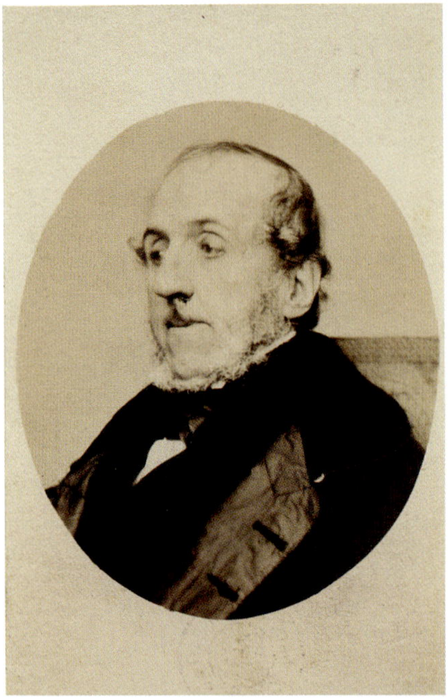

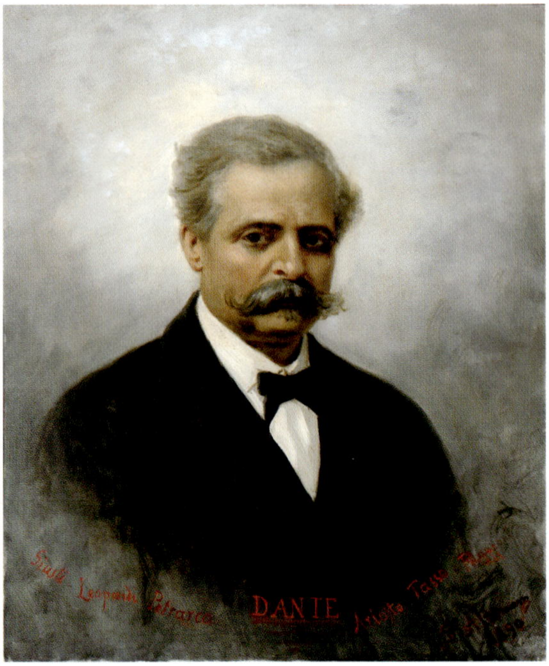

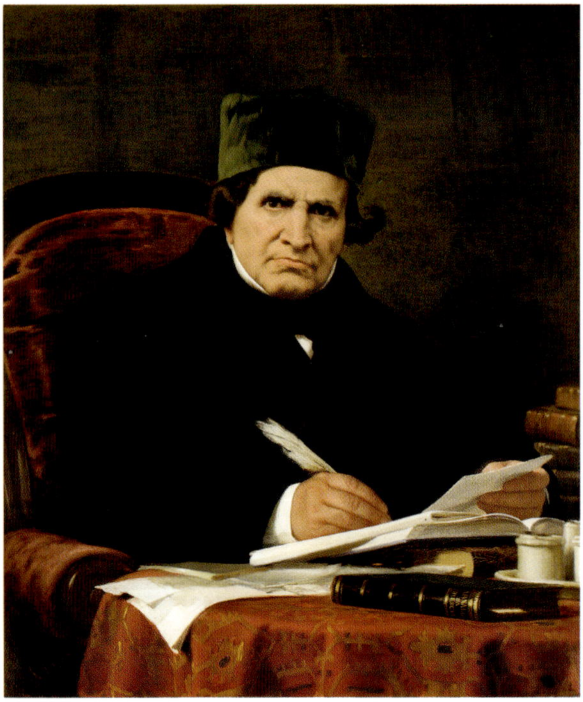

32. Marchese Gino Capponi. Photograph by Alphonse Bernoud, c. 1860s.

33. Francesco Saverio Altamura, Portrait of Francesco De Sanctis, 1890.

34. Stefano Ussi, Portrait of Giovanni Battista Niccolini, 1864.

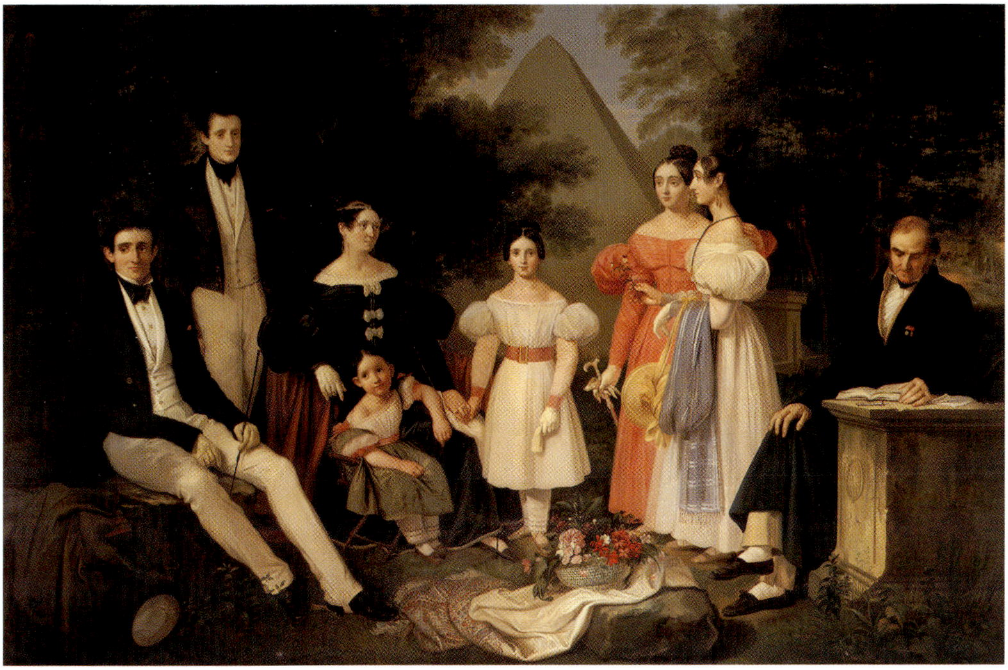

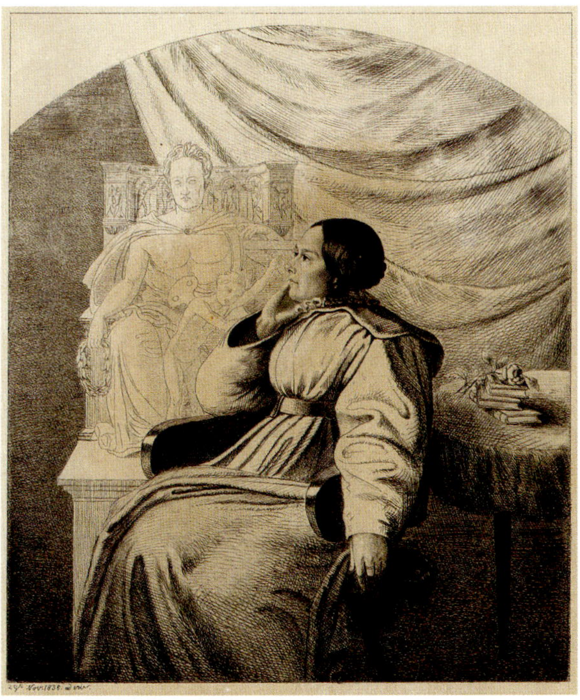

35. Giuseppe Bezzuoli, *La famiglia Antinori*, 1834.

36. Ludwig Emil Grimm, Portrait of Bettina von Arnim, 1838.

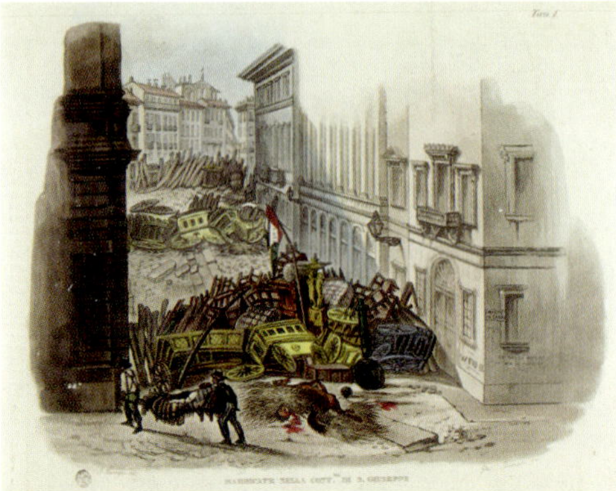

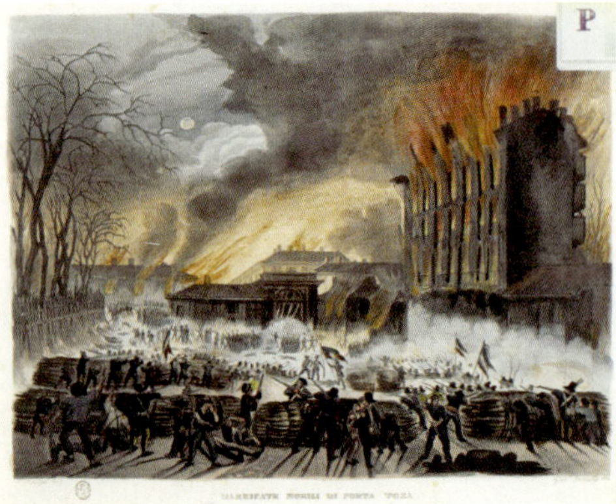

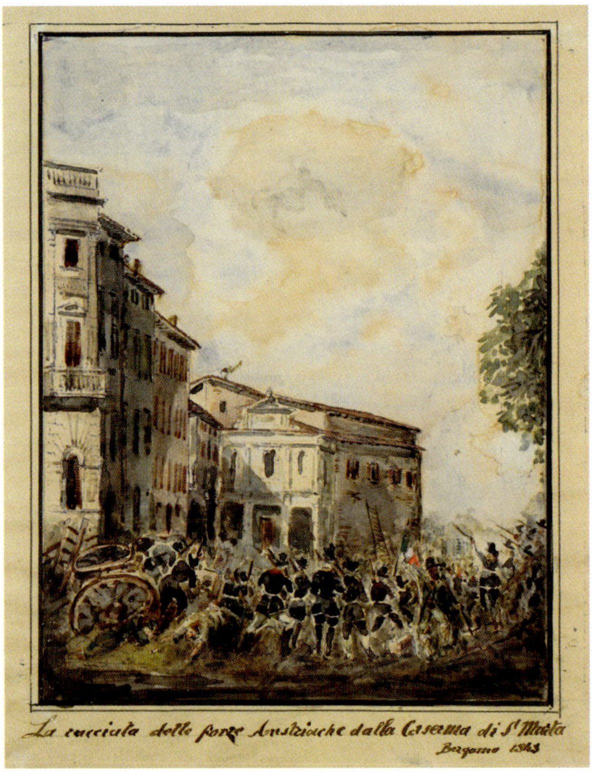

37. Felice Donghi and Gaetano Bonatti, *Barricate nella contrada di S. Giuseppe*, 1848.

38. Felice Donghi and Gaetano Bonatti, *Barricate mobili di Porta Tosa*, 1848.

39. *La cacciata delle forze Austriache dalla Caserma di Santa Marta, Bergamo 1848.*

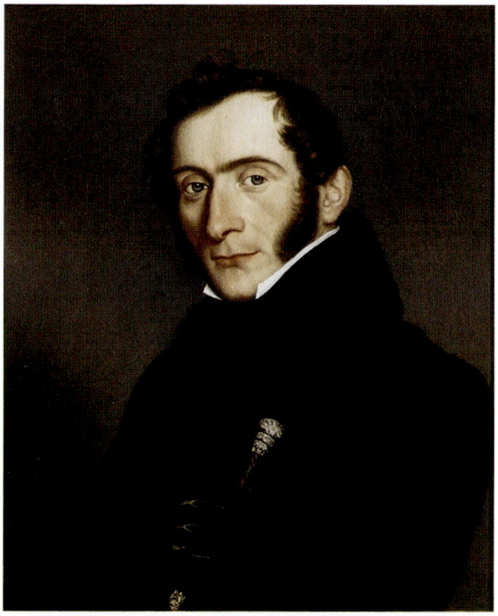

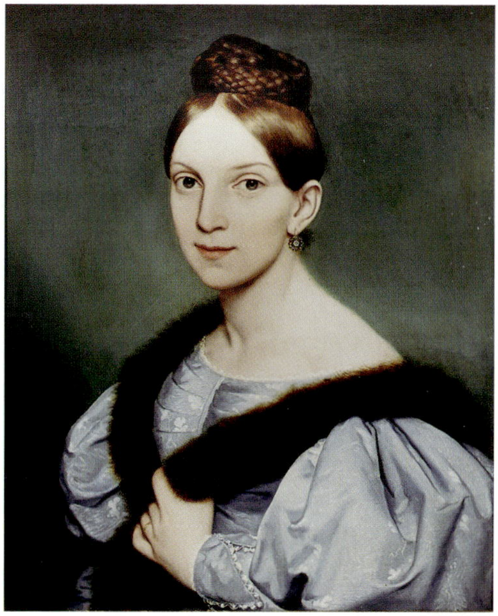

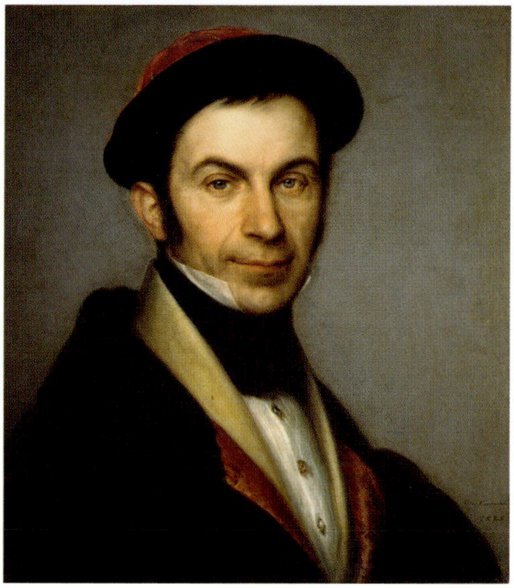

40. Giacomo Trecourt, Portrait of Pietro Luigi Zavaritt, 1842.

41. Giacomo Trecourt, Portrait of Amalia Steiner Zavaritt, 1842.

42. Giovanni Carnovali (Il Piccio), Portrait of Count Guglielmo Lochis, 1835.

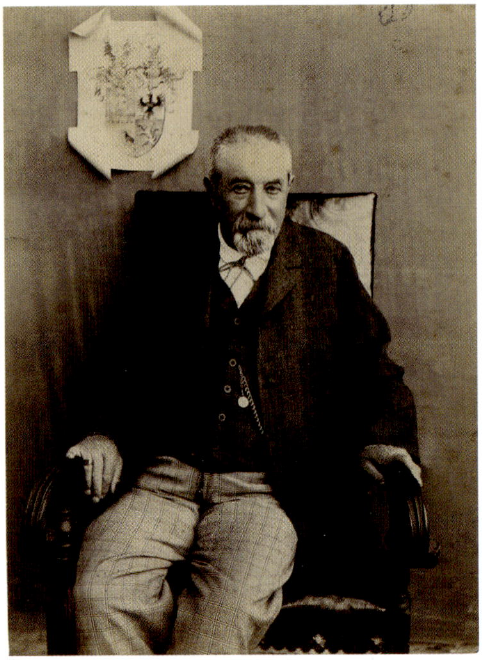

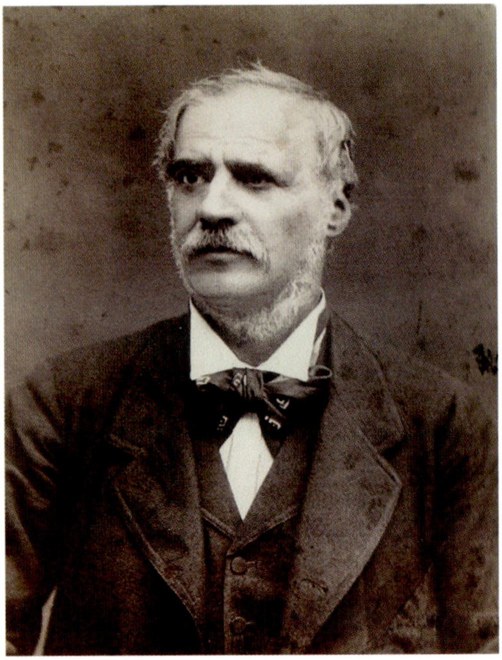

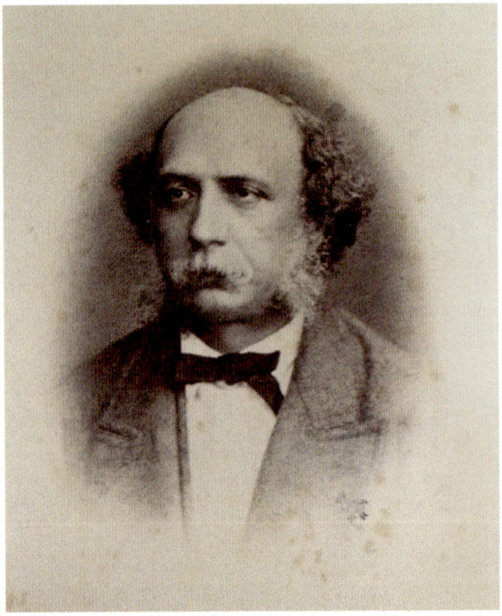

43. Giovanni Battista Camozzi Vertova.

44. Conte Alessandro Porro.

45. Marchese Anselmo Guerrieri Gonzaga.

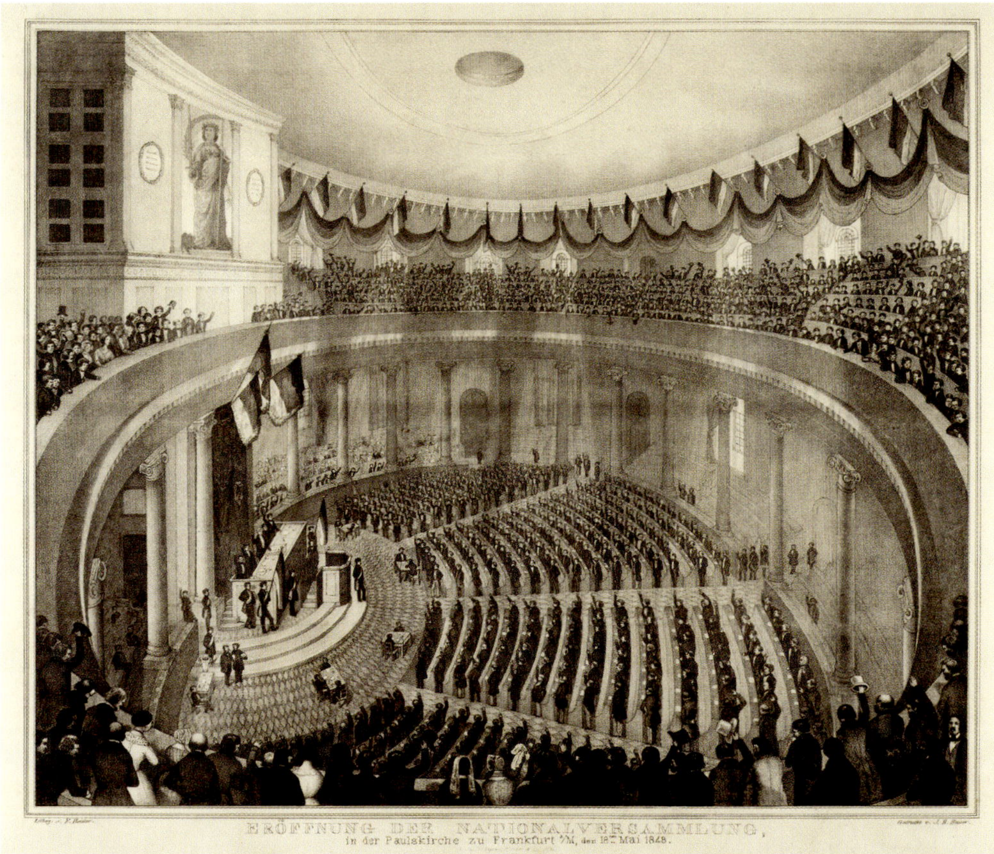

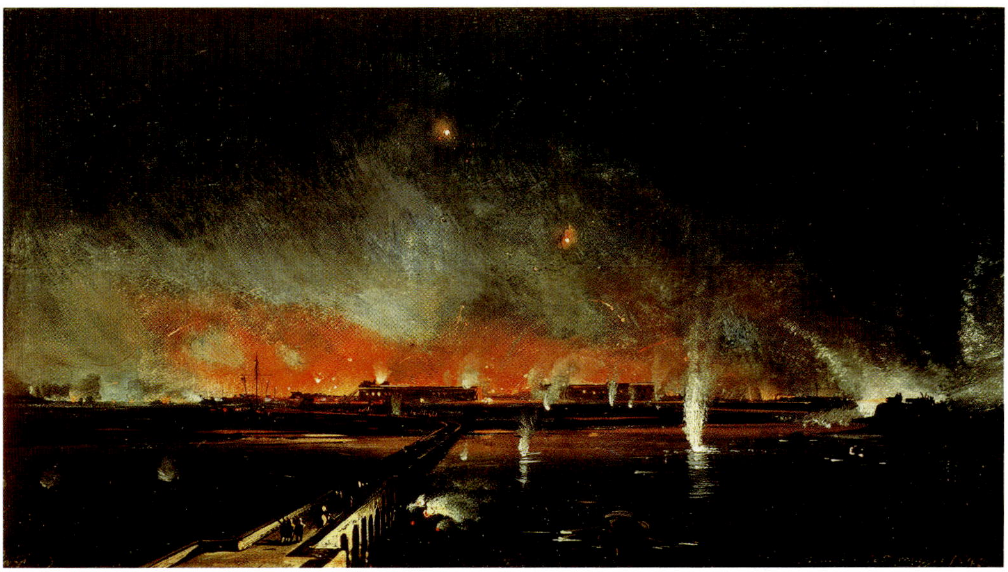

46. Franz Heister and J. B. Bauer, *Eröffnung der NationalVersammlung … 1848.*

47. Ippolito Caffi, *Bombardment of Marghera by the Austrians*, 1849.

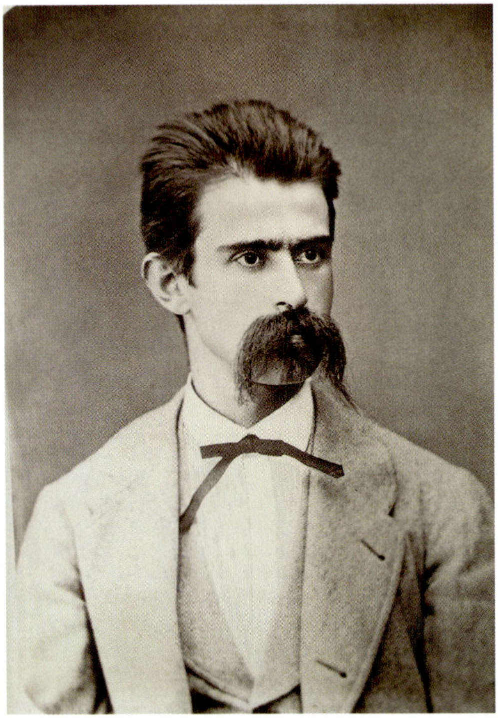

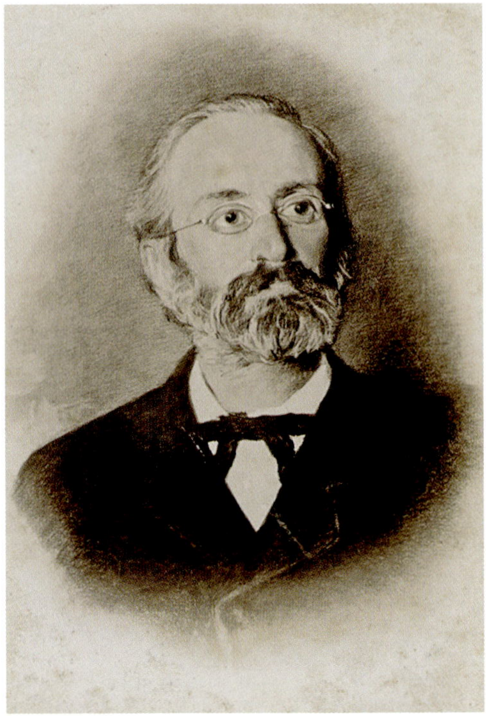

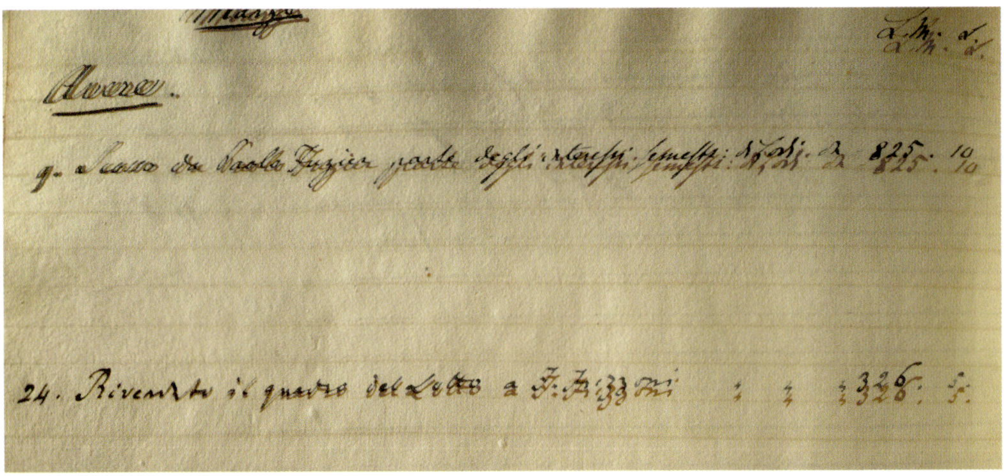

Avere.

9. Incasso da Paolo Frizzoni parte degli interessi semestrali [illegible] 825. 10

24. Rivenduto il quadro del Lotto a T. Frizzoni [illegible] 326. 5.

48. Giovanni Leonardo Frizzoni. Photograph by A. Mauri.

49. Teodoro Frizzoni. Photograph by A. Mauri.

50. Page from Morelli's household account book.

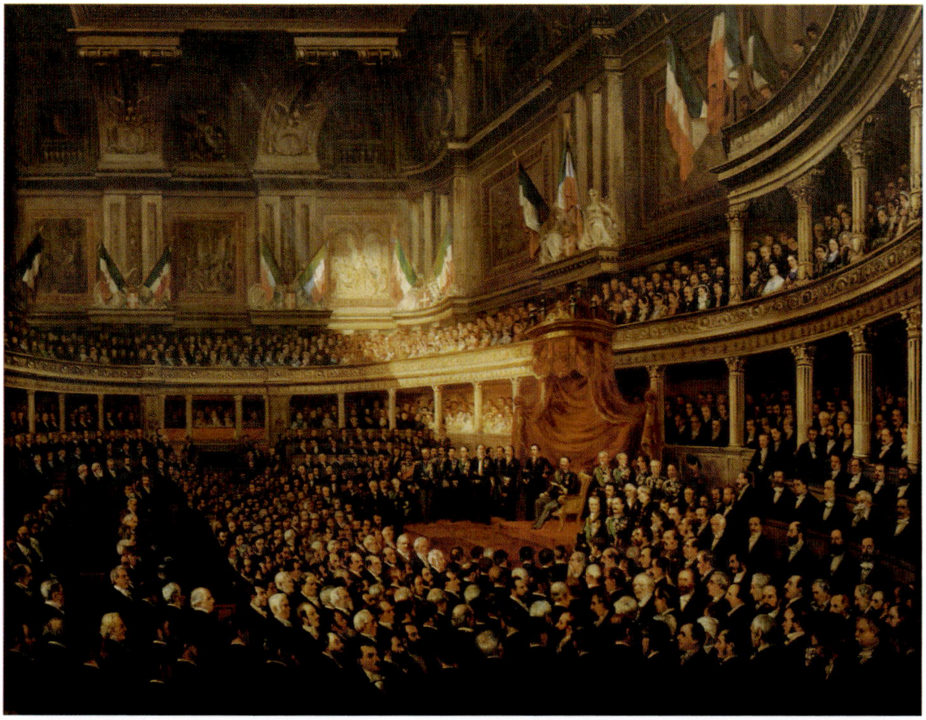

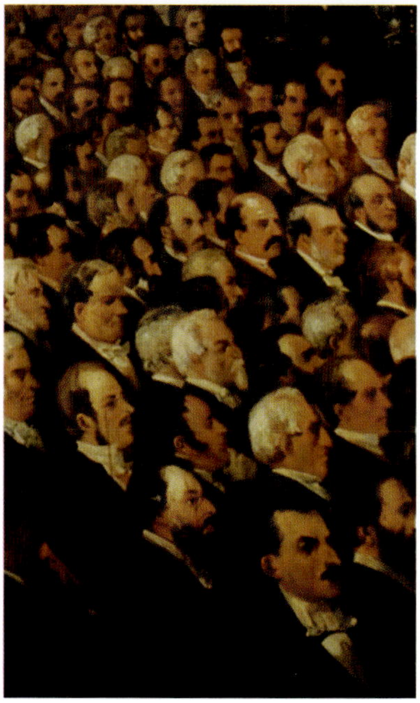

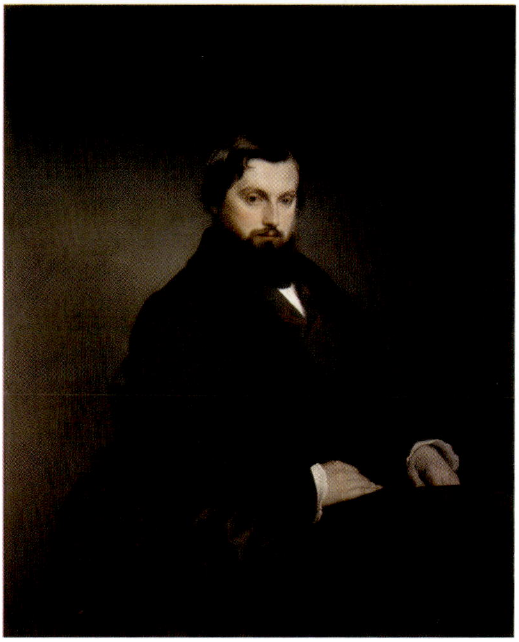

51. Peter Tetar van Elven, *Inaugurazione del Parlamento il 2 aprile 1860*, 1860.

52. Detail of Morelli in Fig. 51, among the Cavouriani.

53. Francesco Hayez, Portrait of Gian Giacomo Poldi Pezzoli, 1851.

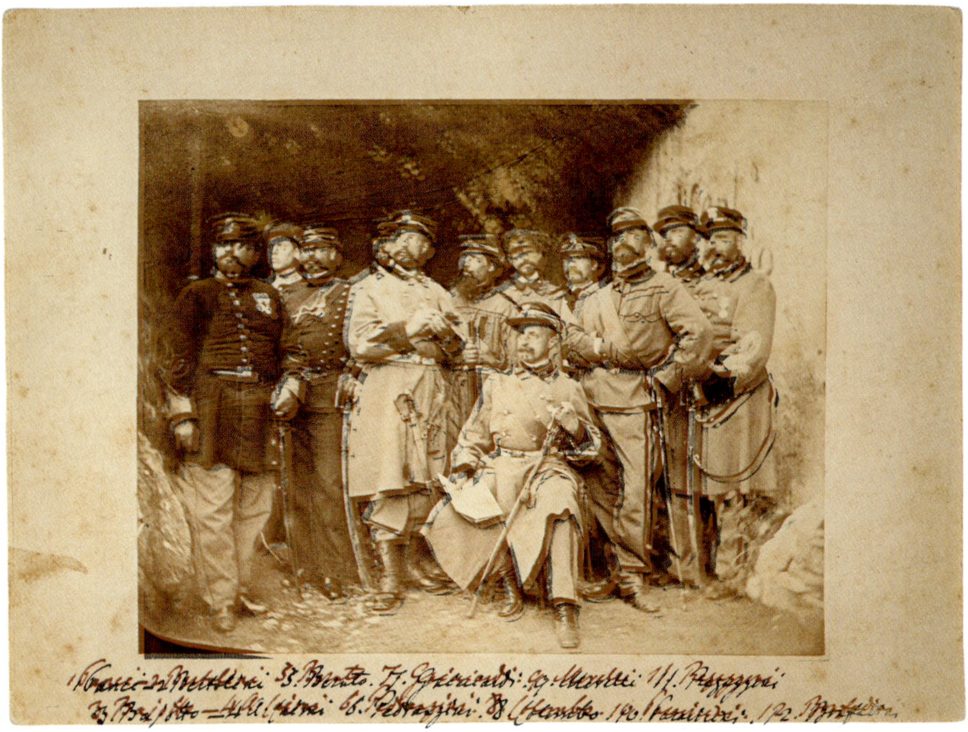

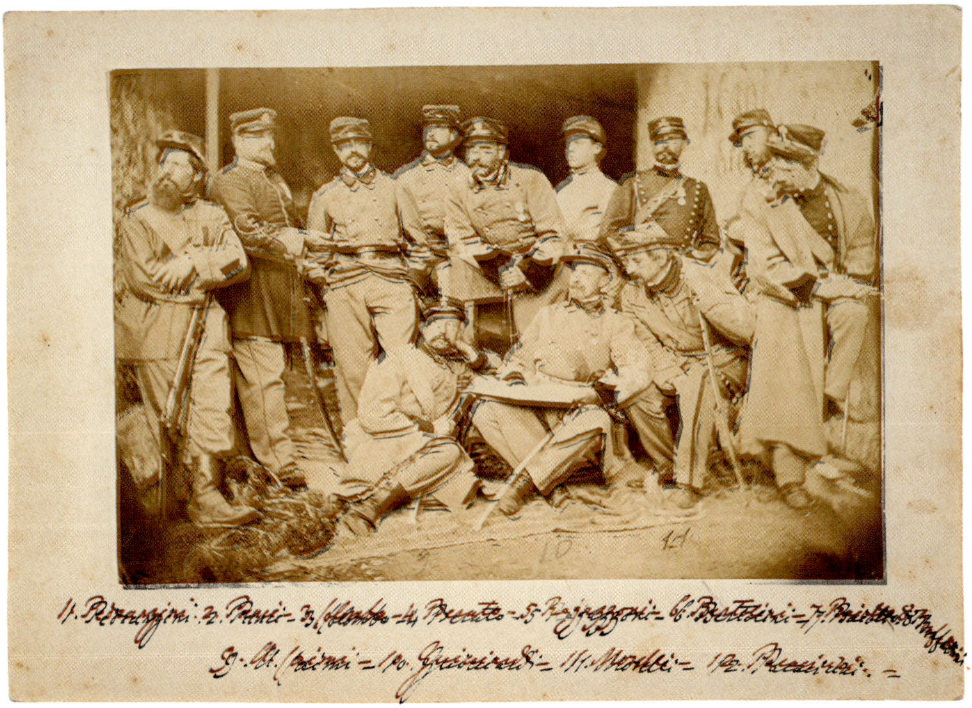

54–55. Colonel Enrico Guicciardi with his troops, including Morelli, 1866.

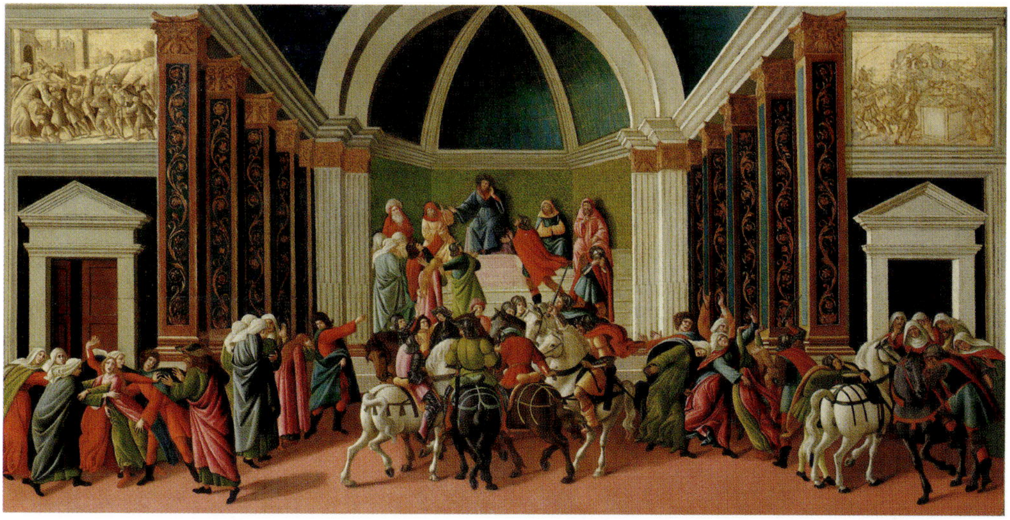

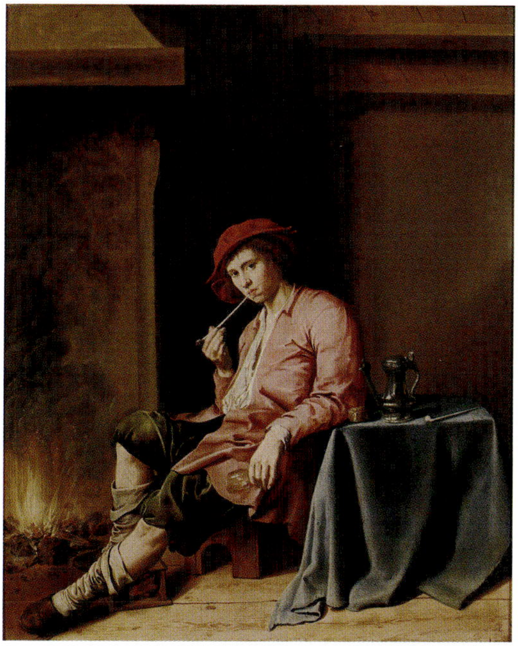

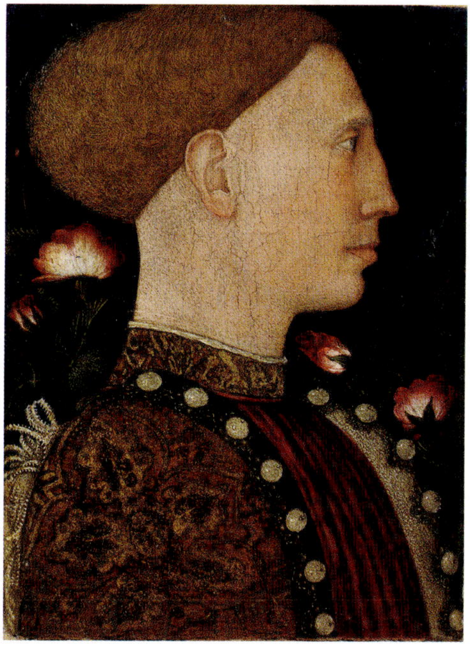

56. Sandro Botticelli, *The History of Virginia the Roman*, c. 1500.

57. Jan Miense Molenaer, *Young Man Smoking*, c. 1635.

58. Antonio Pisano, called Pisanello, Portrait of Leonello d'Este, c. 1441.

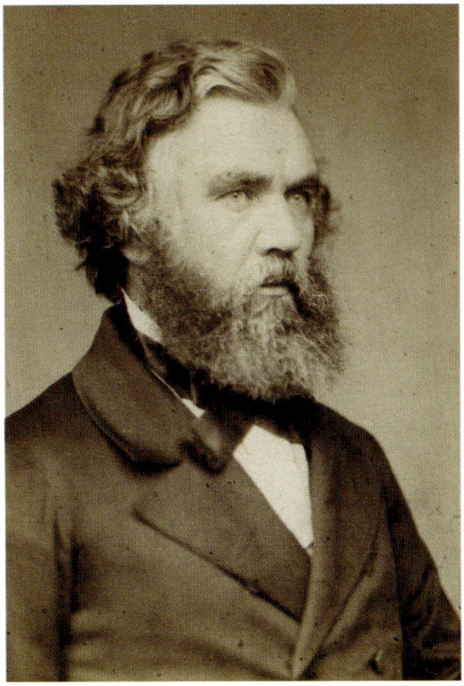

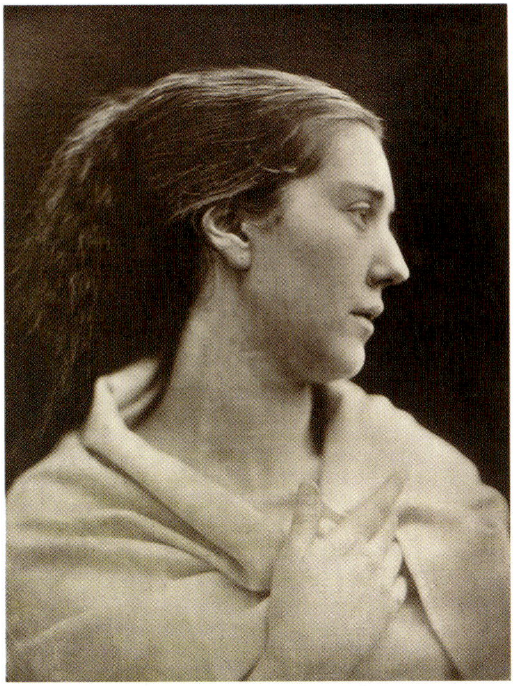

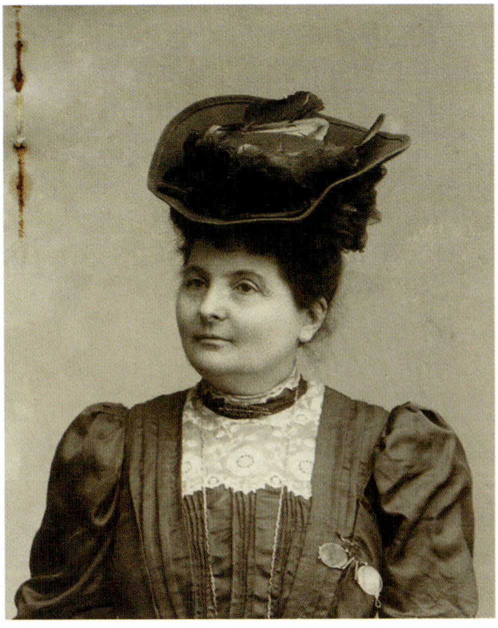

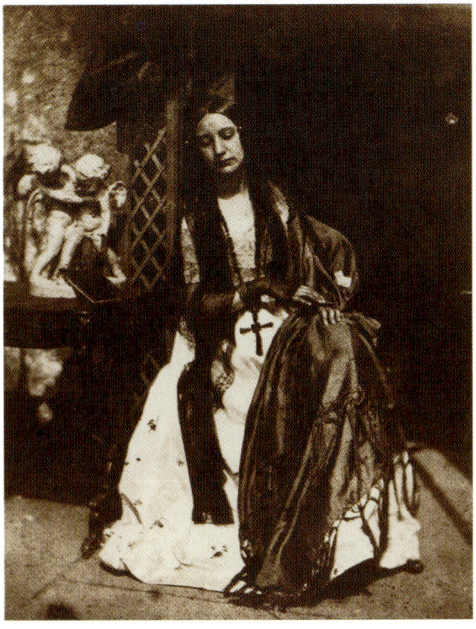

59. Sir Austen Henry Layard. Photograph by Maull & Polyblank, London, c. 1860.

60. Lady Layard. Photograph by Julia Margaret Cameron, 1869.

61. Louise Marie Richter, c. 1880.

62. Lady Eastlake. Calotype by David Octavius Hill and Robert Adamson, c. 1843–48.

 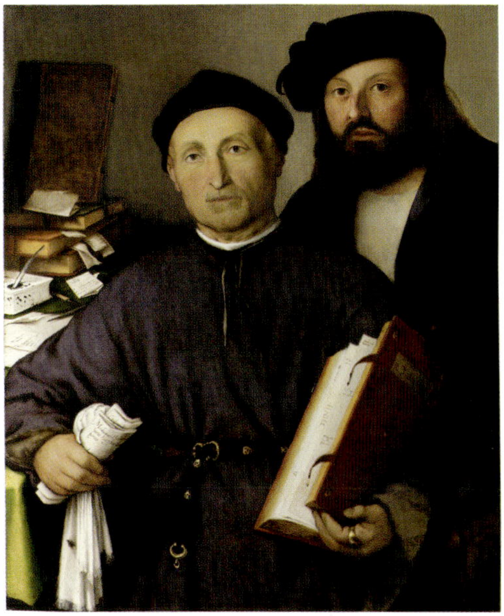

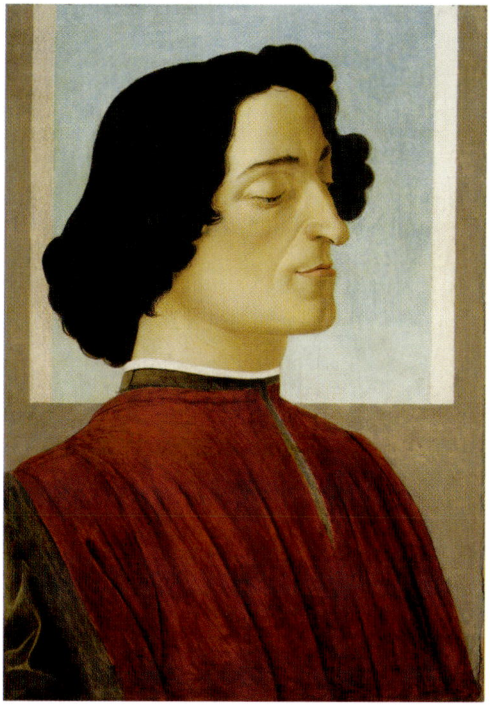

63. Lorenzo Lotto, Giovanni Agostino della Torre and his Son, Niccolò, c. 1515–16. Shown before conservation.

64. Fig. 63 shown after conservation.

65. Sandro Botticelli, Portrait of Giuliano de' Medici, c. 1478–85.

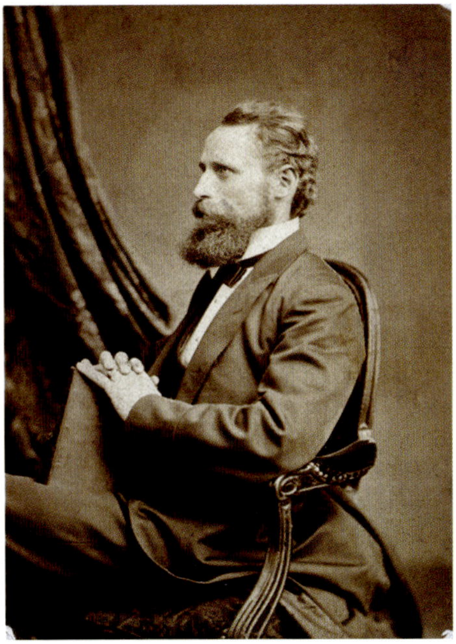

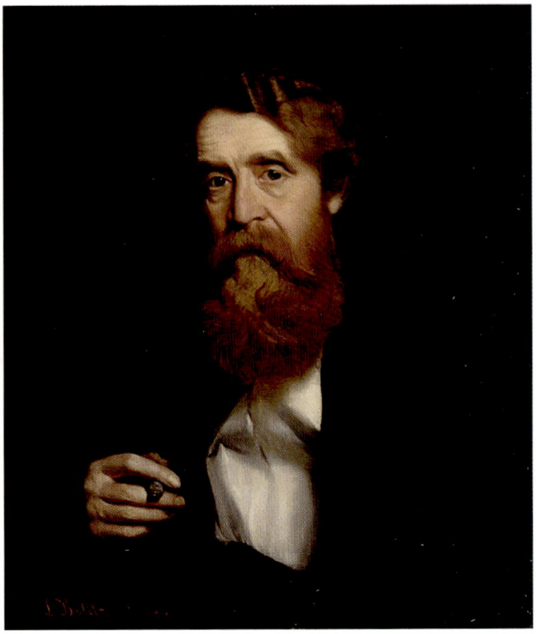

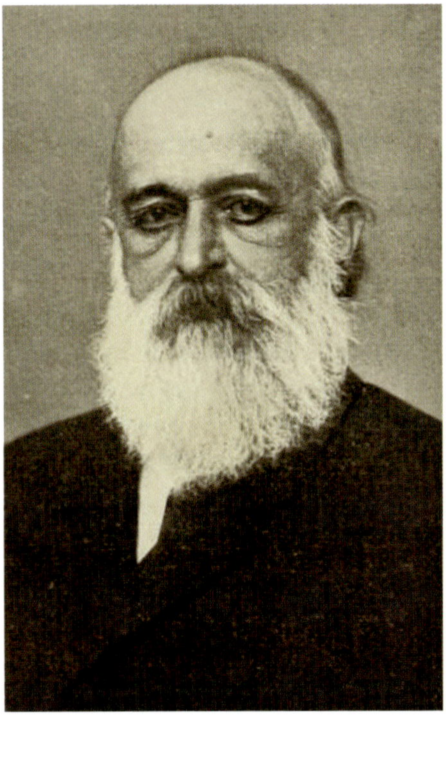

66. Jean Paul Richter, c. 1879.

67. Louis Kolitz, Portrait of Sir Joseph Archer Crowe, 1877.

68. Giovanni Battista Cavalcaselle.

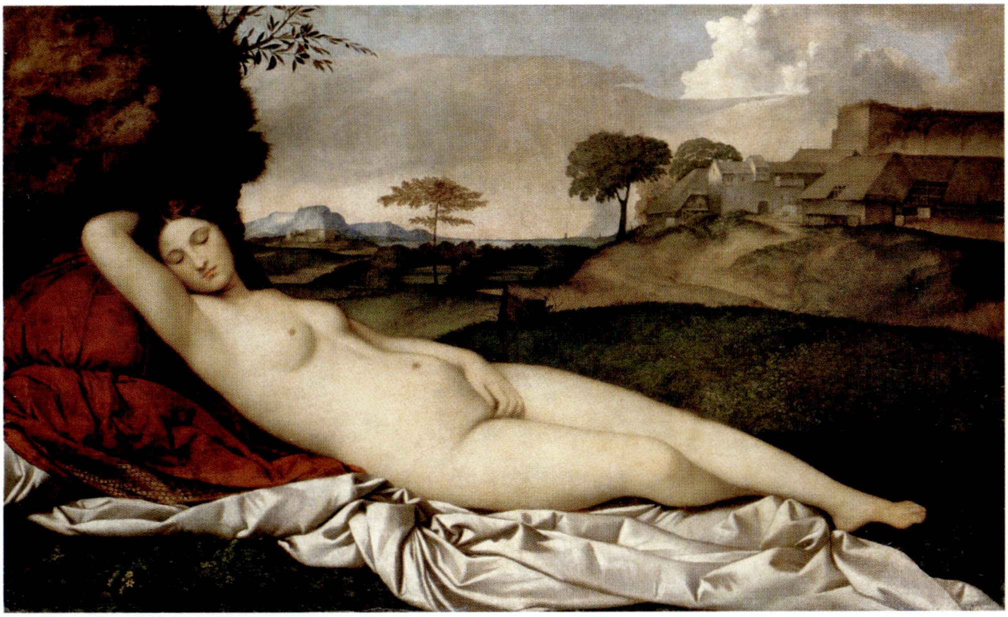

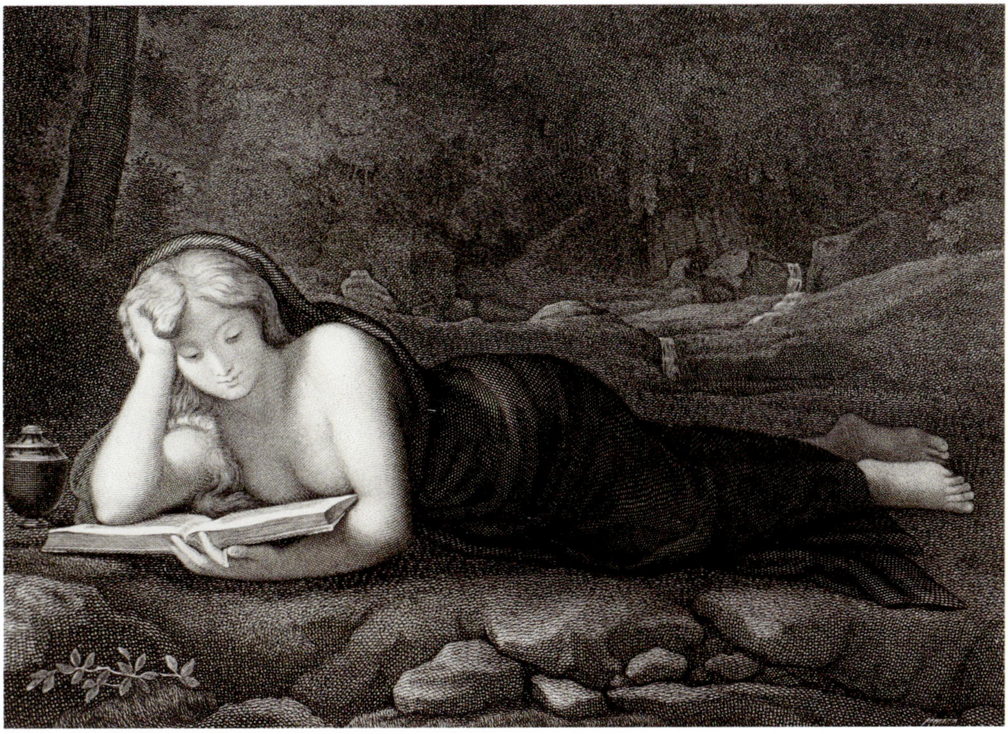

69. Giorgione, *The Sleeping Venus*, c. 1508/10.

70. Engraving after painting attributed to Correggio, *The Reading Magdalen*.

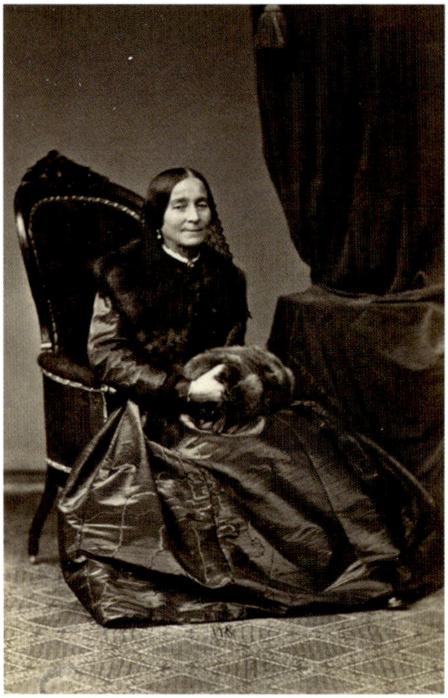

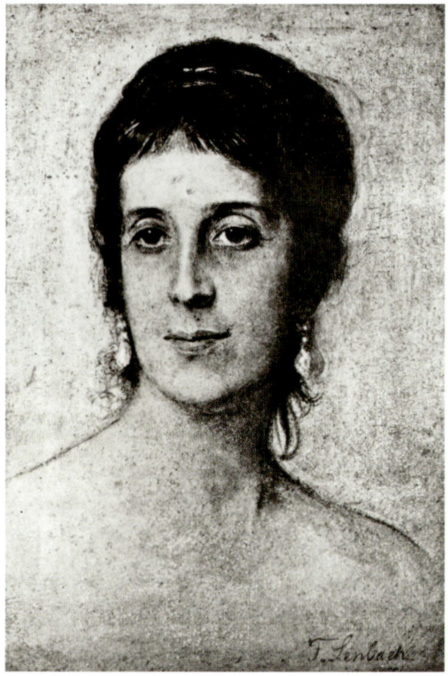

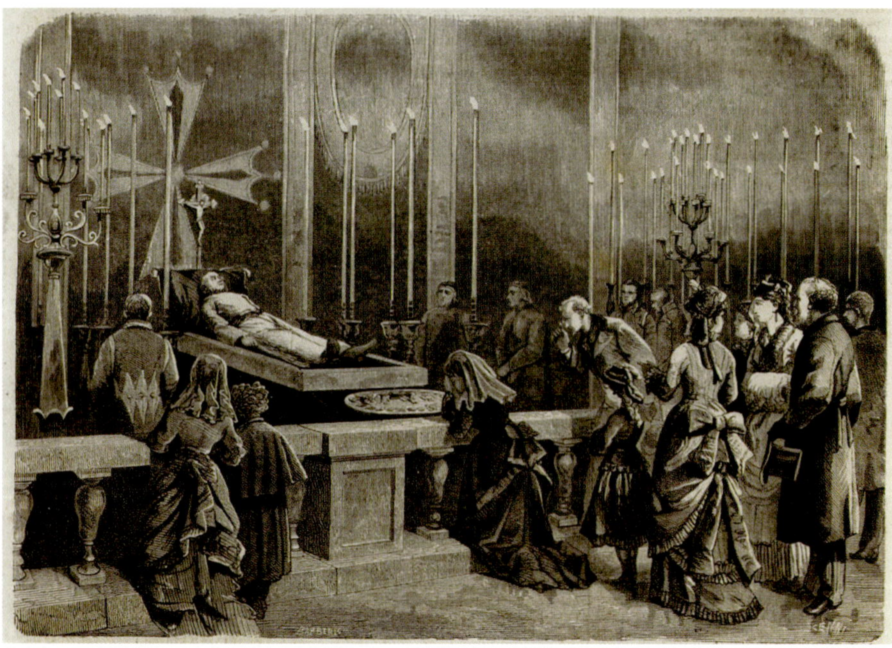

71. Clementina Frizzoni.

72. Franz Seraph von Lenbach, Portrait of Donna Laura Minghetti, 1874.

73. The funeral of Gino Capponi, 1876.

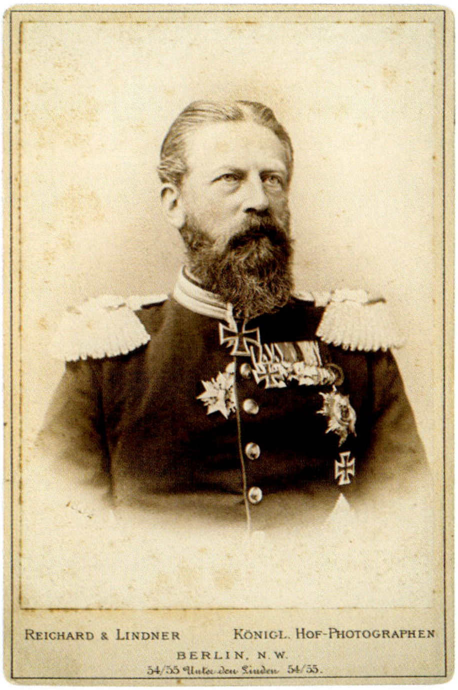

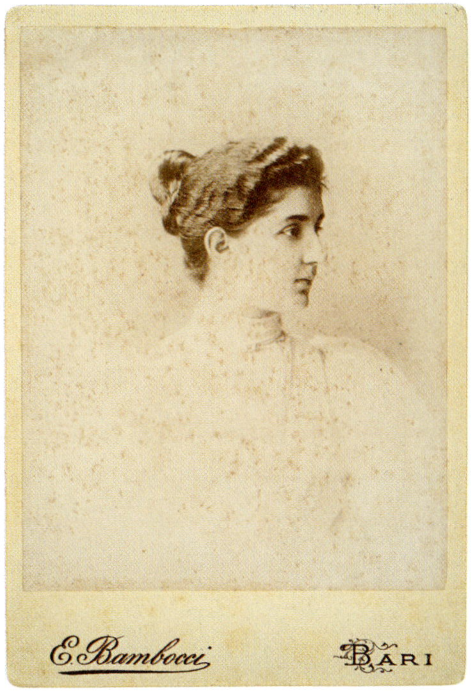

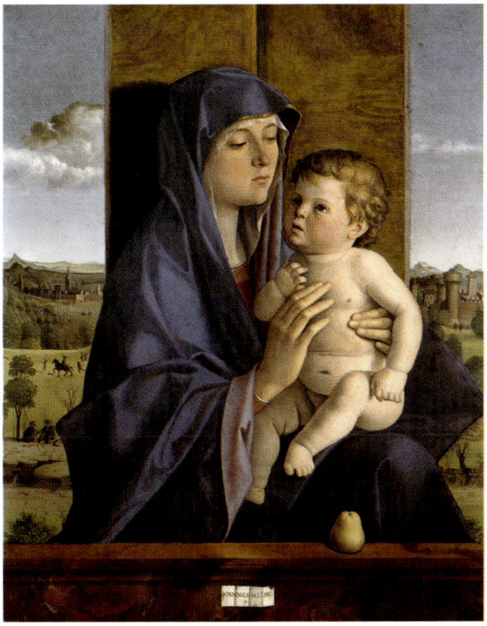

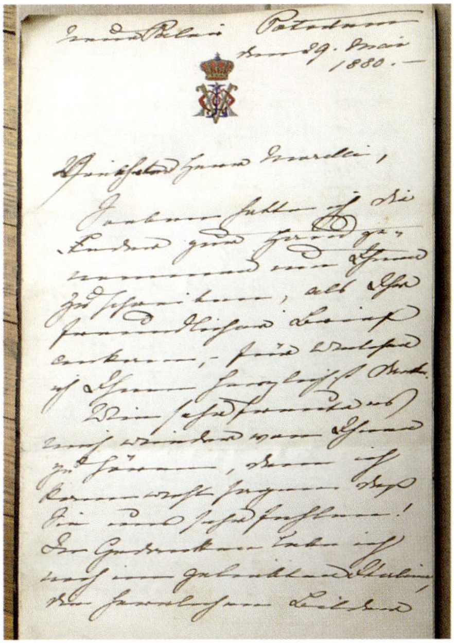

74. Crown Prince Frederick of Prussia. Photograph by Reichard & Lindner, 1879.

75. Crown Princess Victoria of Prussia. Photograph by E. Bambocci, 1879.

76. Giovanni Bellini, *Madonna and Child (The Alzano Madonna)*, c. 1485–87.

77. Crown Princess Victoria, page from letter to Giovanni Morelli, 29 May 1880.

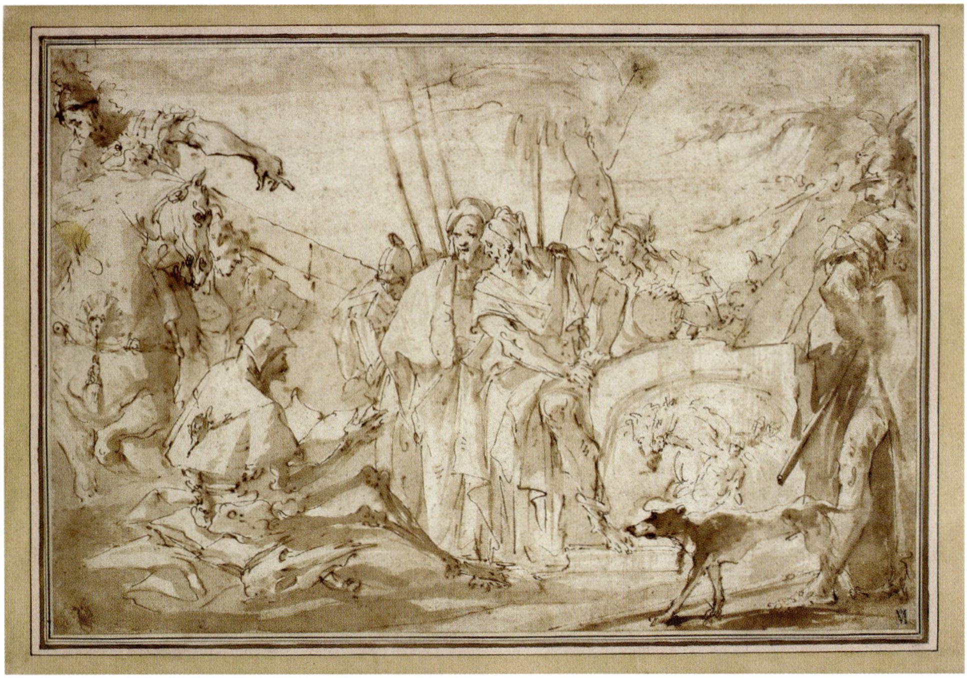

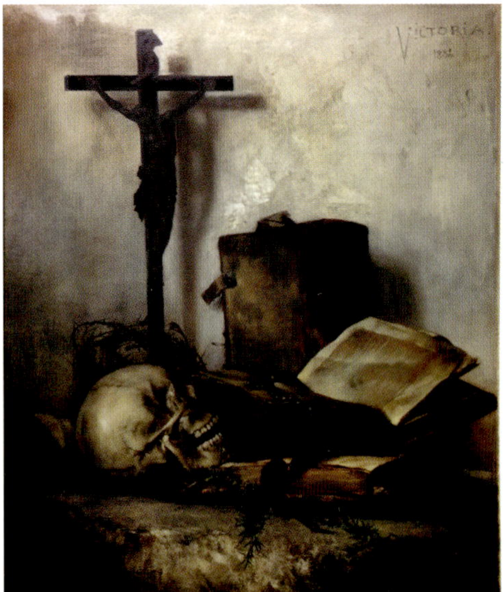

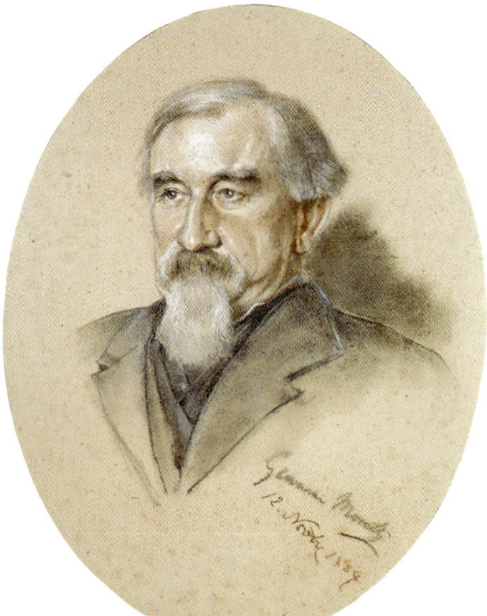

78. Giovanni Battista Tiepolo, *Death Giving an Audience*, c. 1740.

79. Crown Princess Victoria, *Vanitas*, 1884.

80. Crown Princess Victoria, *Giovanni Morelli*, 1884.

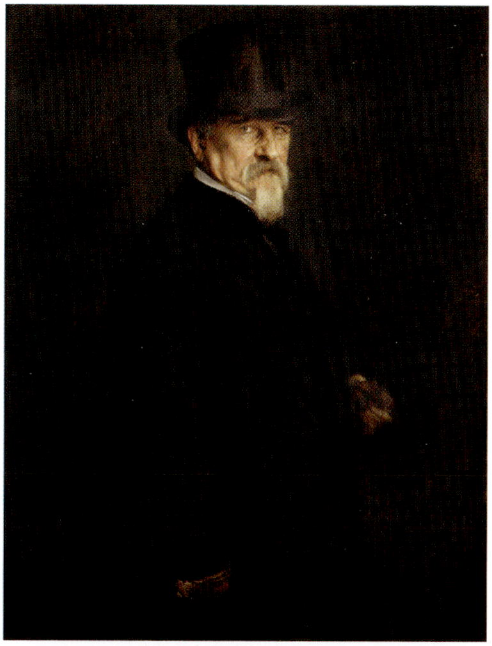
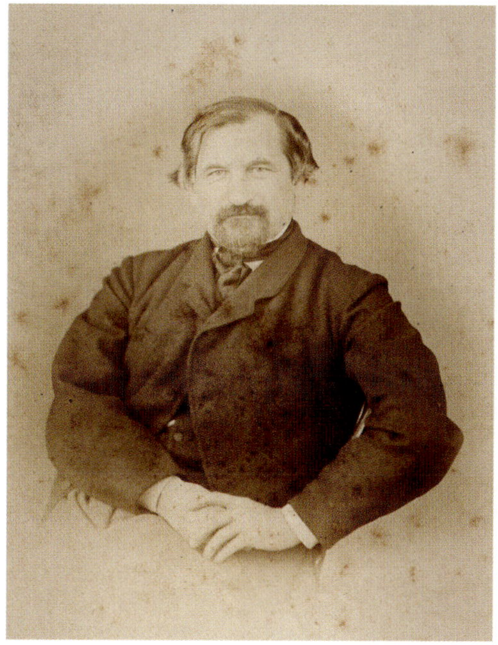
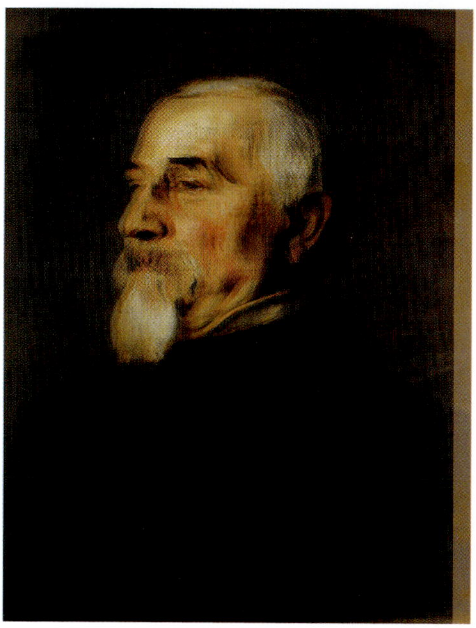
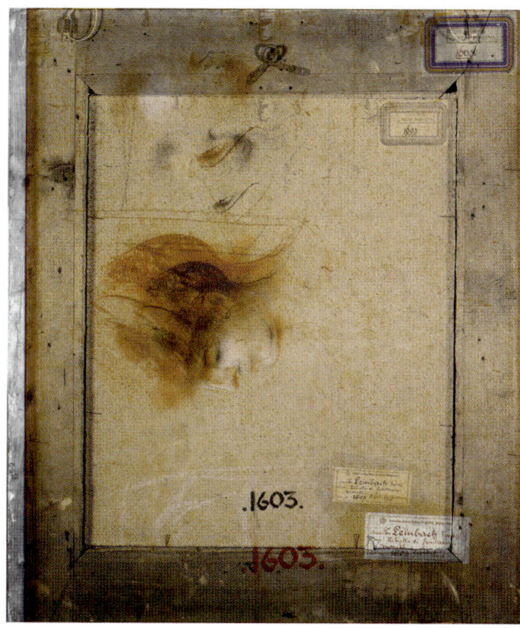

81. Franz Seraph von Lenbach, Portrait of Senator Giovanni Morelli, 1886.

82. Giovanni Morelli. Photograph by Giulio Rossi, c. 1883.

83. Franz Seraph von Lenbach, Portrait of Giovanni Morelli, 1887.

84. Franz Seraph von Lenbach, drawings on verso of Fig. 83.

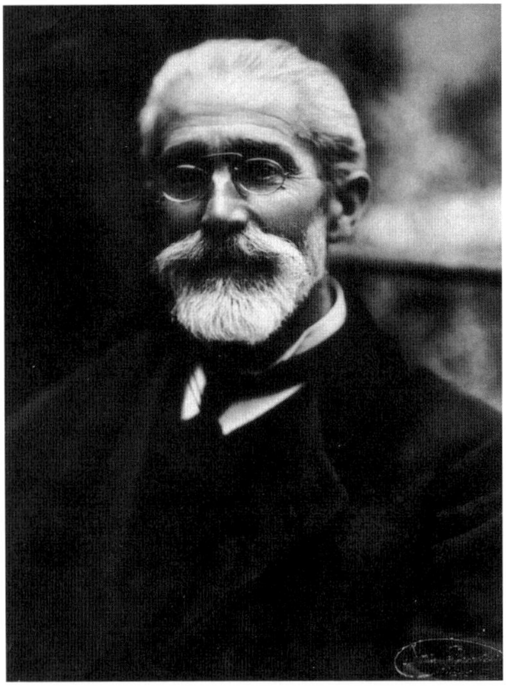

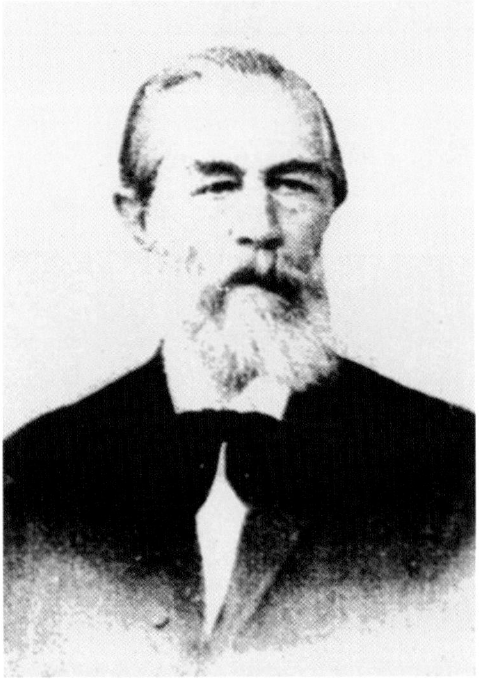

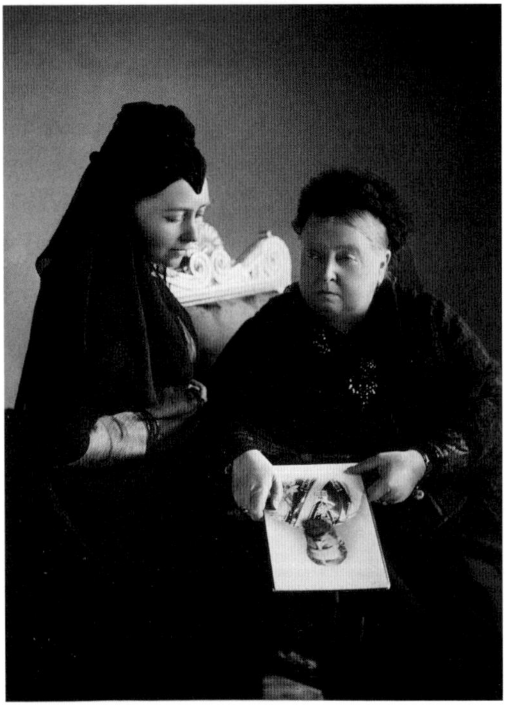

85. Gustavo Frizzoni.

86. Eduard Brockhaus, 1905.

87. Queen Victoria with her eldest daughter, Empress Frederick, in mourning in 1888.

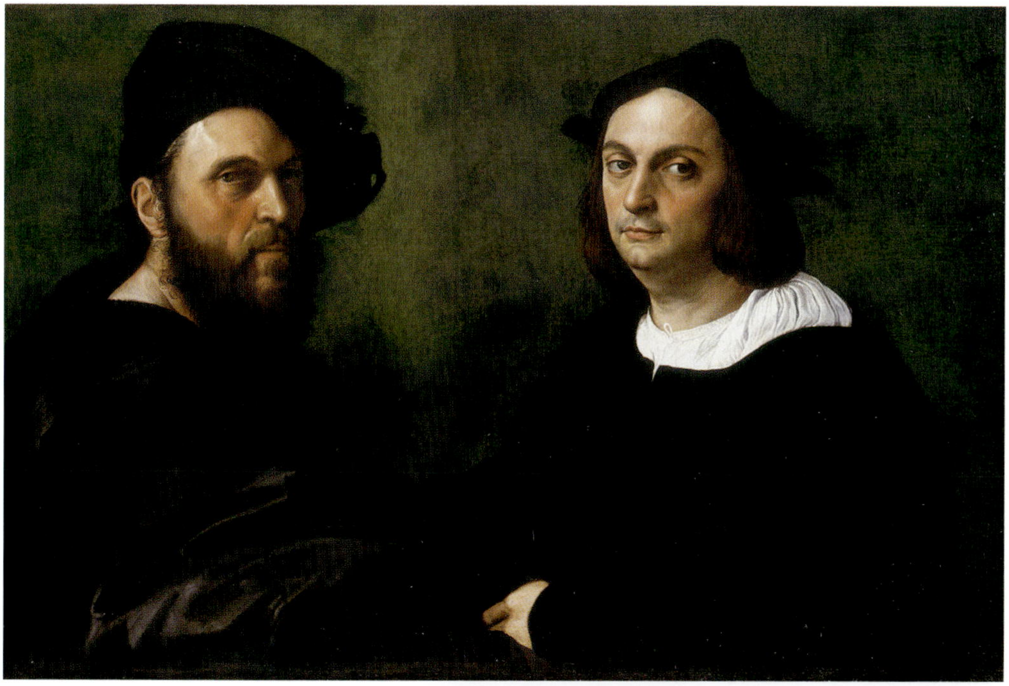

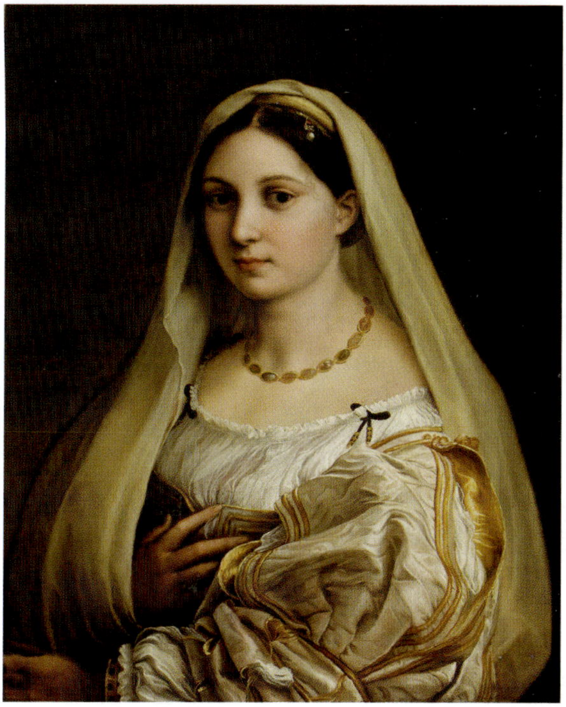

88. Raphael, Double portrait (Andrea Navagero and Agostino Beazzano), 1516.

89. Raphael, *Donna Velata* (Woman with a veil), c. 1512–15.

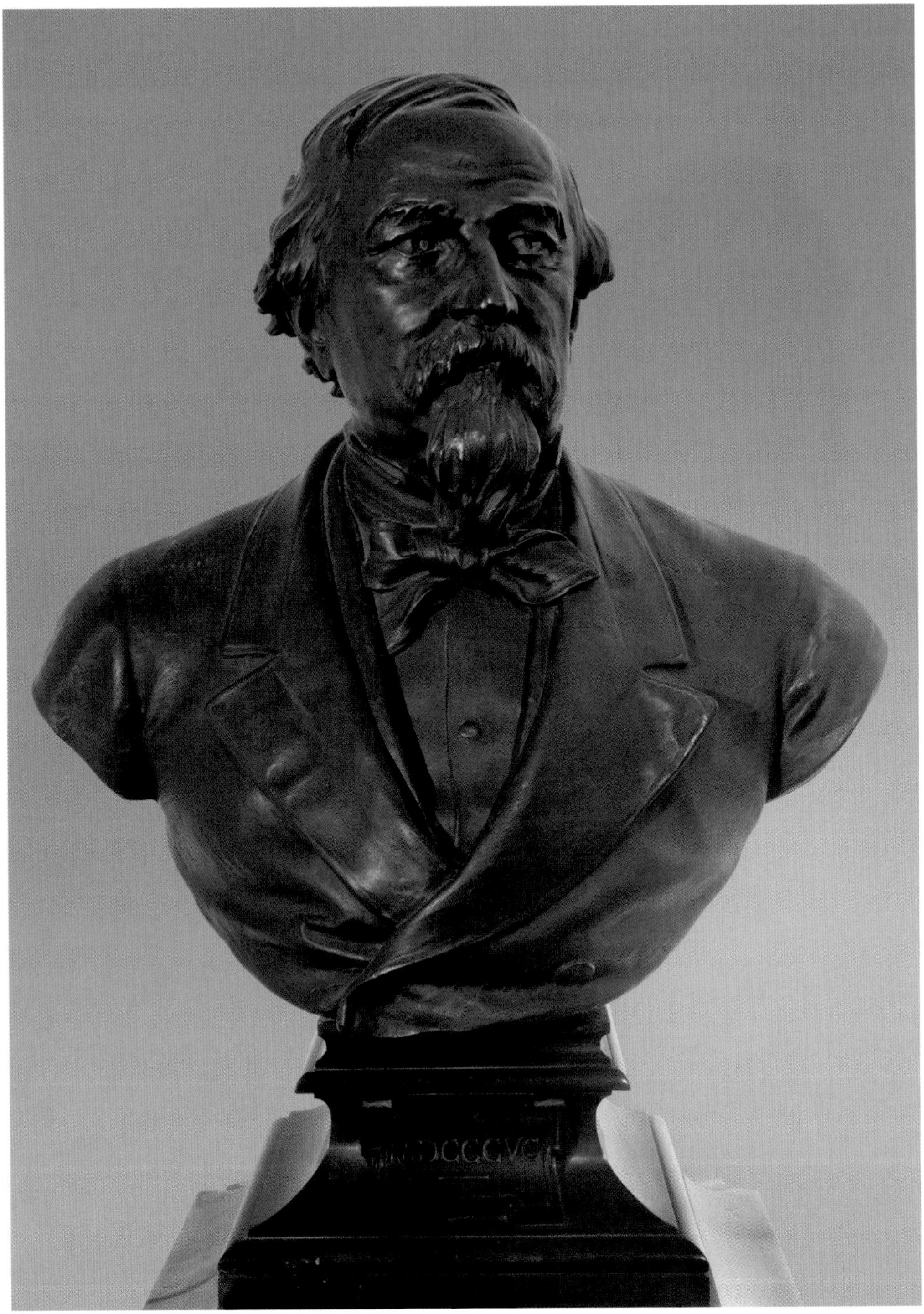

90. Lodovico Pogliaghi, *Giovanni Morelli*, 1895.

Published Writings by Giovanni Morelli

The various pseudonyms used by Morelli are given here as authors' names.

Balvi magnus, das ist kritische Beleuchtung des balvischen Missale. Munich, 1836. Reprinted in Jaynie Anderson, ed. *Balvi magnus und Das Miasma diabolicum: Giovanni Morellis erste pseudonyme Veröffentlichungen: Balvi magnus und Das Miasma diabolicum.* Würzburg: Königshausen und Neumann, 1991.

Johannes Morell. "De regione inguinali. Dissertatio anatomica. Auctore Joanne Morell, medicinae et chirurgiae doctore." Munich: J. Rösl, 1837.

Traugott Gotthilf Schneck, F. Munkeler, and Nicolaus Schäffer. *Das "Miasma diabolicum," das ist ein Aufruf an die christlich germanischen Gemeinen, von Traugott Gotthilf Schneck, mit Hülfe der christlichen Brüder Dr. Jonathan Kappelmeier, Physicus, und Fürchtegott Munkeler, Apotheker, herausgegeben mit Anmerkungen und einem gedrängten Lebensabrisse Schneck's versehen durch Nicolaus Schäffer, cand. Theologiae.* Strasbourg: Schmidt und Grucker, 1839. Reprinted in Jaynie Anderson, ed. *Balvi magnus und Das Miasma diabolicum: Giovanni Morellis erste pseudonyme Veröffentlichungen: Balvi magnus und Das Miasma diabolicum.* Würzburg: Königshausen und Neumann, 1991.

A Dilettante. "Handzeichnungen von Genelli: Von einem Dilettanten." *Kunstblatt* (6 June 1839): 181–82.

"Italienische dramatische Literature: Niccolini's *Arnold von Brescia.*" Part 1: *Allgemeine Zeitung* [Augsburg] 52 (21 February 1844): Beilage, 25–27; Part 2: *Allgemeine Zeitung* [Augsburg] 53 (22 February 1844): Beilage, 419–20.

"Sopra la relazione tra l'arti belle e la natura, discorso di Federigo Schelling tenuto nell'Academia di Monaco, il dì onomastico di S. M. il Re Massimiliano di Baviera, traduzione del dottor G. M." *Lo Spettatore industrial: Studi e notizie di tecnologia, igiene e letterature* 3 (1845): 285–320. Republished by Valentini, Milan, 1845.

"Italienische Briefe I." *Allgemeine Zeitung* [Augsburg] 253 (10 September 1845): Beilage, 2017–19, 2025–27.

"Italienische Briefe II." *Allgemeine Zeitung* [Augsburg] 320 (16 November 1845): Außerordentliche Beilage, 101–2.

"Italiens gegenwärtige politische Verhältnisse." *Allgemeine Zeitung* [Augsburg] 102 (12 April 1846): Beilage, Part I: 809–12; Parte II: 849–52. Parte III: 111 (21 April 1846): Beilage, 881–83.

"Italienische Briefe III." *Allgemeine Zeitung* [Augsburg] 282 (9 October 1846): Beilage, 2249–50.

"Italienische Briefe IV." *Allgemeine Zeitung* [Augsburg] 287 (14 October 1846): Beilage, 2289–90.

"Italienische Briefe V." *Allgemeine Zeitung* [Augsburg] 288 (15 October 1846): Beilage, 2617–18.

"Italienische Briefe VI." *Allgemeine Zeitung* [Augsburg] 298 (25 October 1846): Beilage, 2379–80.

"Italienische Briefe VII." *Allgemeine Zeitung* [Augsburg] 328 (24 November 1846): Beilage, 2617–18.

"Politisches Program der National Partei in Italien." *Allgemeine Zeitung* [Augsburg] 258 (15 September 1847): Beilage, 2057–59; 265 (22 September 1847): Beilage, 2144–16; 268 (25 September 1847): Beilage, 2140–42.

Worte eines Lombarden an die Deutschen. Frankfurt am Main: Streng und Schneider, 1848. (A unique copy in the Biblioteca Civica Angelo Mai, Bergamo; Italian translation in manuscript by D. Cairoli, in the same library).

"Considerazioni filosofiche di F. G. G. Schelling sopra Dante." In *Opere di G. B. Niccolini*. Florence: Le Monnier, 1858. (Translation of F. W. Schelling's *Über Dante in philosophischer Beziehung*, published anonymously in the collected works of Niccolini, with the notice: "Queste considerazioni filosofiche sopra Dante vennero scritte dal più célèbre filosofo della Germania, F. G. G. Schelling, quando era nel vigor degli anni. Un amico mi fu tanto cortese, che volle farne una traduzione in italiano, e concedermi di renderla colle stampe di pubblica ragione. Egli temendo alterare la sostanza dell'idee non pose cura all'eleganza della lingua, confortandosi coll'autorità dell'Alighieri che scrisse 'e qui mi scusi/La novità, se fior la lingua aborre."

"Necrologia di Giuseppe Molteni." *Allgemeine Zeitung* 91 (1 April 1867): 1491–92.

"Raffaello d'Urbino, colla sua 'Madonna del libro'." *La Perseveranza* (1 May 1871): 1.

Iwan [*sic*] Lermolieff. "Die Galerien Roms. Ein kritischer Versuch von Iwan Lermolieff. I: Die Galerie Borghese. Aus dem Russischen übersetzt von Dr. Johannes Schwarze. Mit Illustrationen." *Zeitschrift für bildende Kunst* 9 (1874): 1–11, 73–81, 171–78, 249–53; 10 (1875): 97–106, 207–11, 264–73, 329–34; 11 (1876): 132–37, 168–73.

Iwan [*sic*] Lermolieff. "Über Sebastiano del Piombo und Giulio Romano von Iwan Lermolieff." *Zeitschrift für bildende Kunst* Beiblatt 13 (1878): coll. 553–56. (The substance of the article is a long communication from Lermolieff, based on a letter of 20 March 1878 to Jean Paul Richter; see Giovanni Morelli and Jean Paul Richter, *Italienische Malerei der Renaissance im Briefwechsel von Giovanni Morelli und Jean Paul Richter 1876–1891* (below): 34–38.

Ivan Lermolieff. *Die Werke italienischer Meister in den Galerien von München, Dresden und Berlin. Ein kritischer Versuch von Ivan Lermolieff. Aus dem Russischen übersetzt von Dr. Johannes Schwarze.* Leipzig: E. A. Seemann, 1880.

Ivan Lermolieff, "Perugino oder Raphael? Einige Worte der Abwehr. Von Ivan Lermolieff. Mit Illustrationem." *Zeitschrift für bildende Kunst* 11 (1881): 243–52, 273–82.

Ivan Lermolieff, "Raphaels Jugendentwickelung: Worte der Verständigung gerichtet an Herrn Prof. Springer in Leipzig. Von Ivan Lermolieff." *Reportorium für Kunstwissenschaft* 5 (1882): 147–78.

Giovanni Morelli. "Discussione del disegno di legge concernente il trasporto della Pinacoteca di Torino dal Palazzo Madama al Palazzo di Musei." In *Atti del Parlamento Italiano. Sessione del 1861–1862: Discussioni della Camera dei Deputati*, edited by G. Giuseppe and T. Paolo, 3413–23. Rome, 1882.

Giovanni Morelli. *Italian Masters in German Galleries: A Critical Essay on the Italian Pictures in the Galleries of Munich, Dresden, Berlin, by Giovanni Morelli, Member of the Italian Senate. Translated from the German by Mrs Louise M. Richter.* London: George Bell and Sons, 1883.

Giovanni Morelli and Gino Capponi. *Nozze Ferrari-Gini* (printed in thirty copies only).

Iwan Lermolieff. *Le opere dei maestri italiani nelle gallerie di Monaco, Dresda e Berlino: Saggio critico di Iwan Lermolieff tradotto dal Russo in Tedesco per cura del Dottore Giovanni Schwarze e dal Tedesco in Italiano dalla Baronessa di K. A.* Bologna: Nicola Zanichelli, 1886.

Iwan Lermolieff. "Noch einmal das venezianische Skizzenbuch." *Zeitschrift für bildende Kunst* 22 (1887): 143–55.

Ivan Lermolieff. *Kunstkritische Studien über italienische Malerei: Die Galerien Borghese und Doria Panfili in Rom; Von Ivan Lermolieff. Mit 62 Abbildungen*. Leipzig: F. A. Brockhaus, 1890.

Ivan Lermolieff, *Kunstkritische Studien über italienische Malerei: Die Galerien zu München und Dresden; Mit 41 Abildungen*. Leipzig: F. A. Brockhaus. 1891.

"Handzeichnungen italienischer Meister in photographischen Aufnahmen von Braun & Co. in Dornach, kritisch gesichtet von Giovanni Morelli (Lermolieff). Mitgeteilt von E. Habich." *Kunstchronik* n.s. no. 3 (1891–92): 289–94, 373–78, 441–46, 487–90, 505–508, 524–28, 543–47, 571–74, 590–93; n.s. no. 4 (1893–94): 53–56, 84–90, 155–62, 207–10, 237–40.

Giovanni Morelli. *Italian Painters: Critical Studies of their Works*. Translated by Constance Jocelyn Ffoulkes, with an introduction by Sir Austen Henry Layard. Vol. 1: *The Borghese and Doria Pamfili Galleries in Rome*. London: John Murray, 1892.

Giovanni Morelli. *Italian Painters: Critical Studies of their Works*. Translated by Constance Jocelyn Ffoulkes, with an introduction by Sir Austen Henry Layard. Vol. 2: *The Galleries of Munich and Dresden*. London: John Murray, 1893.

Kunstkritische Studien über italienische Malerei: Die Galerie zu Berlin. Von Ivan Lermolieff. Nebst einem Lebensbilde Giovanni Morelli's herausgegeben von Dr. Gustav Frizzoni. Mit Porträt und 66 Abbildungen. Leipzig: F. A. Brockhaus, 1893. (The volume also contains three essays on Raphael: "Perugino oder Raffael?," "Raffael's Jugendentwickelung," and "Noch einmal das venetianische Skizzenbuch").

Gustavo Frizzoni. "Appunti del senatore Giovanni Morelli a proposito della Galleria del Prado e dell'arte spagnuola." *Archivio storico dell'arte* 7, fasc. I (1894): 63–66.

Giovanni Morelli and Giovanni Battista Cavalcaselle. "Catalogo delle opera d'arte nelle Marche e nell'Umbria." Edited by Adolfo Venturi. *Le Gallerie nazionali italiane* 2 (1894–95): 191–349.

Giovanni Morelli. *Della pittura italiana: Studii storico-critici di Giovanni Morelli (Ivan Lermolieff); Le Gallerie Borghese e Doria-Pamphili in Roma. Prima edizione italiana preceduta dalla biografia e dal ritratto dell'autore, e illustrata da 81 incisioni*. Milan: Fratelli Treves, 1897.

Giovanni Morelli and Jean Paul Richter. *Italienische Malerei der Renaissance im Briefwechsel von Giovanni Morelli und Jean Paul Richter 1876–1891*. Edited by Irma Richter and Gisela Richter. Foreword by Paola della Pergola. Baden-Baden: Bruno Grimm, 1960.

Giacomo Agosti, ed. "Giovanni Morelli corrispondente di Antinori," in *Studi e ricerche di collezionismo e museografia, Firenze 1820–1920*, 1–83. Quaderni del Seminario di Storia della Critica dell'Arte 2 (Pisa: Scuola normale superior di Pisa, 1985).

Jaynie Anderson, ed. *Giovanni Morelli, Dellá pittura italiana. Studii storico-critici di Giovanni Morelli (Ivan Lermolieff). Le Gallerie Borghese e Doria Pamphili in Roma*. Milan: Adelphi, 1991.

Jaynie Anderson, ed. *Balvi magnus und Das Miasma diabolicum: Giovanni Morellis erste pseudonyme Veröffentlichungen: Balvi magnus und Das Miasma diabolicum*. Würzburg: Königshausen und Neumann, 1991.

Jaynie Anderson, ed. *Giovanni Morelli, De la peinture italienne: Les fondements de la theorie de l'attribution en peinture a propos de la collection des Galeries Borghese et Doria-Pamphili*. French translation by Nadine Blamoutier. Paris: Éditions de la Lagune, 1994.

Jaynie Anderson. *Collecting, Connoisseurship and the Art Market in Risorgimento Italy: Giovanni Morelli's Letters to Giovanni Melli and Pietro Zavaritt (1866–1872)*. Venice: Istituto Veneto di Scienze, Lettere ed Arti, 1999.

Jaynie Anderson, ed. *I taccuini manoscritti di Giovanni Morelli*. Le Marche Disperse, Fonti 1. Milan: Motta, 2000.

Jaynie Anderson. *Giuseppe Molteni in Correspondence with Giovanni Morelli: The Restoration of Renaissance Painting in Mid Nineteenth-Century Milan*. Teoria e Storia del Restauro 20. Florence: Edizioni Edifir, 2014.

Selected Bibliography

Archival sources

Anna Flora Eynard, Bergamo
Archivio Antinori, Florence
Archivio di Stato di Verona, Verona
Archivio di Stato di Venezia, Venice
Archivio Ginoulhiac, Milan
Archivio Secco Suardo, Lurano
Archivio Zavaritt, Gorle
Bayerische Staatsbibliothek, Munich
Biblioteca Ambrosiana, Milan
Biblioteca Civica Angelo Mai, Bergamo
Biblioteca Comunale, Forlì
Biblioteca Comunale dell'Archiginnasio, Bologna
Biblioteca dell'Accademia di Belle Arti di Brera, Milan
Bibliotheca Hertziana, Rome
Biblioteca Marciana, Venice
Biblioteca Marucelliana, Florence
Biblioteca Nazionale Centrale di Firenze, Florence
British Library, London
Duke University, North Carolina
Fondazione Cavour, Santena
Fondazione Museo Storico del Trentino, Trento
Frizzoni family archives, Bergamo
Gian Carlo Eynard
Giovanni Frizzoni, Bergamo
John Murray Archive, London (now in the National Library of Scotland, Edinburgh)
Kantonsbibliothek, Aarau
Ludwig-Maximilians-Universität, Munich
Metropolitan Museum of Art New York, Onassis Library for Hellenic and Roman Art in the Department of Greek and Roman Art
Museo del Risorgimento, Milan
Museo Poldi Pezzoli, Milan
Muséum National d'Histoire Naturelle, Paris
National Gallery, London
Piero Malvezzi, Milan
Private archive, Bergamo
Royal Archives, Windsor Castle
Sächsisches Staatsarchiv, Leipzig
Schloss Fasanerie, Eichenzell
Staatsarchiv, Frauenfeld
Tate Gallery Archive, London
Universitäts-Archiv der Friedrich-Alexander-Universität, Erlangen
Universitätsbibliothek, Leipzig
Victoria and Albert Museum, London

Published sources

Agassiz, Elizabeth Cary, ed. *Louis Agassiz: His Life and Correspondence. Vol. 1*. Cambridge, MA: Macmillan, 1885.

Agassiz, Louis. *Études sur les glaciers*. Neuchâtel: Jent et Gassmann, 1840.

Agosti, Giacomo. "Giovanni Morelli corrispondente di Niccolò Antinori." In *Studi e ricerche di collezionismo e museografia Firenze 1820–1920*, 1–84. Quaderni del Seminario di Storia della Critica d'Arte 2. Pisa: Scuola Normale Superiore, 1985.

Agosti, Giacomo, Maria Luisa Negri, and Cinzia Solza. "Il fondo Morelli nella Biblioteca dell'Accademia di Brera." In *G. Morelli: Materiali di Ricerca*, edited by Eleonora Bairati, 115–204. Bergamo: Biblioteca Angelo Mai, 1987.

Agosti, Giacomo. "Un 'italiano d'animo e tedesco di studi' a Firenze: Giovanni Morelli e i suoi interlocutori in Toscana." In *L'Idea di Firenze: Temi e interpretazioni nell'arte strainera dell'Ottocento*, edited by Maurizio Bossi, Lucia Tonini, and Francis Haskell, 117–26. Florence: Centro Di, 1989.

Anderson, Jaynie, ed. *Balvi magnus und Das Miasma diabolicum: Giovanni Morellis erste pseudonyme Veröffentlichungen: Balvi magnus und Das Miasma diabolicum*. Würzburg: Königshausen und Neumann, 1991.

Anderson, Jaynie. *Collecting, Connoisseurship and the Art Market in Risorgimento Italy: Giovanni Morelli's Letters to Giovanni Melli and Pietro Zavaritt (1866–1872)*. Venice: Istituto Veneto di Scienze, Lettere ed Arti, 1999.

Anderson, Jaynie. "'Die geniale Bettina': Giovanni Morelli in Conversation with Bettina von Arnim." *Oxford German Studies* 18–19 (1989/90): 45–59.

Anderson, Jaynie. "The Fascination of an Art Historian at I Tatti: Bernard Berenson and Jacqueline Kennedy." In *Renaissance Studies in Honor of Joseph Connors*, edited by Maechtelt Israaëls and Louis A. Waldman, 737–42, 981–82. Florence: Leo S. Olschki, 2013.

Anderson, Jaynie. "The First Cleaning Controversy at the National Gallery, 1846–1853." In *Appearance, Opinion, Change: Evaluating the Look of Paintings*, edited by Victoria Todd, 3–7. London: United Kingdom Institute of Conservation, 1990.

Anderson, Jaynie. "Frizzoneria in Bergamo." In *Ex Fumo Lucem: Baroque Studies in Honour of Klára Garas: Presented on her Eightieth Birthday*, edited by Zsuzsanna Dobos and Peter Ujvari, vol. 2, 233–52. Budapest: Museum of Fine Arts, 1999.

Anderson, Jaynie. *Giorgione: The Painter of Poetic Brevity*. Paris and New York: Flammarion, 1997.

Anderson, Jaynie. "Giovanni Morelli and the French." In *Histoire de l'histoire de l'art en France au XIXe siècle*, contribution au colloque du 2 au 5 juin 2004, Paris, edited by Roland Recht, Philippe Sénéchal, Claire Barbillon, and François-René Martin, 447–61. France: La Documentation Française, 2008.

Anderson, Jaynie. "Giovanni Morelli et la collection Arconati-Visconti." *La revue du Louvre et des musées de France* 40, no. 3 (1990): 205–211.

Anderson, Jaynie. "Giovanni Morelli et sa définition de 'la scienza dell'arte'." *Revue de l'art* 75 (1987): 49–55.

Anderson, Jaynie. "Giovanni Morelli For and Against Piero della Francesca." In *Piero interpretato: Copie, giudizi e musealizzazione di Piero della Francesca*, edited by Cecilia Preti and Ranieri Varese, 85–88. Ancona: Il Lavoro, 1998.

Anderson, Jaynie. "Giovanni Morelli, museologo del Risorgimento." In *Giovanni Morelli: Collezionista di disegni; La donazione al Castello Sforzesco*, edited by Giulio Bora, 25–39. Catalogue of an exhibition at the Castello Sforzesco, Milan, 9 November 1994–8 January 1995. Milan: Silvana, 1994.

Anderson, Jaynie. "Giovanni Santi e Giovanni Morelli." In *Giovanni Santi: Atti del convegno internazionale di studi; Urbino, Convento di Santa Chiara, 1–19 marzo 1995*, edited by Raniere Varese, 193–97. Milan: Electa, 1999.

Anderson, Jaynie. *The Restoration of Renaissance Painting in Mid Nineteenth-Century Milan: Giuseppe Molteni in Correspondence with Giovanni Morelli*. Teoria e Storia del Restauro 21. Florence: Edifir, 2014.

Anderson, Jaynie. "I taccuini marchigiani di Giovanni Morelli." In *Giovanni Battista Cavalcaselle: Conoscitore e conservatore; Atti del convegno*, edited by Anna Chiara Tommasi, 81–96. Venice: Marsilio, 1998.

Anderson, Jaynie. "Layard and Morelli." In *Austen Henry Layard tra l'oriente e Venezia*. Conference Proceedings, Venice, 26–28 October 1983, edited by Federick M. Fales and Bernard J. Hickey, 109–37, plates VIII–XXI. Rome: "L'Erma" di Bretschneider, 1987.

Anderson, Jaynie. "'Modern Connoisseurship' and the Role it Played in Shaping American Collectors' Taste in Italian Renaissance Art." In *A Market for Merchant Princes: Collecting Italian Renaissance Paintings in America*, edited by Inge Jackson Reist, 28–37. Frick Collection Studies in the History of Art Collecting in America 2. Philadelphia: Pennsylvania State University Press, 2015.

Anderson, Jaynie. "Morelli." In *The Oxford Companion to Western Art*, edited by Hugh Brigstocke, 490. Oxford: Oxford University Press, 2001.

Anderson, Jaynie. "Morelli e Genelli." In *Giovanni Morelli: Collezionista di disegni; La donazione al Castello Sforzesco*, edited by Giuolio Bora, 93–99. Catalogue of an exhibition at the Castello Sforzesco, Milan, 9 November 1994–8 January 1995. Milan: Silvana, 1994.

Anderson, Jaynie. "Morelli e i suoi amici." In *Giovanni Morelli: Collezionista di disegni; La donazione al Castello Sforzesco*, edited by Giuolio Bora, 79–92. Catalogue of an exhibition at the Castello Sforzesco, Milan, 9 November 1994–8 January 1995. Milan: Silvana, 1994.

Anderson, Jaynie. "'A Most Improper Picture': Transformations of Bronzino's Erotic Allegory." *Apollo: The International Magazine of Arts* 139 (February 1994): 19–28.

Anderson, Jaynie. "National Museums, the Art Market and Old Master Paintings." In *Kunst und Kunsttheorie 1400–1900*, edited by Peter Ganz, 375–404. Wölfenbütteler Forschungen 48. Wölfenbüttel: Herzog August Bibliothek, 1991.

Anderson, Jaynie. "Introduction: Otto Mündler and his Travel Diary." In *The Travel Diaries of Otto Mündler 1855–1858*, edited by Carol Togneri Dowd. The Volume of the Walpole Society 51 (London: The Walpole Society, 1985): 7–64.

Anderson, Jaynie. "The Rediscovery of Ferrarese Renaissance Painting in the Risorgimento." *The Burlington Magazine* 135, no. 1085 (August 1993): 539–49.

Anderson, Jaynie. "Salvare gli affreschi del Rinascimento italiano: La missione di Henry Layard." In *Austen Henry Layard, Giovanni Santi e l'affresco di Cagli*, edited by Ranieri Varese, 51–61. Epigrammi 3. Florence: Centro Di, 1994.

Anderson, Jaynie. "Sir Charles Eastlake e i suoi restauratori italiani: Giuseppe Molteni e Raffaele Pinti." In *Giovanni Secco Suardo: La cultura del restauro tra tutela e conservazione dell'opera d'arte*. Acts of the conference at Bergamo, 9–11 March 1995, published as a supplement to *Bollettino d'Arte* 98 (1996): 57–62.

Anderson, Jaynie, Ron Radford, Attilio Pizzigoni, Giovanni Valagussa, and David Wise, *Renaissance: 15th & 16th Century Italian Paintings from the Accademia Carrara, Bergamo*. Exhibition catalogue. Canberra: National Gallery of Australia, 2011.

Angelini, Gianpaolo. *La fratellanza raffaellesca: Fortuna e ricezione del metodo morelliano nell'Italia postunitaria*. Quaderni di Artes 4. Pisa: Edizioni ETS, 2018.

Angelini, Gianpaolo. *La patria e le arti: Emilio Visconti Venosta patriota, collezionista e conoscitore*. Pisa: Edizioni ITS, 2013.

Arrighi, Cletto [Carlo Righetti]. *I 450 deputati del presente e i deputati dell'avvenire per una società di egregi uomini politici, leterati e giornalisti diretta da Cletto Arrighi*. Vol. 6. Milan: Presso gli Editori; E presso l'ufficio della Cronaca grigia, 1865.

Avery-Quash, Susanna, *The Travel Notebooks of Sir Charles Eastlake*. The Volume of the Walpole Society 2011/73. London: The Walpole Society, 2011.

Baker, Christopher. "Connoisseurs at Christ Church: Morelli, Fry and Berenson." *Journal of the History of Collections* 13, no. 2 (2001): 163–73.

Banti, Alberto Mario, and Paul Ginsborg, eds. *Il Risorgimento*. Storia d'Italia, Annali 22. Torino: Giulio Einaudi, 2007.

Barracco, Giovanni. *La Maddalena di Pier di Cosimo*. Rome: Forzani e C., tipografi del Senato, 1910.

Bartuschat, Johannes. "Dante in Germania in età romantica." In *Letture e lettori di Dante: L'età moderna e contemporanea*, edited by Marcello Ciccuto, 47–70. Letture classensi 39. Ravenna: Longo, 2011.

Bassi Rathgeb, Roberto. "Le postille di Antonio Piccinelli alle 'Vite dei pittori, scultori ed architetti bergamaschi di F. M. Tassi'." *L'Arte* 58 (1959): 123–24.

Belgum, Kirsten. "Documenting the Zeitgeist: How the *Brockhaus* Recorded and Fashioned the World for Germans." In *Publishing Culture and the "Reading Nation": German Book History in the Long Nineteenth Century*, edited by Lynne Tatlock, 89-117. Rochester, NY: Camden House, 2010.

Belotti, Bortolo. *Storia di Bergamo e dei Bergamaschi*. Bergamo: Poligrafiche Bolis, 1959.

Benini, Laura. "Descrizione della Quadreria Costabili." *Musei Ferraresi: Bolletino annuale* 7 (1977): 79–96.

Benvenuti, Sergio. *Le lettere di Tommaso Gar negli archivi e nelle biblioteche del Trentino*. Trento: Istituto per la storia del Risorgimento italiano, 1963.

Beretta, Giovanni. *Gorle: La sua storia*. Gorle: La Stamperia di Gorle, 1983.

Bonsanti, Giorgio. "The Art of Conservation: VIII. From Guizzardi to Cavenaghi: Nineteenth-Century Italian Conservators." *The Burlington Magazine* 158, no. 1365 (December 2016): 968–78.

Bora, Giulio. *I disegni della collezione Morelli*. Cinisello Balsamo: Amilcare Pizzi, 1988.

Bosi Maramotti, Giovanna. "Gli anni bolognesi di Corrado Ricci." *Annali della Scuola Normale Superiore di Pisa: Classe di lettere e filosofia*, series 4, vol. 5, no. 2 (2000): 489–99.

Braham, Allan. *Giovanni Battista Moroni: 400th Anniversary Exhibition*. London: National Gallery, 1978.

Brofferio, Sergio, Anna Flora Eynard Ginoulhiac, and Sandra Zavaritt Frizzoni, *Da Celerina a... Bergamo: Biografia e carteggio di Antonio Frizzoni (1754–1835)*. Bergamo: privately printed, 2004.

Buckle, George Earle, ed. *The letters of Queen Victoria. Series 2: A Selection from her Majesty's Correspondence and Journal Between the Years 1862 and 1878. Vol. 1: 1862–1869*. London: John Murray, 1930.

Burckhardt, Jacob. *Der Cicerone: Eine Anleitung zum Genuss der Kunstwerke Italiens*. Basel: Schweighauser'sche Verlagsbuchhandlung, 1855.

Cagnoli, Ottavio. *Verona con cenni statistici e con tavole a tutto il 1851 nel cimitero che fu a san Bernardino*. Verona: Vicentini e Franchini, 1852.

Caimi, Aristide. *Giornale delle operazioni di guerra eseguite dalla Legione di Guardia Nazionale Mobile a Difesa dello Stelvio e Tonale nella campagna del 1866, redatto da Aristide Caimi già Capitano aiutante maggiore in primo della Legione*. Turin: G. Cassone, 1868.

Caimi, Aristide. *Giornale delle operazioni di guerra eseguite dalla Legione di Guardia Nazionale Mobile a Difesa dello Stelvio e Tonale nella campagna del 1866, redatto da Aristide Caimi già Capitano aiutante maggiore in primo della Legione, seconda edizione corredata da documenti aggiunti dal già Comandante della Legione Senatore Enrico Guicciardi*. Rome: Tipografia dell'Opinione, 1881.

Candolle, A. P. *Regni vegetabilis: Systema naturale sive ordines genera et species plantarum secundum methodi naturalis normas digestorum et descriptorum*. Paris, 1818.

Capponi, Gino. *Sull'educazione: Frammento, 1841*. Lugano: Tipografia della Svizzera Italiana, 1845.

Chabod, Federico. *Italian Foreign Policy: The Statecraft of the Founders*, translated by William McCuaig. Princeton, N. J.: Princeton University Press, 1996.

Chaudonneret, Marie-Claude. "Historicism and 'Heritage' in the Louvre, 1820–1840: From the Musée Charles X to the Galerie d'Apollon." *Art History* 14, no. 4 (December 1991): 488–510.

Christiansen, Keith, and Stefan Weppelmann, eds, *The Renaissance Portrait from Donatello to Bellini*. New York: The Metropolitan Museum of Art, 2011.

Cooper, Robyn. "The Popularization of Renaissance Art in Victorian England: The Arundel Society." *Art History* 1, no. 3 (September 1978): 263–92.

Corgnati, Maurizio. *Soldati e pittori nel Risorgimento italiano*. Milan: Fabbri, 1987.

Cova, Alberto. *Storia economica e sociale di Bergamo. Vol. 4: Dalla fine del Settecento all'avvio dello stato unitario*. Bergamo: Fondazione per la Storia Economica e Sociale di Bergamo, 1994.

Crowe, Joseph Archer. *Reminiscences of Thirty-Five Years of My Life*. London: John Murray, 1895.

Curato, Federico. "Profilo biografico di Sir James Hudson, G. C. B." In *Le relazioni diplomatiche tra la Gran Bretagna ed il Regno di Sardegna dal 1852 al 1856: Il carteggio diplomatico di Sir James Hudson*. Vol. 1, xi–cl. Turin: Industria Libraria tip. ed., 1956.

da Persico, Giovanni Battista. *Descrizione di Verona e della sua provincia*. Verona: Società Tipografica Editrice, 1820.

Darwin, Charles. *The Origin of Species*. London: John Murray, 1859.

Davies, Martin. *The Early Italian Schools Before 1400*. National Gallery Catalogues. London: National Gallery, 1961.

de Chapeaurouge, Donat. "Das Milieu als Porträt." *Wallraf-Richarts-Jahrbuch* 22 (1960): 137–59.

De Sanctis, Francesco. *Epistolario (1859–1860)*, edited by Giuseppe Talamo and Carlo Muscetta. Opere di Francesco De Sanctis 20. Turin: Giulio Einaudi, 1965.

De Sanctis, Francesco. *Lettere dall'esilio (1853–1860)*, edited by Benedetto Croce. Bari: G. Laterza, 1938.

degli Alfieri, Giovanni Treccani. *Storia di Milano*. Milan: Treccani, 1960.

Doughty, Oswald, and John Robert Wahl, eds. *Letters of Dante Gabriel Rossetti*. Oxford: Clarendon Press, 1965.

Duggan, Christopher. *The Force of Destiny: A History of Italy since 1796*. London: Penguin, 2007.

Ebert, Hans. *Buonaventura Genelli (Maler und Werk)*. Dresden: Verlag der Kunst, 1987.

Eyck, Frank. *The Frankfurt Parliament 1848–1849*. London: Macmillan, 1968.

Facchinetti, Simone. *Dittico Morelliano*. Arrigoniana 8. Bergamo, 2018.

Farago, Claire. "Re-Reading Richter and MacCurdy: Lessons in Translation." In *Leonardo in Britain: Collections and Reception*, edited by Susanna Avery-Quash and Juliana Barone. Florence: Olschki, 2019.

Ferino Pagden, Sylvia. *Disegni umbri*. Milano: Electa, 1984.

Ferino Pagden, Sylvia. "Raffaello come *test case* della validità del metodo morelliano." In *Giovanni Morelli e la cultura dei conoscitori*. Atti del Convegno Internazionale, Bergamo, 4–7 giugno 1987, edited by Giacomo Agosti, Maria Elisabetta Manca, and Matteo Panzeri, vol. 2, 331–49. Bergamo: Pierluigi Lubrina, 1993.

Fleming, John. "Art Dealing and the Risorgimento: I." *The Burlington Magazine* 115, no. 838 (January–April 1973): 4–17.

Foratti, Aldo. "Gli studi d'arte di Marco Minghetti." *Atti e Memorie della Reale Deputazione di storia patria per l'Emilia e la Romagna* 15, no. 2 (1936–37): 111–33.

Frizzoni, Gustavo. "Appunti del senatore Giovanni Morelli a proposito della Galleria del Prado e dell'arte spagnuola." *Archivio storico dell'arte* 7 (1894): 63–66.

Frizzoni, Gustavo. "Cenni biografici intorno a Giovanni Morelli." In Giovanni Morelli. *Della Pittura Italiana: Studii storico critici di Giovannni Morelli (Ivan Lermolieff); Le Gallerie Borghese e Doria Pamphili in Roma*. Milan: Fratelli Treves Editori, 1897.

Frizzoni, Gustavo. *Collezione di quaranta disegni scelti dalla raccolta del senatore Giovanni Morelli riprodotti in eliotipia descritti ed illustrate dal Dr. Gustavo Frizzoni*. Milan: Hoepli, 1886.

Frizzoni, Gustavo. "Dall'epistolario di due benemeriti dell'arte." *Il Marzocco* 15, no. 40 (1910).

Frizzoni, Gustavo. "Giovanni Morelli: Ein Lebensbild." In *Kunstkritische Studien über italienische Malerei: Die Galerie zu Berlin. Von Ivan Lermolieff. Nebst einem Lebensbilde Giovanni Morelli's herausgegeben von Dr. Gustav Frizzoni. Mit Porträt und 66 Abbildungen*, xi–lxiii. Leipzig: F. A. Brockhaus, 1893.

Frizzoni, Gustavo. *In qual modo si possa impedire, senza ledere il diritto dei privati, che opere d'arte pregevoli continuino ad essere portate via dall'Italia. Relazione svolta al Congresso Artistico Internazionale di Venezia, 1905*. Venice: Garzia, 1908.

Frizzoni, Gustavo. "Jacob Burckhardt nella persona, nei pensieri, nelle opere." *Nuova Antologia* 160 (1898): 660–85.

Frizzoni, Gustavo. "La Galerie Layard." *Gazette des Beaux-Arts* 16, no. 2 (1896)" 461.

Frizzoni, Gustavo. "Lettere di Giacomo Burckhardt ad un'architetto." *Rassegna bibliografica dell'arte italiana* 16 (1903): 149–51.

Frizzoni, Gustavo. *Raccolta di disegni originali dei più celebri artisti tratti dalla scelta collezione del senatore Giovanni Morelli in Milan*. Venice: Gio. Batta Brusa, 1882.

Frosinini, Cecilia, and Maria Cristina Rodeschini, eds. *Il ritratto di Leonello d'Este*. Florence: Edifir, 2016.

Fulford, Roger, ed. *Dearest Mama: Letters Between Queen Victoria and the Crown Princess of Prussia, 1861–1864*. London: Evans Brothers, 1968.

Galasso, Giuseppe, ed. *Antologia degli scritti politici di Carlo Cattaneo*. Vol. 2. Bologna: Mulino, 1962.

Galli Michero, Lavinia M., and Fernando Mazzocca, eds. *Gian Giacomo Poldi Pezzoli: L'uomo e il collezionista del Risorgimento*. Exhibition at the Museo Poldi Pezzoli, Milan. Turin: Allemandi, 2011.

Garin, Eugenio. "Il pensiero di Gino Capponi." in *Gino Capponi: Linguista, storico, pensatore*, edited by Giovanni Nencioni, 41–45. Studi (Accademia toscana di scienze e lettere La Colombaria) 50 (Florence: Olschki, 1977).

Giannini, Cristina. "Giovanni Morelli e il Conte Suardo." In *Giovanni Morelli e la cultura dei conoscitori*. Atti del Convegno Internazionale, Bergamo, 4–7 giugno 1987, edited by Giacomo Agosti, Maria Elisabetta Manca, and Matteo Panzeri, vol. 1, 199–220. Bergamo: Pierluigi Lubrina, 1993.

Giebe, Marlies. "Die 'Schlummernde Venus' von Giorgione und Tizian: Bestandaufnahme und Konservierung—neue Ergebnisse der Röngenanalyse." *Jahrbuch der Staatlichen Kunstsammlungen Dresden* (1992): 91–105.

Ginsborg, Paul. *Daniele Manin and the Venetian Revolution of 1848–49*. London: Cambridge University Press, 1979.

Ginzburg, Carlo. "Spie: Radici di un paradigma indiziario." *Rivista di storia contemporanea* 7 (1978): 1–14.

Ginzburg, Carlo. *Wooden Eyes: Nine Reflections on Distance*. New York: Columbia University Press, 1998.

Giovanni Morelli: Da collezionista a conoscitore: Catalogo della mostra, Bergamo 4 giugno–31 luglio 1987. Bergamo: Accademia Carrara, 1987.

Girardet Soggin, Maria G., Thomas Soggin, Rita Gay, and Salvatore Ricciardi. *Una presenza riformata a Bergamo: La Comunità cristiana evangelica nel corso di due secoli*. Bergamo: Sestante, 2007.

Gregori, Mina. *Giovan Battista Moroni (1520–1578)*. Bergamo: Azienda autonoma di turismo, 1975.

Hadley, Rollin van N., ed. *The Letters of Bernard Berenson and Isabella Stewart Gardner 1887–1924, with Correspondence by Mary Berenson*. Boston: Northeastern University Press, 2016.

Haskell, Francis. "Un martyr de l'attribution: Morris Moore et *l'Apollon et Marsyas* du Louvre." *Revue de l'art* 42 (1978): 77–88.

Henning, Andreas. "Il *San Sebastiano* di Antonello da Messina a Dresda. Iconografia e restauro." In *Antonello da Messina*, edited by Mauro Lucco and Giovanni Carlo Federico Villa, 75–89 Milan: Silvana Editoriale, 2006.

Herre, Franz. *Kaiserin Friedrich, Victoria, eine Engländerin in Deutschland*. Stuttgart-Leipzig: Hohnheim Verlag, 2006.

Hinterding, Erik, and Femy Horsch. "'A Small but Choice Collection': The Art Gallery of King Willem II of the Netherlands (1792–1849)." *Simiolus: Netherlands Quarterly for the History of Art* 19, nos 1–2 (1989): 5–122.

Hogrebe, Wolfram. "Schelling und Dante." *Deutsches Dante-Jahrbuch* 62 (1987): 7–31.

Honegger, Silvio. *Gli Svizzeri di Bergamo: Storia della comunità svizzera di Bergamo dal Cinquecento all'inizio del Novecento*. Storia Sociale della Bergamasca. Bergamo: Edizioni Junior, 1997.

Hopkins, Andrew. "Heinrich Wölfflin's Annotated Books." *Getty Research Journal* 17 (2015): 177–84.

Koopmann, Wilhelm. *Raffaels Handzeichnungen in der Auffassung von W. Koopmann*. Marburg: N. G. Elwert, 1897.

Kultzen, Rolf. "Giovanni Morelli als Briefpartner von Otto Mündler." *Zeitschrift für Kunstgeschichte* 52 (1989): 373–401.

Kultzen, Rolf. "Otto Mündler als Briefpartner Wilhelm von Bodes." In *Martin Gosebruch zu Ehren: Festschrift anlasslich seines 65. Geburtstages am 20. Juni 1984*, edited by Frank Neidhart Steigerwald, 184–191. Munich: Hirmer, 1984.

Kultzen, Rolf. "Otto Mündler als Freund und Förderer des jungen Bode." *Jahrbuch der Berliner Museen*, Beiheft, *"Kennerschaft": Kolloquium zum 150sten Geburtstag von Wilhelm von Bode* (1996): 49–55.

Lechi, Fausto. *I quadri della Collezione Lechi in Brescia*. Florence: Olschki, 1968.

Levey, Michael. "A Little-known Director: Sir William Boxall." *Apollo: The International Magazine of Arts* 101 (1975): 354–59.

Levi, Donata. "Appunti su Corrado Ricci e la sua attività museografica." In *Corrado Ricci: Storico dell'arte tra esperienza e progetto*, edited by Andrea Emiliani and Donatino Domini, 51–63. Ravenna: Longo, 2004.

Levy, Evonne. *Baroque and the Political Language of Formalism (1845–1945): Burckhardt, Wölfflin, Guurlitt, Brinckmann, Sedlmayr*, Basel: Schwabe, 2015.

Lloyd, Christopher. *Art and its Images: An Exhibition of Printed Books Containing Engraved Illustrations after Italian Painting*. Oxford: Bodleian Library, 1975.

Locatelli, Valentina. "Italian Painters: Critical Studies of their Works. The Gemäldegalerie Alte Meister in Dresden: An overview of Giovanni Morelli's attributions." *Journal of Art Historiography* 13 (2015): 1–22.

Locatelli Milesi, Giuseppe. "Gli ostaggi nella caserma di S. Agostino: Episodio della rivoluzione di Bergamo del marzo 1848." *Rivista di Bergamo* (1922): 447–51.

Lützow, Carl. *Die Kunstschätze Italiens in geographische-historischer Übersicht*. Stuttgart: Engelhorn, 1884.

Mattaliano, Emanuele, and Amalia Mezzetti. *Indice ragionato delle "Vite de' pittori e sculturi ferraresi" di Gerolamo Baruffaldi*. Ferrara: Cassa di risparmio di Ferrara, 1981.

Mazzocca, Fernando. "La rappresentazione della guerra nella pittura risorgimentale." In *Storia d'Italia, Annali 22, Il Risorgimento*, edited by Alberto Mario Banti and Paul Ginsborg, 721–43. Turin: Giulio Einaudi, 2007.

Mollisi, Giorgio, ed. *Svizzeri a Bergamo nella storia nell'arte nella cultura nell'economia dal '500 ad oggi*. Lugano: Società Editrice Management, 2009.

Moretti, Lino. *G. B. Cavalcaselle: Disegni da antichi maestri*. Vicenza: Pozza, 1973.

Mottola Molfino, Alessandra. *Museo Poldi Pezzoli: Storia del museo*. Musei e gallerie di Milano. Milan: Electa, 1982.

Müller-Bechtel, Susanne. *Die Zeichnungen als Forschungsinstrument: Giovanni Battista Cavalcaselle (1819–1897) und seine Zeichnungen zur Wandmalerei in Italien vor 1550*. Berlin: Deutscher Kunstverlag, 2009.

Pakula, Hannah. *An Uncommon Woman: The Empress Frederick, Daughter of Queen Victoria, Wife of the Crown Prince of Prussia, Mother of Kaiser Wilhelm*. New York: Simon and Schuster, 1995.

Pantazzi, Sybille. "The Donna Laura Minghetti Leonardo: An International Mystification." *English Miscellany* 16 (1965): 321–48.

Patriarca, Silvana, and Lucy Riall, eds. *The Risorgimento Revisited: Nationalism and Culture in Nineteenth-Century Italy*. New York: Palgrave Macmillan, 2012.

Pau, Richard. "Le origini scientifiche del metodo Morelliano." In *Giovanni Morelli e la cultura dei conoscitori: Atti del convegno internazionale, Bergamo, 4–7 giugno 1987*, edited by Giacomo Agosti, Maria Elisabetta Manca, and Matteo Panzeri, vol. 2, 301–19. Bergamo: Pierluigi Lubrina, 1993.

Pedrotti, Pietro, Enrico Brol, and Bice Rizzi. *L'Azione parlamentare del Trentino nel 1848–49 a Francoforte e a Vienna*. Trento: Tipografia Editrice Mutilati e Invalidi, 1948.

Peluffo, Paolo, Maria Canella, and Paola Zatti. *Cronaca di una rivoluzione: Immagini e luoghi delle Cinque giornate di Milano*. Milan: Silvana, 2011.

Pertile, Lino. "A Text in Movement: Trifon Gabriele's *Annotationi nel Dante*, 1527–1565." In *Interpreting Dante: Essays on the Tradition of Dante Commentary*, edited by Paola Nasti and Claudia Rossignoli, 341–58. Notre Dame, IND: University of Notre Dame, 2013.

Pertile, Lino. "Un testo in movimento: Le 'Annotationi nel Dante' di Trifon Gabriele dal 1527 al 1565." *Rivista di studi danteschi* 6 (2006): 142–53.

Peters, Dorothea. "Reproduced Art: Early Photographic Campaigns in European Collections." In *The Museum is Open: Towards a Transnational History of Museums 1750–1940*, edited by Andrea Meyer and Bénédicte Savoy, 45–58. Berlin: De Gruyter, 2014.

Petrò, Gianmario. "Il castello vescovile di Gorle." *La Rivista di Bergamo* n.s, no. 1 (May 1995): 12–21.

Plant, Margaret. *Venice: Fragile City*. New Haven and London: Yale University Press, 2002.

Podro, Michael. *The Critical Historians of Art*. New Haven and London: Yale University Press, 1982.

Ponsonby, Frederick, ed. *The Letters of the Empress Frederick*. London: Macmillan, 1928.

Ramm, Agatha, ed. *Beloved & Darling Child: Last Letters Between Queen Victoria & Her Eldest Daughter, 1886–1901*. Stroud, UK: Sutton, 1990.

Ricci, Corrado. "Critica d'Arte." *Cronaca Bizantina* (17 January 1886): 3–4.

Richter, Irma, and Gisela Richter, eds. *Italienische Malerei der Renaissance im Briefwechsel von Giovanni Morelli und Jean Paul Richter, 1876–1891*. Vol. I. Baden-Baden: Grimm, 1960.

Richter, Jean Paul. *The Literary Works of Leonardo da Vinci: Compiled and Edited from the Original Manuscripts*. London: Sampson Low, Marston, Searle & Rivington, 1883.

Richter, Jean Paul. Obituary of Giovanni Morelli. *Beilage zur Allgemeinen Zeitung* (6 April 1891): 1–4.

Riva, Cecilia. "La Collezione Layard nel catalogo dattiloscritto 1896." *Predella: Journal of the Visual Arts* 35 (2014): 53–78.

Roberts, Jane. *Royal Artists from Mary Queen of Scots to the Present Day*. London and Glasgow: Grafton Books, 1987.

Robertson, David. *Sir Charles Eastlake and the Victorian Art World*. Princeton, NJ: Princeton University Press, 1978.

Ross, Janet. *Three Generations of Englishwomen: Memoirs and Correspondence of Mrs John Taylor, Mrs Sarah Austin and Lady Duff Gordon*. London: John Murray, 1888.

Rossi, Giuseppe M. *Nuova guida di Verona e della sua provincial*. Verona: Tip. Friziero, 1854.

Rouet, Philippe. "De l'anatomie compare au *connoisseurship* 'scientifique': Cuvier and Morelli." In *L'artiste savant à la conquête du monde moderne*, edited by Anne Lafont, 65–75. Strasbourg: Presses Universitaires, 2010.

Rovetta, Alessandro. "Tracce del 'doppio catalogo' di Giovanni Morelli nei manoscritti di Gustavo Frizzoni all'Ambrosiana: Le collezioni milanesi." *Arte Lombarda*, Nuova serie, No. 146/148 (1–3), 50 anni (2006): 220–26.

Rückert, Rüdiger, ed. *Briefe an und über Friedrich Rückert: Korrespondenz insbesondere von Familienmitgliedern*. Vol. 2. Schweinfurt: Stadt Schweinfurt, 1987.

Rudwick, Martin J. S. *Georges Cuvier, Fossil Bones, and Geological Catastrophes*. Chicago: University of Chicago Press, 1997.

Ryckwert, Joseph. "Semper and the Conception of Style." In *Gottfried Semper und die Mitte des 19. Jahrhunderts: Symposion vom 2. bis 6. Dezember 1974*, edited by Eva Börsch-Supan, 68–81. Basel: Birkhäuser, 1976.

Santini, Luigi. *La comunità evangelica di Bergamo: Vicende storiche*. Torre Pellice: Claudiana, 1960.

Sarti, Telesforo. *Il Parlamento subalpino e nazionale: Profili e cenni biografici di tutti i deputati e senatori eletti e creati dal 1848 al 1890*. Terni: Tipografia Editrice dell'Industria, 1890.

Schutte, Anne. *Pier Paolo Vergerio: The Making of an Italian Reformer*. Geneva: Édition Droz, 1977.

Schwab, Raymond. *La Renaissance orientale*. Paris: Payot, 1950.

Seybold, Dietrich. *Das Schlaraffenleben der Kunst: Eine Biografie des Kunstkenners und Leonardo da Vinci-Forschers Jean Paul Richter (1847–1937)*. Munich: Wilhelm Fink Verlag, 2014.

Sheldon, Julie. "'His Best Successor': Lady Eastlake and the National Gallery." *Museums and Biographies: Stories, Objects, Identities*, edited by Kate Hill, 61–74. London: Boydell & Brewer, 2012.

Spellanzon, Cesare. *Storia del Risorgimento e dell'unità d'Italia*. Milan: Rizzoli, 1936.

Spini, Giorgio. *Risorgimento e protestanti*. Milan: Arnaldo Mondadori, 1980.

Tabarrini, Marco. *Gino Capponi: I suoi tempi, i suoi studi, i suoi amici; Memorie raccolte*. Florence: Barbèra, 1879.

Vannucci, Atto. *Ricordi della vita e delle opere di G. B. Niccolini*. Florence: Felice Le Monnier, 1866.

Venturi, Adolfo. "La formazione della Galleria Layard a Venezia" *L'Arte* 15 (1912): 449–51.

Venturi, Adolfo. *Memorie autobiografiche*. Milan: Hoepli, 1911.

Venturi, Adolfo. "Unbekannte oder vergessene Künstler der Emilia." *Jahrbuch der Königlich Preussischen Kunstsammlungen* 11 (1890): 183–94.

Venuto, Francesca. "Giardini a Verona e provincia nell'Otto e nel Novecento." In *L'architettura a Verona dal periodo napoleonico all'età contemporanea*, edited by Pierpaolo Brugnoli and Arturo Sandrini. Verona: Mondadori, 1994.

von Bode, Wilhelm. *Mein Leben*. Edited by Thomas Gaehtgens and Barbara Paul. Berlin: Nicolaische Verlagsbuchhandlung, 1997.

von Schlosser, Julius. "Die Wiener Schule der Kunstgeschichte." *Mitteilungen des Österreichischen Instituts für Geschichtforschung* 13, no. 2 (1934): 145ff.

von Schlosser, Julius. *La storia dell'arte nelle esperienze e nei ricordi di un suo cultore*. Bari: G. Laterza e Figli, 1936.

von Stockhausen, Tilmann. *Gemäldegalerie Berlin: Die Geschichte ihrer Erwerbungspolitik 1830–1904*. Berlin: Nicolai, 2000.

von Stockhausen, Tilmann. "Otto Mündler als Agent der Berliner Gemäldegalerie." *Jahrbuch der Berliner Museen* 39 (1997): 99–113.

Wölfflin, Heinrich. *Die Jugendwerke des Michelangelo*. Munich: Ackermann, 1891.

Wölfflin, Heinrich. *Heinrich Wölfflin, 1864–1945: Autobiographie, Tagebücher und Briefe*. Edited by Joseph Gantner. Basel: Schwabe, 1984.

Wornum, Ralph Nicholson, and Charles Lock Eastlake. *Descriptive and Historical Catalogue of the Pictures in the National Gallery: With Biographical Notices of the Painters*. London: W. Clowes and Sons, 1847.

Zavaritt, Willi Alberto. *Zavaritt: Cinquecento anni di storie e memorie*. Bergamo: Privately printed, 2017.

Zeri, Federico, and Francesco Rossi. *La raccolta Morelli nell'Accademia Carrara*. Milan: Amilcare Pizzi, 1986.

Index

Printed in the month of October 2019
on the presses of Monotipia Cremonese, Cremona

Ex Officina Libraria Jellinek et Gallerani